SPEECH TECHNOLOGIES

Edited by **Ivo Ipšić**

Speech Technologies
Edited by Ivo Ipšić

CBS, Edition **2016**

Published by InTech
Janeza Trdine 9, 51000 Rijeka, Croatia

Publishing Process Manager Iva Lipovic

Technical Editor Teodora Smiljanic

Cover Designer InTech Design Team

Image Copyright George Nazmi Bebawi, 2010. Used under license from Shutterstock.com

Additional hard copies can be obtained from orders@intechopen.com

Speech Technologies, Edited by Ivo Ipšić
p. cm.
ISBN 978-953-307-996-7

Contents

Preface

The book "Speech Technologies" addresses different aspects of the research field and a wide range of topics in speech signal processing, speech recognition and language processing. The chapters are divided in three different sections: Speech Signal Modeling, Speech Recognition and Applications. The chapters in the first section cover some essential topics in speech signal processing used for building speech recognition as well as for speech synthesis systems: speech feature enhancement, speech feature vector dimensionality reduction, segmentation of speech frames into phonetic segments.

The chapters of the second part cover speech recognition methods and techniques used to read speech from various speech databases and broadcast news recognition for English and non-English languages. The third section of the book presents various speech technology applications used for body conducted speech recognition, hearing impairment, multimodal interfaces and facial expression recognition.

I would like to thank to all authors who have contributed research and application papers from the field of speech and language technologies.

Ivo Ipšić
University of Rijeka,
Croatia

Part 1

Speech Signal Modeling

Multi-channel Feature Enhancement for Robust Speech Recognition

Rudy Rotili, Emanuele Principi, Simone Cifani, Francesco Piazza and
Stefano Squartini
Università Politecnica delle Marche
Italy

1. Introduction

In the last decades, a great deal of research has been devoted to extending our capacity
of verbal communication with computers through automatic speech recognition (ASR).
Although optimum performance can be reached when the speech signal is captured close
to the speaker's mouth, there are still obstacles to overcome in making reliable distant speech
recognition (DSR) systems. The two major sources of degradation in DSR are distortions,
such as additive noise and reverberation. This implies that speech enhancement techniques
are typically required to achieve best possible signal quality. Different methodologies have
been proposed in literature for environment robustness in speech recognition over the past
two decades (Gong (1995); Hussain, Chetouani, Squartini, Bastari & Piazza (2007)). Two main
classes can be identified (Li et al. (2009)).

The first class encompasses the so called model-based techniques, which operate on the
acoustic model to adapt or adjust its parameters so that the system fits better the distorted
environment. The most popular of such techniques are multi-style training (Lippmann et al.
(2003)), parallel model combination (PMC) (Gales & Young (2002)) and the vector Taylor series
(VTS) model adaptation (Moreno (1996)). Although model-based techniques obtain excellent
results, they require heavy modifications to the decoding stage and, in most cases, a greater
computational burden.

Conversely, the second class directly enhances the speech signal before it is presented to the
recognizer, and show some significant advantages with respect to the previous class:

- independence on the choice of the ASR engine: there is no need of intervening into the
  (HMM) of the ASR since all modifications are accomplished at the feature level, which has
  a significant practical mean;

- ease of implementation: the algorithm parameterization is extremely simpler than in the
  model-based case study and no adaptation is requested to find the optimal one;

- lower computational burden, surely relevant in real-time applications.

The wide variety of algorithms in this class can be further divided based on the number of
channels used in the enhancing stage.

Single-channel approaches encompass classical techniques operating in the frequency domain
such as Wiener filtering, spectral subtraction (Boll (1979)) and Ephraim & Malah (logMMSE
STSA) (Ephraim & Malah (1985)), as well as techniques operating in the feature domain such

as the MFCC-MMSE (Yu, Deng, Droppo, Wu, Gong & Acero (2008)) and its optimizations (Principi, Cifani, Rotili, Squartini & Piazza (2010); Yu, Deng, Wu, Gong & Acero (2008)) and VTS speech enhancement (Stouten (2006)). Other algorithms belonging to the single-channel class are feature normalization approaches as cepstral mean normalization (CMN) (Atal (1974)), cepstral variance normalization (CVN) (Molau et al. (2003)), higher order cepstral moment normalization (HOCMN), histogram equalization (HEQ) (De La Torre et al. (2005)) and parametric feature equalization (Garcia et al. (2006)).

Multi-channel approaches use the benefits of the additional informations carried out by the presence of multiple speech observations. In most cases the speech and noise sources are in different spatial locations, thus a multi-microphone system is theoretically able to obtain a significant gain over single-channel approaches, since it may exploit the spatial diversity.

This chapter will be devoted to illustrate and analyze multi-channel approaches for robust ASR in both the frequency and feature domain. Three different subsets will be addressed highlighting advantages and drawbacks of each one: beamforming techniques, bayesian estimators (operating at different level of the feature extraction pipeline) and histogram equalization.

In ASR scenario, beamforming techniques are employed as pre-processing stage. In (Omologo et al. (1997)) the delay and sum beamformer (DSB) has been successfully used coupled with a talker localization algorithm but its performance are poor when the number of microphones is small (less than 8) or when it operates in a reverberant environment. This motivated the scientific community to develop more robust beamforming techniques e.g. generalized sidelobe canceler (GSC) and transfer function GSC (TF-GSC). Among the beamforming techniques, likelihood maximizing beamforming (LIMABEAM) is an hybrid approach that uses informations from the decoding stage to optimize a filter and sum beamformer (Seltzer (2003)).

Multi-channel bayesian estimators in frequency domain has been proposed in (Lotter et al. (2003)) where both minimum mean square error (MMSE) and maximum a posteriori (MAP) criteria were developed. The feature domain counterpart of the previous algorithms has been presented in (Principi, Rotili, Cifani, Marinelli, Squartini & Piazza (2010)). The simulations conducted on the Aurora 2 database showed performance similar to the frequency domain ones with the advantage of a reduced computational burden.

The last subset that will be addressed, is the multi-channel variant of histogram equalization (Squartini et al. (2010)). Here the presence of multiple audio channels is exploited to better estimate the histograms of the input signal and so making the equalization processing more effective.

The outline of this chapter is as follows: section 2 describe the feature extraction pipeline and the adopted mathematical model. Section 3 gives a brief review of the beamforming concept mentioning some of most popular beamformer. Section 4 is devoted to illustrate the multi-channel MMSE and MAP estimators both in frequency and feature domain while section 5 proposes various algorithmic architectures for multi-channel HEQ. Section 6 presents and discuss recognition results in a comparative fashion. Finally, section 7 draws conclusions and proposes future developments.

2. ASR front-end and mathematical background

In the feature-enhancement approach, the features are enhanced before the ASR decoding stage, with the aim of making them as close as possible to the clean-speech environment condition. This means that some extra-cleaning steps are performed into or after the feature extraction module. As shown in figure 1, the feature extraction pipeline has four possible insertion points, each one being related to different classes of enhancement algorithms. Traditional speech enhancement in the discrete-time Fourier transform (DFT) domain (Ephraim & Malah (1984); Wolfe & Godsill (2003)), is performed at point 1, mel-frequency domain algorithms (Yu, Deng, Droppo, Wu, Gong & Acero (2008); Rotili et al. (2009)), operate at point 2 and log-mel or MFCC (mel frequency cepstral coefficients) domain algorithms (Indrebo et al. (2008); Deng et al. (2004)), are performed at point 3 and 4 respectively. Since the focus of traditional speech enhancement is on the perceptual quality of the enhanced signal, the performance of the former class is typically lower than the other classes. Moreover, the DFT domain has a much higher dimensionality than mel or MFCC domains, which leads to an higher computational cost of the enhancement process. Let us

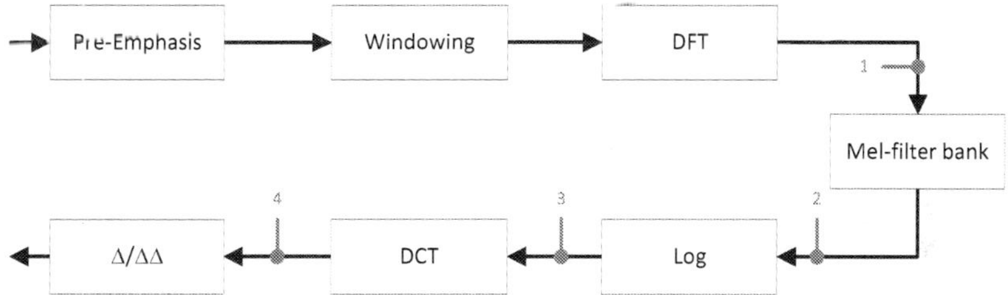

Fig. 1. Feature extraction pipeline.

consider M noisy signals $y_i(t)$, M clean speech signals $x_i(t)$ and M uncorrelated noise signals $n_i(t), i \in \{1, \ldots, M\}$, where t is a discrete-time index. The i-th microphone signal is given by:

$$y_i(t) = x_i(t) + n_i(t). \tag{1}$$

In general, the signal $x_i(t)$ is the convolution between the speech source and the i-th room impulse response. In our case study the far-field model (Lotter et al. (2003)) that assumes equal amplitude and angle-dependent TDOAs (Time Difference Of Arrival) has been considered:

$$x_i(t) = x\left(t - \tau_i(\beta_x)\right), \qquad \tau_i = d\sin\left(\beta_x/c\right) \tag{2}$$

where τ_i is the i-th delay, d is the distance between the source and the microphone array, θ_x is the angle of arrival and c is the speed of sound.

According to figure 1, each input signal $y_i(t)$ is firstly pre-emphasized and windowed with a Hamming window. Then, the fast Fourier transform (FFT) of the signal is computed and the square of the magnitude is filtered with a bank of triangular filters equally spaced in the mel-scale. After that, the energy of each band is computed and transformed with a logarithm operation. Finally, the discrete cosine transform (DCT) stage yields the static MFCC coefficients, and the $\Delta/\Delta\Delta$ stage compute the first and second derivatives.

Given the additive noise assumption, in the DFT domain we have

$$Y_i(k,l) = X_i(k,l) + N_i(k,l) \tag{3}$$

where $X(k,l)$, $Y(k,l)$ and $N(k,l)$ denote the short-time Fourier transforms (STFT) of $x(t)$, $y(t)$ and $n(t)$ respectively, where k is the frequency bin index and l is the time frame index. Equation (3) can be rewritten as follows:

$$Y_i = R_i e^{j\phi_i} = A_i e^{j\alpha_i} + N_i, \qquad 1 \le i \le M \tag{4}$$

where R_i, ϕ_i, A_i and α_i are the amplitude and phase terms of Y_i and X_i respectively. For simplicity of notation, the frequency bin and time frame indexes have been omitted.
The mel-frequency filter-bank's output power for noisy speech is

$$m_{y_i}(b,l) = \sum_k w_b(k)|Y_i(k,l)|^2 \tag{5}$$

where $w_b(k)$ is the b-th mel-frequency filter's weight for the frequency bin k. A similar relationship holds for the clean speech and the noise. The j-th dimension of MFCC is calculated as

$$c_{y_i}(j,l) = \sum_b a_{j,b} \log m_{y_i}(b,l) \tag{6}$$

where $a_{j,b} = \cos((\pi b/B)(j - 0.5))$ are the DCT coefficients. The output of equation (3) denotes the input of the enhancement algorithms belonging to class 1 (DFT domain) and that of equation (5) the input of class 2 (mel-frequency domain). The logarithm of the output of equation (5) is the input for the class 3 algorithms (log-mel domain) while that of equation (6) the input of class 4 (MFCC domain) algorithms.

3. Beamforming

Beamforming is a method by which signals from several sensors can be combined to emphasize a desired source and to suppress all other noise and interference. Beamforming begins with the assumption that the positions of all sensors are known, and that the positions of the desired sources are known or can be estimated as well.
The simplest of beamforming algorithms, the delay and sum beamformer, uses only this geometrical knowledge to combine the signals from several sensors. The theory of DSB originates from narrowband antenna array processing, where the plane waves at different sensors are delayed appropriately to be added exactly in phase. In this way, the array can be electronically steered towards a specific direction. This principle is also valid for broadband signals, although the directivity will then be frequency dependent.
A DSB aligns the microphone signals to the direction of the speech source by delaying and summing the microphone signals.
Let us define the steering vector of the desired source as

$$\mathbf{v}(\mathbf{k}_d, \omega) = \left[\exp\{j\omega\tau_{d,0}\}, \exp\{j\omega\tau_{d,1}\}, \cdots, \exp\{j\omega\tau_{d,M-1}\}\right]^H, \tag{7}$$

where $\mathbf{k}_d$ is the wave number and $\tau_{d,i}, i \in \{1,,\ldots,M\}$ is the delay relative to the i-th channels. The sensor weights $\mathbf{w}_f(\omega)$ are chosen as the complex conjugate steering vector $\mathbf{v}^*(\mathbf{k}_d, \omega)$, with the amplitude normalized by the number of sensors M:

$$\mathbf{w}_f(\omega) = \frac{1}{M}\mathbf{v}^*(\mathbf{k}_d, \omega). \tag{8}$$

The absolute value of all sensor weights is than equal to $1/M$ (uniform weighting) and the phase is equalized for signals with the steering vector $\mathbf{v}(\mathbf{k}_d, \omega)$ (beamsteering).
The beampattern $B(\omega; \theta, \phi)$ of the DSB with uniform sensor spacing d is obtained as

$$B(\omega; \theta, \phi) = \frac{1}{M}\mathbf{v}^H(\mathbf{k}_d, \omega)\mathbf{v}(\mathbf{k}, \omega) = \frac{1}{M}\sum_{m=0}^{M-1} \exp\left\{j\omega\left(\frac{M-1}{2} - m\right)\frac{d}{c}(\cos\theta_d - \cos\theta)\right\}. \tag{9}$$

This truncated geometric series may be simplified to a closed form as

$$B(\omega;\theta,\phi) = \frac{1}{M}\frac{sin(\omega M\tau_b/2)}{sin(\omega\tau_b/2)} \tag{10}$$

$$\tau_b = \frac{d}{c}(cos\theta_d - cos\theta). \tag{11}$$

This kind of beamformer is proved to perform well when the number of microphones is relatively high, and when the noise sources are spatially white. On the contrary, performance degrade since noise reduction is strongly dependent on the direction of arrival of the noise signal. As a consequence, DSB performance on reverberant environments is poor.

In order to increase the performance, more sophisticated solution can be adopted. In particular, adaptive beamformers can ideally attain high interference reduction performance with a small number of microphones arranged in a small space. GSC (Griffiths & Jim (1982)) attempt to minimize the total output power of an array of sensor under the constraint that the desired source must be unattenuated.

The main drawback of such beamformer is the target signal cancellation that occurs in the presence of steering vector errors. They are caused by errors in microphone positions, microphone gains, reverberation, and target direction. Therefore, errors in the steering vector are inevitable with actual microphone arrays, and target signal cancellation is a serious problem. Many signal processing techniques have been proposed to avoid signal cancellation. In (Hoshuyama et al. (1999)), a robust GSC (RGSC) able to avoid these difficulties, has been proposed, which uses an adaptive blocking matrix consisting of coefficient-constrained adaptive filters. Such filters exploit the reference signal from the fixed beamformer to adapt themselves and adaptively cancel the undesirable influence caused by steering vector errors. The interference canceller uses norm-constrained adaptive filters (Cox et al. (1987)) to prevent target-signal cancellation when the adaptation of the coefficient-constrained filters is incomplete. In (Herbordt & Kellermann (2001); Herbordt et al. (2007)) a frequency domain implementation of the RGSC has been proposed in conjunction with acoustic echo cancellation.

Most of the GSC based beamformers rely on the assumption that the received signals are simple delayed versions of the source signal. The good interference suppression attained under this assumption is severely impaired in complicated acoustic environments, where arbitrary transfer functions (TFs) may be encountered. In (Gannot et al. (2001)), a GSC solution which is adapted to the general TF case (TF-GSC) has been proposed. The TFs are estimated by exploiting the nonstationarity characteristics of the desired signal, as reported in (Shalvi & Weinstein (1996); Cohen (2004)), and then used to calculate the fixed beamformer and the blocking matrix coefficients.

However, in case of incoherent or diffuse noise fields, beamforming alone does not provide sufficient noise reduction, and postfiltering is normally required. Postfiltering includes signal detection, noise estimation, and spectral enhancement.

Recently, a multi-channel postfilter was incorporated into the TF-GSC beamformer (Cohen et al. (2003); Gannot & Cohen (2004)). The use of both the beamformer primary output and the reference noise signals (resulting from the blocking branch of the GSC) for distinguish between desired speech transient and interfering transient, enables the algorithm to work in nonstationary noise environments. The multi-channel postfilter, combined with the TF-GSC, proved the best for handling abrupt noise spectral variations. Moreover, in this algorithm, the decisions made by the postfilter, distinguishing between speech, stationary noise, and transient noise, might be fed back to the beamformer to enable the use of the method in real-time applications. Exploiting this information will also enable the tracking of the acoustical transfer functions, caused by the talker movements.

A perceptually based variant of the previous architecture have been presented in (Hussain, Cifani, Squartini, Piazza & Durrani (2007); Cifani et al. (2008)) where a perceptually-based multi-channel signal detection algorithm and a perceptually-optimal spectral amplitude (PO-SA) estimator presented in (Wolfe & Godsill (2000)) have been combined to form a perceptually-based postfilter to be incorporated into the TF-GSC beamformer

Basically, all the presented beamforming techniques outperform the DSB. Recalling the assumption of far-field model (equation (2)) where no reverberation is considered and the observed signals are a simple delayed version of the speech source, the DSB is well suited for our purpose and it is not required to take into account more sophisticated beamformers.

4. Multi-channel bayesian estimators

The estimation of a clean speech signal x given its noisy observation y is often performed under the Bayesian framework. Because of the generality of this framework, x and y may represent DFT coefficients, mel-frequency filter-bank outputs or MFCCs. Applying the standard assumption that clean speech and noise are statistically independent across time and frequency as well as from each other, leads to estimators that are independent of time and frequency.

Let $\epsilon = x - \hat{x}$ denote the error of the estimate and let $C(\epsilon) \triangleq C(x, \hat{x})$ denote a non-negative function of ϵ. The average cost, i.e. $E[C(x, \hat{x})]$, is known as Bayes risk $\mathcal{R}$ (Trees (2001)), and it is given by

$$\mathcal{R} \triangleq E[C(x, \hat{x})] = \int \int C(x, \hat{x}) p(x, y) dx dy \tag{12}$$

$$= \int p(y) dy \int C(x, \hat{x}) p(x|y) dx, \tag{13}$$

in which Bayes rule has been used to separate the role of the observation y and the a priori knowledge.

Minimizing $\mathcal{R}$ with respect to $\hat{x}$ for a given cost function results in a variety of estimators. The traditional mean square error (MSE) cost function,

$$C^{MSE}(x, \hat{x}) = |x - \hat{x}|^2, \tag{14}$$

gives the following expression:

$$\mathcal{R}^{MSE} = \int p(y) dy \int |x - \hat{x}|^2 p(x|y) dx. \tag{15}$$

$\mathcal{R}^{MSE}$ can be minimized by minimizing the inner integral, yielding the MMSE estimate:

$$\hat{x}^{MMSE} = \int x p(x|y) dx = E[x|y]. \tag{16}$$

The log-MMSE estimator can be obtained by means of the cost function

$$C^{log-MSE}(x, \hat{x}) = (\log x - \log \hat{x})^2 \tag{17}$$

thus yielding to:

$$\hat{x}^{log-MMSE} = \exp\left\{E[\ln x|y]\right\}. \tag{18}$$

By using the uniform cost function,

$$C^{MAP}(x,\hat{x}) = \begin{cases} 0, & |x - \hat{x}| \leq \Delta/2 \\ 1, & |x - \hat{x}| > \Delta/2 \end{cases} \tag{19}$$

we get the maximum a posteriori (MAP) estimate:

$$\hat{x}^{MAP} = \underset{x}{\arg\max}\, p(x|y). \tag{20}$$

In the following several multi-channel bayesian estimators are addressed. First the multi-channel MMSE and MAP estimators in frequency domain, presented in (Lotter et al. (2003)), are briefly reviewed. Afterwards, the feature domain counterpart of the MMSE and MAP estimators respectively is proposed. It is important to remark that feature domain algorithms are able to exploit the peculiarities of the feature space and produce more effective and computationally more efficient solutions.

4.1 Speech feature statistical analysis

The statistical modeling of the process under consideration is a fundamental aspect of the Bayesian framework. Considering DFT domain estimators, huge efforts have been spent in order to find adequate signal models. Earlier works (Ephraim & Malah (1984); McAulay & Malpass (1980)), assumed a Gaussian model from a theoretical point of view, by invoking the central limit theorem, stating that the distribution of the DFT coefficients will converge towards a Gaussian probability density function (PDF) regardless of the PDF of the time samples, if successive samples are statistically independent or the correlation is short compared to the analysis frame size. Although this assumption holds for many relevant acoustic noises, it may fail for speech where the span of correlation is comparable to the typical frame sizes (10-30 ms). Spurred by this issue, several researchers investigated the speech probability distribution in the DFT domain (Gazor & Zhang (2003); Jensen et al. (2005)), and proposed new estimators leaning on different models, i.e., Laplacian, Gamma and Chi (Lotter & Vary (2005); Hendriks & Martin (2007); Chen & Loizou (2007)).

In this section the study of the speech probability distribution in the mel-frequency and MFCC domains is reported, so as to open the way to the development of estimators leaning on different models in these domains as well.

The analysis has been performed either on the TiDigits (Leonard (1984)) and on the Wall Street Journal (Garofalo et al. (1993)) database using one hour clean speech segments built by concatenation of random utterances. DFT coefficients have been extracted using a 32 ms Hamming window with 50% overlap. The aforementioned Gaussian assumption models the real and imaginary part of the clean speech DFT coefficient by means of a Gaussian PDF. However, the relative importance of short-time spectral amplitude (STSA) rather than phase has led researchers to re-cast the spectral estimation problem in terms of the former quantity. Moreover, amplitude and phase are statistically less dependent than real and imaginary parts, resulting in a more tractable problem. Furthermore, it can be shown that phase is well modeled by means of a uniform distribution $p(\alpha) = 1/2\pi$ for $\alpha \in [-\pi, \pi)$. This has lead the authors to investigate the probability distribution of the STSA coefficients.

For each DFT channel, the histogram of the corresponding spectral amplitude was computed and then fitted by means of a nonlinear least-squares (NLLS) technique to six different PDFs:

$$\text{Rayleigh:} \quad p = \frac{x}{\sigma} \exp\left(\frac{-x^2}{2\sigma}\right)$$

$$\text{Laplace:} \quad p = \frac{1}{2\sigma} \exp\left(\frac{-|x-a|}{\sigma}\right)$$

$$\text{Gamma:} \quad p = \frac{1}{\theta^k \Gamma(k)} |x|^{k-1} \exp\left(\frac{-|x|}{\theta}\right)$$

$$\text{Chi:} \quad p = \frac{2}{\theta^k \Gamma(k/2)} |x|^{k-1} \exp\left(\left(\frac{-|x|}{\theta}\right)^2\right)$$

$$\text{Approximated Laplace:} \quad p = \frac{\mu^{\nu+1}}{\Gamma(\nu+1)} |x|^\nu \exp\left(\frac{-\mu|x|}{\sigma}\right), \mu = 2.5 \text{ and } \nu = 1$$

$$\text{Approximated Gamma:} \quad p = \frac{\mu^{\nu+1}}{\Gamma(\nu+1)} |x|^\nu \exp\left(\frac{-\mu|x|}{\sigma}\right), \mu = 1.5 \text{ and } \nu = 0.01$$

The goodness-of-fit has been evaluated by means of the Kullback-Leibler (KL) divergence, which is a measure that quantifies how close a probability distribution is to a model (or candidate) distribution. Choosing p as the N bins histogram and q as the analytic function that approximates the real PDF, the KL divergence is given by:

$$D_{KL} = \sum_{n=1}^{N} (p(n) - q(n)) \log \frac{p(n)}{q(n)}. \tag{21}$$

D_{KL} is non-negative (≥ 0), not symmetric in p and q, zero if the distributions match exactly and can potentially equal infinity. Table 1 shows the KL divergence between measured data and model functions. The divergences have been normalized to that of the Rayleigh PDF, that is, the Gaussian model. The curves in figure 2 represent the fitting results, while

STSA Model	TiDigits	WSJ
Laplace	0.15	0.17
Gamma	0.04	0.04
Chi	0.23	0.02
Approximated Laplace	0.34	0.24
Approximated Gamma	0.31	0.20

Table 1. Kullback-Leibler divergence between STSA coefficients and model functions.

the gray area represents the STSA histogram averaged over the DFT channels. As the KL divergence highlights, the Gamma PDF provides the best model, being capable of adequately fit the histogram tail as well. The modeling of mel-frequency coefficients has been carried out using the same technique employed in the DFT domain. The coefficients have been extracted by applying a 23-channel mel-frequency filter-bank to the squared STSA coefficients. The divergences, normalized to that of the Rayleigh PDF, have been reported in table 2. Again,

Mel-frequency Model	TiDigits	WSJ
Laplace	0.21	0.29
Gamma	0.08	0.07
Chi	0.16	0.16
Approximated Laplace	0.21	0.22
Approximated Gamma	0.12	0.12

Table 2. Kullback-Leibler divergence between mel-frequency coefficients and model functions.

figure 3 represents the fitting results and the mel-frequency coefficient histogram averaged

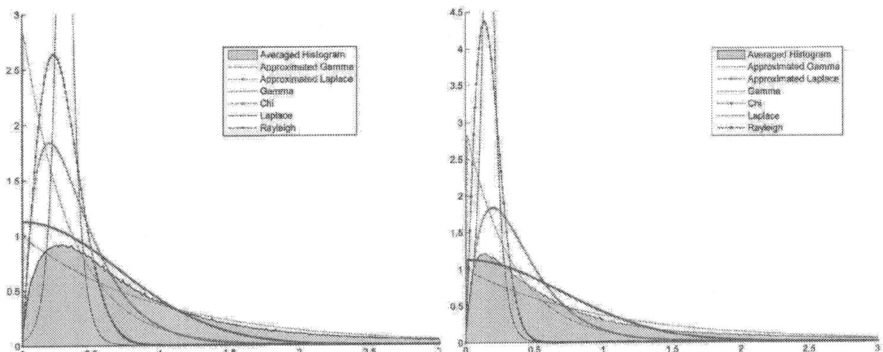

Fig. 2. Averaged Histogram and NLLS fits of STSA coefficients for the TiDigits (left) and WSJ database (right).

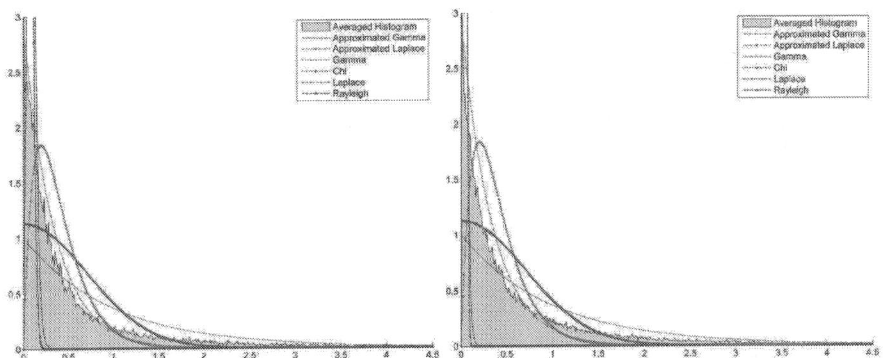

Fig. 3. Averaged Histogram and NLLS fits of mel-Frequency coefficients for the TiDigits (left) and WSJ database (right).

over the filter-bank channels. The Gamma PDF still provides the best model, even if the difference with other PDFs are more modest.

The modeling of log-mel coefficients and MFCCs cannot be performed using the same technique employed above. In fact, the histograms of these coefficients, depicted in figure 4 and 5, reveal that their distributions are multimodal and cannot be modeled by means of unimodal distributions. Therefore, multimodal models, such as Gaussian mixture models (GMM) (Redner & Walker (1984)) are more appropriate in this task: finite mixture models and their typical parameter estimation methods can approximate a wide variety of PDFs and are thus attractive solutions for cases where single function forms fail. The GMM probability density function can be designed as a weighted sum of Gaussians:

$$p(x) = \sum_{c=1}^{C} \alpha_c \mathcal{N}(x; \mu_c, \Sigma_c), \quad \text{with } \alpha_c \in [0,1], \quad \sum_{c=1}^{C} \alpha_c = 1 \tag{22}$$

where α_c is the weight of the c-th component. The weight can be interpreted as a priori probability that a value of the random variable is generated by the c-th source. Hence, a GMM PDF is completely defined by a parameter list $\rho = \{\alpha_1, \mu_1, \Sigma_1, \ldots, \alpha_C, \mu_C, \Sigma_C\}$.

A vital question with GMM PDF's is how to estimate the model parameters ρ. In literature exists two principal approaches: maximum-likelihood estimation and Bayesian estimation. While the latter has strong theoretical basis, the former is simpler and widely used in practice. Expectation-maximization (EM) algorithm is an iterative technique for calculating maximum-likelihood distribution parameter estimates from incomplete data. The Figuredo-Jain (FJ) algorithm (Figueiredo & Jain (2002)) represents an extension of the EM which allows not to specify the number of components C and for this reason it has been adopted in this work. GMM obtained after FJ parameter estimation are shown in figure 4 and 5.

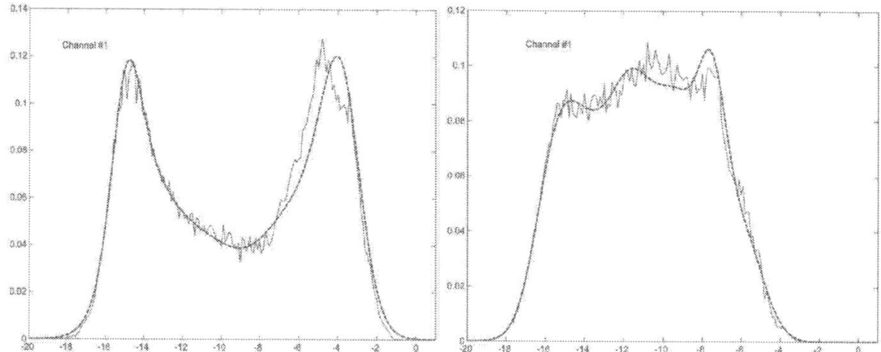

Fig. 4. Histogram (solid) and GMM fit (dashed) of the first channel of LogMel coefficients for TiDigits (left) and WSJ database (right).

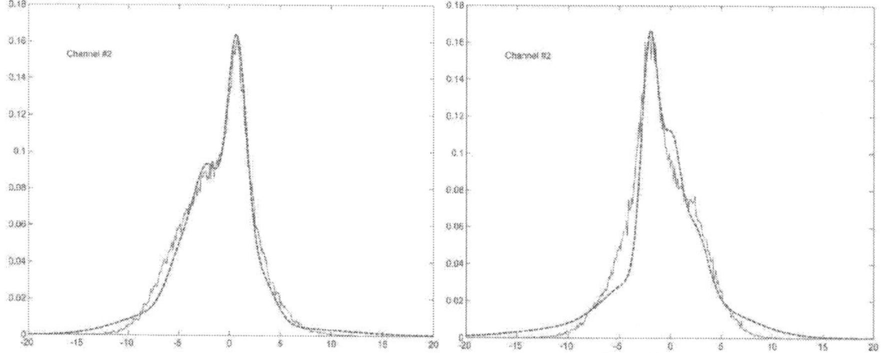

Fig. 5. Histogram (solid) and GMM fit (dashed) of the second channel of MFCC coefficients for TiDigits (left) and WSJ database (right).

4.2 Frequency domain multi-channel estimators

Let us consider a model of equation (4). It is assumed that the real and imaginary parts of both the speech and noise DFT coefficients have zero mean Gaussian distribution with equal variance. This results in a Rayleigh distribution for speech amplitudes A_i, and in Gaussian and Ricians distributions for $p(Y_i|A_i,\alpha_i)$ and $p(R_i|A_i)$ respectively. Such single-channel distributions are extended to the multi-channel ones by supposing that the correlation between the noise signals of different microphones is zero. This leads to

$$p(R_1,\ldots,R_M|A_n) = \prod_{i=1}^{M} p(R_i|A_n), \tag{23}$$

$$p(Y_1,\ldots,Y_M|A_n,\alpha_n) = \prod_{i=1}^{M} p(Y_i|A_n,\alpha_n), \tag{24}$$

$\forall n \in \{1,\ldots,M\}$. The model assumes also that the time delay between the microphones is small compared to the short-time stationarity of the speech. Thus, $A_i = c_i A_r$ and $\sigma_{X_i}^2 = E[|X_i|^2] = c_i \sigma_X^2$ where c_i is a constant channel dependent factor. In addition

$$E[N_i N_j^*] = \begin{cases} \sigma_{N_i}^2, & i = j, \\ 0, & i \neq j. \end{cases}$$

These assumptions give the following probability density functions:

$$p(A_i,\alpha_i) = \frac{A_i}{\pi \sigma_{X_i}^2} \exp\left(-\frac{A_i^2}{\sigma_{X_i}^2}\right), \tag{25}$$

$$p(Y_1,\ldots,Y_M|A_n,\alpha_n) = \prod_{i=1}^{M} \frac{1}{\pi \sigma_{N_i}^2} \exp\left(-\sum_{i=1}^{M} \frac{|Y_i - (c_i/c_n)A_i e^{j\alpha_i}|^2}{\sigma_{N_i}^2}\right) \tag{26}$$

$$p(R_1,\ldots,R_M|A_n) = \exp\left(-\sum_{i=1}^{M} \frac{R_i^2 + (c_i/c_n)^2 A_n^2}{\sigma_{N_i}^2}\right) \prod_{i=1}^{M} \frac{2R_i}{\sigma_{N_i}^2} I_0\left(\frac{2(c_i/c_n)A_n R_i}{\sigma_{N_i}^2}\right). \tag{27}$$

where $\sigma_{X_i}^2$ and $\sigma_{N_i}^2$ are the variance of the clean speech and noise signals in channel i, and I_0 denotes the modified Bessel function of the first kind and zero-th order. As in (Ephraim & Malah (1984)), the a priori SNR $\xi_i = \sigma_{X_i}^2/\sigma_{N_i}^2$ and a posteriori SNR $\gamma_i = R_i^2/\sigma_{N_i}^2$ are used in the final estimators, and ξ_i is estimated using the decision directed approach.

4.2.1 Frequency domain multi-channel MMSE estimator (F-M-MMSE)

The multi-channel MMSE estimate of the speech spectral amplitude is obtained by evaluating the expression:

$$\hat{A}_i = E[A_i|Y_1,\ldots,Y_M] \qquad \forall i \in \{1,\ldots,M\}. \tag{28}$$

By mean of Bayes rule, and supposing that $\alpha_i = \alpha\ \forall i$, it can be shown (Lotter et al. (2003)) that the gain factor for channel i is given by:

$$G_i = \Gamma(1.5)\sqrt{\frac{\xi_i}{\gamma_i(1 + \sum_{r=1}^{M}\xi_r)}} F_1\left(-0.5, 1, \frac{|\sum_{r=1}^{M}\sqrt{\gamma_r \xi_r}e^{j\phi_r}|^2}{1 + \sum_{r=1}^{M}\xi_r}\right), \tag{29}$$

where F_1 denotes the confluent hypergeometric series, and Γ is the Gamma function.

4.2.2 Frequency domain multi-channel MAP estimator (F-M-MAP)

In (Lotter et al. (2003)), in order to remove the dependency from the direction of arrival (DOA) and obtain a closed-form solution, MAP estimator has been used. The assumption $\alpha_i = \alpha$ $\forall i \in \{1, \ldots, M\}$ is in fact only valid if $\beta_x = 0°$, or after perfect DOA correction. Supposing that the time delay of the desired signal is small respect to the short-time stationarity of speech, the noisy amplitudes R_i are independent from β_x.

MAP estimate was obtained extending the approach described in (Wolfe & Godsill (2003)). The estimate $\hat{A}_i$ of the spectral amplitude of the clean speech signal is given by

$$\hat{A}_i = \arg\max_{A_i} p(A_i | R_1, \ldots, R_M) \tag{30}$$

The gain factor for channel i is given by (Lotter et al. (2003)):

$$G_i = \frac{\sqrt{\xi_i/\gamma_i}}{2 + 2\sum_{r=1}^{M} \zeta_r} \mathrm{Re}\left[\sum_{r=1}^{M} \sqrt{\gamma_r \zeta_r} + + \sqrt{\left(\sum_{i=r}^{M} \sqrt{\gamma_r \zeta_r}\right)^2 + (2 - M)\left(1 + \sum_{r=1}^{M} \zeta_r\right)}\right]. \tag{31}$$

4.3 Feature domain multi-channel bayesian estimators

In this section the MMSE and the MAP estimators in the feature domain, recently proposed in (Principi, Rotili, Cifani, Marinelli, Squartini & Piazza (2010)), are presented. They extend the frequency domain multi-channel algorithms in (Lotter et al. (2003)) and the single-channel feature domain algorithm in (Yu, Deng, Droppo, Wu, Gong & Acero (2008)). Let assume again the model of section 2. As in (Yu, Deng, Droppo, Wu, Gong & Acero (2008)), for each channel i it is useful to define three artificial complex variables M_{x_i}, M_{y_i} and M_{n_i} that have the same modulus of m_{x_i}, m_{y_i} and m_{n_i} and phases θ_{x_i}, θ_{y_i} and θ_{n_i}. Assuming that the artificial phases are uniformly distributed random variables leads to consider M_{x_i} and $M_{y_i} - M_{n_i}$ as random variables following zero mean complex Gaussian distribution. High correlation between m_{x_i} of each channel is also supposed in analogy with the frequency domain model (Lotter et al. (2003)). This, again, results in $m_{x_i} = \lambda_i m_x$, with λ_i a constant channel dependent factor.

These statistical assumptions result in probability distributions similar to the frequency domain ones (Lotter et al. (2003)):

$$p\left(m_{x_i}, \theta_{x_i}\right) = \frac{m_{x_i}}{\pi \sigma_{x_i}^2} \exp\left[-(m_{x_i})^2 / \sigma_{x_i}^2\right], \tag{32}$$

$$p\left(M_{y_r} | m_{x_i}, \theta_{x_i}\right) = \frac{1}{\pi \sigma_{d_r}^2} \exp\left[-|\Psi|^2 / \sigma_{d_r}^2\right], \tag{33}$$

where $\sigma_{x_i}^2 = E\left[|M_{x_i}|^2\right]$, $\sigma_{d_r}^2 = E\left[|M_{y_r} - M_{x_r}|^2\right]$, $\Psi = M_{y_r} - \Lambda_{ri} m_{x_i} e^{j\theta_{x_i}}$ and $\Lambda_{ri} = (\lambda_r / \lambda_i)^2$. In order to simplify the notation, the following vectors can be defined:

$$\begin{aligned}
\mathbf{c}_y(p) &= \left[c_{y_1}(p), \ldots, c_{y_M}(p)\right], \\
\mathbf{m}_y(b) &= \left[m_{y_1}(b), \ldots, m_{y_M}(b)\right], \\
\mathbf{M}_y(b) &= \left[M_{y_1}(b), \ldots, M_{y_M}(b)\right].
\end{aligned} \tag{34}$$

Each vector contains respectively the MFCCs, mel-frequency filter-bank outputs and artificial complex variables of all channels of the noisy signal $y(t)$. Similar relationships hold for the speech and noise signals.

4.3.1 Feature domain multi-channel MMSE estimator (C-M-MMSE)

The multi-channel MMSE estimator can be found by evaluating the conditioned expectation $\hat{c}_{x_i} = E\left[c_{x_i}|c_y\right]$. As in the single-channel case, this is equivalent to (Yu, Deng, Droppo, Wu, Gong & Acero (2008)):

$$\hat{m}_{x_i} = \exp\left\{E\left[\log m_{x_i}|\mathbf{m}_y\right]\right\} = \exp\left\{E\left[\log m_{x_i}|\mathbf{M}_y\right]\right\}. \tag{35}$$

Equation (35) can be solved using the moment generating function (MGF) for channel i:

$$\hat{m}_{x_i} = \exp\left(\left.\frac{d}{d\mu}\Phi_i(\mu)\right|_{\mu=0}\right), \tag{36}$$

where $\Phi_i(\mu) = E\left[(m_{x_i})^\mu \mid \mathbf{M}_y\right]$ is the MGF for channel i. After applying Bayes rule, $\Phi_i(\mu)$ becomes:

$$\Phi_i(\mu) = \frac{\int_0^{+\infty}\int_0^{2\pi}(m_{x_i})^\mu \, p\left(\mathbf{M}_y|m_{x_i},\theta_x\right)p\left(m_{x_i}|\theta_x\right)d\theta_x dm_{x_i}}{\int_0^{+\infty}\int_0^{2\pi}p\left(\mathbf{M}_y|m_{x_i},\theta_x\right)d\theta_x dm_{x_i}}. \tag{37}$$

Supposing the conditional independence of each component of the $\mathbf{M}_y$ vector, we can write

$$p\left(\mathbf{M}_y|m_{x_i},\theta_x\right) = \prod_{r=1}^{M}p\left(M_{y_r}|m_{x_i},\theta_x\right), \tag{38}$$

where it was supposed that $\theta_{x_i} = \theta_x$, i.e. perfect DOA correction. The final expression of the MGF can be found by inserting (32), (33) and (38) in (37).

The integral over θ_x has been solved applying equation (3.338.4) in (Gradshteyn & Ryzhik (2007)), while the integral over m_{x_i} has been solved using (6.631.1). Applying (36), the final gain function $G_i(\xi_i,\gamma_i) = G_i$, for channel i is obtained:

$$G_i = \frac{\left|\sum_{r=1}^{M}\sqrt{\xi_r\gamma_r}e^{j\theta_{y_r}}\right|}{1+\sum_{r=1}^{M}\xi_r}\sqrt{\frac{\xi_i}{\gamma_i}}\exp\left(\frac{1}{2}\int_{v_i}^{+\infty}\frac{e^{-t}}{t}dt\right), \tag{39}$$

where

$$v_i = \frac{\left|\sum_{r=1}^{M}\sqrt{\xi_r\gamma_r}e^{j\theta_{y_r}}\right|^2}{1+\sum_{r=1}^{M}\xi_r}, \tag{40}$$

and $\xi_i = \sigma_{x_i}^2/\sigma_{n_i}^2$ is the a priori SNR and $\gamma_i = m_{y_i}^2/\sigma_{n_i}^2$ is the a posteriori SNR of channel i.

The gain expression is a generalization of the single-channel cepstral domain approach shown in (Yu, Deng, Droppo, Wu, Gong & Acero (2008)). In fact, setting $M = 1$ yields the single-channel gain function. In addition, equation (39) depends on the fictitious phase terms introduced to obtain the estimator. Uniformly distributed random values will be used during computer simulations.

4.3.2 Feature domain multi-channel MAP estimator (C-M-MAP)

In this section, a feature domain multi-channel MAP estimator is derived. The followed approach is similar to (Lotter et al. (2003)) in extending the frequency MAP estimator to the multi-channel scenario. The use of the MAP estimator is useful because the computational complexity can be reduced respect to the MMSE estimator and DOA independence can be achieved.

A MAP estimate of the MFCC coefficients of channel i can be found by solving the following expression:

$$\widehat{c}_{x_i} = \arg\max_{c_{x_i}} p(c_{x_i}|c_y).$$

(41)

As in Section 4.3.1, MAP estimate on MFCC coefficients is equivalent to an estimate on mel-frequency filter-bank's output power. By means of Bayes rule, the estimate problem becomes

$$\widehat{m}_{x_i} = \arg\max_{m_{x_i}} p(\mathbf{m}_y|m_{x_i})p(m_{x_i}).$$

(42)

Maximization can be performed using (32) and knowing that

$$p(\mathbf{m}_y|m_{x_i}) = \exp\left\{-\sum_{i=1}^{M} \frac{m_{y_i} + (\lambda_i/\lambda_r)^2 (m_{x_i})^2}{\sigma_{n_i}^2}\right\} \prod_{i=1}^{M}\left[\frac{2m_{y_i}}{\sigma_{n_i}^2} I_0\left(\frac{2(\lambda_i/\lambda_r)m_{y_i}m_{x_i}}{\sigma_{n_i}^2}\right)\right],$$

(43)

where conditional independence of m_{y_i} was supposed.

A closed form solution can be found if the modified Bessel function I_0 is approximated as $I_0(x) = (1/\sqrt{2\pi x})e^x$. The final gain expression is:

$$G_i = \frac{\sqrt{\xi_i/\gamma_i}}{2 + 2\sum_{r=1}^{M}\xi_r} \cdot \mathrm{Re}\left[\sum_{r=1}^{M}\sqrt{\xi_r\gamma_r} + \sqrt{\left(\sum_{r=1}^{M}\sqrt{\xi_r\gamma_r}\right)^2 + (2 - M)\left(1 + \sum_{r=1}^{M}\xi_r\right)}\right].$$

(44)

5. Multi-channel histogram equalization

As shown in the previous sections, feature enhancement approaches improve the test signals quality to produce features closer to the clean training ones. Another important class of feature enhancement algorithms is represented by statistical matching methods, according to which feature are normalized through suitable transformations with the objective of making the noisy speech statistics as much close as possible to the clean speech one. The first attempt in this sense has been made with CMN and cepstral mean and variance nomalization (CMVN) (Viikki et al. (2002)). They employ linear transformations that modify the first two moments of noisy observations statistics. Since noise induces a nonlinear distortion on signal feature representation, other approaches oriented to normalize higher-order statistical moments have been proposed (Hsu & Lee (2009); Peinado & Segura (2006)).

In this section the focus is on those methods based on histogram equalization (Garcia et al. (2009); Molau et al. (2003); Peinado & Segura (2006)): it consists in applying a nonlinear transformation based on the clean speech cumulative density function (CDF) to the noisy statistics. As recognition results confirm, the approach is extremely effective but suffers of some drawbacks, which motivated the proposal of some different variants in the literature. One important issue to consider is that the estimation of noisy speech statistics cannot usually rely on sufficient amount of data.

Up to the author's knowledge, no efforts have been put to employ the availability of multichannel acoustic information, coming from a microphone array acquisition, to augment the amount of useful data for statistics modeling and therefore improve the HEQ performances. Such a lack motivated the present work, where original solutions to combine multichannel audio processing and HEQ at a feature-domain level are advanced and experimentally tested.

5.1 Histogram equalization

Histogram equalization is the natural extension of CMN and CVN. Instead of normalizing only a few moments of the MFCCs probability distributions, histogram equalization normalizes all the moments to the ones of a chosen reference distribution. A popular choice for the reference distribution is the normal distribution.

The problem of finding a transformation that maps a given distribution in a reference one is difficult to handle and it does not have a unique solution in the multidimensional scenario. For the mono-dimensional case an unique solution exists and it is obtained by coupling the original and transformed CDFs of the reference and observed feature vectors.

Let y be a random variable with probability distribution $p_y(y)$. Let also x be a random variable with probability distribution $p_x(x)$ such that $x = T_y(y)$, where $T_y(\cdot)$ is a given transformation. If $T_y(\cdot)$ is invertible, it can be shown that the CDFs $C_y(y)$ and $C_x(x)$ of y and x respectively coincide:

$$C_y(y) = \int_{-\infty}^{y} p_y(v)\partial v = \int_{-\infty}^{x=T_y(y)} p_x(v)\partial v = C_x(x). \tag{45}$$

From equation (45), it is easy to obtain the expression of $x = T_y(y)$ from the CDFs of observed and transformed data:

$$C_y(y) = C_x(x) = C_x(T_y(y)), \tag{46}$$

$$x = T_y(y) = C_x^{-1}(C_y(y)). \tag{47}$$

Finally, the relationship between the probability distributions can be obtained from equation (47):

$$p_y(y) = \frac{\partial C_y(y)}{\partial y} = \frac{\partial C_x(T_y(y))}{\partial y} =$$

$$= p_x(T_y(y))\frac{\partial T_y(y)}{\partial y} = p_x(x)\frac{\partial T_y(y)}{\partial y}. \tag{48}$$

Since $C_y(y)$ and $C_x(x)$ are both non-decreasing monotonic functions, the resulting transformation will be a non-linear monotonic increasing function (Segura et al. (2004)).

The CDF $C_x(x)$ can be obtained from the histograms of the observed data. The histogram of every MFCC coefficient is created partitioning the interval $[\mu - 4\sigma, \mu + 4\sigma]$ into 100 uniformly distributed bins B_i, $i = 1, 2, \ldots, 100$, where μ and σ are respectively the mean and standard deviation of the MFCC coefficient to equalize (Segura et al. (2004)). Denoting with Q the number of observations, the PDF can be approximated by its histogram as:

$$p_y(y \in B_i) = \frac{q_i}{Qh} \tag{49}$$

and the CDF as:

$$C_y(y_i) = C_y(y \in B_i) = \sum_{j=1}^{i} \frac{q_j}{Q}, \tag{50}$$

where q_i is the number of observations in the bin B_i and $h = 2\sigma/25$ is the bin width. The center y_i of every bin is then transformed using the inverse of the reference CDF function, i.e. $x = C_x^{-1}(y_i)$. The set of values (y_i, x_i) defines a piecewise linear approximation of the desired transformation. Transformed values are finally obtained by linear interpolation of such tabulated values.

5.2 Multi-channel histogram equalization

One of the well-known problems in histogram equalization is represented by the fact that there is a minimum amount of data per sentence necessary to correctly calculate the needed cumulative densities. Such a problem exists both for reference and noisy CDFs and it is obviously related to the available amount of speech to process. In the former case, we can use the dataset for acoustic model training: several results in literature (De La Torre et al. (2005); Peinado & Segura (2006)) have shown that Gaussian distribution represents a good compromise, specially if the dataset does not provide enough data to suitably represent the speech statistics (as it occurs for Aurora 2 database employed in our simulations). In the latter, the limitation resides in the possibility of using only the utterance to be recognized (like in command recognition task), thus introducing relevant biases in the estimation process. In conversational speech scenarios, is possible to consider a longer observation period, but this inevitably would have a significant impact not only from the perspective of computational burden but also and specially in terms of processing latency, not always acceptable in real-time applications. Of course, the amount of noise presence makes the estimation problem more critical, likely reducing the recognition performances.

The presence of multiple audio channels can be used to alleviate the problem: indeed occurrence of different MFCC sequences, extrapolated by the ASR front-end pipelines fed by the microphone signals, can be exploited to improve the HEQ estimation capabilities. Two different ideas have been investigated on purpose:

- MFCC averaging over all channels;
- alternative CDF computation based on multi-channel audio.

Starting from the former, it is basically assumed that the noise captured by microphones is highly incoherent and far-field model with DOA equal to $0°$ applied to speech signal (see section 6); therefore it is reasonable to suppose of reducing its variance by simply averaging over the channels.

Consider the noisy MFCC signal model (Moreno (1996)) for the i-th channel

$$\mathbf{y}_i = \mathbf{x} + \mathbf{D}\log(1 + \exp(\mathbf{D}^{-1}(\mathbf{n}_i - \mathbf{x})), \tag{51}$$

where $\mathbf{D}$ is the discrete cosine transform matrix and $\mathbf{D}^{-1}$ its inverse: it can be easily shown that the averaging operation reduces the noise variance w.r.t the speech one, thus resulting in an SNR increment. This allows the subsequent HEQ processing, depicted in figure 6, to improve its efficiency.

Coming now to the alternative options for CDF computation, the multi-channel audio information availability cab be exploited as follows (figure 7):

1. histograms are obtained independently for each channel and then all results averaged (CDF Mean);
2. histograms are calculated on the vector obtained concatenating the MFCC vectors of each channel (CDF Conc).

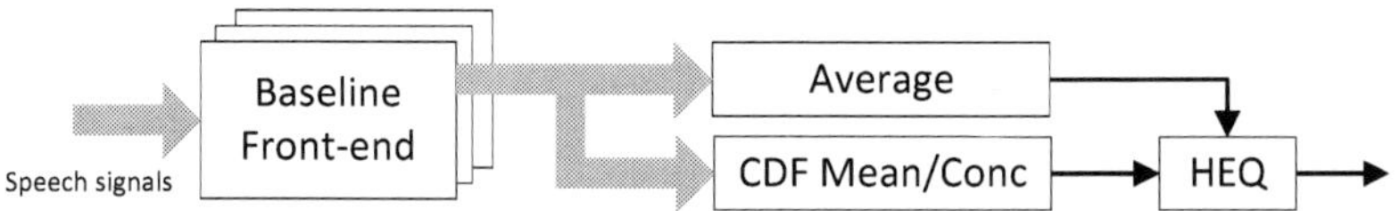

Fig. 7. HEQ MFCCmean CDF mean/conc: HEQ based on averaged MFCCs and mean of CDFs or concatenated signals.

Fig. 6. HEQ MFCCmean: HEQ based on averaged MFCCs.

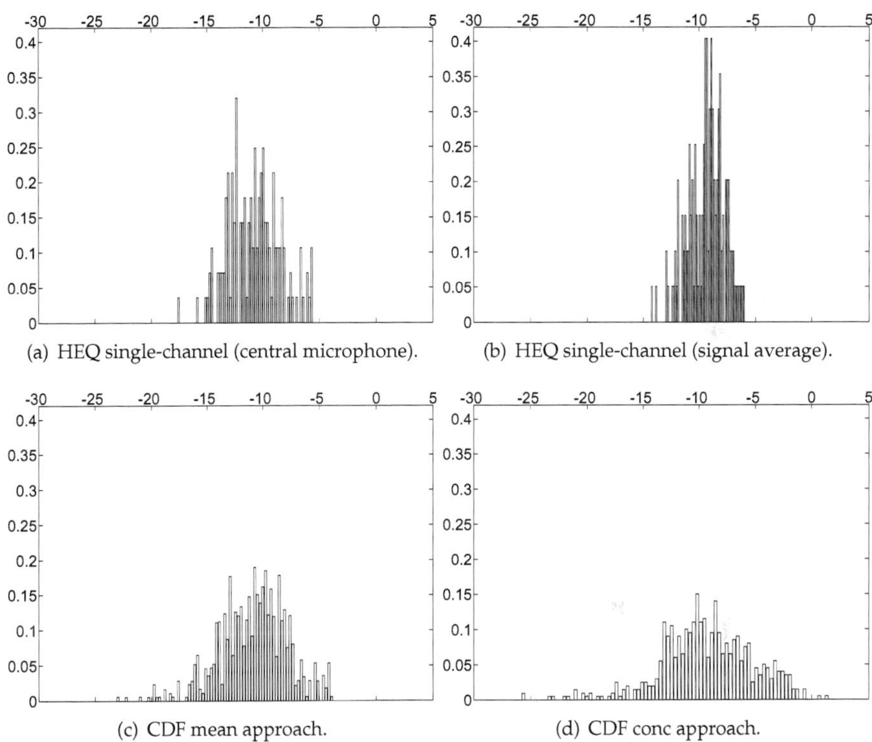

(a) HEQ single-channel (central microphone).

(b) HEQ single-channel (signal average).

(c) CDF mean approach.

(d) CDF conc approach.

Fig. 8. Histograms of cepstral coefficient c_1 related utterance FAK_5A corrupted with car noise at SNR 0 dB. CDF mean and CDF con histograms are estimated using four channels.

The two approaches are equivalent if the bins used to build the histogram coincide. However, in the CDF Mean approach, taking the average of the bin centers as well, gives slightly smoother histograms which helps the equalization process. Whatever the estimation algorithm, equalization has to be accomplished taking into account that the MFCC sequence used as input in the HEQ transformation must fit the more accurate statistical estimation performed, otherwise outliers occurrence due to noise contribution could degrade the performance: this explains the usage of the aforementioned MFCC averaging.

Figure 8 shows histograms of single-channel and multi-channel approaches of the first cepstral coefficient using four microphones in far-field model. Bins are calculated as described in section 5.1. A short utterance of length 1.16 s has been chosen to emphasize the difference in histogram estimation in single and multi-channel approaches. Indeed, histograms of multi-channel configurations depicted in figure 7 better represent the underlying distribution (figure 8(c)-(d)) specially looking at the distribution tails, not properly rendered by the other approaches. This is due to availability of multiple signals corrupted by incoherent noise, which augments the observations available for the estimation of noisy feature distributions. Such a behavior is particularly effective at low SNRs, as recognition results in section 6 will demonstrate.

Note that operations described above are done independently for each cepstral coefficient: such an assumption is widely accepted and used among scientist working with statistics normalization for robust ASR.

6. Computer Simulations

In this section the computer simulations carried out to evaluate the performance of the algorithms previously described are reported. The work done in (Lotter et al. (2003)) has been taken as reference: simulations have been conducted considering the source signal in far-field model (see equation (2)) with respect to an array of $M = 4$ microphones with distance $d = 12$ cm. The source is located at 25 cm from the microphone array. The near-field and reverberant case studies will be considered in future works.

Three values of θ_x have been tested: $0°$, $10°$ and $60°$. Delayed signals have been obtained by suitably filtering the clean utterances of tests A, B and C of the Aurora 2 database (Hirsch & Pearce (2000)). Subsequently, noisy utterances in test A, B and C were obtained from the delayed signals by adding the same noises of Aurora 2 test A, B and C respectively. For each noise, signals with SNR in the range of 0-20 dB have been generated using tools (Hirsch & Pearce (2000)) provided with Aurora 2.

Automatic speech recognition has been performed using the Hidden Markov Model Toolkit (HTK) (Young et al. (1999)). Acoustic models structure and recognition parameters are the same as in (Hirsch & Pearce (2000)). The feature vectors are composed of 13 MFCCs (with C0 and without energy) and their first and second derivatives. Acoustic model training has been performed in a single-channel scenario and applying each algorithm in its insertion point of the ASR front-end pipeline as described in section 2. "Clean" and "Multicondition" acoustic models have been created using the provided training sets.

For the sake of comparison, in table 3 are reported the recognition results using the baseline feature extraction pipeline and the DSB. In using DSB the exact knowledge of the DOAs which leads to a perfect signal alignment is assumed. Recalling the model assumption made in section 2, since the DSB performs the mean over all the channels it reduces the variance of the noise providing higher performance than the baseline case. The obtained results can be employed to better evaluate the improvement arising from the insertion of the feature enhancement algorithms presented in this chapter.

	Test A		Test B		Test C		A-B-C AVG	
	C	M	C	M	C	M	C	M
baseline ($\beta_x = 0°$)	63.56	83.18	65.87	84.91	67.93	86.27	65.79	84.78
DSB	76.50	93.12	79.86	94.13	81.47	94.96	79.27	94.07

Table 3. Results for both baseline feature-extraction pipeline and DSB

6.1 Multi-channel bayesian estimator

Tests have been conducted on algorithms described in Sections 4.2 and 4.3, as well as on their single-channel counterpart. The results obtained with the log-MMSE estimator (LSA) and its cepstral extension (C-LSA), and those obtained with frequency and feature domain MAP single-channel estimators are also reported for comparison purpose.

Frequency domain results in table 4 show as expected that the multi-channel MMSE algorithm gives the best performance when $\beta_x = 0°$, while accuracy degrades as β_x increases. Results in table 5 confirm the DOA independence of multi-channel MAP: averaging on β_x and acoustic models, recognition accuracy is increased of 11.32% compared to the baseline feature extraction pipeline. Good performance of multi-channel frequency domain algorithms confirm the segmental SNR results in (Lotter et al. (2003)).

On clean acoustic model, feature domain multi-channel MMSE algorithm gives a recognition accuracy around 73% regardless of the value of β_x (table 6). Accuracy is below the single-channel MMSE algorithm, and differently from its frequency domain counterpart it is DOA independent. This behaviour is probably due to the presence of artificial phases in the gain expression. The multi-channel MAP algorithm is, as expected, independent of the value of β_x, and while it gives lower accuracies respect to F-M-MMSE and F-M-MAP algorithms, it outperforms both the frequency and feature domain single-channel approaches (table 7).

	Test A		Test B		Test C		A-B-C AVG	
	C	M	C	M	C	M	C	M
F-M-MMSE ($\beta_x = 0°$)	84.23	93.89	83.73	92.19	87.10	94.71	85.02	93.60
F-M-MMSE ($\beta_x = 10°$)	80.91	92.61	81.10	91.19	84.78	93.78	82.26	92.53
F-M-MMSE ($\beta_x = 60°$)	70.83	88.29	71.84	86.50	76.68	91.67	73.12	88.82
LSA	76.83	87.02	77.06	85.24	78.97	88.48	77.62	86.91

Table 4. Results of frequency domain MMSE-based algorithms

	Test A		Test B		Test C		A-B-C AVG	
	C	M	C	M	C	M	C	M
F-M-MAP ($\beta_x = 0°$)	82.52	89.62	82.13	88.29	86.11	91.30	83.59	89.73
F-M-MAP ($\beta_x = 10°$)	82.20	89.46	81.93	88.00	85.84	90.39	83.32	89.28
F-M-MAP ($\beta_x = 60°$)	82.39	89.36	82.07	88.05	86.13	90.38	83.53	89.26
MAP	75.95	84.97	76.29	82.81	77.75	85.72	76.66	84.44

Table 5. Results of frequency domain MAP-based algorithms

	Test A		Test B		Test C		A-B-C AVG	
	C	M	C	M	C	M	C	M
C-M-MMSE ($\beta_x = 0°$)	70.80	89.94	73.00	88.75	75.37	92.02	72.96	90.23
C-M-MMSE ($\beta_x = 10°$)	70.40	89.68	72.88	88.72	75.21	91.89	72.83	90.10
C-M-MMSE ($\beta_x = 60°$)	70.72	89.69	72.77	88.80	75.19	91.93	72.89	90.14
C-LSA	75.68	87.81	77.06	86.85	76.94	89.25	76.56	87.97

Table 6. Results of feature domain MMSE-based algorithms

	Test A		Test B		Test C		A-B-C AVG	
	C	M	C	M	C	M	C	M
C-M-MAP ($\beta_x = 0°$)	78.52	91.51	79.28	89.99	81.63	93.04	79.81	91.51
C-M-MAP ($\beta_x = 10°$)	78.13	91.22	79.04	89.94	81.59	92.68	79.52	91.28
C-M-MAP ($\beta_x = 60°$)	78.23	91.22	79.04	90.07	81.38	92.68	79.55	91.32
C-MAP	74.62	88.44	76.84	87.67	75.61	89.58	75.69	88.56

Table 7. Results of feature domain MAP-based algorithms

To summarize, computer simulations conducted on a modified Aurora 2 speech database showed the DOA independence of the C-M-MMSE algorithm, differently from its frequency domain counterpart, and poor recognition accuracy probably due to the presence of random phases in the gain expression. On the contrary, results of the C-M-MAP algorithm confirm, as expected, its DOA independence and show that it outperforms single-channel algorithms in both frequency and feature domain.

6.2 Multi-channel histogram equalization

Experimental results for all tested algorithmic configurations are reported in tables 8 and 9 in terms of recognition accuracy. Table 10 shows results for different values of β_x and number of channels for the MFCC CDF Mean algorithm: since the other configurations behave similarly, results are not reported. Focusing on "clean" acoustic model results, the following conclusions can be drawn:

- No significant variability with DOA is registered (table 8): this represents a remarkable result, specially if compared with the MMSE approach in (Lotter et al. (2003)) where such a dependence is much more evident. This means that no delay compensation procedure have to be accomplished at ASR front-end input level. A similar behaviour can be observed both in the multi-channel mel domain approach of (Principi, Rotili, Cifani, Marinelli, Squartini & Piazza (2010)), and in the frequency domain MAP approach of (Lotter et al. (2003)), where phase information is not exploited.

- Recognition rate improvements are concentrated at low SNRs (table 9): this can be explained by observing that the MFCC averaging operation significantly reduces the feature variability leading to computational problems in correspondence of CDF extrema values when nonlinear transformation (47) is applied.

- As shown in table 10, the average of MFCCs over different channels is beneficial when applied with HEQ: in this case we can also take advantage of the CDF averaging process or of the CDF calculation based on MFCC channel vectors concatenation. Note that the improvement is proportional to the number of audio channels employed (up to 10% of accuracy improvement w.r.t. the HEQ single-channel approach).

In the "Multicondition" case study, the MFCCmean approach is the best performing and improvements are less consistent than the "Clean" case but still significative (up to 3% of accuracy improvement w.r.t. the HEQ single-channel approach). For the sake of completeness, it must be said that similar simulations have been performed using the average on the mel coefficients, so before the log operation (see figure 1): the same conclusions as above can be drawn, even though performances are approximatively and on the average 2% less than those obtained with MFCC based configurations.

In both "Clean" and "Multicondition" case the usage of the DSB as pre-processing stage for the HEQ algorithm leads to a sensible performance improvement with regard to the only single-channel HEQ. The configuration with the DSB and the single channel HEQ have been tested in order to compare the effect of averaging the channels in the time domain or in the MFCC domain. As shown in table 8, the DSB + HEQ outperform the HEQ MFCCmean CDFMean/CDFconc algorithms but it must be pointed out that in using the DSB a perfect DOAs estimation is assumed. In this sense the obtained results can be seen as reference for future implementations, where a DOA estimation algorithm is employed with the DSB.

(a) Clean acoustic model

	$\beta_x = 0°$	$\beta_x = 10°$	$\beta_x = 60°$
HEQ MFCCmean	85.75	85.71	85.57
HEQ MFCCmean CDFMean	90.68	90.43	90.47
HEQ MFCCmean CDFconc	90.58	90.33	91.36
HEQ Single-channel	81.07		
DSB + HEQ Single-channel	92.74		
Clean signals	99.01		

(b) Multicondition acoustic model

	$\beta_x = 0°$	$\beta_x = 10°$	$\beta_x = 60°$
HEQ MFCCmean	94.56	94.45	94.32
HEQ MFCCmean CDFMean	93.60	93.54	93.44
HEQ MFCCmean CDFconc	92.51	92.48	92.32
HEQ Single-channel	90.65		
DSB + HEQ Single-channel	96.89		
Clean signals	97.94		

Table 8. Results for HEQ algorithms: accuracy is averaged across Test A, B and C.

	0 dB	5 dB	10 dB	15 dB	20 dB	AVG
HEQ MFCCmean	66.47	82.63	89.96	93.72	95.96	85.74
HEQ MFCC CDFmean	73.62	89.54	95.09	97.02	98.18	90.69
HEQ MFCCmean CDFconc	72.98	89.42	95.23	97.16	98.14	90.58
HEQ Single-channel	47.31	76.16	89.93	94.90	97.10	81.78

Table 9. Recognition results for Clean acoustic model and $\beta_x = 0°$: accuracy is averaged across Test A, B and C.

	2 Channels		4 Channels		8 Channels	
	C	M	C	M	C	M
0°	88.27	93.32	90.68	93.60	91.44	93.64
10°	87.97	93.18	90.39	93.44	91.19	93.46
60°	87.81	92.95	90.43	93.43	91.32	93.52

Table 10. Results for different values of β_x and number of channels for the HEQ MFCC CDFmean configuration. "C" denotes clean whereas "M" multi-condition acoustic models. Accuracy is averaged across Test A, B and C.

7. Conclusions

In this chapter, different multi-channel feature enhancement algorithms for robust speech recognition were presented and their performances have been tested by means of the Aurora 2 speech database suitably modified to deal with the multi-channel case study in a far-field acoustic scenario. Three are the approaches here addressed, each one operating at a different level of the common speech feature extraction front-end, and comparatively analyzed: beamforming, bayesian estimators and histogram equalization.

Due to the far-field assumption, the only beamforming technique here addressed is the delay and sum beamformer. Supposing that the DOA is ideally estimated, DSB improves recognition performances both alone as well as coupled with single-channel HEQ. Future works will investigate DSB performances when DOA estimation is carried out by a suitable algorithm.

Considering bayesian estimators, the multi-channel feature-domain MMSE and MAP estimators extend the frequency domain multi-channel approaches in (Lotter et al. (2003)) and generalize the feature-domain single-channel MMSE algorithm in (Yu, Deng, Droppo, Wu, Gong & Acero (2008)). Computer simulations showed the DOA independence of the C-M-MMSE algorithm, differently from its frequency domain counterpart, and poor recognition accuracy probably due to the presence of random phases in the gain expression. On the contrary, results of the C-M-MAP algorithm confirm, as expected, its DOA independence and show that it outperforms single-channel algorithms both in frequency and feature-domain.

Moving towards the statistical matching methods, the impact of multi-channel occurrences of same speech source in histogram equalization has been also addressed. It has been shown that averaging both the cepstral coefficients related to different audio channels and the cumulative density functions of the noisy observations allow augmenting the equalization capabilities in terms of recognition performances (up to 10% of word accuracy improvement using clean acoustic model), with no need of worrying about the speech signal direction of arrival.

Further works are also intended to establish what happens in near-field and reverberant conditions. Moreover, the promising HEQ based approach could be extended to other histogram equalization variants, like segmental HEQ (SHEQ) (Segura et al. (2004)), kernel-based methods (Suh et al. (2008)) and parametric equalization (PEQ) (Garcia et al. (2006)), which the proposed idea can be effectively applied.

Finally, due to the fact of operating in different domains, it is possible to envisage of suitably merge the three approaches here addressed in a unique performing noise robust speech feature extractor.

8. References

Atal, B. (1974). Effectiveness of linear prediction characteristics of the speech wave for automatic speaker identification and verification, *the Journal of the Acoustical Society of America* 55: 1304.

Boll, S. (1979). Suppression of acoustic noise in speech using spectral subtraction, *IEEE Transactions on Acoustics, Speech and Signal Processing* 27(2): 113–120.

Chen, B. & Loizou, P. (2007). A Laplacian-based MMSE estimator for speech enhancement, *Speech communication* 49(2): 134–143.

Cifani, S., Principi, E., Rocchi, C., Squartini, S. & Piazza, F. (2008). A multichannel noise reduction front-end based on psychoacoustics for robust speech recognition in highly noisy environments, *Proc. of IEEE Hands-Free Speech Communication and Microphone Arrays*, pp. 172–175.

Cohen, I. (2004). Relative transfer function identification using speech signals, *Speech and Audio Processing, IEEE Transactions on* 12(5): 451–459.

Cohen, I., Gannot, S. & Berdugo, B. (2003). An integrated real-time beamforming and postfiltering system for nonstationary noise environments, *EURASIP Journal on Applied Signal Processing* 11: 1064?1073.

Cox, H., Zeskind, R. & Owen, M. (1987). Robust adaptive beamforming, *Acoustics, Speech, and Signal Processing, IEEE Transactions on* 35: 1365–1376.

De La Torre, A., Peinado, A., Segura, J., Perez-Cordoba, J., Benítez, M. & Rubio, A. (2005). Histogram equalization of speech representation for robust speech recognition, *Speech and Audio Processing, IEEE Transactions on* 13(3): 355–366.

Deng, L., Droppo, J. & Acero, A. (2004). Estimating Cepstrum of Speech Under the Presence of Noise Using a Joint Prior of Static and Dynamic Features, *IEEE Transactions on Speech and Audio Processing* 12(3): 218–233.
    URL: *http://ieeexplore.ieee.org/lpdocs/epic03/wrapper.htm?arnumber=1288150*

Ephraim, Y. & Malah, D. (1984). Speech enhancement using a minimum-mean square error short-time spectral amplitude estimator, *Acoustics, Speech and Signal Processing, IEEE Transactions on* 32(6): 1109–1121.

Ephraim, Y. & Malah, D. (1985). Speech enhancement using a minimum mean-square error log-spectral amplitude estimator, *IEEE Transactions on Acoustics, Speech, and Signal Processing* 33(2): 443–445.

Figueiredo, M. & Jain, A. (2002). Unsupervised learning of finite mixture models, *Pattern Analysis and Machine Intelligence, IEEE Transactions on* 24(3): 381 –396.

Gales, M. & Young, S. (2002). An improved approach to the hidden Markov model decomposition of speech and noise, *Acoustics, Speech, and Signal Processing, 1992. ICASSP-92., 1992 IEEE International Conference on*, Vol. 1, IEEE, pp. 233–236.

Gannot, S., Burshtein, D. & Weinstein, E. (2001). Signal enhancement using beamforming and nonstationarity with applications to speech, *Signal Processing, IEEE Transactions on* 49(8): 1614–1626.

Gannot, S. & Cohen, I. (2004). Speech enhancement based on the general transfer function gsc and postfiltering, *Speech and Audio Processing, IEEE Transactions on* 12(6): 561–571.

Garcia, L., Gemello, R., Mana, F. & Segura, J. (2009). Progressive memory-based parametric non-linear feature equalization, *INTERSPEECH*, pp. 40–43.

Garcia, L., Segura, J., Ramirez, J., De La Torre, A. & Benitez, C. (2006). Parametric nonlinear feature equalization for robust speech recognition, *Proc. of ICASSP 2006*, Vol. 1, pp. I –I.

Garofalo, J., Graff, D., Paul, D. & Pallett, D. (1993). CSR-I (WSJ0) Complete, *Linguistic Data Consortium* .

Gazor, S. & Zhang, W. (2003). Speech probability distribution, *Signal Processing Letters, IEEE* 10(7): 204 – 207.

Gong, Y. (1995). Speech recognition in noisy environments: A survey, *Speech communication* 16(3): 261–291.

Gradshteyn, I. & Ryzhik, I. (2007). *Table of Integrals, Series, and Products, Seventh ed.*, Alan Jeffrey and Daniel Zwillinger (Editors) - Elsevier Academic Press.

Griffiths, L. & Jim, C. (1982). An alternative approach to linearly constrained adaptive beamforming, *Antennas Propagation, IEEE Transactions on* 30(1): 27–34.

Hendriks, R. & Martin, R. (2007). MAP estimators for speech enhancement under normal and Rayleigh inverse Gaussian distributions, *Audio, Speech, and Language Processing, IEEE Transactions on* 15(3): 918–927.

Herbordt, W., Buchner, H., Nakamura, S. & Kellermann, W. (2007). Multichannel bin-wise robust frequency-domain adaptive filtering and its application to adaptive beamforming, *Audio, Speech and Language Processing, IEEE Transactions on* 15(4): 1340–1351.

Herbordt, W. & Kellermann, W. (2001). Computationally efficient frequency-domain combination of acoustic echo cancellation and robust adaptive beamforming, *Proc. of EUROSPEECH*.

Hirsch, H. & Pearce, D. (2000). The aurora experimental framework for the performance speech recognition systems under noise conditions, *Proc. of ISCA ITRW ASR, Paris, France*.

Hoshuyama, O., Sugiyama, A. & Hirano, A. (1999). A robust adaptive beamformer for microphone arrays with a blocking matrix using constrained adaptive filters, *Signal Processing, IEEE Transactions on* 47(10): 2677–2684.

Hsu, C.-W. & Lee, L.-S. (2009). Higher order cepstral moment normalization for improved robust speech recognition, *Audio, Speech, and Language Processing, IEEE Transactions on* 17(2): 205 –220.

Hussain, A., Chetouani, M., Squartini, S., Bastari, A. & Piazza, F. (2007). Nonlinear Speech Enhancement: An Overview, *in* Y. Stylianou, M. Faundez-Zanuy & A. Esposito (eds), *Progress in Nonlinear Speech Processing*, Vol. 4391 of *Lecture Notes in Computer Science*, Springer Berlin / Heidelberg, pp. 217–248.

Hussain, A., Cifani, S., Squartini, S., Piazza, F. & Durrani, T. (2007). A novel psychoacoustically motivated multichannel speech enhancement system, *Verbal and Nonverbal Communication Behaviours, A. Esposito, M. Faundez-Zanuy, E. Keller, M. Marinaro (Eds.), Lecture Notes in Computer Science Series, Springer Verlag* 4775: 190–199.

Indrebo, K., Povinelli, R. & Johnson, M. (2008). Minimum Mean-Squared Error Estimation of Mel-Frequency Cepstral Coefficients Using a Novel Distortion Model, *Audio, Speech, and Language Processing, IEEE Transactions on* 16(8): 1654–1661.

Jensen, J., Batina, I., Hendriks, R. & Heusdens, R. (2005). A study of the distribution of time-domain speech samples and discrete fourier coefficients, *Proceedings of SPS-DARTS 2005 (The first annual IEEE BENELUX/DSP Valley Signal Processing Symposium)*, pp. 155–158.

Leonard, R. (1984). A database for speaker-independent digit recognition, *Acoustics, Speech, and Signal Processing, IEEE International Conference on ICASSP '84.*, Vol. 9, pp. 328 – 331.

Li, J., Deng, L., Yu, D., Gong, Y. & Acero, A. (2009). A unified framework of HMM adaptation with joint compensation of additive and convolutive distortions, *Computer Speech & Language* 23(3): 389–405.

Lippmann, R., Martin, E. & Paul, D. (2003). Multi-style training for robust isolated-word speech recognition, *Acoustics, Speech, and Signal Processing, IEEE International Conference on ICASSP'87.*, Vol. 12, IEEE, pp. 705–708.

Lotter, T., Benien, C. & Vary, P. (2003). Multichannel direction-independent speech enhancement using spectral amplitude estimation, *EURASIP Journal on Applied Signal Processing* pp. 1147–1156.

Lotter, T. & Vary, P. (2005). Speech enhancement by MAP spectral amplitude estimation using a super-Gaussian speech model, *EURASIP Journal on Applied Signal Processing* 2005: 1110–1126.

McAulay, R. & Malpass, M. (1980). Speech enhancement using a soft-decision noise suppression filter, *Acoustics, Speech and Signal Processing, IEEE Transactions on* 28(2): 137 – 145.

Molau, S., Hilger, F. & Ney, H. (2003). Feature space normalization in adverse acoustic conditions, *Acoustics, Speech, and Signal Processing, 2003. Proceedings.(ICASSP'03). 2003 IEEE International Conference on*, Vol. 1, IEEE.

Moreno, P. (1996). *Speech recognition in noisy environments*, PhD thesis, Carnegie Mellon University.

Omologo, M., Matassoni, M., Svaizer, P. & Giuliani, D. (1997). Microphone array based speech recognition with different talker-array positions, *Proc. of ICASSP*, pp. 227–230.

Peinado, A. & Segura, J. (2006). Speech recognition with hmms, *Speech Recognition Over Digital Channels*, pp. 7–14.

Principi, E., Cifani, S., Rotili, R., Squartini, S. & Piazza, F. (2010). Comparative evaluation of single-channel mmse-based noise reduction schemes for speech recognition, *Journal of Electrical and Computer Engineering* 2010: 1–7.
URL: *http://www.hindawi.com/journals/jece/2010/962103.html*

Principi, E., Rotili, R., Cifani, S., Marinelli, L., Squartini, S. & Piazza, F. (2010). Robust speech recognition using feature-domain multi-channel bayesian estimators, *Circuits and Systems (ISCAS), Proceedings of 2010 IEEE International Symposium on*, pp. 2670 –2673.

Redner, R. A. & Walker, H. F. (1984). Mixture densities, maximum likelihood and the em algorithm, *SIAM Review* 26(2): 195–239.

Rotili, R., Principi, E., Cifani, S., Squartini, S. & Piazza, F. (2009). Robust speech recognition using MAP based noise suppression rules in the feature domain, *Proc. of 19th Czech & German Workshop on Speech Processing*, Prague, pp. 35–41.

Segura, J., Benitez, C., De La Torre, A., Rubio, A. & Ramirez, J. (2004). Cepstral domain segmental nonlinear feature transformations for robust speech recognition, *IEEE Signal Process. Lett.* 11(5).

Seltzer, M. (2003). *Microphone array processing for robust speech recognition*, PhD thesis, Carnegie Mellon University.

Shalvi, O. & Weinstein, E. (1996). System identification using nonstationary signals, *Signal Processing, IEEE Transactions on* 44(8): 2055–2063.

Squartini, S., Fagiani, M., Principi, E. & Piazza, F. (2010). Multichannel Cepstral Domain Feature Warping for Robust Speech Recognition, *Proceedings of WIRN 2010, 19th Italian Workshop on Neural Networks May 28-30, Vietri sul Mare, Salerno, Italy.*

Stouten, V. (2006). Robust automatic speech recognition in time-varying environments, *KU Leuven, Diss* .

Suh, Y., Kim, H. & Kim, M. (2008). Histogram equalization utilizing window-based smoothed CDF estimation for feature compensation, *IEICE - Trans. Inf. Syst.* E91-D(8): 2199–2202.

Trees, H. L. V. (2001). *Detection, Estimation, and Modulation Theory, Part I*, Wiley-Interscience.

Viikki, O., Bye, D. & Laurila, K. (2002). A recursive feature vector normalization approach for robust speech recognition in noise, *Acoustics, Speech and Signal Processing, 1998. Proceedings of the 1998 IEEE International Conference on*, Vol. 2, IEEE, pp. 733–736.

Wolfe, P. & Godsill, S. (2000). Towards a perceptually optimal spectral amplitude estimator for audio signal enhancement, *Proc. of IEEE ICASSP*, Vol. 2, pp. 821–824.

Wolfe, P. & Godsill, S. (2003). Efficient alternatives to the ephraim and malah suppression rule for audio signal enhancement, *EURASIP Journal Applied Signal Processing* 2003: 1043–1051.

Young, S., Kershaw, D., Odell, J., Ollason, D., Valtchev, V. & Woodland, P. (1999). *The HTK Book. V2.2*, Cambridge University.

Yu, D., Deng, L., Droppo, J., Wu, J., Gong, Y. & Acero, A. (2008). Robust speech recognition using a cepstral minimum-mean-square-error-motivated noise suppressor, *Audio, Speech, and Language Processing, IEEE Transactions on* 16(5): 1061–1070.

Yu, D., Deng, L., Wu, J., Gong, Y. & Acero, A. (2008). Improvements on Mel-frequency cepstrum minimum-mean-square-error noise suppressor for robust speech recognition, *Chinese Spoken Language Processing, 2008. ISCSLP'08. 6th International Symposium on*, IEEE, pp. 1–4.

2

Real-time Hardware Feature Extraction with Embedded Signal Enhancement for Automatic Speech Recognition

Vinh Vu Ngoc, James Whittington and John Devlin
La Trobe University
Australia

1. Introduction

The concept of using speech for communicating with computers and other machines has been the vision of humans for decades. User input via speech promises overwhelming advantages compared with standard input/output peripherals, such as, mouse, keyboard, and buttons. To make this vision a reality, considerable effort and investment into automatic speech recognition (ASR) research has been conducted for over six decades. While current speech recognition systems perform very well in benign environments, their performance is rather limited in many real-world settings. One of the main degrading factors in these systems is background noise collected along with the wanted speech.

There are a wide range of possible uncorrelated noise sources. They are generally short lived and non-stationary. For example in the automotive environments, noise sources can be road noise, engine noise, or passing vehicles that compete with the speech. Noise can also be continuous, such as, wind noise, particularly from an open window, or noise from a ventilation or air conditioning unit.

To make speech recognition systems more robust, there are a number of methods being investigated. These include the use of robust feature extraction and recognition algorithms as well as speech enhancement. Enhancement techniques aim to remove (or at least reduce) the levels of noise present in the speech signals, allowing clean speech models to be utilised in the recognition stage. This is a popular approach as little-or-no prior knowledge of the operating environment is required for improvements in recognition accuracy.

While many ASR and enhancement algorithms or models have been proposed, an issue of how to implement them efficiently still remains. Many software implementations of the algorithms exist, but they are limited in application as they require relatively powerful general purpose processors. To achieve a real-time design with both low-cost and high performance, a dedicated hardware implementation is necessary.

This chapter presents the design of a Real-time Hardware Feature Extraction System with Embedded Signal Enhancement for Automatic Speech Recognition appropriate for implementation in low-cost Field Programmable Gate Array (FPGA) hardware. While suitable for many other applications, the design inspiration was for automotive applications, requiring real-time, low-cost hardware without sacrificing performance. Main components of this design are: an efficient implementation of the Discrete Fourier Transform (DFT), speech enhancement, and Mel-Frequency Cepstrum Coefficients (MFCC) feature extraction.

2. Speech enhancement

The automotive environment is one of the most challenging environments for real-world speech processing applications. It contains a wide variety of interfering noise, such as engine noise and wind noise, which are inevitable and may change suddenly and continually. These noise signals make the process of acquiring high quality speech in such environments very difficult. Consequently, hands-free telephones or devices using speech-recognition-based controls, operate less reliably in the automotive environment than in other environments, such as in an office. Hence, the use speech enhancement for improving the intelligibility and quality of degraded speech signals in such environments has received increasing interest over the past few decades (Benesty et al., 2005; Ortega-Garcia & Gonzalez-Rodriguez, 1996).

The rationale behind speech enhancement algorithms is to reduce the noise level present in speech signals (Benesty et al., 2005). Noise-reduced signals are then utilized to train clean speech models, and as a result, effective and robust recognition models may be produced for speech recognizers. Approaches of this sort are common in speech processing since they require little-to-no prior knowledge of the operating environment to improve the recognition performance of the speech recognizers.

Based on the number of microphone signals used, speech enhancement techniques can be categorized into two classes, single-channel (Berouti et al., 1979; Boll, 1979; Lockwood & Boudy, 1992) and multi-channel (Lin et al., 1994; Widrow & Stearns, 1985). Single channel techniques utilize signals from a single microphone. Most techniques on noise reduction belong to this category, including spectral subtraction (Berouti et al., 1979; Boll, 1979) which is one of the traditional methods.

Alternatively, multi-channel speech enhancement techniques combine acoustic signals from two or more microphones to perform spatial filtering. The use of multiple microphones provides the ability to adjust or steer the beam to focus the acquisition on the location of a specific signal source. Multi-channel techniques can also enhance signals with low signal to noise ratio due to the inclusion of multiple independent transducers (Johnson & Dudgeon, 1992). Recently, dual microphone speech enhancement has been applied to many cost sensitive applications as it has similar benefits to schemes using many microphones, while still being cost-effective to implement (Aarabi & Shi, 2004; Ahn & Ko, 2005; Beh et al., 2006).

With the focus on the incorporation of a real-time low-cost but effective speech enhancement system for automotive speech recognition, two speech enhancement algorithms are discussed in this chapter. These are Linear Spectral Subtraction (LSS) and Delay-and-Sum Beamforming (DASB). The selection was made based on the simplicity and effectiveness of the algorithms for automotive applications. The LSS works well for speech signals contaminated with stationary noise such as engine and road noise, while the DASB can perform effectively when the location of signal sources (speakers) are specified, for example, the driver. Each algorithm can work in standalone mode or cascaded.

Before discussing these speech enhancement algorithms in detail, common speech preprocessing is first described.

2.1 Speech preprocessing and the Discrete Fourier Transform
2.1.1 Speech preprocessing

Most speech processing algorithms perform their operations in the frequency domain. In these cases, speech preprocessing is required. Speech preprocessing uses the DFT to transform speech from a time domain into a frequency domain. A general approach for processing speech signals in the frequency domain is presented in Figure 1.

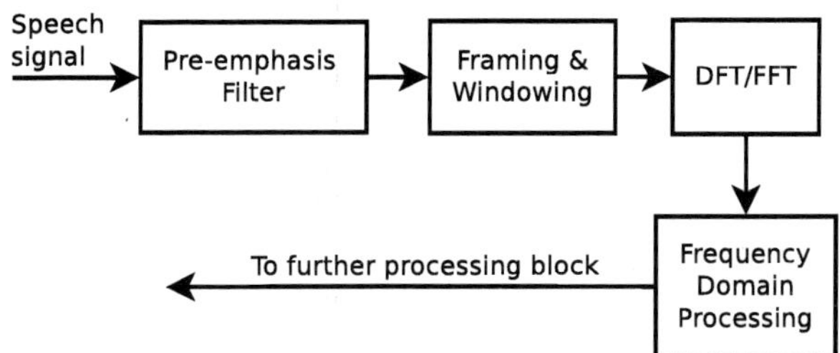

Fig. 1. Block diagram of basic speech processing in the frequency domain

Speech signals, acquired via a microphone, are passed through a pre-emphasis filter, which is normally a first-order linear filter. This filter ensures a flatter signal spectrum by boosting the amplitude of high frequency components of the original signals.
Each boosted signal from the pre-emphasis filter is then decomposed into a series of frames using square sliding windows with frame advances typically being 50% of the frame length. The length of a frame is normally $32ms$ which has 512 samples at 16Khz sampled rate. To attenuate discontinuities at frame edges, a cosine window is then applied to each overlapping frame. A common window used in speech recognition is the Hamming window.
The framing operation is followed by the application of the DFT, in which time-domain acoustic waveforms of the frames are transformed into discrete frequency representations. The frequency-domain representation of each frame in turn is then used as inputs of the Frequency Domain Processing (FDP) block, where signals are improved by speech enhancement techniques and a speech parametric representation is extracted by the speech recognition front-end.

2.1.2 DFT algorithm
The discrete transform for the real input sequence x $\{x(0), x(1), \cdots, x(N-1)\}^T$ is defined as:

$$X(k) \sum_{n=0}^{N-1} x(n)e^{\frac{-j2\pi kn}{N}}, k = 0, 1, \ldots, N-1. \tag{1}$$

In practice, the above DFT formula is composed of *sine* and *cosine* elements:

$$X_{Re}(k) = \sum_{n=0}^{N-1} x(n)\cos(\frac{2\pi kn}{N}), \tag{2}$$

$$X_{Im}(k) = \sum_{n=0}^{N-1} x(n)\sin(\frac{2\pi kn}{N}), \tag{3}$$

where *Re* and *Im* represent the real and imaginary parts of DFT coefficients.
The two formulas (2) and (3) can be implemented directly in FPGA hardware using two MAC (Multiplier and Accumulator) blocks which are embedded in many low-cost FPGA devices. Figure 2 shows the structure of this implementation for either a real or imaginary component. As shown in the figure, the multiplier and the accumulator are elements of one MAC hardware primitive. Therefore, the direct implementation of the DFT formula on FPGA hardware results in a simple design requiring only modest hardware resources. However, it does result in a considerably long latency ($2N^2$ multiplications and $2N^2$ additions).

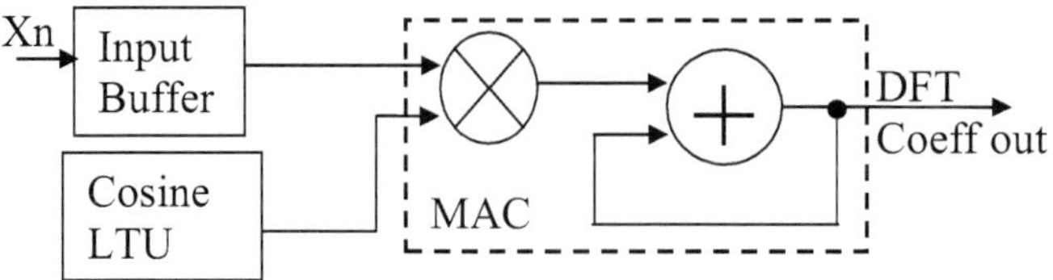

Fig. 2. Hardware structure of direct DFT implementation

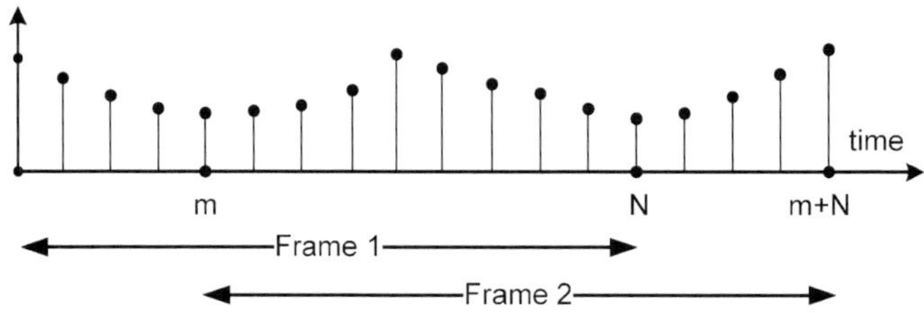

Fig. 3. Overlapped frames

2.1.3 Utilizing overlapping frames property in DFT to reduce latency

Figure 3 shows an example of two overlapped frames: F_1 and F_2. F_2 overlaps $N - m$ samples with the previous frame (F_1). It is expected that computations for those $N - m$ samples from the previous frame (F_1) can be reused for the current frame (F_2). In this way, significant computation, and thus latency, can be saved.

Based on frame F_1 and F_2 mentioned above (Figure 3), the algorithm can be described simply as follows.

In order to utilize the 50% overlapping frames feature, the DFT of Frame F_1 is

$$X_1(k) = \sum_{n=0}^{\frac{N}{2}-1} x(n)e^{\frac{-j2\pi kn}{N}} + \sum_{n=\frac{N}{2}}^{N-1} x(n)e^{\frac{-j2\pi kn}{N}}. \tag{4}$$

Similarly, the DFT of Frame F_2 is

$$X_2(k) = \sum_{n=0}^{\frac{N}{2}-1} x(n+\frac{N}{2})e^{\frac{-j2\pi kn}{N}} + \sum_{n=\frac{N}{2}}^{N-1} x(n+\frac{N}{2})e^{\frac{-j2\pi kn}{N}}. \tag{5}$$

In short, formulas (4) and (5) can be respectively inferred as:

$$X_1(k) = A + B, \tag{6}$$

and

$$X_2(k) = C + D. \tag{7}$$

If n in term C is substituted by $n = i - \frac{N}{2}$, then:

$$C = \sum_{i=\frac{N}{2}}^{N-1} x(i)e^{\frac{-j2\pi k(i-\frac{N}{2})}{N}} = e^{j\pi k}\sum_{i=\frac{N}{2}}^{N-1} x(i)e^{\frac{-j2\pi ki}{N}}. \tag{8}$$

By observation, C now clearly has a similar formula to B except for $e^{j\pi k}$ factor. Also, all the samples used in B will be elements of C, as frame F_1 and frame F_2 are 50% overlapped. So the DFT of Frame F_2 is:

$$X_2(k) = e^{j\pi k}B + D. \tag{9}$$

If we generally call term B and D as $X_{half\_old}(k)$ and $X_{half\_new}(k)$ respectively, the DFT of each frame can be presented as:

$$X(k) = e^{j\pi k}X_{half\_old}(k) + X_{half\_new}(k), \tag{10}$$

where the calculation of $X_{half\_old}(k)$ is performed on the $\frac{N}{2}$ overlapped samples that already appear in the previous frame, while that of $X_{half\_new}(k)$ is performed on the $\frac{N}{2}$ new samples in the current frame. Recursively, $X_{half\_new}(k)$ will become $X_{half\_old}(k)$ in the next frame. The expressions $X_{half\_new}(k)$ are computed by the term D formula, with the index running from 0:

$$X_{half\_new}(k) = \sum_{i=0}^{\frac{N}{2}} x(i)e^{\frac{-j2\pi k(i+\frac{N}{2})}{N}}. \tag{11}$$

In practice, term $e^{j\pi k}$ only takes a value of either $+1$ or -1, thus, the computation of $\frac{N}{2}$ overlapped samples can be directly reused. So, only $X_{half\_new}(k)$ needs to be computed, and thus, the DFT computation requirement is reduced by 50%.

Resulting from this saving in computation, a novel simple hardware structure has been developed and compares well to the simpleness of the direct DFT implementation.

2.1.4 Efficient DFT hardware implementation

This section presents an efficient hardware implementation of the previous described overlapping DFT (OvlDFT) algorithm. This algorithm and implementation are subjected to patent (Vu, 2010).

Firstly, assuming that the input samples, $x(i)$, are real, the output of the DFT is symmetric, then as a result, only values k from 0 to $\frac{N}{2} - 1$ are required. Also, as described in the previous section, only X_{half_new} is required to be computed. To simplify the formula, the real (X_{Re}) and imaginary (X_{Im}) parts of X_{half_new} are computed individually, as presented in equation (12) and (13). By doing this, the term $e^{j\pi k}$ in (10) only takes values of either 1 or -1 depending on k.

$$X_{Re}(k) = \sum_{i=0}^{\frac{N}{2}-1} x(i)\cos\left(\frac{2\pi k(i+\frac{N}{2})}{N}\right), \tag{12}$$

$$X_{Im}(k) = \sum_{i=0}^{\frac{N}{2}-1} x(i)\sin\left(\frac{2\pi k(i+\frac{N}{2})}{N}\right). \tag{13}$$

The structure of the proposed hardware DFT algorithm is shown in Figure 4. In order to achieve the 50% computational saving, additional memory (the RAM block) is required to buffer appropriate results from the computation of the previous frame.

The heart of this hardware structure lies in the novel implementation of this RAM buffer memory. By using RAM blocks which are commonly embedded in low-cost FPGA devices and configured as dual port memory in our proposed hardware structure, the content of

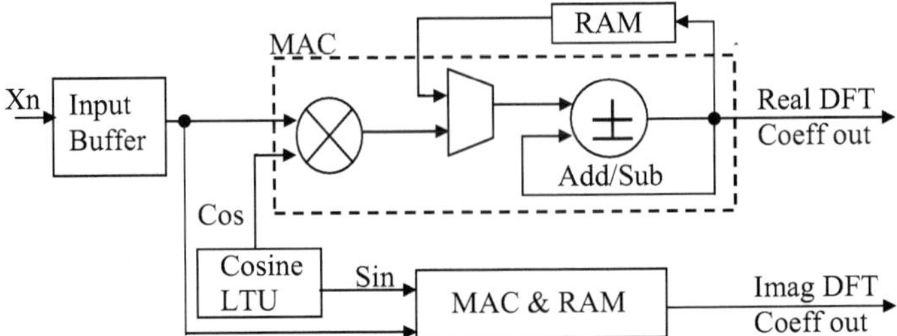

Fig. 4. OvlDFT hardware structure-Components within dashed box belong to one FPGA MAC primitive

the buffer memory slot can be read and written to simultaneously via two different ports as illustrated by the RAM blocks in Figure 4.

As shown in Figure 4, each frame sample in the input buffer is firstly multiplied (MUL block) with a cosine or sine element and then the multiplication results are accumulated (ADD block). After every $\frac{N}{2}$ samples, the current value in the accumulator ($X_{half\_new}(k)$ of current frame) is stored in the RAM at address k (k is the DFT bin index) in order to be used as $X_{half\_old}(k)$ for the upcoming frame.

Simultaneously, the previously stored value in RAM ($X_{half\_old}(k)$, at the same address k) is read via the second port of the dual port RAM and added to (or subtracted from) the current $X_{half\_new}(k)$ in the accumulator by the same ADD block before being replaced by the current value $X_{half\_new}(k)$. The decision between addition or subtraction is dependent on value k, due to the term $e^{j\pi k}$, previously mentioned. The result produced by the ADD element at this time is latched as a DFT coefficient at bin k as follows from Equation (10).

When the next frame arrives, half of the computation of DFT for this new frame is already available from the DFT computation of the previous frame stored in the RAM buffer, hence reducing the calculation latency by half. The process is repeated until the last DFT bin is reached.

The MUL (multiplier) block is a dedicated hardware block common on current FPGA devices. Moreover, the MUL, MUX, and ADD blocks are elements of one primitive MAC block embedded in many low-cost FPGAs. Thus, the proposed hardware architecture can be implemented with simple interconnection and minimum resources on such devices.

The above hardware implementation requires $\frac{N}{2}$ clock cycles to compute each DFT bin. Thus all $\frac{N}{2}$ required frequency bins require only $\frac{N^2}{4}$ clock cycles. If a 50% overlapped frame has 512 samples, with a typical FPGA clock frequency of 100MHz, this represents a latency of 0.16384ms. This is well within the new frame generation rate of 16ms for a 16KHz sample rate. Therefore, the OvlDFT is easily fast enough for speech preprocessing tasks.

2.1.5 Windowing and frame energy computation

In order to reduce spectral leakage, a *window* on the time-domain input signal is usually applied. However, windowing in the time-domain would compromise the symmetry properties utilized by the proposed algorithm and the saved calculation from the previous frame would no longer be valid.

The alternative to applying a window in the time domain is to use convolution to perform the windowing function in the frequency domain (Harris, 1978). Although, as convolution is typically a very time consuming operation, windowing in the frequency domain is

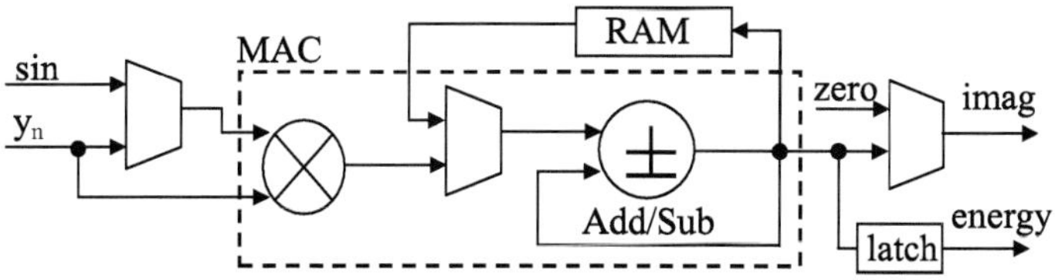

Fig. 5. Modification of the imaginary part of Fig. 4 for energy computation.

only generally used when the window function produces a short sequence of convolution coefficients. Fortunately, this desired property is present in some commonly used window functions such as Hamming and Hann windows. The Hann window produces three values $(-0.25, 0.5,$ and $-0.25)$ which can be easily implemented in the convolution processing by shift registers instead of the more expensive multipliers.

Furthermore, the frame energy power required by the MFCC block (discussed later) can be computed with almost no cost by modifying the first DFT bin calculation phase in the OvlDFT design. In contrast, the energy value must be calculated separately if a normal time-domain window is applied, hence, the OvlDFT algorithm will result in further resource savings when used in a MFCC hardware design.

The frame energy is computed follows. In the DFT computation, the imaginary part of the first frequency component is always zero. This can be exploited to compute the frame energy with a modest amount of additional hardware. The imaginary part of the proposed DFT implementation is modified to embed the frame energy computation by adding two multiplexers and a latch, as shown in Fig. 5.

When the first frequency component of a frame is computed, the input frame sample is fed to the imaginary MAC instead of the sine value (sin). Thus, the input sample will be squared and accumulated in the MAC. Consequently, the final output of this imaginary MAC, when calculating the first component, is the energy of the frame while the actual imaginary part of the first frequency component is tied to zero. For other components, the normal procedure described in Section 2.1.4 is performed.

This method of frame energy computation can only be used in conjunction with frequency-domain windowing. If windowing is performed in the time domain, the frame will be altered, and thus, the frame energy will not be computed correctly.

2.2 Linear spectra subtraction
2.2.1 Algorithm

In an environment with additive background noise $r(n)$, the corrupted version of the speech signal $s(n)$ can be expressed as:

$$y(n) = s(n) + r(n). \tag{14}$$

Following the preprocessing procedure, the captured signal is framed and transformed to the frequency domain by performing the discrete Fourier transform (DFT) on the framed signal $y(n)$:

$$Y(i,\omega) = S(i,\omega) + R(i,\omega), \tag{15}$$

where i is the frame index.

Before the spectral subtraction is performed, a scaled estimate of the amplitude spectrum of the noise $|\hat{R}(i,\omega)|$ must be obtained in a silent (i.e. no speech) period. An estimate of the amplitude spectrum of the clean speech signal can be calculated by subtracting the spectrum of the noisy signal with the estimated noise spectrum:

$$\left|\hat{S}(i,\omega)\right|^{\gamma} = \left|Y(i,\omega)\right|^{\gamma} - \alpha(i,\omega)\left|\hat{R}(i,\omega)\right|^{\gamma}, \tag{16}$$

where γ is the exponent applied to the spectra, with $\gamma = 1$ for amplitude spectral subtraction and $\gamma = 2$ for power spectral subtraction. The frequency-dependent factor, $\alpha(i,\omega)$, is included to compensate for under-estimating or over-estimating of the instantaneous noise spectrum. Should the subtraction in Equation (16) give negative values (i.e. the scaled noise estimate is greater than the instantaneous signal), a flooring factor is introduced. This leads to the following formulation of spectral subtraction:

$$\left|\hat{S}_t(i,\omega)\right|^{\gamma} = \left|Y(i,\omega)\right|^{\gamma} - \alpha(i,\omega)\left|\hat{R}(i,\omega)\right|^{\gamma},$$

and

$$\left|\hat{S}(i,\omega)\right|^{\gamma} = \begin{cases} \left|\hat{S}_t(i,\omega)\right|^{\gamma} & \left|\hat{S}_t(i,\omega)\right|^{\gamma} > \beta\left|Z(i,\omega)\right|^{\gamma}, \\ \beta\left|Z(i,\omega)\right|^{\gamma} & \text{otherwise,} \end{cases} \tag{17}$$

where $\left|Z(i,\omega)\right|$ is either the instantaneous noisy speech signal amplitude or the noise amplitude estimate, β is the noise floor factor ($0 < \beta \ll 1$). Common values for the floor factor range between 0.005 and 0.1 (Berouti et al., 1979).

The enhanced amplitude spectrum $\left|\hat{S}(i,\omega)\right|$ is recombined with the unaltered noisy speech phase spectrum to form the enhanced speech in the frequency domain and ready to be fed to the further speech processing blocks.

2.2.2 Linear spectral subtraction implementation

A generalized hardware implementation of the spectral subtraction derived directly from the previous description is shown in Figure 6.

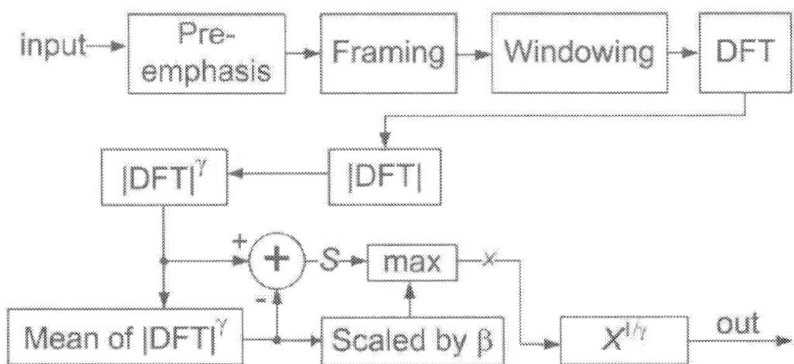

Fig. 6. The block diagram of the generalized implementation of spectral subtraction.

The estimated noise is calculated from the first N frames and stored in an internal buffer by the *Mean of* $|DFT|^{\gamma}$ block. The essence of the spectral subtraction technique occurs through subtracting the stored estimated noise from the subsequent magnitude spectrum for each frame as stated in Equation (17). The result of this subtraction is then compared with a scaled version of the average noise magnitude (known as the noise floor), with the larger of the two chosen as the output, denoted by $|X|$.

To recover the normal magnitude level, $|X|$ is raised to the power of $1/\gamma$. The output of this block, *out*, is ready to be used as the magnitude part of the enhanced signal to be fed into the speech recognition engine.

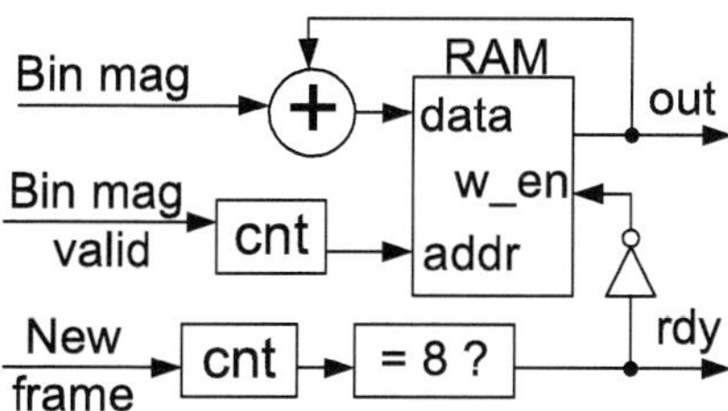

Fig. 7. Noise calculation block

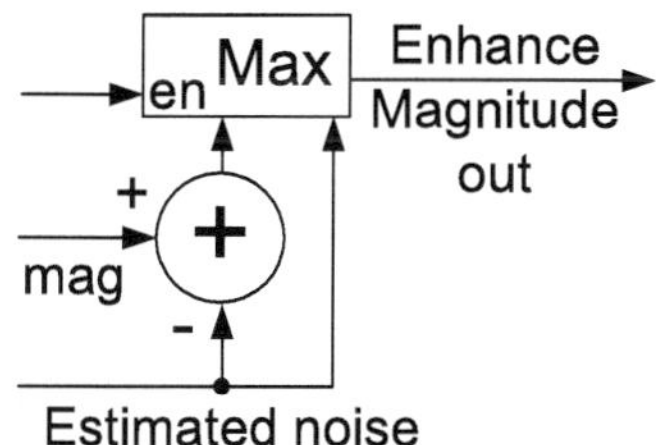

Fig. 8. Noise subtraction block

Algorithm refinement for in-car speech enhancement

For cost-effective automotive speech enhancement, we make the assumption that the noise characteristics $|\hat{R}(i,\omega)|$ can be accurately estimated during a silent period before the speech, for example 8 frames; and $|\hat{R}(i,\omega)|$ remains unchanged during the entire speech. Therefore, we can set $\alpha(i,\omega) = 1$ for all the values of i and ω. We also use the noise estimate for the calculation of the noise floor, that is $|Z(i,\omega)| = |\hat{R}(\omega)|$.

Typically, the parameters γ and β are set to optimize the signal-to-noise ratio (SNR). However, for the best speech recognition performance optimization, we may choose these two parameters differently from their common values (Kleinschmidt, 2010; Kleinschmidt et al., 2007).

It has been shown that magnitude spectral subtraction provides better speech recognition accuracy than power spectral subtraction (Whittington et al., 2008). Therefore, $\gamma = 1$ is selected for our implementation. One important benefit of this selection is that the resource requirement of the implementation is significantly reduced because the need for resource-intensive square and square root operations is avoided.

With $\gamma = 1$, experiments using floating-point software (Whittington et al., 2009) have been used to determine the optimal value of β on part of the AVICAR database (Lee et al., 2004). It has been shown that maximum recognition accuracy can be obtained by setting $\beta = 0.55$ and that the performance is only marginally worse (approximately 0.1%) if we set $\beta = 0.5$. Therefore, $\beta = 0.5$ was selected for the implementation because of its simplicity.

Efficient noise estimation and subtraction

An inefficient design covering the steps to estimate the noise and apply noise subtraction can result in significant additional hardware resources due to the requirement of a complex control flow and data buffering. To achieve low hardware resource usage, a pipeline design is proposed. The design requires no control mechanism as the data is processed in an orderly fashion due to the simple pipeline structure.

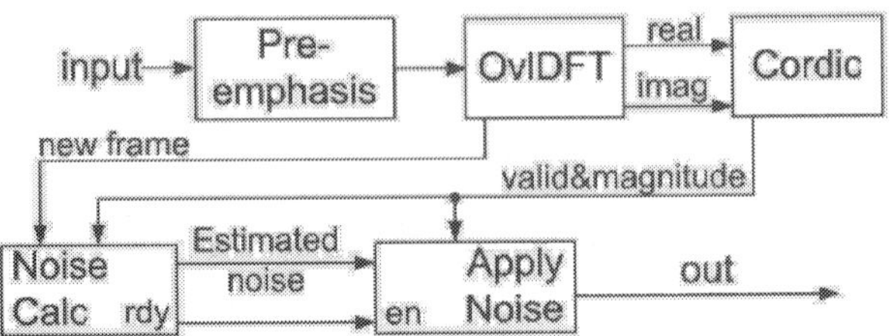

Fig. 9. The block diagram for the FPGA design

The first 8 frames of the input signal are used to compute the estimated noise magnitude spectrum by the structure shown in Figure 7. From frame 9, the noise subtraction is applied by a cascaded structure, as shown in Figure 8.

The magnitude valid pulse, *Bin_mag_valid*, drives an 8-bit counter as the memory location in RAM for the current sample. Concurrently, to perform the noise calculation, the magnitude value is accumulated and stored to the same memory location as long as the signal *rdy* is not set. If *rdy* is set, the same counter will function as the read address to access the estimated noise in the RAM buffer, thus eliminating the need for the complex feedback control from the subsequent block, the *Noise Subt* block.

Similarly, the *New frame* pulse, indicating a new frame, drives a frame counter during noise estimation. When the frame counter reaches 8, the *rdy* signal will be set, indicating the end of the noise estimation process. Signal *rdy* is also used to disable the frame counter and the RAM writing function.

The noise subtraction is applied by a structure shown in Figure 8 and the cascaded wiring in Figure 9. The subtraction result is compared with the associated estimated noise scaled by $\beta = 0.5$. To perform this, the *MAX* block simply re-interprets the estimated noise signal by moving the fraction point of the value one bit to the left, eliminating a shift register.

The proposed structure of the overall system.
The structure of the proposed FPGA implementation of spectral subtraction is shown in Figure 9, with the detail is described below.

The input signal first passes through the speech preprocessing block. In addition to the DFT real and imaginary components, a pulse output signal, *new frame*, is generated to indicate that a frame has been processed. The DFT coefficients are then fed to the Cordic block (a core supplied by Xilinx (Xilinx, 2010) to produce the magnitude of each coefficient.

The essence of the spectral subtraction technique occurs through the *Noise Calc* and the cascaded *Noise Subt* blocks which estimate the noise and perform noise subtraction respectively, as detailed in Section 2.2.2.

2.3 Dual-channel array beam-forming
2.3.1 Algorithm
Beamforming is an effective method of spatial filtering that differentiates the desired signals from noise and interference according to their locations. The direction where the microphone array is steered is called the look direction.

One beamforming technique is the delay-and-sum beamformer which works by compensating signal delay to each microphone appropriately before they are combined using an additive operation. The outcome of this delayed signal summation is a reinforced version of the desired signal and reduced noise due to destructive interference among noises from different channels.

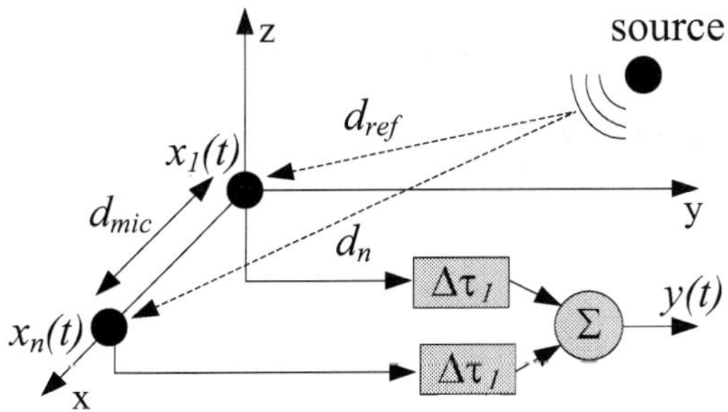

Fig. 10. Dual-microphone delay-and-sum beamforming

As illustrated in Figure 10, consider a desired signal received by N omni-directional microphones at time t, in which each microphone output is an attenuated and delayed version of the original signal $a_n s(t - \tau_n)$ with added noise v_n, is given by:

$$x_n(t) = a_n s(t - \tau_n) + v_n(t). \tag{18}$$

In the frequency domain, the array signal model is defined as:

$$\mathbf{X}(\omega) = S(\omega)\mathbf{d} + \mathbf{V}(\omega), \tag{19}$$

where $\mathbf{X} = [X_1(\omega), X_2(\omega), \cdots, X_N(\omega)]^T$, $\mathbf{V} = [V_1(\omega), V_2(\omega), \cdots, V_N(\omega)]^T$. The vector $\mathbf{d}$ represents the array steering vector which depends on the actual microphone and source locations.

For a source located near the array, the wavefront of the signal impinging on the array should be considered a spherical wave and the source signal is said to be located within the near-field of the array instead of a planar wave commonly assumed for a source located far from the array. In the near field, $\mathbf{d}$ is given by (Bitzer & Simmer, 2001):

$$\mathbf{d} = [a_1 e^{-j\omega\tau_1}, a_2 e^{-j\omega\tau_2}, ..., a_N e^{-j\omega\tau_N}]^T, \tag{20}$$

$$a_n = \frac{d_{ref}}{d_n}, \tau_n = \frac{d_n - d_{ref}}{c}, \tag{21}$$

where d_n and d_{ref} denote the Euclidean distance between the source and the microphone n, or the reference microphone, respectively, and c is the speed of sound.

To recover the desired signal, each microphone output is weighted by frequency domain coefficients $w_n(\omega)$. The beamformer weights are designed to maintain the beam at the look direction to be constant (e.g. $\mathbf{w}^H\mathbf{d} = 1$). For a dual-microphone case, the beamformer output is the sum of each weighted microphone:

$$Y(\omega) = \sum_{n=1}^{2} w_n^*(\omega)X_n(\omega). \tag{22}$$

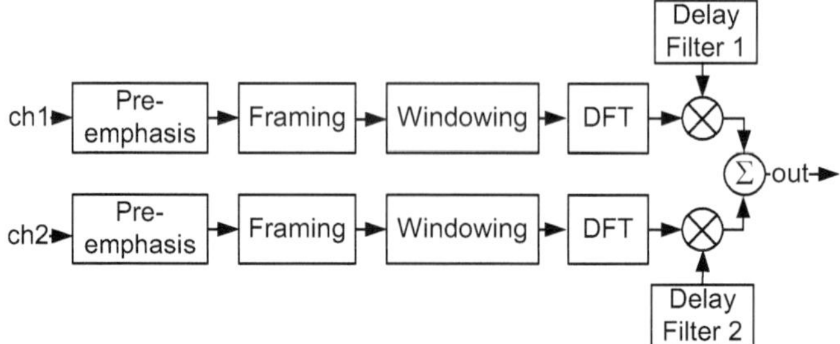

Fig. 11. General diagram of the DASB

The beamformer output $Y(\omega)$ is enhanced speech in the frequency domain and is ready to be fed to the following speech processing blocks. In digital form, the whole process of DASB can be summarized in Figure 11 where the delay filters are defined by the weighting coefficients $w_n(\omega)$.

For fixed microphone positions, the array steering vector d and therefore the weighting coefficients $w_n(\omega)$ will be fixed. Hence, $w_n(\omega)$ can be pre-computed and stored in read-only memory (ROM) to save real-time computation.

2.3.2 Dual-channel array beam-forming implementation

In this section, the duplicated processing sections of the general DASB structure shown in Figure 11 are identified and some efficient sharing mechanisms are proposed.

Sharing between two input channels

The sharing of one hardware block for both input channels can be achieved with a novel and simple modification to the *OvlDFT* structure presented previously (Vu, Ye, Whittington, Devlin & Mason, 2010).

As all the intermediate computations between segments of *OvlDFT* are stored in RAM, the computation of the second input channel can be added by simply doubling the memory space of the Input Buffer as well as the RAM blocks to convert them to "ping-pong" buffers, as illustrated in Figure 12. With the double size buffer, data for Channel 1 and Channel 2 can be located on the lower and upper half of the memory respectively. When a segment of Channel 1 is finished, the Input Buffer's address is increased, and the most significant bit of each memory address will be automatically set so that the second half of the memory is examined. Thus, Channel 2 will then be processed automatically.

Assuming the speech input is a sequence of N real samples, only $\frac{N}{2}$ frequency bins are needed. The output of the system will be sequences of $\frac{N}{2}$ DFT coefficients of the first channel, followed by an equivalent sequence of the second channel.

Delay filter sharing

In the frequency domain, the process of filtering is simply the multiplication of the DFT coefficients of the input signal with the corresponding delay filter coefficients. Delay filter coefficients are pre-computed and stored in read only memory (ROM).

As discussed previously, the overlapping DFT produces DFT coefficients of the two channels alternatively in one stream. Thus, to make the structure simple and easy to implement, the coefficients of the two delay filters are stored in one block of ROM; one filter is located in the lower half of address space while the other is located in the upper half. These filter coefficients

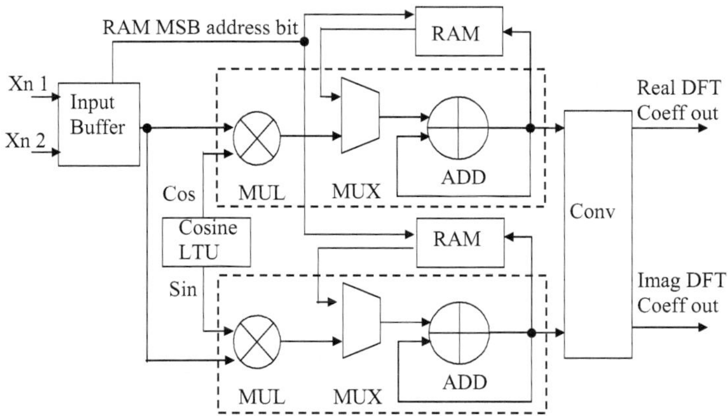

Fig. 12. Dual channel overlapping DFT hardware structure

can be read independently by the most significant bit of the ROM address, which changes automatically when the address is increased.

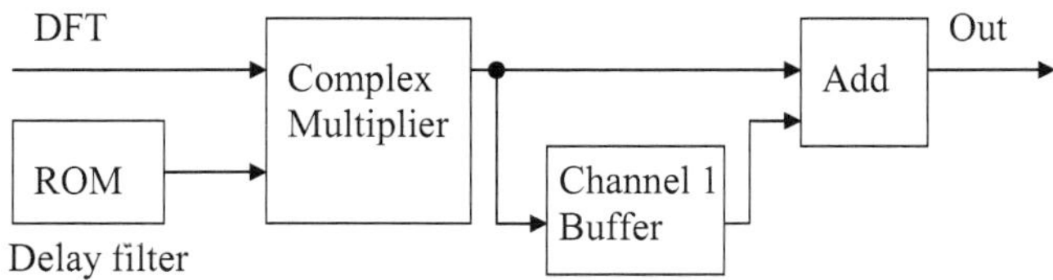

Fig. 13. DASB Delay Filter Diagram

Figure 13 shows the diagram of the Delay filter used for both channels. The product of the filter coefficient (from the lower half of the ROM) and the corresponding DFT coefficient (from the sequence of channel 1) is buffered at the same address of the Channel 1 Buffer block memory. When the DFT coefficients of Channel 2 are calculated and multiplied with filter coefficients from the upper half of the ROM, the product will be added to the Channel 1 delay filter product (already stored in the buffer) to produce the final DASB output.

FPGA implementation
The FPGA design consists of three main blocks as illustrated in Figure 14.

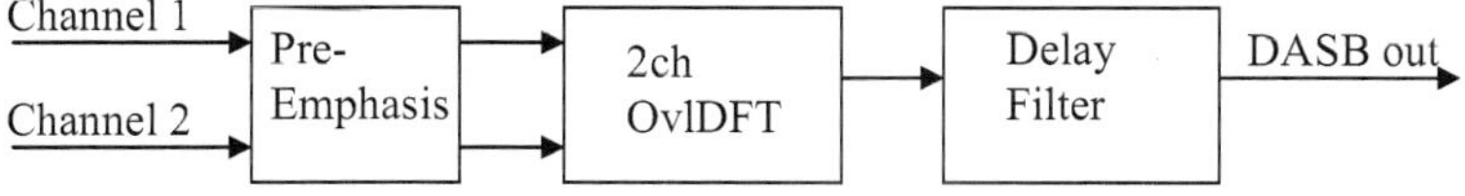

Fig. 14. FPGA design diagram of DASB

The first block is the pre-emphasis filter. The common practice for setting this pre-emphasis filter is given by $y(i) = x(i) - 0.97x(i-1)$, where $x(i)$ and $y(i)$ are the ith input and output samples, respectively. Its implementation requires a delay block, a multiplier and an adder.
The second block is the dual-channel overlapping frame DFT as presented in Section 2.3.2 with Hann windowing. The Input Buffer using dual-port BlockRAM is configured as a circular

buffer. Two input channels are multiplexed so that they are stored into the same circular buffer at the lower and upper memory location, respectively.

The third block is the delay filter as presented in Section 2.3.2 and shown in Figure 13. As there is a large time gap between any two DFT coefficients, only one MAC primitive is used to perform the complex multiplication through 4 clock cycles. This provides further saving of hardware resources.

The FPGA design of the DASB can easily process dual 16 bit inputs at 16 KHz sample rate in real-time with the master clock as low as 8.2 MHz.

3. Speech recognition feature extraction front-end

The speech recognition front-end transforms a speech waveform from input devices, such as a microphone, to a parametric representation which can be recognized by a speech decoder. Thus, the front-end process, known as feature extraction, plays a key role in any speech recognition system. In many systems, the feature extraction front-end is implemented using a high-end floating-point processor, however, this type of implementation is expensive both in terms of computer resources and cost.

This section discusses a new small footprint *Mel-Frequency Cepstrum Coefficients* front-end design for FPGA implementation that is suitable for low-cost speech recognition systems. By exploiting the overlapping nature of the input frames and by adopting a simple pipeline structure, the implemented design only utilizes approximately 10% of the total resources of a low-cost and modest-size FPGA device. This design not only has a relatively low resource usage, but also maintains a reasonably high level of performance.

3.1 Mel-frequency cepstrum coefficients

Following the speech preprocessing and enhancement, the signal spectrum is calculated and filtered by F band-pass triangular filters equally spaced on the Mel-frequency scale, where F is a number of filters. Specifically, the mapping from the linear frequency to the Mel-frequency is according to the following formula:

$$Mel(f) = 1127 \ln(1 + \frac{f}{700}). \tag{23}$$

The cepstral parameters are then calculated from the logarithm of the filter banks amplitude, m_i, using the discrete cosine transform (DCT) (Young et al., 2006):

$$c_k = \sqrt{\frac{2}{F}} \sum_{i=1}^{F} m_i \cos\left[\frac{\pi k}{F}(i - 0.5)\right]. \tag{24}$$

where index k runs from 0 to $K - 1$ (K is the number of cepstral coefficients).

The higher order cepstral coefficients are usually quite small so that there is a large variation of cepstral coefficients between the low-order and high-order coefficients. Therefore, it is handy to re-scale the cepstral coefficients to achieve similar magnitudes. This is done by using a lifter scheme as follows (Young et al., 2006):

$$c_k' = (1 + \frac{L}{2} \sin \frac{\pi k}{L}) c_k, \tag{25}$$

where c_k' is the rescaled coefficient for the c_k value.

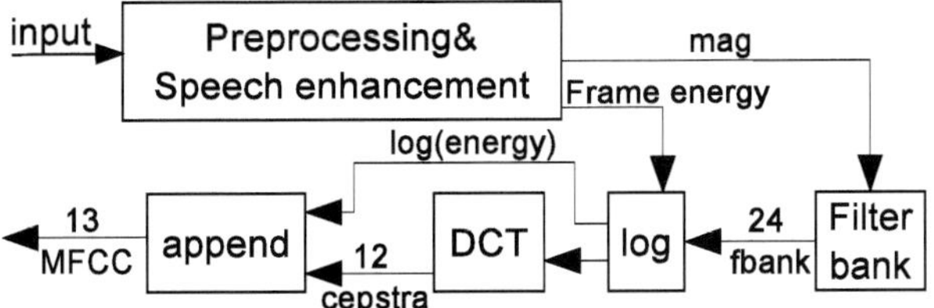

Fig. 15. Block diagram of the overall FPGA design

An energy term is normally appended with the cepstra. The energy (E) is computed as the logarithm of the signal energy, that is, for speech frame $\{y(n), n = 0, 1, \cdots, N-1\}$.

$$E = \log \sum_{n=0}^{N-1} y^2(n). \tag{26}$$

Optionally, time derivatives, Delta and Acceleration Coefficients, can be added to the basic static parameters which can greatly enhance the performance of a speech recognition system. The delta coefficients are computed using the following regression formula

$$d_t = \frac{\sum_{\theta=1}^{\Theta} \theta(c_{t+\theta} - c_{t-\theta})}{2 \sum_{\theta=1}^{\Theta} \theta^2}, \tag{27}$$

where d_t is a delta coefficient at time t computed in terms of the corresponding static coefficients $c_{t-\Theta}$ to $c_{t+\Theta}$, and the value of Θ is the window size. Acceleration coefficients are obtained by applying the same formula to the delta coefficients.

3.2 MFCC front-end implementation

In many applications, such as an in-car voice control interface, low power consumption is important, but low cost is vital. Therefore, the design will first attempt to save resources and then reduce latency for low-power consumption (Vu, Whittington, Ye & Devlin, 2010).

3.2.1 Top-level MFCC front-end design

The new front-end design consists of 5 basic blocks as illustrated in Fig. 15, which has 24 Mel-frequency filter banks and produces 39 observation features: 12 cepstra coefficient and one frame energy value, plus their delta and accelerator time derivatives.
The core MFCC blocks include: *Filter-bank*, Logarithm, *DCT* block (combining DCT and the lifter steps), and Append-Deltafy (computing Delta and Accelerator time derivatives) blocks are described in later sections.

3.2.2 A note on efficient windowing by convolution

As noted previously, the speech preprocessing with OvlDFT performs windowing by convolution with an embedded frame energy computation. Although the circular convolution is simple, significant hardware resources are specifically required to compute the first and the last frequency bins.
Each of the other output frequency bins depend on three input components: the previous bin, itself and the following bin. However, the first frequency bin requires the last frequency bin to compute the circular convolution and via versa. This incurs an additional hardware resource cost for buffering and control.

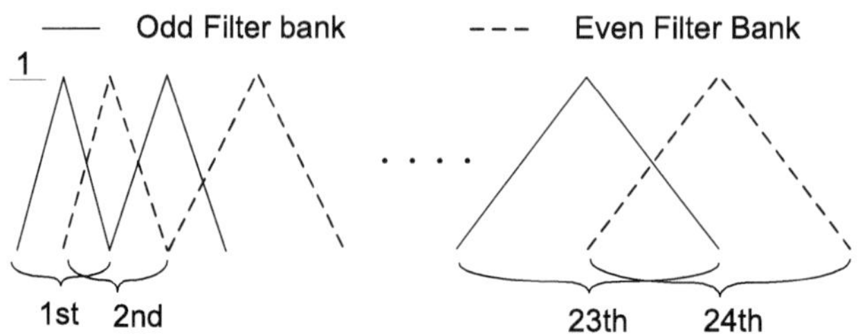

Fig. 16. Triangular Mel frequency filter bank

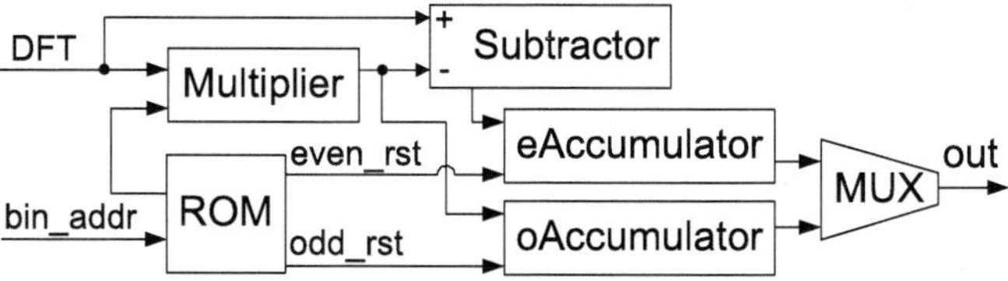

Fig. 17. Block diagram for Mel frequency bank calculation

These hardware resource costs can be saved if band-limiting is applied. Very low and very high frequencies might belong to regions in which there is no useful speech signal energy. As a result, a few frequency bins at the beginning and the end of the frequency range can be rejected without a significant loss of performance. Thus hardware used for the additional buffering and control can be saved.

In related work, Han et al. proposed an MFCC calculation method involving half-frames (Han et al., 2006). However, in their method, the windowing is performed in the time domain and the Hamming window is applied to the half-frames instead of the full-frames in the original calculation. As the method presented here applies the window function on the full-frames, in theory, the output of this method should have a smaller error from the original calculation than the method of Han et al.

3.2.3 Mel filter-bank implementation

The signal spectrum is calculated and filtered by 24 band-pass triangular filters, equally spaced on the Mel-frequency scale. Dividing the 24 filters into 12 odd filters and 12 even filters as shown in Figure 16 leads to a simplification in the required hardware structure.

As the maximum magnitude of each filter is unity and aligned with the beginning of the next filter (due to the equal separation in the Mel-frequency scale), the points of the even filter banks can be generated by subtracting each of the odd filter bank samples from 1. Thus, only the odd-numbered filters need to be calculated and stored, leading to the saving of significant memory space.

More specifically, if the weighted odd power spectrum, E_{odd}, is calculated first then the weighted even power spectrum, E_{even}, can be easily computed as:

$$E_{even} = X_k(1 - W_{odd}^k) = X_k - E_{odd}, \tag{28}$$

where X_k is the power of the frequency bin k; and W_{odd}^k is the associated weight values from the stored odd filter.

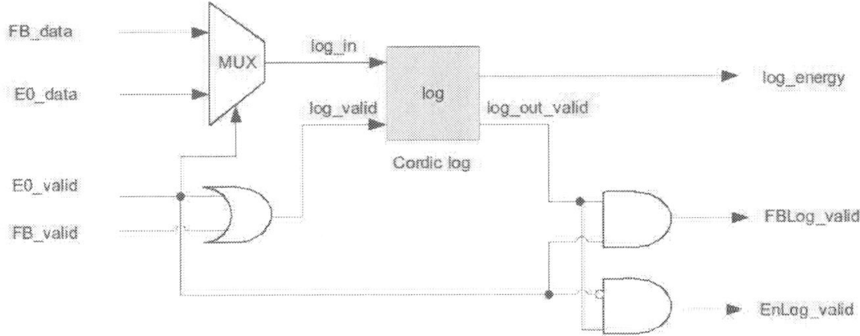

Fig. 18. Sharing scheme for logarithm calculation

The above observation leads to efficient implementation of the filter bank algorithm shown in Figure 17. The data from speech preprocessing is processed in a pipelined fashion through the Multiplier blocks. The Multiplier block multiplies each data sample with the odd filter value at the corresponding sample location (according to the frequency bin address, bin_addr) producing E_{odd}, while E_{even} is an output of the $Subtractor$ block. These products are then added to the value in the odd and even accumulators ($oAccumulator$ and $eAccumulator$ blocks) successively. The resulting either odd or even filter-bank data values are then merged into the out stream by the multiplexer (MUX).

The ROM stores the frequency bin address where the accumulators need to be reset in order to start a fresh calculation. The same process is repeated until 24 filterbank values have been calculated.

Equation (28) was also investigated by Wang et al. (Wang et al., 2002), although, without the distinction of the odd and the even filter, where a complex Finite State Machine (FSM) for control is required as described in (Wang et al., 2002). This complex FSM normally generates a long latency as well as requiring significant hardware resources.

In contrast, the work presented here results in a much simpler pipeline implementation (with only 1 multiplier, 1 ROM and 3 adders/subtractors) and thus saves more hardware resources. Furthermore, this implementation runs in a pipeline fashion with a much smaller latency; it requires only $N + 4$ (where N is the number of frequency bins) clock cycles to compute any number of filters.

3.2.4 Logarithm calculation

Two different data points in the MFCC design, triangle filter banks and frame energy output, are required to perform the logarithm. Figure 18 shows a structure of sharing one logarithm block to compute both data streams alternatively.

A multiplexer is needed to select if either the incoming energy data or filter bank data are to be processed by the log block which is implemented by using CORDIC logic core provided by Xilinx (Xilinx, 2010).

From this block, the logarithmic operation is applied to the input data so long as valid signals are active high. Log_valid is activated if either E0_valid or FB_valid signals are high. If the logarithmic value is available at the output, then the log_out _valid signal will go high. Energy_valid indicates when the logarithmic value of the E0 energy is available at the output. This signal will only be high when both log_out_valid and E0_valid are true. Similarly,

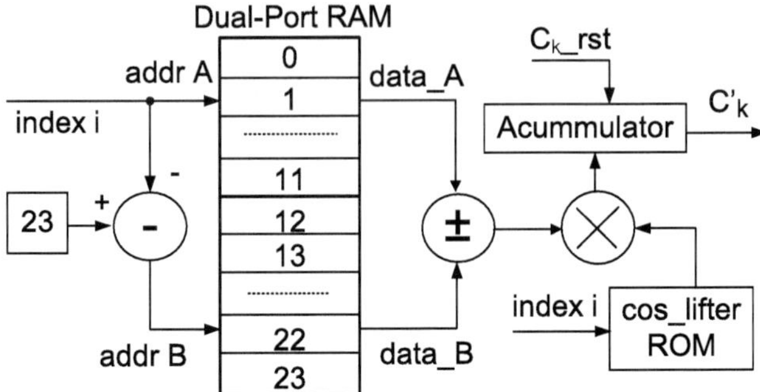

Fig. 19. Block diagram for cepstra and lifter calculation

FBLog_valid indicates if the logarithmic value of the filter bank coefficient is available at the output.

3.2.5 Cepstra and lifter computation

The Mel-Frequency Cepstral Coefficients (MFCCs) are calculated from the log filter bank's amplitude m using the DCT defined in Equation (24). The cosine values are multiplied with the constant $\sqrt{\frac{2}{F}}$ (F is 24 in this example) and are stored in a ROM, prior to the summation operation. This yields the following equation:

$$c_k = \sum_{i=1}^{24} m_i r_i,\tag{29}$$

where $r_i = \sqrt{\frac{2}{F}} \cos\left[\frac{\pi k}{F}(i - 0.5)\right]$.

Due to the symmetry of the cosine values, the summation can be reduced to a count from 1 to 12 according to the following formula:

$$c_k = \sum_{i=1}^{12} \left[m_i r_i + (-1)^{i-1} m_{25-i} r_i \right]$$

$$= \sum_{i=1}^{12} r_i \left[m_i + (-1)^{i-1} m_{25-i} \right].\tag{30}$$

As discussed previously, it is advantageous to re-scale the cepstral coefficients to have similar magnitudes by using the lifter in Equation (25). A separate calculation of this lifter formula is essential, although it requires time and resources. However, by combining the lifter formula with the pre-computed DCT matrix, r_i, the lifter can be calculated without any extra time or hardware cost. Thus, r_i now becomes:

$$r_i = \sqrt{\frac{2}{F}} \cos\left[\frac{\pi k}{F}(i - 0.5)\right] \left(1 + \frac{L}{2} \sin\frac{\pi k}{L}\right).\tag{31}$$

The block diagram of cepstra and lifter computation is presented in Fig. 19. A dual-port RAM is first filled with the 24 log filter bank amplitudes. Then, two symmetrical locations are read from the RAM via two independent ports. The RAM data outputs are added to,

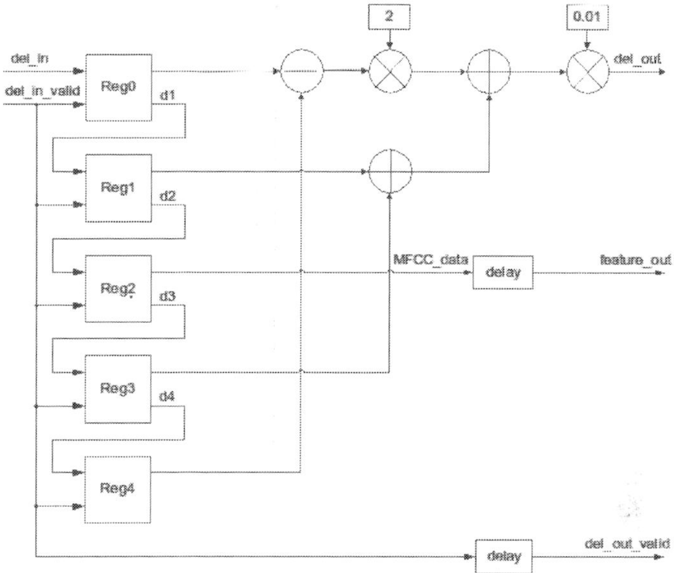

Fig. 20. Deltafy block diagram

or subtracted from, each other respectively. The computation results and the constant values from the ROM are then processed by a MAC which performs a multiplication and accumulates the resulting values. The accumulator of the MAC is reset by C_{k_rst} at the beginning of every new c'_k computation.

3.2.6 Deltafy block

In this work, both delta and accelerator coefficients have a window size of 2, so they can share the same formula (Equation 27) and the same hardware structure. With the window size having a value of 2 ($\Theta = 2$ in Equation 27), the derivative d_t of element c_t is calculated by the following formula

$$d_t = \frac{(c_{t+1} - c_{t-1}) + 2 \times (c_{t+2} + c_{t-2})}{10}. \tag{32}$$

Figure 20 shows the corresponding hardware structure of both delta and accelerator computation. The thirteen elements of MFCC data (12 DCT coefficient appended by one frame energy value) are shifted from register Reg0 to Reg4. When all four registers have one valid element, the signal del_in_valid enables the derivative calculation for the element in Reg2 only, performing the computation shown in Equation 32.

The del_out_valid signal then enables the MFCC data and its derivative to be available at the output. Then, the MFCC elements in each register are shifted forward by one register and the above process is repeated.

The accelerator coefficients are computed by cascading the same hardware after the delta computation hardware.

4. Performance evaluation

Having constructed the new OvlDFT hardware design and integrated it into a speech recognition feature extraction front-end with two embedded speech enhancement techniques, it is necessary to validate their performance. For this work there are four aspects of interest: (i) is the OvlDFT is an effective DFT processing block; (ii) how well does the fixed-point hardware MFCC feature extraction front-end match a floating-point software equivalent; (iii) do the embedded speech enhancement techniques improve speech recognition performance; and (iv) how effective in terms of hardware resource usage and hardware processing are these implementations.

4.1 Testing and resource usage of FPGA design

The small footprint fixed-point hardware MFCC feature extraction with embedded speech enhancement design has been implemented on a Xilinx Spartan 3A-DSP 1800 development board. As this is a low-cost and modest-size FPGA device the, the design's resource utilization can illustrate the advantages of this hardware implementation. The development of the FPGA design was conducted block by block, based on equivalent floating-point MATLAB implementation. Each block was tested after it was completed to ensure correct operation before the next block was developed.

To verify key sections and the complete design, test data signals were fed into the system with the output data passed to a computer for analysis. This output was then compared with that from a floating-point model of the system. To determine relative quantization error range, both the FPGA and the floating-point model outputs were converted back into the time domain.

Testing of the OvlDFT design

To test the OvlDFT, the same speech files from the AVICAR database (Lee et al., 2004) were fed to the OvlDFT and a floating-point Matlab DFT. The power spectrum of the both versions was then compared side by side. The comparison result showed that the two output data sets are identical to the fourth or fifth digit following the decimal point. This experiment was repeated using other AVICAR speech files used in the later speech recognition experiments with corresponding results.

Testing of the LSS design

Figure 21 shows an example of the input (speech from the AVICAR, AF2_35D_P0_C2_M4.wav file), corresponding output, and quantization error of the hardware system compared to the floating point model output. It can be seen that the enhanced output is much cleaner than the inputs and that the quantization error is of the order of 10^{-4}. This test was repeated with similar AVICAR speech files used in the later speech recognition experiments and resulted in a consistent quantization error.

Testing of the DASB design

Two speech files from microphone 2 and 6 of the AVICAR (AF2_35D_P0_C2 records) were chosen for Channel 1 and Channel 2 respectively. Figure 22 shows the test inputs and output of the fixed-point FPGA system and the difference between the FPGA output and that of the floating-point model. Here it can be seen that the enhanced output is clean and the error is within the range of $\pm 10^{-4}$. This test was repeated with a range of AVICAR data sets used later in the performance experiments with all cases exhibiting a consistent error of $\pm 10^{-4}$.

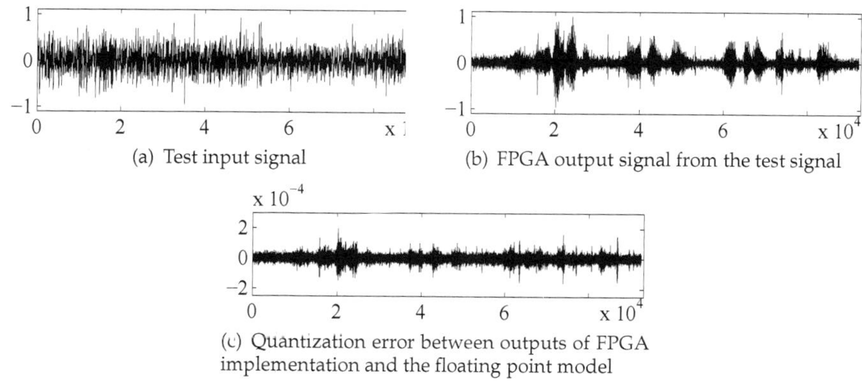

(a) Test input signal

(b) FPGA output signal from the test signal

(c) Quantization error between outputs of FPGA
implementation and the floating point model

Fig. 21. An example of input and output signals of the LSS FPGA design

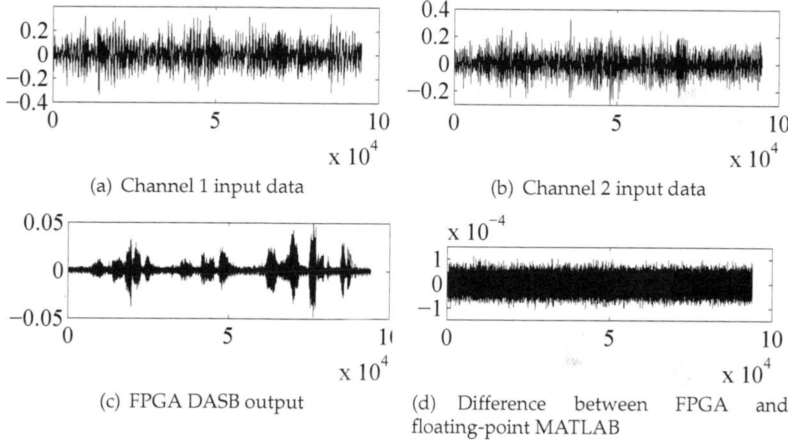

(a) Channel 1 input data

(b) Channel 2 input data

(c) FPGA DASB output

(d) Difference between FPGA and floating-point MATLAB

Fig. 22. The input, output and FPGA quantization error of DASB on the test files

Testing of the MFCC design

To test the quantization error of the MFCC design, a comparison of the fixed-point FPGA output was made with the output from the equivalent floating-point Hidden Markov Model Toolkit (HTK) (Young et al., 2006). The configurations of both HTK and the FPGA design are: 512 samples per 50% overlapped frame, 50Hz-7950Hz cut-off frequency, 24-filter filter bank, 12 cepstra coefficients and lifted by a parameter $L = 22$. Using the same speech input, the quantization error is 10^{-3} which is still consistent over the AVICAR test set.

FPGA resource usage

Table 1 shows the resource usage of the MFCC front-end with embedded DASB and then LSS speech enhancement. With the LSS applied first, the hardware is slightly larger due to the application on both channels. However, due to the low working clock rate, the hardware

Resources	Available	Enhanced MFCC resources	Usage
Slices	16640	3401	20.44%
BRAMs	84	28	33.33%
Multiplier	84	12	14.28%

Table 1. Resource usage on Spartan-3A DSP 1800 device of the MFCC feature extraction design with embedded speech enhancement

resource can be share between the two channels, thus, the additional hardware is mainly input/output buffer generated using BRAM blocks.

The FPGA resource utilisation for the design at present is only around 14% to 33%, thus only a modest portion of the target FPGA resources have been utilised, giving significant space for other future designs, such as, the implementation of a speech recognition decoder.

The MFCC implementation with speech enhancement processes data in pipeline. This pipeline requires only a 4.1Mhz clock, which is the required clock of the slowest component (the OvlDFT), to process a 16KHz sample rate speech in real-time. Hence, if a significant higher clock was used, say 100Mhz, the resulting spare processing capacity could be applied to addition tasks, such as, enabling input from a large microphone array.

4.2 Recognition performance

Validation of speech enhancement performance in this context can only be measured through statistical analysis of speech recognition rates for various enhancement scenarios, including the no enhancement case, using data sets containing a variety of speakers. Experiments for this work were conducted using the phone numbers task of the AVICAR database (Lee et al., 2004).

AVICAR database

AVICAR is a multi-channel Audio-Visual In-CAR speech database collected by the University of Illinois, USA. It is a large, publicly available speech corpus designed to enable low-SNR speech recognition through combining multi-channel audio and visual speech recognition. For this collection, an array of eight microphones was mounted on the sun visor in front of the speaker who was positioned on the passenger's side of the car. The location of the speaker's mouth was estimated to be 50 cm behind, 30 cm below and horizontally aligned with the fourth microphone of the array (i.e. 58.3cm in a direct line). The microphones in the array are spaced 2.5 cm apart. Utterances for each speaker were recorded under five different noise conditions which are outlined in Table 2 (Lee et al., 2004)

Condition	Description
IDL	Engine running, car stopped, windows up
35U	Car travelling at 35 mph, windows up
35D	Car travelling at 35 mph, windows down
55U	Car travelling at 55 mph, windows up
55D	Car travelling at 55 mph, windows down

Table 2. AVICAR noise conditions

The speech recognition experiments involved passing sets of the AVICAR speech waveforms through the hardware feature extraction unit (incorporating the OvlDFT and embedded speech enhancement) followed by the HTK speech decoder. This was repeated for each of the various enhancement scenarios in turn, as well as the no enhancement case to provide a baseline reference. All speech recognition results quoted below are word correction (in %), calculated as:

$$WordCorrection = \frac{N - D}{N}.100\% \tag{33}$$

Where:

- N represents the total number of words in the experiment;

- D the number of correct words omitted in the recogniser output;

Performance experiments

To evaluate the designs, A baseline speech recognition is first set up for comparison. For this work, the HTK software is used as a recognition engine for both of the baseline and the FPGA system.

In these experiments, the baseline used HCopy supplied by HTK as the speech recognition front-end, while the the FPGA design produces the MFCC features which are then fed directly to the HTK recognition engine. In both cases, the HTK recognition engine uses an acoustic model trained by HTK tools from a Wall Street Journal corpus with 16 Gaussians per state. To simplify the evaluation steps, the continuous speech phone numbers task (i.e. digit sequences) has been used with the following grammar:

$digit = one | two | three | four | five |
six | seven | eight | nine | oh | zero;
(SENT-START <$digit> SENT-END)

There are about 60 sentences in the test set of each noise condition. Each sentence is a speech of 10 digit phone number, thus, there are around 600 digits in total to be recognised for each noise condition. For the speech recognition experiments of the LSS enhancement alone, speech file from microphone 4 (central to the speaker) were used. While for evaluation of other scenarios which all include DASB, speech files from microphone 2 and 6 (equal distant on either side of the speaker) were used.

This experiment was designed to provide an indicative measure of the speech recognition performance of the hardware design. What is important here is to show that there is an improvement in speech recognition performance using hardware speech enhancement techniques, not the absolute value of the speech recognition performance. To conduct such a test, a huge speech database and complex language model would be required with test conducted across a wide range of scenarios, this is beyond the scope of this work.

	IDL	35U	35D	55U	55D	Average
Baseline	88.0	67.8	56.1	58.8	29.0	59.9
FPGA LSS	90.8	70.7	58.6	64.4	47.0	66.3

Table 3. Word correction of FPGA LSS-MFCC design

The Linear Spectral Subtraction scenario demonstrates clear improvement over the no enhancement baseline case under all noise conditions. Although the improvement is a rather modest 2-3% for the lower noise conditions, becoming a more substantial 18% for the noisiest condition, 55MPH, windows down (Table 3).

The Delay-Sum Beamforming scenario provides a substantial improvement over the baseline of between 17-20% for all but the lowest noise (idle) condition where the improvement is still over 5% (Table 4). The DASB also provides greater recognition improvement than the Linear Spectral Subtraction alone for all cases apart from the noisiest condition, where the improvement is basically the same for both techniques.

	IDL	35U	35D	55U	55D	Average
Baseline	88.0	67.8	56.1	58.8	29.0	59.9
FPGA DASB	93.6	86.1	74.0	78.1	46.5	75.6

Table 4. Word correction of FPGA DASB-MFCC design

	IDL	35U	35D	55U	55D	Average
Baseline	88.0	67.8	56.1	58.8	29.0	59.9
FPGA DASB-LSS	94.2	87.8	77.5	81.4	62.3	80.6

Table 5. Word correction of FPGA DASB-LSS-MFCC design

	IDL	35U	35D	55U	55D	Average
Baseline	88.0	67.8	56.1	58.8	29.0	59.9
FPGA LSS-DASB	94.6	88.4	78.3	82.7	62.3	81.2

Table 6. Word correction of FPGA LSS-DASB-MFCC design

Cascading the two enhancement techniques results in even greater performance improvement than either scenario operating alone. As shown in Table 5 and 6, the improvement is over 20% in all but the lowest noise case which has an improvement of more than 6%. While the recognition rate for highest noise case, 55MPH windows down, has more than doubled. The order in which the hardware enhancement blocks cascaded doesn't seem to exhibit any significant difference for this test. While the recognition performance of the Linear Spectral Subtraction followed by Delay-Sum Beamforming is between 0 and 1.3% higher than the reverse case this difference is likely to be within the limitation of the test.

5. Discussion and conclusions

In this chapter, a small footprint FPGA hardware implementation of a MFCC feature extraction front-end with embedded speech enhancement has been presented. The two speech enhancement techniques were chosen because of their simpleness and effectiveness for the example in-car application.

By exploiting the overlapping nature of the input frames and other redundancy in data and control processes, the design has achieved a modest hardware resource usage on a low-cost FPGA. The patented OvlDFT is a key to this small hardware utilization, and along with other optimization has resulted in only about 20% utilisation of a Spartan 3A DSP 1800 device.

In addition, the design is able to work in real time with a clock of only 4.1 Mhz which is very much slower than a typical FPGA clock of 100 Mhz. These two factors illustrate how little of the FPGA's speech processing potential is actually used, leaving significant room for addition designs, such as, a hardware speech decoder. Furthermore, with the sharing of speech preprocessing hardware between the MFCC feature extraction and the two speech enhancement designs, the embedded speech enhancement feature is provided almost for free. Speech recognition experiments using noisy files from the AVICAR database indicates the speech enhancement provides clear improvement in recognition performance, particularly for cases where the speech enhancement techniques are combined.

However, it should be noted that this speech recognition test is rather limited in scope. In that, it only uses the AVICAR phone numbers task and microphones in limited positions. To gain a more accurate measurement of speech recognition performance, comprehensive experiments would be required using many speech databases and vocabularies. To do this requires considerable time and processing power which was beyond the range of this work where the

focus was on the hardware design. Also, tests using different microphone positions relative to the speaker should be conducted as microphone position may impact on performance.
In conclusion, the real-time hardware feature extraction with embedded signal enhancement for automatic speech recognition design has been demonstrated to be effective and equivalent in performance to a comparable software system. Furthermore, it exhibits characteristic suitable for application in low-cost automotive applications, although it may also be used in other noisy environments.

6. Acknowledgment

The authors gratefully acknowledge the Cooperative Research Centre for Advance Automotive Technologies (AutoCRC) for their partial support of this work.

7. References

Aarabi, P. & Shi, G. (2004). Phase-based dual-microphone robust speech enhancement, *IEEE Transactions on Systems, Man, and Cybernetics, Part B* 34(4): 1763–1773.

Ahn, S. & Ko, H. (2005). Background noise reduction via dual-channel scheme for speech recognition in vehicular environment, *IEEE Transaction on Consumer Electronics* 51(1): 22–27.

Beh, J., Baran, R. H. & Ko, H. (2006). Dual channel based speech enhancement using novelty filter for robust speech recognition in automobile environment, *IEEE Transaction on Consumer Electronics* 52(2): 583–589.

Benesty, J., Makino, S. & Chen, J. (2005). *Speech Enhancement*, Springer.

Berouti, M., Schwartz, R. & Makhoul, J. (1979). Enhancement of speech corrupted by acoustic noise, *Proc. IEEE Int. Conf. on Acoustics, Speech, and Signal Processing*, pp. 208–211.

Bitzer, J. & Simmer, K. U. (2001). Superdirective microphone arrays, *in* M. S. Brandstein & D. B. Ward (eds), *Microphone Arrays*, Springer, chapter 2, pp. 19–38.

Boll, S. (1979). Suppression of acoustic noise in speech using spectral subtraction, *Acoustics, Speech and Signal Processing, IEEE Transactions on* 27(2): 113 – 120.

Han, W., Chan, C.-F., Choy, C.-S. & Pun, K.-P. (2006). An efficient mfcc extraction method in speech recognition, *Circuits and Systems, 2006. ISCAS 2006. Proceedings. 2006 IEEE International Symposium on*, pp. 4 pp.–.

Harris, F. (1978). On the use of windows for harmonic analysis with the discrete fourier transform, *Proceedings of the IEEE* 66(1): 51–83.

Johnson, D. H. & Dudgeon, D. E. (1992). *Array Signal Processing: Concepts and Techniques*, Simon & Schuster.

Kleinschmidt, T. (2010). *Robust Speech Recognition using Speech Enhancement*, PhD thesis, Queenslan University of Technology. http://eprints.qut.edu.au/31895/1/Tristan_Kleinschmidt_Thesis.pdf.

Kleinschmidt, T., Dean, D., Sridharan, S. & Mason, M. (2007). A continuous speech recognition evaluation protocol for the avicar database, *1st International Conference on Signal Processing and Communication Systems*, Gold Coast, Australia, pp. 339–344.

Lee, B., Hasegawa-johnson, M., Goudeseune, C., Kamdar, S., Borys, S., Liu, M. & Huang, T. (2004). Avicar: Audio-visual speech corpus in a car environment, *in Proc. Conf. Spoken Language, Jeju, Korea*, pp. 2489–2492.

Lin, Q., Jan, E.-E. & Flanagan, J. (1994). Microphone arrays and speaker identification, *Speech and Audio Processing, IEEE Transactions on* 2(4): 622 –629.

Lockwood, P. & Boudy, J. (1992). Experiments with a nonlinear spectral subtractor (nss), hidden markov models and the projection, for robust speech recognition in cars, *Speech Commun.* 11(2-3): 215–228.

Ortega-Garcia, J. & Gonzalez-Rodriguez, J. (1996). Overview of speech enhancement techniques for automatic speaker recognition, *Spoken Language, 1996. ICSLP 96. Proceedings., Fourth International Conference on*, Vol. 2, pp. 929 –932.

Vu, N., Whittington, J., Ye, H. & Devlin, J. (2010). Implementation of the mfcc front-end for low-cost speech recognition systems, *Circuits and Systems (ISCAS), Proceedings of 2010 IEEE International Symposium on*, pp. 2334 –2337.

Vu, N., Ye, H., Whittington, J., Devlin, J. & Mason, M. (2010). Small footprint implementation of dual-microphone delay-and-sum beamforming for in-car speech enhancement, *Acoustics Speech and Signal Processing (ICASSP), 2010 IEEE International Conference on*, pp. 1482 –1485.

Vu, N. (2010). Method and device for computing matrices for discrete Fourier transform (DFT) coefficients, *Patent No. WO/2010/028440*.

Wang, J.-C., Wang, J.-F. & Weng, Y.-S. (2002). Chip design of mfcc extraction for speech recognition, *Integr. VLSI J.* 32(1-3): 111–131.

Whittington, J., Deo, K., Kleinschmidt, T. & Mason, M. (2008). Fpga implementation of spectral subtraction for in-car speech enhancement and recognition, *Signal Processing and Communication Systems, 2008. ICSPCS 2008. 2nd International Conference on*, pp. 1–8.

Whittington, J., Deo, K., Kleinschmidt, T. & Mason, M. (2009). Fpga implementation of spectral subtraction for automotive speech recognition, *Computational Intelligence in Vehicles and Vehicular Systems, 2009. CIVVS '09. IEEE Workshop on*, pp. 72–79.

Widrow, B. & Stearns, S. D. (1985). *Adaptive Signal Processing*, Prentice-Hall.

Xilinx (2010). Cordic v4.0 product specification.
    URL: *http://www.xilinx.com/support/documentation/ip_documentation/cordic_ds249.pdf*

Young, S. J., Evermann, G., Gales, M. J. F., Hain, T., Kershaw, D., Moore, G., Odell, J., Ollason, D., Povey, D., Valtchev, V. & Woodland, P. C. (2006). *The HTK Book, version 3.4*, Cambridge University Engineering Department, Cambridge, UK.

3

Nonlinear Dimensionality Reduction Methods for Use with Automatic Speech Recognition

Stephen A. Zahorian and Hongbing Hu
Binghamton University, NY,
USA

1. Introduction

For nearly a century, researchers have investigated and used mathematical techniques for reducing the dimensionality of vector valued data used to characterize categorical data with the goal of preserving "information" or discriminability of the different categories in the reduced dimensionality data. The most established techniques are Principal Components Analysis (PCA) and Linear Discriminant Analysis (LDA) (Jolliffe, 1986; Wang & Paliwal, 2003). Both PCA and LDA are based on linear, i.e. matrix multiplication, transformations. For the case of PCA, the transformation is based on minimizing mean square error between original data vectors and data vectors that can be estimated from the reduced dimensionality data vectors. For the case of LDA, the transformation is based on minimizing a ratio of "between class variance" to "within class variance" with the goal of reducing data variation in the same class and increasing the separation between classes. There are newer versions of these methods such as Heteroscedastic Discriminant Analysis (HDA) (Kumar & Andreou, 1998; Saon et al., 2000). However, in all cases certain assumptions are made about the statistical properties of the original data (such as multivariate Gaussian); even more fundamentally, the transformations are restricted to be linear.

In this chapter, a class of nonlinear transformations is presented both from a theoretical and experimental point of view. Theoretically, the nonlinear methods have the potential to be more "efficient" than linear methods, that is, give better representations with fewer dimensions. In addition, some examples are shown from experiments with Automatic Speech Recognition (ASR) where the nonlinear methods in fact perform better, resulting in higher ASR accuracy than obtained with either the original speech features, or linearly reduced feature sets.

Two nonlinear transformation methods, along with several variations, are presented. In one of these methods, referred to as nonlinear PCA (NLPCA), the goal of the nonlinear transformation is to minimize the mean square error between features estimated from reduced dimensionality features and original features. Thus this method is patterned after PCA. In the second method, referred to as nonlinear LDA (NLDA), the goal of the nonlinear transformation is to maximize discriminability of categories of data. Thus the method is patterned after LDA. In all cases, the dimensionality reduction is accomplished with a Neural Network (NN), which internally encodes data with a reduced number of dimensions. The differences in the methods depend on error criteria used to train the network, the architecture of the network, and the extent to which the reduced dimensions are "hidden" in the neural network.

The two basic methods and their variations are illustrated experimentally using phonetic classification experiments with the NTIMIT database and phonetic recognition experiments with the TIMIT database. The classification experiments are performed with either a neural network or Bayesian maximum likelihood Mahalanobis distance based Gaussian assumption classifier For the phonetic recognition experiments, the reduced dimensionality speech features are the inputs to a Hidden Markov Model (HMM) recognizer that is trained to create phone level models and then used to recognize phones in separate test data. Thus, in one sense, the recognizer is a hybrid neural network/Hidden Markov Model (NN/HMM) recognizer. However, the neural network step is used for the task of nonlinear dimensionality reduction and is independent of the HMM. It is shown that the NLDA approach performs better than the NLPCA approach in terms of recognition accuracy. It is also shown that speech recognition accuracy can be as high as or even higher using reduced dimensionality features versus original features, with "properly" trained systems.

2. Background

Modern automatic speech recognition systems often use a large number of spectral/ temporal "features" (i.e., 50 to 100 terms) computed with typical frame spaces on the order of 10 ms. Partially because of these high dimensionality feature spaces, large vocabulary continuous speech automatic speech recognition often have several million parameters that must be determined from training data (Zhao et al., 1999). In this scenario, the "curse of dimensionality" (Donoho, 2000) becomes a serious practical issue; for high recognition accuracy with test data, the feature dimensionality should be reduced, ideally preserving discriminability between phonetically different sounds, and/or large databases should be used for training. Both approaches are used. Despite growing computer size and computer storage densities, it should be noted that in principle the amount of data needed for adequate training grows exponentially with the number of features; for example, increasing dimensionality from 40 to 50, increases the need for more data by a factor proportional to $k^{(50-40)} = k^{10}$, where k is some number representing the average number of data samples distributed along each dimension, and almost certainly 2 or larger. Thus, for good training of model parameters, increasing dimensionality from 40 to 50, considered a modest increase, could easily increase the need for more data by a factor of 1000 or more. Therefore it seems unlikely that increased database size alone is a good approach to improved ASR accuracies by training with more and more features.

In this chapter, some techniques are presented for reducing feature dimensionality while preserving category (i.e., phonetic for the case of speech) discriminability. Since the techniques presented for reducing dimensionality are statistically based, these methods also are subject to "curse of dimensionality" issues. However, since this dimensionality reduction can be done at the very front end of a speech recognition system, with fewer model parameters tuned than in an overall recognition system, the "curse" can be less of a problem. We first review some traditional linear methods for dimensionality reduction before proceeding to the nonlinear transformation, the main subject of this chapter.

2.1 Principal Components Analysis (PCA)

Principal Components Analysis (PCA), also known as the Karhunen-Loeve Transform (KLT), has been known of and in use for nearly a century (Fodor, 2002; Duda et al., 2001), as a linear method for dimensionality reduction. Operationally, PCA can be described as follows:

Let $\mathbf{X} = [x_1, x_2, ..., x_n]^T$ be an n-dimensional (column) feature vector, and $\mathbf{Y} = [y_1, y_2, ..., y_m]^T$ be an m-dimensional (column) feature vector, obtained as the linear transform of $\mathbf{X}$, using the n by m transformation matrix $\mathbf{A}$, i.e. $\mathbf{Y} = \mathbf{A}^T\mathbf{X}$.

Let $\hat{\mathbf{X}} = \mathbf{BY}$ be an approximation to $\mathbf{X}$. Note that $\mathbf{X}, \mathbf{Y}$ and $\hat{\mathbf{X}}$ can all be viewed as (column) vector-valued random variables. The goal of PCA is to determine $\mathbf{A}$ and $\mathbf{B}$, such that $E\{(\mathbf{X}-\hat{\mathbf{X}})^2\}$ is minimized. That is, $\hat{\mathbf{X}}$ should approximate $\mathbf{X}$ as well as possible, in a mean square error sense. As has been shown in several references (for example, Duda et al., 2001), this seemingly intractable problem has a very straightforward solution, provided $\mathbf{X}$ is zero mean and multivariate Gaussian. The rows of transformation $\mathbf{A}^T$ have been shown to be the eigenvectors of the covariance matrix of $\mathbf{X}$, corresponding to the m largest eigenvalues of this matrix. The columns of $\mathbf{B}$ are also the same eigenvectors. Thus the "forward" and "reverse" transformations are transposes of each other. The components of $\mathbf{Y}$ are uncorrelated. Furthermore the expected value of this normalized mean square error between original and re-estimated $\mathbf{X}$ vectors can be shown to equal the ratio of the sum of "unused" eignevalues to the sum of all eigenvalues. The columns of $\mathbf{A}$ are called the principal components basis vectors and the components of $\mathbf{Y}$ are called the principal components.

If the underlying assumption of zero mean multivariate Gaussian random variables is satisfied, then this method of feature reduction generally performs very well. The principal components are also statistically independent for the Gaussian case. The principal components "account for" or explain the maximum amount of variance of the original data. Figure 1 shows an example of scatter plot of 2-D multivariate data and the resulting orientation of the first primary principal components basis vector. As expected this basis vector, represented by a straight line, is oriented along the axis with maximum data variation.

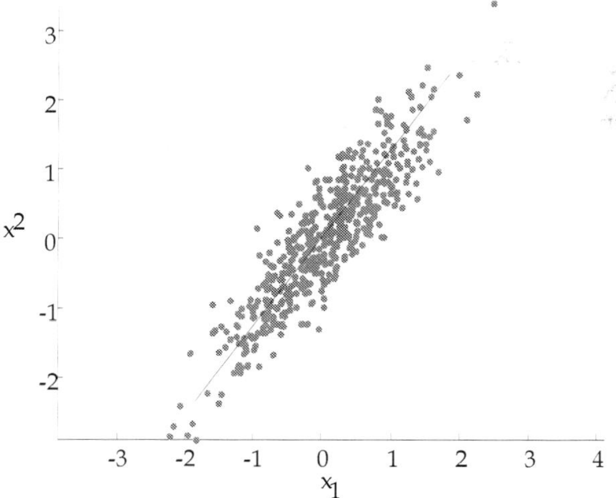

Fig. 1. Scatter plot of 2-D multivariate Gaussian data and first principal components basis vector. Line is a good fit to data.

Figure 2 depicts data which is primarily aligned with a U shaped curve in a 2-D space, and the resulting straight line (PCA) basis vector fit to this data. Since the original data is not multivariate Gaussian, the PCA basis vector is no longer a good way to approximate the data. In fact, since the data primarily follows a curved path in the 2-D space, no linear transform method, resulting in a straight line subspace, will be a good way to approximate the data with one dimension.

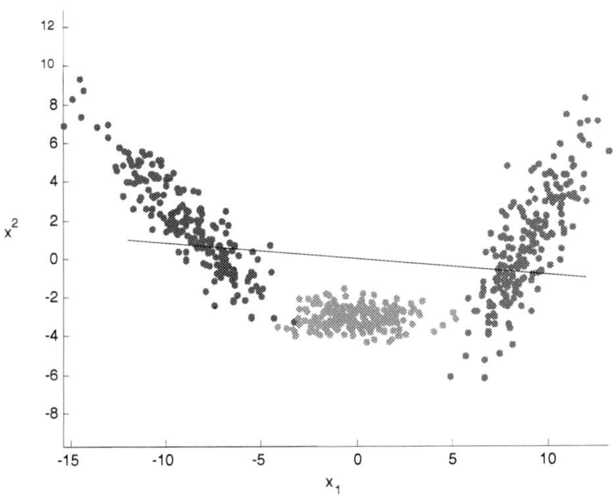

Fig. 2. Scatter plot of 2-D multivariate Gaussian data and first principal components basis vector. No straight line can be a good fit to this data.

2.2 Linear Discriminant Analysis (LDA)

Linear transforms for the purpose of reducing dimensionality while preserving discriminability between pre-defined categories have also long been known about and used (Wang & Paliwal, 2003), and are usually referred to as Linear Discriminant Analysis (LDA). The mathematical usage of this is identical to that for PCA. That is $Y = A^T X$, where X, Y are again column vectors as for PCA.

The big difference is in how A is computed. For LDA, it has been shown that the columns of A correspond to the m largest eigenvalues of $S_W^{-1} S_B$, where S_W is the within class covariance matrix and S_B is the between class covariance matrix.

Often S_B is computed as the covariance of the category means; alternatively, it is sometimes computed as the "grand" covariance matrix over all data, ignoring category labels, identical to the covariance matrix used to compute PCA basis vectors. S_W, the within class covariance matrix, is generally computed by first determining the covariance matrix for each category of data, and then averaging over all categories. The explicit assumption for LDA is that the within class covariance of each category is the same, which is rarely true in practice. Nevertheless, for many practical classification problems, features reduced by LDA often are as effective or even advantageous to original higher dimensional features. Figure 3 depicts 2-D 2-class data, and shows the first PCA basis vector as well as the first LDA basis vector. Clearly, for this example, the two basis vectors are quite different, and clearly the projection of data onto the first LDA basis vector would be more effective for separating the two categories than data projected onto the first PCA basis vector.

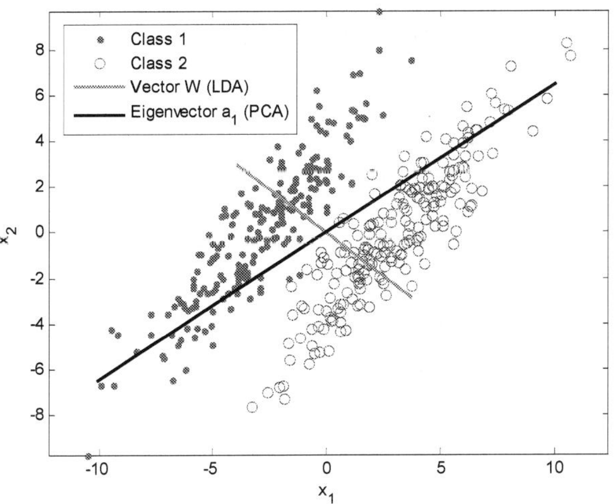

Fig. 3. 2-D 2-class data, along with first LDA basis vector and first PCA basis vector. The classes would be well separated by a projection onto the first LDA basis vector, but poorly separated by a projection onto the first PCA basis vector.

2.3 Heteroscedastic Discriminant Analysis (HDA)

Another linear transformation technique, related to linear discriminant analysis, but which accounts for the (very common) case where within class covariance matrices are not the same for all classes, is called Heterocscedastic Discriminant Analysis (HDA) (Saon et al., 2000). The process for HDA is described in some detail by Saon et al., and illustrated in terms of its ability to better separate (as compared to LDA) data in reduced dimensionality subspaces, when the covariance properties of the individual classes are different.

HDA suffers from two drawbacks. There is no known closed form solution for minimizing the objective function required to solve for the transformation—rather a complex numerically based gradient search is required. More fundamentally, with actual speech data, HDA alone was found to perform far worse than LDA. Nevertheless, if an additional transform, called the Maximum Likelihood Linear Transform (MLLT) (Gopinath, 1998) was used after HDA, then overall performance was found to be the best among the methods tested by Saon et al. However, ASR accuracies obtained with a combination of LDA and MLLT were nearly as good as those obtained with HDA and MLLT. A detailed summary of HDA and MLLT are beyond the scope of this chapter; however, these methods, either by themselves, or in conjunction with the nonlinear methods described in this chapter warrant further investigation.

3. Nonlinear dimensionality reduction

If the data are primarily clustered on curved subspaces embedded in high dimensionality feature spaces, linear transformations for feature dimensionality reduction are not well suited. For example, the data depicted in Figure 2 would be better approximated by its position with respect to a curved U-shape line rather the straight line obtained with linear PCA. (Bishop et al. 1998) discusses several theoretical methods for determining these curved subspaces (manifolds) within higher dimensionality spaces. Another general method, and the one illustrated and explored in more detail in this chapter, is based on a "bottleneck" neural network (Kramer, 1991). This method relies on the general ability of a neural network with nonlinear activation functions at each node, with enough nodes and at least one hidden layer, to be able to determine an arbitrary nonlinear mapping. The general network configuration is shown in Figure 4.

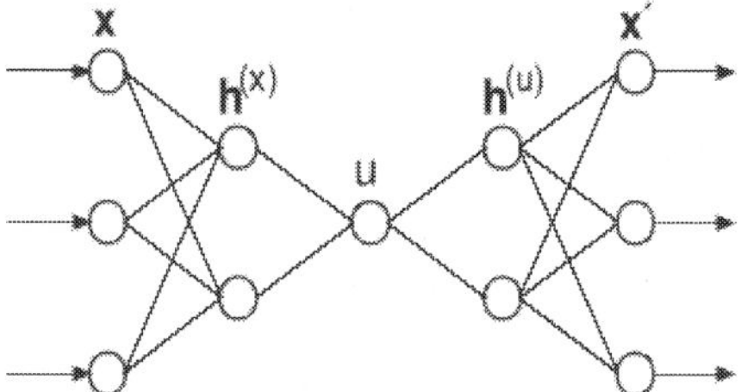

Fig. 4. Architecture of Bottleneck Neural Network.

Presumably, although not necessarily, with enough nodes in each of the hidden layers, and with "proper" training, the network will represent data at the outputs of the bottleneck layer as well as possible in a subspace with a number of dimensions equal to the number of nodes in the bottleneck layer. If data lies along a single curved line in a higher dimensionality space, 1 node in the bottleneck layer should be sufficient. If data lies on a curved surface embedded in a higher dimensionality space, 2 nodes in the bottleneck layer should be sufficient.

3.1 Nonlinear Principal Components Analysis (NLPCA)

If the bottleneck neural network is trained as an identity map, that is with outputs equal to inputs, and using a mean square error objective function, then the neural network can be viewed as performing nonlinear principal components analysis (NLPCA) (Kramer, 1991). Since the final NN outputs are created from the internal NN representations at the bottleneck layer, the bottleneck outputs can be viewed as the reduced dimensionality version of the data. This idea was tested using pseudo-random data generated so as to cluster on curved subspaces.

NLPCA is first illustrated by an example depicted in Figure 5. For this case, 2-D pseudo random data was created to lie along a U shaped curve, similar to the data depicted in Figure 2. A neural network (2-5-1-5-2) was then trained as an identify map. The numbers in parentheses refer to the number of nodes at each layer, proceeding from input to output. All hidden nodes and output nodes had a bipolar sigmoidal activation function. After training with backpropagation, all data were transformed by the neural network. In Figure 5, the original data is shown as blue symbols, and the transformed data is shown by red. Clearly, the data have been projected to a curved U shaped line, as would be expected for the best line fit to the original data.

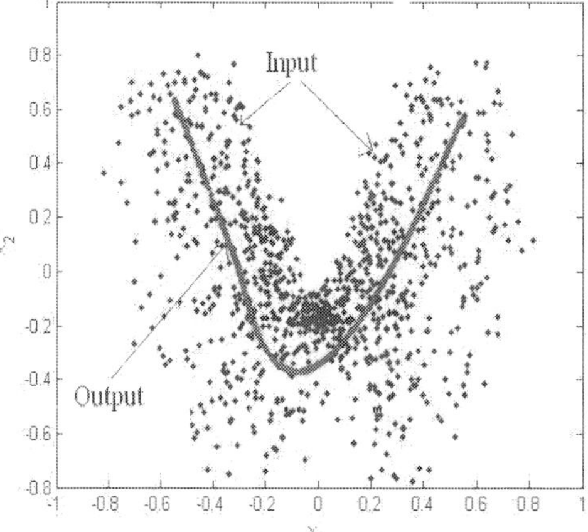

Fig. 5. Plot of input and output data for pseudo-random 2-D data. The output data (red line) is reconstructed data obtained after passing the input data through the trained neural network.

In Figure 6, NLPCA is illustrated by data which falls on a 2-D surface embedded in a 3-D space. For this case, 2-D data pseudo random data are created, but confined to lie on the surface of a 2-D Gaussian shaped surface, as depicted in the left panel of Figure 6. Then a neural network (3-10-2-10-3) was trained as an identity map. After training, the outputs of the neural network are plotted in the right panel of Figure 6. Clearly the neural network "learned" a 2-D internal representation, at the bottleneck layer, from which it could reconstruct the original data.

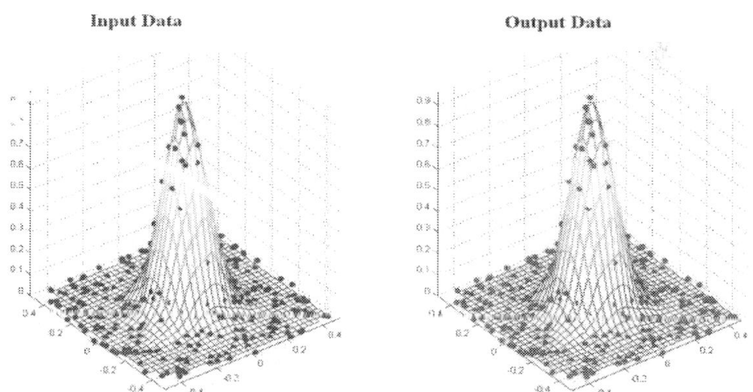

Fig. 6. Input and output plot of the 3-D Gaussian before (left) and after (right) using neural network for NLPCA.

4. Nonlinear Discriminant Analysis (NLDA)

Despite the apparent ability of a neural network to well represent data from reduced dimensions, as illustrated by the examples depicted in Figure 5 and Figure 6, for applications to machine pattern recognition, including automatic speech recognition, a nonlinear feature reduction analogous to linear discriminant analysis might be advantageous to NLPCA. Fortunately, only a minor modification to NLPCA is needed to form NLDA. The same bottleneck network architecture is used, but trained to recognize categories rather than as an identity map. In the remaining part of this chapter, two versions of NLDA based on this strategy are described, followed by a series of experimental evaluations for the phonetic classification and recognition tasks.

4.1 Nonlinear dimensionality reduction architecture

In a previous work (Zahorian et al., 2007), NLPCA was applied to an isolated vowel classification task, and the nonlinear method based on neural networks was experimentally compared with linear methods for reducing the dimensionality of speech features. It was demonstrated that NLPCA which minimizes mean square reconstruction error from a reduced dimensionality space can be very effective for representing data which lies in curved subspaces, but did not appear to offer any advantages over linear dimensionality reduction methods such as PCA and LDA, for a speech classification task. A summary of this work is presented in Section 4.5. In contrast, the nonlinear technique NLDA based on minimizing classification error was quite effective for improving accuracy.

The general form of the NLDA transformer and its relationship to the HMM recognizer are depicted in Figure 7. NLDA is based on a multilayer bottleneck neural network and performs a nonlinear feature transformation of the input data. The outputs of the network are further (optionally) processed by PCA to create transformed features to be the inputs of an HMM recognizer. Note that in this usage, "outputs" may be from the final outputs or from one of the internal hidden layers.

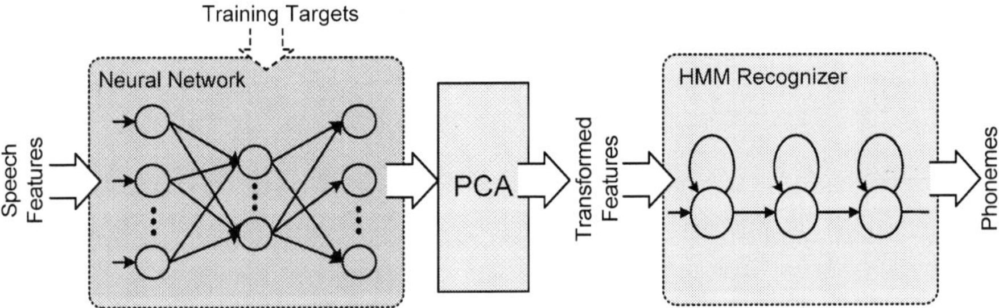

Fig. 7. Overview of the NLDA transformation for speech recognition.

The multilayer bottleneck neural network employed in NLDA contains an input layer, hidden layers including the bottleneck layer, and an output layer. The numbers of nodes in the input and output layers respectively correspond to the dimensions of the input features and the number of categories in the training target data. The targets were chosen as the 48 (collapsed) phones in the training data. The number of hidden layers was experimentally determined as well as the number of nodes included in those layers. However, most typically three hidden layers were used. Two NLDA approaches were investigated as different layers of networks are used to obtain dimensionality reduced data.

4.2 NLDA1

In the first approach, which is referred to as NLDA1, the transformed features are produced from the final output layer of the network. This approach is similar to the use of tandem neural networks used in some automatic speech recognition studies (Hermansky & Sharma, 2000; Ellis et al., 2001). Figure 8 illustrates the use of network outputs in NLDA1.

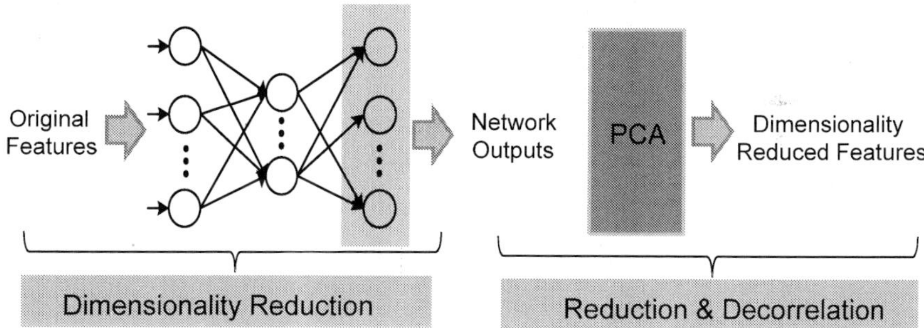

Fig. 8. Use of network outputs in NLDA1.

4.3 NLDA2

Since the activations of the middle layer represent the internal structure of the input features, in the second approach named NLDA2, the outputs of the middle hidden layer, with fewer nodes than the input layer, are used as transformed features to form reduced but more discriminative dimensions. Figure 9 illustrates the use of network outputs in NLDA2. These two versions of NLDA were experimentally tested, with and without PCA following the neural network transformer, with some variations of the nonlinearities in the networks.

The dimensionality of the reduced feature space is determined only by the number of nodes in the middle layer. Therefore, an arbitrary number of reduced dimensions can be obtained, independent of the input feature dimensions and the nature of the training targets. A lower dimensional representation of the input features is easily obtained by simply deploying fewer nodes in the middle layer than the input layer. This flexibility allows dimensionality to be adjusted so as to optimize overall system performance (Hu & Zahorian, 2008; Hu & Zahorian, 2009; Hu & Zahorian, 2010).

In contrast with NLDA1 where dimensionality reduction is assigned to PCA, for NLDA2, since the dimensionality reduction can be accomplished with the neural network only, the linear PCA is used specifically for reducing the feature correlation.

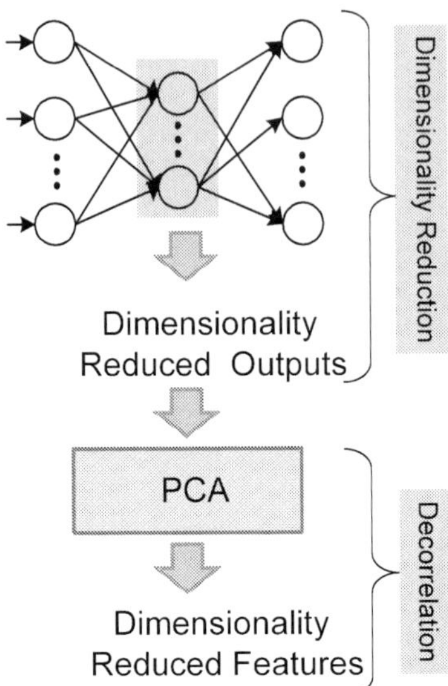

Fig. 9. Middle layer outputs used as dimensionality reduced features in NLDA2.

4.4 Neural networks

In optimizing the design of a neural network, an important consideration is the number of hidden layers and an appropriate number of hidden nodes in each layer. A neural network with no hidden layers can form only simple decision regions, which is not suitable for highly nonlinear and complex speech features. Although it has been shown that a neural network with a single hidden layer is able to represent any function with a sufficient number of hidden nodes (Duda et al., 2001), the use of multiple hidden layers generally provides a flexible configuration such as distributed deployment of hidden nodes, and diverse nonlinear functions for different layers. On the number of hidden nodes, a small number reduces the network's computational complexity. However, the recognition accuracy is often degraded. The more hidden nodes a network has, the more complex a decision surface can be formed, and thus better classification accuracy can be expected (Meng, 2006). Generally, the number of hidden nodes is empirically determined by a combination of accuracy and computational considerations, as applied to a particular application.

Another important consideration is selecting an activation function, or the nonlinearity of a node. Typical choices include a linear activation function, a unipolar sigmoid function and a bipolar sigmoid function as illustrated in Figure 10.

The activation function should match the characteristic of the input or output data. For example, with training targets assigned the values of "0" and "1", a sigmoid function with the outputs in the range of [0, 1] is a good candidate for the output layer. Most typically a mean square error, between the desired output and actual output of the NN, is the objective function that is minimized in NN training. As another powerful approach, the softmax function takes all the nodes in a layer into account and calculates the output of a node as a posterior probability. When the outputs of the network are to be used as transformed features for the HMM recognition, a linear function or a softmax function is appropriate to generate the data with a more diverse distribution, such as one that would be well-modeled with a GMM. Moreover, equipped with various nonlinearities, the neural network is expected to have a stronger discriminative capability and thus it is enabled to cope with more complex data.

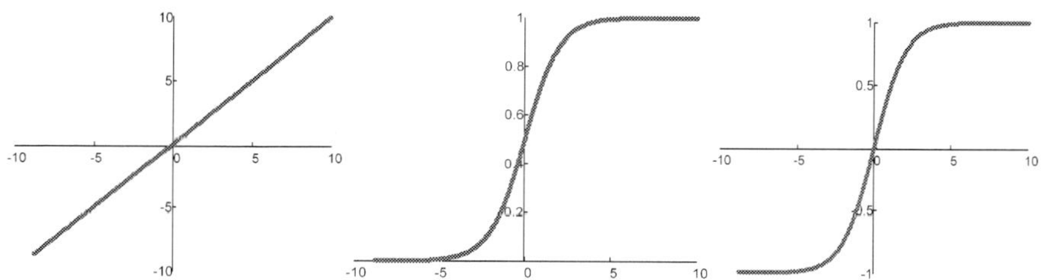

Fig. 10. Illustrations of a linear activation function (left), a unipolar sigmoid function (middle) and a bipolar sigmoid function (right).

The weights of the neural network are estimated using the backpropagation algorithm to minimize the distance between the scaled input features and target data. The update of the weights in each layer depends on the activation function of that layer, thus the network learning can be designed to perform different updates when dissimilar activation functions are used. In addition, a difficulty in neural network training is that the input data has a wide range of means and variances for each feature component. In order to avoid this, the input data of neural networks is often scaled so that all feature components have the same mean (zero) and variance (so that range of values is approximately ± 1).

4.5 Investigation of basic issues

Before performing a series of time consuming phonetic recognition experiments involving the entire TIMIT database, extensive neural network training, and HMM training and evaluation, a more limited set of phonetic classification experiments was conducted using only the vowel sounds extracted from NTIMIT, the telephone version of TIMIT. Note that unlike phonetic recognition experiments, for the case of classification, the timing labels in the database are explicitly used for both training and testing. Thus classification is "easier" than recognition, and accuracies typically higher, since phone boundaries are known in advance and used. In this first series of experiments, classification experiments were conducted using PCA, LDA, NLPCA, and NLDA2 transformations, as well as the original features.

The 10 steady-state vowels /ah/, /ee/, /ue/, /ae/, /ur/, /ih/, /eh/, /aw/, /uh/, and /oo/ were extracted from the NTIMIT database (see section 5.1) and used.

All the training sentences (4620 sentences) were used to extract a total of 31,300 vowel tokens for training. All the test sentences (1680 sentences) were used to extract a total of 11,625 vowel tokens for testing. For each vowel token, 39 DCTC-DCS features were computed using 13 DCTC terms and 3 DCS terms.

For all cases, including original features, and all versions of the transformed features, a neural network classifier with 100 hidden nodes and 10 output nodes, trained with backpropagation, was used as the classifier. In addition, a Bayesian maximum likelihood Mahalanobis distance based Gaussian assumption classifier (MXL) was used for evaluation.

For the neural network transformation cases, the first and third hidden layers had 100 nodes (empirically determined). The number of hidden nodes in the second hidden layer was varied from 1 to 39, according to the dimensionality being evaluated. For the case of NLDA2, the network used for dimensionality reduction was also a classifier. For the sake of consistency, the outputs of the hidden nodes from the bottleneck neural network were used as features for a classifier, using either another neural network or the MXL classifier. [1] In these initial experiments, the bottleneck neural network outputs were not additionally transformed with PCA.

4.5.1 Experiment 1

In the first experiment, all training data were used to train the transformations including LDA, PCA, NLPCA, and NLDA2, and the classifiers. Figure 11 shows the results based on the neural network and MXL classifiers for each transformation method in terms of classification accuracy, as the number of features varies from 1 to 39.

For both the neural network and MXL classifiers, highest accuracy was obtained with NLDA2, especially with a small numbers of features. For the MXL classifier, NLDA2 features result in approximately 10% higher classification accuracies as compared to all other features. For both the neural network and MXL classifiers, accuracy with NLPCA features was very similar to that obtained with linear PCA. For reduced dimensionality features and/or a MXL classifier, the NLDA2 transformation was clearly superior to original features or any of the other feature reduction methods. However, with a neural network classifier and much higher dimensionality features, all feature sets perform similarly in terms of classification accuracy.

As just illustrated, dimensionality reduction is not necessarily advantageous in terms of accuracy for classifiers trained with enough data and the "right" classifier. However, for the case of complex automatic speech recognition systems, there is generally not enough training data.

4.5.2 Experiment 2

To simulate lack of training data, another experiment was conducted. In this experiment, the training data was separated into two groups, with about 50% in each group. One group of data (group 1) was used for "training" transformations while the other data (group 2) was used for training classifiers. In contrast to experiment 1 for which all the training data was used for both the training of transformations and classifiers, for experiment 2, a fixed 50% of the training data was used for "training" transformations and a variable percentage, ranging from 1% to 100% of the other half of the training data, was used for training classifiers.

---

[1] It was, however, experimentally verified that classification results obtained directly from the bottleneck neural network were nearly identical to those obtained with this other network.

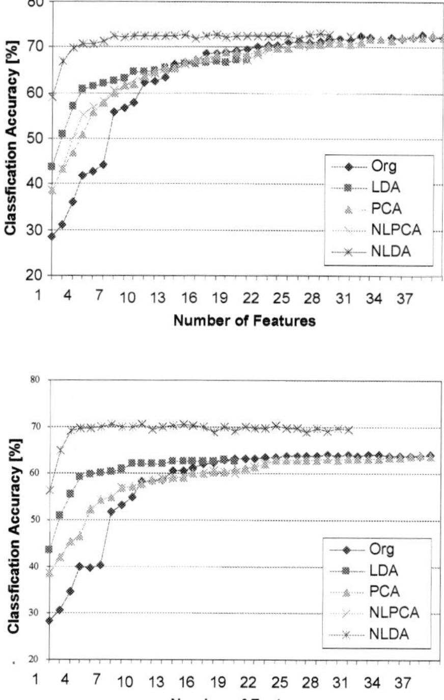

Fig. 11. Classification accuracies of neural network (top panel) and MXL (bottom panel) classifiers with various types of features.

The results obtained with the neural network and MXL classifiers using 10% of the group 2 training data (that is, 5% of the overall training data) are shown in Figure 12. The numbers of features evaluated are 1, 2 4, 8, 16 and 32. For both the neural network and MXL classifiers, NLDA2 clearly performs much better than the other transformations or the original features. However, the advantage of NLDA2 decreases with an increasing number of features, and as the percentage of group 2 data increases (not shown in figure).

4.6 Category labels for discriminatively based transformations

For all discriminatively based transformations, either linear or nonlinear, an implicit assumption is that training data exists which has been labeled according to category. For the case of classification, such as the experiments just described, this labeled data is needed anyway, for both training and test data, to conduct classification experiments; thus the need for category labeled data is not any extra burden. However, for other cases, such as the phonetic recognition experiments described in the remainder of this chapter, there may or may not be easily available and suitable labeled training data. This issue of category labels is described in more detail in the following two subsections.

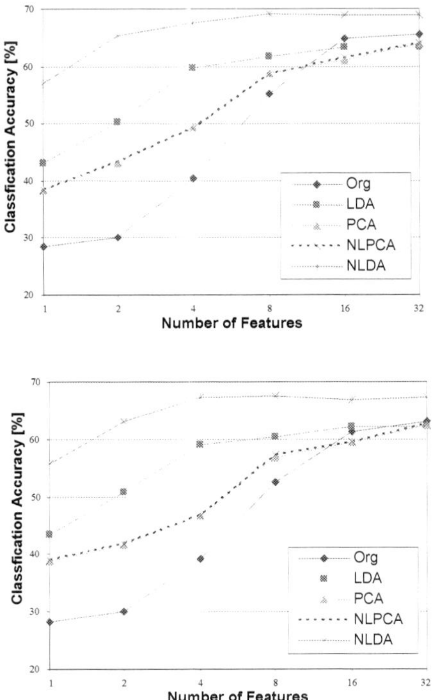

Fig. 12. Classification accuracies of neural network (top panel) and MXL (bottom panel) classifiers using 10% of group 2 training data for training classifier.

4.6.1 Phonetic-level targets

The training of the neural network (NLDA1 and NLDA2) requires category information for creating training targets. For the case of databases such as TIMIT, the data is labeled using 61 phone categories, and the starting point for training discriminative transformations would seem to be these phonetic labels. In the neural network training, these are referred to as targets. Ideally, the targets are uncorrelated, which enables quicker convergence of weight updates. The targets can also be viewed as multidimensional vectors, with a value of "1" for the target category and "0s" for the non-target categories.

Figure 13 illustrates a sequence of phoneme training targets for the TIMIT database using 48 phoneme categories. These vectors have 48 dimensions and each vector consists of only one peak value to indicate the category. Note that, in the TIMIT case, other reasonable choices for targets would be 61 (the number of phone label categories), or 39 (the number of collapses phone categories). However, empirically, the choice of 48 categories, with only some phones combined, seemed to be the best choice for both neural network training targets and for the creation of HMM phone models.

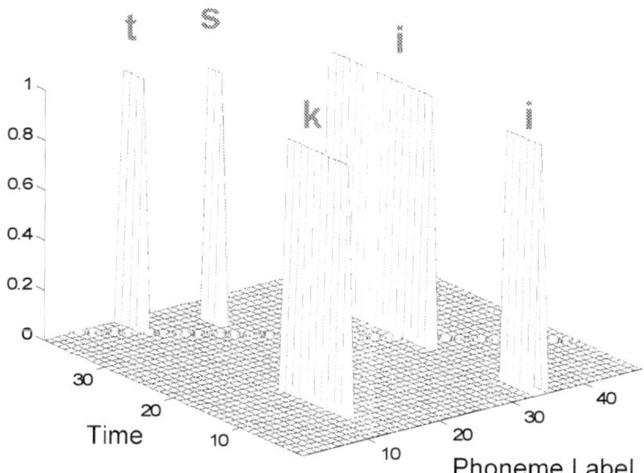

Fig. 13. Training target vectors of the neural network.

4.6.2 State-level targets

Due to the nonstationarity of speech signals, a speech signal varies even in a very short time interval (e.g. a phoneme). For speech recognition tasks, instead of phone level training targets, state (as in hidden states of an HMM) dependent targets could be advantageous in training a versatile network for more highly discriminative speech features. However, the boundaries between states in a phoneme are likely to be indistinct; even more importantly, from a practical perspective is that, unlike phonemes, the (HMM) state boundaries are unknown in advance of training. Thus the estimation of state boundary information is required. This boundary information may be in error due to the nature of unclear state boundaries and the lack of a reliable estimation approach. Therefore, in the discriminative training process, "don't cares" were used to account for this lack of precision in determining state boundaries. In the neural network training process, the errors of output nodes corresponding to "don't cares" are not computed and thus these "don't cares" have no effect on weight updates.

The state training targets with "don't cares" uses "don't care" states for each phoneme model, so that one neural network trained with the targets can generate state dependent outputs. As illustrated in Figure 15, the phone-specific training targets in Figure 14 are expanded to 144 dimensions by duplicating the phoneme specific target by the required number of the states. In the training process, for each point in time, one state target is considered as a "1," and the other two state targets for that point in time are considered as a "don't care," and the state targets for all other categories are considered as "0" value targets. As time progresses during a phone, the "1" moves from state 1 to state 2, to state 3.

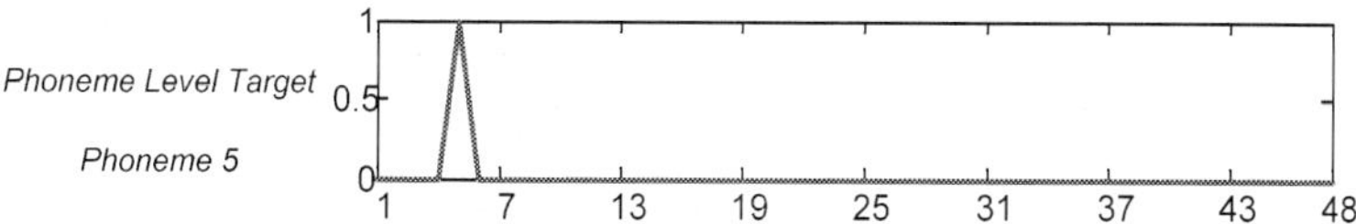

Fig. 14. Illustration of a phoneme level target.

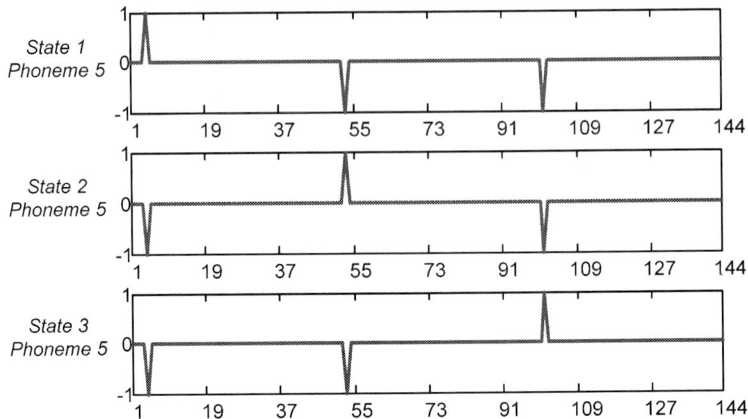

Fig. 15. Illustration of the state level training targets with "don't cares." The -1 values are used to denote "don't cares."

Two approaches are used to determine state boundaries. The first approach uses a fixed state length ratio for all phonemes, with typically about the first 1/6 of each phoneme considered as state 1, the central 2/3 as state 2, and the final 1/6 as state 3 (assuming a 3-state model for each phoneme). The second approach determines state boundaries using the HMM-based Viterbi alignment based on already trained HMMs. As illustrated in one of the experiments presented later, the state dependent targets were shown to perform better than phone level targets. The simpler approach of using fixed ratios for state boundaries was as good as using the Viterbi alignment approach.

5. Evaluation of feature reduction methods with phonetic recognition experiments

Given the high dimensionality of speech feature spaces used for automatic speech recognition, typically 39 or more, it is not feasible to visualize the distribution of data in feature space. It is possible that a reduced dimensionality subspace obtained by linear methods, such as PCA or LDA, forms an effective, or at least adequate subspace for implementing automatic speech recognition systems with a reduced dimensionality feature space. Note that if PCA or LDA do perform well, these methods would be preferred to the nonlinear methods, due to the much simpler implementation methods and the corresponding need for less data. However, it is also possible that one of the nonlinear methods for feature reduction is more effective, that is enable higher ASR accuracy, than any of the linear methods. The comparisons of these various methods can only be done experimentally.

5.1 TIMIT database

The database used for all experiments reported in the remainder of this chapter is TIMIT. The TIMIT database was developed in the early 1980's for expediting acoustic-phonetic ASR research (Garofolo et al., 1993; Zue et al, 1990). It consists of recordings of 10 sentences from each of 630 speakers, or 6300 sentences total. Of the text material in the database, two dialect sentences (SA sentences) were designed to expose the specific variants of the speakers and were read by all 630 speakers. There are 450 phonetically-compact sentences (SX sentences) which provide a good coverage of pairs of phones. Each speaker read 5 of these sentences and each text was spoken by 7 different speakers. A total of 1890 phonetically-diverse sentences (SI sentences) were selected from existing text sources to add diversity in sentence types and phonetic contexts. Each speaker read 3 of these sentences, with each text being read only by a single speaker. All sentences are phonetically labeled with start and stop times for each phoneme.

The database is further divided into a suggested training set (4620 sentences, 462 speakers) and suggested test set (1680 sentences, 168 speakers). The training and test sets are balanced in terms of representing dialect regions and male/female speakers. Although a total of 61 phonetic labels were used in creating TIMIT, due to the great similarity of many of these phonemes (both from a perception point of view and acoustically), most ASR researchers, ever since the work reported by Lee and Hon (Lee & Hon, 1989) have combined these very similar sounding phones, and collapsed the phone set to 39 total. Similarly, most researchers have not used the SA sentences for ASR experiments, since the identical phonetic contexts (every speaker read the same sentences for the SA sentences), were thought be non representative of everyday speech.[2] Most, but not all researchers, have used the recommended training and test sets. For all ASR experiments reported in this chapter, the SA sentences were removed, the recommended training and test sets were used, and the phone set was collapsed to the same 39 phones used in most ASR experiments with TIMIT. The NTIMIT database, used for the classification experiments described in section 4.5, is the same one as TIMIT, except the data was transmitted over phone lines and re-recorded. Thus NTIMIT is more bandlimited (approximately 300Hz to 3400 Hz), more noisy, but has the identical "raw" speech.

5.2 DCTC/DCSC speech features

For both training and testing data, the modified Discrete Cosine Transformation Coefficients (DCTC) and Discrete Cosine Series Coefficients (DCSC) (Zahorian et al. 1991; Zahorian et al., 1997; Zahorian et al., 2002; Karnjanadecha & Zahorian, 1999) were extracted as original features. The modified DCTC is used for representing speech spectra, and the modified DCSC is used to represent spectral trajectories. Each DCTC is represented by a DCSC expansion over time; thus the total number of features equals the number of DCTC terms times the number of DCSC terms. The number of DCTCs used was 13, and number of DCS terms was varied from 4 to 7, for a total number of features ranging from 52 to 91. These numbers are given for each experiment. Additionally, as a control, one experiment was conducted with Mel-frequency Cepstral Coefficients (MFCCs) (Davis & Mermelstein, 1980), since these MFCC features are most typically used in ASR experiments. A total of 39 features including 13 MFCC features, delta terms, and delta-delta terms were extracted from both the training and test data.

5.3 Hidden Markov Models (HMMs)

Left-to-right Markov models with no skip were used and a total of 48 monophone HMMs were created from the training data using the HTK toolbox (Verion 3.4) (Young et al., 2006).

---

[2]With all else identical, the use of SA sentences typically improves ASR accuracy by about 2%.

The bigram phone information extracted from the training data was used as the language model. Various numbers of states and mixtures were evaluated as described in the following experiments. In all cases diagonal covariance matrices were used. For final evaluations of accuracy, some of these 48 monophones were combined to create the "standard" set of 39 phone categories.

5.4 Experiment with various reduced dimensions

The first experiment was conducted to evaluate the two NLDA versions with various dimensions in the reduced feature space with and without the use of PCA. As input features, 13 DCTCs, computed with 8 ms frames and 2 ms spacing, were represented with 6 DCSCs over a 500 ms block, for a total of 78 features (13 DCTCs x 6 DCSCs). The 48-dimensional outputs of the neural network were further reduced by PCA in NLDA1, while the dimensionality reduction was controlled only by the number of nodes in the middle layer in NLDA2. The features which were dimensionality reduced by PCA and LDA alone were also evaluated for the purpose of comparison. Figure 16 shows recognition accuracies of dimensionality reduced features using 1-state and 3-state HMMs with 3 mixtures per state. Note that the NLDA1 features without the PCA process are always 48 dimensions. Compared to the PCA and LDA reduced features, the NLDA1 and NLDA2 features performed considerably better for both the 1-state and 3-state HMMs.

For the case of 3-state HMMs, the transformed features reduced to 24 dimensions resulted in the highest accuracy of 69.3% for NLDA1. A very similar accuracy of 69.2% was obtained with NLDA2 using 36-dimensional features. The recognition accuracies were further improved by about 3% with PCA reduced dimensionality features versus the NLDA features for most cases, showing the effectiveness of PCA in de-correlating the network outputs. The accuracies obtained with the original 78 features, and 3 mixture HMMs, are approximately 58% (1 state models) and 63% (3 state models).

5.5 NLDA1 and NLDA2 experiment with various HMM configurations

The aim of the second experiment is a more thorough evaluation of NLDA1 and NLDA2 using a varying number of states and mixtures in HMMs. The 78 DCTC/DCSCs (computed as mentioned in previous section) were reduced to 36 dimensions based on the results of the previous experiment. The 48 phoneme level targets were used in the training of the network. The features which are the direct outputs of the network without PCA processing were also evaluated.

Figure 17 shows accuracies using 1-state and 3-state HMMs with a varying number of mixtures per state. NLDA2 performed better than NLDA1 for all conditions--approximately 2% higher accuracy. The NLDA2 transformed features resulted in the highest accuracy of 73.4% with 64 mixtures, which is about 1.5% higher than the original features for the same condition. The use of PCA improves accuracy on the order of 2% to 10%, depending on the conditions. Although not shown explicitly by the results depicted in Figure 17, it was also experimentally determined that for NLDA1, highest accuracies were obtained using a nonlinearity in the output nodes of the NN for training, but replacing this with a linear node for transforming the features for use with the HMM. In contrast, for NLDA2, best performance was obtained with the nonlinearities used for both training and final transformations. The superiority of the NLDA transformed features is more significant when a small number of mixtures are used. For example, the NLDA2 features modeled by 3-

state HMMs with 3 mixtures resulted in an accuracy of 69.4% versus 63.2% for the original features.

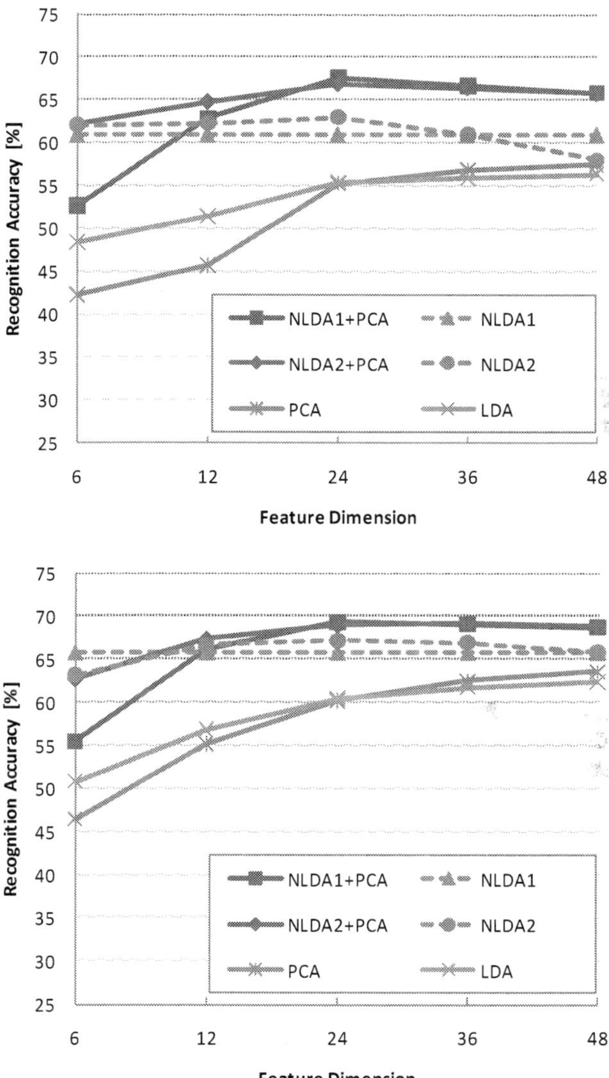

Fig. 16. Accuracies of NLDA1 and NLDA2 with various dimensionality reduced features based on 1-state (top panel) and 3-state HMMs (bottom panel). The NLDA1 features without PCA are always 48 dimensions.

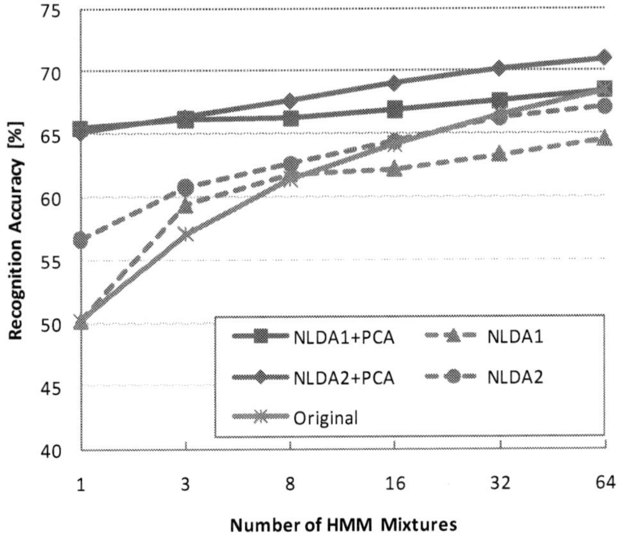

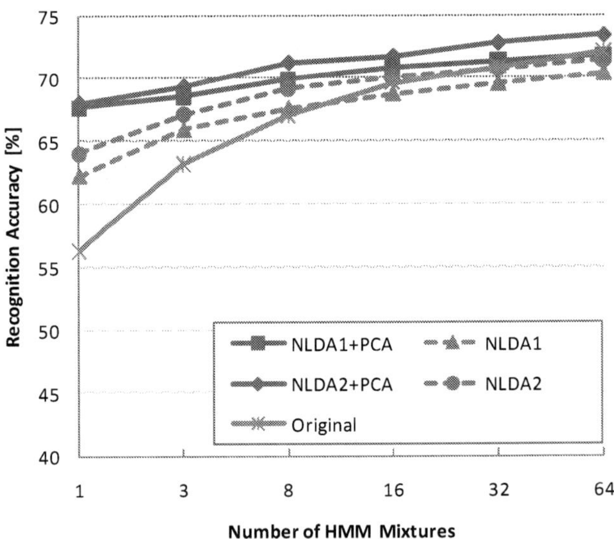

Fig. 17. Accuracies of the NLDA1 and NLDA2 features using 1-state (top panel) and 3-state HMMs (bottom panel) with various numbers of mixtures.

These results imply that the middle layer outputs of a neural network are able to better represent original features in a dimensionality-reduced space than are the outputs of the final output layer. The configuration of HMMs can be largely simplified by incorporating NLDA.

5.6 Experiments with large network training

The results of the previous experiment showed large performance advantages for NLDA2 over NLDA1 and the original features, when using either a small number of features, or a "small" HMM. However, if all original features were used, and a 3- state HMM with a large number of mixtures were used, there was very little advantage of NLDA2, in terms of phonetic recognition accuracy. Therefore, an additional experiment was performed, using the state level targets with "don't cares," as mentioned previously, and a very large neural network for transforming features. The state targets were formed using either a constant length ratio (ratio for 3 states: 1:4:1) or a Viterbi forced alignment approach, as described in Section 4.5. The expanded neural networks had 144 output nodes and were iteratively trained. For both NLDA1 and NLDA2, the networks were configured with 78-500-36-500-144 nodes, going from input to output.

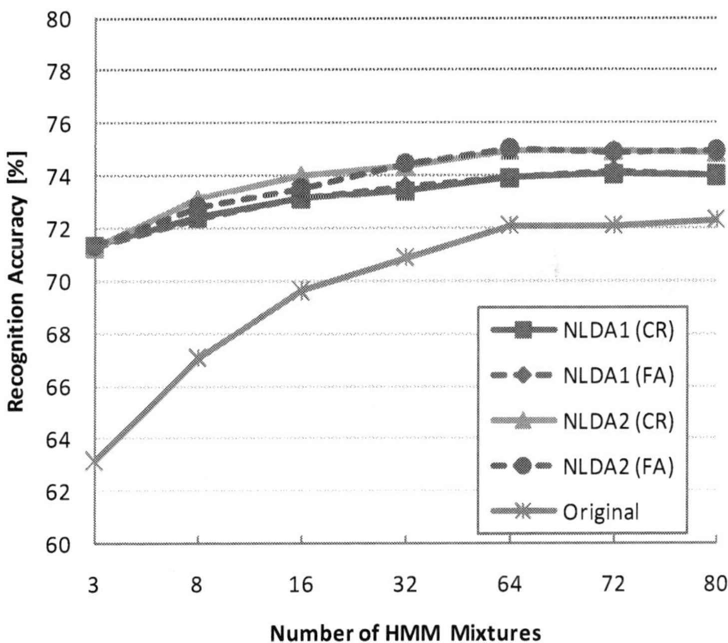

Fig. 18. Recognition accuracies of the NLDA dimensionality reduced features using the state level targets. "(CR)" and "(FA)" indicate the training targets obtained with the constant length ratio and forced alignment respectively.

As shown in Figure 18, both NLDA1 and NLDA2 using the expanded targets lead to a significant increase in accuracy. The NLDA2 accuracies are typically about 2% higher than NLDA1 accuracies. The use of forced alignment for state boundaries resulted in the highest accuracy of 75.0% with 64 mixtures. However, the best result using the much simpler constant ratio method is only marginally lower at 74.9%. Similar experiments, with all identical conditions except using either phone level targets, or state level targets without "don't cares" resulted in about 2% lower accuracies. These results imply that the use of "don't cares" is able to reduce errors introduced by inaccurate determination of state boundaries.

Comparing these results with those from Figure 17, the NLDA2 features in a reduced 36-dimensional space achieved a substantial improvement versus the original features, especially when a small number of mixtures were used. These results show the NLDA methods based on the state level training targets are able to form highly discriminative features in a dimensionality reduced space.

5.7 MFCC experiments

For comparison, 39-dimensional MFCC features (12 coefficients plus energy with the delta and acceleration terms) were reduced to 36 dimensions with the same configurations and evaluated. The results followed the same trend, but the accuracies were about 4% lower than those of the DCTC-DCSC features for all cases, for example, 70.7% with NLDA2 using forced alignment and 32 mixtures.

6. Conclusions

Nonlinear dimensionality reduction methods, based on the general nonlinear mapping abilities of neural networks, can be useful for capturing most of the information from high dimensional spectral/temporal features, using a much smaller number of features. A neural network internal representation in a "bottleneck" layer is more effective than the representation at the output of a neural network. The neural network features also should be linearly transformed with a principal components transform in order to be effective for use by a Hidden Markov Model. For use with a multi-hidden-state Hidden Markov Model, the nonlinear transform should be trained with state-specific targets, but using "don't cares," to account for imprecise information about state boundaries. In future work, linear transforms other than principal components analysis, such as heteroscedastic linear transforms followed by maximum likelihood linear transforms, should be explored for post processing of the nonlinear transforms. Alternatively, the neural network architecture and/or training constraints could be modified so that the nonlinearly transformed features are more suitable as input features for a Hidden Markov Model.

7. References

Bishop, C. M.; Svensén, M. & Williams, C. K. I. (1998). GTM: The generative topographic mapping. *Neural Computation*, 10 (1): 215-234, 1998.

Davis, S. B. & Mermelstein, P. (1980). Comparison of parametric representations for monosyllabic word recognition in continuously spoken sentences, *IEEE Trans. on Acoustics, Speech and Signal Processing* , 28, 357-366.

Donoho, D. L. (2000). *Aide-Memoire. High-Dimensional Data Analysis: The Curses and Blessings of Dimensionality*. Department of Statistics, Stanford University.

Duda, R. O.; Hart, P. E. & Stork, D. G. (2001). *Pattern Classification*. (R. O. Duda, Ed.) New York: A Wiley-Interscience Publication.

Ellis, D.; Singh, R. & Sivadas, S. (2001). Tandem Acoustic Modeling In Large-Vocabulary Recognition. *Proc. ICASSP '01*, pp. 517-520, Salt Lake City, USA, May 7-11, 2001.

Fodor, I. (2002). *A Survey of Dimension Reduction Techniques*. Technical Report, Center for Applied Scientific Computing, Lawrence Livermore National Laboratory.

Garofolo, J. S.; Lamel, L. F.; Fisher, W. M.; Fiscus, J. G.; Pallett, D. S. & Dahlgren, N. L. (1993). TIMIT Acoustic-Phonetic Continuous Speech Corpus, http://www.ldc.upenn.edu/Catalog/LDC93S1.html. *TIMIT Acoustic-Phonetic Continuous Speech Corpus*.

Hermansky, H.; Ellis D. P. W. & Sharma, S. (2000). Tandem connectionist feature extraction for conventional HMM systems. *Proc. ICASSP '00*, *3*, pp. 1635-1638. Istanbul, Turkey, June 5-9, 2000.

Hu, H. & Zahorian, S. A. (2008). A Neural Network Based Nonlinear Feature Transformation for Speech Recognition. *Proc. INTERSPEECH '08*, pp. 533-1536, Brisbane, Australia, Sept. 22-26, 2008.

Hu, H. & Zahorian, S. A. (2009). Neural Network Based Nonlinear Discriminant Analysis for Speech Recognition. *Proc. ANNIE 2009*.

Hu, H. & Zahorian, S. A. (2010). Dimensionality Reduction Methods for HMM Phonetic Recognition. *Proc. ICASSP 2010*, pp. 4854 – 4857, Dallas, Texas, March 14-19, 2010.

Jolliffe, I. (1986). *Principal Component Analysis*. New York: Springer-Verlag.

Karnjanadecha, M. & Zahorian, S. A. (1999). Signal modeling for isolated word recognition. *Proc. ICASSP '99*. pp. 293-296, Phoenix, Arizona, March 15-19, 1999.

Kramer, M. A. (1991). Nonlinear principal component analysis using autoassociative neural networks. *AIChE Journal*, *37*, 233-243.

Kumar, N. & Andreou, A. G. (1998). Heteroscedastic discriminant analysis and reduced rank HMMs for improved speech recognition. *Speech Communication*, *26*, 283-297.

Lee, K.-F. & Hon, H. W. (1989). Speaker-independent phone recognition using hidden Markov models. *IEEE Transactions on Acoustics, Speech, and Signal Processing*, *37*, 1641-1648.

Meng, F. (2006). *Whole Word Phonetic Displays for Speech Articulation Training*. Ph.D. Dissertation, Old Dominion University, Norfolk, VA.

Saon, G.; Padmanabhan, M.; Gopinath, R. & Chen, S. (2000). Maximum likelihood discriminant feature spaces. *Proc. ICASSP '00*, pp. II1129--II1132, Istanbul, Turkey, June 5-9, 2000.

Wang, X. & Paliwal, K. K. (2003). Feature extraction and dimensionality reduction algorithms and their applications in vowel recognition. *Pattern Recognition*, *36*, 2429-2439.

Young, S.; Evermann, G.; Gales, M.; Hain, T.; Kershaw, D.; Liu, X.; Moore, G.; Odell, J.; Ollason, D.; Povey, D.; Valtchev, V. & Woodland, P. (2006). *The HTK Book (for HTK Version 3.4)*, Cambridge University Engineering Department.

Zahorian, S. A.; Qian, D. & Jagharghi, A. J. (1991). Acoustic-phonetic transformations for improved speaker-independent isolated word recognition. *Proc. ICASSP'91*, pp. 561-564. Toronto, Ontario, Canada, May 14-17, 1991.

Zahorian, S.; Silsbee, P. & Wang, X. (1997). Phone Classification with Segmental Features and a Binary-Pair Partitioned Neural Network Classifier. *Proc. ICASSP '97*, pp. 1011-1014, Munich, Germany, April 21-24, 1997.

Zahorian, S. A.; Zimmer, A. M. & Meng, F. (2002). Vowel Classification for Computer-based Visual Feedback for Speech Training for the Hearing Impaired, *Proc. ICSLP 2002*, pp. 973-976, Denver, CO, Sept. 16-20, 2002.

Zahorian, S. A.; Singh, T. & Hu, H. (2007). Dimensionality Reduction of Speech Features using Nonlinear Principal Components Analysis. *Proc. INTERSPEECH '07*, pp. 1134-1137, Antwerb, Belgium, Aug. 27-31, 2007.

Zhao, J.; Zhang, X.; Ganapathiraju, A.; Deshmukh, N. & Picone, J. (1999). Decision Tree-Based State Tying For Acoustic Modeling. *A Tutorial*, Institute for Signal and Information Processing, Department of Electrical and Computer Engineering, Mississippi State University.

Zue, V.; Seneff, S. & Glass, J. (1990). Speech database development at MIT: Timit and beyond. *Speech Communication*, 9, 351-356.

4

Determination of Spectral Parameters of Speech Signal by Goertzel Algorithm

Božo Tomas[1,2,3] and Darko Zelenika[2,3]
[1]Croatian Telecom d.d. Mostar
[2]University "Herzegovina", Faculty of Social Sciences Dr. Milenko Brkić
[3]University of Mostar, Faculty of Mechanical Engineering and Computing
Bosnia and Herzegovina

1. Introduction

The speech is a sound different from all other sounds, and information transmission by speech is a basic mechanism of human communication. The study of speech as one of the main factors of human communication is a multidisciplinary problem thus different fields of science deal with particular aspects of this phenomenon. At the beginning of 21st century the biggest scientific challenge in the segment of speech technologies is the realization of spontaneous communication between human and computer. Technology's solution of recognition and synthesis of speech can't compare with human perceptions and production of the speech. That means our nature, God given, emotion and acts aren't still enough explored, and we have here a lot of space for learning, watching and scientific exploring.

With talking we can transmit to our surroundings complicated information expressed by linguistic contents, but that aren't the least level communication's possibility of speech sound. Sound, which transfers speech signal, carries many information which speech signal contains and decodes that information as well as their production is spontaneous and very simple for human perception (Tomas, 2006). Furthermore, identification, evaluation and selection of certain information contents from a total audio picture are at a consciousness level. Besides linguistic information, the speech signal contains a variety of non-linguistic information from which a listener can get a great deal of information that is not contained in the linguistic information, such as: gender, speaker's age, intentions, a psychological state, and situation the speaker is in; an emotional state of the speaker; surrounding the speaker is in, etc (Tomas et al., 2007a; 2007b; 2009).

Emotions are definitely one of the most important non-linguistic speech attributes (Dellaert & Waibel, 1996). Speaker's emotional state has influence on the articulation and phonation pronounced phonemes. A vocal fold vibration and articulators movement depends on emotional state of speaker. Each speaker's emotion forms vocal chords and vocal system that is acoustically shown through variations of the speech signal parameters. The main problem is to define the parameters that create certain illusions in a speech signal, namely to define correlations between emotions and measurable variations of speech signal parameters (Amir & Ron, 1998; Ramamohan & Dandapt, 2006; Tao et al., 2006). In last few years, numerous investigations have been done in order to determine correlation of the speech parameters and the speaker's emotional state (Amir, 2001; Amir & Ron, 1998; Cowie et al., 2001; Lee & Narayanan, 2005; Morrison et al., 2007; Petrushin, 2000; Scherer, 2003; Ser et al., 2008; Ververidis & Kotropoulos, 2006; Wiliams & Stevens, 1972).

In this chapter, the spectral parameters during the pronouncing of vowels /a/ and /e/ in Croatian (Serbian, Bosnian) language in different emotional conditions has been analyzed. This is done by analyzing structure of vowels /a/ and /e/ spectral parameters for three emotional states: neutral, anger and speech under stress. Impact of emotions on speech signals parameters was analyzed: formant frequencies structure, pitch frequency, dynamics of pitch parameters and pitch harmonics structure. This chapter also describes the Goertzel algorithm and its implementation with speech signal spectral analysis. It describes the method of formant analysis of vowels as well as the vowel harmonics analysis of Goertzel algorithm. The Goertzel algorithm provides fast and simple determination of speech signal structure and precisely determines speech signal frequency values independently of speaker. In analysis of certain speech signal parameters, non-linguistic speech signal attributes can be recognized. The purpose of introducing Goertzel algorithm into the frequency analysis of the digital speech signal is a fast signal processing, and determining of spectral energy from the digital signal in desired frequency bins on the basis of pre-defined coefficient m.

The chapter is organized as follows. In Section 2 the phonetic characteristics of the Croatian language are shortly presented. In Section 3 recording of speech sound materials as well as Goertzel algorithm are shortly presented. Spectral energy analysis of isolated vowels and formant vowel structure tracking by Goertzel algorithm is presented in Section 4. In Section 5, the glottal speech during the pronouncing vowel /a/ has been analyzed. The correlation of certain pitch harmonics parameters and speaker's emotional states were investigated. In Section 6, an imaginary idealized futurist communication model of speech transmission is presented. Section 7 concludes the chapter with final remarks.

2. The basic phonetic properties of the Croatian language

The knowledge of linguistics and phonetics is of great importance in a large number of applications of digital speech processing, such as synthesis and speech recognition (Delic et al., 2010; Flanagan, 1972; Ipsic & Martincic-Ipsic, 2010 & Pekar et al., 2010). The study of linguistics deals with language rules and their impact on human communication, while phonetics deals with the study and classification of sounds in speech.

Language is the basic human communication and it can be transferred by speech or writing-reading. The smallest segment of speech sound is the phoneme. The voice (phoneme) in written language is a letter (grapheme). The voice is the smallest spoken unit that can be isolated from a word of some language, i.e. the voice represents the smallest noticeable discrete segment of sound in continuous speech flow. It is defined as articulated sound in speech which represents the material realization of an abstract linguistic unit - phoneme.

The phonemes are language-specific units and thus each language needs a declaration of its own phonetic alphabet (Sigmund, 2009). The number of phonemes commonly in use in each literary language varies between 30 and 50.

The number of phonemes and graphemes (letter) in Croatian language is the same (30) and they are in alphabetic order: a, b, c, č, ć, d, dž, đ, e, f, g, h, i, j, k, l, lj, m, n, nj, o, p, r, s, š, t, u, v, z, ž. In Croatian as well as kindred South Slavic language (Serbian, Bosnian) any word can be graphically represented using 30 letters (grapheme). Acoustic realization i.e. pronunciation of graphemes is very simple in Croatian language. Each written symbol (letter i.e. grapheme) has its own phoneme and vice versa. This rule stands for all words in Croatian language. Therefore reading and writing in Croatian language is very simple.

Based on the configuration and the opening of the vocal tract, Croatian sounds are divided into three basic groups. These are:

- vowels ('open' sounds): a, e, i, o, u
- semi vowels (sonants): j, l, lj, m, n, nj, r, v
- consonants: b, c, č, ć, d, dž, đ, f, g, h, k, p, s, š, t, z, ž

Semi vowels and consonants when used less specifically are put into the same group, i.e., the consonants.

There are several classifications of the sounds in Croatian language. There are voiced speech sounds and unvoiced speech sounds. Voiced speech sounds classification is the most important in speech technologies. In speech, pitch is not present in all sounds (Ahmadi & McLoughlin, 2010). Pitch harmonics are of a very high intensity in vowels, less high intensity in semi vowels and the least intensity in voiced consonants (b, d, dž, đ, g, z, ž). The rest of the consonants (c, č, ć, f, h, k, p, s, š, t) are unvoiced speech sounds and they have no pitch.

In spoken language the vowels are sound that carry the most information. Vowels constitute the most important speech sounds group and are characterized by the fact that these are the sounds of the greatest energy. When the vowels are produced the majority of the vocal tract is open and in the course of the entire duration of pronunciation the vocal cords vibrate. The primary purpose of vowels is to connect the consonants into the syllables, i.e., the formation of utterable words. In written language, the records of vowels often carry little information, i.e., in most cases the recognition of text messages is possible even when they are completely eliminated out of words.

2.1 The remaining phonetic properties of the Croatian language

Croatian orthographic rules are based on the phonological-morphological principle which enables automatisation of phonetic transcription. Standard definition of orthographic to phonetic rules, one grapheme to one phonetic symbol (Ipsic & Martincic-Ipsic, 2010). Although there are only 30 different sounds in the language, a far greater number of modifications of the same appear in a real speech. The manner of articulation of each sound depends significantly on its context, i.e., the sounds on its left and right side. This phenomenon is called coarticulation. Therefore, high-quality synthetic speech cannot be obtained by simply merging the 30 discreet sounds. Also it is important to emphasize that the transitions from one sound to another are not sudden (step), but are very gradual and are defined by the gradual transition of the articulator from the initial position corresponding the first sound towards the new position corresponding to the next sound. In this process, the vocal tract passes a series of inter-states, which causes the formation of a series of transitive sounds of relatively short duration. The elimination of these transitions significantly disrupts the naturalness of a synthetic speech.

For the purpose of solving this problem, and with the simpler speech synthesizers, the removed pairs of phonemes or so called diphthongs recorded from the actual speech are used as the basic elements of synthesis. In this way, among the basic elements, there are present and also the transitions mentioned above.

2.2 The segmenting of sounds in a continuous natural speech

The uttering of vowels takes from 50 to 300 ms. Consonants are only the processes of in-vibrating and out-vibrating of the previous and the following vowels, with a duration of 2 to

40 ms. The shortest speech sounds last only as it's necessary for the ear to recognize the tonal pitch. The sounds in speech and music should be long enough for the ear to analyze them tonally, about at the same time they must not follow each other too fast so as to prevent masking of the next by the previous masked.

For the research of the variations of the duration of sounds in speech segments during the expression of speech emotions, it is indispensable to analyze the uttered segments on the words as the units of the linguistic context as well as segment sounds from the isolated uttered words. Since there have been noted problems of dichotomy between spoken words and words as units of context in the speech continuum, together with the problems of phonetic positions, the communication situation, individual variations and the like, it is important for the needs of analysis of the manifestations of speech expressions of emotions, though preliminary, to establish criteria for the segmentation of sounds in a continuous speech.

3. Analysis procedure

3.1 Speech material

Twenty students were chosen for this research (all male). The acoustic recordings were made in speech recording and processing Croatian Telecom Mostar studio on mixing board (16-channel MIC/LINE mixer Mackie 1604-VLZ PRO). Each student was asked to pronounce five speech phrases. They are four words: "mama", "ma", "je", "ne" and loudly pronounced vowel "a". A Croatian word "mama" consists of two equal syllables "ma" and it means mother i.e. mum. Word "ma" is a mono syllable word and it is often used to express anger. Word "je" means OK and word "ne" means NO. A certain emotional state was simulated for each speech phrase. The word "mama" was pronounced in a neutrally emotional mode with a bit of sadness, while the word "ma" was pronounced simulating anger and surprise. Also, the pronunciation of the word "je" was without emotions i.e. neutral voice while in pronouncing the word "ne" anger was simulated. Loudness as the expression of stress was simulated by loudly pronounced vowel /a/ in the "Jako A" speech file. Recording of vowel /a/ in the "Jako A" speech file was realized in different conditions due to dynamic of the loudly pronounced vowel (less sensitive microphone). The stress conditions considered in this study include simulated anger and loudness (Bou-Ghazale & Hansen, 2000).

The best speaker was chosen by audio testing. Each speech phrase of all 20 speakers (students) was assessed on a scale from 1 to 5. Points were determined for each speaker by taking the sum of the marks for each of his/her five speech phrases. The speaker with the highest score needed to record given speech material another four times. (This consisted of 20 files, 5 for each speech phrase) Finally the best recording of each speech phrase was chosen for a sample. Speech files "Jako A", "MAMA", "MA", "JE" and "NE", were being recorded in Sound Recorder program with sampling frequency of f_u=8000 Hz and 16 bits of mono-configuration and resolution of quantization. Further, the vowel /a/ was isolated from the MAMA and MA files. That is the first /a/ in the word MAMA. In the same way vowel /e/ was isolated from the files JE and NE.

3.2 Spectral analysis

Each temporal signal carries certain frequency contents. The presentation of temporal signals in the frequency domain is very significant. Frequency representation of a signal mostly enables better analysis of appearance which the signal represents. The speech is signal with time-dependent spectral content. Time–frequency representations are often used for the analysis of speech signals due to their non-stationary nature. For a practical application the speech signal can be processed in various ways, other than time- domain, to extract useful information. A classical tool is the Fourier transform (FT) which offers perfect spectral resolution of a signal (Shafi et al., 2009).

Fourier techniques have been a popular analytical tool in the study of physics and engineering for more than two centuries and it is the prime method used to transfer a temporal signal into frequency domain. With the arrival of digital computers, it became theoretically possible to calculate the Fourier series and Fourier transform of a function numerically (Dutt, 1991). A major break-through in overcoming this difficulty was the development of the Fast Fourier Transform (FFT) algorithm in the 1960s which established Fourier analysis as a useful and practical numerical tool. The FFT converts a time-domain sequence x(n) into an equivalent sequence X(k) in the frequency- domain. Spectral analysis of the speech signal in most of published studies was obtained by applying a Fast Fourier Transform (FFT). In this study Goertzel algorithm is used in speech signal spectral analysis.

3.2.1 The application of Goertzel algorithm at the analysis of speech signal

Goertzel algorithm is often applied technique at the realization of digital DTMF (Dual –Tone Multiple Frequency) receivers. DTMF signalling, the so-called tone dialling, is done running audio tones that transmitter generates and that needs to be decoded on the receiver's side for the purpose of the further processing. DTMF transmitter (encoder) generates a compound audio signal formed of two mutually harmonically independent frequencies by combining of eight given frequencies. Receiver needs to decode the frequency contents of the received audio signal.

DFT plays an important role in the implementation of algorithms into the systems for digital signal processing. The usage of the FFT algorithm significantly reduces the computation time of Fourier transformation. If you need to detect one or more tones in the audio signal or only one or a few frequencies, there is a lot faster method. The Goertzel's algorithm allows decoding of a tone (frequency) with much less processor load compared to the Fast Fourier Transform (FFT).

Since the speech is also a complex audio signal, we draw the same conclusions, which means that at the processing of digital voice signal, we can apply the same technologies and algorithms that we will, of course, adapt to the needs of the analysis of speech signal. It is evident that for the analysis of digital voice signal Goertzel's algorithm can be used. The main advantage of this algorithm is that the coefficients in the equation for a particular frequency are fixed, what makes the calculation much simpler. At the analysis of speech we use the algorithm that at the exit, instead of decoding of levels at the desired frequencies, gives the spectral energy of the analyzed frequency band, i.e. Goertzel's algorithm is used for filtering. When determining spectral energy of digital signal it is necessary to remember only two previously calculated values, from the last step N, difference equations of Goertzel's algorithm, which we calculate by the 'step by step' method, while for the detection is required to determine the signal spectrum at the end of filtering.

The purpose of introducing Goertzel algorithm into the frequency analysis of the digital voice signal is a fast signal processing, and determining of spectral energy from the digital signal in desired frequency bins on the basis of pre-defined coefficients m. Then, by the analysis of the calculated energies, for particular bins, we can get a lot of information contained in the speech signal. Also, since using the Goertzel's algorithm we can determine the parameters required for the recognition of speech, the speaker, emotions and other non-linguistic attributes, it is logical that Goertzel's algorithm can be implemented for the realization of these activities.

3.2.2 Basic Goertzel algorithm

The basic Goertzel transform was derived from the discrete Fourier transform (DFT). Algorithm was introduced by Gerald Goertzel (1920-2002) in 1958 (Goertzel, 1958). It's an extremely efficient method of detecting a single frequency component in a block of input data. Figure 1 depicts the signal flow for the basic Goertzel algorithm as each sample is processed (Kiser, 2005).

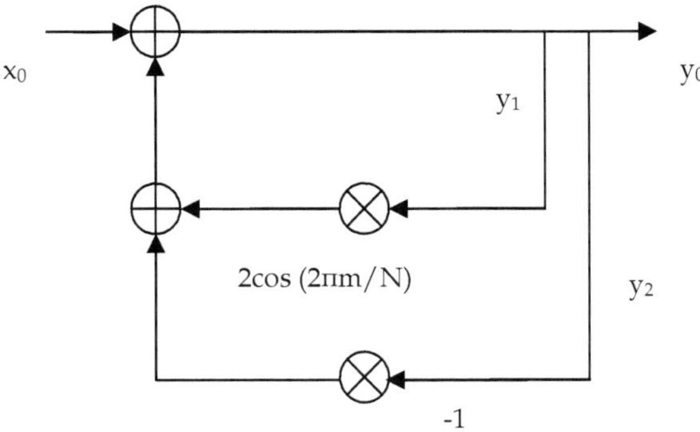

Fig. 1. Signal flow of the Goertzel algorithm

The signal flow of the algorithm produces an output y_0 for each sample processed. The output is a combination of the current ADC sample added to the product of the previous output y_1 multiplied by a constant minus the previous output y_2. Figure 1 may be written as:

$$y_0 = x_0 + y_1 \times 2\cos\left(\frac{2\pi m}{N}\right) - y_2 \tag{1}$$

y_0 is the current processed output, x_0 is the current ADC sample, y_1 is the previously output, and y_2 is the next previously processed output, m is the frequency domain bin number. N is the sample block size. Input samples are processed on a sample-by-sample basic. Processing continues over a block of input data length N.

The Goertzel transform is normally executed at a fixed sample rate and a fixed value of N. To detect multiple frequencies (i.e. *frequency bins*), each frequency must be assigned its own coefficient and then the value is used in equation (1). Depending on the number of desired detection frequencies, there will be an equal number of equations like equation (1) that must be executed once during each sample. At the end of a block of data, the spectral energy of each frequency bin will be computed and validated.

3.2.3 Spectral energy of Goertzel bins

The Goertzel algorithm is a filter bank implementation that directly calculates one Discrete Fourier transform (DFT) coefficient. The Goertzel algorithm is a second-order filter that extracts the energy present at a specific frequency (Bagchi & Mitra, 1995; Felder et al., 1998). Therefore, for the analysis of digital speech signal a system that will give a spectral energy of the analyzed (filtered) signal bandwidth (bin) is suitable. Such system is shown in Figure 2.

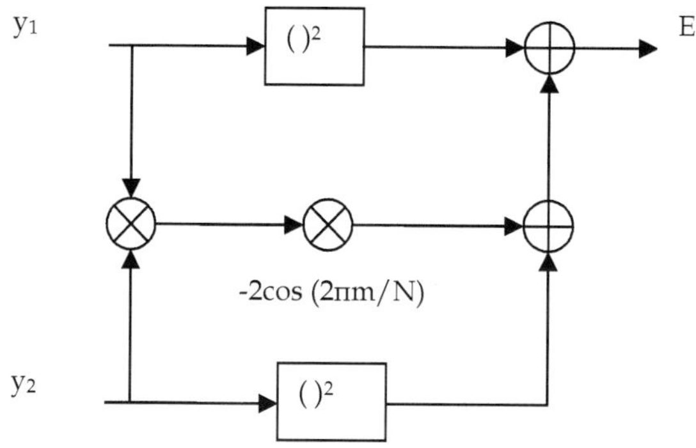

Fig. 2. Determination of spectral energy bin

Figure 2 may be written as:

$$E_m = y_1^2 + y_2^2 - 2y_1y_2 \cos\left(\frac{2\pi m}{N}\right)$$
(2)

After a block of data has been processed, spectral energy for the signal of interest (frequency bin) is determined by y_1 and y_2 variables. The sum of the squares of y_1 and y_2 are computed to determine the spectral energy of a particular frequency bin. One of the advantages of the Goertzel transform is that spectral energy computation needs to be performed only at the end of a block of data. After a block of data has passed through equation (1) (filter part), the spectral energy of Goertzel bins (frequency bin) is simply determined by equation (2) (energy part).

The Goertzel algorithm implementation has the tremendous advantage that it can process the input data as it arrives. The output value is only needed for the last sample in the block. The FFT has to wait until the entire sample block has arrived. Therefore, the Goertzel algorithm reduces the data memory required significantly.

In the analyses, spectral energy distribution of isolated vowel /a/ is in the final invariant time position during its pronunciation. Our software built for these researches allows selecting of sample, from the analyzed file, from which it will start loading samples in the equation (1). The analyses (all five speech files of chosen speaker) begin from sample k=50 which mean that the first 6,25 ms of speech file are skipped. Thereby, beginning transition of vowel pronunciation was avoided. The speech file is first loaded into the software, after that frequencies tuning coefficients – m are loaded, followed by sensing start sample – k and number of samples – N that is number of Goertzel transform iteration i.e. the equation (1).

4. Formant vowel structure tracking by Goertzel algorithm

In many science papers from this area, for the most significant parameters of speech signal which fertilized change under emotions and stress there has been defined basic frequency and energetic structure of pronounced words. Also, and analysis of formants show that exist considerable departure in formants structure at pronounced speech in different emotion's state or under impact of stress. Spectral energy analysis of isolated vowels by applying Goertzel's algorithm gives a proper illustration that enables classification of emotions by comparing the energy, and their formants.

Formant frequencies structure gives a good view to determine linguistic as well as non-linguistic speech meaning and it represents a significant parameter within the synthesis and speech recognition procedure. In fact formants are groups of harmonics enhanced by the vocal tract resonance. There is a resonance i.e. the enhancement of spectral energy in speech signal spectrum at formant frequencies (Tomas & Obad, 2009).

The difference between formant frequency structures of vowel /a/ is very informative about the speaker's emotional state. The dominant influence of emotions is on the first formant. Frequencies of the first formant are increased in expression of the emotions of anger and happiness but decreased in case of fear and sadness. Therefore, changes of vowel /a/ formant structure are not sufficient for separation of primary emotions: anger, happiness, fear and sadness.

4.1 The determination of the formant vowels structure using the Goertzel algorithm

We will analyze the speech signal, vowel / a /, recorded with the "Sound Recorder" software with the sampling frequency fu = 8000Hz, and stored under the title "Jako A". If the Goertzel's transformation, equation (1), is performed on the time segment of the recorded speech signal of 25ms duration, we have N = 200 samples of speech signal, which we process by the algorithms described by the equation (1) and the equation (2). From f_u = 8000Hz and N = 200 result's the frequency band for each Goertzel's bin: B = f_u / N = 40 Hz. The first formant will be sought in the frequency band (400 - 720) Hz. This frequency band is divided in the next 8 bins. The frequency bands of the eight bins, as well as their central frequencies, on which we base the calculation of the coefficients of tuning the frequency domain m, are shown in Table 1.

Bin	1	2	3	4	5	6	7	8
B (Hz)	400-440	440-480	480-520	520-560	560-600	600-640	640-680	680-720
f_{bins}	420	460	500	540	580	620	660	700

Table 1. The division of frequency band into bins

Now we will calculate the coefficients of tuning the frequency domain m for each bin, which will be included in the expression 2cos(2πm/N) and the value of that expression, that is a constant - different for each bin, will be stored on particular memory locations, so that the processor spends less time for the calculation of the equation (1), since the equation is executed in 200 steps. We will illustrate this for bin 1:

$$f_{bins}^{(1)} = 420 \Rightarrow m_1 = f_{bins}^{(1)} \frac{N}{f_u} = f_{bins}^{(1)} \frac{200}{8000} = \frac{f_{bins}^{(1)}}{40} = \frac{420}{40} = 10,5 \tag{3}$$

The coefficient of tuning the frequency domain, the k-th bin m_k, with the sampling frequency f_u = 8000Hz, and the length of block of time samples N = 200, we calculate by the following equation:

$$f_{bins}^{(k)} = define \Rightarrow m_k = f_{bins}^{(k)} \frac{N}{f_u} = f_{bins}^{(k)} \frac{200}{8000} = \frac{f_{bins}^{(k)}}{40} \tag{4}$$

By the inclusion of the obtained values m_k in the expression of $2\cos(2\pi m_k/N)$, we get for each bin its coefficient $k_{m(k)}$ for the calculation of the equation (1). The outline of all values is given in Table 2 (Tomas & Obad, 2008).

Now we have all the necessary input constants for the calculation of equations (1) and (2). The samples of speech signals are entered in the same order that they are sampled in the equation (1), sample by sample, i.e. the equation is performed step by step until the last step N = 200. The calculated values of the equation in the last two steps N = 200 and N = 199 are stored and entered into the equation (2). For each bin we calculate the spectral energy by entering the coefficients of the bin into the equation (1). In fact, in this way we determine the spectral energy on the frequency of f_{bin} in its corresponding Goertzel's bin.

Bin	1	2	3	4	5	6	7	8
f_{bins}	420	460	500	540	580	620	660	700
m_k	10,5	11,5	12,5	13,5	14,5	15,5	16,5	17,5
$k_{m(k)}$	1,8921	1,8477	1,8477	1,8228	1,7960	1,7675	1,7372	1,7052
E	4,3561	4,6030	69,4686	74,4163	48,7836	144,986	**416,102**	58,0926

Table 2. Display of parameters, coefficients and spectral energy of bins

The same procedure is for other formants, which would be searched for in higher frequency bands. Also, we do not have to take bins in a row. Also, by the simple choice of constants we calculate the bins that overlap. In addition, if we need greater selectivity of bins we are able to accomplish that by increasing the number of input samples N with unchanged sampling frequency, or vice versa.

From Table 2 it can be seen that the first formant of the vocal /a/ is positioned in the bin 7 in the frequency band (640-680) Hz. Also, based on the value of energies in bins 6 and 8 we read that the formant is positioned at the beginning of the bin 7, i.e. that it is in the frequency band (640-660) Hz. However, for the majority of analysis it is not necessary to determine the exact frequency positions of formants but the division of the bins is quite enough. The conclusions about the emotional states of speakers, as well as the recognition of speech and speaker can be drawn on the basis of relations between the energies of selected bins.

For more precise determination of the frequency of the first formant we can carry out the following procedure of Goertzel's transformation on bins 6 and 7. To do that we would increase the number of samples of speech signal (e.g. N=400) for that frequency band so that the frequency band for new Goertzel's bin would be: B= f_u/N=8000/400 =20 Hz. The analyzed frequency band (620-680) Hz can be divided into three new bins and for these three new bins we can calculate spectral energies. However, with N = 400, i.e. 50ms of speech signal we would come out of the frame of quasistationariness. On the other hand we could with N = 200 by selecting m-coefficient of tuning of a segment of frequency domain, analyse the bands with overlapping of neighbouring bins, e.g. 50% and get the spectral energy on the analysed frequency band with the distance of 20 Hz instead of 40 Hz as in Table 2 where the bins are in a row with no overlapping.

4.2 Influence of emotions to the formant structure of vowel /a/

Using the results of the (Vojnović, 2004) for Serbian language with the PRAAT program for male speakers, we shall make an analysis applying the Goertzel algorithm. Achieved results of the influence of emotional state of males to the formant structure of vowel /a/ are displayed in the Table 3. A similar analysis was done for German language (Kienast & Sendlmeier, 2000). Hence, with male speakers, no matter the emotional state of a speaker, while pronouncing vowel /a/ formants should be looked for in the following frequency bandwidths:
-    Formant 1 in the bandwidth of (400-700) Hz
-    Formant 2 in the bandwidth of (1350-1500) Hz
-    Formant 3 in the bandwidth of (2500-2700) Hz

EMOTIONS	Frequency (Hz) of 1st formant	Frequency (Hz) of 2nd formant	Frequency (Hz) of 3rd formant
N -Neutral	539	1393	2560
A- Anger	651	1436	2604
H- Happiness	605	1458	2600
F- Fear	538	1466	2599
S- Sadness	455	1422	2672

Table 3. Average middle frequency of the first three formants of male speakers for different emotional states

Figure 3 illustrate the comparison of spectral energies of the vowel /a/ within expected ranges of the first three formants (the red line is isolated vowel /a/ from "MA" speech file, and the blue line is isolated vowel /a/ from "MAMA" speech file). In comparison of energy values for emotions classifications, in equations (1) and (2) we adjust the bins of wider frequency bandwidth. At the sampling frequency of 8 kHz it is convenient to use N=100 or N=200 and so get the bins in bandwidth of 80Hz and 40 Hz respectively.

4.3 Influence of emotions to the frequency composition of vowels /a/ and /e/

Figure 4 and Figure 5 illustrate the comparison of spectral energies of isolated vowels /a/ and /e/ in neutral pronouncing (MAMA and JE) and in simulated anger (MA and NE) at the bandwidth of Goertzel's bins of 80 Hz (N=100) and 40 Hz (N=200) respectively. While

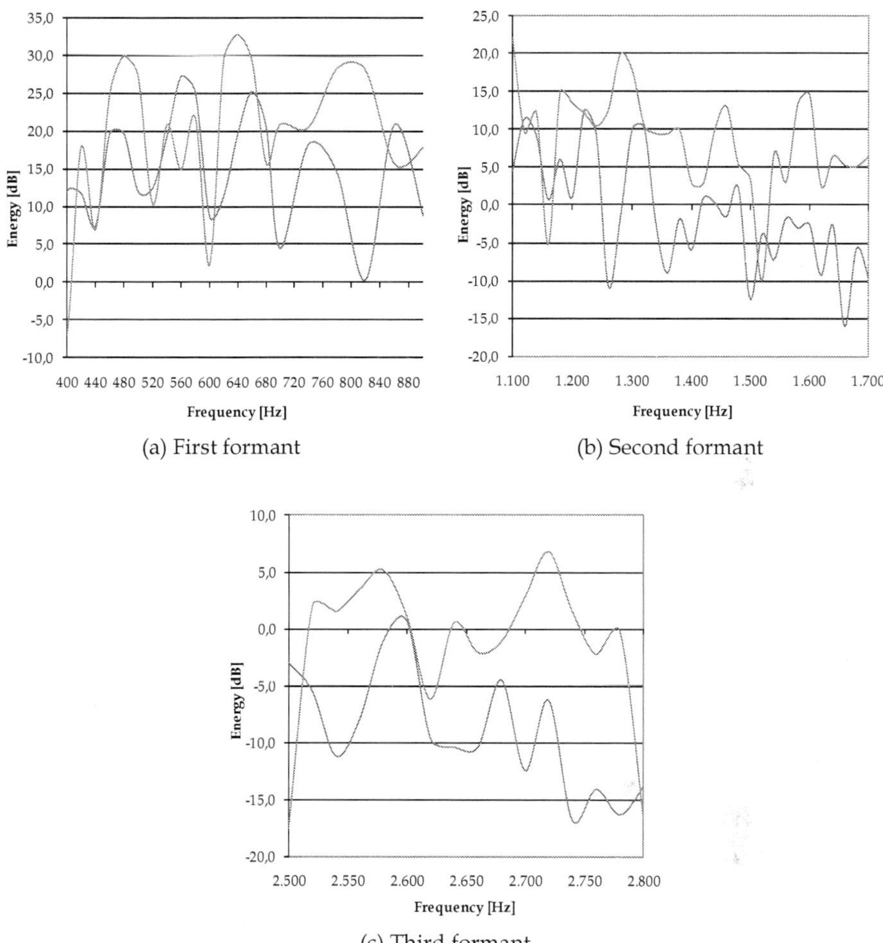

(a) First formant

(b) Second formant

(c) Third formant

Fig. 3. Bandwidth of the first three formants "A" N=200, f=8 kHz, overlapping of bins 50%

pronouncing /a/ from MA in anger, positions of formants frequency are higher than while pronouncing it without emotions in articulation of word MAMA, which affirms the researches illustrated by the Table 3. Also, it is obvious that the energy of spectrum /a/ from MA, of articulation in anger, is higher that the energy of the neutral articulation of vowel /a/ from MAMA within all three frequency bandwidths observed. Also, as we positioned the first formant for "JakoA" in the bandwidth of 640-660 Hz, we may conclude that "JakoA" has been articulated in the emotional state that might be anger, happiness or some stressful emotion, since F1> 600 Hz (Tomas & Obad, 2009).

On the following figures the blue line is neutral articulation (vowel /a/ is isolated from "MAMA" speech file and vowel /e/ is isolated from "JE" speech file), the red line is articulation that expresses anger (vowel /a/ is isolated from "MA" speech file and vowel /e/ is isolated from "NE" speech file).

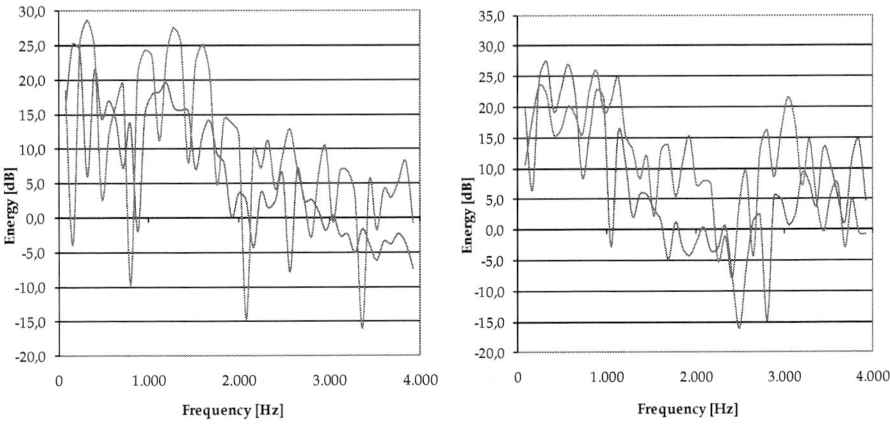

(a) Comparison of two articulations of /a/   (b) Comparison of two articulations of /e/

Fig. 4. Comparison of spectral energies of isolated vowels /a/ and /e/, N=100

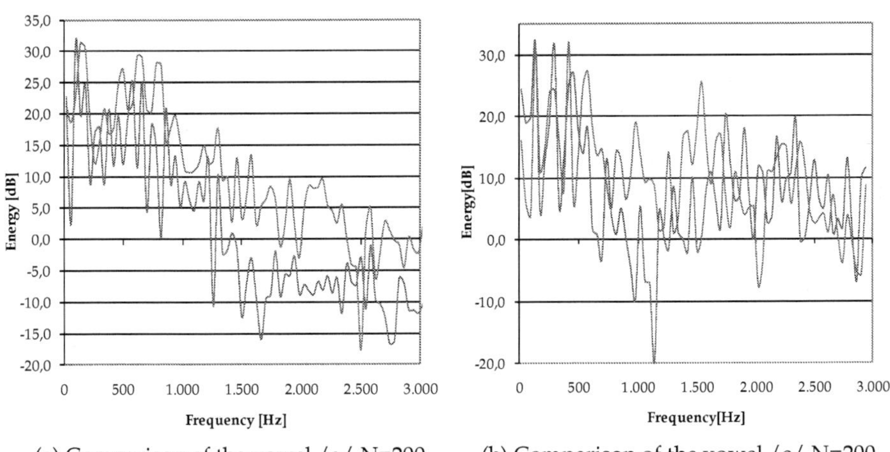

(a) Comparison of the vowel /a/ N=200   (b) Comparison of the vowel /e/ N=200

Fig. 5. Comparison of the spectral energy of isolated /a/ and /e/, N=200

Generally speaking, with spectral analysis of isolated vowels /a/ and /e/ from words: MA, MAMA , JE and NE by applying Goertzel's transformation, we may recognize the emotions of the speaker by comparing following parameters of voice signals received spectrums (Tomas & Obad, 2009):

- in articulation without emotions and with sadness and sorrow, spectral energy is mostly lower (in almost all bandwidths) than in articulation with expression of emotions (A,H,F) with exception of bandwidths of low frequencies of the first harmonics.
- hence, one of the ways to identify emotions for one speaker at analysis of spectrum of vowel /a/ by Goertzel's algorithm, is comparison of the spectral energy of isolated vowel /a/ in frequency bandwidth (above the first harmonic) of few bins (depending on the bandwidth of bin) with the energy of referent signal of vowel /a/ neutral i.e. without emotions. Here we compare the ratio of sum of energy bins of analyzed /a/ (Ean) with the sum of energy bins of neutral referent /a/ (Er). If Ean > Er we then have the expression of A, II or F, and if the ratio Ean/Er <1 we have then the expression of (S- sadness) or (Sr-Sorrow). We may achieve the same results with tabular view. The similar conclusions may be applicable for vowel/e/.
- in neutral articulation and with emotions (S and Sr) the frequencies of the first formant of vowel /a/ are lower than in articulation with expression of emotions (A and H). With Goertzel's algorithm we affirm the results achieved by other methods: F1>600 Hz A or H and for F1 <600 Hz, it is the case of S or Sr (for males).
- in case of vowel /e/ the formants frequencies for different emotions are more distanced than it is the case for /a/ , which is shown by Figure 4 and Figure 5.

For comparison of spectral energies and formants in classification of emissions we may use the bins of wider frequency bandwidth. For the case of sampling frequency of 8kHz presented bandwidths of 40 Hz and 80Hz defined by the numbers of samples N=200 and N=100 respectively give a proper graphical overview and good results. Advantage of using bins of wider bandwidth is that we cover the analyzed bandwidth with small number of bins that program may process in one cycle since it uses the same input samples. Of course each bin has different coefficients and final values of spectral energy.

It is obvious from the Figure 4 and Figure 5 that the spectral energy of isolated vowel /a/ from MA in articulation that expressed the anger is much higher compared to /a/ from MAMA in neutral articulation that expresses no emotions. It is noticeable as well that in the ranges of lower frequencies that difference of energy is less expressed, while in the range of middle frequencies in the bandwidth of 1-4 kHz the energy difference is expressed the most. It is illustrated by Figure 6, where there are precisely calculated spectral energies in that frequency bandwidth with distance points of 12,5 Hz (N=320, f= 8 kHz, overlapping of bins 50%).

Figure 6 (a) illustrates the comparison of spectral energies of isolated vowels /a/ digitalized with sampling frequency of 8 kHz, while Goertzel's transformation was applied with 320 samples of digitalized signal so that the bins were of 25 Hz bandwidths.

Except this, the neighbouring bins are overlapping 50% so the spectral energy was calculated for the frequency bandwidth of 1-2 kHz with calculating distance points of 12,5 Hz. Figure 6 (b) illustrates the comparison of spectral energies of isolated vowel /a/ in the bandwidth of 2-3 kHz. Hence, if we perform the identification and classification of emotions with only energy comparisons of isolated vowels /a/, we may do a quick analysis by selecting several bins in string from the frequency bandwidth of middle frequencies (1-4 kHz) and to compare the sums of the energies of those bins as it was explained earlier (Tomas & Obad, 2009).

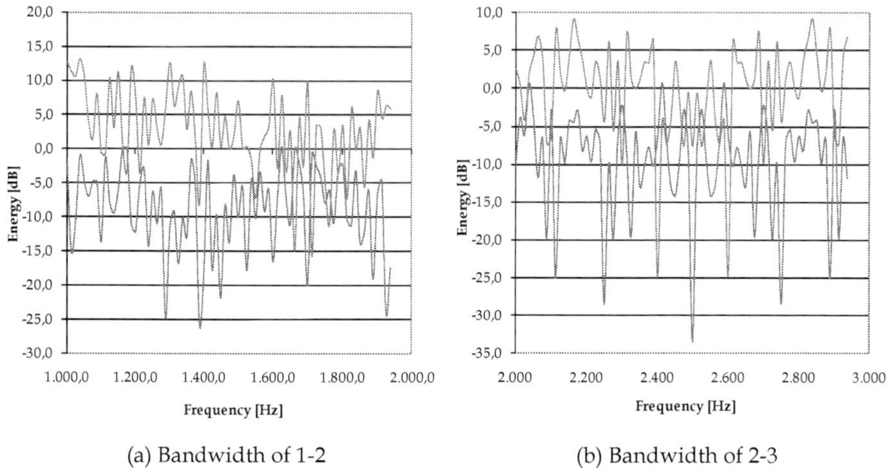

(a) Bandwidth of 1-2	(b) Bandwidth of 2-3

Fig. 6. Comparison of spectral energies of vowels /a/ in the bandwidth of 1-2 kHz and 2-3 kHz

5. Pitch harmonic parameters

Spectral energy analysis of isolated vowels by applying Goertzel's algorithm enables classification of emotions by comparing their harmonics (Tomas et al., 2007b). For selected number of samples $N=320$ duration of time frame is 40 ms, which still satisfies quasistationary speech conditions. Harmonics parameters of vowel /a/ isolated from "Jako A", "MAMA" and "MA" speech files are shown in Table 4.

Emotions	H1	H 2	H 3	H 4	H 5	$D=H_{max}-H_{min}$	F (Hz)
MAMA	1	3	2	5	4	3332,5-47,8=3184,7	58,75
MA	1	5	4	2	3	7855,7-270,1=7585,6	97,5
Jako A	2	4	5	3	1		80,9

Table 4. Structure, dynamics and basic frequency of vowel /a/ harmonics depend on emotions

Conclusions of the first five harmonics parameters analysis are:
- Harmonics frequencies depend on speaker's emotions
- Distribution of harmonics energy amplitudes (harmonics amplitude structure) depend on emotions (1st harmonic has the highest energy value, 2nd harmonic has the second high energy value, and energy value declines respectively, so 5th harmonic has the lowest energy value.
- Histograms and dynamics of harmonics energy amplitudes depend on emotions.

Recording of vowel /a/ in the "Jako A" speech file, was realized in different conditions (less sensitive microphone), therefore absolute and decibel measurements values are not identical to values of vowel /a/ in "MAMA" and "MA" speech files. Thus, their dynamic and histogram bands are not comparable. However, these changes do not influence frequency and harmonic structure.

The following Figures illustrate vowel /a/ harmonics. There is dB and absolute amount of spectral energy in Figure 7 and Figure 8. Figure 7 shows frequency band 0-600 Hz, N=320 and frequency bin overlap of 50 %. Sampling frequency is 8 kHz, thus bin width is 25 Hz, and spectral energy results are shown by 12,5 Hz points distance. On Figure 7 the blue line is neutral articulation (vowel /a/ is isolated from "MAMA" speech file), the red line is articulation that expresses anger (vowel /a/ is isolated from "MA" speech file).

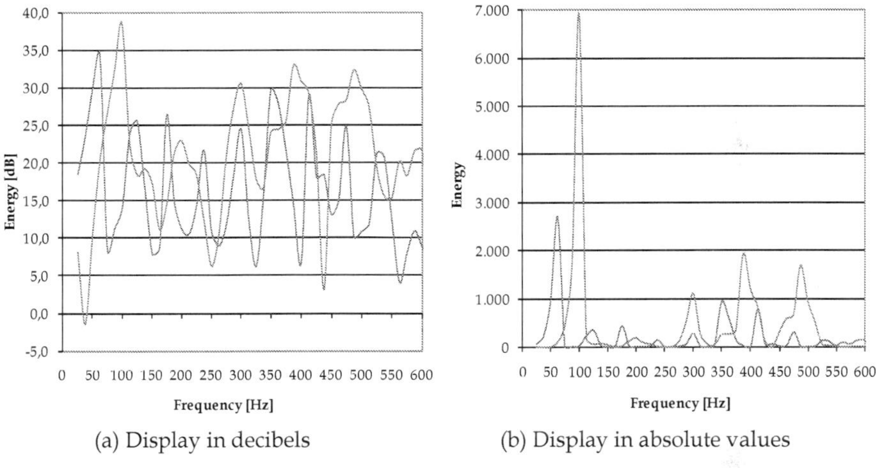

(a) Display in decibels   (b) Display in absolute values

Fig. 7. Comparison of vowel /a/ harmonics

Figure 8 shows spectral energy diagram in frequency band of the first ten harmonics of vowel /a/ in the "JakoA" file. Spectral energy is shown in dB (10 logEaps).

Figure 7 and Figure 8 illustrate correlation of harmonics amplitude, dynamic and base frequency with emotions. In Table 4, the lowest basic frequency has vowel /a/ isolated from the MAMA file, spoken in a neutral emotional condition, while the highest basic frequency has vowel /a/ isolated from the MA file, spoken with angry and surprise simulation. Amplitudes dynamic in angry is higher than in neutral emotional speech. Also, amplitudes dynamic of "Jako A" file would have been higher too if it had been recorded in the same conditions. Harmonics structure in all three emotional conditions is different indicating emotional influence, but for determination of correlations more analyses are required. It is necessary to import parameters – indexes that will clearly describe harmonics structure.

The Goertzel algorithm provides fast and simple determination of speech signal structure and precisely determination of speech signal frequency values independently of speaker. In analyzes of certain speech signal parameters, non-linguistic speech signal attributes can be recognized (Tomas et al., 2007b).

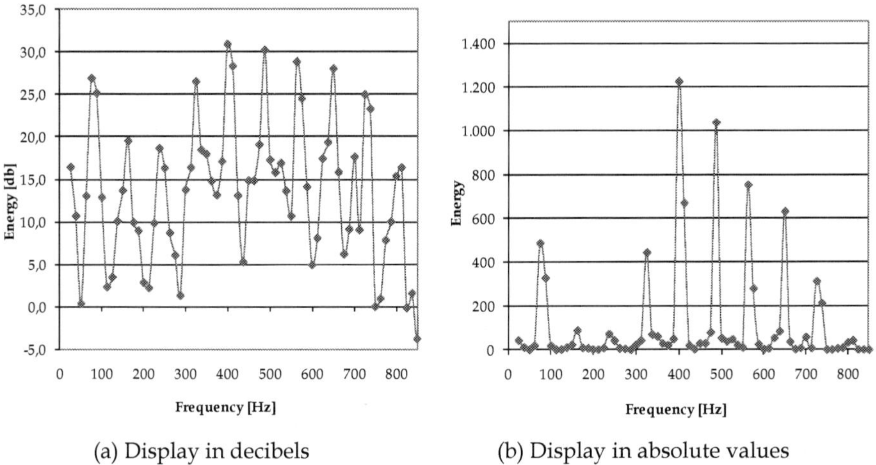

(a) Display in decibels   (b) Display in absolute values

Fig. 8. Harmonics diagram of "Jako A" file

5.1 Harmonics structure normed indexes (HSNI)

Implementation of parameters provides fast, efficient and clear overview of analyzed speech files harmonics structure. HSNI are parameters that are fast and simply calculated and they provide articulate and fast classification of emotions (Tomas et al., 2007a). Table 4 shows structure of the first five harmonics. Numbers, that defined intercomparison of the absolute mounts of energies, are assigned to harmonics. Energies are identified by Goertzel algorithm with 12,5 Hz distance frequency, at the harmonic frequency. If energies are identified with higher calculating precision of 2,5 Hz, for our speech files amounts are shown in the Tables 5, 6 and 7. In the Tables there are exact amount of frequencies at which spectral energies amount are maximal. It is evident that harmonics structure in Tables 5. and 7. are changed after more precise calculations with harmonics structure in the Table 4. There are permutations of the harmonics H2 and H3 in the Table 3 and H4 and H5 in the Table 7 respectively.

Harmonics	H1	H2	H3	H4	H5
Structure	1	2	3	5	4
Freq. (Hz)	58,75	120	176,25	236,75	297,5
Energy	3332,5	523,4	443,2	147,8	315,4
Index	1	0,157	0,132	0,044	0,095

Table 5. The first five harmonics structure of the vowel /a/ from "MAMA" file

Harmonics	H1	H2	H3	H4	H5
Structure	1	5	4	2	3
Freq. (Hz)	97,5	195	297,5	390	487,5
Energy	7855,7	270,1	1172,6	1941,8	1688,4
Index	**1**	**0,0344**	**0,1493**	**0,2472**	**0,2149**

Table 6. The first five harmonics structure of the vowel /a/ from "MA" file

Harmonics	H1	H2	H3	H4	H5
Structure	2	5	4	3	1
Freq. (Hz)	80,6	161,25	242,5	325	400
Energy	713,3	91,2	113,8	445,6	1227,2
Index	**0,581**	**0,0743**	**0,093**	**0,363**	**1**

Table 7. The first five harmonics structure of the vowel /a/ from " Jako A " file.

Harmonics	H1	H2	H3	H4	H5
MAMA Index I_k	**1**	**0,157**	**0,132**	**0,044**	**0,095**
MA Index I_k	**1**	**0,0344**	**0,1493**	**0,2472**	**0,2149**
"Jako A"Index I_k	**0,581**	**0,0743**	**0,093**	**0,363**	**1**

Table 8. The first five HSNI of the vowel /a/

Absolute amounts of spectral energies are normed thus spectral energies amounts of every harmonics divide with maximal amount harmonic spectral energy. That defines parameters shown in the last rows of Tables 5., 6. and 7 . These parameters are called HSNI and they are easily defined by equation (5):

$$I_k = \frac{E(H_k)}{E(H_{max})} \tag{5}$$

I_k is index of the H_k harmonic, $E(H_k)$ is spectral energy amount of the H_k harmonic and $E(H_{max})$ is spectral energy amount with the highest absolute amount. In the Tables 5, 6 and 7 calculated amount of I_k index are shown in the last rows and amount of $E(H_k)$ are shown in the next to last rows of the Tables. These indexes are parameters for recognition and classification of emotions and others non-linguistic speech attributes (Tomas et al., 2007a). Graphs of HSNI linear interpolation are shown on the Figure 9.

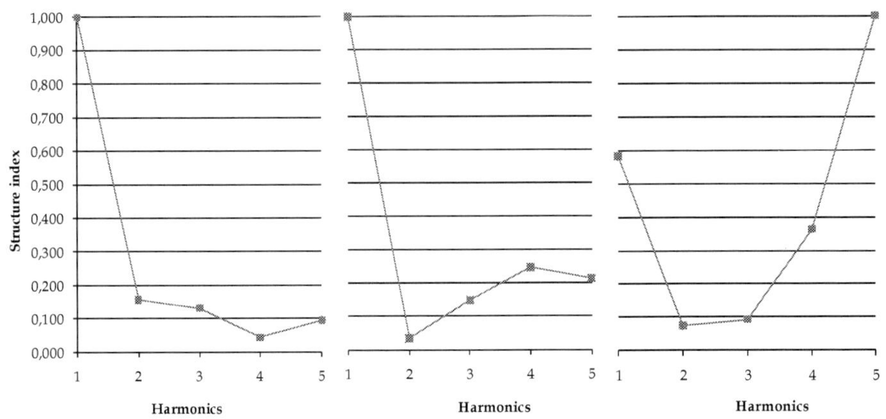

(a) /a/ from "MAMA" file   (b) /a/ from "MA" file   (c) /a/ from "Jako A" file

Fig. 9. Graphs of HSNI of vowel /a/

HSNI of vowel /a/ from "MAMA", "MA" and "Jako A" speech files are shown in Table 8. Also, graph of indexes linear interpolation is shown in Figure 10.
The graphs confirmed that implementation and analyze of these indexes provide recognition and classification and others non-linguistic speech attributes.

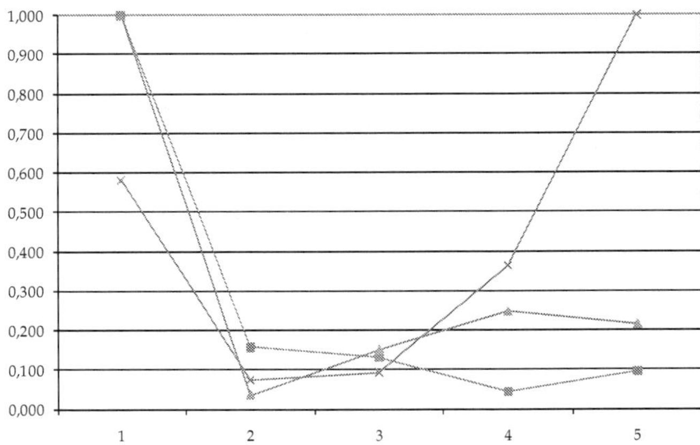

Fig. 10. HSNI of vowel /a/ from "MAMA", MA" and "Jako A" file

5.2 The area of stress

The lines on figures 9 and 10 show graphs of HSNI of vowel /a/ for our chosen speaker. The graph (lines) of indexes linear interpolation of vowel /a/ is different depending on the speaker's emotional state. One can assume that the graphs of other vowels will behave similarly. That means that the curves of all five vowels, articulated by one speaker, for a certain emotion will almost overlap. Therefore, we will have areas of emotions. The area of stress and the expected areas of articulation without emotions (without stress) for our speaker are shown on the following figure.

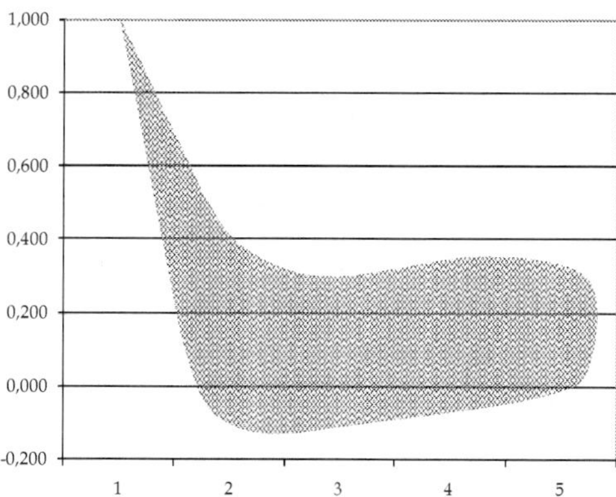

(a) Tracking the speaker "without stress"   (b) Tracking the speaker "with stress"

Fig. 11. Expected areas of the articulation

If we track a speaker's HSNI graph during continuous speech, (without emotions and stress), the graph will be in the blue area. However, if for any reason the speaker experiences stress (ex. A pilot experiencing stress because of an unexpected situation on flight) the HSNI graph will no longer be in the blue area but rather in the red area which is the area of stress.

In this chapter, HSNI, the lines of emotions, and the area of stress are presented on the basis of the first five harmonics. To get better results, it would be desirable to work with a larger number of harmonics. In order to detect stress in our speaker, only the first and higher (4 and 5) harmonics indexes are relevant, while the second and third indexes stay in the same area whether the speaker experiences stress or not. Therefore, by tracking the shape of HSNI lines and the area in which the lines are located, stress of a speaker can be detected. When tracking the area of stress, instead of tracking the lines we can track HSNI points only. As far as our speaker is concerned we should track when the first, fourth and fifth HSNI point enters the red area. Expected areas with and without stress for our speaker are shown on Figure 12.

In many applications the emotional state of one speaker (the pilot) is tracked. It is especially very important to determine when that speaker undergoes stress (Hansen et al., 2000; Zhou et al., 2001). It is shown how the harmonic frequencies change if the speaker changes emotional states. Besides that, during speech in one emotional state the basic speech frequency is not fixed. Therefore, the HSNI and the areas of emotions are practical for the classification of emotions and especially for stress detection.

It is known that the frequencies of basic harmonics are different for male, female and child speakers. The main feature which can speaker's sex distinguish is fundamental frequency $F0$ with typical values of 110 Hz for male speech and 200 Hz for female speech. The pitch of

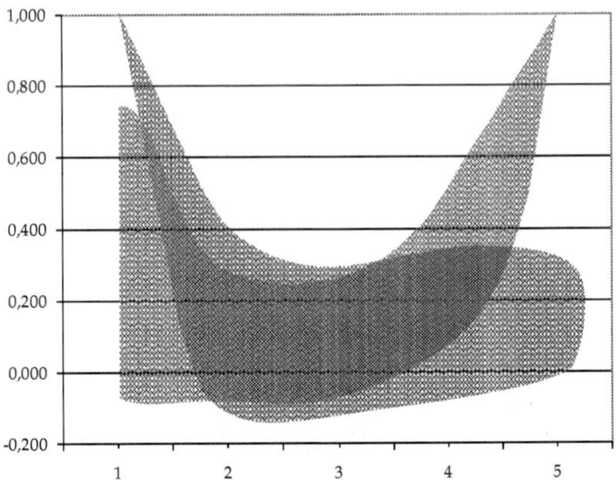

Fig. 12. Expected areas "without stress" and "with stress"

children is so different that they are often treated as "the third sex". Most values of *F0* among people aged 20 to 70 years lie between 80-170 Hz for men, 150-260 Hz for women and 300-500 Hz for children (Sigmund, 2008). Therefore, in many applications in speech technologies these three groups of speakers must be programmed separately. HSNI can probably help to overcome this problem.

6. The voice communication channel model

Communication with computers, by means of speech has been a topic frequently regarded as a science fiction. In the last thirty years technology that has enabled speech recognition and its synthesis has made exceptional developments. At the same time, we are witnesses of explosion in systems used for recognition and synthesis of speech with an additional dimension: emotions.

If standard voice communication channels are enhanced by compatible ASR and speech synthesisers, which code linguistic and non-linguistic speech parameters with common protocol we get communication model with negligibly short link engagement in comparison to duration of the actual conversation (Tomas et al., 2007a). Transfer of voice information content down the line would take short time, whereas voice through the microphone terminal on the side of speaker and voice through the synthesiser on the side of listener are in real time. Actually, at transfer we use coded indexes of non-linguistic attributes of the speaker's voice (speaker's voice characteristics) and coded indexes of linguistic information content from voice database. These indexes are coded data of linguistic and non-linguistic information with which are passed on the linguistic meaning of the conversation textual content and non-linguistic attributes of the speaker.

This model would have been more practical and simpler in an enclosed system, where the number of participants in communication is limited as well as the pool of words and expressions which are used in communication. Naturally, improvement of systems for synthesis and recognition of voice will enable implementation of this model in open communication systems.

A statement is a pronunciation of one or more words that have a single meaning to the computer. A statement can be one word, several words, a sentence or several sentences. The representation of the described voice communication model is shown in Figures 13 and 14. The Figure 13 shows speaker's side of the model, whereas Figure 14 shows receiving end, i.e. the listener's side.

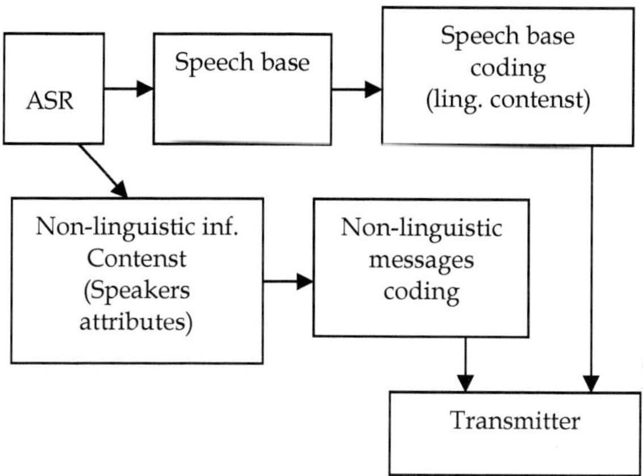

Fig. 13. A part of communication channel, speaker side

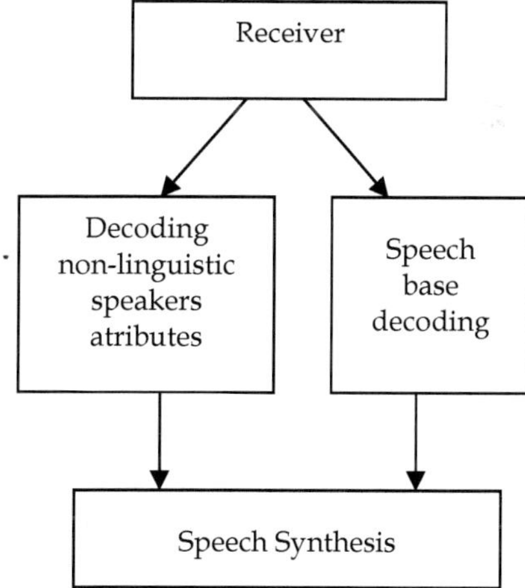

Fig. 14. A part of communication channel, listener side

Let us presume that we have closed communication system with 1000 participants. Every participant have stored and coded relevant non-linguistic characteristics of his voice. After link connection, non-linguistic information coder forwards characteristics to transmitter, which transmits them.   On the receive side non-linguistic information decoder recognize speaker and send information about non-linguistic parameters of speakers voice to a synthesizer.

After non-linguistic information exchange, transmitter ASR recognizes spoken words and statements. They are coded in the speech base coder and are forwarded to receiver like coded indexes. On the receiver side, speech base decoder decodes received words and statements. A speech synthesizer produces them with recognized speaker voice. Of course, this basic model can be upgrade depending of communication requirements i.e. (military, police, etc.).

6.1 Model application possibilities

A telephone PSTN channel was used only as an illustration and packet networks would be suitable for speech transmission by this model. It would also be very convenient to divide the information part of the packet into two parts where linguistic speech information could be transmitted through one part and nonlinguistic information could be transmitted through the other, as shown in Figure 15. Due to nature of speech itself, it is not necessary for each packet to contain the nonlinguistic part, so it possible to get even a better efficiency of this model. This is very important with the realization of speech communication through networks with reduced speed and capacity channels such as VoIP that is the most current one today but also the other packet networks and their protocol.

Linguistic Information	Nonlinguistic Information	Header packet

Fig. 15. Packet structure

Application possibilities of this model are multiple and we will presume mention some of them:

- Closed communication system
- Open communication system
- Speech to text
- Conversation of different languages speakers if an interpreter is within the model
- An aid for persons with special needs
- VOiP
- Speech message transformation systems
- Automatic speech translation from Croatian intro other world-wide languages and via versa
- E-mail and SMS messages reading
- Text to speech
- Etc.

Finally, stress and emotions classification can also be employed in forensic speech analysis by law enforcement to assess the state of telephone callers or as an aid in suspect interviews.

The majority of studies in the field of speaker stress and emotion analysis have concentrated on pitch, with several considering spectral features derived from a linear model of speech production.

7. Conclusion

Each speech message, besides linguistic information content (semantic meaning of spoken text), contains non-linguistic characteristics of speaker. The non-linguistic characteristics are correlated to certain acoustic characteristics of speech signal. Studying non-linguistic information's contents in speech signal is quality jump in speech analyses. The aim of many future researches will be finding suitable acoustic characteristics of speech signal that, besides the linguistic contents, will be used for a reliable determination of many non-linguistic contents in speech signal.

In this chapter the correlation of certain spectral parameters and speaker's emotional states are investigated. It has been reported that the spectral parameters vary with different emotions. A detailed study of all the spectral parameters can provide information on their dependence on different emotions. Defining and valuation of the parameters that are relevant for recognizing emotional speech attributes is the newest element of research in speech scientific discipline and also qualitative improvement in speech technologies. It is clear that we are at the beginning of the process of research of the one complex scientific field that will open a lot of new segments in many scientific disciplines.

8. References

Ahmadi, F. & McLoughlin, I. (2010). The Use of Low-Frequency Ultrasonics in Speech Processing, In: *Signal Processing*, Sebastian Miron, pp. 503-528, InTech, Retrieved from: http://www.intechopen.com/articles/show/title/the-use-of-low-frequency-ultrasonics-in-speech-processing

Amir, N. (2001). Classifying Emotions in Speech: A Comparison of Methotds, *Proceedings of 7th European Conference on Speech Communication and Technology EUROSPEECH*, pp.127-130, Holon, Israel, September 2001

Amir, N. & Ron, S. (1998). Toward an Automatic Classification of Emotions in Speech, *Proceedings of the 4th Int. Conf. on Spoken Language Processing*, Sydney, Australia, Nov-Dec 1998

Bagchi, S. & Mitra, S.K. (1995). An efficient algorithm for DTMF decoding using the subband NDFT. *IEEE Int. Symp. On Circuits and Systems*, Vol. 3, (May 1995), pp. 1936-1939, ISSN 0271-4310

Bou-Ghazale, S.E., & Hansen, J.H.L. (2000). A Comparative Study of Traditional and Newly Proposed Features for Recognition of Speech Under Stress. *IEEE Trans. on Speech and Audio Processing*, Vol. 8, No. 4, (July 2000), pp. 429-442, ISSN 1063-6676

Cowie, R.; Douglas-Cowie, E.; Tsapatsoulis, N.; Votsis, G.; Kollias, S.; Fellenz, W.; et al (2001). Emotion recognition in human-computer interaction. *IEEE Signal Processing Magazine*, Vol. 18, No. 1, (January 2001), pp. 32-80, ISSN 1053-5888

Delic, V.; Secujski, M.; Jakovljevic, N.; Janev, M.; Obradovic, R. & Pekar, D. (2010). Speech Technologies for Serbian and Kindred South Slavic Languages, In: *Advances in Speech Recognition*, Noam Shabtai, pp. 141-164, Sciyo, Retrieved from:

http://www.intechopen.com/articles/show/title/speech-technologies-for-serbian-and-kindred-south-slavic-languages

Dellaert, F.; Polzin, T. & Waibel, A. (1996). Recognizing Emotion in Speech, *Proceedings of Conf. on Spoken Language Processing ICSLP*, pp.1970-1973, Philadelphia, PA, October 1996

Dutt, A. (1991). A Fast Algorithm for the Evaluation of Trigonometric Series, *YALE UNIV NEW HAVEN CT DEPT OF COMPUTER SCIENCE*, January 1991

Felder,M. D.; Mason,J. C. & Evans, B.L. (1998). Efficient ITU-Compliant Dual-Tone Multiple-Frequency Detection Using the Non-Uniform Discrete Fourier Transform. *IEEE Signal Processing Letters*, Vol. 3, No. 7, (July 1988), pp. 160-163, ISSN 1070-9908

Flanagan, J. (May 1972). *Speech Analysis Synthesis and Perception*, Springer, Verlag, ISBN-13 978-0387055619, Berlin

Goertzel, G. (1958). An algorithm for the evaluation of finite trigonometric series. *American Mathematics Monthly*, Vol. 65, No. 1, (January 1958), pp. 34-35, ISSN 0002-9890

Hansen, J.H.L; Swail, C.; South, A.J.; Moore, R.K.; Steeneken, H.; Cupples, E.J.; Andreson, T.; Vloeberghs, C.R.A.; Trancoso, I. & Verlinde, P. (2000). The impact of speech under 'stress' on military speech technology. *NATO Res. Technol. Org. RTO-TR-10, AC/323 (IST) TP/5 IST/TG-01*, (March 2000), ISBN 92-837-1027-4

Ipsic, I. & Martincic-Ipsic, S. (2010). Croatian Speech Recognition, In: *Advances in Speech Recognition*, Noam Shabtai, pp. 123-140, Sciyo, Retrieved from: http://www.intechopen.com/articles/show/title/croatian-speech-recognition

Kienast, M. & Sendlmeier, W.F. (2000). Acoustical Analysis of Spectral and Temporal Changes in Emotional Speech, *Proceedings of the ISCA ITRW on Speech and Emotion*, pp. 92-97, Newcastle, Northern Ireland, UK, September 2000

Kiser, E. (2005). Digital Decoding Simplified Sequential Exact-Frequency Goertzel Algorithm. *CIRCUIT CELLAR*, No. 182, (September 2005), pp. 22-26, ISSN 1528-0608

Lee, C. & Narayanan, S. (2005). Toward detecting emotions in spoken dialogs. *IEEE Transactions on Speech and Audio Processing*, Vol. 13, No. 2, (March 2005), pp. 293-303, ISSN: 1063-6676

Morrison, D.; Wang, R. & Liyanage C.D.S. (2007). Ensemble Methods for Spoken Emotion Recognition in Call-centres. *Speech Communication*, Vol. 49, No. 2, (February 2007), pp. 98-112, ISSN 0167-6393

Pekar, D.; Miskovic, D.; Knezevic, D.; Vujnovic-Sedlar, N.; Secujski, M. & Delic, V. (2010). Applications of Speech Technologies in Western Balkan Countries, In: *Advances in Speech Recognition*, Noam Shabtai, pp. 105-122, Sciyo, Retrieved from: http://www.intechopen.com/articles/show/title/applications-of-speech-technologies-in-western-balkan-countries

Petrushin, V.A. (2000). Emotion recognition in speech signal: Experimental study, development, and application, *Proceedings of the 6th International Conference on Spoken Language Processing*, Beijing, China, October 2000

Ramamohan, S. & Dandapat, S. (2006). Sinousoidal Model-Based Analysis and Classification of Stressed Speech. *IEEE Trans. on Audio, Speech, and Language Processing*, Vol. 14, No. 3, (May 2006), pp. 737-746, ISSN 1558-7916

Scherer, K.R. (2003). Vocal Communication of Emotion: A Review of research paradigms. *Speech Commun.*, Vol. 40, No.1, (April 2003), pp. 227-256, ISSN 0167-6393

Ser, W.; Cen, L. & Yu. Z.L. (2008). A Hybrid PNN-GMM Classification Scheme for Speech Emotion Recognition, *Proceedings of the 19th International Conference on Pattern Recognition (ICPR)*, ISBN 978-1-4244-2175-6, Florida, USA, December 2008

Shafi, I.; Ahmad, J.; Shah, S.I. & Kashif, F. M. (2009). Techniques to Obtain Good Resolution and Concentrated Time-Frequency Distributions: A Review. *EURASIP Journal on Advances in Signal Processing*, Vol. 2009, Article ID 673539, 43 pages, 2009.doi:10.1155/2009/673539, ISSN 1687-6172

Sigmund, M. (2008). Automatic Speaker Recognition by Speech Signal, In: *Frontiers in Robotics, Automation and Control*, Alexander Zemliak, pp. 41-54, InTech, Retrieved from:
http://www.intechopen.com/articles/show/title/automatic_speaker_recognition_by_speech_signal

Sigmund, M. (2009). Information Mining from Speech Signal, In: *Recent Advances in Signal Processing*, Ashraf A Zaher, pp. 297-319, InTech, Retrieved from:
http://www.intechopen.com/articles/show/title/information-mining-from-speech-signal

Tao, J.; Kang, Y., & Li A., (2006). Prosody Conversion From Neutral Speech to Emotional Speech. *IEEE Trans. on Audio, Speech, and Language Processing*, Vol. 14, No. 4 (July 2006), pp. 1145-1154, ISSN 1558-7916

Tomas,B. (2006). Recognition of Linguistic and Nonlinguistic Information Contents in Speech Signal (in Croatian), *Proceedings of the 6th International Conference on Telecommunication BIHTEL*, Sarajevo, Bosnia and Herzegovina, October-November 2006

Tomas, B. & Obad M. (2008). Speech Signal Analysis by Goertzel Algorithm (In Serbian), *Proceedings of 16th Telecommunications Forum TELFOR 2008*, ISBN 978-86-7466-337-0, Belgrade, Serbia, November 2008

Tomas, B. & Obad M. (2009). Formant Vowel Structure Tracking by Goertzel Algorithm, *Proceedings of 4th International Conference on Digital Telecommunications*, ISBN 978-0-7695-3695-8, Colmar, France, July 2009

Tomas, B.; Maletić, M. & Obad, M. (2007a). Recognition and Implementation of Emotions in Speech Communications Model, *Proceedings of the 3rd Congress of the Alps Adria Acoustics Association*, JOANNEUM RESEARCH, Graz, Austria, September 2007

Tomas, B.; Maletić, M. & Raguž, Z. (2007b). Influence of Emotions to Pitch Harmonics Parameters of Vowel /a/, *Proceedings of the 49th International Symposium ELMAR-2007*, ISBN 978-953-7044-05-3, Zadar, Croatia, September 2007

Ververidis, D. & Kotropoulos, C. (2006). Emotional speech recognition: resources, features, and methods. *Speech Communication*, Vol. 48, No.9, (Sep. 2006) pp. 1163-1181, ISSN 0167-6393

Vojnović, M. (2004). Influence of Emotional State of the Speaker to Formant Structure of Vowel /a/ (in Serbian), *Proceedings of the 5th Congress DOGS*, Sombor, Serbia, September 2004

Wiliams, C.E. & Stevens, K.N. (1972). Emotions and Speech: Some Acoustical Correlates, *J.Acoust. Soc. Amer.*, Vol. 52, No. 4, (October 1972), pp. 1238-1250, ISSN 0001-4966
Zhou, G.; Hansen, J.H.L. & Kaiser, J.F. (2001). Nonlinear Feature Based Classification of Speech Under Stress. *IEEE Transactions on Speech and Audio Processing*, Vol. 9, No. 3, (March 2001), pp. 201-216, ISSN 1063-6676

5

Blind Segmentation of Speech Using Non-linear Filtering Methods

Okko Räsänen, Unto K. Laine and Toomas Altosaar
Aalto University School of Science and Technology
Finland

1. Introduction

Automated segmentation of speech into phone-sized units has been a subject of study for over 30 years, as it plays a central role in many speech processing and ASR applications. While segmentation by hand is relatively precise, it is also extremely laborious and tedious. This is one reason why automated methods are widely utilized. For example, phonetic analysis of speech (Mermelstein, 1975), audio content classification (Zhang & Kuo, 1999), and word recognition (Antal, 2004) utilize segmentation for dividing continuous audio signals into discrete, non-overlapping units in order to provide structural descriptions for the different parts of a processed signal.

In the field of automatic segmentation of speech, the best results have so far been achieved with semi-automatic HMMs that require prior training (see, e.g., Makhoul & Schwartz, 1994). Algorithms using additional linguistic information like phonetic annotation during the segmentation process are often also effective (e.g., Hemert, 1991). The use of these types of algorithms is well justified for several different purposes, but extensive training may not always be possible, nor may adequately rich descriptions of speech material be available, for instance, in real-time applications. Training of the algorithms also imposes limitations to the material that can be segmented effectively, with the results being highly dependent on, e.g., the language and vocabulary of the training and target material. Therefore, several researchers have concurrently worked on blind speech segmentation methods that do not require any external or prior knowledge regarding the speech to be segmented (Almpanidis & Kotropoulos, 2008; Aversano et al., 2001; Cherniz et al., 2007; Esposito & Aversano, 2005; Estevan et al., 2007; Sharma & Mammone, 1996). These so called blind segmentation algorithms have many potential applications in the field of speech processing that are complementary to supervised segmentation, since they do not need to be trained extensively on carefully prepared speech material. As an important property, blind algorithms do not necessarily make assumptions about underlying signal conditions whereas in trained algorithms possible mismatches between training data and processed input cause problems and errors in segmentation, e.g., due to changes in background noise conditions or microphone properties. Blind methods also provide a valuable tool for investigating speech from a basic level such as phonetic research, they are language independent, and they can be used as a processing step in self-learning agents attempting to make sense of sensory input where externally supplied linguistic knowledge cannot be used (e.g., Räsänen & Driesen, 2009; Räsänen et al., 2008).

This paper introduces a novel method for blind phonetic segmentation of speech that utilizes novel non-linear filtering methods and a short-term FFT representation of signal spectra. The method is compared to existing methods reported in literature and is shown to achieve a very similar level of performance despite the large methodological differences. A careful analysis of errors occurring in the segmentation is performed, shedding light to the question why all blind algorithms fall short of ideal segmentation performance in a similar manner.

2. A novel methodological approach to segmentation

The algorithm is based on the assumption that phonetically meaningful units are manifested as spectrally coherent, relatively steady stretches of a speech signal. To divide a speech signal into non-overlapping units, a segmentation algorithm needs to utilize parameters with specific distance metrics to estimate the similarity or changes in the signal's spectral content. The algorithm introduced here utilizes temporally integrated cross-correlation distances of feature vectors. In the basic version of the algorithm, features are produced by the Fourier transform from speech segments provided by short-term windowing. The straightforward use of FFT coefficients instead of many other possible parametric choices (e.g., MFCC or PLP) was motivated by preliminary findings made during in-house vowel-classification experiments under extremely noisy conditions. The computational simplicity of the FFT was also an influencing factor. In order to compare the effects of auditory modeling to a pure FFT representation, the use of MFCCs was tested and is reported in section 3.5.

In contrast to many prevailing approaches (e.g., Almpanidis & Kotropoulos, 2008; Aversano et al., 2001; Estevan et al., 2007), the FFT analysis is performed in a short (6 ms Hamming) window with a small window shift (2 ms) in order to detect the location of the main vocal tract excitation (after the glottal closure) for voiced sounds. These window locations provide high energy with sharp formants (good spectral contrast), which further improves the detection of formant movements at the segment boundaries as well as the noise robustness of the process. A short window also reduces the smoothing effect of formant frequency modulation during pitch periods and removes the unwanted influence of the fundamental frequency from the features.

The incoming speech signal is first pre-emphasized with a 2nd order FIR filter:

$$y[n] = b_0 x[n] + b_1 x[n-1] + b_2 x[n-2] \tag{1}$$

where values $b_0 = 0.3426$, $b_1 = 0.4945$ and $b_2 = -0.64$ are used according to (Nossair et al., 1995) in order to set the formants to an approximately equal amplitude level. The signal is then windowed with a 6 ms Hamming window and shifted by 2 ms steps. The linear-scale absolute value FFT is then calculated from these 96 samples in the window to create a spectral representation at each frame location, yielding a total of 48 coefficients for 16 kHz signals. The short-term energy (STE) of each 2 ms frame is also stored for further use. The FFT coefficients in each frame are then divided by the mean of their values within the frame and all coefficients are compressed using a hyperbolic tangent mapping in order to simulate the non-linear sensitivity of human hearing:

$$f'[m] = \tanh(\alpha \cdot f[m]) \tag{2}$$

where $\alpha = 0.45$ and $f[m,c]$ is the c'th coefficient at time m.
Once the entire signal has been transformed, a cross-correlation matrix $\mathbf{C}$ is calculated from the frames, i.e., each element $\mathbf{C}(m_1,m_2)$ indicates the cross-correlation of feature vectors at time m_1 and m_2:

$$C(m_1,m_2) = \frac{f'(m_1) \cdot f'(m_2)}{\|f'(m_1)\| \|f'(m_2)\|} \tag{3}$$

Now the diagonal of the correlation matrix can be considered as the linear time axis that runs through the signal, i.e., from the top-left towards the bottom-right.

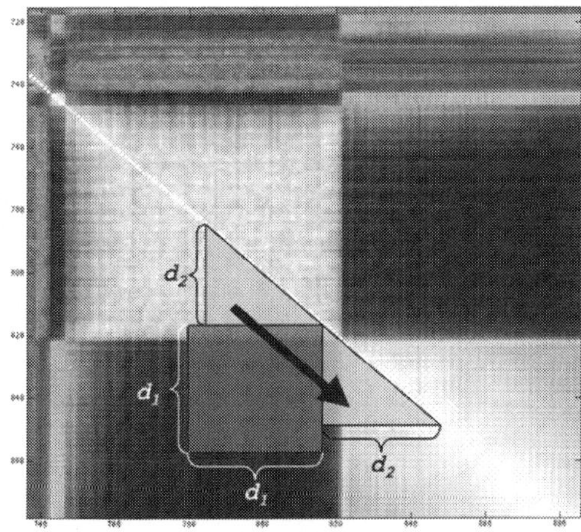

Fig. 1. Part of the correlation-matrix with a superimposed 2D-filter moving along the diagonal. The area under the square at time m corresponds to $a[m]$ and the area under the triangles corresponds to $b[m]$. Signal frame indices are marked on both axes.

A special 2D-filter is applied to the correlation matrix that is composed of one square region $a[m]$ of size $d_1 \times d_1$ with its top-right corner placed against the diagonal, as well as two identical triangles $b[m]$ with side lengths of d_2 where each hypotenuse is placed next to the diagonal (refer to fig. 1). As the filter moves downwards along the diagonal, the sum of the cross-correlation matrix elements under the triangles $b[m]$ is subtracted from the sum of the elements under the square $a[m]$ at each time step.

$$s[m] = a[m] - b[m] \tag{4}$$

This produces a representation $s[m]$ of the speech signal where large negative peaks reflect significant spectral changes and thus indicate potential segment boundary locations, refer to fig. 2. The resolving capability of $s[m]$ can be adjusted by varying the parameters d_1 and d_2, which is, in the end, basically a trade-off between the temporal accuracy and boundary detection reliability.
Signal $s[m]$ can be noisy especially when using small values of d_1 and d_2 and often results in an overly detailed analysis. The application of a so-called *minmax*-filter is therefore warranted to refine the representation (the minmax-filter is a conceptual modification of the

well known maxmin-filter). As the filter passes through the signal, at each point it takes n_{mm} subsequent samples from $s[m]$ and determines the maximum v_{max} and minimum v_{min} values of this sliding window subvector. The difference of this method compared to common maxmin-filtering is that the filter produces the difference $d_{max}=v_{max}-v_{min}$ as an output at the point where the minimum value was located instead of the center of the time window (note that deep valleys in $s[m]$ indicate the location of segment boundary candidates). The filtering removes small fluctuations and retains only the largest (local) changes in the signal $s[m]$ at the points of local minima. The following pseudo-code describes the functionality of the filter:

$$d_{max} = \max(s[m : m + n_{mm}]) - \min(s[m : m + n_{mm}])$$
$$I = find\_index(\min(s[m : m + n_{mm}])) \tag{5}$$
$$s'[m + I] = d_{max}$$

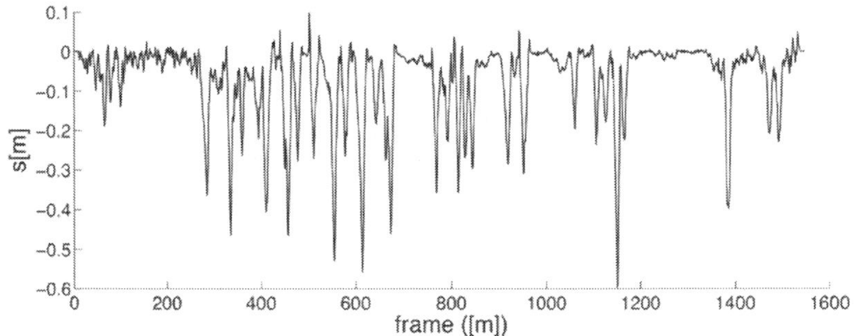

Fig. 2. Signal s[m] produced by the sliding 2D-filter of figure 1. Valleys indicate potential segment boundary locations.

As a result of filtering, signal $s'[m]$ is obtained, refer to fig. 3, in which the estimated segment boundary locations are now represented as easily identifiable positive peaks. Peak heights are normalized to a scalar value ranging from 0 to 1 to provide a probability classification for each boundary: the higher the peak, the larger the local change in the spectral properties, and the more probable it is that a phone transition has occurred.

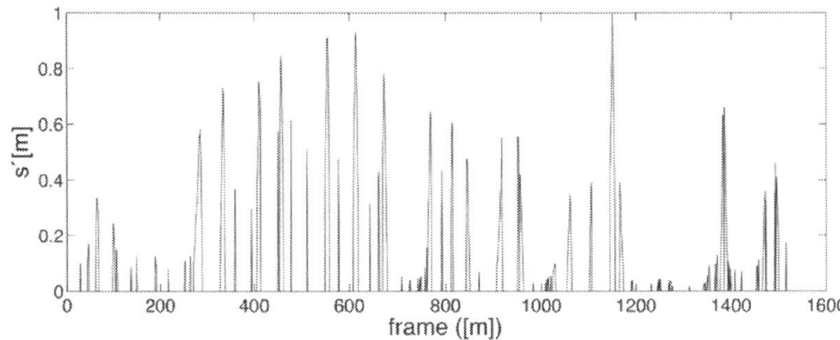

Fig. 3. s'[m] generated by minmax-filtering of s[m].

Another special operation that mimics a form of temporal masking is applied to the representation $s'[m]$ to ensure that only the most prominent points of change are reported. For example, in the case of long spectral transitions between two adjacent phones, or due to non-correlating noise, several peaks may appear very close to one other. The inclusion of multiple points of change from several nearby frames is prevented by the following procedure: the distance between each peak in $s'[m]$ that crosses a manually chosen threshold level p_{min} is calculated. If two or more peaks are closer than t_d to each other, the probability ratings of the peaks are compared. Only the most probable (highest) peak is retained, while its location is slightly adjusted towards the removed peak(s). The new location is situated between the old peaks and directly proportional to the ratio of probability ratings of the peaks in the region. As a result, a further refined $s_r[m]$ is obtained.

In theory, a list of detected segments can now be created by choosing all the peaks that exceed the minimum peak probability threshold p_{min}. In practice however, this leads to splitting of the silent or quiet sections of the signal into several small segments. This can be avoided by comparing the energy of the original signal at each peak location to a minimum energy threshold e_{min} before a final decision is made. In terms of different energy thresholding mechanisms that were studied, the optimal results were obtained by using the mean energy value from –8 ms to +30 ms around the estimated boundary location for comparison to a fixed threshold, which was set to +6 dB from the minimum signal level. This asymmetry resembles the temporal masking effect present in hearing, in which effective backward masking is limited to approximately –10 ms whereas forward masking extends to a much longer time period (see page 78 in Zwicker & Fastl, 1999). All peaks exceeding the silence threshold are used as segmentation output. Figure 4 shows a schematic overview of the algorithm.

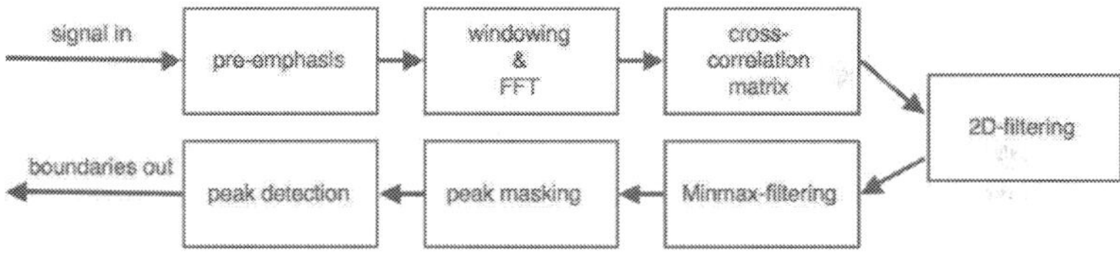

Fig. 4. Block diagram of the segmentation algorithm showing subsequent processing steps.

3. Experiments

The aim of the experiments was to obtain a good understanding of the overall performance of the algorithm so that it could be compared to earlier results found in other publications related to blind segmentation. Furthermore, determining the general effects of different parameters on segmentation results was desired. The results are presented for both genders separately in order to analyze whether gender specific differences exist, and a comparison of the obtained results to those found in existing literature is made. Additionally, noise robustness is evaluated. These results, with a brief analysis of the underlying statistics, will be covered in this section.

3.1 Evaluation measures

In order to evaluate segmentation quality, it is necessary to have a reference to which the output of the algorithm is compared. Since many well-known speech corpora are provided with a manual annotation, including TIMIT and our in-house Finnish speech corpus, a comparison to annotated segment boundaries was chosen as the primary evaluation metric. While manual segmentation is prone to the variability present in individual judgments, it is often considered as a reliable baseline for quality if it is carefully produced (Wesenick & Kipp, 1996). In addition, manual inspection of the segmentation output was performed in several phases of development and testing, yielding a more detailed insight into the phonetic details of the underlying signal in relation to the behavior of the algorithm.

A standard way to measure hits and misses in the literature is to detect whether the segmentation algorithm produces a segment boundary within a ±20 ms window (*search region*) centered around each reference boundary (Almpanidis & Kotropoulos, 2008; Aversano et al., 2001; Estevan et al., 2007; Kim & Conkie, 2002; Sarkar & Sreenivas, 2005; Scharenborg et al., 2007; Sjölander, 2003). If overlapping search regions exist, that is, adjacent regions with their reference boundaries are closer than 40 ms to each other, then the regions are asymmetrically shrunk to divide the space between two reference boundaries into two equal-width halves (see Räsänen et al., 2009). This will prevent ambiguous situations associated with overlapping search regions. Now each region can be searched for algorithmically generated boundaries: a boundary within a search region is considered as a *hit* and all additional boundaries within the same search region are counted as *insertions*. Empty regions are the source of *deletions* (or *misses*). Using this approach, the total number of hits N_{hit}, detected boundaries N_f, and reference boundaries N_{ref} are computed over the entire test material in order to derive the measures defined in table 1.

Overall segmentation accuracy is defined in terms of hit rate (HR). For some finite section of speech let N_{hit} be the number of boundaries correctly detected and N_{ref} be the total number of boundaries in the reference. HR can then be calculated using equation 6 in table 1 (Aversano et al., 2001). HR is inversely proportional to the miss (or error) rate, which is also sometimes used to indicate segmentation accuracy. Another central measure, especially in the case of blind methods, is the over-segmentation (OS) rate (7), which can be obtained if the total number of algorithmically produced boundaries N_f is included in the analysis (Petek et al., 1996). Different authors have used varying symbols for the above measures, originating from, e.g., signal detection theory. However, they have been found non-descriptive and are therefore replaced in this work by the new symbols *HR* and *OS*.

$$HR = \frac{N_{hit}}{N_{ref}} * 100 \quad (6) \qquad OS = (\frac{N_f}{N_{ref}} - 1) * 100 \quad (7)$$

$$PRC = \frac{N_{hit}}{N_f} \quad (8) \qquad RCL = \frac{N_{hit}}{N_{ref}} \quad (9)$$

$$F = \frac{2.0 * PRC * RCL}{PRC + RCL} \quad (10)$$

Table 1. Standard quality measures used to evaluate segmentation

Precision (8) describes the likelihood of how often the algorithm identifies a correct boundary whenever a boundary is detected. Recall (9) is the same as HR (6) but without scaling to a percentage. In order to describe the overall quality of the segmentation with a single scalar between 0 and 1, the F-value can be computed from precision and recall (Ajmera et al., 2004). However, it has been shown that the F-value is not sensitive to so-called stochastic over-segmentation, where the hit rate of the algorithm can be increased by allowing higher levels of over-segmentation while the algorithm is actually producing new boundaries at random locations without any true reference to the underlying signal (Räsänen et al., 2009). A quality measure called R-value has been proposed to overcome this problem (Räsänen et al., 2009), and was therefore utilized in the evaluation process as a main criterion of quality, although the other quality measures are also reported for comparison. The R-value measures the distance between the current point of operation and the ideal performance (100% HR, 0% OS) in the HR/OS-plane (12), and the distance between the current point of operation and the case where the number of insertions is zero (12). These distances r_1 and r_2 are combined into a single scalar value between 0 and 1 according to (13), with unity indicating ideal performance.

$$r_1 = \sqrt{(100 - HR)^2 + (OS)^2} \tag{11}$$

$$r_2 = \frac{-OS + HR - 100}{\sqrt{2}} \tag{12}$$

$$R = 1 - \frac{abs(r_1) + abs(r_2)}{200} \tag{13}$$

Some authors also compute insertion rates (Cherniz et al., 2007) or ROC curves based on the ratio of insertions and total number of frames in the system (Esposito & Aversano, 2005). However, we find this type of methodology problematic since the number of frames is directly affected by the window step size, whereas the number of insertions and hits are not greatly affected since the temporal parameters (e.g., masking distance) are defined in temporal units (seconds) instead of number of frames. For example, changing the step size from 2 ms to 1 ms would basically halve the number of insertions per frame, providing very little information about the performance of the algorithm itself.

3.2 Material

The segmentation algorithm was tested on clean speech using the TIMIT speech corpus covering several American-English dialects. Additionally, a set of experiments was conducted using Finnish speech from a smaller and speaker-limited in-house corpus to detect possible language dependencies. The Finnish speech consisted of two male speakers each uttering 81 sentences of read speech, each sentence containing 28 phones on average. The sentences had been phonetically designed so that all of the naturally occurring diphones in Finnish were covered. A single phonetician then carefully segmented and labeled this material manually to produce about 4500 phones in total as well as 1680 segments (e.g., closures and releases indicated separately).

3.3 Results

Table 2 contains the evaluation results for the TIMIT test set using settings that provide optimal performance in terms of R-value (see section 3.4 for parameter dependencies). The full test set (560 female and 1120 male sentences) was used, containing utterances from a total of 168 different speakers. A hit rate of 71.9% with -6.9% over-segmentation was obtained as a mean for both genders. The results also show that the results from both genders are nearly similar, the performance on female data being slightly higher (table 2).

gender	HR (%)	OS (%)	F-value	R-value
female	72.84	-7.9	0.78	0.79
male	71.37	-6.4	0.76	0.77
male+female	71.9	-6.9	0.76	0.78

Table 2. Segmentation results for the TIMIT test set.

The reader should note that by accepting higher values of over-segmentation (something that is not always desirable), higher hit rates are possible. The most straightforward manner to increase the over-segmentation level of the described algorithm is to adjust the length of the minmax-filter and the probability threshold p_{min} of the peak detector. Table 3 shows the results for the entire test set of TIMIT at an over-segmentation level of 54.3%. Although the overall HR has now increased notably, a large degradation of the R-value (and a relatively smaller degradation of the F-value) reflects the fact that this is simply due to an extremely high number of produced segment boundaries that start to hit search regions by chance.

gender	HR (%)	OS (%)	F-value	R-value
male+female	85.5	54.3	0.69	0.48

Table 3. Segmentation results for the TIMIT test set at a higher level of over-segmentation (male and female combined).

In general, the obtained results are well in line with the other results reported in literature regarding blind segmentation algorithms (table 4). More importantly, it seems that different blind algorithms achieve very similar levels of accuracy in terms of F- and R-values despite their methodological differences. The algorithm by Estevan et al. (2007) seems to obtain the highest R-values, but since we did not implement all of the algorithms shown in the table, it is impossible to conclude anything due to the fact that the differences in accuracy are of the same scale as the possible deviations in quality measures caused by ambiguities in evaluation methods (see Räsänen et al., 2009). The similarity of results is a topic that shall be returned to in the discussion section.

For the Finnish in-house corpus, the speech of two male speakers was automatically segmented independently to gain insight to both a) single speaker dependency, and b) the difference between rather swiftly spoken English material compared to very carefully articulated Finnish speech. The algorithm achieved 73.1% and 74.0% hit rates with over-segmentation values of 1.4% and -1.4% (F = 0.73, R = 0.77, and F = 0.75, R = 0.78, respectively) for the two Finnish speakers using the same parameters as in the TIMIT tests. These findings support the language and gender independency supposition of the algorithm and verify that excessive parameter tweaking is not necessary between languages.

Algorithm	HR (%)	OS (%)	F-value	R-value
Räsänen et al. (2009, this paper)	71.9	-6.90	0.76	0.78
Almpanidis and Kotropoulos (2008)	80.72	11.31	0.76	0.78
Aversano et al. (2001)	73.58	0.00	0.74	0.77
Esposito and Aversano (2005)	79.30	9.00	0.76	0.78
Estevan et al. (2007)	76.00	0.00	0.76	0.80

Table 4. Blind segmentation results on TIMIT from different authors.

3.4 Parameter dependency

In order to determine the impact of each parameter on overall performance in the described algorithm, parameters were adjusted and tested independently. Data used in the experiments were a randomly chosen subset of the TIMIT test set (N = 200 utterances), a set size considered sufficiently large to describe the behavior of the quality measures as a function of the parameter values. The most important parameters controlling the algorithm's behavior were the length n_{mm} of the minmax-filter, the peak masking distance t_d, and the boundary probability threshold p_{min}.

First it was verified that the FFT window length of 96 samples leads to the best performance (this corresponds to 6 ms at a 16 kHz sampling rate). As the purpose was to perform an FFT-analysis in which the window location regularly matches the location of the maximum energy of pitch periods (see section 2), this 6 ms window approximately satisfies the condition for both male and female speakers. Since the performance degraded for smaller and larger window sizes, the window length was fixed to 6 ms for the remaining parameter experiments.

During the development of the algorithm it was observed that the length n_{mm} of the minmax-filter, the threshold p_{min}, and the masking distance t_d of the final peak selector, were the most dominating parameters in the performance of the algorithm. As for n_{mm}, the value is mainly a tradeoff between over-segmentation and hit-rate, where approximately $n_{mm} = 34$ frames (68 ms) was used in most of the tests to produce approximately OS = 0% for the entire TIMIT test material (note that the parameter experiments were performed with a subset of the test section and led to slightly different results due to a reduced set size). In the experiments it was observed that while the length n_{mm} controls the tradeoff between OS and HR, the F- and R-values are not greatly affected by these changes when OS levels are low. On the contrary, the peak selection threshold value p_{min} has a more dramatic effect on the F value. This is an expected result since it resembles the probability threshold for boundary detection: as more probable peaks are chosen, the obtained precision improves. However, when using higher values of p_{min} the algorithm starts to miss less probable boundaries (in terms of the algorithm), decreasing the recall.

For masking distance t_d, an optimal point can be found in the proximity of $t_d = 25$ ms. This is a reasonable result since the rate of articulation in normal speech rarely exceeds four phones per 100 ms. There are still, e.g., some very short plosives that may exhibit bursts shorter than 20 ms, resulting in a decreased HR with longer masking distances than burst durations. On the other hand, by using values of tens of milliseconds, segmenting longer bursts into several small segments is avoided since the cross-correlation of the spectral coefficients may vary considerably within such variable transitions.

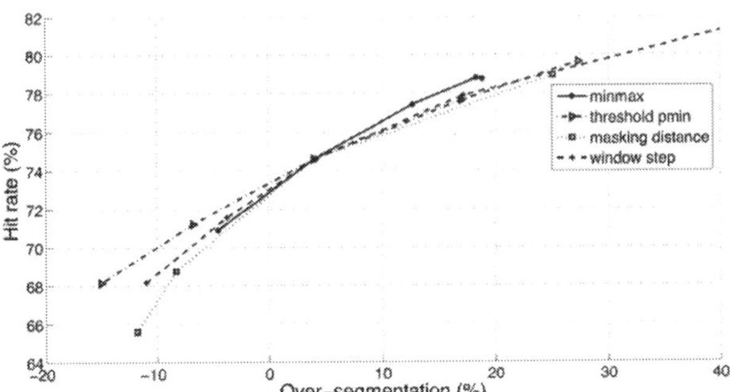

Fig. 5. Effects of different parameter values on segmentation results tested independently of each other. Parameter ranges are n_{mm} = 20-100 ms, t_d = 5-45 ms, ws = 1-3 ms and p_{min} = 0.02-0.1. Adjustment of the values changes the trade-off balance between hit-rate and over-segmentation, but the slope decreases as the value of over-segmentation increases.

To summarize, it was noted that most parameters control the tradeoff between over-segmentation and hit rate in a parallel fashion, while no parameter alone has a clear impact on improving the results (see fig. 5). Also, since many of the parameters are complementary, there are many possible combinations that achieve very similar results. Each value of choice for a parameter limits the maximum hit-rate by some amount in order to keep the over-segmentation at a reasonable level. It is possible to achieve much higher hit-rates by allowing over-segmentation to grow to very high values (see table 2). However, a large number of insertions is not usually desirable if the goal is to perform phonetic segmentation. It should be noted that once the parameters were set, the algorithm performed equally well for both genders and also for English and Finnish speech without any need for language specific optimization.

3.5 FFT versus MFCC in noise

While the FFT spectrum is a straightforward choice for use in algorithms for segment boundary detection, more popular alternative methods to describe spectral information also exist. One well-established choice in the field of speech processing is to use a parametric representation called Mel-frequency cepstral coefficients (MFCC) to obtain a simple auditory representation of the spectrum. To determine whether MFCCs enhance the performance of the segmentation algorithm when compared to the FFT, comparison tests were carried out. The first 20 static cepstral coefficients (ignoring the zeroth one) were chosen to represent the speech signal, since a further increase in their number did not yield any improvements.

Tests showed that the application of MFCCs to a 10 ms Hamming window with 2 ms steps led to optimal results in terms of windowing properties. Further increases in window size led to blurred temporal accuracy and therefore missed boundaries. Very similar results, as compared to the FFT, were obtained with noise-free signals, and led to values of HR = 74.7%, OS = 1.1% (F = 0.74, R = 0.78).

White noise and babble noise robustness of these two representations were tested with a subset of the TIMIT corpus by introducing additive white noise and babble noise to the original signals. The babble noise was generated from TIMIT data by summing together speech signals from five different speakers speaking different utterances. Figure 6 displays the behavior of the R-value as a function of SNR. A decrease in SNR in the white noise condition leads to a small increase in the hit-rate with the FFT, but since this also starts to increase the over-segmentation level, the overall R-value drops dramatically. The hit-rate increase is explained as an increase in unintentional hits to the search regions due to increased OS (see Räsänen et al., 2009). MFCC segmentation preserves a much more conservative OS-rate at reasonable white noise levels when compared to the FFT.

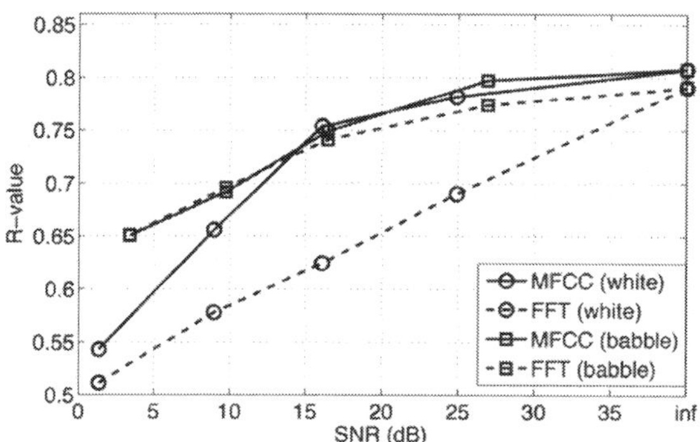

Fig. 6. The effects of white and babble noise on FFT and MFCC representations. FFT is shown with dashed lines and MFCC with solid lines. Circles denote white noise and squares babble noise.

In the case of babble noise, the difference between MFCC and FFT representations is very small. Over-segmentation at a near zero SNR level is more than 10% lower with babble noise when compared to the white noise situation, yielding much higher R-values. This is slightly surprising, since babble noise has its energy and spectral transients concentrated at the same frequency bands as the test signals.

The overall conclusion from comparing FFT and MFCC representations is that the difference is small, but MFCC seems to behave in a more stable manner especially when there is noise at the higher frequencies (e.g., white noise). This is due to the reduced spectral resolution of the MFCC's at the higher frequencies. With more natural babble noise, this difference is diminished.

4. Segmentation error analysis

4.1 Phone class-specific accuracies

Boundaries that automatic segmentation fails to detect are highly dependent on the underlying phonetic content. Some phone transitions are easy to detect due to sudden changes in the spectrum, whereas, e.g., glides and liquids may be more difficult to separate from their neighboring phones. In order to understand why and how the algorithm differs from manually produced references in the evaluated material, segmentation accuracy was estimated separately for each possible type of diphone transition defined in the reference annotation. Evaluation was performed using the FFT signal representation and TIMIT test set, yielding overall performances as reported in table 4. In order to capture an overview of the performance and to reduce sparseness of diphone data in TIMIT, the 62 ARPABET phone classes used in TIMIT annotation were grouped into 7 larger phone classes according to Hasegawa-Johnson (2009).

		To							
		Tense vowels	Lax vowels	Glides and liquids	Nasals	Fricatives	Stops and affricates	Closures	Mean
From	Tense vowels	48.6	25.4	44.5	85.2	94.8	N/A	65.5	60.7
	Lax vowels	80.0	17.1	37.0	82.4	89.7	N/A	76.3	63.8
	Glides and liquids	52.7	45.4	56.8	79.8	91.3	N/A	63.5	64.9
	Nasals	91.0	82.8	69.3	51.9	86.6	89.7	56.5	75.4
	Fricatives	87.8	82.1	88.4	90.5	68.1	N/A	83.7	83.4
	Stops and affricates	58.1	64.5	70.8	87.1	44.6	N/A	72.6	66.3
	Closures	45.1	34.7	58.2	73.8	77.3	80.3	55.6	60.7
	Mean	66.2	50.3	60.7	78.7	78.9	85.0	67.7	**68.8**

Table 5. Segmentation accuracy (%) for diphone transitions. Rows indicate the preceding phone while columns indicate the posterior phone of each pair. Pairs with less than 5 occurrences are excluded from the statistics.

As can be seen from table 5, there are extensive differences in accuracy between different diphone transitions. Especially problematic are across-class transitions between closures and vowels, vowels and glides, and stops and fricatives. This is understandable due to the spectral similarities of the phones in these pairs. Many sound classes also have very different segmentation accuracies depending on their relative position in the diphone. This is partly due to the fact that language specific structures impose constraints regarding which phones can precede or follow the current one. This yields different pre- and post-phone distributions for each single phone class, which is not seen in the table since it contains averaged results over entire phone groups. Another affecting factor is coarticulation that causes the segments to lose some of their spectral contrast.

Figure 7 shows histograms of segment output deviations from reference boundaries. This type of presentation reveals that transitions between spectrally contrasting segments lead to sharp distributions around, or near to, zero deviations, whereas similar speech sounds (e.g., transitions inside a phone group, the diagonals in figures and tables) have very broad distributions and low accuracies. Distributions of the majority of well-detected transitions are unimodal and fit well inside the ±20 ms time window used as an evaluation criterion.

The overall distribution of all correctly detected segment boundaries relative to the reference fits well with a normal distribution with a mean of zero and variance of approximately $\sigma_n^2 = 0.1^2$. This shows that approximately 35% of the boundaries would be located outside the search region if the deviation threshold was changed from 20 ms to 10 ms. This provides support for the convention of the ±20 ms deviation allowance that is typically found in literature (Almpanidis & Kotropoulos, 2008; Aversano et al., 2001; Estevan et al., 2007; Kim & Conkie, 2002; Sarkar & Sreenivas, 2005; Scharenborg et al., 2007; Sjölander, 2003), since the algorithm reacts very systematically to changes in the signal in a time window of this size but rarely at larger distances.

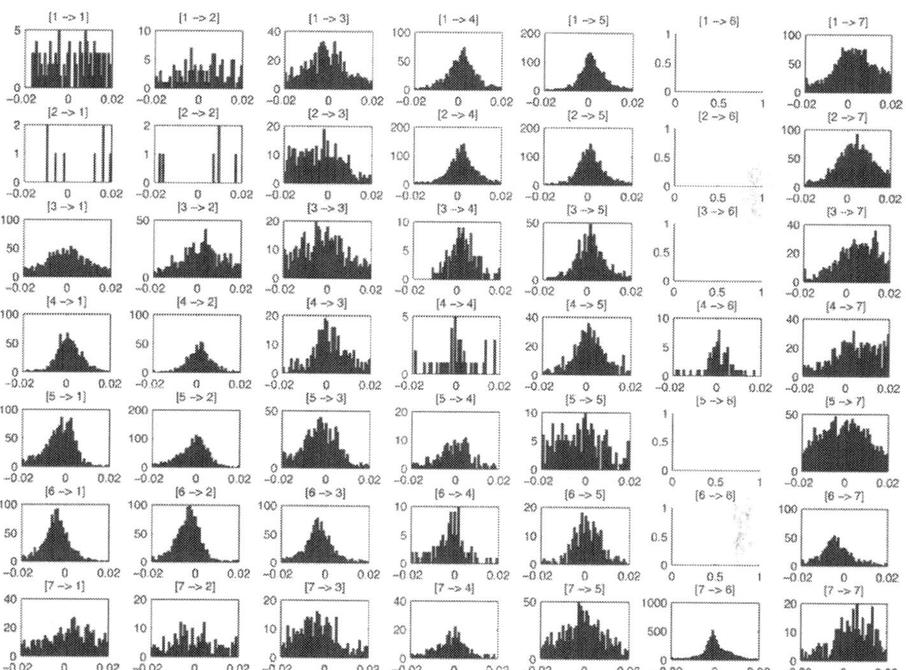

Fig. 7. Segmentation accuracy for phone classes found in Table 5 shown as temporal error distributions (seconds). Error is defined as the distance (in seconds) between produced segment boundaries and reference annotation (male + female speakers). 1: Tense vowels, 2: lax vowels, 3: glides and liquids, 4: nasals, 5: fricatives, 6: stops and affricates, 7: closures.

		To					
		Tense vowels	Lax vowels	Glides and liquids	Nasals	Fricatives	Stops and affricates	Closures
FROM	Tense vowels	4.2	2.1	-0.5	-3.6	0.2	N/A	-4.9
	Lax vowels	-25.0	-14.3	9.7	-1.8	-1.1	N/A	-2.4
	Glides and liquids	-0.5	0.4	-2.2	-10.7	-3.1	N/A	-7.4
	Nasals	-5.4	-7.5	4.6	11.3	1.4	-4.9	1.4
	Fricatives	-4.3	-1.1	-6.5	0.9	1.1	N/A	-3.4
	Stops and affricates	-9.5	-4.4	-1.4	3.1	-1.4	N/A	-1.8
	Closures	2.9	6.1	-1.5	-4.8	-5.6	2.3	-7.8

Table 6. Segmentation accuracy difference (%) between male and female speakers (positive value = male performance better, negative value = female performance better).

Accuracy differences for phone transitions between male and female speakers were also estimated using the FFT representation (table 6). The differences in accuracy show that some transitions (e.g., from lax vowels to tense vowels and between lax vowels) are significantly more accurately detected in female speech, whereas some others (e.g., nasal-to-nasal and lax vowel-to-glide) transitions are more readily detected in male speech. The reason for such differences is not clear, but they may arise from cross-gender differences in the anatomy of the vocal apparatus. The role of very short-term windowing in FFT may also have an impact, since the ratio of window length and one pitch period is different for the two genders.
Phone specific performance was also studied between the FFT and MFCC. It was determined that these two representations produce different results for some phone categories. The FFT segmentation performs especially well on fricatives, stops and affricates, whereas MFCC is more sensitive to vowels, glides and liquids. The FFT based segmentation seems to be much more accurate for the beginnings of stops and affricates (+14% compared to MFCC; e.g., [bcl]-[b]) whereas MFCC exhibits slightly more accuracy with post-phone transitions of the same phone classes (e.g., from [b] to [a]). These differences are somewhat expected, as the FFT has a high resolution also at the higher frequencies (fricatives and quick transitions, e.g., bursts) whereas Mel-filtering weights the low frequency range more. Despite the differences noted for different speech sound categories, both spectral representations end up exhibiting very similar results for overall segmentation accuracy (see section 3.3).

4.2 Inspection of problematic segments

As the detection of some vowel transitions is problematic for the algorithm, further studies were made to gain a deeper insight into these cases. Figure 8 illustrates an example of why it may not be possible to achieve extremely high accuracies with bottom-up approaches in general. In this example the word *"water"* is spoken by a female speaker: the time waveform is shown in the top pane while the linear-frequency spectrogram is shown below. The manually determined boundaries for phone [ao]'s transitions are indicated by dashed lines.

The segmentation algorithm is able to detect the [ao]-[dx] transition while the [w]-[ao] transition remains undetected, causing a deletion to be registered. There is no noticeable change in the spectrum, waveform, pitch, or even in signal energy, so the only possible way to place a boundary at such a location would be based on perceptual judgment. An automatic algorithm using such features, and working in a bottom-up manner, probably cannot detect such types of changes in speech.

There are also onsets of phones that do not contain sudden spectral changes but their waveform shape changes radically when compared to that of their neighbors. One such phone that is especially difficult for the present algorithm to detect is the pharyngeal fricative [q], which often contains a similar formant structure to the preceding vowel but where pitch and signal energy suddenly drop causing a perceptually creaky voice. These changes can be seen in the waveform as areas of significantly decreased amplitude and shifted phase. One example of this situation can be seen in figure 9 where a transition is occurring at the end of the word *"misquote"* and leading into *"was"*. These types of deletions could be avoided by including a supplementary module with the algorithm that could track, e.g., changes in the waveform shape, pitch, or phase of the speech signal.

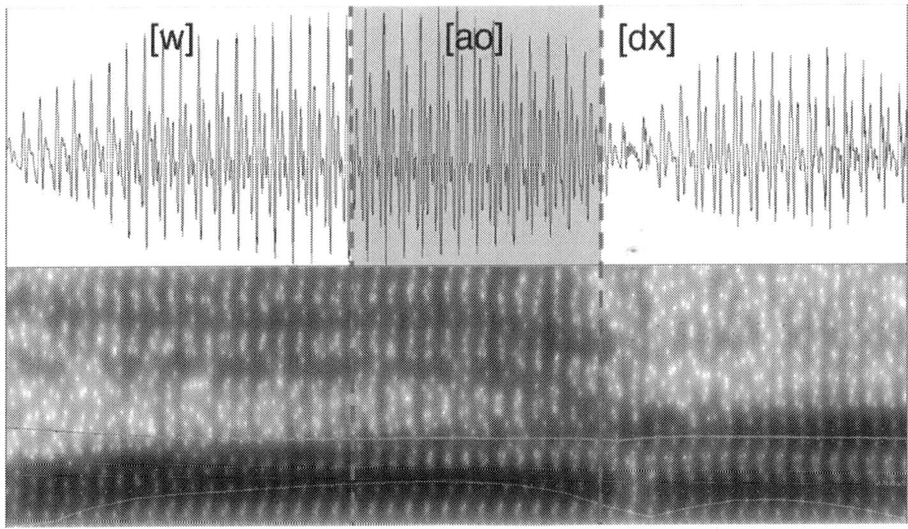

Fig. 8. A partial waveform for the word *"water"* spoken by a female speaker as well as a related spectral representation that includes F0 (upper line) and energy contours (lower line). Dashed lines indicate reference phone boundaries. The [w]-[ao] transition boundary is practically impossible to detect with the bottom-up segmentation algorithm described in this paper due to lack of changes in the feature space. Images were created using Praat software.

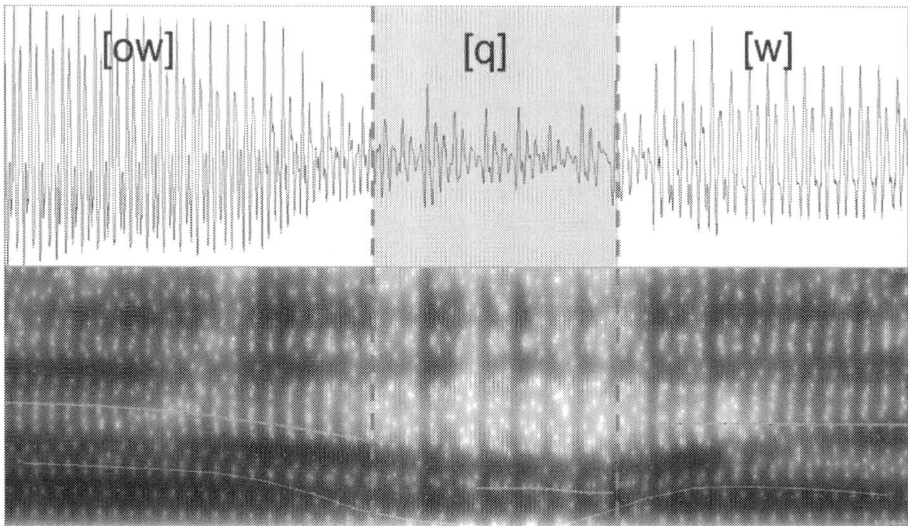

Fig. 9. The transition from [ow] to pharyngeal fricative [q] at the end of the word *"misquote"* and also from [q] to [w] in the beginning of word *"water"* are difficult to detect using spectral analysis, while changes in waveform shape are easily perceived visually.

Another general characteristic difference between the algorithm's output and the reference annotations can be found at the endings of speech signals: it is often difficult to determine where the final phone ends, and very often the perceptual ending (and annotated boundary) takes place earlier, while the spectrum of the breathy ending keeps fading away for a moment longer. As the algorithm reacts most prominently to the point where there is a structural discontinuity point in the spectrum (i.e., the signal changes from a correlating formant structure to a silence), it places a boundary where the spectrum of the exhalation finally fades to a non-existent level. This effect was observed with both English and Finnish data.

The implicit assumption underlying this work is that "optimal" automatic segmentation of continuous speech should lead to results where preferably only one phone occupies one segment. However, there seems to be a large number of cases where effective segmentation of continuous speech to phonetic units is difficult using blind bottom-up approaches. For some transitions, the changes in the features representing the signal may be gradual (e.g., in diphthongs) or almost non-existent (fig. 8), although a human listener still perceives a change from one articulatory position to another due to learned distinctions. In some other cases, like at the endings of the signals, the points of change simply cannot be unanimously defined. Real speech also contains situations where phones are spectrally split into two or more "subphones". This occurs, e.g., when an oral vowel is nasalized or a nasalized vowel is "oralized" causing rapid spectral changes to occur at first formant as well as nasal formant locations. Another example of this type of splitting is a liquid or a fricative situated between front and back vowels or some other changing phonetic context. This type of phenomena may cause the first part of such a segment to differ considerably from its remainder.

Thus, the implicit assumption behind the chosen segmentation methodology and the preferred goal is partially conflicting with the natural operation of articulatory mechanisms. Spectral change alone is not a sufficient cue for phone segment boundaries since some intra-segmental changes can be larger than some transitions from one phone class to another. This leads to an inevitable tradeoff between segmentation accuracy and over-segmentation. If more comprehensive blind phone-segmentation is required then problematic cases should be studied in more detail in order to handle them in a correct and language-universal manner. This question is left as a topic for further studies.

5. Conclusions

This paper introduced a novel blind speech segmentation algorithm that utilizes the cross-correlations of adjacent spectral representations of the signal. Local changes in the spectrum are detected using a two-dimensional filter on the cross-correlation matrix. Output from the filter is then reduced using a non-linear minmax-filtering technique, and finally a temporal masking operation is applied to the detected signal changes. The results obtained by this algorithm are comparable to those found in literature (Almpanidis & Kotropoulos, 2008; Aversano et al., 2001; Esposito & Aversano, 2005; Estevan et al., 2007; Scharenborg et al., 2007). The performed experiments also give support for the language and gender independency of the algorithm, although further evaluation on several other languages would be required to confirm this.

Experiments from several authors seem to indicate that a maximum level of segmentation accuracy with a purely bottom-up approach is already being achieved and falls below available HMM-solutions in terms of reference evaluation. The results reported by Almpanidis and Kotropoulos (2008), Aversano et al. (2001), Esposito and Aversano (2005), and Estevan et al. (2007) all produce very similar results for the TIMIT corpus material while using totally different approaches for phone segmentation - a striking discovery already noted briefly by Estevan et al. (2007). Interestingly enough, the algorithm introduced in this paper also achieves a very similar level of accuracy with yet another methodological approach. The observed asymptotic behavior from these five different methods may indicate that further improvements may not be possible without introducing linguistic or contextual knowledge, even when working in noise-free conditions. Analyzing the instantaneous properties of speech signals systematically falls short of ideal performance.

More evidence for the suggested accuracy 'limit' existing in the bottom-up approaches can be found by analyzing the results of Cherniz et al. (2007), who attempted to improve the algorithm presented by Esposito & Aversano (2005) by replacing the original Melbank signal representation with continuous multiresolution entropy (CME) and continuous multiresolution divergence (CMD). Although the use of CMD had a statistically significant effect by lowering the number of insertions (from OS = 16.61% to OS = 13.87%), the number of detected boundaries did not change significantly ($Pr(\varepsilon < \varepsilon_{ref}) > 80.57\%$) despite employing totally different parametric representations. Similarly, here we have studied the use of FFT and MFCC in the blind segmentation task and showed that already the simple short-time FFT leads to comparable segmentation accuracy with the MFCCs ($R = 0.78$). One may ask whether part of the observed inaccuracies would result from the variability of the underlying reference annotation. However, the role of manual biases in overall performance should be small if ± 20 ms search regions are used for evaluation (see Wesenick & Kipp, 1996, for reliability of manual transcriptions). The boundary deviation distributions obtained in this study also support the suitability of the standard ±20 ms search regions used in evaluation.

Based on the given evidence and work already performed in the field of blind segmentation, we hypothesize that it is extremely difficult to construct a blind algorithm that analyzes the local properties of speech with universal decision parameters that could achieve notably higher segmentation accuracies than those already developed and reported in the cited literature and in this paper. In practice this would mean that grossly 70-80% of phone boundaries can be automatically and reliably detected and pinpointed in time by tracking changes in spectrotemporal features extracted from speech. The remaining 20-30% seem to be defined by changes that are too small to be detected unless the system really knows what type of signal changes it should look for in a given context. This may be the price that has to be paid with algorithms that do not learn from data or utilize expert knowledge from proficient language users.

Finally, it should also be kept in mind that perfectly matching reference boundaries is not (always) the ultimate goal of speech segmentation. In the end, the purpose of the segmentation algorithm depends on the entire speech processing system in which it is implemented, and the most important evaluation method would be then to observe and measure the functionality of the system in its entirety.

6. Acknowledgements

This research was conducted as part of the work in the Acquisition of Communication and Recognition Skills (ACORNS) project, funded by the Future and Emerging Technologies, in the Information Society Technologies thematic priority in the 6th Framework Programme of the European Union. The authors wish to thank Prof. Lou Boves from the Language and Speech Unit of Radboud University and Prof. Paavo Alku from the Dept. of Signal Processing and Acoustics of Helsinki University of Technology for giving valuable comments on this work.

7. References

Ajmera, J., McCowan, I., & Bourlard, H. (2004). Robust Speaker Change Detection. *IEEE Signal Processing Letters*, Vol. 11, No. 8, pp. 649-651

Almpanidis, G., & Kotropoulos, C. (2008). Phonemic segmentation using the generalized Gamma distribution and small sample Bayesian information criterion. *Speech Communication*, Vol. 50, pp. 38-55

Antal, M. (2004). Speaker Independent Phoneme Classification in Continuous Speech. *Studia Univ. Babes-Bolyai, Informatica*, Vol. 49, No. 2, pp. 55-64

Aversano, G., Esposito, A., Esposito, A., & Marinaro, M. (2001). A New Text-Independent Method for Phoneme Segmentation, *Proceedings of the IEEE international Workshop on Circuits and Systems*, Dayton, Ohio, USA, August, 2001

Cherniz, A.S., Torres, M.E., Rufiner, H.L., & Esposito A. (2007). Multiresolution Analysis Applied to Text-Independent Phone Segmentation. *Journal of Physics: Conference Series*, Vol. 90, pp. 1-7

Esposito, A., & Aversano, G. (2005). Text Independent Methods for Speech Segmentation, In: *Lecture Notes in Computer Science: Nonlinear Speech Modeling,* Chollet G. et al. (Eds.), pp. 261-290, Springer Verlag, Berlin Heidelberg

Estevan, Y.P., Wan, V., & Scharenborg, O. (2007). Finding Maximum Margin Segments in Speech, *Proceedings IEEE International Conference on Acoustics, Speech, and Signal Processing (ICASSP '07)*, Honolulu, Hawaii, USA, April, 2007

Hasegawa-Johnson, M. (2005). Phonetic and Prosodic Transcription Codes, In: *Lecture Notes in Speech Recognition Tools,* Page accessed in Dec. 15th, 2010, Available from: http://www.isle.illinois.edu/sst/courses/minicourse/2005/transcriptions.pdf

Hemert, J.P. (1991). Automatic Segmentation of Speech. *IEEE Trans. Signal Processing,* Vol. 39, No. 4, pp. 1008-1012

Kim, Y.-J., & Conkie, A. (2002). Automatic segmentation combining an HMM-based approach and spectral boundary correction, *Proceedings of International Conference on Spoken Language Processing (ICSLP'02)*, Denver, Colorado, September, 2002

Makhoul, J., & Schwartz, R. (1994). State of the Art in Continuous Speech Recognition, In: *Voice Communication Between Humans and Machines,* D.B. Roe & J.G. Wilpon (Eds.), pp. 165-198, National Academy Press, Washington D.C.

Mermelstein, P. (1975). Automatic segmentation of speech into syllabic units. *J. Acoust. Soc. Am.,* Vol. 58, No. 4, pp. 880-883

Nossair, Z.B., Silsbee, P.L., & Zahorian, S.A. (1995). Signal Modeling Enhancements for Automatic Speech Recognition, *Proceedings IEEE International Conference on Acoustics, Speech, and Signal Processing (ICASSP'95)*, Detroit, Michigan, USA, May 1995

Petek, B., Andersen, O., & Dalsgaard, P. (1996). On the Robust Automatic Segmentation of Spontaneous Speech, *Proceedings of International Conference on Spoken Language Processing (ICSLP'96)*, Philadelphia, USA, October, 1996

Räsänen, O., Laine, U.K., & Altosaar, T. (2008). Computational language acquisition by statistical bottom-up processing, *In Proceedings of 9th Annual Conference of the International Speech Communication Association (Interspeech '08)*, Brisbane, Australia, September, 2008

Räsänen, O., Laine, U.K., & Altosaar, T. (2009). An Improved Speech Segmentation Quality Measure: the R-value, *Proceedings of 10th Annual Conference of the International Speech Communication Association (Interspeech '09)*, Brighton, England, September, 2009

Räsänen, O., & Driesen, J. (2009). A comparison and combination of segmental and fixed-frame signal representations in NMF-based word recognition, *Proceedings of 17th Nordic Conference on Computational Linguistics (NODALIDA)*, Odense, Denmark, May, 2009

Sarkar, A., & Sreenivas, T.V. (2005). Automatic speech segmentation using average level crossing rate information, *Proceedings of IEEE International Conference on Acoustics, Speech, and Signal Processing (ICASSP'05)*, Philadelphia, USA, March, 2005

Scharenborg, O., Ernestus, M., & Wan, V. (2007). Segmentation of speech: Child's play? *Proceedings of 8th Annual Conference of the International Speech Communication Association (Interspeech '07)*, Antwerp, Belgium, August, 2007

Sharma, M., & Mammone, R. (1996). 'Blind' speech segmentation: automatic segmentation of speech without linguistic knowledge, *Proceedings of International Conference on Spoken Language Processing (ICSLP'96)*, Philadelphia, USA, October, 1996

Sjölander, K. (2003). An HMM-based system for automatic segmentation and alignment of speech, *Proceedings of Fonetik 2003, the XVI Swedish Phonetics Conference 9*, Lövånger, Sweden, June, 2003

Wesenick, M.-B., & Kipp, A. (1996). Estimating the Quality of Phonetic Transcriptions and Segmentations of Speech Signals, *Proceedings of International Conference on Spoken Language Processing (ICSLP'96)*, Philadelphia, USA, October, 1996

Zhang, T., & Kuo, C.-C.J. (1999). Hierarchical classification of audio data for archiving and retrieving, *Proceedings of the IEEE International Conference on Acoustics, Speech, and Signal Processing (ICASSP'99)*, Phoenix, Arizona, March, 1999

Zwicker, E., & Fastl, H. (1999). *Psychoacoustics: Facts and Models* (2nd ed.), Springer Series in Information Sciences, Springer, Berlin

6

Towards a Multimodal Silent Speech Interface for European Portuguese

João Freitas[1,2,3], António Teixeira[3], Miguel Sales Dias[1,2] and Carlos Bastos[3]
[1]Microsoft Language Development Center, Tagus Park, Porto Salvo,
[2]ISCTE-Lisbon University Institute/ADETTI-IUL,
[3]Departamento de Electrónica Telecomunicações e Informática/IEETA,
Universidade de Aveiro
Portugal

1. Introduction

Automatic Speech Recognition (ASR) in the presence of environmental noise is still a hard problem to tackle in speech science (Ng et al., 2000). Another problem well described in the literature is the one concerned with elderly speech production. Studies (Helfrich, 1979) have shown evidence of a slower speech rate, more breaks, more speech errors and a humbled volume of speech, when comparing elderly with teenagers or adults speech, on an acoustic level. This fact makes elderly speech hard to recognize, using currently available stochastic based ASR technology. To tackle these two problems in the context of ASR for Human-Computer Interaction, a novel Silent Speech Interface (SSI) in European Portuguese (EP) is envisioned.

A SSI performs ASR in the absence of an intelligible acoustic signal and can be used as a human-computer interface (HCI) modality in high-background-noise environments such as, living rooms, or in aiding speech-impaired individuals such as elderly persons (Denby et al., 2010). By acquiring sensor data from elements of the human speech production process – from glottal and articulators activity, their neural pathways or the brain itself – an SSI produces an alternative digital representation of speech, which can be recognized and interpreted as data, synthesized directly or routed into a communications network.

The aim of this work, is to identify possible multimodal solutions that address the issues raised by adapting existing work on SSIs to a new language. For that motive, a brief state-of-the-art review including current SSI techniques, along with the EP language characteristics that have implications in the capabilities of the different techniques, is provided. The work here presented, describes an initial effort in developing a SSI HCI modality which targets all users (universal HCI) including elderly, for EP. This SSI will then be used as a HCI modality to interact with computing systems and smartphones, respectively, in indoor home scenarios and mobility environments. This paper focuses on the approaches of Visual Speech Recognition (VSR) and Acoustic Doppler Sensors (ADS) for speech recognition, evaluating novel methodologies in order to cope with EP language characteristics. The work here presented describes the initial stage of a novel approach to VSR based on feature tracking using the FIRST algorithm for information extraction. FIRST stands for Feature

Invariant to Rotation and Scale Transform and has been successfully applied to other areas of research (Bastos & Dias, 2008). Regarding the Doppler approach, several examples of this technique are presented for the first time for EP, analyzing important language characteristics such as, nasality.

This paper is structured as follows: next section presents a brief critical review of the state-of-the-art, updating and complementing in depth recent reviews regarding SSIs (Denby et al., 2010); sections 3 and 4 provide a state-of-the art background for the two selected approaches – VSR and ADS ; in section 5 several alternative approaches are described; section 6 discusses the specificities of EP and how these relate to SSI; section 7 presents two experiments aiming at assessing the potential/limitations of some of the techniques in EP specific problems, particularly on identifying the nasal sounds (vowels and consonants).

2. Silent speech interfaces

A Silent Speech Interface comprises a system that interprets human signals other than the audible acoustic signal enabling speech communication (Denby et al., 2010). The SSI paradigm, in the context of speech technologies related research, has rose from the need of aiding speech-handicapped, communications that require the absence of sound or noise such as the ones used in military scenarios, or to increase the robustness of speech recognition in environments with a high level background noise. A SSI system is commonly characterized by the acquisition of information from the human speech production process such as, articulators, facial muscle movement or brain activity. Although further research is still needed in this field, the concept present in a SSI holds a potential solution for a more natural interface for those with disabilities at the vocal tract level, such as people who have undergone a laryngectomy and seniors with speaking difficulties. Informally, one can say that a SSI extends the human speech production model by the use of sensors, ultrasonic waves or vision. This provides a more natural approach than currently available speech pathology solutions like, electrolarynx, tracheo-oesophageal speech, and cursor-based text-to-speech systems (Denby et al., 2010).

Outside biomedical research, the communications sector, has known great expansion in the last years, and has also become interested on SSIs. The increasing number of mobile devices worldwide has spawned the need for privacy in cell phone conversations. In public environments where silence is often required such as, meetings, cinema or talks, someone talking on the cell phone is usually considered annoying, thus providing the ability to perform an urgent call in this situations has become a point of common interest. Likewise, disclosure of private conversations can occur by performing a phone call in public places, which leads to embarrassing situations from the caller point of view or even to information leaks.

2.1 SSIs and the speech production chain

The speech production model can divided into several stages. According to Levelt (Levelt, 1989), the communicative intention phase is the first phase of each speech act and consists in converting patterns of goals into messages followed by the grammatical encoding of the preverbal message to surface structure. The next phase of the speech production is the passage from the surface structure to the phonetic plan, which, informally speaking is the sequence of phones that are fed to the articulators. This can be divided between the electrical impulse fed into the articulators and the actual process of articulating. The final phase consists on the consequent effects of the previous phases.

The existent experimental SSI systems described in the literature, cover extraction of information from all the stages of speech production, from intention to articulation to effects of articulation, as depicted on Fig. 1. The current approaches can be divided as follows:

- **Intention level** (brain / Central Nerve System): Interpretation of signals from implants in the speech-motor cortex (Brumberg et al., 2010) , Interpretation of signals from electro-encephalographic (EEG) sensors (Porbadnigk et al., 2009);
- **Articulation control** (muscles): surface Electromyography (sEMG) of the articulator muscles or the larynx (Wand et al., 2009 & Maier-Hein et al., 2005);
- **Articulation** (articulators): Capture of the movement of fixed points on the articulators using Electromagnetic Articulography (EMA) sensors (Fagan et al., 2008); Real-time characterization of the vocal tract using ultra-sound (US) and optical imaging of the tongue and lips (Denby & Stone, 2004; Hueber et al., 2008); Capture movements of a talker's face through ultrasonic sensing devices (Srinivasan et al., 2010; Kalgaonkar et al. 2008);
- **Articulation effects**: Digital transformation of signals from a Non-Audible Murmur (NAM) microphone (a type of stethoscopic microphone) (Toda et al., 2009) , Analysis of glottal activity using electromagnetic (Ng et al., 2000; Quatieri et al., 2006), or vibration (Patil et al., 2010) sensors;

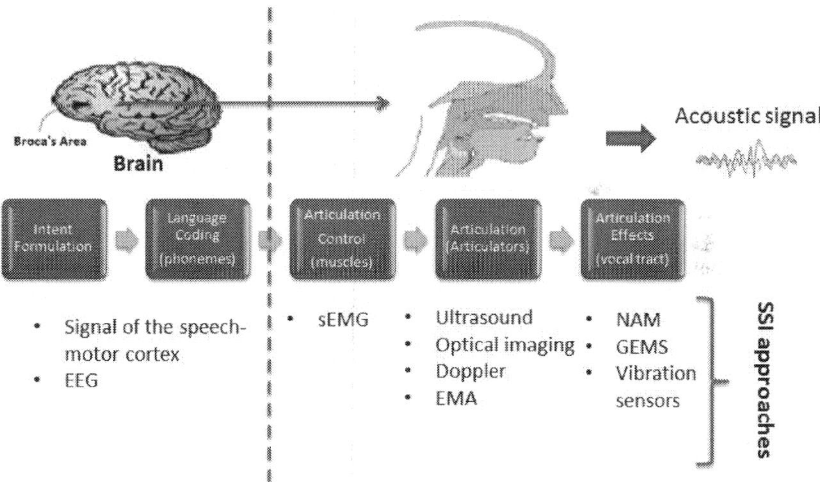

Fig. 1. Phased speech production model with the correspondent SSIs

The taxonomy presented above and illustrated in Fig. 1 allows associating each type of SSI to a stage of the human speech production model providing a better understanding from where the speech information is extracted.

Existent SSI approaches only consider VSR used as a complement for other approaches such as, ultrasound imaging. Furthermore, only lips are considered in the region of interest (ROI), not taking into account information extracted from jaws and cheeks.

2.2 Challenges

In the work presented by Denby and coworkers (Denby et al., 2009) several challenges to the development of SSIs can be found, such as:

- Sensor positioning – In order to achieve speaker independence and higher usability rates a more robust method for positioning the sensors must be found. Currently, the results of several approaches such as, EMA, EMG and EEG, are highly sensible to the position of the sensors requiring previous training or very accurate deployment.
- Speaker Independence – Many of the SSIs extracted features depend on the user's anatomy, experience and even his/her synaptic coding.
- Lombard and silent speech effects – The effects adverting from silent speech articulation and the Lombard effect (different articulation when no auditory feedback is provided) are not yet clear and require further investigation.
- Prosody and nasality – The extraction of speech cues for prosody (in systems where output synthesis is envisaged) and nasality in SSIs is also an issue. Due to the modified or absent speech signal, the information for these parameters must be obtained by other means.

These categories represent areas in this field where further research is required in order to reach an optimal SSI solution. In the work here presented we focus on a new challenge of adapting an SSI to a new language – European Portuguese – which involves addressing some of the issues referred above, such as, nasality.

3. Automatic visual speech recognition

Automatic Speech Recognition (ASR) has suffered a considerable evolution in the last years, especially, in well-defined applications with controlled environments. However, results clearly show that speech recognizers are still inferior to humans and that the human speech perception clearly outperforms state-of-the art ASR systems (Lippman, 1997). Likewise, in order to achieve a pervasive and natural human-computer interface further improvements are needed in channel robustness, ASR in uncontrolled situations and speakers (e.g. elderly) with environment noise (Potamianos et al., 2003).The human speech perception is bimodal in nature, and the influence of the visual modality over speech intelligibility has been demonstrated by the McGurk effect (Stork & Hennecke, 1996; MacGurk & MacDonald, 1976), which states the following: Vision affects the performance of the human speech perception because it permits to identify the source location; it allows a better segmentation of the audio signal; and it provides information about the place of articulation, facial muscle and jaw movement (Potamianos et al., 2003). This fact has motivated the development of audio-visual ASR (AV-ASR) systems and automatic visual speech recognition (AVSR) systems, as depicted on Fig. 2.

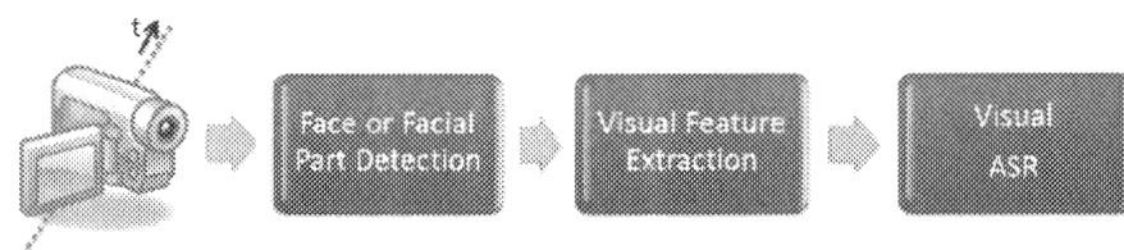

Fig. 2. Visual Speech Recognition system pipeline.

In visual-only ASR systems, a video composed of successive frames is used as an input for the system. Relatively to audio front-end, the VSR system adds a new step before the feature extraction, which consists of segmenting the video and detect the location of the speaker's face, including the lips. After this estimation, suitable features can be extracted. The majority of the systems that use multiple simultaneous input channels such as, audio plus video, have a better performance when compared with systems that depend on a single visual or audio only channel (Liang et al., 2010). This has revealed to be true for several languages such as, English, French, German, Japanese and Portuguese; and for various cases such as, nonsense words, isolated words, connected digits, letters, continuous speech, degradation due to speech impairment, etc. (Potamianos et al., 2003).

3.1 Feature extraction techniques

According to the literature (Liang et al., 2010) there are three basic methodologies to extract features in a face and lip reading system: appearance-based; shape-based; or a fusion of both. The first method is based on information extracted from the pixels in the whole image or from some regions of interest. This method assumes that all pixels contain information about the spoken utterance, leading to high dimensionality issues. Shape-based approaches base the extraction of features in the lip's contours and also parts of the face such as, cheek and jaw. This method uses geometrical and topological aspects of the face in order to extract features, like the height, width and area of the mouth image moment descriptors of the lip contours, active shape models or lip-tracking models. Shape-based methods require accurate and reliable facial and lip feature detection and tracking, which reveal to be complex in practice and hard at low image resolution (Zhao et al., 2009). The third method is a hybrid version of the first and second methods and combines features from both previous methodologies either as a joint shape appearance vector or as a cooperative statistical model learned from both sets of features. Appearance-based methods, due to its simplicity and efficiency, are the most popular (Liang et al., 2010). A comprehensive overview of these methodologies can be found in (Potamianos et al., 2003).

The challenge in extracting features from video, resides in collecting required information from the vast amounts of data present in image sequences. Each video frame contains a large number amount of pixels and is obviously too large to model as a feature vector. In order to reduce dimensionality and to allow better feature classification, techniques based on linear transformations are commonly used such as, PCA - Principal Component Analysis, LDA- Linear Discriminant Analysis, DCT- Discrete Cosine Transform and DWT - Dynamic Time Warping, Haar transforms, LSDA- Locality Sensitive Discriminant Analysis, or a combination of these methods (Potamianos et al., 2003; Liang et al., 2010). In our work we have followed an appearance-based approach using vision-based feature extraction and tracking. This type of approach has proliferated in the area of computer vision due to its intrinsic low computational cost, allowing real time solutions. To fully address our problem, we need a robust feature extraction and tracking mechanism and the Computer Vision community provides us different alternatives, such as (Harris & Stephens, 1988), SIFT – Scale Invariant Feature Transform (Lowe, 2004), PCA-SIFT (Ke & Sukthankar, 2004), SURF - Speeded Up Robust Features (Bay et al., 2006) or FIRST-Fast Invariant to Rotation and Scale Transform (Bastos & Dias, 2009). In terms of VSR, the concepts behind these techniques have been used for the elimination of dependencies on affine transformations by (Gurbuz et al., 2001) and promising results, in terms of robustness, have been achieved. These methods have shown high matching accuracy on the presence of affine transformations. However, some limitations in real-time applications were found. For example, an objective analysis in (Bastos & Dias, 2009), showed that SURF took 500 milliseconds to compute and extract 1500 image features on images with resolution of 640x480 pixel, while PCA-SIFT took 1300 ms, SIFT took 2400 ms and FIRST only 250 ms (half of the second most efficient, SURF). As for matching the same 1500 features against themselves, the figures for SURF, PCA-SIFT, SIFT and FIRST were, respectively, 250 ms, 200 ms, 800 ms and 110 ms, as observed by (Bastos & Dias, 2009).Given these results, we have selected FIRST as the technique to be used in this work to extract and match features, since the real-time requirement is essential in practical VSR systems.

The selected approach, FIRST, can be classified as a corner-based feature detector transform for real-time applications. Corner features are based on points and can be derived by finding rapid changes in edge's direction and analyzing high levels of curvature in the image gradient. FIRST features are extracted using minimum eigenvalues and are made scale, rotation and luminance invariant (up to some extent of course, since with no luminance, no vision in the visible domain is possible), using real-time computer vision techniques. A more detailed description of the algorithm is provided in section 7.1. The FIRST feature transform was mainly developed to be used in application areas of Augmented Reality, Gesture Recognition and Image Stitching. However, to our knowledge this approach has not yet been explored in VSR and the potential for extracting information, such as nasality, using this technique is still novelty.

4. Doppler signals for SSI

Ultrasound Doppler sensing of speech is one of the approaches reported in the literature that is also suitable for implementing a SSI (Srinivasan et al., 2010). This technique is based on the emission of a pure tone in the ultrasound range towards the speaker's face that is received by an ultrasound sensor tuned to the transmitted frequency. The reflected signal will contain Doppler frequency shifts proportional to the movements of the speaker's face. Based on the analysis of the Doppler signal, patterns of movements of the facial muscles, lips, tongue, jaw, etc., can be extracted (Toth et al., 2010). The ADS have been previously used in voice activity detection (Kalgaonkar et al., 2007), speaker identification (Kalgaonkar & Raj, 2008), speech recognition (Zhu et al., 2007; Srinivasan et al., 2010) and synthesis (Toth et al., 2010). When using ADS for speech recognition, the sensor has been placed either at 6-8 inches or 16 inches from the speaker, being the second more realistic. The results for ultrasound-only approaches are still far from audio-only performance. Best results in speech recognition (Srinivasan et al., 2010) show a recognition accuracy of 33% in speaker independent digit recognition, using HMMs trained with recordings of 6 speakers, revealing viability and margin for improvement of this approach.

4.1 The Doppler Effect

The Doppler Effect is the change in frequency of an emitted wave perceived by a listener moving relative to the source of the wave. If we consider the scenario depicted on Fig. 3, where the source T emits a wave with frequency f_0 that is reflected by the moving object, in this case the speaker's face. The reflected signal is then given by Eq. 1, with v being the velocity of the moving object based on the transmitter T and v_s is the velocity of the sound in the medium.

$$f = f_0 \left(\frac{v_s + v}{v_s - v} \right) \tag{1}$$

Since articulators move at different velocities when a person speaks, the reflected signal will have multiple frequencies each one associated with the moving component (Toth et al., 2010).

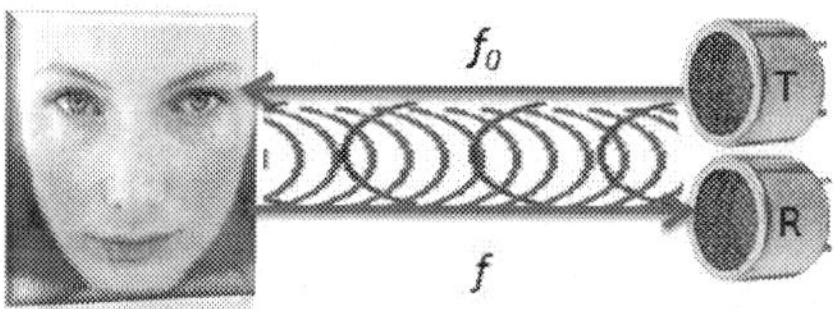

Fig. 3. Doppler Effect representation (T – Transmitter, R- Receptor).

To our knowledge, only recently Doppler has been applied to speech recognition in (Srinivasan et al., 2010) and no research of this technique regarding EP has yet been published. Below, a first example of the Doppler signal and the correspondent audio signal applied to an EP word *canto* [kɐ̃tu] (corner), is depicted on Fig. 5.

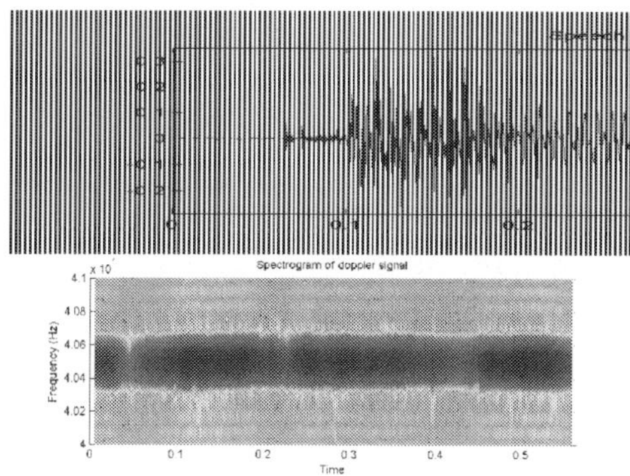

Fig. 5. Audio signal (above) and spectrogram of the Doppler signal (below) for the word *canto*.

This approach, like it was stressed before, still has margin for improvement especially when applied for Silent Speech recognition and the potential for detecting characteristics such as, nasality is still unknown. For that reason, and for being an example of very recent work, a first approach to EP using this technology is described on section 7.2. Future research in this area will need to address issues such as, changes in pose and distance of the speaker variation that affect the ultrasound performance.

5. Other SSI approaches

In this section alternative technologies to ADS and VSR, for silent speech recognition, are described according to the several stages of the speech production model and it is explained in what way information can be collected at all stages, starting by the intention phase to the articulation effects.

5.1 Brain computer interfaces used for silent speech recognition

The goal of a Brain Computer Interface (BCI) is to interpret thoughts or intentions and convert them into a control signal. The evolution of cognitive neuroscience, brain-imaging and sensing technologies has provided means to understand and interpret the physical processes in the brain. BCI's has a wide scope of application and can be applied to several problems like, assistance to subjects with physical disabilities (e.g. mobility impairments), detection of epileptic attacks, strokes, or to control computer games (Nijholt et al., 2008). A BCI can be based in several types of changes that occur during mental activity, such as, electrical potentials, magnetic fields, or metabolic/hemodynamic recordings. Current SSI approaches have been based on electrical potentials, more exactly on the sum of the postsynaptic potentials in the cortex. Two types of BCI's have been used for unspoken speech recognition, one invasive approach based on the interpretation of signals from intra-cortical microelectrodes in the speech-motor cortex and a non-invasive approach based on the interpretation of signals from electro-encephalographic sensors. Unspoken speech recognition tasks have also been tried based on magnetoencephalograms (MEG), which measures the magnetic fields caused by current flows in the cortex. However, results have shown no significant advantages over EEG-based systems (Suppes et al., 1997). A wide overview of BCI's can be found in (Nijholt et al., 2008).

5.1.1 Intra-cortical microelectrodes

Due to the invasive nature, increased risk and medical expertise required, this approach is only applied as a solution to restore speech communication in extreme cases such as, subjects with the locked-in syndrome medically stable and presenting normal cognition. When comparing with EEG sensors this type of systems present a better performance enabling real-time fluent speech communication (Brumberg et al., 2010). This technique consists in the implantation of an extracellular recording electrode and electrical hardware for amplification and transmission of brain activity. Relevant aspects of this procedure include: the location for implanting the electrodes; the type of electrodes; and the decoding modality. Results for this approach in the context of a neural speech prosthesis show that a subject is able to correctly perform a vowel production task with an accuracy rate up to 89% after a several month training period (Brumberg et al. 2009).

5.1.2 EEG sensors

A SSI based on unspoken speech is particularly suited for subjects with physical disabilities such as, the locked-in syndrome. The term unspoken speech refers to the process where the subject imagines speaking a given word without moving any articulatory muscle or producing any sound. Results from this approach have achieved accuracies significantly above chance (4 to 5 times higher) and indicate that the Broca's and Wernicke's areas as the most relevant in terms of sensed information (Wester & Schultz, 2006). Other studies (DaSalla et al., 2009) were performed using vowel speech imagery, regarding the classification of the vowels /a/ and /u/ and achieved overall classification accuracies ranged from 68 to 78%, indicating the use of vowel speech as a potential speech prosthesis controller.

5.2 Surface EMG

According to the speech production model, the articulator's muscles are activated through small electrical currents in the form of ion flows, originated in the central and peripheral nervous systems. The electrical potential generated by the resistance of muscle fibers, during speech, leads to patterns that occur in the region of the face and neck, which can be measured by a bioelectric technique called surface electromyography. This technique consists in the study of the muscle activity through its electrical properties. Currently, there are two sensing techniques to measure electromyography signals: invasive indwelling sensing and non-invasive sensing. In this work, as in most of the sEMG-based ASR research the latter approach is used (Betts & Jorgensen, 2006). Since this approach only relies on the analysis of the resulting myoelectric signal pattern related with muscle activity, it allows overcoming the main limitations of current ASR technology such as, robust ASR in the presence of environmental noise, and use of ASR near bystanders and for private actions (Denby et al., 2010). This technology has been used for solving communication in acoustically harsh environments, such as the cockpit of an aircraft (Chan et al., 2001) or when wearing a self-contained breathing apparatus or a hazmat suit (Betts & Jorgensen, 2006). Latest studies show that recognition rates up to 90% can be achieved, for a 100-word vocabulary in a speaker dependent scenario (Jou et al. ,2007; Schultz & Wand, 2010), or for small vocabularies scenarios where only one pair of surface electrodes is used (Jorgensen et al., 2003).

5.3 Electromagnetic articulography

By monitoring the movement of fixed points in the articulators using EMA sensors, this approach collects information from the articulation stage (referred on Fig. 1) of the speech production model. It is based on implanted coils or magnets attached to the vocal apparatus (Fagan et al., 2008), which can be electrically connected to external equipment or coupled with magnetic sensors positioned around the user's head. The movements of the sensors are then tracked and associated with the correspondent sound. For example, in Fagan (Fagan et al., 2008), magnets were placed on the lips, teeth and tongue of a subject and were tracked by 6 dual axis magnetic sensors incorporated into a pair of glasses. Results from this laboratory experiment show an accuracy of 94% for phonemes and 97% accuracy for words, considering very limited vocabularies (9 words and 13 phonemes).

5.4 Ultrasound and optical imaging of the tongue and lips

One of the limitations found in VSR process described earlier is the visualization of the tongue, a vital articulator for speech production. In this approach this limitation is overcome by placing beneath the chin, an ultrasound transducer, thus providing a partial view of the tongue surface in the mid-sagittal plane (Denby et al., 2010). This type of approaches is commonly combined with frontal and side optical imaging of the user's lips. For this type of systems the ultrasound probe and the video camera are usually fixed to a table or a helmet to ensure that no head movement is performed or that the ultrasound probe is correctly oriented in regard to the palate and the camera is kept at a fixed distance (Florescu et al., 2010). Latest work in the US/Video approach relies on a global coding approach in which images are projected onto a more fit space regarding the vocal tract configuration – the EigenTongues. This technique encodes not only tongue information but also information about other structures that appear in the image such as, hyoid bone and muscles (Hueber et al., 2007). Results for this technique show that for an hour of continuous speech, 60% of the phones are correctly identified in a sequence of tongue and lip images, showing that better performance can be obtained using more limited vocabularies or using isolated word in silent speech recognition tasks, still considering realistic situations (Hueber et al., 2009).

5.5 Non-audible murmur microphones

Non-audible murmur is the term given by research community to low amplitude speech sounds produced by laryngeal airflow noise resonating in the vocal tract (Denby et al., 2010). This type of speech is not perceptible to nearby listeners, but can be detected using the NAM microphone, introduced by (Nakajima et al., 2003). This microphone can be used in the presence of environmental noise, enables some degree of privacy and can be a solution for subjects with speaking difficulties or laryngeal disorders such as, the elderly. The device consists on a condenser microphone covered with soft silicone or urethane elastomer, which helps to reduce the noise caused by friction to skin tissue or clothing (Otani et al., 2008). The microphone diaphragm is exposed and the skin is in direct contact with the soft silicone. This device has a frequency response bandwidth of about 3 kHz, with peaks at 500-800 Hz and some problems concerning small spectral distortions and tissue vibration have been detected. However, the device remains as an acceptable solution for robust speech recognition (Denby et al., 2010). The best location for this microphone was determined by (Nakajima, 2005) to be on the neck surface, more precisely below the mastoid process on the large neck muscle. This technology has also been tried in a multimodal approach in (Tran et al., 2010) where this approach is combined with a visual input. In terms of recognition accuracy, Herucleous (Herucleous et al., 2003) has reported values around 88% using an iterative adaptation of normal-speech to train HMM's, requiring only a small amount of NAM data.

5.6 Electromagnetic and vibration sensors

The development of this type of sensors was motivated by several military programs in Canada, EUA and European Union to evaluate non-acoustic sensors in acoustically harsh environments such as, interiors of military vehicles and aircrafts. In this case, by non-acoustic it is meant that the sound is propagated through tissue or bone, rather than air (Denby et al., 2010). The aim of these sensors is then to remove noise by correlating the acquired signal with the one obtained from a standard close-talk microphone. These sensors have presented good results in terms of noise attenuation with gains up to 20 db (Dupont & Ris, 2004; Quatieri et al., 2006) and word error rate (WER) significant improvements (Jou et al., 2004). It has also been presented by (Quatieri et al., 2006) that these sensors can be used to measure several aspects of the vocal tract activity such as low-energy, low-frequency and events such as, nasality, which is strong characteristic of EP as described in section 6.1. Based on these facts, the use of these technologies is being considered by Advanced Speech Encoding program of DARPA for non-acoustic communication (Denby et al., 2010). These types of sensors can be divided into two categories, electromagnetic and vibration. Regarding electromagnetic sensors the following types can be found: Electroglottograph (EGG); General Electromagnetic Motion System (GEMS) and Tuned Electromagnetic Resonating Collar (TERC). In terms of vibration microphones the following types can be found: Throat Microphone, Bone microphone, Physiological microphone (PMIC) and In-ear microphone.

6. SSI for European Portuguese

The existing SSI research has been mainly developed by groups from EUA (Hueber et al., 2009), Germany (Calliess & Schultz, 2006), France (Tran et al., 2009) and Japan (Toda et al.,

2009), which have focused their experiments on their respective languages. There is no published work for European Portuguese in the area of SSIs, although there are previous research on related areas, such as the use of EMA (Rossato et al., 2006), Electroglotograph and MRI (Martins et al., 2008) for speech production studies, articulatory synthesis (Teixeira & Vaz, 2000) and multimodal interfaces involving speech (Teixeira et al., 2005; Dias et al., 2009). There are also several studies on lip reading systems for EP that aim at robust speech recognition based on audio and visual streams (Pêra et al., 2004; Sá et al., 2003). However, none of these addresses European Portuguese distinctive characteristics, such as nasality.

6.1 European Portuguese characteristics
According to Strevens (Strevens, 1954), when one first hears European Portuguese (EP), the characteristics that distinguishes it from other Western Romance languages are, the large amount of diphthongs, nasal vowels and nasal diphthongs, frequent alveolar and palatal fricatives and the dark diversity of the l-sound. Although, EP presents similarities in vocabulary and grammatical structure to Spanish, the pronunciation significantly differs. Regarding co-articulation, which is "the articulatory or acoustic influence of one segment or phone on another"(Magen, 1997), results show that European Portuguese stops, revealed less resistant to co-articulatory effects than fricatives.

6.1.1 Nasality
Although nasality is present in a vast number of languages around the world, only 20% have nasal vowels (Rossato et al., 2006). In EP there are five nasal vowels ([ĩ], [ẽ], [ɐ̃], [õ], and [ũ]); three nasal consonants ([m], [n], and [ɲ]); and several nasal diphthongs [wɐ̃] (quando), [wẽ] (aguentar), [jɐ̃] (fiando), [wĩ] (ruim) and triphthongs [wɐ̃w] (enxaguam).
Nasal vowels in EP diverge from other languages with nasal vowels, such as French, in its wider variation in the initial segment and stronger nasality at the end (Trigo, 1993; Lacerda & Head, 1966).
Doubts still remain regarding tongue positions and other articulators during nasals production in EP, namely, nasal vowels (Teixeira et al., 2003). Martins (Martins et al., 2008) have detected differences at the pharyngeal cavity level and velum port opening quotient when comparing EP and French nasal vowels articulation.

7. Experiments analysis

In our research we have designed experiments to analyze and explore two SSI approaches – VSR and ADS – applied to EP. The paper addresses an important research question, regarding the capability of two different approaches to distinguish nasal sounds from oral ones. To tackle this objective, we have designed a scenario where we want to recognize/distinguish words possibly differing only by the presence or absence of nasality in one of its phones. In EP, nasality can distinguish consonants (e.g. the bilabial stop consonant [p] becomes [m], with nasality creating minimal pairs such as [katu]/[matu]) and vowels (in minimal pairs such as [titu]/[tĩtu]).

7.1 Experiment I – visual speech recognition FIRST-based
The visual speech experiment here presented aims at demonstrating a hypothesis, according to which the skin deformation of the human face, caused by the pronunciation of words, can

be captured by studying the local time-varying displacement of skin surface features distributed across the different areas of the face, where the deformation occurs. We can abstract these image features as particles, and here we are interested in studying the kinematic motion of such particles and specially, its displacements in time, in relation to a given reference frame. Differently from authors that focus their research solely in the analysis of lip deformation (Zhao et al., 2009), in our approach we are interested in other areas of the face, in addition to the lip area. It´s worth recalling that this experiment was designed having in mind its further applicability in real-time speech recognition. Due to previous evidence of the superiority of FIRST, if we compare it SIFT, PCA-SIFT and SURF (Bastos & Dias, 2009), in applications, like augmented reality, that require real-time behavior while keeping sufficient precision and robust scale, rotation and luminance invariant behavior, we have decided to use the FIRST features in our experiment.

The envisioned experiment is divided into the phases depicted in Fig.6.

Fig. 6. The phases of our Visual Speech Recognition experiment.

To put our experiment into practice, we have specified, developed and tested a prototype VSR system. It receives an input video containing a visually spoken utterance. We ask the speaker to be quiet for a few moments, so that we are able to extract FIRST features from the video sequence. After just some frames, the number of detected features stabilizes and we refer to those as the calibration features and their position is stored. The number of calibration features remains constant for the full set of the pronounced words, which, in our case is 40.

After calibration, we assume that the speaker is pronouncing a word and therefore, in each frame, we need to track the new position of each feature in the image plane. In our current experiment we are just performing, in each frame, FIRST feature extraction and subsequently template matching with the calibration features. Further optimizations towards real-time behavior are possible, by using the tracking approach of (Bastos & Dias, 2009), which uses optical flow and feature matching in smaller image regions. If the template matching normalized cross correlation is higher that a predefined threshold, then we assume that the feature was matched and its new u, v image position is updated. Then, the Euclidian distance between the new updated feature position in the current frame and its position in the previous frame, is computed. For each feature, the resulting output will be a law in time of the displacement (distance) of each, relatively to the calibration position. During the feature matching process several outliers may occur and are later removed in a post-processing phase (Fig.6).

In each frame, we are able to compute the displacement of each of the human face surface features that we are tracking. These feature displacements, will then be used as input feature vectors for a following machine classification stage. By analyzing these feature vectors during the full story of the observed word pronunciation and comparing these analysis with the remaining examples, we can chose the one with the closest distance, consequently being able to classify that observation as a recognized word. The distance is obtained by applying Dynamic Time Warping (DTW) (Rabiner & Juang, 1993). In the following sections, we provide a detailed description of the process.

7.1.1 Feature extraction

The feature extraction process follows the work of (Bastos & Dias, 2008) and is performed using Minimum Eigen Values (MEV), as described in the (Shi & Tomasi, 1994) detector. The reason for choosing this detector is related with its robustness in the presence of affine transformations. For feature extraction, the image is first converted to gray scale. Then, a block of 3x3 pixels is taken at every image position and the first derivatives in the direction of x (Dx) and y (Dy) are computed using the Sobel operators Ox and Oy (Eq. 2), for convolution with the 3x3 pixels block. The convolution will result in evaluation of the mentioned first derivatives in direction of x and y. With the computed derivatives, we can construct matrix C, where the sum is evaluated in all elements of the 3x3 block. The Eigen Values are found by computing Eq. 4, where I is the identity matrix and λ the column vector of Eigen Values.

$$O_x = \begin{bmatrix} -1 & 0 & 1 \\ -2 & 0 & 2 \\ -1 & 0 & 1 \end{bmatrix} \quad O_y = \begin{bmatrix} 1 & 2 & 1 \\ 0 & 0 & 0 \\ -1 & -2 & -1 \end{bmatrix} \tag{2}$$

$$C = \begin{bmatrix} \sum D_x^2 & \sum D_x D_y \\ \sum D_x D_y & \sum D_y^2 \end{bmatrix} \tag{3}$$

$$det(C - \lambda I) = 0 \tag{4}$$

Two solutions (λ_1, λ_2) will result from the equation and the minimum Eigen Value ($min(\lambda_1, \lambda_2)$) will be retained. In order to perform feature identification and determine strong corners, a threshold is applied to the resulting MEV's. Only features that satisfy the threshold value of 1% of the global maximum in the current MEV spectrum are selected. Non-maximum suppression is also performed by evaluating if the candidate corner's MEV is the maximum in a neighborhood of 3x3 pixels. After the features position in the image plane have been found, several computer vision techniques are applied in order to make such features scale, rotation and luminance invariant, while at the same time maintaining the efficiency requirements. The algorithm for this procedure is already described in (Bastos & Dias, 2008), and for this reason we will only refer which techniques were used.

To make the FIRST features scale invariant it is assumed that every feature has its own intrinsic scale factor. Based on the results of the Sobel filters, the edges length can be directly correlated with the zooming distance. By finding the main edge length of the derivatives an intrinsic scale factor can be computed. The scale factor will then enable for the intrinsic feature patch to be normalized and consequently make it scale invariant. Only a surrounding area of 7x7 pixels relatively to the feature center is considered in order to deal with other derivatives that may appear resultant from zooming in/out.

In order to achieve rotation invariance the highest value of the feature's data orientation is determined. Assuming that the feature's data is an $n \times n$ gray scale image patch (g_i) centered at (c_x, c_y), already scale invariant, the function that find the main orientation angle of the feature g_i is given by:

$$\theta(g_i) = b \max(H(g_i)) \tag{5}$$

Where $H(g_i)$ gives the highest value of orientation of g_i based on an orientation histogram composed by b elements (each element corresponds to $360°/b$ degrees interval). The max function returns the $H(g_i)$ histogram vector index. After obtaining the result of Eq. 5, a rotation of $\theta(g_i)$ degrees is performed to the g_i gray scale patch.

Luminance Invariance is accomplished by using a template matching technique that uses invariant image gray scale templates (Bastos & Dias, 2009). This technique is based on the image average and standard deviation to obtain a normalized cross correlation value between features. A value above 0.7 (70%) is used as correlation factor.

7.1.2 Feature matching

The FIRST feature transformation here presented is not as distinctive as SIFT or PCA-SIFT, for that reason, a method based on feature clustering is used. The method groups features into clusters through a binary identification value with low computation cost. The identification signature is obtained by evaluating three distinct horizontal and vertical regions of Difference of Gaussians patches (Davidson & Abramowitz, 2006). Difference of Gaussians is a gray scale image enhancement algorithm, which involves the subtraction of one blurred version of an original gray scale image from another, which is a less blurred version of the original. The blurred gray scale images are obtained by convolving the original image with Gaussian kernels with different standard deviations. The signature will be composed of 8 digits and only features that correspond to a specified feature's binary signature are matched, thus reducing the overall matching time. For positive or null regions a value of 1 will be assigned. Negative regions will be assigned with 0. When a FIRST feature patch is processed and created, this evaluation is performed and this feature is inserted in the corresponding cluster using the obtained binary identification. When matching a feature, we also compute the binary identification of the candidate feature, which allow us to only match with potential candidates instead of matching with all the calibration features collected in a previous phase. For each feature, when a matching is found, the displacement (standard Euclidian distance (Eq. 6)) is computed between the updated feature position and the initial (calibrated) position, given by:

$$d(p, q) = \sqrt{(p_x - q_x)^2 + (p_y - q_y)^2} \tag{6}$$

The result from this process is bi-dimensional pattern as the one depicted on Fig.8 for the words *cato* [katu] (cact) and *canto*. The horizontal axis represents the video frame (i.e. time) and the vertical axis represents the 40 features displacements, observed in the respective examples of word pronunciation. These images provide us with a view of how features vary in time for different words.

The input videos for these results were recorded under approximately the same conditions and a clear difference between these two words can be noticed in the patterns. Each feature will have a different behavior in its displacement across time, as depicted on Fig. 9, which shows two features from different human face regions for the same word.

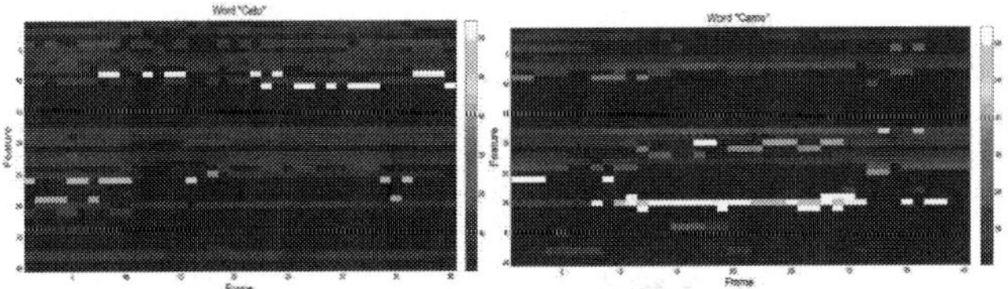

Fig. 8. Image graph for the words *cato* (above) and *canto* (below).

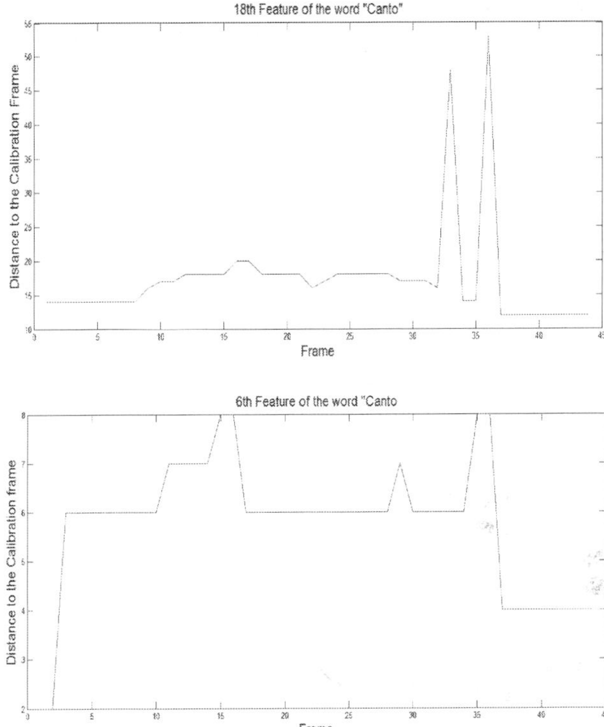

Fig. 9. Temporal behavior of the feature number 18 (right) and number 6 (left) for the word *canto*.

7.1.3 Post-processing

In the post-processing phase outliers have been removed using Chauvenet's criterion (Chauvenet, 1960) with a 0.5 threshold. This approach, although being simple, has shown good results demonstrated by empirical measures. A value is considered to be an outlier when the matching between two features is incorrect, i.e. the matching feature is not the original one. This situation is highlighted on Fig. 10 were the outlier is marked with a red circle on both frames.

Fig. 10. Matching between two frames with an outlier highlighted by a red circle.

7.1.4 Classification

For this initial stage of research the Dynamic Time Warping (DTW) technique was used to find an optimal match between a sufficient number of observations. DTW addresses very well one of the characteristics of our problem: it provides temporal alignment to time-varying signals that have different durations. This is precisely our case, since even observations of the pronunciation of the same word will certainly have different elapsed times. In Fig. 11 the DTW is applied to several pairs of words observations and we depict the DTW distance results, by means of gray scale coding of such results. For the *cato*/*canto* DTW computation we have, in the horizontal axis, the number of frames of *canto* production, whereas in the vertical axis, we have the number of frames for *cato* pronunciation. These diagrams can be simply interpreted as follows: The similarity between two words is given by the smallest DTW distance between them across time, thus when two words are the same, as shown in the comparison between canto and canto (upper-left graph), the lowest distance will lay in the image's diagonal. The red line represents the lower DTW distances found across time. In the upper-left panel the control case is represented by comparing a word observation with itself originating a straight diagonal line (i.e. all DTW distances in the diagonal are zero). Furthermore, as expected, a certain similarity with the word *Cato* (upper-right panel) can be noticed, since the only difference relies on a nasal phoneme instead of an oral one. It is also visible that the word *tinto* [tĩtu] (red) (bottom-left) presents the highest discrepancy regarding *canto*.

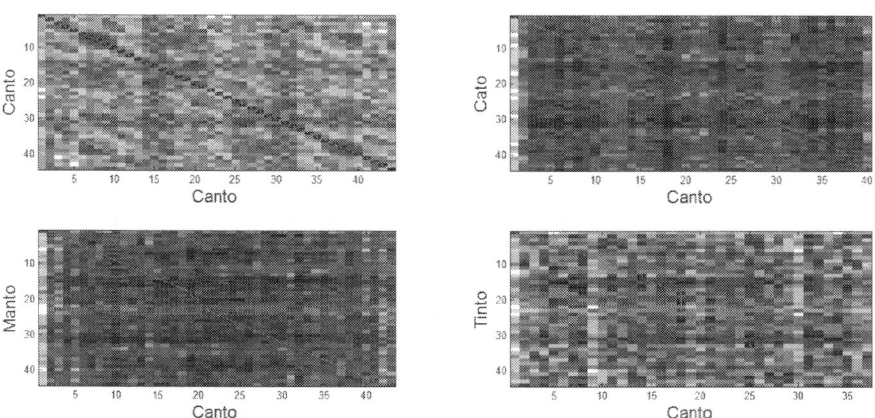

Fig. 11. Distance comparison between the word *canto* and *manto* [mẽtu] (cloak) /*tinto*/*cato* using the Matlab algorithm from (Ellis, 2003).

7.1.5 Experimental setup

The input videos were recorded by one of the authors (JF) using a webcam video of 2 megapixel during daytime with some exposure to daylight. In these videos the user exhibits some spaced facial markings in areas surrounding the lips, chin and cheeks. These fiduciary markers were made with a kohl pencil.

7.1.6 Corpus

For this experiment a database containing 112 video sequences was built from scratch. The videos contain a single speaker uttering 8 different words in European Portuguese, with 14 different observations of each word. These words were not randomly selected and represent four pairs of words containing oral and nasal vowels (e.g. *cato/canto*) and sequences of nasal consonant followed by nasal or oral vowel (e.g. *mato/manto*). In Table 1 the pairs of words and their respective phonetic transcription is provided.

Word Pair	Phonetic Transcription
cato/ canto	ˈkatu / ˈkẽtu
peta / penta	ˈpetɐ / ˈpẽtɐ
mato / manto	ˈmatu / ˈmẽtu
tito / tinto	ˈtitu / ˈtĩtu

Table 1. Pairs of words used in the VSR experiment

7.1.7 Results and discussion

In order to classify the results the following algorithm based on DTW was applied:

1. Randomly select K observations from each word in the Corpus (see table 1) that will be used as the reference (training) pattern, while the remaining ones will be used for testing.
2. For each observation from the test group:
   a. Compare each observation with the representative examples.
   b. Select the word that provides the minimum distance.
3. Compute WER, which is given by the number of incorrect classifications over the total number of observations considered for testing.
4. Repeat the procedure N times.

Considering this algorithm with N = 20 and K varying from 1 to 10, the following results in terms of Word Error Rate (WER) are achieved:

K	Mean	σ	Best	Worst
1	32.98	5.43	25.00	45.19
2	26.93	4.84	19.79	41.67
3	22.95	5.20	15.91	36.36
4	17.94	4.73	11.25	26.25
5	16.04	3.99	9.72	22.22
6	12.81	3.53	7.81	20.31
7	13.04	4.26	3.57	19.64
8	12.08	3.68	6.25	22.92
9	8.63	4.01	2.50	17.50
10	9.22	3.28	3.13	15.63

Table 2. WER classification results for 20 trials (N = 20).

For this experiment, based on the results from Table 2, the best result was achieved when K = 9, having an average WER of 8.63% and 2.5% WER for the best run. When analyzing the mean WER values across the K values, a clear improvement can be noticed, when the amount of representative examples of each word increases, suggesting that improving the training set might be beneficial for our technique. Additionally, the discrepancy found between the best and worst values suggest that further research is required on how to select the best representation for a certain word.

If we analyze the results from a different perspective, a value stabilization of WER when K = 6 can be observed in the boxplot from Fig. 12. However, considering the available corpora it is important to highlight that when K is higher the amount of test data becomes reduced. For example, when K = 10 only 4 observations from each word are considered. In this graph outliers can also be observed for K = 2, K = 7 and K = 8.

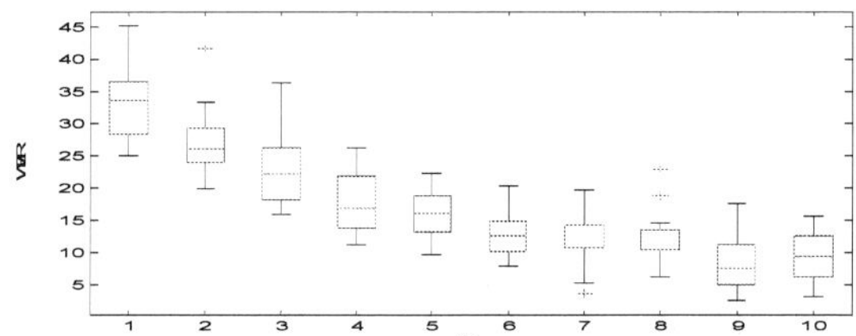

Fig. 12. Boxplot of the WER results for the several K values.

In order to further analyze the quality of the experiment several confusion matrixes are presented (Fig. 13) for the most relevant runs. Each input represents the actual word and each output represents the classified word. The order presented in Table 1 is applied for each word. When analyzing the confusion matrixes for the several trials, errors can be found between the following pairs: [kẽtu] as [katu] (Fig. 13 b)); [matu] as [mẽtu] and vice-versa (Fig. 13 a) and b)); [tĩtu] as [titu] (Fig. 13 a) and b)); and [kẽtu] as [matu] (Fig. 13 c)). As expected, confusion is more often between words where the only difference relies in the nasal sounds (consonants and vowels).

7.2 Experiment II - Doppler-based nasal phonemes detection

In this experiment a Doppler-based sensing (see section 4) system was used, composed by a Doppler emitter connected to a signal generator tuned to 40 kHz and a Dopler receptor tuned to that frequency. Doppler receptor and emitter were placed on both sides of the microphone as described in previous experiments by (Kalgaonkar et al., 2007). Microphone speech signal and Doppler receiver signals were acquired using a 96 kHz sampling rate. The process of demodulation was performed in Matlab and essentially consisted on applying amplitude demodulation to the derivative of the Doppler signal and applying a low pass filter (as in (Kalgaonkar et al., 2007)).

The same set of words used in the previous experiment (see Table 1) was recorded in different conditions by varying distance from speaker to receptor and microphone and silent or normal production. The subject was one of the authors (AT). Below are representative examples of the obtained signals as spectrograms. Fig. 14 presents the results for the minimal pair of words *cato/canto*, essentially differing in the nasality of the first vowel.

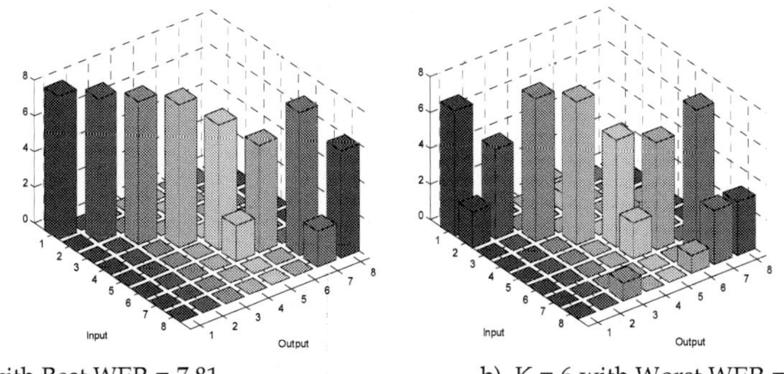

a) K = 6 with Best WER = 7.81   b) K = 6 with Worst WER = 20.31

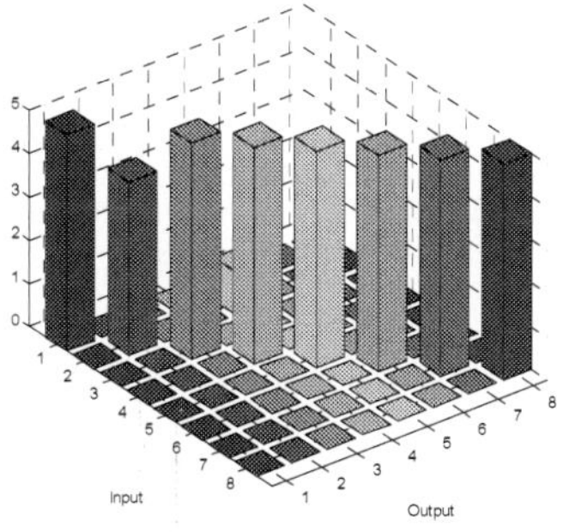

c) K=9 with WER = 2.5%

Fig. 13. Confusion matrix for best and worst run of K = 6 and best run of K = 9. Input and output axis values have the following correspondence with the words from the Corpus: *cato* = 1, *canto* =2, *peta* = 3, *penta* = 4, *mato* = 5, *manto* = 6, *tito* = 7 and *tinto* = 8. The vertical axis corresponds to the number of word classifications.

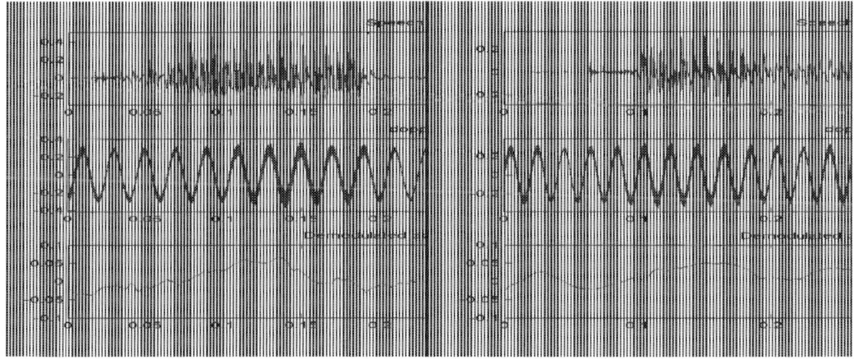

Fig. 14. Speech signal, Doppler signal and demulated signal for the words *cato* and *canto*.

By looking at the speech signal plus the spectral information between 20 and 200 Hz of the demodulated signal in Fig. 15 a clear difference between words can be empirically observed. However, despite the promising look of this approach further research needs to be performed.

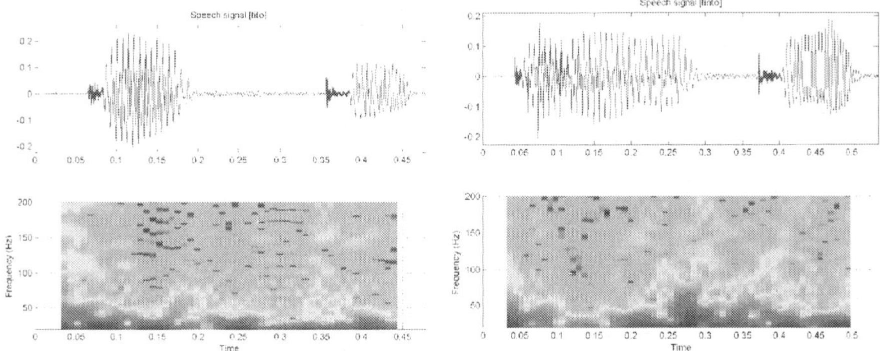

Fig. 15. Speech signal and spectrogram of the demulated signal for the pair *tito/tinto*.

7.2.1 Noticeable differences

This preliminary experiment shows for the first time ADS applied to EP and represents an initial promising step for the development of a SSI based on Doppler for EP. The resulting spectrograms for the several pairs of words show that a clear difference can be subjectively depicted from the obtained spectrograms and time-varying signals, even when the comparison is performed between similar words where the only difference resides in a nasal sound versus an oral one. Further signal processing analysis is needed, to derive new feature vectors towards the improvement of the word classification scheme presented in the previous sections.

8. Conclusion

8.1 Summary of paper and main conclusions from the two experiments

The aim of this work is to identify possible technological solutions and methodologies that enable the development of a multimodal SSI, specially targeted for EP. For that reason a brief analysis of the state-of-the-art was presented and we have proposed a new taxonomy, based on the speech production model. This paper also introduced a novel technique for feature extraction and classification in the VSR domain. This technique is based on an existing robust scale, rotation and luminance invariant feature detection transform in computer vision (FIRST), which has been applied in the past for real-time applications, such as Augmented Reality. The novelty of our approach is the application of FIRST to extract skin features spread across different regions of a speakers' face and to track their displacement, during the time that elapses while the speaker utters a word. By collecting a training set and a test set, totaling 4 minimal pairs of European Portuguese words, with 14 different observations of each word, we were able to classify the silent pronunciation of such words, using a classification scheme based in Dynamic Time Warping (DTW) technique.

DTW was used to find an optimal match between a sufficient number of observations and, in our experiments, we were able to calculate a mean Word Error Rate (WER) of 8.63% (STD 4.01%) with the best figure of 2.5% WER for the best run. As expected, error analysis detected recognition problems between similar words were the only difference is a nasal phoneme instead of an oral one. This demonstrates the difficulty on distinguishing pairs of words that only differ on nasal sounds. However, in this experiment many of these pairs were successfully discriminated, supporting our hypothesis that the skin deformation of the human face, caused by the pronunciation of words, can be captured by studying the local time-varying displacement of skin surface features, using FIRST, and that this framework can be applied to a successful vision-based SSI system for EP. Additionally, first experiments using Doppler signals for EP were reported. In this second experiment, an initial spectral analysis demonstrates a clear difference between the minimal pairs of words mentioned on Table 1. The results from both experiments are promising and motivate the development of a multimodal SSI based on these two technologies.

8.2 Future work

For the VSR modality, we expect to improve the system pipeline, by addressing several approaches. One of such activities is the adoption of the full optimal use of FIRST feature tracking, for real-time silent speech recognition. Additionally, we plan to perform facial segmentation into several regions of interest and the use of a second camera for a lateral perspective of the face, since the experiments carried so far, included only a frontal image from a single camera. We will also consider the use of one or more depth cameras (such as Microsoft Kinect (Kinect, 2011)), along with a parallel research of generalizing FIRST for 3D image features. Regarding the Doppler modality, a complete feature extraction, tracking and classification scheme, similar to the one presented for VSR, needs to be developed and tested. We also plan to carry silent speech recognition experiments in EP involving, the Doppler modality approach. In terms of classification techniques, DTW will be further exploited, but other models that capture the temporal behavior of the signals, such as Hidden Markov Models, could be considered. For statistically significant analysis, we plan to collect and analyze a more extensive corpus in EP, allowing a more concrete investigation of which tracking measures can be extracted during speech. More long term goals include the fusion of both approaches in a single multimodal SSI continuing the studies of how well can both approaches complement one another.

9. References

Bastos, R. & Dias, M. S. (2008). Automatic Camera Pose Initialization, using Scale, Rotation and Luminance Invariant Natural Feature Tracking, in *The Journal of WSCG*

Bastos, R. & Dias, M. S. (2009). FIRST - Fast Invariant to Rotation and Scale Transform: Invariant Image Features for Augmented Reality and Computer Vision. VDM Verlag 2009.

Bay, H.; Tuytelaars, T. & Gool, L. V. (2006). SURF: Speeded Up Robust Features. In *Proceedings of the 9th European Conference on Computer Vision*, Springer LNCS volume 3951, part 1, pp 404-417

Brumberg, J. S.; Kennedy, P. R. & Guenther, F. H. (2009). Artificial speech synthesizer control by brain-computer interface. In *Proceedings of Interspeech 2009*, Brighton, UK.

Brumberg, J. S.; Nieto-Castanonf, A.; Kennedye, P. R. & Guenther. F. H. (2010). Brain–computer interfaces for speech communication. Speech Communication, Volume 52, Issue 4, April 2010, Pages 367-379

Calliess, J.-P. & Schultz, T. (2006). Further Investigations on Unspoken Speech. Studienarbeit, Universita¨ t Karlsruhe (TH), Karlsruhe, Germany

Chan, A.D.C.; Englehart, K.; Hudgins, B.; & Lovely, D.F. (2001). Hidden Markov model classification of myoelectric signals in speech. *Proceedings of the 23rd Annual International Conference of the IEEE Engineering in Medicine and Biology Society*, vol. 2, 2001, pp. 1727–1730

Chauvenet, W. (1960). A Manual of Spherical and Practical Astronomy Volume II. 1863. Reprint of 1891. 5th ed. Dover, N.Y.: 1960. pp. 474 - 566

DaSalla, C.S.; Kambara, H.; Sato, M. & Koike, Y. (2009). Spatial filtering and single-trial classification of EEG during vowel speech imagery. In: Proc. *3rd Internat. Convention on Rehabilitation Engineering and Q4 Assistive Technology* (i-CREATe 2009), Singapore

Davidson, M. W. & Abramowitz, M. (2006). Molecular Expressions Microscopy Primer: Digital Image Processing - Difference of Gaussians Edge Enhancement Algorithm. In Olympus America Inc. and Florida State University

Denby, B. & Stone, M. (2004). Speech synthesis from real time ultrasound images of the tongue. In: *Proc. IEEE Internat. Conf. on Acoustics, Speech, and Signal Processing*, (ICASSP"04), Montre´al, Canada, 17–21 May 2004, Vol. 1, pp. I685–I688.

Denby, B.; Schultz, T.; Honda, K.; Hueber, T.; Gilbert, J.M. & Brumberg, J.S.(2010), Silent speech interfaces. Speech Communication, v.52 n.4, p.270-287, April, 2010

Dias, M. S.; Bastos, R.; Fernandes J.; Tavares, J. & Santos, P. (2009). Using Hand Gesture and Speech in a Multimodal Augmented Reality Environment, GW2007, LNAI 5085, pp.175-180

Dupont, S. & Ris, C. (2004). Combined use of close-talk and throat microphones for improved speech recognition under non-stationary background noise. *In: Proc. Robust 2004, Workshop (ITRW) on Robustness Issues in Conversational Interaction*, Norwich, UK, August 2004

Ellis, D. (2003). Dynamic Time Warp (DTW) in Matlab Web resource, last visited on 26-02-2011, available from:
http://www.ee.columbia.edu/~dpwe/resources/matlab/dtw

Fagan, M.J.; Ell, S.R.; Gilbert, J.M.; Sarrazin, E. & Chapman, P.M. (2008). Development of a (silent) speech recognition system for patients following laryngectomy. Med. Eng. Phys. 30 (4), 419–425

Florescu, V-M.; Crevier-Buchman, L.; Denby, B.; Hueber, T.; Colazo-Simon, A.; Pillot-Loiseau, C.; Roussel, P.; Gendrot, C. & Quattrochi, S. (2010). Silent vs Vocalized Articulation for a Portable Ultrasound-Based Silent Speech Interface", *Proceedings of Interspeech*, Makuari, Japan

Gurbuz, S., Z. Tufekci, Patterson, E. & Gowdy, J.N. (2001). Application of affine-invariant Fourier descriptors to lipreading for audio-visual speech recognition. *IEEE*

International Conference on Acoustics, Speech, and Signal Processing 2001. Proceedings. (ICASSP '01),

Harris, C. & Stephens, M. (1988). A combined corner and edge detector. *In Proceedings of the 4th Alvey Vision Conference*, pp 147-151

Helfrich, H. (1979). Age markers in speech. In: Scherer, K. & Giles, H.: Social markers in speech. Cambridge: University Press

Heracleous, P.; Nakajima, Y.; Lee, A.; Saruwatari, H. & Shikano, K. (2003). Accurate hidden Markov models for non-audible murmur (NAM) recognition based on iterative supervised adaptation. *Automatic Speech Recognition and Understanding, 2003.* ASRU '03. 2003 IEEE Workshop on , vol., no., pp. 73- 76, 30 Nov.-3 Dec. 2003

Hueber, T.; Aversano, G.; Chollet, G.; Denby, B.; Dreyfus, G.; Oussar, Y.; Roussel, P. & Stone, M. (2007). Eigentongue feature extraction for an ultrasound-based silent speech interface. Proceedings of ICASSP (Honolulu, USA), pp. 1245-1248

Hueber, T.; Chollet, G.; Denby, B.; Dreyfus, G. & Stone, M. (2008). Phone Recognition from Ultrasound and Optical Video Sequences for a Silent Speech Interface. Interspeech, Brisbane, Australia, pp. 2032-2035

Hueber T.; Benaroya, E. L.; Chollet, G.; Denby, B.; Dreyfus, G.; Stone, M. (2009). Visuo-Phonetic Decoding using Multi-Stream and Context-Dependent Models for an Ultrasound-based Silent Speech Interface. *In Proceedings of Interspeech 2009*, Brighton, UK

Jorgensen, C.; Lee D.D. & Agabon, S. (2003). Sub auditory speech recognition based on EMG signals. In: Proc. Internat. Joint Conf. on Neural Networks (IJCNN), pp. 3128–3133

Jou, S.; Schultz, T. & Waibel, A. (2004). Adaptation for Soft Whisper Recognition Using a Throat Microphone. International Conference of Spoken Language Processing (ICSLP-2004), Jeju Island, South Korea, October 2004.

Jou, S.; Schultz, T. & Waibel, A. (2007). Multi-stream articulatory feature classifiers for surface electromyographic continuous speech recognition. In: Internat. Conf. on Acoustics, Speech, and Signal Processing. IEEE, Honolulu, Hawaii

Kalgaonkar K.; Raj B. & Hu R. (2007). Ultrasonic doppler for voice activity detection. IEEE Signal Processing Letters, vol.14(10), pp. 754–757,

Kalgaonkar K. & Raj B. (2008). Ultrasonic doppler sensor for speaker recognition," in ICASSP'08

Ke, Y. & Sukthankar, R. (2004). PCA-SIFT: A more distinctive representation for local image descriptors. In *Proceedings of IEEE Computer Society Conference on Computer Vision and Pattern Recognition* (CVPR), pp 506-513

Kinect (2011). Last visited on 27-02-2011, Available from: http://www.xbox.com/pt-PT/kinect

Lacerda, A. & Head, B. F. (1966). Análise de sons nasais e sons nasalizados do Português. Revista do Laboratório de Fonética Experimental (de Coimbra), VI:5_70.

Levelt, W. (1989). Speaking: from Intention to Articulation. Cambridge, Mass.: MIT Press.

Liang, Y.; Yao, W.; Minghui, D. (2010). Feature Extraction Based on LSDA for Lipreading. International Conference on Multimedia Technology (ICMT)

Lippmann, R. P. (1997). Speech recognition by machines and humans. *Speech Communication* 22(1): 1-15

Lowe, D. G. (2004). Distinctive Image Features from Scale-Invariant Keypoints, *International Journal of Computer Vision 60*, pp. 91-110

MacGurk, H. & MacDonald, J. (1976). *Hearing lips and seeing voices*, Nature, Vol. 264, pp. 746–748

Maier-Hein, L.; Metze, F.; Schultz, T. & Waibel, A. (2005). Session independent non-audible speech recognition using surface electromyography, *IEEE Workshop on Automatic Speech Recognition and Understanding*, pp. 331–336, San Juan, Puerto Rico

Magen, H.S. (1997). *The extent of vowel-to-vowel coarticulation in English*, J. Phonetics 25 (2), 187–205

Martins, P.; Carbone, I.; Pinto, A.; Silva, A. & Teixeira, A. (2008). European Portuguese MRI based speech production studies, *Speech Communication. NL: Elsevier*, Vol.50, No.11/12, (December 2008), pp. 925–952, ISSN 0167-6393

Nakajima, Y.; Kashioka, H.; Shikano, K. & Campbell, N. (2003). Non-audible murmur recognition input interface using stethoscopic microphone attached to the skin, In: Proc. IEEE ICASSP, pp. 708–711

Nakajima, Y. (2005). Development and evaluation of soft silicone NAM microphone. Technical Report IEICE, SP2005-7, pp. 7–12

Ng, L.; Burnett, G.; Holzrichter, J. & Gable, T. (2000). Denoising of human speech using combined acoustic and EM sensor signal processing. In: *Internat. Conf. on Acoustics, Speech, and Signal Processing (ICASSP)*, Istanbul, Turkey, 5–9 June 2000, Vol. 1, pp. 229–232

Nijholt, A.; Tan, D.; Pfurtscheller, G.; Brunner, C.; R. Millán, J.; Allison, B.; Graimann, B.; Popescu, F.; Blankertz, B. & Müller, K. (2008). Brain-Computer Interfacing for Intelligent Systems, IEEE Intelligent Systems, Vol.23 No.3, pp.72-79, (May 2008)

Otani, M.; Shimizu, S. & Tatsuya, H. (2008). Vocal tract shapes of non-audible murmur production, Acoustical Science and Technology, 29(2): 195-198

Patil, S. A. & Hansen, J. H. L. (2010). The physiological microphone (PMIC): A competitive alternative for speaker assessment in stress detection and speaker verification, Speech Communication 52(4): 327-340

Pêra, V.; Moura, A. & Freitas, D. (2004). LPFAV2: a new multi-modal database for developing speech recognition systems for an assistive technology application, In SPECOM-2004, 73-76

Porbadnigk, A.; Wester, M.; Calliess, J. & Schultz, T. (2009). EEG-based speech recognition impact of temporal effects, In: Biosignals 2009, Porto, Portugal, (January 2009), pp. 376–381

Potamianos, G.; Neti, C.; Gravier, G.; Garg, A. & Senior, A. W. (2003). Recent advances in the automatic recognition of audiovisual speech, Proceedings of the IEEE 91(9): 1306-1326

Quatieri, T.F.; Messing, D.; Brady, K.; Campbell, W.B.; Campbell, J.P.; Brandstein, M.; Weinstein, C.J.; Tardelli, J.D. & Gatewood, P.D. (2006). Exploiting non-acoustic sensors for speech enhancement, IEEE Trans. Audio Speech Lang. Process, 14 (2), 533–544

Rabiner, L. R. & Juang, B. (1993). Fundamentals of speech recognition, Prentice-Hall, Inc., Chapter 4

Rossato, S.; Teixeira, A. & Ferreira, L. (2006). Les Nasales du Portugais et du Français : une étude comparative sur les données EMMA. *In XXVI Journées d'Études de la Parole*. Dinard, FR, Jun. 2006.

Sá, F.; Afonso, P.; Ferreira, R. & Pera, V. (October 2003). Reconhecimento Automático de Fala Contínua em Português Europeu Recorrendo a Streams Audio-Visuais, In: The Proceedings of COOPMEDIA'2003 - Workshop de Sistemas de Informação Multimédia, Cooperativos e Distribuídos, Porto, Portugal, October 8, 2003

Schultz, T. & Wand, M. (2010). Modeling coarticulation in large vocabulary EMG-based speech recognition, Speech Communication, Vol. 52, Issue 4, April 2010, pp. 341-353

Shi, J. & Tomasi, C. (1994). Good Features to Track, In IEEE Conference on CVPR

Srinivasan, S.; Raj, B. & Ezzat, T. (2010). Ultrasonic sensing for robust speech recognition, In ICASSP

Strevens, P. (1954). Some observations on the phonetics and pronunciation of modern Portuguese, Rev. Laboratório Fonética Experimental, Coimbra II, 5–29

Stork, D. G. & Hennecke, M. E. (1996). Eds., Speechreading by Humans and Machines, Berlin, Germany: Springer-Verlag

Suppes, P.; Lu, ZL. & Han, B. (1997). Brain wave recognition of words, Proc Natl Acad Sci USA 94:14965–14969

Teixeira, A. & Vaz, F. (2000). Síntese Articulatória dos Sons Nasais do Português, Anais do V Encontro para o Processamento Computacional da Língua Portuguesa Escrita e Falada (PROPOR), pp. 183-193, ICMC-USP, Atibaia, São Paulo, Brasil

Teixeira, A.; Castro Moutinho, L. & Coimbra, R.L. (2003). Production, acoustic and perceptual studies on European Portuguese nasal vowels height, In: Internat. Congress Phonetic Sciences (ICPhS), pp. 3033–3036

Teixeira, A.; Martinez, R.; Silva, L. N.; Jesus, L..; Príncipe, J. C.; Vaz, F. (2005). Simulation of Human Speech Production Applied to the Study and Synthesis of European Portuguese. *Eurasip Journal on Applied Signal Processing*. Hindawi Publishing Corporation, vol. 2005, n° 9, p. 1435-1448

Tran, V.-A.; Bailly, G.; Loevenbruck, H. & Toda, T. (2009). Multimodal HMM-based NAM-to-speech conversion, In Proceedings of Interspeech 2009, Brighton, UK

Tran, V.-A.; Bailly, G.; Loevenbruck, H. & Toda, T. (2010). Improvement to a NAM-captured whisper-to-speech system, Speech Communication, Vol.52, Issue 4, (April 2010), pp.314-326

Trigo, R. L. (1993). The inherent structure of nasal segments, In M. K. Huffman e R. A. Krakow (editores), Nasals, Nasalization, and the Velum, Phonetics and Phonology, Vol. 5, pp.369-400, Academic Press Inc.

Toda T.; Nakamura K.; Nagai T.; Kaino T.; Nakajima Y. & Shikano, K. (2009). Technologies for Processing Body-Conducted Speech Detected with Non-Audible Murmur Microphone. *In Proceedings of Interspeech 2009*, Brighton, UK; September 2009.

Toth, A.R.; Kalgaonkar, K.; Raj, B. & Ezzat, T. (2010). Synthesizing speech from Doppler signals. *IEEE International Conference* on *Acoustics Speech and Signal Processing* (ICASSP), vol., no., pp.4638-4641, 14-19 March 2010

Wand, M.; Jou, S.; Toth, A. R. & Schultz, T. (2009). Synthesizing Speech from Electromyography using Voice Transformation Techniques. *In Proceedings of Interspeech 2009*, Brighton, UK

Wester, M. & Schultz, T. (2006). Unspoken speech – speech recognition based on electroencephalography. Master's Thesis, Universita"t Karlsruhe (TH), Karlsruhe, Germany

Zhao, G.; Barnard, M. & Pietikäinen, M. (2009). Lipreading with local spatiotemporal descriptors. Trans. Multi. 11(7): 1254-1265

Zhu, B.; Hazen, T.; J. & Glass, J. R. (2007). Multimodal speech recognition with ultrasonic sensors. In Eurospeech

7

The Influence of Lombard Effect on Speech Recognition

Damjan Vlaj and Zdravko Kačič
University of Maribor, Faculty of Electrical Engineering and Computer Science
Slovenia

1. Introduction

The origin of Lombard effect dates back one hundred years. In 1911 Etienne Lombard discovered the psychological effect of speech produced in the presence of noise (Lombard, 1911). The Lombard effect is a phenomenon in which speakers increase their vocal levels in the presence of a loud background noise and make several vocal changes in order to improve intelligibility of the speech signal (Anglade & Junqua, 1990; Bond et al., 1989; Dreher & O'Neill, 1957; Egan, 1971; Junqua, 1996; Junqua & Anglade, 1990; Van Summers et al., 1988). In nowadays speech recognition applications appearance of Lombard effect can be expected in various domains, where spontaneous and conversational speech communication will take place in uncontrolled acoustic environments.

Two main interpretations of the Lombard effect have been proposed. The first argues that the effect is a physiological audio-phonatory reflex (Lombard, 1911), the second that Lombard changes are motivated by compensation on the part of the speaker for decreased intelligibility (Lane & Tranel, 1971). Some authors have also argued that both mechanisms may contribute to the changes made by the speaker in noisy environments (Junqua, 1993).

Detailed surveys of the literature on the Lombard effect phenomenon was made in (Lane & Tranel, 1971) and more recently in (Junqua, 1996). The conducted research showed that Lombard speech is different from normal speech in a number of ways. The main changes of characteristics of Lombard speech can be seen in increase in voice level, fundamental frequency and vowel duration, and a shift in formant center frequencies for F1 and F2 (Anglade & Junqua, 1990; Applebaum et al., 1996; Junqua, 1996; Junqua & Anglade, 1990). It was also reported in (Hanley & Steer, 1949) that speaking rate may be reduced when speech is produced in a noisy environment. A detailed acoustic and phonetic analysis of speech under different types of stress including the Lombard effect was carried out also in (Hansen, 1988). The studies showed that under the Lombard effect, duration of vowels increase while that of unvoiced stops and fricatives decrease. Also, spectral tilt decreases implying an increase in high-frequency components under the Lombard effect. An increase in pitch and first formant location also occurs in both cases. Also, energy migration from low and high frequency to the middle range for vowels, and movement from low to higher bands for unvoiced stops and fricatives was observed. In addition to the above, differences between male and female speakers was noted in (Junqua, 1993). Lombard changes are on the other hand greater in adults than in children and in spontaneous speech than in reading tasks (Amazi & Garber, 1982; Lane & Tranel, 1971).

It was concluded in (Bond et al., 1989) that the above mentioned changes of speech characteristics in Lombard speech are made to increase the vocal effort and to articulate in a more precise manner for better communication in a noisy condition.

Researchers (Pickett, 1956; Dreher & O'Neill, 1957; Ladgefoged, 1967) studied intelligibility of utterances under the Lombard effect. It was shown that the intelligibility of Lombard speech increases up to a certain level of noise, when presented at a constant speech-to-noise ratio, and sharply decreases when speech becomes shouted. It was also demonstrated that the presence of auditory feedback of speech is necessary to maintain the intelligibility of Lombard speech, as the primary purpose of Lombard effect is to increase speech intelligibility in communication with other speakers in noisy environments.

It was reported in (Junqua, 1996) and in (Van Summers et al., 1988) that acoustic changes that occur in speech in a noisy environment are different from person to person and are highly speaker-dependent (Junqua, 1996). This was confirmed also in (Van Summers et al., 1988), where the authors reported a significant increase in fundamental frequency for one male speaker, but not for the second, when they spoke in quiet and in different levels of noise. The characteristics of Lombard speech may also vary with the type of ambient noise, and with the language of the speaker (Junqua, 1996).

It was suggested in (Lane & Tranel, 1971) that the magnitude of the speakers' response to noise is likely to be governed by the desire to achieve intelligible communication. As an argument to support this idea they argue that in a noisy condition, speakers would not change their voice level when talking to themselves. In (Bond et al., 1989) the idea was confirmed as the authors observed that the magnitude of the Lombard effect is greater when speakers believe they are communicating with interlocutors. Encountering these Lombard reflex cannot be considered as an all-or-none response with some threshold level (Junqua, 1996; Lane & Tranel, 1971). According to (Junqua, 1996), the variability in Lombard speech appears to be distributed along a continuum. The acoustic differences that can be observed between Lombard speech and normal speech are believed to have an effect on intelligibility. As reported in (Junqua, 1993; Van Summers et al., 1988; Dreher & O'Neill, 1957) the speech produced in noise is more intelligible than speech produced in quiet, when both types of speech are presented in noise at an equivalent signal-to-noise ratio. It was also shown in (Junqua, 1996) that the type of masking noise and the gender of the speakers used for the experiment are crucial to the difference in intelligibility of speech produced in noise-free and in noisy conditions. In (Junqua, 1993) it was also demonstrated that the babble noise degrades the intelligibility of English digit vocabulary more than white noise. He also showed that in such case the female Lombard speech is more intelligible than the male Lombard speech. It was further revealed that breathiness decreases the intelligibility of speech. In this sense it seems that female speakers tend to decrease the breathiness in their productions more than male speakers do (Junqua, 1993).

In this chapter we want to present the influence of Lombard effect on speech recognition, which presence can be expected in contemporary speech recognition application in numerous application domains. For this reason, we will use the Slovenian Lombard Speech Database, which was recorded in studio environment. Slovenian Lombard Speech Database will be presented in Section 2. The changes of Lombard speech characteristics will be presented in Section 3. With the experiments we want to confirm the influence of Lombard effect on speech recognition. In section 4, the experimental design for speech recognition will be presented. The results of experiments will be given in Section 5 and the conclusion will be drawn in Section 6.

2. Lombard speech database

For the analysis of the speech characteristics and speech recognition experiments, we used Lombard speech database recorded in Slovenian language. The Slovenian Lombard Speech Database[1] (Vlaj et al., 2010) was recorded in studio environment. In this section Slovenian Lombard Speech Database will be presented in more detail. Acquisition of raw audio material recorded in studio conditions is described in Subsection 2.1. Annotation of speech material and conversion of the audio material to the final format are presented in Subsection 2.2. The structure of Slovenian Lombard Speech Database is presented in Subsection 2.3.

2.1 Acquisition of raw audio material

The Slovenian Lombard Speech Database was recorded in studio environment. Each speaker pronounced a set of eight corpuses in two recording sessions with at least one week pause between recordings. Approximately 30 minutes of speech material per speaker and per session was recorded.

The recordings were performed using a hands-free microphone AKG C 3000 B, close talking microphone Shure Beta 53 and two channel electroglottograph EG2. Four channel recordings were performed:

* hands free microphone,
* close talking microphone,
* laryngograph and
* recordings of noise mixed with speaker's speech that was played on speaker's headphones during recordings.

The recording platform consisted of Audigy 4 PRO external audio card for 4 channel audio recording, Phonic MU244X mixer, and using 96 kHz sampling frequency, 24-bit linear quantization.

Two types of noises were used in recordings: babble and car noise. The noises were taken from the Aurora 2 database (Hirsch & Pearce, 2000) and were normalized. The noises were played to speaker's headphones AKG K271.

At the beginning of each recording the level of the reproduced background noise was adjusted according to the scheme proposed in (Bořil et al., 2006). The required noise level was adjusted by setting the corresponding effective voltage of the sound card open circuit VRMS OL. Noise levels of 80 dB SPL[2] and 95 dB SPL at a virtual distance of 1–3 meters were used for the Lombard speech recordings.

Three recordings of all corpuses were made within one recording session:

* without noise (reference recording),
* at 80 dB SPL and
* at 95 dB SPL.

A short pause was made between recordings of items of particular corpus (word, number, number string, and sentence) to allow speaker's recovery. After the complete corpus was recorded a longer pause was made to allow for speaker's recovery.

There was an interaction between the "Lombard" speaker and a listener. The listener heard the attenuated speech mixed with non attenuated noise, evaluated the intelligibility and reacted accordingly. The reaction of the listener was mediated to the speaker by means of

---

[1] The owner of the database is SVOX·

[2] SPL is abbreviation for Sound Pressure Level·

message displayed on the LCD display, where the speaker was notified that the pronunciation was intelligible or she/he was asked to repeat the pronunciation as it was not intelligible enough.

2.2 Annotation of speech material

The manual annotation of speech material is performed by the LombardSpeechLabel tool (Figure 1) developed at the University of Maribor. The program tool is written in the Tcl/Tk/Tix language, which is suitable for visual programming. It was developed on the Microsoft Windows platform and can be incorporated into other operating system platforms with small modifications.

The LombardSpeechLabel tool window is divided into three fields. The upper field contains four waveform views (hands free microphone, close talking microphone, laryngograph and recordings played on speaker's headphones) of the signal that have been captured during recording of the database. By clicking the buttons on the right hand side of the upper field, each signal can be played individually. The bottom of the tool window is divided into two parts. On the left hand side the information about the speaker and the recording is given. On the right hand side, the additional data of the recording and the orthographic transcription are presented.

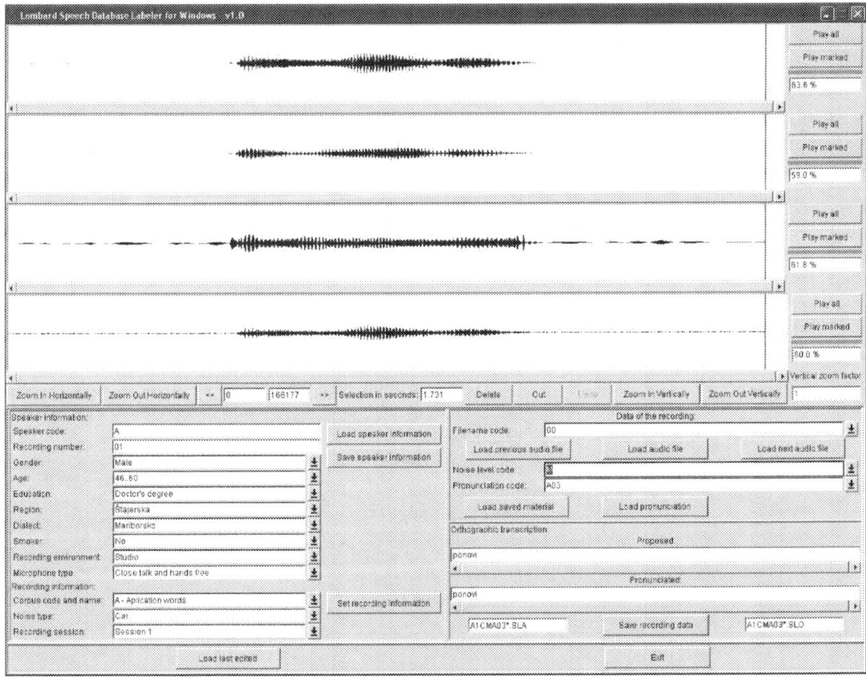

Fig. 1. LombardSpeechLabel tool for manual annotation of speech material.

The conversion of the audio material to the final format, which was set to 96 kHz sampling frequency, 16-bit linear quantization is also made with the LombardSpeechLabel tool.

2.3 The structure of the database

The Slovenian Lombard Speech Database consists of recordings of 10 Slovenian native speakers. Five males and five females were recorded. As we already mentioned, each speaker pronounced a set of eight corpuses in two recording sessions with at least one week pause between recordings. The corpus's structure is similar to SpeechDat II database (Kaiser & Kačič, 1997). In the following subsections more information about the database will be given.

2.3.1 Audio and label file format

Audio files are stored as sequences of 16-bit linear quantization at the sampling frequency of 96 kHz. They are saved in Intel format. Each prompted utterance is stored in a separate file. Each speech file has an accompanying SAM label file with UTF-8 symbols.

A	Speaker code (A-Z)
S	Session code (1-9) – used only 1 and 2
T	Code of the noise type: • R: without noise • C: Car noise • B: Babble noise
R	Code of the recording: • N: recording of the reference signal without presence of noise • L: recording of the signal without presence of noise • M: recording of the signal with presence of noise level of 80 dB SPL • H: recording of the signal with presence of noise level of 95 dB SPL
NNN	Code of the corpus (A00 – Z99): A – application words, B – connected digits, D – dates, I – isolated digits, N – natural numbers, S – phonetically rich sentences, T – times, W – phonetically rich words
C	Code of the recording channel: • 1: hands-free microphone • 2: close talk microphone • 3: signal captured by laryngograph • 4: signal in headphones that was heard by a speaker
LL	Two letter ISO 639 language code
F	File type code O=Orthographic label file, A=audio speech file

Table 1. Description of file nomenclature.

2.3.2 File nomenclature

File names follow the ISO 9660 file name conventions (8 plus 3 characters) according to the main CD ROM standard. Owing to the large amounts of audio material, the data were stored on a DVD-ROM media.

The following template for file nomenclature is used:

```
A S T R NNN C. LL F
```

The file nomenclature is described in Table 1.

2.3.3 Directory structure

The directory structure is set so that each speaker is located on his own DVD-ROM volume. Each speaker has two sessions. In each session the reference condition and two noise conditions are included. Each condition includes eight corpses. The following five levels directory structure is defined:

```
\<database>
  \<speaker>
    \<session>
      \<condition>
        \<corpus>
```

The Lombard speech database directory structure is presented in Table 2.

<database>	Defined as: <name><language code> i.e. LOMBSPSL Where: <name> is LOMBSP indicating Lombard Speech <LL> is the ISO 2-letters code SL for Slovenian
<speaker>	Defined as: SPK_<a> Where <a> is a progressive letter from A to Z. This letter is the same as the first letter used in file names (see subsection 2.3.2).
<session>	Defined as: SES_<s> Where <s> is a progressive number in the range 1 to 9. This number is the same as the second number used in file names (see subsection 2.3.2).
<condition>	Tree types of conditions are defined: • REF: recording of the reference signal without presence of noise, • CAR: recording of the signal with presence of car noise and • BABBLE: recording of the signal with presence of babble noise
<corpus>	Defined as: CORPUS_<c> Where <c> is a letter for one of corpus defined: A – application words, B – connected digits, D – dates, I – isolated digits, N – natural numbers, S – phonetically rich sentences, T – times, W – phonetically rich words

Table 2. Lombard speech database directory structure.

2.3.4 Corpus code definition

As it is useful for users to clearly identify the speech file contents by looking at the filename, we have specified the corpus code to support one letter corpus identifier and two numbers identifier. The corpus code definition is described in Table 3.

3. Changes of Lombard speech characteristics

In this section, we will present changes of three Lombard speech characteristics: mean value of pitch, phoneme duration and frequency envelope. To demonstrate changes of Lombard speech characteristics we used recordings of Slovenian Lombard Speech Database presented in Section 2.

In the analysis, the Lombard speech characteristics were measured for different voiced phonemes for the utterances of three words: "ustavi" (stop), "ponovi" (repeat) and "predhodni" (previous). In this paper only the selected results of Lombard speech analysis will be presented.

Corpus identifier	Item identifier	Corpus contents
A	00-29	application words (30 words)
B	00-04	connected digits (10 digits sequence pronounced 5 times)
D	00-04	dates (5 dates)
I	00-11	isolated digits (12 digits)
N	00-04	natural numbers (5 numbers)
S	00-29	phonetically rich sentences (30 sentences)
T	00-06	times (7 times)
W	00-49	phonetically rich words (50 words)

Table 3. Corpus code definition.

3.1 Mean value of pitch

According to the literature, the value of pitch increases in Lombard speech compared to normal speech. In this section the results of mean pitch values of the first phoneme "O" of the word "ponovi" (Repeat) will be presented. Figures 2 and 3 show the mean pitch values of voiced speech (vowel "O") for five speakers, for two sessions and two noise types. Speakers 1 and 2 were male speakers, whereas speakers 3 to 5 were female speakers.

Significant increase of pitch in first vowel "O" of the word "ponovi" (repeat) compared to reference pronunciations can be seen on Figures 2 and 3 for Lombard speech recorded under 95dB noise level for all five speakers. The increase can be observed in both recording sessions and for both noise types, although the extent varies among speakers. The increase is almost the same for the first, second and the fifth speaker and varies most for the third speaker in case of babble background noise. In case of car background noise the difference is bigger for the first and the forth speaker. For utterances recorded under 80 dB noise level the increase of pitch is significant in case of babble noise (except for third speaker) but is less clear in case of car noise for most speakers

3.2 Phoneme duration

In this section the results of the duration of the vowel "A" of the word "ustavi" (stop) for all five speakers are presented. Figures 4 and 5 show the results of the analysis. It can be seen that the duration varies among speakers, but is more consistent per speaker regarding different recording sessions, background noise type and noise level. However, there is no clear distinction in phoneme duration concerning different recording sessions, background noise level or noise type. Figures 4 and 5 indicate that speakers tend to increase the phoneme duration at higher level of background noise, but this seems to be not as consistent as the increase of pitch.

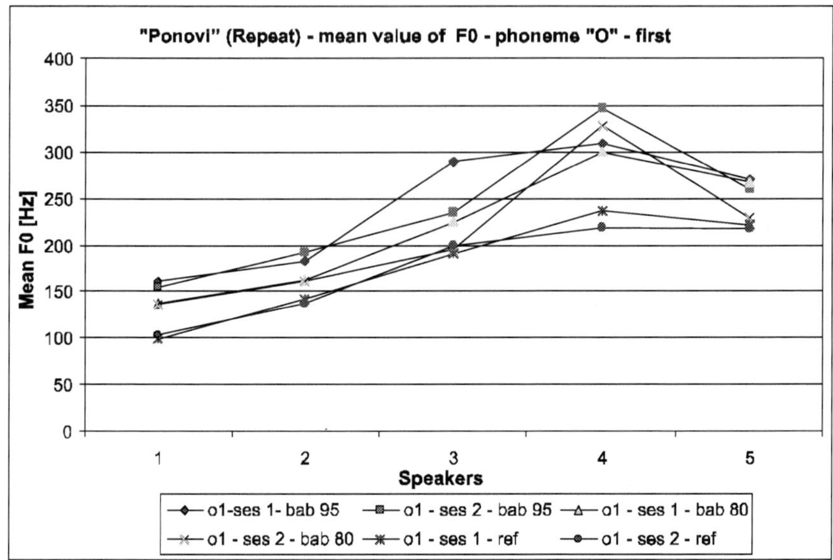

Fig. 2. Mean pitch values of the first phoneme "O" of the word "ponovi" (Repeat) recorded at different noise levels and at babble background noise.

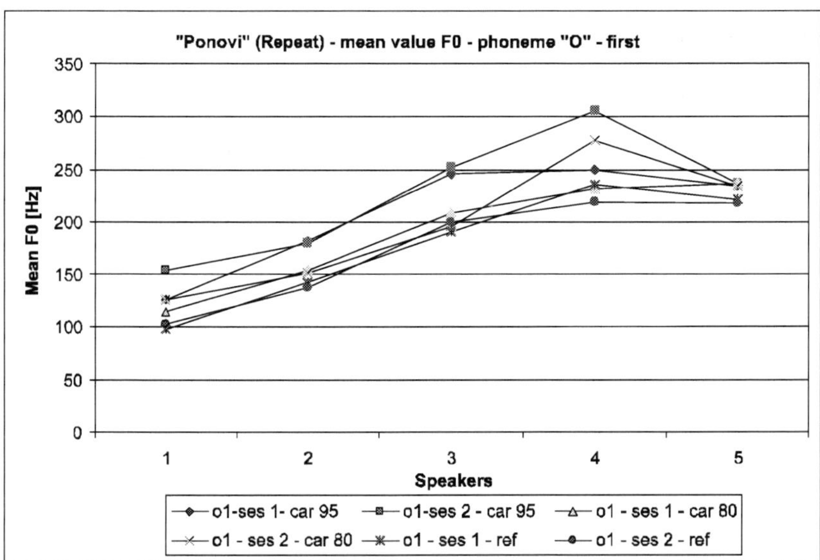

Fig. 3. Mean pitch values of the first phoneme "O" of the word "ponovi" (Repeat) recorded at different noise levels and at car background noise.

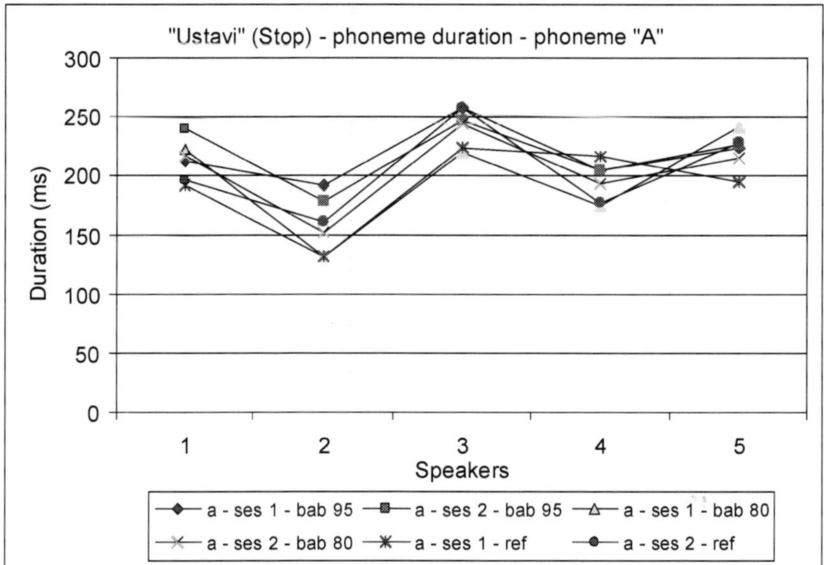

Fig. 4. Duration of the phoneme "A" of the word "ustavi" (Stop) recorded at babble background noise and at different noise levels.

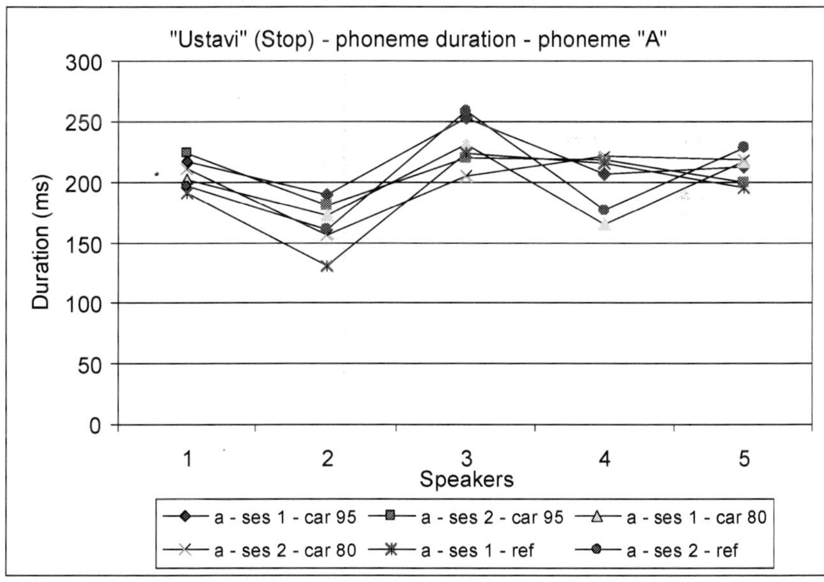

Fig. 5. Duration of the phoneme "A" of the word "ustavi" (Stop) recorded at car background noise and at different noise levels.

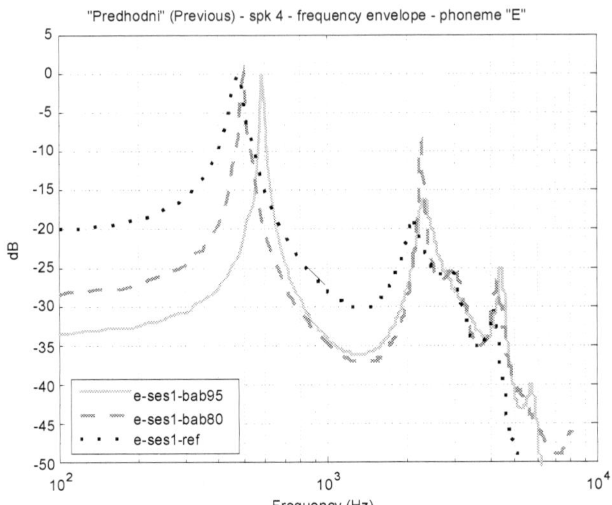

Fig. 6. Frequency envelope of phoneme "E" of the word "Predhodni" (Previous) recorded at babble background noise and at different noise levels for female speaker (speaker 4) and for the first recording session.

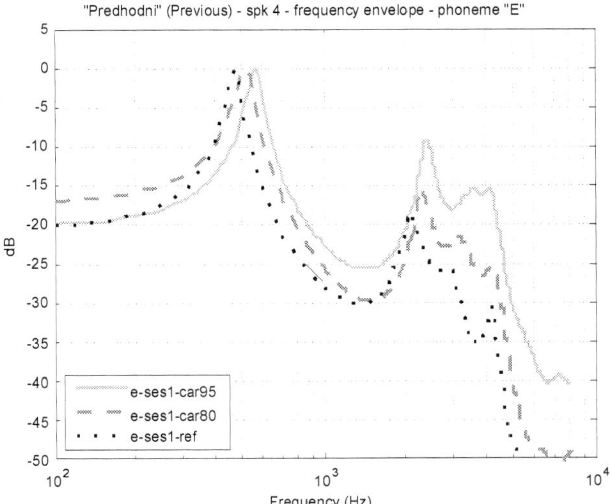

Fig. 7. Frequency envelope of phoneme "E" of the word "Predhodni" (Previous) recorded at car background noise and at different noise levels for female speaker (speaker 4) and for the first recording session.

3.3 Frequency envelope

In this section the results of frequency envelope of phoneme "E" of the word "Predhodni" (Previous) recorded at different background noises and at different noise levels for female speaker (speaker 4) are presented. Figures 6 and 7 show these results of the analysis. The increase of the first formant frequency is evident for both background noise types. Also an increase of energy in higher frequency range can be seen. Both features are known to occur in Lombard speech. The changes of these features are less obvious for utterance uttered at 80 dB background noise.

4. Experimental design

We created experimental design, which showed the influence of Lombard effect on speech recognition. It was carried out on the Slovenian Lombard Speech Database. The experimental design for acoustic modeling was based on continuous Gaussian density Hidden Markov Models. For hidden Markov modeling the HTK toolkit was used (Young et al., 2000). For training only recordings of the signal without presence of noise on speaker headphones (see code L of the recording in Table 1) were used. The training was done with monophone acoustical models. The reason why we decided to use monophone acoustical models and not triphone or word acoustical models lays in the content of the Slovenian Lombard Speech Database. For the training of triphone acoustical models the speech material of the Slovenian Lombard Speech Database is not big enough. Looking from the point of view of word acoustical models, the Slovenian Lombard Speech Database has too many various words to be trained well enough. The training procedure for monophone acoustical models is presented in Figure 8. The Gaussian mixtures were increased by power of 2 up to 32 mixtures per state. Monophone acoustical models were trained on all eight corpuses from the Slovenian Lombard Speech Database (see Table 3). For this reason 2880 recorded files with 9474 pronounced words were used. In the next paragraph we will shortly present the HTK tools, which were used in the training procedure.

The HTK tool *HCompV* scans a set of data files, computes the global mean and variance and sets all of the Gaussians in a given HMM to have the same mean and variance. The HTK tool *HERest* is used to perform a single re-estimation of the parameters of a set of HMMs using an embedded training version of the Baum-Welch algorithm. *HHEd* is a script driven editor for manipulating sets of HMM definitions. Its basic operation is to load in a set of HMMs, apply a sequence of edit operations and then output the transformed set. We used this program tool to add short pause model and for increasing the number of Gaussian mixture components for each state.

For the testing three types of the recordings were used:

- recordings of the signal without presence of noise on the speaker headphones,
- recordings of the signal with presence of noise level of 80 dB SPL on the speaker headphones and
- recordings of the signal with presence of noise level of 95 dB SPL on the speaker headphones.

The Slovenian Lombard Speech Database is recorded in two recording sessions with at least one week pause between recordings. For the training of monophone acoustical models the speech material of the first session was used and for the testing the speech material of the second session was used. We also made cross experiments, so that we trained monophone acoustical models on the second session and tested them on the first session. The tests were made on four corpuses (application words, phonetically rich words, isolated digits and connected digits) from the Slovenian Lombard Speech Database. The test on application words contained 320 words and the test on phonetically rich words contained 500 words. The corpuses isolated digits and connected digits were combined in one test with 620 digits/words. Word loop was used in all tests, which simply puts all words of the vocabulary in a loop and therefore allows any word to be followed by any other word. The results will be presented in Section 5.

For the experimental design, we used Mel-cepstral coefficients and energy coefficient as features. We also used first and second derivative of the basic features. The features were created with the front-end using the basic distributed speech recognition standard from ETSI (ETSI ES 201 108, 2000).

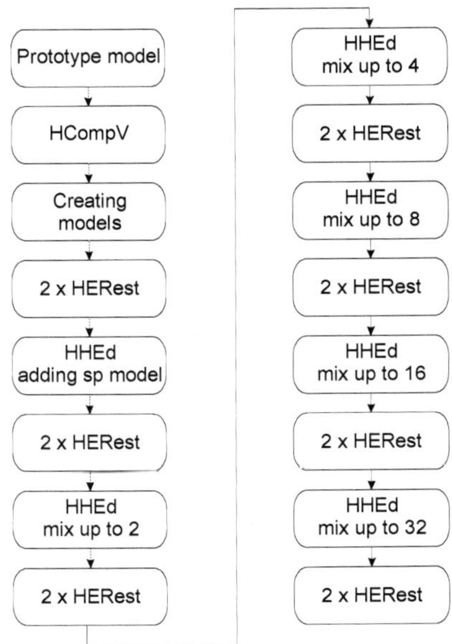

Fig. 8. The procedure for training of monophone acoustical models.

5. Results

The results obtained by the experiments will be presented in this section. Figures 9 to 14 present charts, which show the results on speech recognition accuracy. There are twelve groups with three speech recognition results presented on all charts. The first column in each group of results presents speech recognition accuracy when there was no noise played on the speaker headphones. The second column presents speech recognition accuracy when car or babble noise was played on the speaker headphones with the noise level of 80 dB SPL. The last third column presents speech recognition accuracy, when car or babble noise was played on the speaker headphones with the noise level of 95 dB SPL. At this point we must point out that recordings used for training of monophone acoustical models and testing have no noise present. The noise mentioned was played on speaker headphones to encourage the speaker to speak louder. Speech recognition experiments were made on six different Gaussian mixtures per state. In the charts this is indicated by mix1 to mix 32. The speech recognition results are presented for both training scenarios. In the first scenario the monophone acoustical models were trained on the first session of the Slovenian Lombard Speech Database and then tested on the second one. In the second scenario the monophone acoustical models were trained on the second session and then tested on the first one. Bellow the title of the charts there is a row beginning with "Trained on" that indicates in which session monophone acoustical models were trained.

Figures 9 and 10 show speech recognition accuracy tested on corpus A (application words) with presence of car and babble noise on the speaker's headphones. Figures 11 and 12 show speech recognition accuracy tested on corpus W (phonetically rich words) with presence of car and babble noise on the speaker's headphones. And last two Figures 13 and 14 show speech recognition accuracy tested on corpuses B (connected digits) and I (isolated digits) with presence of car and babble noise on the speaker's headphones.

From the speech recognition results we can conclude that the Lombard effect is present in the recordings, which were recorded with noise present on the speaker's headphones. When the noise level on the speaker's headphones was increased from 80 dB SPL to 95 dB SPL, the speech recognition accuracy decreased.

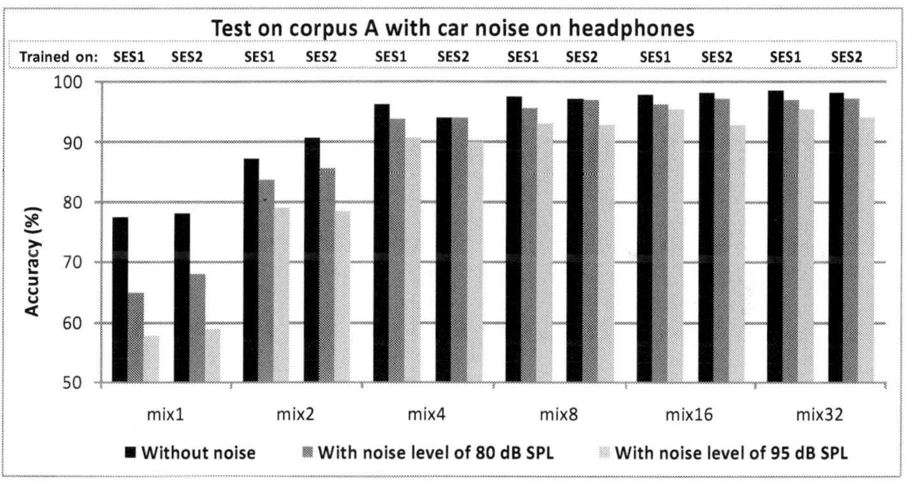

Fig. 9. Speech recognition accuracy tested on application words (corpus A) with presence of car noise on the speaker headphones.

The speech recognition accuracy was almost always better when the monophone acoustical models were trained on first sessions and tested on second session. The reason for this could lay in better trained monophone acoustical models on the first session or better acoustical environment in the second session of the Slovenian Lombard Speech Database. Should the second answer be correct, it could be concluded that speakers have adapted. Namely, when speakers recorded the second session, they had already known what to expect.

The best speech recognition results were achieved, when the tests were made on phonetically rich words (corpus W). The results were the worst, when the tests were made on connected and isolated digits (corpuses B & I). If we analyze speech recognition results at only 32 Gaussian mixtures per state, we can see that the smallest differences between the tests when no noise was present on speaker's headphones and the tests when the noise level of 95 dB SPL was present on speaker's headphones were obtained on corpuses A (application words) and W (phonetically rich words).

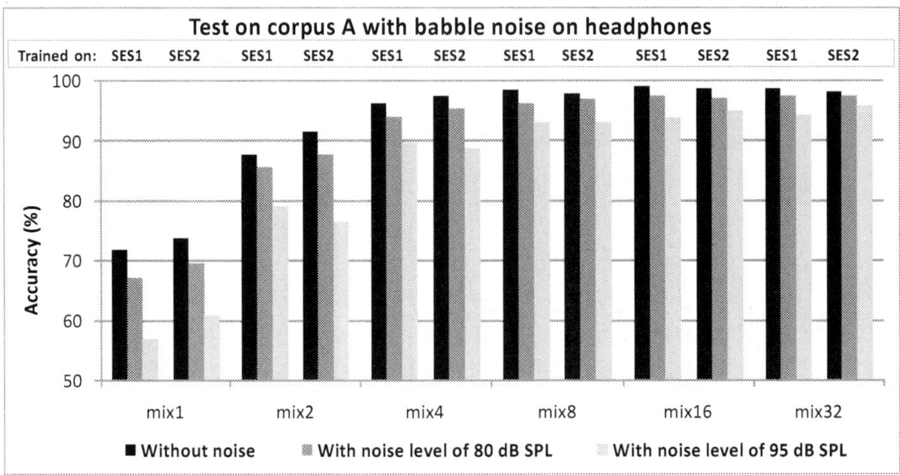

Fig. 10. Speech recognition accuracy tested on application words (corpus A) with presence of babble noise on the speaker headphones.

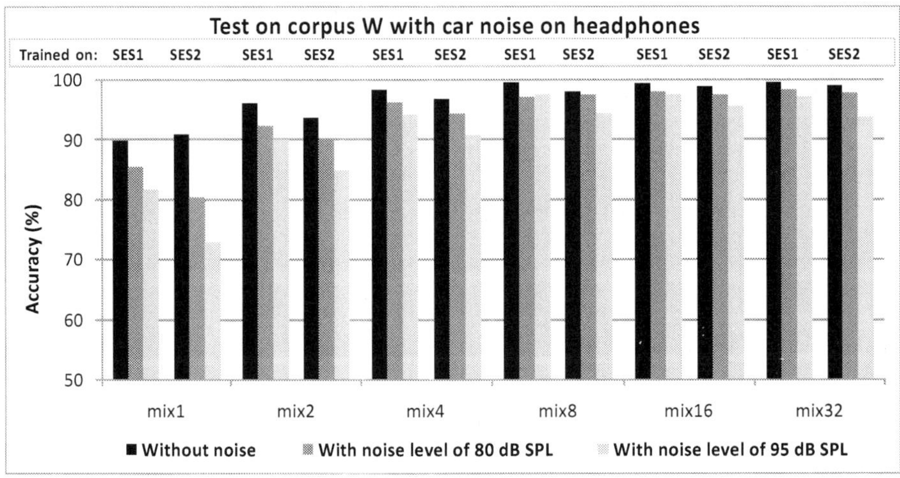

Fig. 11. Speech recognition accuracy tested on phonetically rich words (corpuses W) with presence of car noise on the speaker headphones.

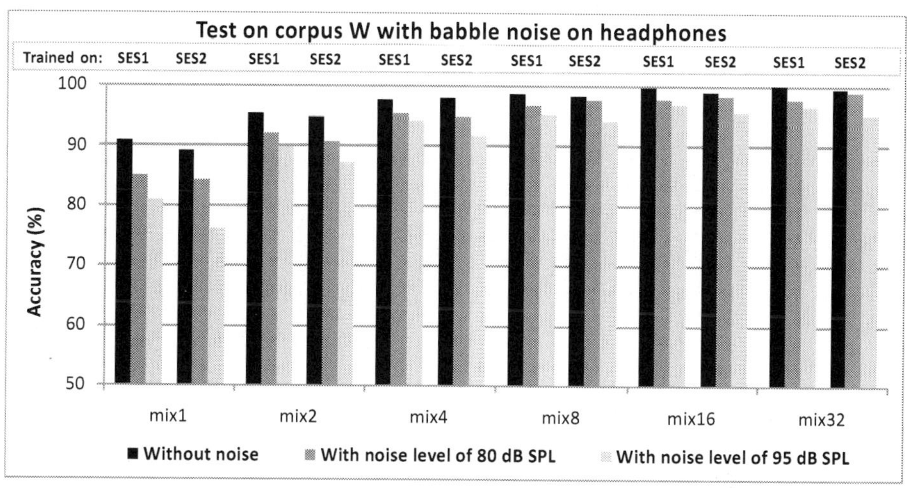

Fig. 12. Speech recognition accuracy tested on phonetically rich words (corpuses W) with presence of babble noise on the speaker headphones.

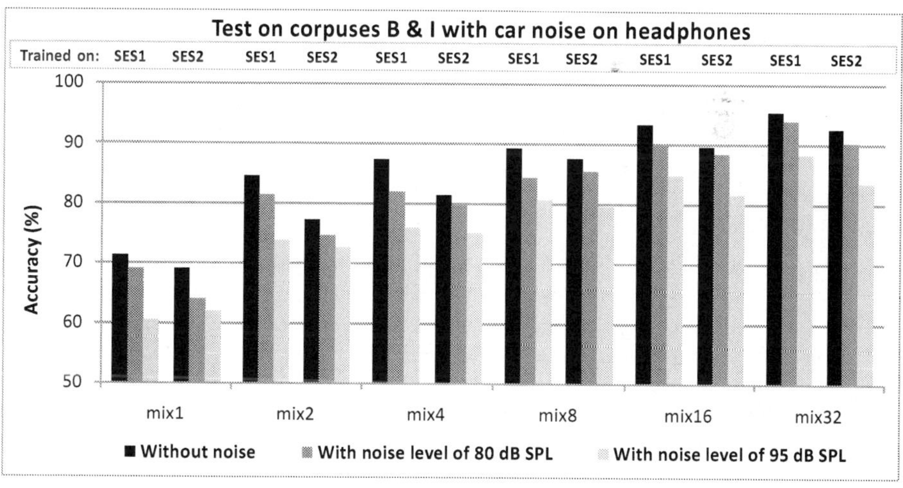

Fig. 13. Speech recognition accuracy tested on connected and isolated digits (corpuses B & I) with presence of car noise on the speaker headphones.

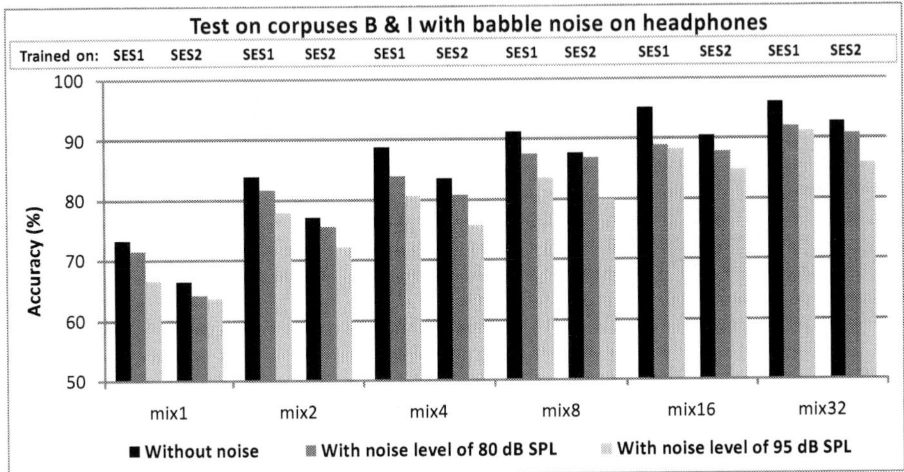

Fig. 14. Speech recognition accuracy tested on connected and isolated digits (corpuses B & I) with presence of babble noise on the speaker headphones.

By increasing the number of Gaussian mixtures per state, the speech recognition accuracy was also increased. If we look at the speech recognition accuracy presented in the charts, we can see that the influence of Lombard effect is smaller at 32 Gaussian mixtures per state than at lower number of Gaussian mixtures per state. This can be concluded from the fact that the difference of the speech recognition accuracy under different conditions (without noise, with noise level of 80 dB SPL and with noise level of 95 dB SPL) is the smallest at 32 Gaussian mixtures per state.

Considering the average of the obtained speech recognition results at 32 Gaussian mixtures per state, we can conclude that speech recognition accuracy was reduced by 1.59 %, when the noise level of 80 dB SPL was present on speaker's headphones and by 4.60 %, when the noise level of 95 dB SPL was present on speaker headphones.

6. Conclusion

In this chapter we made a short review of papers covering the topic of the Lombard effect, which were written by researchers in last hundred years. Nowadays, the presence of Lombard effect can be expected in contemporary speech recognition applications in numerous application domains. We made experiments to present the influence of Lombard effect on speech recognition. In order to do so, we used the Slovenian Lombard Speech Database, which was presented in Section 2. The Slovenian Lombard Speech Database was recorded in studio environment. In Section 3, we presented changes of three Lombard speech characteristics: mean value of pitch, phoneme duration and frequency envelope. In Section 4, the experimental design was presented. Results were presented in Section 5. With the experiments we confirmed the influence of Lombard effect on speech recognition accuracy.

7. References

Amazi, D. K. & Garber, S. R. (1982). The Lombard sign as a function of age and task. *The Journal of Speech and Hearing Research*, Vol. 25, No. 4, pp. 581–585.

Anglade, Y. & Junqua, J-C. (1990). Acoustic-phonetic study of Lombard speech in the case of isolated-words. *STL Research Reports*, Vol. 2, pp. 129-135.

Applebaum, T.; Hanson, B. & Morin, P. (1996). Recognition strategies for Lombard speech. *STL Research Reports*, Vol. 5, pp. 69-75.

Bond, Z.; Moore, T. & Gable, B. (1989). Acoustic-phonetic characteristics of speech produced in noise and while wearing an oxygen mask. *Journal of the Acoustical Society of America*, Vol. 85, No. 2, pp. 907 -912.

Bořil H., Bořil T. & Pollák P. (2006). Methodology of Lombard speech database acquisition: Experiences with CLSD, *Proceedings of the fifth Conference on Language Resources and Evaluation - LREC'06*, Genoa, Italy, pp. 1644-1647.

Dreher, J. & O'Neill, J. (1957). Effects of ambient noise on speaker intelligibility for words and phrases. *Journal of the Acoustical Society of America*, Vol. 29, No. 12, pp. 1320-1323.

Egan, J. (1971). The Lombard reflex: Historical perspective. *Archives of otolaryngology*, Vol. 94, pp. 310-312.

ETSI ES 201 108 v1.1.1 (2000). *Speech Processing, Transmission and Quality aspects (STQ), Distributed speech recognition, Front-end feature extraction algorithm, Compression algorithm*, ETSI standard document, Valbonne, France.

Hanley, T. & Steer, M. (1949). Effect of level of distracting noise upon speaking rate, duration and intensity. *Journal of Speech and Hearing Disorders*, Vol. 14, No. 4, pp. 363-368.

Hansen J. H. L. (1988). *Analysis and Compensation of Stressed and Noisy Speech with Application to Robust Automatic Recognition*, Ph.D. dissertation, School of Elect. Eng., Georgia Inst. of Technol., Atlanta.

Hirsch H. G. & Pearce D. (2000). The Aurora experimental framework for the performance evaluation of speech recognition systems under noisy conditions, *Proceedings of the ISCA ITRW ASR'00*, Paris, France.

Junqua, J-C. (1993). The Lombard reflex and its role on human listeners and automatic speech recognizers. *Journal of the Acoustical Society of America*, Vol. 1, pp. 5 10-524.

Junqua, J-C. (1996). The influence of acoustics on speech production: A noise-induced stress phenomenon known as the Lombard reflex. *Speech Communication*, Vol. 20, No 1-2, pp. 13-22.

Junqua, J-C. & Anglade, Y. (1990). Acoustic and perceptual studies of Lombard speech: Application to isolated-words automatic speech recognition. *STL Research Reports*, Vol. 2, pp. 73-81.

Kaiser J. & Kačič Z. (1997). *SpeechDat Slovenian Database for the Fixed Telephone Network*, University of Maribor, Maribor, Slovenia.

Ladgefoged, P. (1967). *Three Areas of Experimental Phonetics*. Oxford Univ. Press., London, U.K.

Lane, H. & Tranel, B. (1971). The Lombard sign and the role of hearing in speech. *Journal of Speech and Hearing Research*, Vol. 14, pp. 677-709.

Lombard, E. (1911). Le signe de l'elevation de la voix, *Annals maladiers oreille, Larynx, Nez, Pharynx*, Vol. 37, pp. 101-119.

Pickett J. M. (1956). Effects of vocal force on the intelligibilty of speech sounds, *Journal of the Acoustical Society of America*, Vol. 28, No. 5, pp. 902–905.
Van Summers, W.; Pisoni, D.; Bernacki, R.; Pedlow, R. & Stokes M. (1988). Effects of noise on speech production: acoustic and perceptual analyses. *Journal of the Acoustical Society of America*, Vol. 84, No. 3, pp. 917-928.
Vlaj, D.; Zögling Markuš, A.; Kos, M. & Kačič, Z. (2010). Acquisition and Annotation of Slovenian Lombard Speech Database, *Proceedings of the seventh Conference on International Language Resources and Evaluation – LREC'10*, Valletta, Malta, pp. 595-600.
Young, S.; Kershaw, D.; Odell, J.; Ollason, D.; Valtchev, V. & Woodland, P. (2000). *The HTK book*, Version 3.0, Microsoft Corporation, USA.

Suitable Reverberation Criteria for Distant-talking Speech Recognition

Takanobu Nishiura and Takahiro Fukumori
Ritsumeikan University
Japan

1. Introduction

The recognition of distant-talking speech has rapidly improved in recent years, because many novel speech-recognition techniques have been proposed that are robust against noise and reverberance. The signal to noise ratio (SNR) is generally used as a common criterion in speech-recognition techniques that are robust against noise. SNR is an effective noise criterion for estimating the recognition of speech in noisy environments. As an algorithm based on the perceptual evaluation of speech quality (PESQ) (T. Yamada et al. (2006)) has also been proposed to achieve the same target, we can roughly estimate the recognition of speech in noisy environments. However, no common reverberation criteria have been proposed to attain robust reverberant-speech recognition. It has therefore been difficult to estimate the recognition of reverberant speech. The reverberation time, T_{60}, (M. R. Schroeder (1965)) is currently generally used to recognize distant-talking speech as a reverberation criterion. It is unique and does not depend on the position of the source in a room. However, distant-talking speech recognition greatly depends on the location of the talker relative to that of the microphone and the distance between them. Therefore, T_{60} is unsuitable for measuring the recognition of distant-talking speech. We propose newly reverberation criteria for measuring the recognition of distant-talking speech to overcome this problem. We first investigate suitable reverberation criteria to enable distant-talking speech to be recognized. We calculated automatic speech recognition with early and late reflections based on the impulse response between a talker and the microphone. We then evaluated it based on ISO3382 acoustic parameters (ISO3382 (1997)). Based on above investigation, we finally propose novel reverberation criteria RSR-D_n (Reverberant Speech Recognition criteria with D_n) which utilise ISO3382 acoustic parameters for robustly estimating reverberant speech recognition performance.

2. Conventional reverberation criteria for recognition of distant-talking speech

2.1 Reverberation time, (T_{60})
2.1.1 Reverberation time based on theory of room acoustics
Reverberation time (M. R. Schroeder (1965)) is the most fundamental concept for evaluating indoor acoustical fields and is a parameter that expresses the duration of sound. Reverberation time is the time required for a sound in a room to decay by 60 dB (called T_{60}). As the theory assumes a diffusible sound field in a room, the effect does not change even if sound-absorbing material is placed in any position in the room. The reverberation time is

constant for all positions of the sound source and the microphone in the room. However, it alone is insufficient as the criterion for the recognition of distant-talking speech because this depends on the distance between a talker and the microphone in the same environment.

2.1.2 Method of measuring reverberation time

Schroeder developed a basic method (M. R. Schroeder (1965)) of measuring reverberation by integrating the square of the impulse response. The reverberation time is easily measured with his method. The reverberation curves are derived from Eq. (1) with impulse response $h(\lambda)$.

$$< y_d^2(t) >= N \int_t^\infty h^2(\lambda)d\lambda \tag{1}$$

where $< >$ is the ensemble average, and N is the power of the unit frequency of random noise. The reverberation time in this reverberation curve is the time it takes to drop 60 dB below the original level.

2.2 Total amplitude of reflection signals (A value)

The A value (H. Kuttruff (2000)) is used as a reverberation criterion as often as reverberation time for the recognition of distant-talking speech. It is derived from Eq. (2).

$$A = \sqrt{\int_\epsilon^n h^2(t)dt \ / \ \int_0^\epsilon h^2(t)dt,} \tag{2}$$

where ϵ represents the duration of direct sound within approximately $3 - 5$ ms. The A value indicates the energy ratio between direction and reflections on the captured signal, and it depends on the distance between the talker and microphone in the same room. However, it does not distinguish early reflections from late reverberations.

3. Relation between early reflections and distant-talking speech recognition

We define early reflections as high-correlation signals with direct sound, especially those that arrive within a few milliseconds of direct sound in this paper. Late reverberations are defined as low or no correlation signals with direct sound, especially those that arrive over a few milliseconds after direct sound.

3.1 Early reflections in distant-talking speech recognition

Early reflections, especially those that arrive within 50 ms of direct sound, are useful to humans when listening to speech (H. Kuttruff (2000)). However, the higher the reflection energy becomes, the less effectively speech is recognized, subject to clean acoustic phoneme models. However, it was previously unclear whether early reflections were useful for recognizing speech in the recognition of distant-talking speech because the reverberation time and A values were used as reverberation criteria. We evaluated what relation there was between early reflections and the recognition of distant-talking speech on the basis of impulse responses between a talker and the microphone to develop more suitable reverberation criteria for distant-talking speech recognition.

3.2 Evaluation experiment
3.2.1 Recording conditions

We measured impulse responses in actual environments. The impulse responses were measured in $T_{60} = 0.2$ and 0.7 s environments, subject to distances of 0.1 and 0.5 m between

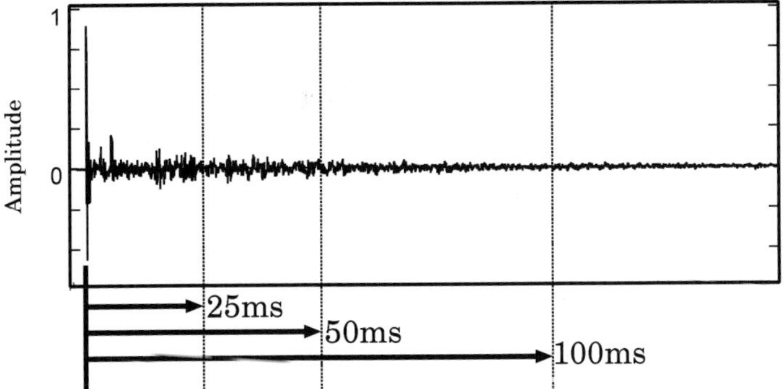

Fig. 1. *Example of impulse response extraction for three evaluation periods.*

Decoder	Julius (A. Lee et al. (2001))
HMM	IPA monophone model
	(Gender-dependent)
Feature vectors	12 orders MFCC +
	12 orders ΔMFCC +
	1 order ΔPower
Frame length	25 ms. (Humming window)
Frame interval	10 ms.

Table 1. Experimental conditions for speech recognition.

the talker and the microphone. A time stretched pulse (Y. Suzuki et al. (1995)) was used to measure the impulse responses. The recordings were made with 16 *kHz* sampling and 16 *bit* quantization.

3.2.2 Experimental conditions
An ATR phoneme-balanced set (K. Takeda et al. (1987)) was employed as the speech samples that were made up of 216 isolated Japanese words that were uttered by 14 speakers (7 females and 7 males). We evaluated the relation between early reflections and the recognition of distant-talking speech by convolving speech samples and impulse responses. Impulse responses were extracted during each period of evaluation as shown in Figure 1 to evaluate the relation between reflections and the recognition of distant-talking speech for all evaluation periods. Table 1 lists the experimental conditions for speech recognition.

3.2.3 Experimental results
Figure 2 plots the experimental results, where T_{60} is the reverberation time, *Dis.* is the distance between the talker and the microphone, and *WRR* is the word recognition rate. The *A* value is the energy ratio between the direction and reflections from the duration of direct sound to each evaluation period. We confirmed that early reflections within about 12.5 *ms* after direct sound only contributed slightly to the recognition of distant-talking speech in quiet environments on the basis of these results, although early reflections within about 50 *ms* from the duration of direct sound contributed greatly to human hearing ability. We also confirmed that late

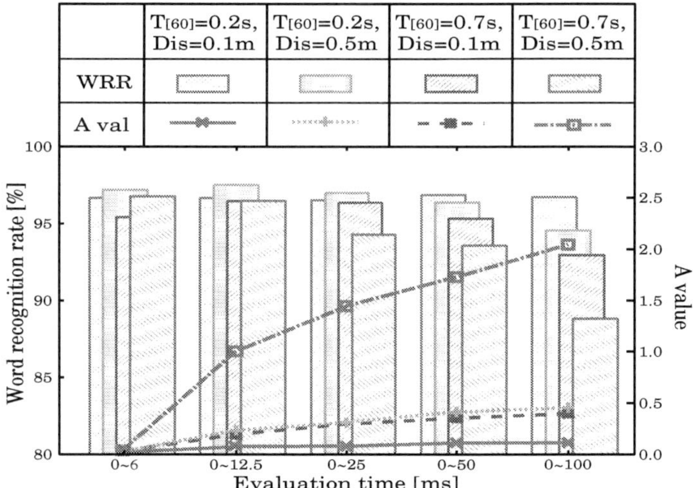

Fig. 2. *Effects of early reflections on distant-talking speech recognition.*

reflections over about 12.5 *ms* after direct sound decreased the recognition of distant-talking speech. The higher the *A* value becomes in Figure 2, the greater the number of reflections. However, we confirmed that the ability to recognize speech can be improved de spite a higher *A* value. Therefore, we again found that suitable reverberation criteria were necessary for the recognition of distant-talking speech on the basis of our evaluation experiments.

4. Toward suitable reverberation criteria

4.1 ISO3382 acoustic parameters

ISO3382 (ISO3382 (1997)) proposed parameters for measuring room acoustics. The ISO3382 standard defines measurements of reverberation times in rooms with reference to other acoustical parameters. Acoustics parameters are classified into four categories on the basis of this standard:

1. Sound level

2. Reverberation time

3. Balance between early and late arriving energies (Clarity, Definition, and Center time)

4. Binaural parameters (IACC, Lateral Fraction)

These parameters are directly calculated based on measured impulse responses. We focused on the third category (balance between early and late arriving energies), because it has a high correlation with clarity and the reverberance of the acoustic sound field.

4.2 Balance between early and late arriving energy

"Clarity," "Definition," and "Center time" are defined as the acoustic parameters of balance between early and late arriving energies in the ISO3382 standard. The *C* value expresses the clarity of acoustics and is derived from Eq. (3). The *D* value expresses the definition of acoustics and is derived from Eq. (4). Center time expresses the center time based on a square impulse response and is derived from Eq. (5).

$$C_n = 10 \log_{10} \left(\int_0^n h^2(t)dt \, / \, \int_n^\infty h^2(t)dt \right), \tag{3}$$

$$D_n = \int_0^n h^2(t)dt \, / \, \int_0^\infty h^2(t)dt, \tag{4}$$

$$T_s = \int_0^\infty t\, h^2(t)dt \, / \, \int_0^\infty h^2(t)dt, \tag{5}$$

where, n is the border time between early and late arriving energies. The C value measure and the condition of music are highly correlated with $n = 80\ ms$, and the D value measure and the condition of speech are highly correlated with $n = 50\ ms$ based on the ISO3382 standard. In addition, the larger T_s becomes, the more late reverberations there are.

4.3 Evaluation experiments
We evaluated the relation of the ISO3382 acoustic parameters and the recognition of distant-talking speech to determine suitable reverberation criteria. We also compared all acoustic parameters with regression analysis based on ordinary least squares.

4.3.1 Recording conditions
We measured impulse responses in six environments, i.e., a "Living room" (LV, $T_{60} = 250\ ms$), a "Conference room" (CR, $T_{60} = 350\ ms$), a "Corridor" (CC, $T_{60} = 600\ ms$), a "Prefabricated bath" (PB, $T_{60} = 700\ ms$), an "Elevator hall(lobby)" (EV, $T_{60} = 700\ ms$), and "Standard stairs" (SS, $T_{60} = 800\ ms$). The distances between the talker and the microphone were between 10 cm and 500 cm in all environments. We measured 307 impulse responses in all. A time-stretched pulse was used to measure the impulse responses as in Section 3.2.1. The recordings were conducted with 16 kHz sampling and 16 bit quantization.

4.3.2 Experimental conditions
The speech recognition experiments were conducted under the same conditions as in Section 3.2.2. An ATR phoneme-balanced set was employed as the speech samples that were made up of 216 isolated Japanese words that were uttered by 14 speakers (7 females and 7 males). Table 1 lists the experimental conditions for speech recognition.

4.3.3 Experimental results
Figures 3-6 plot the experimental results. The horizontal axes represent the word recognition rate, and the vertical axes represent the A value, C_{80}, D_{50}, and T_s. Table 2 lists the results for all acoustic parameters with regression analysis based on ordinary least squares. We found that the ISO3382 acoustic parameters were strong candidates for the reverberation criteria based on these results because the regression coefficients for the C, D, and T_s values were higher than that for the A value.

4.3.4 Discussion
The results from the evaluation experiments proved the ISO3382 acoustic parameters were strong candidates as the reverberation criteria for the recognition of distant-talking speech. We therefore assumed that the early reflection signal, which is the most important factor in

	LV	CR	CD	PB	EV	SS	AVE.
A	0.81	0.93	0.79	0.89	0.81	0.69	**0.82**
C_{80}	0.82	0.86	0.85	0.96	0.91	0.89	**0.88**
D_{50}	0.73	0.91	0.93	0.95	0.92	0.91	**0.89**
T_s	0.82	0.87	0.95	0.97	0.91	0.77	**0.88**

Table 2. Regression coefficients for all acoustic parameters.

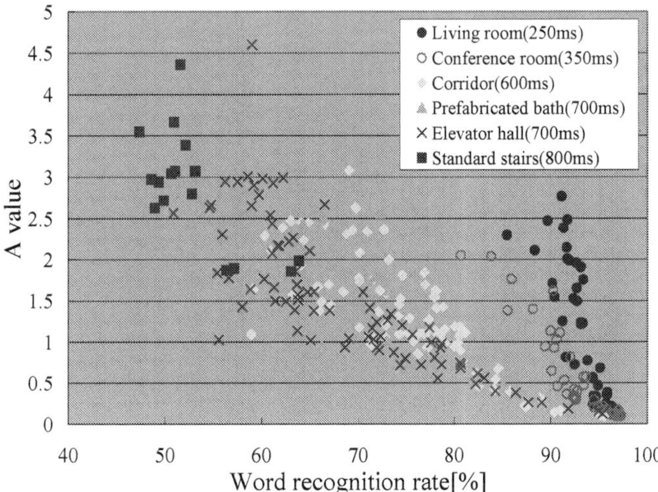

Fig. 3. *A value.*

the recognition of reverberant speech, does not depend on the total amount of reflection, but on the balance between early and late arriving energies. Our next challenge is to examine the use of suitable reverberation criteria based on the C_n and D_n values of ISO3382 acoustic parameters with a suitable border time, n, between early and late arriving energies to prove this hypothesis. If suitable border time n can be estimated, we can easily estimate the recognition of reverberant speech with one impulse response between the talker and microphone.

5. Performance estimation of reverberant speech recognition based on reverberation criteria

5.1 Performance estimation based on reverberation time

Reverberation time is usually used to estimate reverberant speech recognition performance. However, other reverberant features are altered by the difference between assumption of a diffusible sound field in a room and an actual sound field. Thus, it is difficult to estimate speech recognition performance with only reverberation time. In this section, we conducted an evaluation experiment in three reverberant environments shown in Table 3(b) to investigate the relation between reverberation time and speech recognition performance. We first

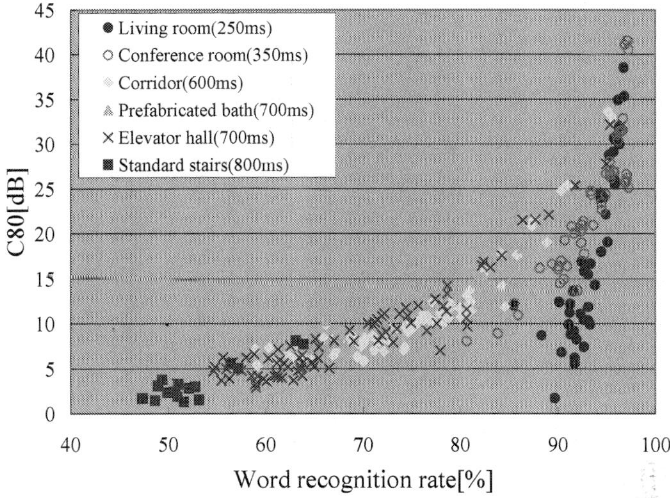

Fig. 4. *Clarity (C$_{80}$).*

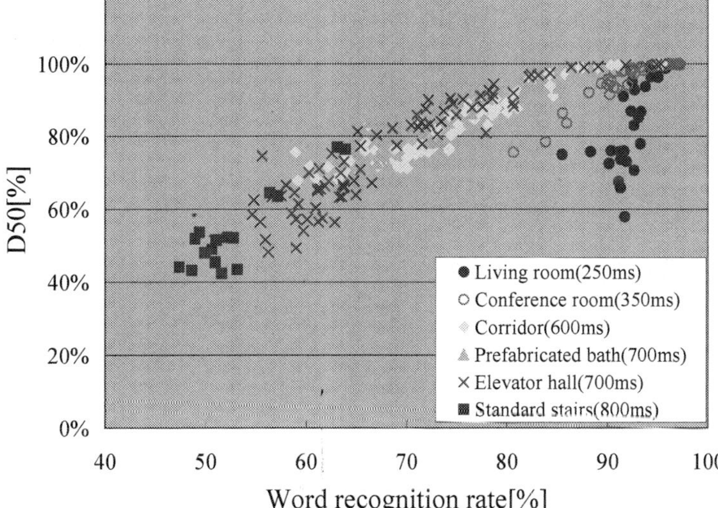

Fig. 5. *Definition (D$_{50}$).*

measured several impulse responses in each environment. After that, we acquired speech recognition performance with a speech recognition engine (A. Lee et al. (2001)) by using the training data convolved speech sample and each measured impulse response. Figure 7

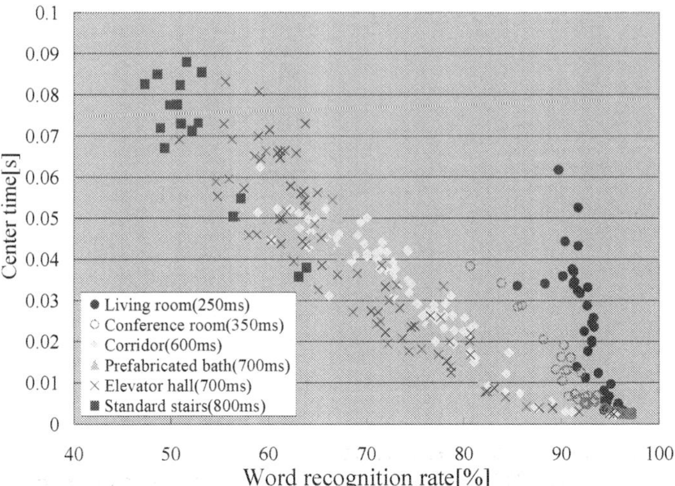

Fig. 6. *Center time (T_s).*

shows the obtained result. The line in Figure 7 represents the average of speech recognition performance in each reverberant environment.   We confirmed the speech recognition performance degradation and the variance increase in heavy reverberant environment. As a result, we could confirm that it is significantly difficult to estimate speech recognition performance in heavy reverberation environment in comparison with light reverberant environment.

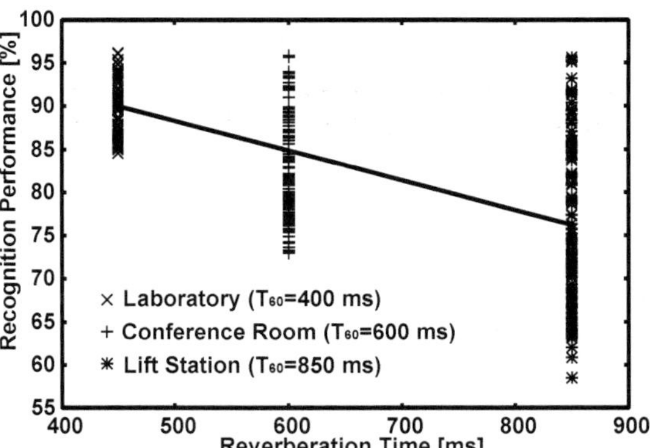

Fig. 7. Reverberant speech recognition performance in three reverberant environments.

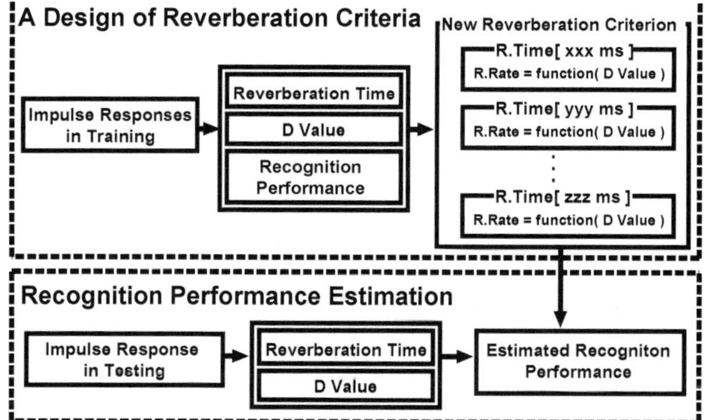

Fig. 8. Overview of the proposed method.

5.2 Performance estimation based on new reverberation criteria RSR-D_n

5.2.1 Early reflections in reverberant speech recognition

In previous section 3.2.3, we confirmed two facts about reverberant speech recognition. One is that early reflections within about 12.5 ms after direct sound contributed slightly to the recognition of reverberant speech in quiet environments, although early reflections within about 50 ms from the duration of direct sound contributed greatly to human hearing ability. The other is that late reflections over about 12.5 ms after direct sound decreased the recognition of reverberant speech. Based on these results, we confirmed that it is difficult to estimate the reverberant speech recognition performance using only reverberation time, since it does not take these factors into consideration. Therefore, we concluded that we would need to use the experimental results we had previously obtained to determine suitable reverberation criteria for recognizing reverberant speech.

5.2.2 New reverberation criteria with RSR-D_n

We attempted to design the new reverberation criteria RSR-D_n to estimate reverberant speech recognition performance as shown at the top of Figure 8. First, we investigated the relation between the D value and reverberant speech recognition performance. We then used regression analysis based on the correlation coefficients for these to design the RSR-D_n to cover each reverberation time. We used four steps in our approach, explained in detail as follows.

Step.1: We measured many impulse responses in a number of environments to obtain training data. Using the measured impulse responses as a basis, we used Eq. (1) to calculate reverberation times.

Step.2: We next calculated the D value with Eq. (4) after performing Step 1. In Eq. (4), the border time n is essential for determining the maximum value of the relation between D value and speech recognition performance. Thus, we determined the suitable border time n as described in Section 5.3.1 and then used the value to calculate D_n.

Step.3: We then acquired speech recognition performance with a speech recognition engine (A. Lee et al. (2001)) by using the training data obtained using dry data and measured impulse responses as described in Step 1.

(a) Training environments
Soundproof room (T_{60} = 100 ms, 72 RIRs)
Japanese style room (T_{60} = 400 ms, 72 RIRs)
Laboratory (T_{60} = 450 ms 72 RIRs)
Conference room (T_{60} = 600 ms, 120 RIRs)
Living room (T_{60} = 600 ms, 72 RIRs)
Corridor (T_{60} = 600 ms, 120 RIRs)
Bath room (T_{60} = 650 ms, 28 RIRs)
Lift station (T_{60} = 850 ms, 120 RIRs)
Standard stairs (T_{60} = 850 ms, 56 RIRs)
(b) Environments to calculate speech recognition performance
Laboratory (T_{60} = 450 ms, 72 RIRs)
Conference room (T_{60} = 600 ms, 120 RIRs)
Lift station (T_{60} = 850 ms, 120 RIRs)
(c) Environments to calculate a suitable n
Japanese style room (T_{60} = 400 ms, 72 RIRs)
Conference room (T_{60} = 600 ms, 120 RIRs)
Standard stairs (T_{60} = 850 ms, 56 RIRs)
(d) Environments to design RSR-D_n
Japanese style room (T_{60} = 400 ms, 72 RIRs)
Conference room (T_{60} = 600 ms, 120 RIRs)
Standard stairs (T_{60} = 850 ms, 56 RIRs)
(e) Test environments
Laboratory (T_{60} = 450 ms, 72 RIRs)
Bath room (T_{60} = 650 ms, 28 RIRs)
Lift station (T_{60} = 850 ms, 120 RIRs)

Table 3. Experimental conditions(RIRs : Room Impulse Responses)

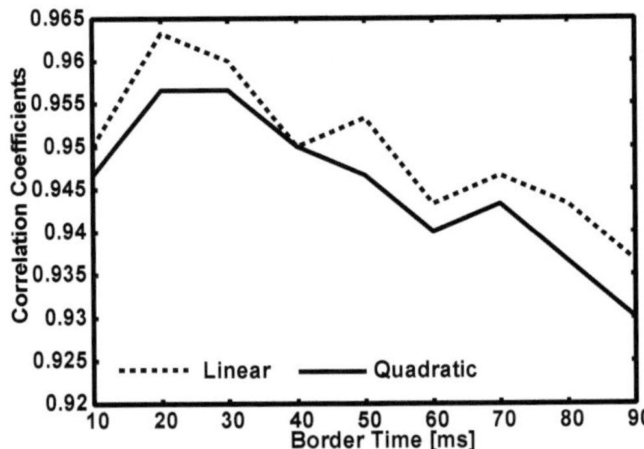

Fig. 9. Relation between correlation coefficient in each regression curve and border time n

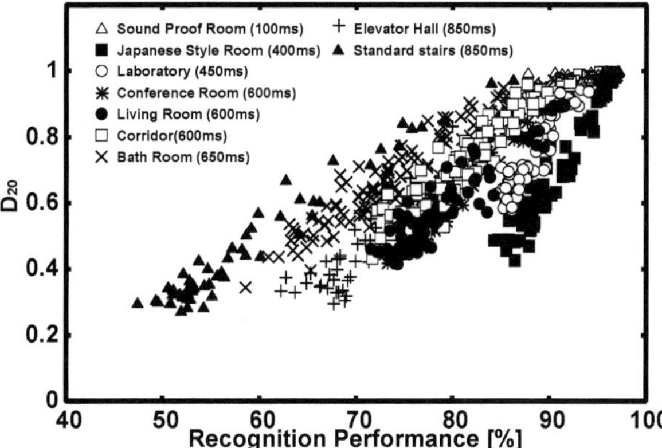

Fig. 10. Relation between D_{20} and speech recognition performance (Overall)

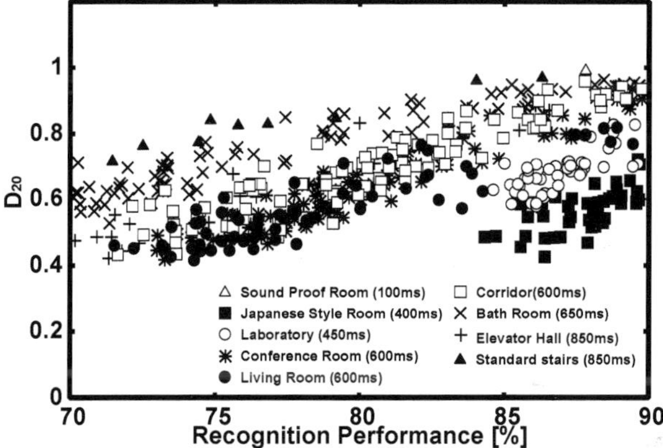

Fig. 11. Relation between D_{20} and speech recognition performance (Close-up)

Step.4: Finally, we conducted regression analysis based on the D value calculated from Steps 1 and 2 and the speech recognition performance calculated in Step 3. We used linear and quadratic functions as regression curves calculated with regression analysis based on ordinary least squares.

5.2.3 Performance estimation of reverberant speech recognition with RSR-D_n

As shown at the bottom of Figure 8, we will try to estimate the speech recognition performance with the RSR-D_n. We first calculate the reverberation time and the D value based on impulse responses in test environments. Based on them, we try to estimate the speech recognition performance with the RSR-D_n in same reverberation time.

5.3 Evaluation experiments

We used the proposed criteria to estimate the reverberant speech recognition performance. Initially, we measured 732 impulse responses to design the reverberant criteria RSR-D_n in the nine training environments shown in Table 3(a). A time-stretched pulse was used to measure the impulse responses. The recordings were conducted with 16 *kHz* sampling and 16 *bit* quantization. All impulse responses were measured for distances ranging between $100 \sim 5,000$ mm. For estimation of speech recognition performance, we used an ATR phoneme-balanced set as the speech samples that were made up of 216 isolated Japanese words that were uttered by 14 speakers (7 females and 7 males). In addition, the recognition performance varies largely depending on the recognition task. Thus, RSR-D_{20} design and performance estimation should be conducted in the same recognition task.

5.3.1 Suitable border time n for reverberant criteria RSR-D_n

In Eq. (4), the border time n is essential for determining the maximum value of the relation between D value and speech recognition performance. Thus, we conducted evaluation experiments in the three environments shown in Table 3(c), using the D value and two regression functions (linear and quadratic) to determine the most suitable border time n. Figure 9 shows the results we obtained. From linear and quadratic regression analysis, it was determined that 20 msec was the most suitable border time value. We therefore used 20 msec as the border time for calculating D_n and designing RSR-D_{20}.

5.3.2 Suitable RSR-D_{20} design

Figure 10 and 11 show the relation between speech recognition performance and D_{20} for the nine training environments shown in Table 3(a). These figures also show the regression analysis results for the three environments shown in Table 3(d). Figure 12 shows the relation between RSR-D_{20} and speech recognition performance based on the regression analysis results in three environments(Japanese room, Conference room and Standard stairs). Table 4 shows correlation coefficients with their respective regression functions for these three environments. We defined that RSR-D_{20}L represents RSR-D_{20} with a linear regression function, and RSR-D_{20}Q represents RSR-D_{20} with a quadratic regression function. As a result of Table 4, we confirmed that both RSR-D_{20}L and RSR-D_{20}Q are much the most suitable criteria for estimation of reverberant speech recognition.

5.3.3 Performance estimation with RSR-D_{20}Q

Finally, we attempted to estimate the reverberant speech recognition performance for the three test environments shown in Table 3(e). Both closed and open tests were carried out for this purpose. In closed test, we estimated speech recognition performance on known condition with RSR-D_n designed in the same environment. On the other hand, in open test, we estimated recognition performance on unknown condition with RSR-D_n designed in the other environments including same reverberation time. Figure 13 shows the obtained results. Standard deviations are given in Table 5. The results showed that average estimation error of less than 5% was achieved with RSR-D_{20}Q in all environments. Table 4 shows the correlation coefficients obtained with RSR-D_{20}L and RSR-D_{20}Q. As the table shows, both the RSR-D_{20}L and RSR-D_{20}Q coefficients are higher than 0.93 in all environments. Thus, it can be concluded that the RSR-D_{20} criteria provides much better estimation performance than conventional reverberation criteria and that it is a particular strong candidate for suitably recognizing reverberant speech.

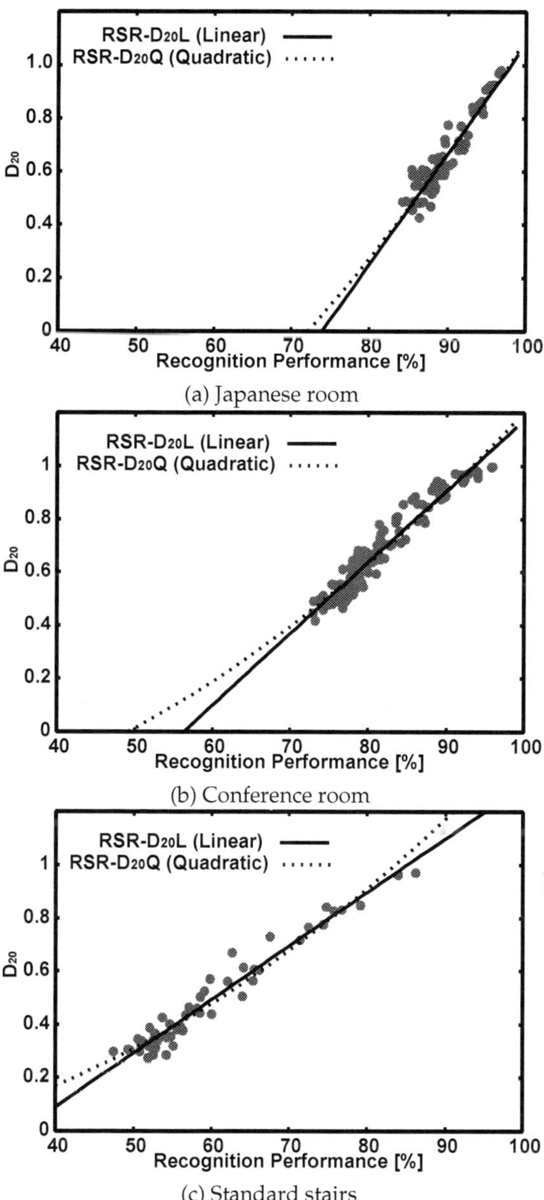

(a) Japanese room

(b) Conference room

(c) Standard stairs

Fig. 12. Relation between RSR-D_{20} and speech recognition performance

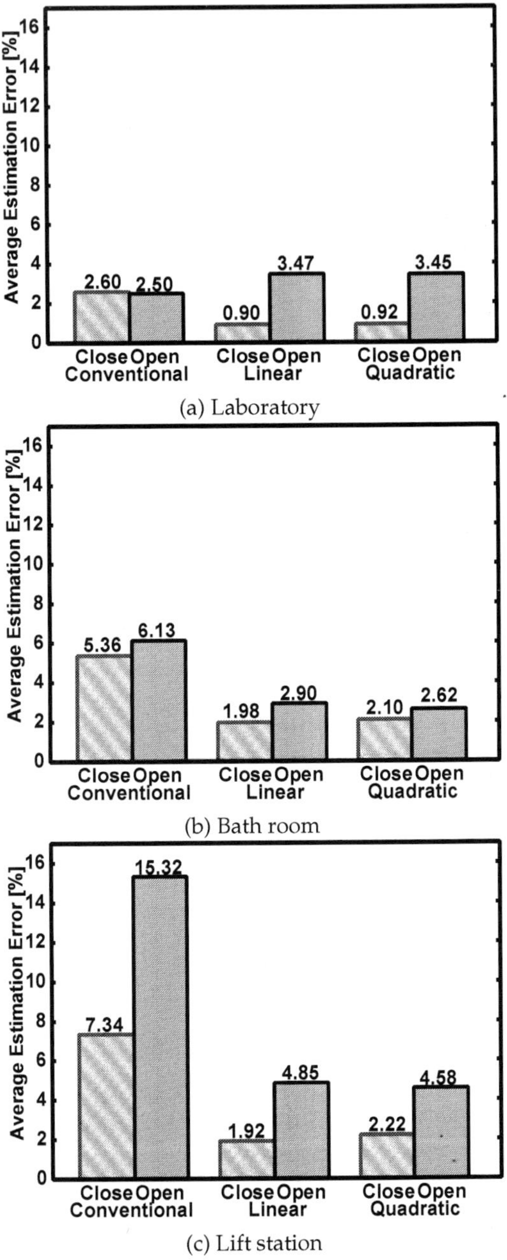

(a) Laboratory

(b) Bath room

(c) Lift station

Fig. 13. Average estimation error

	RSR-D_{20}L (Linear)	RSR-D_{20}Q (Quadratic)
Env.	---	---
T_{60} = 400 ms	0.937	**0.939**
T_{60} = 600 ms	**0.966**	0.963
T_{60} = 850 ms	**0.977**	0.972

Table 4. Correlation coefficients

Env.	Conventinal Method Close / Open	RSR-D_{20}L (Linear) Close / Open	RSR-D_{20}Q (Quadratic) Close / Open
T_{60} = 450 ms	3.10 / 3.26	1.10 / 3.62	1.13 / 3.60
T_{60} = 650 ms	6.92 / 7.18	2.46 / 3.49	2.59 / 3.14
T_{60} = 850 ms	8.80 / 17.64	2.41 / 5.35	2.81 / 5.23

Table 5. Standard deviations

6. Conclusions

We first evaluated the relation between early reflections and the recognition of distant-talking speech toward suitable reverberation criteria to enable distant-talking speech to be recognized. As a result, we found that early reflections within about 12.5 *ms* from the duration of direct sound contributed slightly to the recognition of distant-talking speech in non-noisy environments. We also confirmed that the C and D values of ISO3382 were strong candidates for the reverberation criteria of distant-talking speech recognition as a result of evaluation experiments with ISO3382 acoustic parameters. Therefore, to facilitate the recognition of reverberant speech, we then proposed new reverberation criteria RSR-D_{20} (Reverberant Speech Recognition criteria with D_{20}), which calculates recognition performance based on D_{20} for ISO3382 acoustic parameters. Experiments conducted in actual environments confirmed that the proposed criteria (particularly RSR-D_{20}Q) provide much better estimation performance than conventional reverberation criteria. We also intend to investigate suitable reverberation criteria in the frequency domain for distant-talking speech recognition with the Modulation Transfer Function (MTF) (T. Houtgast et al. (1980)) in future work.

7. Acknowledgments

This work was partly supported by Global COE and Grants-in-Aid for Scientific Research funded by Japan's Ministry of Education, Culture, Sports, Science, and Technology of Japan. This work was also partly supported by the "Ono Acoustics Research Fund".

8. References

T. Yamada, M. Kumakura, and N. Kitawaki, "Performance estimation of speech recognition system under noise conditions using objective quality measures and artificial voice," IEEE Trans. on ASLP, Vol. 14, No. 6, pp. 2006-2013, Nov. 2006.

M. R. Schroeder, "New method of measuring reverberation time," J. Acoust. Soc. Am., Vol. 37, pp. 409-412, 1965.

ISO3382: Acoustics- Measurement of the reverberation time of rooms with reference to other acoustical parameters. International Organization for Standardization, 1997.

H. Kuttruff, "Room Acoustics," Spon Press, 2000.

Y. Suzuki, F. Asano, H.-Y. Kim, and Toshio Sone, "An optimum computer-generated pulse signal suitable for the measurement of very long impulse responses", J. Acoust. Soc. Am. Vol. 97 (2), pp. 1119-1123, 1995.

K. Takeda, Y. Sagisaka, and S. Katagiri, "Acoustic-Phonetic Labels in a Japanese Speech Database," Proc. European Conference on Speech Technology, Vol. 2, pp. 13-16, Oct. 1987.

A. Lee, T. Kawahara, and K. Shikano, "Julius - an open source real-time large vocabulary recognition engine," In Proc. European Conf. on Speech Communication and Technology, pp. 1691-1694, 2001.

T. Houtgast, H.J.M. Steeneken, and R. Plomp, "Predicting speech intelligibility in room acoustics," Acustica, Vol. 46, pp. 60-72, 1980.

9

The Importance of Acoustic Reflex in Speech Discrimination

Kelly Cristina Lira de Andrade[1], Silvio Caldas Neto[2]
and Pedro de Lemos Menezes[3],
[1]Sinus - Otorhinolaringology Clinic,
[2]Universidade Federal de Pernambuco,
[3]Universidade Estadual de Ciências da Saúde de Alagoas,
Acoustic Instrumentation Laboratory
Brazil

1. Introduction

Communication is essential for social interaction and may interfere significantly with school, professional performance or social communication. When we speak we allow others to know our thoughts, feelings and needs and them to know ours.

Hearing, in turn, is the main sense responsible for acquiring speech and language in children. Impairment of this function may compromise not only language, but also social, emotional and cognitive aspects (Tiensoli et al., 2007).

2. Noise

The word noise comes from the latin "rugitus", which means roar. Acoustically it is composed of various sound waves in relation to anarchically distributed amplitude and phase, causing an unpleasant sensation, in contrast to music. It is any undesirable sound disturbance that interferes with what one wishes to hear. From the physics standpoint, noise is defined as a sound composed of a large number of randomly distributed acoustic vibrations with amplitude and phase relationships (Ferreira, 1975).

Noise can be divided into two categories: impact or impulsive and continuous or intermittent. In the first case, it represents peaks of acoustic energy of less than one second, at intervals greater than one second. Intermittent noise is all and any noise that is not classified as impact or impulsive.

Nepomuceno (1994) defines noise as an audible phenomenon whose frequencies cannot be discriminated because they differ between one another by lower values than those detected by the auditory device. It is responsible for the production of unpleasant auditory sensations and therefore different from sound. Noise is an interesting study subject because it directly affects the health of people, disqualifies the environment in which they live and causes social problems, in that its effects alter and degrade social relationships (Souza, 2004).

Speech intelligibility is defined as the relationship between words spoken and understood, expressed in percentage. For communication to be effective and intelligible, speech intelligibility must be higher than 90% (Nepomuceno, 1994). In noisy environments such as companies, schools, means of transportation, recreation areas or any other place with a large number of people, communication is significantly compromised.

3. Acoustic reflex

The hearing mechanism is described as consisting of three divisions: outer, middle and inner ear. Each compartment of the ear has the particular function of allowing sound to be transmitted, amplified and finally transformed into electrical stimulus that are conveyed to the cortex by the auditory nerve. Middle ear structures include the tensor tympani muscle and the stapedius muscle, the smallest striated muscles in the body.

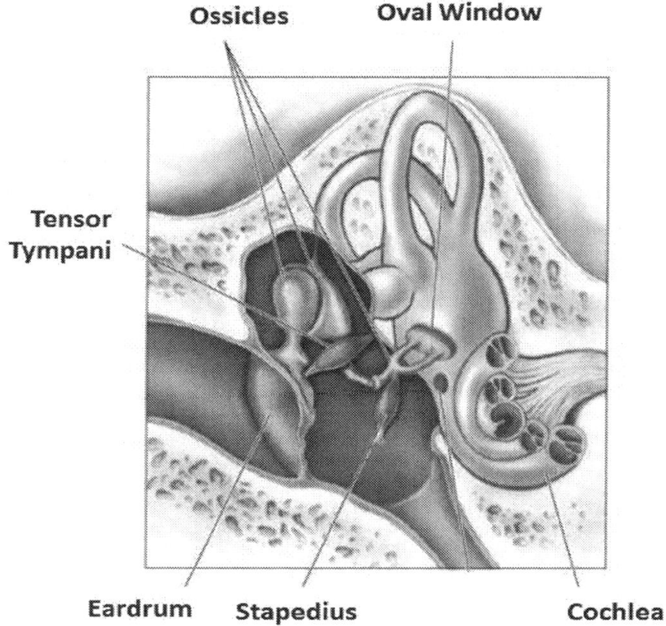

Fig. 1. Middle ear

Contraction of stapedius and tympani muscles may also occur by extra acoustic excitation such as painful and tactile sensations. Voluntary contraction might occur in some subjects. Bujosa (1978) found that stimuli triggering stapedius muscle reflexes can be sonorous (unilateral, contralateral, ipsilateral and bilateral), tactile (in the skin of the tragus and upper eyelid) and electric (these are not observable in otitis media, osteosclerosis, facial paralysis, and sonorous cases). Stimuli that trigger tensor tympani reflexes are sonorous, tactile (airflow) and nasal mucosa stimulation with ammonia vapors.

Several studies have been conducted on the function of intratympanic muscles and some correlate it with activities of hearing centers. Lidén, Peterson & Hartford (1970) state that for acoustic stimuli, the primary response is from the stapedius muscle and that it exhibits lower reflex threshold to sound pressures than the tympani tensor. Observing the activity of the middle ear muscles is the function of the method used and, using imitanciometry, only stapedius muscle function can be determined with precision. For this reason, the acoustic reflex is denominated the stapedius reflex (Lopes Filho, 1975).

The neural complex of the acoustic reflex is located in the lowest part of the brainstem. In the ipsilateral pathway, the acoustic stimulus is transmitted from the cochlea to the acoustic nerve and then to the ipsilateral ventral cochlear nuclei, and in turn, through the trapezoid body to the facial motor nucleus and ipsilateral stapedius. In the contralateral pathway, transmission is from the ventral cochlear nuclei to the medial superior olivary complex, crossing to the facial motor nucleus, then proceeding to the facial nerve and contralateral stapedius. It is believed that this description, although the most accepted, involves much more complex multisynaptic connections, where upper auditory pathways act on the acoustic reflex, inhibiting or increasing it (Borg, 1973; Robinette & Brey, 1978; Downs & Crum, 1980; Northern, Gabbard, Kinder, 1989; Northern & Downs, 1989).

Motor neurons are located near, but not within the facial nucleus. They are separated anatomically into functional bundles and are capable of ipsi, contra or bilateral stimulus responses. By stimulating one ear, these connections can obtain bilateral responses from the facial nerve and consequently from the stapedius. In 1992, Colleti et al observed that pathologies of the ascending auditory pathways may interfere in the acoustic reflex, where activity is also thought to be regulated by cortical and subcortical structures. Thus, the acoustic reflex and the cochlear-olivary system would receive tonic facilitative influence from hearing centers (Carvallo, 1997a). Therefore, for acoustic reflex to occur, there must be integrity of the afferent, association and efferent pathway.

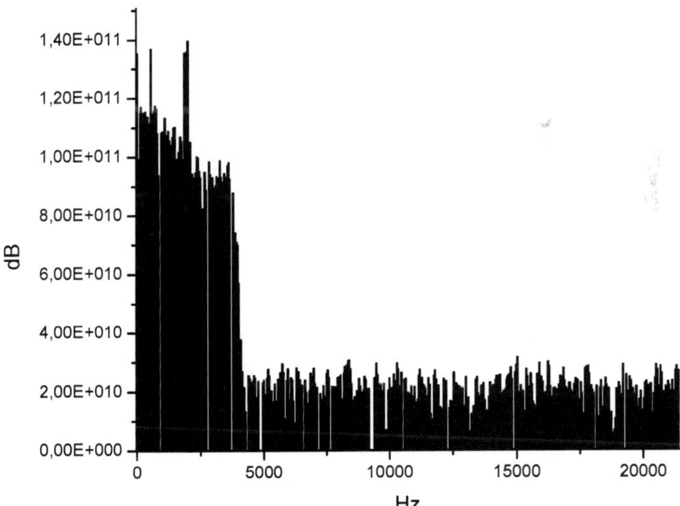

Fig. 2. Noise spectrum of speech

Andrade et al (2011) conducted a study involving 18 female participants, divided into two groups: acoustic reflexes present (20 ears) and absent (16 ears). A total of 180 disyllabic words were presented, 90 for each ear, randomly emitted at a fixed intensity of 40 dB above the three-tone average. At the same time, three types of noise were presented ipsilaterally (white, pink and speech), one at a time, at three intensities: 40, 50 and 60 dB above the three-tone average.

The three types of noises presented at intensities of 40 and 50 dB above the three-tone average showed better efficiency in discriminating speech in the group with acoustic reflexes present. For the intensity of 60 dB, using white and pink noise, a similar percentage of hits was observed between the two study groups. The better performance in discriminating at all intensities, including at 60dB, was found with the use of speech noise. The study concluded that the presence of reflex helps discriminate among speech sounds, especially in noisy environments.

White noise, described in the aforementioned study, consists of frequencies between 10 and 10,000 Hz, with equal intensity and energy maintained at high frequencies and efficient up to 6000 Hz. Pink noise is filtered white noise composed of frequencies between 500 and 4000 Hz, a band where it is most effective (Menezes, 2005).To construct speech noise, a recording was made in which several individuals were talking at the same time, simulating a noisy environment. Frequencies ranged only from 0 to 4 kHz. The noise spectrum was analyzed and fast Fourier transform is shown below.

4. New findings

A recent study conducted by Andrade et al (2011) compared three groups of normal hearers with pure-tone auditory threshold up to 20 dBHL for frequencies of 250, 500, 1000, 2000, 4000, 6000 and 8000 Hz dBNA (ANSI -1969), with inter-ear differences for frequencies less than or equal to 10 dB and age between 18 and 55 years. The following exclusion criteria were established: exposure to occupational or leisure noise, ear surgery, more than three ear infections within the last year, use of ototoxic medication and hereditary cases of deafness. In the control group the subjects showed reflexes up to 90 dBSPL (70 to 90 dB). In the second group, the normal hearers exhibited reflexes between 95 and 110 dBSPL (Group 2) and in the third group, the subjects had no stapedius reflex (Group 3). Each group consisted of 8 female participants, totaling 16 ears per group. As with Andrade (2011), speech noises were used at intensities of 40, 50 and 60 dB above the three-tone average.

Using TDH39 headphones in acoustic cabin, words and noises were emitted ipsilaterally and only hits were considered, that is, words correctly repeated. This test used 120 disyllable words, 60 for each ear. These were emitted randomly at a fixed intensity of 40dB above the three-tone average. Noise was used at intensities of 40, 50 and 60 dB above the three-tone average, that is, 20 words per intensity were presented. The responses characterized as distortions were stored in a databank and will be analyzed in future studies. If the participant did not respond or responded incorrectly, the word was repeated once again after the following word on the list was presented.

The sample studied was composed of 24 female volunteers. The age of control group subjects varied from 28.5 to 39.5 years, with mean age of 32.1 years and standard deviation of 9.8. In the second group, the age range was between 27.1 and 40 years, with mean age o 33.1 years and standard deviation of 10.8. In the group with no reflexes present, the age range was between 26.3 and 37.2 years, with mean age of 30.7 years and standard deviation of 6.5.

An evaluation of the different intensities of speech sound showed similar behavior to that of the means presented. Thus, it was decided to only show these mean results.

The results of this new study, as illustrated in graph 1, show a slightly higher mean percentage of hits for the control group (normal hearers with reflexes up to 90 dBSPL), as compared to Group 2 (normal hearers with reflexes between 95 and 110 dBSPL). However, the Mann Whitney U test did not reveal statistically significant differences (p=0.28). However, when the two aforementioned groups were compared (Control and 2) with the group of normal hearers with no stapedius reflexes (Group 3), the difference was significant, with p-values of 0.005, 0.000 and 0.031, as shown in the following table:

	Noise (+40 dB)	Noise (+50 dB)	Noise (+60 dB)
Mann-Whitney U	83.500	54.000	103.000
Wilcoxon W	219.500	190.000	239.000
Z	-3.533	-3.639	-2.193
P value	0.005	0.000	0.031

Table 1. P-value for noise intensities

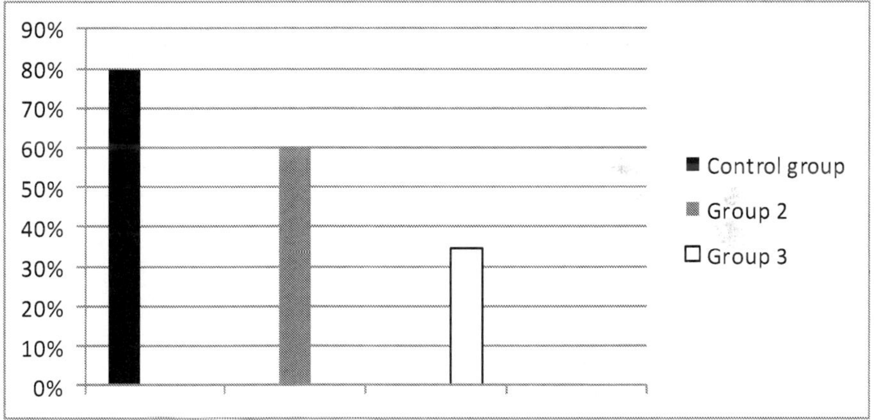

Graph 1. Mean percentage of hits per group in the speech discrimination test with noise, irrespective of ear or noise intensity used.

Thus, enhanced discrimination ability can be observed at all intensities, using speech noise, including at 60 dB, for the group with reflexes present, regardless of intensity, as compared to Group 3, with no reflexes present. That is, a significant difference occurs only when we compare groups of individuals without acoustic reflex in discriminating sounds in the presence of speech noise (Andrade, 2011).

5. Speech tests

Based on the previously described studies, it is important to point out that word recognition tests are very important in audiological diagnosis. The audiological battery is considered incomplete without measures of speech recognition.

The ability to understand speech is one of the most important measurable aspects of human auditory function. Logoaudiometry is a means to evaluate speech recognition under adequately controlled conditions (Penrod, 1999). The tests used to measure auditory performance of individuals performing speech recognition tasks use isolated stimuli, monosyllable and disyllable words being the most widely used (Lacerda, 1976).

Speech recognition is accompanied by a combination of acoustic, linguistic, semantic and circumstantial cues (Gama, 1994). However, when an excess of some of these cues are heard under favorable conditions, they can be disregarded. For message transmission to be effective, there must be redundancy of the acoustic cues that the hearer draws on, according to the situation and context of the communication. This is what occurs, for example, with conversations in noisy environments.

In audiological practice, it is common to find subjects with the same degree and configuration of sensorineural auditory loss who exhibit substantially different skills with respect to speech perception. There is a relatively weak relationship between tone auditory thresholds and speech intelligibility for individuals with sensorineural auditory loss. Factors other than auditory sensitivity likely interfere in speech perception (Yoshioka, 1980).

The following have been offered to explain the difficulty in understanding speech in noise, for patients with sensorineural auditory loss: noise, which has a masking function; loss of binaural integration, which increases the signal-to-noise ratio by 3 dB or more; difficulties in temporal resolution and frequencies; decrease in the dynamic field of hearing and the effect of masking low frequency energy (vowels) on middle and high frequency threshold (consonants). The negative influence of noise may be due to the following factor: the monaural entry to the auditory system does not allow the noise reduction processing possible in a binaural auditory system (Almeida, 2003).

Most individuals with auditory loss at high frequencies (above 3000 Hz) have little or no difficulty in understanding speech in silent environments, since these situations contain a series of excess cues that they can use to understand speech. However, in noisy environments or under adverse conditions, such as when speech is distorted, the subject may have innumerable difficulties regarding speech intelligibility, given that the number of cues falls drastically, leading to the use of only the cues available in the particular situation.

Thus, it is extremely important to study hearing performance less favorable conditions, such as simulating conversation in an environment where several individuals are talking at the same time and determining which processes interfere in the speech perception of these subjects. This justifies the concern about not only measuring speech recognition capacity in situations of acoustic isolation, in which concurrent stimuli are under control, but also in situations resembling real life (Schochat, 1994).

Two types of noise are recommended in the evaluation of speech perception: competitive speech noise and environmental noise, with competitive speech noise exerting a more significant effect on speech perception than environmental noise in general (Sanders, 1982).

In 2004, Caporali & Silva conducted a study to determine the effects of hearing loss and age on speech recognition in the presence of noise, using two types of noise. Three experimental groups were organized, one composed of adults without auditory alteration, another by adult subjects with hearing loss at high frequencies and a third group of elderly with similar audiometric configuration to that of the group with loss. All subjects performed speech recognition task in silence, in the presence of an amplified white noise spectrum and "cocktail party" noise, at the same signal-to-noise ratio (0 dB), in both ears. The results showed that noise interferes negatively on speech recognition in all the groups. Performance of normal-hearing subjects was better than that of the groups with hearing loss. However, the group of elderly performed worse, especially with respect to "cocktail party" noise. It was also observed that all the subjects exhibited better results in the second ear tested, showing a learning effect. Findings demonstrate that both age and hearing loss contributed to the low performance exhibited by the elderly in speech perception in the presence of noise and that "cocktail party" noise was suitable for this investigation.

6. Noise in the work environment

It is well known that physical and mental well being is important for good performance, in both professional and social activities. Many measures have been taken to provide better occupational conditions to workers; however, there are a number of aspects that are not recognized or valued.

It is very important to carry out research to clarify the extra auditory effects of noise on human beings, increase concern and efforts to eliminate this risk agent and adopt effective preventive and curative measures that provide better quality of life to workers.

Hearing loss may result if individuals remain in high noise environments. Given that it occurs slowly and gradually, prevention has not been given proper attention (Ayres & Corrêa, 2011). Recruitment, buzzing and poor speech signal discrimination are also observed in unfavorable environmental conditions. In addition to these auditory problems, other disorders caused by elevated noise may occur, possibly affecting other organs in the body, provoking problems such as: headaches; digestive disorders; restless sleep; lack of sleep; impaired attention and concentration; buzzing in the ears or head; vertigo and loss of balance; cardiac and hormonal alterations; anxiety, nervousness and increased aggressiveness (Kwitko, 2001).

In a retrospective study, Miller (1972) observed that groups of workers with different periods of exposure to noise (in years) showed greater losses at 4000 Hz. These initial alterations would not be detected by individuals themselves. With an increase in exposure time, other frequencies would be involved (500 Hz to 3000 Hz) with damaging consequences for speech reception.

The physical working environment must be well planned, obeying health and safety norms, have adequate illumination and space and be acoustically treated, which does not always occur. In most companies, workers are exposed to an unfavorable acoustic environment owing to background noise generated by different sound sources, such as air conditioning, conversation, movement of people, equipment and non-acoustically treated room, promoting sound reverberation.

For workers with hearing loss, or even for those with normal hearing, attempting to avoid background noise in the work environment is undeniably challenging and often frustrating. Symptoms related to noise exposure include anger, anxiety, irritability, emotional stress, lower morale and motivation, distraction, mental fatigue and sleep disturbances (Kryter, 1971). The performance of tasks may also be significantly affected by the presence of sound. Several studies suggest that sound reduces overall precision instead of total amount of work, and is more apt to affect the performance of complex tasks rather than simple ones (Miller, 1974).

The absence of acoustic reflexes is another negative factor in noisy work environments, given that the speech sound discrimination capacity of individuals with this impairment, added to all the previously described problems, is more affected. It is important that more studies correlating the aforementioned variables be conducted in order to contribute to improved working environments for individuals with abnormal acoustic reflex.

7. Conclusion

Given the recognized importance of acoustic reflex for communication, new studies should make a thorough investigation of the nuances of this relationship, in order to develop new technologies that allow individuals to communicate adequately in noisy work environments, thereby avoiding accidents and ultimately improving their quality of life.

8. Acknowledgment

We are grateful to Professors of UNCISAL for auditory evaluating of the patients and we thank all students of the Acoustic Instrumentation Laboratory.

9. Referencies

ALMEIDA,K. & IORIO, M.C.M. (2003) *Próteses Auditivas. Fundamentos téoricos e Aplicações clínicas.*, Lovise, São Paulo, Brazil.

ANDRADE, K. C.; CALDAS NETO, S.; CAMBOIM, E. D.; SOARES, I. A.; VELERIUS, M. & MENEZES, P. L. (2011) The importance of acoustic reflex for communication. *American journal of Otolaringology.* In press.

AYRES, O. D. & CORRÊA, P. A. J. (2001) *Manual de Prevenção de Acidentes do Trabalho.* Ed. Atlas S.A., São Paulo, Brazil.

BORG, E. (1973) On the neuronal organization of the acoustic middle ear reflex. A physiological and anatomical study *brain research.* Vol. 49, pp 101-23.

BUJOSA, G. C. Impedanciometría. (1978) In: VIÑALS, R. P. *Progresos em otorrinolaringología.* Salvat, Barcelona, Spain, pp.45-54.

CAPORALI, S. A. & SILVA, J. A. (2004) Reconhecimento de fala no ruído em jovens e idosos com perda auditiva. *Rev. Bras. Otorrinolaringol.* vol.70 no.4 São Paulo, Brazil.

CARVALLO, R. M. M. & ALBERNAZ, M. L. P. (1997) Reflexos acústicos em lactentes. *Acta Awho,* vol.16, no. 3, pp 103-08.

COLLETI, V.; FIORINO, F.G., VERLATO, M.D. & CARNER M. (1992) Acoustic Reflex in Frequency Seletivity: Brain Stem Auditory Evoked Response and Speech Discrimination. In: KATZ, K., STECHER, N.A. & HENDERSON, D. Eds. *Central Auditory Processing: A Transdisciplinary* View. St. Louis: Mosby Year Book;

DOWNS, D. W. & CRUM, M. A . (1980) The hyperative acoustic reflex – four case studies. *Arch Otolaryngol.* Vol. 106, pp 401-04.

FERREIRA, A. B. (1975) *Novo dicionário da língua portuguesa.* Rio de Janeiro: Nova Fronteira.

GAMA, M. R. (1994) *Percepção da fala: uma proposta de avaliação qualitativa.* São Paulo: Pancast.

HANDEL, S. The physiology of listening. (1993) In: HANDEL, S. *Listening, An introduction to the perception of auditory events*. Cambridge, Massachusetts: First MIT press paperback edition. Chap. 12, pp. 467 e 468.

KAWASE, T.; HIDAKA, H. & TAKASAKA, T. (1997) Frequency summation observed in the human acoustic reflex. *Hear. Res.*, Amsterdam, v. 108, n. 1-2, pp. 37-45.

KRYTER, K. D. (1971) *The effects of noise on man*. London and New York: Academic Press. 633 pp.

KWITKO, A., (2001) Coletânea: PAIR, PAIRO, RUÍDO, EPI, EPC, PCA, CAT, Perícias.Ed. LTr, São Paulo.

LACERDA, A.P. (1976) *Audiologia Clínica*. Rio de Janeiro: Guanabara Koogan

LIDÉN, G.; PETERSON, J. L. & HARFORD, E. R. (1970) Simultaneous recording of changes in relative impedance and air pressure during acoustic and nonacoustic elicitation of the middle-ear reflexes. *Acta Otolaryngol.*, vol. 263, pp. 208-17.

LINARES. A. E. & CARVALLO, R. M. M. (2004) Latência do reflexo acústico em crianças com alteração do processamento auditivo. *Arq. Otorrinolaringol.*, v. 8, n. 1, pp. 11-18.

LOPES FILHO, O. C. & SCHIEVANO, S. R. (1975) Predição do limiar auditivo por meio da impedanciometria. *Rev. Bras. de Otorrinolaringol.*, vol. 41, pp. 238-46.

MENEGUELLO, J.; DOMENICO, M. L. D.; COSTA, M. C. M.; LEONHARDT, F. D.; BARBOSA, L. H. & PEREIRA, L. D. (2001) Ocorrência de reflexo acústico alterado em desordens do processamento auditivo. *Rev.Bras. Otorrinolaringol.* São Paulo, Brazil, v. 67, pp. 45-8.

MENEZES, P. L., NETO, S. C. & MOTTA, M.(2005) *Biofísica da Audição*. Edition 1, Lovise, São Paulo, Brazil.

METZ, O. (1952) Limiar da contração reflexa dos músculos da orelha média e recrutamento de volume. *Arch Otolaryng (Chic.)*, vol. 55, pp. 536-43.

MILLER, J.D. (1972) *Effects of noise on the quality of human life. Central Institute for the Deaf*, St. Louis (Special Contract Report Prepared for the Environmental Agency, Washington, D.C.) Occupational Exposure to Noise, NIOSH, USA.

MILLER, J. D.(1974) Effects of noise on people. *Journal of the Acoustical Society of America*, vol. 56,pp. 729–769.

NEPOMUCENO, L. (1994) *Elementos de acústica física e psicoacústica*. Edgard Blucher, São Paulo, Brazil.

NORTHERN, J.L.; GABBARD, S. A. & KINDER, D. L. Reflexo acústico. In: KATZ, J.(1989) *Tratado de audiologia clínica*. Manole, São Paulo, Brazil, pp. 483 - 503.

NORTHERN, J. L. & DOWNS, M. P. (1989) *Audição em crianças*. Manole, São Paulo, Brazil.

PENROD, J. P. Testes de Discriminação Vocal. (1999) In: KATZ, J. *Tratado de Audiologia Clínica*. Manole, 4a Ed. São Paulo, Brazil. pp. 146-62.

ROBINETTE, M. S. & BREY, R.H. (1978) Influence of alcohol on the acoustic reflex and temporary threshold shift. *Arch Otolaryngol.*, vol. 104, pp. 31-7.

SANDERS, D.A. (1982) *Aural rehabilitation*. Prentice Hall , New Jersey, USA.

SCHOCHAT, E. (1994) *Percepção de fala: Presbiacusia e perda auditiva induzida pelo ruído*. [Tese de Doutorado]. FFLCH/USP, São Paulo, Brazil.

SIMMONS, F. B. (1994) Perceptual theories of middle ear muscle function. *Ann. Otol. Rhinol. Laryngol.*, Saint Louis, v. 73, n. 1, pp. 724-739.

SOUZA, D. S. (2004) *Instrumentos de gestão da poluição sonora para a sustentabilidade das cidades brasileiras* [Tese]. UFRJ, Rio de Janeiro, Brazil.

TIENSOLI, L. O.; GOULART, L. M. H. F; RESENDE, L.M. & COLOSIMO, E.A. (2007) Triagem auditiva em hospital público de Belo Horizonte, Minas Gerais, Brasil: deficiência auditiva e seus fatores de risco em neonatos e lactentes. *Cad. Saúde Pública*, Rio de janeiro, Brazil, v. 23, n. 6, pp. 1431-1441.

WORMALD, P. J.; ROGERS, C. & GATEHOUSE, S.(1995) Speech discrimination in patients with Bell's palsy and a paralysed stapedius muscle. *Clin. Otolaryngol.*, Oxford, USA, v. 20, n. 1, pp. 59-62.

YOSHIOKA, P. & THORNTON; A.R. (1980) Predicting speech discrimination from audiometric thresholds. *J Speech Hear Res*; vol. 23, pp. 814-27.

ZEMLIN, W. R. (2000) *Princípios de Anatomia e Fisiologia em Fonoaudiologia*. Artmed, Porto Alegre, Brazil. chap. 6, pp. 433-529.

10

Single-Microphone Speech Separation: The use of Speech Models

S. W. Lee
Singapore

1. Introduction

Separation of speech sources is fundamental for robust communication. In daily conversations, signals reaching our ears generally consist of target speech sources, interference signals from competing speakers and ambient noise. Take an example, talking with someone in a cocktail party and making a phone call in a train compartment. Fig. 1 shows a typical indoor environment having multiple sound sources, such as speech from different speakers, sounds from a television set and telephone ringing, etc. These sources are often overlapped in time and frequency. While human attends to individual sources without difficulty, most speech applications are vulnerable and resulted in degraded performance.

This chapter focuses on speech separation for single microphone input, in particular, the use of prior knowledge in the form of speech models. Speech separation for single microphone input refers to the estimation of individual speech sources from the mixture observation. It remains important and beneficial to various applications, namely surveillance systems, auditory prostheses, speech and speaker recognition.

Over the years, extensive effort has been devoted. Speech enhancement and separation are two popular approaches. Speech enhancement (Lim, 1983; Loizou, 2007) generally reduces the interference power, by assuming that certain characteristics of individual source signals are held. There is one speech source at most. In contrast, speech separation (Cichocki & Amari, 2002; van der Kouwe et al., 2001) extracts multiple target speech sources directly.

Fig. 1. Illustration of multiple sound sources present in typical acoustic environments.

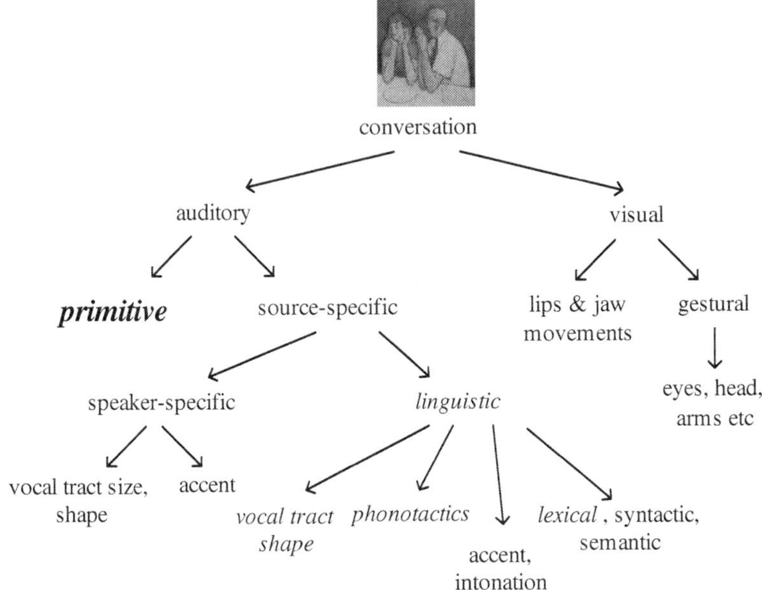

Fig. 2. Potential cues that are useful for separation. This picture is adopted and redrawn from Martin Cooke's NIPS 2006 tutorial presentation.

The differences in source characteristics are exploited, rather than individual characteristics. Consequently, speech separation is suitable for dynamic environments of sources with rapid-changing characteristics.

Computational auditory scene analysis (CASA) is one of the popular speech separation methods that exploits human perceptual processing in computational systems (Wang & Brown, 2006). Human beings have shown great success in speech separation using our inborn capability. Our perceptual organization always gives reliable performance that individual sound sources are resolved, even with a single ear (Bregman, 1990; Cherry, 1953). The separation remains effective, even for sound sources with fast-changing properties, such that appropriate actions can be taken by knowing the present environment around us. All of these suggest that modeling how human being separates mixed sound sources is a possible way for speech separation.

Given an input mixture observation, it is undergone an auditory scene analysis (ASA), which first examines various cues from the mixture observation (Bregman, 1990). Cues are related to the rules that govern how sound components from one source should look like. Take an example, voiced speech source has power always located at multiples of the fundamental frequency (F0). These frequency components are grouped together by using the harmonicity cue (Bregman, 1990). Furthermore, cues are associated with some relevant features. F0 and power distribution are the features for the cue mentioned above. After applying different cues, sound components, which are likely to come from the same origin, are grouped together as one single source. These resultant sources finally constitute the 'scenes' that experienced.

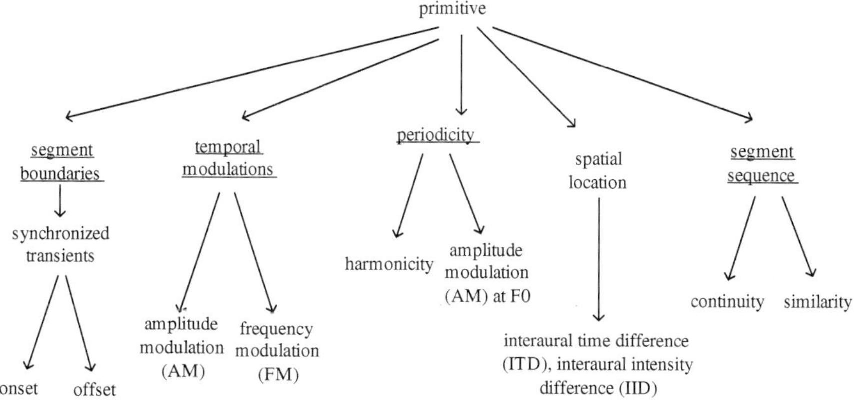

Fig. 3. Primitive cues (This picture is adopted and redrawn from Martin Cooke's NIPS 2006 tutorial presentation). For single-microphone speech separation, cues underlined are available.

A number of cues are applied during ASA. They are either primitive or schema-based. Fig. 2 and 3 depict some potential cues for separation. Primitive cues are global, physical constraints, such as those structural properties of sound sources, source-listener geometry, etc., which lead to certain acoustic consequence. Harmonicity and continuity are two examples. They are independent of the speech source identity and remain valid in a wide variety of auditory scenarios. Schema-based cues are source-specific. They are related to speakers' characteristics and the linguistic aspects of the languages. Examples for schema-based cues are context information, prior knowledge of familiar auditory patterns, etc. (Bregman, 1990). Those in italics (Fig. 2) are cues that adopted in the separation algorithm introduced later.

Regarding linguistic cues, different aspects, namely vocal tract shape, accent, intonation, phonotactics, lexical, syntactic and semantic rules are included. By phonotactics, it refers to a branch of phonology dealing with restrictions in a language on the allowed combinations of phonemes. Lexicon is the vocabulary of a language. Syntactic rules govern the ways of sentences are formed by the combinations of lexical items into phrases. Semantic rules concern about meanings are properly expressed in a given language.

Traditionally, primitive cues are often adopted in separation methods (Brown & Cooke, 1994; Hu & Wang, 2004), due to the use of simple tonal stimuli in perceptual studies and their reliability over time.

The first separation method appeared in 80's. Parsons proposed a frequency-domain approach for extracting target voiced speech sources from a mixture of two competing voices (Parsons, 1976). Strong influence of harmonicity cue on auditory perception (Assmann, 1996; Meddis & Hewitt, 1992) are observed in voiced speech. For two voiced speech sources, the mixture observation is essentially the sum of the comb-like harmonic spectra. This separation process is aimed to compile a set of spectral peak tables which describe the frequency, magnitude, phase and the origin of each spectral peak and reconstruct individual voiced sources accordingly. Overlapped peaks are resolved and source F0s are tracked. As harmonicity is the only cue involved and this method is limited to vowels and fully voiced sentences, separation methods later on move to apply more and more cues on various types of speech, which are present in real conversation.

Weintraub later proposed a CASA system for the separation of simultaneous speech of a male and female speaker (Weintraub, 1985). Harmonicity and continuity are employed. Continuity refers to the auditory behaviour that a continuous trajectory or a discontinuous but smooth trajectory tend to promote the perceptual integration of the changing experience (Bregman, 1990). The change could be in terms of frequency components, pitch contour, intensity, spatial location, etc. On the other hand, an abrupt change indicates that a new source appears. This system consists of three stages:

1. The pitch periods of individual speakers are first determined by dynamic programming (DP). Output power of each frequency channel is inspected and summaized. The pitch period with the strongest peak is selected and assigned to the speaker who has the closest average pitch (Data with annotations are collected from four speakers).

   The resultant pitch periods are potential pitch values only. The next stage determines if the individual sources are voiced or unvoiced at different moments.

2. The number of periodic sources and the associated type are decided by a pair of Markov models by using the continuity cue. One Markov model is dedicated for one speech source, which consists of seven states: silence, periodic, non-periodic, onset, offset, increasing periodicity and decreasing periodicity. The Viterbi algorithm (Jelinek, 1997; Viterbi, 2006) is used to find out when a sound source starts to be periodic and when it becomes non-periodic.

3. After knowing the number and the characteristics of sound sources over time, the magnitude in each channel for a given sound source is estimated. By looking at pre-computed records which store the expected magnitude in each channel with the pitch frequency information, individual magnitudes are estimated.

Shortly after the publication of the CASA tome from Bregman, a series of separation systems for speech sources or music emerged (Brown, 1992; Cooke, 1993; Ellis, 1994; Mellinger, 1991). All of them differed from previous systems in a way that a number of primitive grouping cues are adopted, rather than exploiting harmonicity alone. Table 1 lists out the primitive cues used. These systems basically follow the framework below. After time-frequency analysis and feature extraction, sound components with coherent properties are searched and grouped together, according to the results from a variety of cues. These systems are 'data-driven' such that the separation result solely depends on the primitive cues of the mixture signal. No prior knowledge or learned pattern is involved.

system	harmonicity	continuity	onset	offset	AM	FM
Weintraub (Weintraub, 1985)	✓	✓				
Cooke (Cooke, 1993)	✓	✓			✓	
Mellinger (Mellinger, 1991)		✓	✓			✓
Brown (Brown, 1992)	✓	✓	✓	✓		

Table 1. The use of various primitive cues in different CASA systems.

The study of Brown presents a segregation system that improves from previous systems (Brown, 1992; Brown & Cooke, 1994; 1992). It is aimed to segregate speech from an arbitrary intrusion, such as narrow-band noise, siren and concurrent speech source. Primitive features

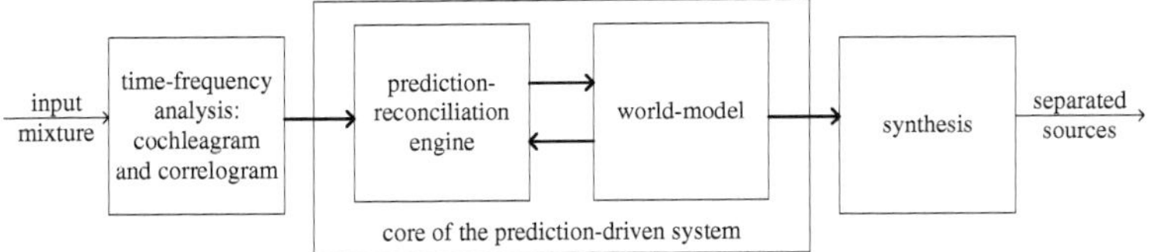

Fig. 4. Block-diagram of Ellis' system, showing the prediction-reconciliation engine looks for a prediction constructed by elements inside the world-model, such that the observations in energy envelope and periodicity are matched.

including harmonicity, continuity, onset and offset are computed from the auditory nerve activity. Segments are derived by identifying contiguous channels having similar local harmonicity. They are then aggregated over time by finding the most probably pitch contour using dynamic programming (Cooper & Cooper, 1981). For segments with synchronous onset or offset, they are likely to be assigned to the same source.

Several years later, a 'prediction-driven' separation system is proposed by Ellis (Ellis, 1996). This is a schema-based system. It comprises a process of reconciliation between the observed low-level acoustic features and the predictions of a world-model. The world-model constructs a simplified representation of an input stimulus (acts as an external world) by using a collection of independent sound elements.

The collection consists of three elements: noise clouds, tonal elements and transients. They are chosen as 'schemas', so as to reasonably model arbitrary signals and give satisfactory expression of subjective experience. The noise cloud class is used to represent 'noise-like' sounds with specific intensity over a range of time and frequency, but without a fine structure. Tonal elements simulate sounds that give perceptible periodicity. They have a pitch track besides the time-frequency energy envelope that characterizes a noise cloud. The third class of sound element is designed to model typical clicks and cracks. These rapid bursts of energy differ from the previous two classes in a way that no periodicity is perceived, being short in duration with a broad spectrum and followed by a fast exponential decay of energy.

If the predicted sound events is found to be consistent with the extracted cues, they will form a scene interpretation, no matter if direct primitive evidence is observed or not. Fig. 4 depicts the basic layout of Ellis' prediction-driven system.

Recently, Barker *et al.* has proposed a recognition algorithm (Barker et al., 2005) which decodes speech signals from a segregation perspective. It is aiming at finding the word sequence, along with the time-frequency segregation mask for a given noisy speech observation, that is,

$$\hat{W}, \hat{S} = \arg\max_{W,S} P(W, S | \mathbf{Y}) \tag{1}$$

where W and S are the word sequence and segregation mask respectively. $\mathbf{Y}$ are the observation features. By including an unknown speech source feature term $\mathbf{X}$, they expressed $P(W, S | \mathbf{Y})$ in terms of a hypothetical segregation term $P(S | \mathbf{Y})$. Barker *et al.* evaluated this extraction algorithm on a connected digit task. The observation features $\mathbf{Y}$ are from corrupted speech with background noise. Comparing with a conventional recognition system, a significant reduction in word error rate is achieved.

Schema-based separation is an emergent and potential direction that research work on separation algorithm is less explored, compared to systems using primitive cues alone (Barker et al., 2005; 2006; Brown, 1992; Brown & Cooke, 1994; Cooke, 1993; Ellis, 1996; Hu & Wang, 2006). Traditional CASA separation systems rely on the use of primitive cues in a data-driven manner, where low-level acoustic features are gradually merged to form the resultant scenes. Nevertheless, schema-based separation is indispensable and advantageous to the underdetermined nature of single-microphone speech separation. Perceptual experiments have shown that using primitive, acoustic features alone in a bottom-up architecture is simply insufficient to achieve the superior performance of the human auditory system that we habitually possess. Schema-based separation with speech modeling is expected to be beneficial and offer linguistic cues in a top-down direction.

Speech signals are much complex than tonal signals. Moreover, the psychoacoustic studies are generally not aimed at designing separation methods. Are these human perceptual principles applicable in automatic speech separation as well? What are their relative strengths in deriving the 'scenes'? What are the appropriate representations for these cues to be incorporated in separation methods? In the following, perceptual cues and the associated psychoacoustic studies are analyzed from the perspective of speech separation. Potential cues are compared and selected based on their merits for separation.

2. Perceptual cues for speech separation

2.1 Harmonicity

Harmonicity refers to the property that if a set of acoustic components are harmonically related, i.e. having frequencies that are multiples of a F0, listeners tend to group these components into a single scene. This property is sometimes referred as periodicity. This demonstrates that the pitch frequency of a speech source is one of the essential factors influencing our separation. A number of work have attempted to study this on perceptual segregation of double (simultaneous) synthetic vowels (Assmann, 1996; Assmann & Paschall, 1998; Assmann & Summerfield, 1990; Meddis & Hewitt, 1992; Scheffers, 1983). In one of Scheffers's experiments, five synthetic vowels with 200 ms duration were involved. It is found that when the vowels were unvoiced, or both with the same F0, listeners were able to identify both constituents significantly better than chance level. Furthermore, when a difference in F0 was introduced, the identification rate of both vowels improved. Identification performance increased with the increase of F0 difference and reached an asymptote at 1-2 semitones. This finding is consistent to many other research work, showing that listeners are able to identify both vowel pairs with a performance is significantly above chance, even when the two vowels are with similar amplitude, starting and ending time and presented to the same ear. From this experiment, the harmonic patterns of periodic sounds is expected to provide proper separation of concurrent sounds. This is particularly useful, because speakers are unlikely to share identical F0 at the same instant.

The above Scheffers' experiments have clearly shown that harmonicity determines the grouping of sound components, as long as the constituent sources are voiced and with distinct F0s. Nevertheless, the identification remains effective and significantly better than chance level, even when the vowels are unvoiced or share the same F0. For this case, harmonicity is inapplicable. This reflects that some other cues are involved, besides harmonicity, where speech models developed over time are likely to contribute.

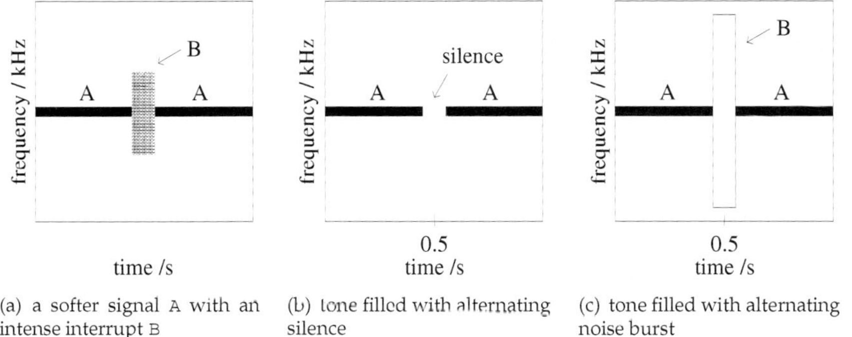

(a) a softer signal A with an intense interrupt B

(b) tone filled with alternating silence

(c) tone filled with alternating noise burst

Fig. 5. An perceptual experiment about the continuity cue, redrawn from (Bregman & Ahad, 1996).

2.2 Continuity

Recall that continuity refers to the auditory behaviour that a continuous trajectory or a discontinuous but smooth trajectory tend to promote the perceptual integration of the changing experience (Bregman, 1990). On the other hand, an abrupt change indicates that a new source appears. The continuity cue is based on the Gestalt principles (Bregman, 1990; Koffka, 1963). Dates back to the last early century, a group of German psychologists formulated a theory of perceptual organization. This theory is aimed to explain why patterns of highly connected visual objects are formed, despite sensory elements seem to be separated. The German word 'Gestalt' means pattern. The Gestalt principles apply not only to images, but also to sounds.

This continuity cue has been investigated by many perceptual experiments (Bregman, 1990; Bregman & Ahad, 1996; Bregman & Dannenbring, 1973; Ciocca & Bregman, 1987; Darwin & Bethell-Fox, 1977). Different types of sound materials were used, including synthetic vowels, alternating tone sequences, tones preceding and following a noise burst and so on. These experiments have demonstrated the effect of continuity on the unitary perception of sound components, regardless of simple tones or complex speech sources.

To explain the principles how continuity is used during ASA, Fig. 5 shows a classical perceptual experiment studying the perceptual continuation of tone through a noise burst (Bregman & Ahad, 1996). Part of a signal A is deleted and replaced by a short, louder interrupting sound B. A simple example would be the following: Signal A is a 1000 Hz pure tone and the interrupting sound B is a burst of white noise. The tone is presented with alternating silence at the beginning (Fig. 5(b)), which consists of 900 ms of tone with 100 ms of silence in one cycle. After several cycles, the noise is introduced and after each group of cycles, the noise intensity is increased. In the final group of cycles (Fig. 5(c)), the spectrum level of the noise is the same as tone A at 1000 Hz. Listeners now hear the tone as continuously unbroken behind the noise burst. Furthermore, this does not happen in any of the previous intensities. This perception of continuity occurs when the neural activity during B includes activity very similar to what normally occur in signal A. Hence, there is evidence that signal A may still be present behind the interrupt. If this evidence is missing, for example, if there is a sudden change at the boundary, then listeners would perceive signal A as a signal that only lasts until the interruption. In the experiment above, continuity comes when the noise level is the same as the tone level in the final group of cycles. During listening, the auditory system tries to detect if the signal A continue inside B or if there is any sudden change that destroys the continuation. In a more complex case, a spoken sentence appears to continue through a short loud noise burst (Bregman, 1990; Warren, 1970; 1982; Warren & Obusek, 1971; Warren et al., 1972). This 'phonemic restoration' is due to the fact that our ASA process often restores the perception of a phoneme, so as to complete the partially deleted word.

The continuity cue has not been widely adopted in current CASA systems. There are only a few examples using it as a supplement to other popular cues, such as harmonicity, onset and offset (Cooke & Brown, 1993; Klapuri, 2001). A possible reason for this is given below, which is related to the natures of signal A in the above perceptual experiment. The continuity principle monitors the degree of restoration of signal A inside the occlusion. This leads to a question: Is it necessary to locate signal A before applying the continuity cue to have restoration? According to the continuity condition described in the perceptual experiment, ASA determines if there is evidence that the on-going signal A presents inside the interrupt. Hence, the boundaries, that is, the occlusion part, and the parts before and after it must be defined first. This becomes a prerequisite and the continuity cue acts as a supplementary cue to predict the missing part only. Since the boundaries of occlusion is already defined, other top-down information, for example, lexicons, phonotactics and syntactic constraints can be derived accordingly and used to replace the continuity cue. Compared with the continuity cue, these source-specific cues are global and statistical modeling is ready made. Furthermore, to define whether a change is with good continuation is not an easy task by itself, in particular, for speech signals with varying properties over time. When compared with other grouping cues, such as harmonicity, the description of continuity is relatively loose. Unlike continuity, constitutive components of a harmonic source share a strong mutual relation which are clearly defined in physical laws. Given a signal A, it remains unknown to decide if the trajectory has a close cubic polynomial fit is continuous or not. It is a relative issue that considers physiological limitations and natures of signal A.

2.3 Onset & offset

This onset & offset cue is under the Gestalt principle of common fate (Bregman, 1990; Koffka, 1963). This principle states that our perceptual system tends to group sensory elements which synchronously change in the same way, acting as a way of organizing simultaneous sounds. In reality, frequency components originated from the same source often vary in a coherent manner. For instance, they tends to start and stop together (sharing an identical time record), change in amplitude or frequency together (results in amplitude or frequency modulation). On the other hand, components from independent sound sources rarely start or end at the same time in normal listening environments. Onset and offset correspond to the beginning and ending time of a sound source respectively. They are especially influential to voiced speech and music (Mellinger, 1991).

Psychoacoustic evidence of the onset and offset principle has been intensively investigated in tone, speech and music stimuli (Bregman & Ahad, 1996; Bregman & Pinker, 1978; Dannenbring & Bregman, 1978; Darwin, 1984; Darwin & Ciocca, 1992; Darwin & Sutherland, 1984; Summerfield & Culling, 1992). In one of the Bregman's experiments (Bregman & Pinker, 1978), a paradigm as shown in Fig. 6 is adopted to illustrate the effect of onset and offset synchrony on streaming.

The stimulus used for the experiment is a repeating cycle composed of a pure tone A alternating with a complex tone with components B and C. A, B and C are pure tones with

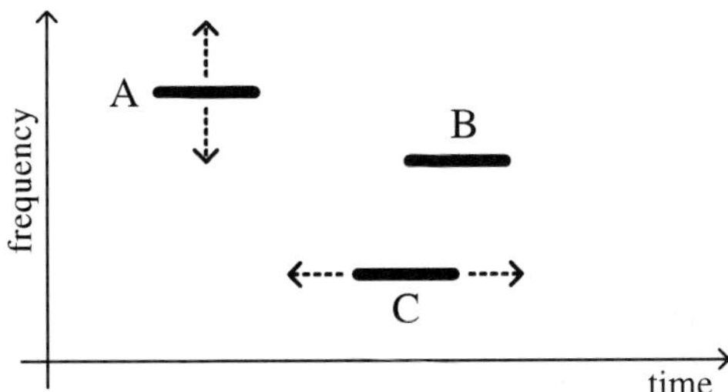

Fig. 6. A demonstration showing the influence of onset and offset synchrony on streaming (redrawn from (Bregman & Pinker, 1978)). Frequency proximity and synchrony of tones determine how the three tones are perceived.

identical amplitude and equal duration. The frequencies of B and C remain unchanged throughout the experiment. From the experimental results, it is shown that simultaneous and sequential groupings compete with each other. Two factors are involved in the competition, namely the frequency proximity of A and B and synchrony of B and C. If B and C share common onset and offset, this synchrony strengthens the force of simultaneous grouping of B and C to become a complex tone (BC-BC-BC-BC), which would otherwise belong to separated streams as in the case of sequential grouping. In this experiment, both onset and offset of B are made to be synchronous or asynchronous with those of C at the same time. If only the offset synchrony is employed alone, its influence is found to be much weaker than the onset synchrony (Brown, 1992; Darwin, 1984; Darwin & Sutherland, 1984).

Although experiments have consistently reported that onset and offset are influential to perceptual grouping, they are not sufficient conditions for grouping the harmonics of a vowel (Barker, 1998; Darwin & Sutherland, 1984). They are not necessary conditions neither. In some cases, the onset and offset cues are not necessary, for example, the experiment described under the harmonicity cue. Concerning whether they are sufficient conditions or not, further experiments on voiced speech illustrate the arguments. Darwin and Sutherland have demonstrated that leading onset of a harmonic can reduce its contribution to the vowel's quality (Darwin & Sutherland, 1984) (as shown in Fig. 7(a)). However, if a tone at the octave of the harmonic which onsets synchronously with the leading harmonic, but stops as the vowel begins is added, the reduced contribution of the leading onset will be canceled. The extent to which an individual harmonic contributes towards the perception of a vowel depends on various factors: (1) whether it starts at the same time as other harmonics; (2) whether it ends at the same time; (3) whether it forms a perceptual group with other sounds. Referring to Fig. 7(b), the additional octave tone and the leading section of the harmonic jointly form a separate stream that ends just before the vowels begins. The remaining section of the harmonic is left to be part of the vowel perception.

Hence, it is believed that other principles and grouping cues are expected to be involved. Take an example, harmonicity acts as a stronger cue and onset and offset are comparatively supplementary in this experiment.

2.4 Amplitude modulation & frequency modulation

The cue that have just been discussed — onset & offset accounts for instantaneous events which happen shortly. A more general Gestalt principle of common fate concerning the

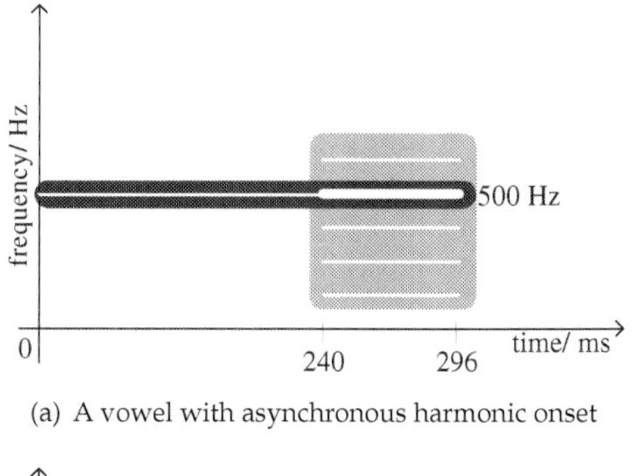

(a) A vowel with asynchronous harmonic onset

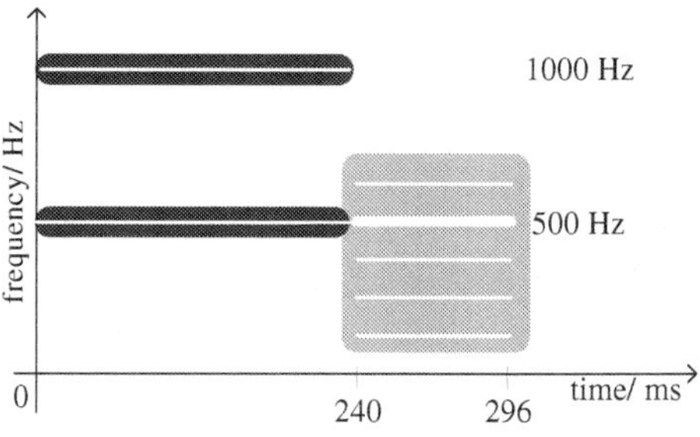

(b) A vowel with asynchronous harmonic onset, together with a octave tone

Fig. 7. Contribution of a leading onset of a harmonic to the vowel perception(redrawn from (Darwin & Sutherland, 1984)). Different streams are highlighted with distinct colors.

change over the course of time is the amplitude and frequency modulation (Bregman, 1990; Darwin, 2001; Koffka, 1963). This cue refers to the tendency that if any subset of elements of an auditory scene changes proportionally and synchronously, it will be segregated from other elements within the scene that are changing in a different way. It is very unlikely to have unrelated elements within an auditory scene undergoing parallel changes by accident. It is much more reasonable to assume that these unrelated elements are arisen from the same source. For a continuous speech source, frequency components will go on and off roughly at the same time, glide up and down in frequency together (called frequency modulation or FM), be amplified and attenuated together (called amplitude modulation or AM) and so on. These latter two types of synchronous changes have been studied in various psychoacoustic experiments with complex tones or vowels (Bregman, 1990; Bregman et al., 1985; Bregman & Ahad, 1996; Bregman et al., 1990; Carlyon, 1991; Darwin, 2001; Gardner et al., 1989; Hall et al., 1984; Kubovy, 1981; Marin & McAdams, 1991; McAdams, 1989; Purwins et al., 2000; Summerfield & Culling, 1992).

There are experiments showing evidence on the use of common AM for grouping, which requires frequency elements to be fused sharing identical modulation frequency and phase. The effects being observed, however, are small (Bregman et al., 1985). Other experiments on amplitude modulation show equivocal evidence. Listeners are found to be unable to take advantage of AM incoherence for slow modulating rates like 2.5 Hz (Darwin & Carlyon, 1995; Summerfield & Culling, 1992).

Concerning frequency modulation, human voice is one of the everyday examples. It is found that the components of all natural sounds with sustained vibration contain small-bandwidth random fluctuations in frequency. Speech voices and sounds from musical instruments share this property (Deutsch, 1999; Flanagan, 1972; Jansson, 1978; Lieberman, 1961; McAdams, 1989). For real speech signals, the pitch frequency varies from time to time. When the vocal cords are tightened, the pitch frequency increases. Simultaneously, all the harmonics rise in a proportional way, so as to maintain their constant ratios to the fundamental. Furthermore, some experiments have shown that both harmonic and inharmonic stimuli are perceived as more fused when coherent modulation is applied (Helmholtz, 1954). Due to this coherence among the frequency components, it is possible that the auditory system employs such coherence frequency modulation as a cue for grouping spectral components together; and conversely treat any spectral components with different frequency modulation as separate streams.

To test this hypothesis, McAdams designed a series of experiments which studied the effect of frequency modulation on segregation of concurrent speech sources (McAdams, 1989). It is found that when frequency modulation is present on a vowel, the perceived prominence of the vowel increases; however, this modulation effect is independent of the modulation states of any accompanying sounds. The prominence is not reduced when accompanying sounds share identical modulation with the vowel. There is no change in vowel prominence if accompanying sounds are modulated incoherently. The last condition is highly similar to the scenario with multiple speech sources. Frequency components of a continuous speech source rise and fall over time and components from different sources are modulated incoherently. Although modulation to the target source aids to promote its prominence, there is no distinction between coherent and incoherent modulation to humans. Therefore, common FM does not help segregation of the components from a speech source from a mixture signal. Subsequent experiments further support the absence of effects of common FM or AM during ASA (Carlyon, 1991; 1992; Deutsch, 1999).

Stimuli consists of three simultaneous vowels (/a/, /i/ and /o/) at different pitches in a chord of two seconds duration. Four conditions of coherent or incoherent frequency modulation have been tested: (1) no vowels are modulated; (2) all vowels are coherently modulated by an identical modulating signal; (3) one vowel is modulated, while the other two are remained steady without any modulation; (4) one vowel is modulated independently against a background of the remaining two vowels, which are modulated coherently with one another. The modulating signal is constituted by both periodic and noise-like components. It has been verified in a pretest that these individual vowels are identifiable in isolation with perfect accuracy, regardless of pitch and the presence or absence of modulation.

Another explanation for the absence of contribution of common FM to segregation is based on the close relationship of FM with harmonicity. Continuous voiced speech with rising or falling F0 exhibits not only common FM, but also the harmonicity over time. Whether the coherent motions of frequency components or their harmonic structure contribute, indicates if they can be used as basis for segregation. Summerfield and Culling has investigated the role of harmonicity and common FM by performing experiments using different F0 and FM (Summerfield & Culling, 1992). They also checked if the harmonicity cue is so strong that most of the segregation is already achieved, leaving nothing for other cues to contribute. Based on the experimental findings, they concluded that common FM cannot help segregation of concurrent sources and harmonicity cue is always dominant.

2.5 Schema-based grouping

The following addresses the use of high-level cues for separating monaural speech. Specifically, the use of linguistic and visual information in speech perception will be discussed. Primitive cues arise from acoustic properties of the environment, however, there exists many observations that are contributed by either attention or learning (Bregman, 1990; Dowling, 1973; Meddis & Hewitt, 1992; Scheffers, 1983; Warren, 1970). To account for the observed human capabilities in these experiments, primitive cuess are inadequate. Dowling showed that the identification of interleaved pairs of melodies is easier when the melodies are familiar or when music training is acquired beforehand (Dowling, 1973). Attention(conscious effort) can also be used to specifically hear out frequency components from complexes that would group together otherwise. Based on these experimental findings, it is evident that some higher-level information other than primitive features is involved.

The double synthetic vowel experiment described under the harmonicity cue also demonstrates that primitive cues alone cannot justify the phenomenon that listeners are able to identify the constituent vowels significantly above chance, even when nearly all primitive features are approximately the same, identical amplitude, onset and offset time and F0. The difference between the two constituent vowels lies only in their spectral shapes. This demonstrates that even when the grouping mechanism is unable to separate the incoming sound using primitive cues, the innate recognition processing is still responsible for recognizing each of the two overlapping constituent vowels and generate separated 'scenes'. Listeners are capable of segregating sound sources, in particular, speech sources under situations where certain primitive features are difficult or impossible to be observed from the input mixture signal. During the perceptual organization, by guessing the missing or occluded information with some high-level information, for example, those linguistic cues that listed in Fig. 3, the estimate is instinctively incorporated as if it has been directly perceived. In the following, evidence of the schema-based grouping from experimental psychoacoustics will be reviewed, which illustrates what logical basis have been adopted.

One of the examples is about this restoration phenomena from Warren (Warren, 1970; 1982; Warren & Obusek, 1971; Warren et al., 1972; Weintraub, 1985). Listeners hear a speech recording. Within the utterance, an entire phoneme has been removed and replaced by a loud noise burst, which sounds like a cough. 'Auditory induction' then occurs, where the missing phoneme is perceived on top of the loud noise. Based on the contextual cues of neighboring regions (linguistic constraints), listeners unconsciously infer the most likely sound. Furthermore, the precise location of the missing part could not be identified.

Subsequent studies have shown that the success of phonemic restoration is contributed by several factors, including repeated listening of the speech utterance, prior knowledge and linguistic skills of listeners, timbres of different sound sources, the characteristics of the noise masker and the associated continuity.

Another way in which the auditory system uses linguistic information, particularly in the application of speech separation, can be seen in the following example. Cherry has performed a set of recognition experiments using speech stimuli, to investigate the ways that we recognize what one person is saying while the others are talking simultaneously (Cherry, 1953). Specifically, the objective is to study if linguistic knowledge promotes speech separation. To focus on linguistic cues, other factors, such as, lip-reading, gestures, spatial geometry and speaker-specific styles are eliminated. This is done by adding pieces of speech recording spoken by the same speaker together to form the stimuli. As a result, only linguistic cues, for example, transitional probabilities between phonemes (phonotactics), subject matter (semantics and lexicon), syntax and intonation and monaural primitive grouping cues remain. The experiments are designed to present two mixed speech passages to a listener and he is asked to separate one of the passages and verbally repeat it word by word or phrase by phrase. Most of the listeners' extracted speech is found to be accurate, with little errors only. There are few transpositions of phrases between passages which are highly probable. In some passage pairs, there is no such transposition exists. Besides, there is no phrase with consecutive two or three words being wrongly recognized.

It is believed that this recognition task requires the knowledge of neighboring events (the events can be phonemes, words and subject matters) and a big storage of probabilities, calculating the probability rankings of various phonemic and lexical combinations. While the knowledge of neighboring events could be resulted from primitive grouping or previous learning, the storage of probabilities enables prediction made on a probabilistic basis, so as to combat any interference or occlusion from competing speech.

Schema-based grouping is powerful, particularly when some critical acoustic features are made to be unobservable by interfering signals. Hypothesis from high-level knowledge compensates any missing components and removes redundant elements according to the relevant continuously-trained models. Comparatively, primitive grouping does not have such compensation or removal functionality, since missing components are simply absent in the mixture input and primitive grouping just assigns (part of or the whole) sound components to either source. Nothing will be added or taken away during grouping.

Nevertheless, schema-based organization is not independent of primitive grouping. They rather collaborate in most sound separation scenarios. Schemas are developed by learning common patterns. At the early stage, primitive grouping provides initial organization, which is then left for the interpretation and 'bootstrap' of the schemas. When familiar patterns are gradually developed, features from primitive grouping cues enable reduction in the hypothesis space that handled in the schema-based organization. After the optimal hypothesis is determined, grouping at primitive level is changed accordingly and this process may be repeated, until a consistent grouping is achieved.

Knowing that harmonicity and prior knowledge of familiar auditory patterns for schema-based grouping are found to be powerful, whereas other cues such as continuity remain relatively inferior. In the following section, a separation algorithm using the idea of recognition models is introduced. It incorporates the statistical distribution of speech sounds in a top-down direction to perform separation and predict target source signals in terms of low-level features. Models of individual speech sounds are employed to supply any missing components and eliminate redundant ones.

3. Speech separation with speech models

A speech separation algorithm for single-microphone mixture input is introduced (Lee et al., 2007). It showcases a potential way to utilize both primitive and schema-based cues in separation systems. The meaning of 'model' is two-folded. First, based on the source-filter model of speech signals, the algorithm reconstructs individual speech sources by estimating their associated spectral envelopes and suppress the interfering source accordingly. Second, with the use of speech models as prior knowledge, trajectories of spectral envelope are

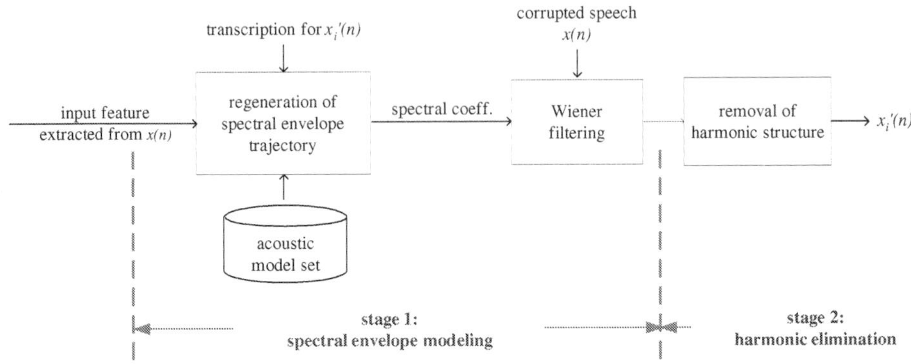

Fig. 8. Block-diagram of the proposed separation system. Same procedure is applied to all speech sources.

regenerated in a top-down, probabilistic manner. Selective primitive cues are incorporated as well to generate smooth source outputs with single periodicity (Lee et al., 2006).

Speech modeling and recognition techniques are adopted to statistically capture this knowledge and 'familiar auditory patterns' are built. They are used to govern the separation process (in a top-down, macroscopic view) and to revise typical primitive features of source estimates (in a bottom-up, microscopic view). These statistics of auditory patterns acts as prior knowledge to the proposed separation system and are gradually updated during the training process for the embedded speech recognition engine of the proposed system.

Fig. 8 depicts the block-diagram of the proposed separation system, where $x_i'(n)$ is the estimate for source i ($i \in [1,2]$). To extract either of the speech sources, $x_1(n)$ or $x_2(n)$, same procedure is applied with slightly different inputs. It is assumed that the text transcription for both speakers are either known or estimated by some means.

1. The first stage is about extracting the spectral envelope of target source. A speech recognition engine is employed inside the block 'regeneration of spectral envelope trajectory', so as to output the optimal model sequence. At the output end, a sequence of spectral coefficients describing the expected spectral envelope trajectory for the target source $x_i(n)$ is estimated.

2. Wiener filtering is then used to remove the interference source, based on the spectral information of the target source obtained from the preceding regeneration block. The resultant spectral envelope behaves properly with peaks at target formant frequencies. This completes the envelope extraction part.

3. Provided that both $x_1(n)$ and $x_2(n)$ are voiced in the current frame, the excitation sources of both target and interference are still present at the Wiener filter output. In the second stage, a comb filtering block is used to remove any harmonic structure associated with the interfering source. This completes the harmonic part and the output waveform will be the estimated source $x_i'(n)$.

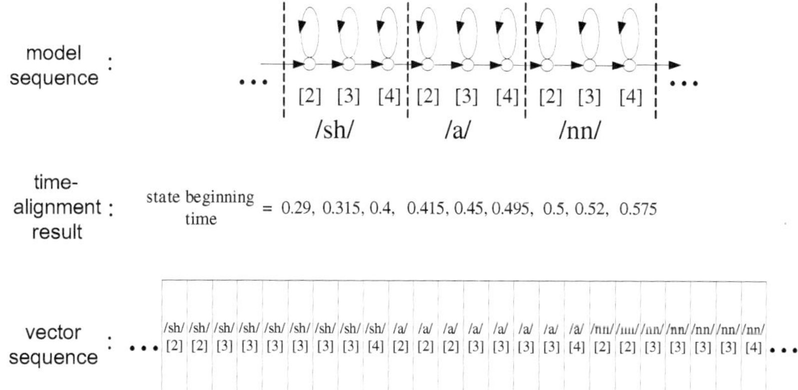

Fig. 9. An example of a time-alignment result and the corresponding vector sequence. The symbols $/\cdot/$ and $[\cdot]$ denote model name and state number respectively. Each HMM contains five states, with state [2], [3] and [4] are emitting states. The longer a state is aligned, the more the mean vector is repeated.

3.1 Regeneration of spectral envelope trajectory

To search for or align with any familiar patterns of the input mixture signal $x(n)$, speech models in the form of reliable feature representation are necessary. Line spectrum pair (LSP) ((Itakura, 1975; Paliwal, 1989; Soong & Juang, 1984; Wakita, 1981)) is employed to parameterize $x(n)$ and a set of hidden Markov models (HMMs) in phone units is trained to model these familiar patterns.

The input mixture signal $x(n)$ is first converted to a sequence of LSP feature vectors. With a given transcription, the 'regeneration of spectral envelope trajectory' block uses the Viterbi algorithm (Jelinek, 1997; Rabiner & Juang, 1993) to perform forced alignment at state level. By storing a set of familiar speech patterns (acoustic models), this regeneration block helps to retrieve the expected spectral shape of a target speech source, $X_i(\omega,t)$. Moreover, the time-alignment defines the boundaries when a particular model state is activated. The mean vectors of associated acoustic models are extracted from the model set and replicated according to the time-alignment. By looking at this vector sequence, the expected spectral shape evolution of the target source, $X_i(\omega,t)$ is illustrated in LSP sense.

Fig. 9 shows an example of a time-alignment result and the respective vector sequence. Suppose acoustic models /sh/, /a/ and /nn/ are retrieved and aligned with the observed sequence of LSP feature vectors. After alignment or recognition, the activation time (time-alignment) of individual model states is output in the form of the beginning time and the ending time. In the current implementation, the state beginning time is used only, but not the state ending time. This is because the beginning time of a model state is just the next time unit of the ending time of the preceding model state. As alternative, the ending time record can be used instead. Referring to the time-alignment result (shown in the middle), state [2] of /sh/ is activated at 0.29 s and state [3] of /a/ is switched on at 0.45 s. Consequently, by putting the speech-pattern describing model mean vectors together accordingly, the longer a state is aligned, the more the model mean vector is repeated, the spectral trajectory is approximated.

The resultant vector sequence will be similar to the one shown at the bottom, which represents the expected spectral shape evolution of the target source, $X_i(\omega, t)$.

The generated trajectories are piecewise constant, since model mean vectors are just kept intact and concatenated together. This, however, introduces (1) discontinuities at state transitions; and (2) conflicts between the static and dynamic coefficients. Hence, based on the statistics of dynamic coefficients modeled by HMMs, individual trajectories of static components are further revised before leaving the 'regeneration of spectral envelope trajectory' block in Fig. 8 and smooth, consistent trajectories are generated. This revision is carried out in the LSP domain, since the LSP representation for ordered and bounded coefficients is robust to interpolation and quantization. Finally, the resultant coefficients representing the expected spectral envelope of a target source are converted back to LPC coefficients $\{a_m\}$ as the output. Familiar speech models, in the form of mean and variance vectors of static and dynamic LSP coefficients, are trained by a set of speech training data. The model set is HMM-based.

The static component of the vector sequence obtained from Viterbi exhibits the spectral shape evolution of a target source. It is also associated to the dynamic component by linear regression. Simple replication of the mean vector from a model state will produce piecewise constant static components in consecutive frames, but non-zero dynamic components. Nevertheless, this inconsistency does not exist in real speech signals. As a result, the dynamic component, including the delta and acceleration coefficients, is used as a constraint in generating the static component, similar to the ways showed in (Lee et al., 2006).

Let $\theta_{im}(n), m = 1, 2, \ldots, M$ be the set of LSP coefficients estimated at frame n for source i. The order of LSP is denoted by M. By putting these θ_{im} vectors together, the spectral shape evolution for source i is exhibited. Consider the m-th dimension of the vector sequence, the temporal trajectory is expressed as

$$\boldsymbol{\theta_{im}} = \begin{bmatrix} \theta_{im}(1) & \theta_{im}(2) & \cdots & \theta_{im}(N) \end{bmatrix}^T \tag{2}$$

where N is the number of frames in total. Similarly, we have

$$\Delta\boldsymbol{\theta_{im}} = \begin{bmatrix} \Delta\theta_{im}(1) & \Delta\theta_{im}(2) & \cdots & \Delta\theta_{im}(N) \end{bmatrix}^T \text{ and} \tag{3}$$

$$\Delta^2\boldsymbol{\theta_{im}} = \begin{bmatrix} \Delta^2\theta_{im}(1) & \Delta^2\theta_{im}(2) & \cdots & \Delta^2\theta_{im}(N) \end{bmatrix}^T \tag{4}$$

where $\Delta\theta_{im}(n)$ and $\Delta^2\theta_{im}(n)$, for $n = 1, 2, \ldots, N$ are the delta coefficients and acceleration coefficients respectively. T represents the transpose operation.

For each LSP dimension, the contour $\boldsymbol{\theta_{im}}$ is generated by finding the maximum-likelihood estimate by the aligned static, delta and acceleration statistics. Equivalently, this is given in Equation (5).

The regenerated trajectory is found by,

$$\boldsymbol{\theta'_{im}} = \begin{bmatrix} \mathbf{W}_{\mathrm{LSP}}{}^T \boldsymbol{\Sigma}_{\mathrm{im}}{}^{-1} \mathbf{W}_{\mathrm{LSP}} \end{bmatrix}^{-1} \mathbf{W}_{\mathrm{LSP}}{}^T \boldsymbol{\Sigma}_{\mathrm{im}}{}^{-1} \boldsymbol{\theta_{im}} \tag{6}$$

where $\boldsymbol{\Sigma}_{\mathrm{im}}$ and $\mathbf{W}_{\mathrm{LSP}}$ are the diagonal covariance matrix and

$$\mathbf{W}_{\mathrm{LSP}} = \begin{bmatrix} \mathbf{I} \\ \mathbf{W} \\ \mathbf{W}^2 \end{bmatrix} \tag{7}$$

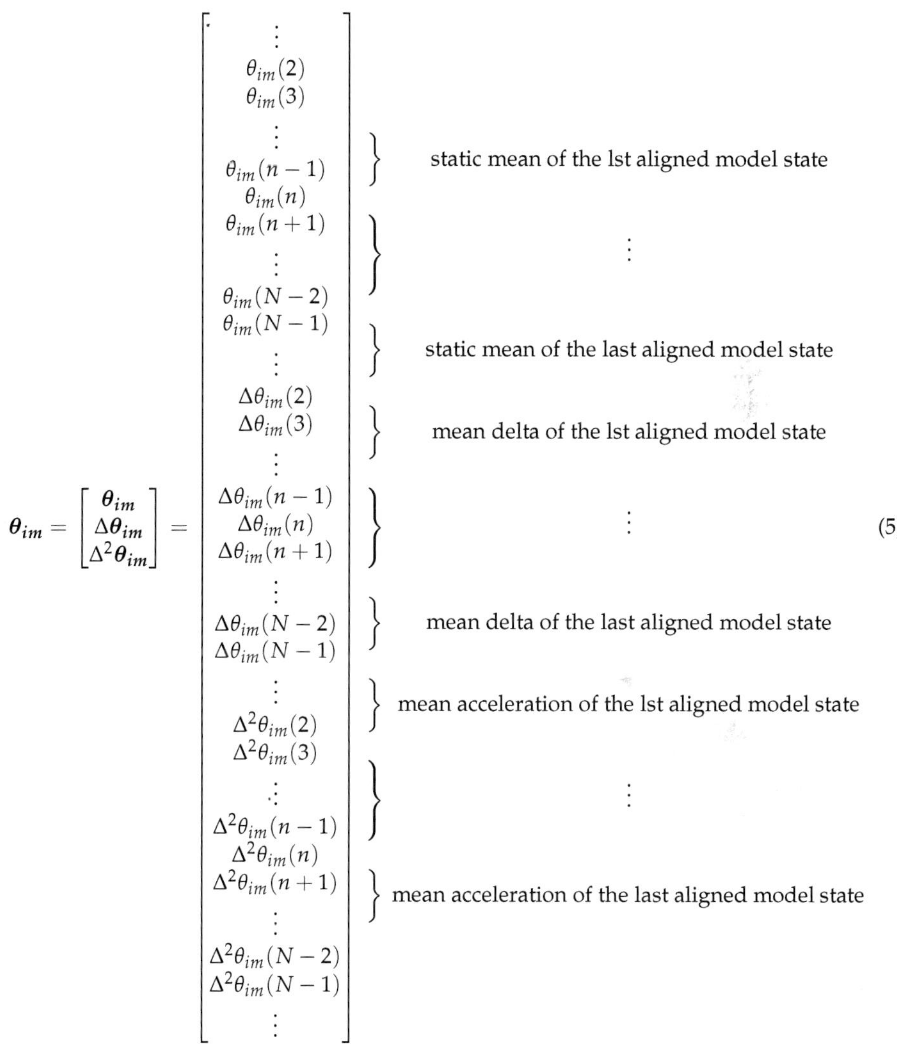

$$
\boldsymbol{\theta}_{im} = \begin{bmatrix} \boldsymbol{\theta}_{im} \\ \Delta\boldsymbol{\theta}_{im} \\ \Delta^2\boldsymbol{\theta}_{im} \end{bmatrix} = \begin{bmatrix} \vdots \\ \theta_{im}(2) \\ \theta_{im}(3) \\ \vdots \\ \theta_{im}(n-1) \\ \theta_{im}(n) \\ \theta_{im}(n+1) \\ \vdots \\ \theta_{im}(N-2) \\ \theta_{im}(N-1) \\ \vdots \\ \Delta\theta_{im}(2) \\ \Delta\theta_{im}(3) \\ \vdots \\ \Delta\theta_{im}(n-1) \\ \Delta\theta_{im}(n) \\ \Delta\theta_{im}(n+1) \\ \vdots \\ \Delta\theta_{im}(N-2) \\ \Delta\theta_{im}(N-1) \\ \vdots \\ \Delta^2\theta_{im}(2) \\ \Delta^2\theta_{im}(3) \\ \vdots \\ \Delta^2\theta_{im}(n-1) \\ \Delta^2\theta_{im}(n) \\ \Delta^2\theta_{im}(n+1) \\ \vdots \\ \Delta^2\theta_{im}(N-2) \\ \Delta^2\theta_{im}(N-1) \\ \vdots \end{bmatrix}
\left.\begin{matrix} \\ \\ \end{matrix}\right\} \text{static mean of the 1st aligned model state}
\quad\vdots
\left.\begin{matrix} \\ \\ \end{matrix}\right\} \text{static mean of the last aligned model state}
\left.\begin{matrix} \\ \end{matrix}\right\} \text{mean delta of the 1st aligned model state}
\quad\vdots
\left.\begin{matrix} \\ \end{matrix}\right\} \text{mean delta of the last aligned model state}
\left.\begin{matrix} \\ \end{matrix}\right\} \text{mean acceleration of the 1st aligned model state}
\quad\vdots
\left.\begin{matrix} \\ \end{matrix}\right\} \text{mean acceleration of the last aligned model state}
\tag{5}
$$

respectively, building from the N-by-N linear regression coefficient matrix $\mathbf{W}$.

Consequently, the regenerated LSP trajectories become continuous and smoothly varying, showing similar dynamic change as $\Delta\theta_{im}$ and $\Delta^2\theta_{im}$ described. Before passing to Wiener filtering, the LSPs are converted back to their corresponding LPC coefficients. At this moment, the spectral shape of a target source is ready. The sequence of LPC coefficients $\{a_m\}$ resulted from the regenerated LSP coefficients θ'_{im} are output to Wiener filtering.

3.2 Wiener filtering and associated LPC formulation

Based on the spectral information of a target source obtained from the preceding trajectory regeneration, Wiener filtering is then used to suppress or to attenuate the interference source. With the LPC coefficients output after trajectory regeneration $\{a_m\}$, the corresponding Wiener filter is derived accordingly. For the present two-source separation problem, the frequency response is

$$H(\omega) = \frac{P_{x,x_i}(\omega)}{P_x(\omega)} \tag{8}$$

where

$$P_{x,x_i}(\omega) = \text{cross power spectral density between } x_1(n) + x_2(n)$$
$$\text{and } x_i(n), \quad i \in [1,2] \tag{9}$$
$$P_x(\omega) = \text{auto power spectral density of mixture input } x(n) \tag{10}$$

Assuming that the two source signals have zero crosscorrelation,

$$P_{x,x_i}(\omega) = P_{x_i}(\omega) \tag{11}$$
$$P_x(\omega) = P_{x_1}(\omega) + P_{x_2}(\omega) \tag{12}$$

In terms of LPC coefficients, $H(\omega)$ corresponding to source i becomes

$$H(\omega) = \frac{G_{x_i}^2 B_{x_i}(\omega)}{G_x^2 B_x(\omega)} \tag{13}$$

where G_{x_i} and G_x are the gains of excitation for $x_i(n)$ and $x(n)$, respectively. Furthermore,

$$B_{x_i}(\omega) = \left| \frac{1}{1 + \sum\limits_{m=1}^{M} a_{mx_i}(e^{j\omega})^{-m}} \right|^2 \tag{14}$$

$$B_x(\omega) = \left| \frac{1}{1 + \sum\limits_{m=1}^{M} a_{mx}(e^{j\omega})^{-m}} \right|^2 . \tag{15}$$

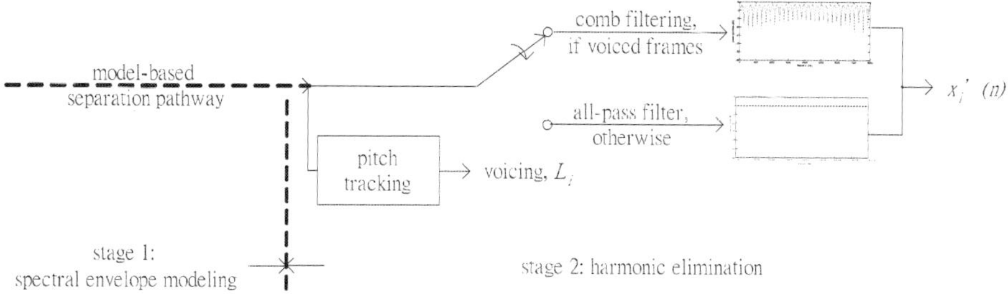

Fig. 10. Block-diagram of harmonic removal of interfering source. For voiced frames, a pitch prediction error filter is used to suppress the harmonics of the interfering source; for unvoiced frames or pauses, an all-pass filter is used instead.

3.3 Harmonic removal of interfering source

A comb filtering in the form of pitch prediction error filter (Ramachandran & Kabal, 1989) is incorporated in the second stage. This stage is used to attenuate harmonic structure associated with the interfering source. For frames where there is no harmonic structure from interfering source, an all-pass filter is applied instead. Fig. 10 depicts the block-diagram. Voicing and pitch information are extracted at the beginning of the second stage.

The impulse response of the pitch prediction error filter $h_p(n)$ is

$$h_p(n) = \delta(n) - \beta_1\delta(n-L) - \beta_2\delta(n-(L+1)) - \beta_3\delta(n-(L+2)) \tag{16}$$

where β_j are the filter coefficients for $j \in [1,2,3]$. L is the lag representing the period of the interfering source.

4. Performance evaluation

Experiments on continuous, real speech utterances are presented below to demonstrate the efficacy of the proposed separation algorithm. It is found that the spectral shape of target speech is retrieved by using the separation algorithm with speech models. Resultant source estimates are close to target speech.

The evaluation set contains 200 mixture signals. These 200 mixture signals are generated by 100 Mandarin source utterances recorded by a female speaker. The signal durations are roughly 3.5 s for each utterance. They are mixed together with equal power, i.e. the signal-to-interference ratio is 0 dB. The evaluation metric used is Itakiura-Saito distortion (d_{IS}).

Itakura-Saito distortion (d_{IS}) concerns about the dissimilarity between a reference speech signal and a test speech signal in an all-pole modeling manner. It represents the degree of spectral matching in terms of general spectral shape and overall gain offset, focusing on the spectral envelope rather than every detail of a speech signal. Fig. 11 depicts the d_{IS} measurements before and after separation.

By comparing the Itakura-Saito distortion values before and after the separation algorithm, the system performance is evaluated. As shown in Fig. 11, most of the IS values of estimated outputs are distributed around IS value = 1 (log value = 0), whereas the IS values of mixture signals are distributed from small to extremely large values. Apart from this, after separation, the mean IS value has been reduced. These confirms that the separation algorithm is effective

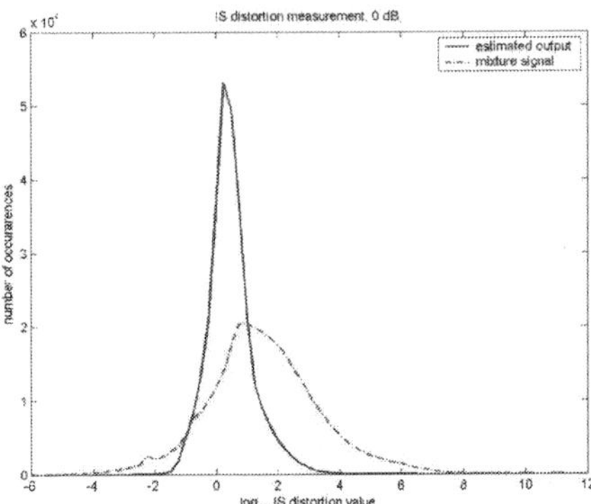

Fig. 11. Measured d_{IS} results before and after separation.

to reduce the Itakura-Saito distortion exhibited in mixture observation and generate source estimate close to target speech source.

Note that there are some extremely small amount of IS values in mixture signals, which probably locate in strong local signal-to-interference regions. After separation, these nearly interference-free regions are filtered and small distortion (as shown by the d_{IS} values after separation) is resulted. In other words, accurate source estimates are achieved.

5. Conclusion

As technologies advance, speech processing applications are no longer limited to controlled usage. More and more applications are designed for daily use, where multiple sound sources with rapidly-changing properties are present. Separation of speech sources become necessary. Over the time, primitive separation cues are often adopted in single-microphone separation algorithms. Nevertheless, schema-based cues are indispensable and critical to separation performance. This chapter first reviews various perceptual cues with the perspective of speech separation. Individual cues are inspected and ranked accordingly to its merits on speech separation. A speech separation algorithm is then introduced to illustrate how primitive and schema-based cues, in particular, in the form of speech models, are incorporated to generate smooth and accurate speech estimates. Experimental results have shown that the effectiveness of this speech model-based separation.

6. References

Assmann, P. F. (1996). Tracking and glimpsing speech in noise: Role of fundamental frequency, *Acoustical Society of America and Acoustical Society of Japan Third Joint Meeting* .

Assmann, P. F. & Paschall, D. D. (1998). Pitches of concurrent vowels, *Journal of the Acoustical Society of America* 103: 1150 – 1160.

Assmann, P. F. & Summerfield, Q. (1990). Modeling the perception of concurrent vowels: Vowels with different fundamental frequencies, *Journal of the Acoustical Society of America* 88: 680 – 697.

Barker, J. (1998). The relationship between speech perception and auditory organization: Studies with spectrally reduced speech, Ph.D. dissertation, University of Sheffield, August 1998.

Barker, J., Cooke, M. P. & Ellis, D. P. W. (2005). Decoding speech in the presence of other sources, *Speech Communication* 45(1): 5–25.

Barker, J., Coy, A., Ma, N. & Cooke, M. (2006). Recent advances in speech fragment decoding techniques, *Proc. ICSLP*, pp. 85 – 88.

Bregman, A. S. (1990). *Auditory Scene Analysis: The Perceptual Organization of Sound*, The MIT Press, Cambridge, Massachusetts.

Bregman, A. S., Abramson, J., Doehring, P. & Darwin, C. J. (1985). Spectral integration based on common amplitude modulation, *Perception & Psychophysics* 37: 483 – 493.

Bregman, A. S. & Ahad, P. A. (1996). *Demonstrations of Auditory Scene Analysis: The Perceptual Organization of Sound*, The MIT Press, Cambridge, Massachusetts.

Bregman, A. S. & Dannenbring, G. L. (1973). The effect of continuity on auditory stream segregation, *Perception & Psychophysics* 13(2): 308 – 312.

Bregman, A. S., Levitan, R. & Liao, C. (1990). Fusion of auditory components: Effects of the frequency of amplitude modulation, *Perception & Psychophysics* 47(1): 68 – 73.

Bregman, A. S. & Pinker, S. (1978). Auditory streaming and the building of timbre, *Canadian Journal of Psychology* 32: 19 – 31.

Brown, G. J. (1992). *Computational Auditory Scene Analysis: A Representational Approach*, PhD thesis, University of Sheffield.

Brown, G. J. & Cooke, M. (1994). Computational auditory scene analysis, *Computer Speech and Language* 8(4): 297–336.

Brown, G. J. & Cooke, M. P. (1992). A computational model of auditory scene analysis, *Proc. ICSLP*, pp. 523 – 526.

Carlyon, R. P. (1991). Discriminating between coherent and incoherent frequency modulation of complex tones, *Journal of the Acoustical Society of America* 89: 329 – 340.

Carlyon, R. P. (1992). The psychophysics of concurrent sound segregation, *Philosophical Transcactions: Biological Sciences* 336: 347 – 355.

Cherry, E. C. (1953). Some experiments on the recognition of speech, with one and with two ears, *Journal of the Acoustical Society of America* 25: 975 – 979.

Cichocki, A. & Amari, S.-i. (2002). *Adaptive Blind Signal and Image Processing: Learning Algorithms and Applications*, John Wiley & Sons, Ltd., Chichester.

Ciocca, V. & Bregman, A. S. (1987). Perceived continuity of gliding and steady-state tones through interrupting noise, *Perception & Psychophysics* 42(5): 476 – 484.

Cooke, M. (1993). *Modelling Auditory Processing and Organisation*, Cambridge University Press.

Cooke, M. P. & Brown, G. J. (1993). Computational auditory scene analysis: Exploiting principles of perceived continuity, *Speech Communication* 13: 391 – 399.

Cooper, L. & Cooper, M. W. (1981). *Introduction to Dynamic Programming*, Pergamon Press Ltd., Oxford.

Dannenbring, G. L. & Bregman, A. S. (1978). Streaming vs. fusion of sinusoidal components of complex tones, *Perception & Psychophysics* 24(4): 369 – 376.

Darwin, C. J. (1984). Perceiving vowels in the presence of another sound: Constraints on formant perception, *Journal of the Acoustical Society of America* 76: 1636 – 1647.

Darwin, C. J. (2001). Auditory grouping and attention to speech, *Proc. of the Institute of Acoustics*, Vol. 23, pp. 165 – 172.

Darwin, C. J. & Bethell-Fox, C. E. (1977). Pitch continuity and speech source attribution, *Journal of Experimental Psychology: Human Perception and Performance* 3(4): 665 – 672.

Darwin, C. J. & Carlyon, R. P. (1995). Auditory grouping, *in* B. C. J. Moore (ed.), *Hearing*, Academic Press, San Diego, California, chapter 11, pp. 387 – 424.

Darwin, C. J. & Ciocca, V. (1992). Grouping in pitch perception: Effects of onset asynchrony and ear of presentation of a mistuned component, *Journal of the Acoustical Society of America* 91: 3381 – 3390.

Darwin, C. J. & Sutherland, N. S. (1984). Grouping frequency components of vowels: When is a harmonic not a harmonic?, *The Quarterly Journal of Experimental Psychology* 36A(2): 193 – 208.

Deutsch, D. (1999). Grouping mechanisms in music, *in* D. Deutsch (ed.), *The Psychology of Music*, second edn, Academic Press, chapter 9, pp. 299 – 348.

Dowling, W. J. (1973). The perception of interleaved melodies, *Cognitive Psychology* 5: 322 – 337.

Ellis, D. P. W. (1994). A computer implementation of psychoacoustic grouping rules, *Proc. 12th International Conference on Pattern Recognition*, Vol. 3, pp. 108 – 112.

Ellis, D. P. W. (1996). *Prediction-driven Computational Auditory Scene Analysis*, PhD thesis, Massachusetts Institute of Technology.

Flanagan, J. (1972). *Speech, Analysis, Synthesis and Perception*, 2nd ed. Springer-Verlag, Berlin.

Gardner, R. B., Gaskill, S. A. & Darwin, C. J. (1989). Perceptual grouping of formants with static and dynamic differences in fundamental frequency, *Journal of the Acoustical Society of America* 85: 1329 – 1337.

Hall, J. W., Haggard, M. P. & Fernandes, M. A. (1984). Detection in noise by spectro-temporal pattern analysis, *Journal of the Acoustical Society of America* 76: 50 – 58.

Helmholtz, H. (1954). *On the sensations of tone as a physiological basis for the theory of music*, 2nd ed. Dover Publications, New York.

Hu, G. & Wang, D. (2004). Monaural speech segregation based on pitch tracking and amplitude modulation, *IEEE Trans. Neural Networks* 15(5): 1135–1150.

Hu, G. & Wang, D. (2006). An auditory scene analysis approach to monaural speech segregation, *in* E. Hänsler & G. Schmidt (eds), *Topics in Acoustic Echo and Noise Control*, Springer, chapter 12, pp. 485 – 515.

Itakura, F. (1975). Line spectrum representation of linear predictor coefficients of speech signals, *Journal of the Acoustical Society of America* 57: S35.

Jansson E. V. (1978). Tone characteristics of the violin, *Svensk Tidskrift för Musikforskning (Swedish Journal of Musicology)* STM 1978:1: 83–105.

Jelinek, F. (1997). *Statistical Methods for Speech Recognition*, The MIT Press, Cambridge, Massachusetts.

Klapuri, A. P. (2001). Multipitch estimation and sound separation by the spectral smoothness principle, *Proc. ICASSP*, pp. 3381 – 3384.

Koffka, K. (1963). *Principles of Gestalt Psychology*, Harcourt, Brace & World, Inc., New York.

Kubovy, M. (1981). Concurrent-pitch segregation and the theory of indispensable attributes, *in* M. Kubovy & J. R. Pomerantz (eds), *Perceptual Organization*, Lawrence Erlbaum Associates, Publishers., chapter 3, pp. 55 – 98.

Lee, S. W., Soong, F. K. & Ching, P. C. (2006). An iterative trajectory regeneration algorithm for separating mixed speech sources, *Proc. ICASSP*, pp. I–157 – I–160.

Lee, S. W., Soong, F. K. & Ching, P. C. (2007). Model-based speech separation with single-microphone input, *Proc. Interspeech*, pp. 850 – 853.

Lieberman P. (1961). Perturbations in vocal pitch, *Journal of the Acoustical Society of America* 33: 597 – 603.

Lim, J. S. (1983). *Speech Enhancement*, Prentice Hall, Englewood Cliffs, New Jersey.

Loizou, P. C. (2007). *Speech Enhancement: Theory and Practice*, CRC Press, Boca Raton.

Marin, C. M. H. & McAdams, S. (1991). Segregation of concurrent sounds. II: Effects of spectral envelope tracing, frequency modulation coherence, and frequency modulation width, *Journal of the Acoustical Society of America* 89: 341 – 351.

McAdams, S. (1989). Segregation of concurrent sounds. I: Effects of frequency modulation coherence, *Journal of the Acoustical Society of America* 86: 2148 – 2159.

Meddis, R. & Hewitt, M. J. (1992). Modeling the identification of concurrent vowels with different fundamental frequencies, *Journal of the Acoustical Society of America* 91: 233 – 245.

Mellinger, D. K. (1991). *Event Formation and Separation in Musical Sound*, PhD thesis, Stanford University.

Paliwal, K. K. (1989). A study of line spectrum pair frequencies for vowel recognition, *Speech Communication* 8: 27 – 33.

Parsons, T. W. (1976). Separation of speech from interfering speech by means of harmonic selection, *Journal of the Acoustical Society of America* 60: 911 – 918.

Purwins, H., Blankertz, B. & Obermayer, K. (2000). Computing auditory perception, *Organised Sound* 5: 159 – 171.

Rabiner, L. & Juang, B.-H. (1993). *Fundamentals of Speech Recognition*, Prentice Hall, Englewood Cliffs, New Jersey.

Ramachandran, R. P. & Kabal, P. (1989). Pitch prediction filters in speech coding, *IEEE Trans. Acoust., Speech, Signal Processing* 37: 467 – 478.

Scheffers, M. T. M. (1983). *Sifting Vowels: Auditory Pitch Analysis and Sound Segregation*, PhD thesis, University of Gröningen, The Netherlands.

Soong, F. K. & Juang, B.-H. (1984). Line spectrum pair (LSP) and speech data compression, *Proc. ICASSP*, pp. 37 – 40.

Summerfield, Q. & Culling, J. F. (1992). Auditory segregation of competing voices: Absence of effects of FM or AM coherence, *Philosophical Transcactions: Biological Sciences* 336: 357 – 366.

van der Kouwe, A. J. W., Wang, D. & Brown, G. J. (2001). A comparison of auditory and blind separation techniques for speech segregation, *IEEE Trans. on Speech and Audio Processing* 9: 189–195.

Viterbi, A. J. (2006). A personal history of the viterbi algorithm, *IEEE Signal Processing Magazine* 23: 120 – 142.

Wakita, H. (1981). Linear prediction voice synthesizers: Line-spectrum pair (LSP) is the newest of several techniques, *Speech Technology* pp. 17 – 22.

Wang, D. & Brown, G. J. (2006). *Computational Auditory Scene Analysis: Principles, Algorithms, and Applications*, John Wiley & Sons, Ltd., Hoboken, New Jersey.

Warren, R. M. (1970). Perceptual restoration of missing speech sounds, *Science* 167: 392 – 393.

Warren, R. M. (1982). *Auditory Perception: A New Synthesis*, Pergamon Press, Elmsford, New York.

Warren, R. M. & Obusek, C. J. (1971). Speech perception and phonemic restorations, *Perception & Psychophysics* 9: 358 – 362.

Warren, R. M., Obusek, C. J. & Ackroff, J. M. (1972). Auditory induction: Perceptal synthesis of absent sounds, *Science* 176: 1149 – 1151.

Weintraub, M. (1985). *A Theory and Computational Tool of Auditory Monaural Sound Separation*, PhD thesis, Stanford University.

Part 2

Speech Recognition

11

Speech Recognition System of Slovenian Broadcast News

Mirjam Sepesy Maučec and Andrej Žgank
University of Maribor, Laboratory for Digital Signal Processing
Slovenia

1. Introduction

Speech is the most natural form of expression which is why it accounts for the majority of communication and information around the world. Media monitoring is a crucial activity today. For the most part today's methods are manual, with human reading, listening and watching, annotating topics and selecting items of interest for the user. The huge amount of data we can access nowadays in different formats (audio, video, text) and through distinct channels revealed the necessity to build systems that can efficiently store this data and retrieve this data automatically. Unavoidable component of such systems is speech recognition engine. Different types of speech and speech environments pose different challenges and, therefore, require different engines to accurately process the speech.

Speech recognition of broadcast news (BN ASR) is designed for news-oriented content from either television or radio and it readily processes broadcasts that include news, multi-speaker roundtable discussions and debates and even open-air interviews outside of the studio. BN ASR is a challenging task for many years and different languages. This chapter summarizes our key efforts to build BN ASR system for Slovenian language.

BN ASR system open the possibility for many applications where the use of automatic transcriptions is a major attribute. One of applications is live subtitling (Brousseau et al., 2003; Imai et al., 2000; Lambourne et al., 2004), were BN ASR system processes audio input and creates closed captions (Figure 1). Another task is speaker tracking, which can be used to find parts of speech belonging to specific speaker (Leggetter et al., 1995) in an audio input (Figure 2). Speech content search and retrieval is also a very useful functionality, which can be applied based on speech recognition. Based on some key terms a user can index audio/video to create a searchable repository to find the exact clip they need and its transcript. Yet another challenging field is topic detection and topic tracking. The goal is to use the system for continuously monitoring a TV channel, and searching inside their news programs for the stories that match the profile of a given user.

The chapter describes in detail our Speech Recognition System of Slovenian Broadcast News (UMB BNSI system), which is still under development. The chapter is organized as follows. First in section 2 we overview research work on broadcast news speech recognition. Properties of the Slovenian language make transcribing Slovenian broadcast news a more challenging task than for example English language. In section 3 basic differences are outlined. Section 4 summarizes the speech and text corpora used for training and testing the system. Section 5 introduces the baseline UMB BNSI system. Section 6 describes advances based on recent improvements on the system. The experimental results are given in section 7. Finally, section 8 states some conclusions.

Fig. 1. Example of live subtitling using the BN ASR system.

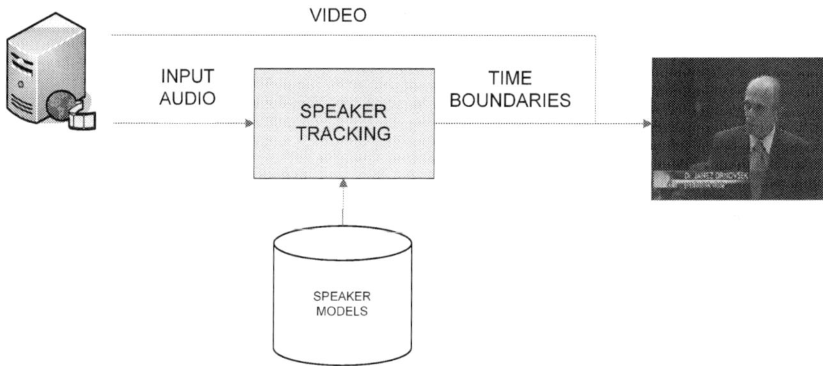

Fig. 2. Example of speaker tracking application designed with the BN ASR system.

2. Overview of research work on broadcast news speech recognition

Speech recognition has intrigued engineers and scientists for centuries. The problem of automatic speech recognition has been approached progressively. Based on major advances in statistical modeling of speech in the 1980s, automatic speech recognition systems have made considerable progress from then.

Broadcast News large vocabulary continuous speech recognition is one of the most challenging tasks today in the research field of language technologies. US agency DARPA was one of the key initiators in the area of Broadcast News system with the HUB campaigns. Several research groups took part in the HUB campaigns. The first experiments were performed for English language, thereafter also experiments for Spanish and Mandarin followed. Two main approaches to modeling BN ASR systems can be observed:

- increasing the complexity of system,
- increasing the amount of data for modeling.

The first approach resulted in increased processing times, therefore a dedicated faster subsystems (1xRT, 10xRT) were also developed. The main topic in increasing the complexity of the BN ASR system is how to model spontaneous speech, which is part of audio stream. Analysis of disfluencies in spontaneous speech that shows their acoustic, prosodic and phonetic features influencing the speech recognition task were presented in (Batliner et al., 1995; Quimbo et al., 1998). First research work on spontaneous speech recognition was performed in (Godfrey et al., 1992; Stolcke et al., 1996). A set of various research works followed, focusing on improvements in different parts of spontaneous speech modeling (Siu et al., 1996; Peters et al., 2003; Stouten et al., 2003). Although permanent improvements were achieved modeling the spontaneous speech, the word error rate is still relatively high. Analyses of errors (Stouten et al., 2006; Rangarajan et al., 2006; Seiichi et al., 2007) that occur during the spontaneous speech recognition indicate the need for further development on this research topic.

The goal of increasing the amount of data available for training is particularly difficult for under-resourced languages. The majority of highly inflectional languages belong to this group. To overcome this problem, additional modeling approaches for highly inflectional languages must be integrated in the BN ASR system. The first research work on subword units for speech recognition in highly inflectional languages were performed for Serbian, Croatian and Czech language (Geutner et al., 1995; Byrne et al., 1999; Byrne et al., 2000). Different topologies of speech recognizer were implemented. Promising results were achieved during these tests. The first research work on subword units modeling for Slovenian language was presented in (Rotovnik et al., 2002). Further research work for Slovenian language followed in (Rotovnik et al., 2003). Achieved results showed that it is possible to achieve statistically significant improvements of results. It was indicated that an increase in the quality of acoustic models will be necessary to further improve the speech recognition results. Short subword units are very similar and consequently the confusability increases.

Another approach in modeling highly inflectional languages is based on increasing the number of words in the vocabulary (Nouza et al., 2004) or its adaptation (Geuntner et al., 1998). In the case when the first approach is used, the increased computational complexity is compensated with usage of simpler acoustic models, which may decrease the recognition results. When the second approach is used, very time consuming generation of new language models must be performed after each adaptation step.

The unsupervised and lightly supervised training of acoustic models was introduced in (Kemp et al., 1999; Lamel et al., 2002). The results confirm that such approach can be effectively used with automatically transcribed speech resources. Similarly effective results were observed, when discriminative training of acoustic models was incorporated (Woodland et al., 2000).

3. Speech recognition in highly inflected languages

Many techniques were first developed for English language and declared as language independent. Highly inflected languages make speech recognition a more difficult task in comparison to English due to their higher complexity (Maučec et al., 2004; Maučec et al., 2009). The concept of word formation is of great importance from the language modelling point of view. The Slovenian language shares its characteristics to varying degrees with many other inflectional languages, especially the Slavic ones. In Slovenian, parts of speech (POS) are divided into two classes according to their inflectionality:

- the inflectional class: noun (substantive words), adjective (adjectival words), verb and adverb;
- the non-inflectional class: preposition, conjunction, particle and interjection.

Slovenian words often exhibit clearer morphological patterns in comparison with English words. A morpheme is the smallest part of a word with its own meaning. In order to form different morphological patterns (declinations, conjugations, gender and number inflections) two parts of a word are distinguished: a stem and an ending. There is one additional feature of the Slovenian language. Morphologically speaking some morphemes alternate in consonants, vowels and some in both simultaneously. Because of inflectionality, for Slovenian, approximately ten times larger recognition vocabulary is needed to assure the same text coverage as for English.

Word order in the Slovenian language does not play such an important role as in other languages (e.g. English language). The reason lies in the grammar of Slovenian language. There is a lot of grammatical information encoded in Slovenian words, which is in English language defined by the position in sentence. A simple sentence is presented as an example (Table 1). All six Slovenian word permutations form semantically logical sentences and are to be expected in spoken language. In contrast, English language does not support such freedom of word order choice. Therefore n-gram modeling, which is a standard in statistical language modeling, results in better language models for English language than for Slovenian language (Maučec et al., 2009).

Slovenian		English	
Maja študira angleščino.	✓	Maja studies English.	✓
Angleščino študira Maja.	✓	English studies Maja.	×
Študira Maja angleščino?	✓	Studies Maja English?	×
Študira angleščino, Maja?	✓	Studies English Maja.	×
Maja, angleščino študira.	✓	Maja English studies.	×
Angleščino Maja študira	✓	English Maja studies.	×

Table 1. Word permutations in Slovenian and English.

4. Speech and language resources

Speech and language resources are crucial in development of speech recognition systems. Speech databases are needed for acoustic modelling, and text databases for language modeling.

The main speech database used in our system was Slovenian BNSI Broadcast News (Žgank et al., 2005) speech database, which consists of two parts. The first part is speech corpus with transcriptions (BNSI-Speech) and the second part is text corpus (BNSI-text).

BNSI-Speech (Table 2) contains speech of news shows (evening news called TV Dnevnik, and late night news shows called Odmevi). It was captured in the archive of RTV Slovenia. Speech signal has different acoustic properties (Figure 3) (Schwartz et al., 1997). Two most frequent focus conditions in database are F0 (36.6%; read studio speech) and F4 (37.6%; read or spontaneous speech with background other than music). The high amount of F4 condition is caused by strict transcribers that very often assigned background, even if its level was very low. 16.2% of speech in the BNSI database is spontaneous (F1), while 6.0% is spoken in presence of background music (F3). Less than one hour of speech originates over the telephone channel (F2). Less than 0.1% of material was spoken by nonnative speakers (F5).

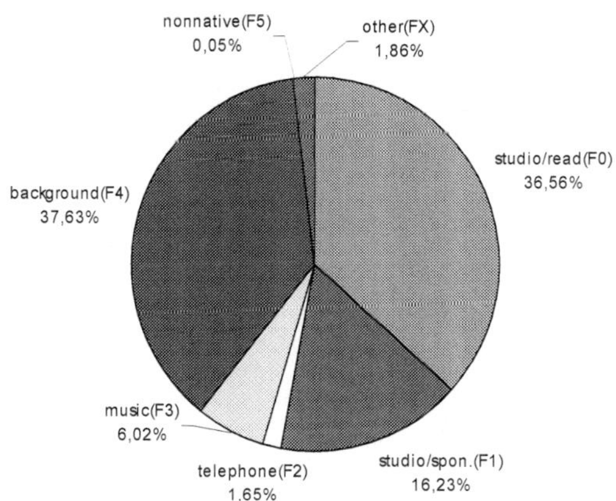

Fig. 3. Ratio of various focus conditions in the BNSI speech database.

The complete speech corpus consists of 36 hours of material (Table 2). The size of the training set is 30 hours. The next 3 hours are used for development set, which function is to fine tune the recogniser's parameters on it. The last 3 hours are used for evaluation set. The average length of a news show in the database is 51:22.

speech corpus:	BNSI-Speech
total length(h)	36
number of speakers	1565
number of words	268k

Table 2. Slovenian BNSI Broadcast News speech database

Table 3 shows some statistics of corpora used to train a language model. Transcriptions of BNSI-Speech corpus were used as the first database. This database was the smallest one. BNSI-text corpus is a collection of different TV scenarios. Some of scenarios were used by reporters and read from a teleprompter during a show. Both databases capture the characteristics of spoken language. Other two databases are collections of samples of written language. The Večer database is a collection of articles of newspaper Večer from 1998 till 2001. The largest database is FidaPLUS corpus (Arhar et al., 2007).

text corpus:	BNSI-Speech	BNSI-text	Večer	FidaPLUS
number of sentences	30k	614k	12M	46M
number of words	573k	11M	95M	621M
number of distinct words	51k	175k	736k	1.6M

Table 3. Slovenian text database

The material dates from the 1996 till 2006. The corpus is a composition of texts from different categories such as newspapers, magazines, books, the internet and other. Table 4 shows the proportion of different categories.

type:	percentage
internet	1.24%
books	8.74%
newspapers	65.26%
magazines	23.26%
other	1.5%

Table 4. Text variety in FidaPLUS corpus

FidaPLUS corpus is linguistically annotated and presented in the form of attributes of the element containing one corpus token. The information about all the possible lemmas and POS-tags is included in the corpus, together with the disambiguated single lemma and POS tag (see example in table 5). Although linguistic information is useful, it was not incorporated in language models discussed in this chapter.

excerpt from the corpus	translation to English
<w lemma="voditi" msd="Gppste--n-----n" lemmas="voditi voda vod" msds="Gppste--n-----n,Gpvsde--------n, Sozed,Sozem,Sozdi,Sozdt Sommi,Sommo" lemmass="voditi voda vod Voda" msdss="Gppste--n-----n,Gpvsde--------n, Sozed,Sozem,Sozdi,Sozdt Sommi,Sommo Slzed,Slzem"> vodi</w>	lead(V) lead(V), water(N), duct(N) lead(V), water(N), duct(N), Voda(NP)

Table 5. The verb …vodi… [to lead] taken from one sample sentence in the FidaPLUS corpus

We are modeling spoken language. There exist large amounts of written texts but we still lack adequate spoken language corpora. In our repository only two corpora are examples of spoken language (BNSI-Speech and BNSI-Text). Other two, Večer and FidaPLUS, are corpora of written language. It can be seen that the collection of texts is significantly diverse. Spoken sentences are short, and written sentences can be very large and complex. Word order in spoken language is much more relaxed than in written language (Duchateau et al., 2004 ; Fitzgerald et al., 2009 ; Honal et al., 2005). We discussed this phenomenon in previous section. Spoken sentences are often not grammatically correct. Written text is in most cases proof-read by professionals in a given language. Diversity of corpora should be taken into account when building a language model.

5. UMB BNSI baseline system

This section contains a description of the components in the UMB BNSI speech recognition system. The system is based on continuous density Hidden Markov Models for acoustic modelling and on n-gram statistical language models. It consists of three main modules, segmentation, features extraction, and decoding. The core module is a speech decoder, which needs three data sources for its operation: acoustic models, language model and lexicon. The block diagram of the baseline system is depicted in figure 4.

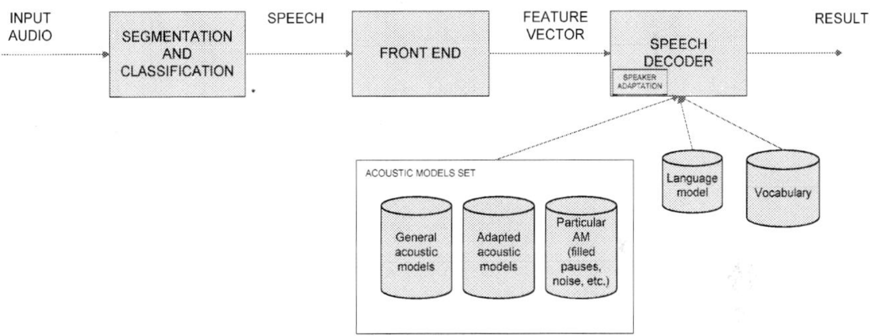

Fig. 4. Block diagram of experimental speech recognition system.

5.1 Segmentation
The main goal of the segmentation module is to produce homogeneous part of input audio stream. The Broadcast News topic can incorporate spoken material in adverse acoustic conditions. One of the most frequent cases is when is the journalist's voice mixed with background audio from the video segment. As a result of segmentation the homogeneous audio parts can be modeled with different acoustic models (wide-band vs. narrow-band), or even with complete separate speech recognition systems.

The three major segmentation criteria, which can be used in a Broadcast News speech recognition system, are:
- channel (narrow-band, wide-band),
- speech/silence/music/noise,
- gender (male, female, unknown).

Different methods can be used for acoustic segmentation: energy based, bandwidth based, Gaussian Mixture Models (GMM), Hidden Markov Models,... UMB BNSI system usually applies automatic acoustic segmentation based on multi-model GMM approach. In tests presented in this paper manual acoustic segmentation based on transcription files was used to exclude the influence of automatic acoustic segmentation on speech recognition results. Prior analysis showed that automatic acoustic segmentation decreases the speech recognition performance by approximately 2% absolute.

5.2 Feature extraction

Features are extracted from overlapping frames of homogeneous speech signal with duration of 32ms and frame shift of 10ms. Two different methods were used for frontend (i.e. feature extraction). The first one was based on mel-cepstral coefficients and energy (12 MFCC + 1 E, delta, delta-delta) and the second one was based on perceptual linear prediction (PLP). The size of baseline feature vector was 39 (Marvi, 2006). Also, the cepstral mean normalization was added to the MFCC feature extraction to reduce the influence of various acoustic channels (Maddi et al., 2006), which can be found in Broadcast News databases. This method significantly improved the speech recognition performance.

5.3 Acoustic modelling

The manually segmented speech material was used for training. This was necessary to exclude any influence of errors that could occur during an automatic segmentation procedure.

The developed baseline acoustic models were gender independent. The training of baseline acoustic models was performed using the BNSI Broadcast News speech database. The procedure was based on common solutions (Žgank et al., 2006). First the context independent acoustic models with mixture of Gaussian probability density function (PDF) were trained and used for force alignment of transcription files. In the second step, the context independent acoustic models were developed once again from scratch, using the refined transcriptions. The context-dependent acoustic models (triphones) were generated next.

The number of free parameters in the triphone acoustic models, which should be estimated during training, was controlled with the phonetic decision tree based clustering. The decision trees were grown from the Slovenian phonetic broad classes that were generated using the data-driven approach based on phoneme confusion matrix (Žgank et al., 2005a). Three final sets of baseline triphone acoustic models with 4, 8 and 16 mixture Gaussian PDF per state were generated. As some additional training data was won from the pool of outliers in comparison with the system described in (Žgank et al., 2008), additional training iterations were applied to context-dependent acoustic models. These transcriptions preprocessing steps showed significant improvement of log-likelihood rate per acoustic model according to an analysis.

5.4 Language modelling and vocabulary

The vocabulary contained the 64K most frequent words in all three corpora. The lowest count of a vocabulary word was 36. The out-of-vocabulary rate on the evaluation set was 4.22%, which is significantly lower than for some other speech recognition systems built for highly inflectional Slovenian language (Žgank et al., 2001; Rotovnik et al., 2007). A possible reason for this is the usage of text corpora with speech transcriptions for language modelling.

However in highly-inflected languages the number of possible word forms is very high. Many valid word forms are missing from the 64K vocabulary. If we enlarge the vocabulary, the complexity of a language model increases, which is demanding from a computational point of view. The vocabulary problem can be alleviated considerably by using sub-word units instead of words as basic vocabulary units. In our research this idea served as a starting point as well (Rotovnik et al., 2002), but did not bring any improvement in broadcast news domain.

Baseline language model was word-based bigram language model. All bigrams were included in the model. Katz back-off with Good-Turing discounting was used for smoothing. Language models were trained using SRI LM Toolkit (Stolcke, 2002).

A language model generated only from largest databases, Večer and FidaPLUS, would be too much adapted to the type of written language. When this language model is used in a UMB BNSI system it will not perform well. The sentences spoken in broadcast news do not match the style of the written sentences. A language model built only from Broadcast News transcriptions would probably be the most appropriate. The problem is that we do not have enough BN transcriptions to generate a satisfactory language model.

Baseline language model was built on first three text corpora. If we would merge all corpora into one big corpus, the influence of much smaller corpus of spoken language (BNSI-Speech) would be lost. Each text corpus was used for construction of one language model component. Individual components were then interpolated using BNSI-Devel set. The interpolation weights were: 0.26 (BNSI-Speech), 0.29 (BNSI-Text), and 0.45 (Večer). Final model contained 7.37M bigrams and resulted in perplexity of 410 on BNSI-Eval set.

5.5 Decoding

The standard one-pass Viterbi decoder with pruning and limited number of active models was used for speech recognition experiments in the next section. We applied additional fine tuning of decoder parameters on combined development set in comparison to the system described in (Žgank et al., 2008), to further improve the performance of speech recognition system.

The main characteristics of the baseline UMB BNSI system are summarized in table 6.

Baseline system	
Features extraction	MFCC, PLP
Features characteristics	window size: 32ms with 10ms frame shift
Acoustic model (AM)	inter-word context dependent trigraphemes
AM complexity	16 mixture Gaussian
Language model	interpolated bigram model
Vocabulary size	64000

Table 6. Characteristics of the baseline system

The baseline speech recognition system achieved 66.0% speech recognition accuracy when used with manual segmentation. This result is comparable to speech recognition system of similar complexity, which is used for highly inflected languages.

6. Improvements in the UMB BNSI system

This section describes recent improvements on the UMB BNSI system. The improvements in the area of acoustic modeling were mainly focused in the feature extraction module. MFCC and PLP feature vectors were used for all experiments, as they showed slightly different performance in various conditions. Beside the speech recognition accuracy also the decoding time can be significantly influenced by the feature vector type.

The influence of feature extraction characteristics on speech recognition performance was analyzed in the experiments. The characteristics observed were: frame length (32 ms versus 25 ms), size of filter bank (26 and 42) and number of MFCC coefficients (12 and 8). When acoustic models for the last two characteristics were developed, the clustering threshold for decision tree based clustering was modified to produce context dependent acoustic models of comparable complexity.

The main improvement in the language modeling procedure was introduction of FidaPLUS text corpus, which significantly increased the number of words in set. Having large text corpus makes transition from bigram to trigram reasonable.

7. Results of comparative experiments

Bigram and trigram language models were built. Independent language model components were constructed, using each database in separation for counting n-grams. If we will use all corpora together as one huge training corpus, the statistical dependencies typical for spoken language and represented by first two corpora, will be weaken by dependencies typical for written language and expressed by much larger training material. In each component Katz back-off with Good-Turing discounting was used for smoothing. Experiments with modified Kneser-Ney smoothing were also performed, but did not bring any improvements. Individual components were then interpolated using the BNSI-Devel corpus of 4 broadcast shows. Optimal interpolation weights for the corresponding 4 models were iteratively computed to minimize the perplexity of an interpolated model on BNSI-Devel corpus. Two interpolated models were build, bigram and trigram models. Table 7 contains interpolation weights for both of them.

component:	bigram	trigram
BNSI-Speech	0.20	0.18
BNSI-Text	0.28	0.24
Večer	0.15	0.12
FidaPLUS	0.37	0.46

Table 7. Interpolation weights for bigram and trigram models.

Perplexity on BNSI-Eval set of final bigram model was 359, and the perplexity of trigram model was 246. The number of bigrams redoubled in comparison to baseline system. As the result of adding the fourth language component the perplexity of bigram model improved by 12%. In trigram model 33.6M trigrams were added. Transition from bigram to trigram model brought 40% of improvement in perplexity. The transition was reasonable because of the size of FidaPLUS corpus. At the same time the language model increased in size and slows down the decoding process.

Several experiments were performed to evaluate the improvements introduced in the UMB BNSI system. The first test was focused on evaluation of using MFCC or PLP feature extraction module in combination with the trigram language models (see Table 8). The results of bigram language models were used as a baseline value.

system:	Correct [%]	Accuracy [%]
bigram, MFCC	69.0	65.7
bigram, PLP	69.6	66.0
trigram, MFCC	70.7	67.5
trigram, PLP	71.4	68.0

Table 8. Recognition results obtained with bigram and trigram language models and MFCC and PLP features.

The more complex trigram language models improved the speech recognition performance by approximately 2%. The accuracy increased from 65.7% to 67.5% when MFCC feature extraction was used and from 66.0% to 68.0% when PLP feature extraction was applied. The disadvantage of using trigram language models is the increased complexity of speech recognition system, which results in increased decoding time.

The second evaluation step was focused on including the FidaPLUS text corpus to language modeling. The results are presented in table 9.

system:	Correct [%]	Accuracy [%]
bigram1, MFCC	70.0	67.4
trigram1, MFCC	73.6	71.0
bigram2, MFCC	60.9	57.7
trigram2, MFCC	73.4	71.1

Table 9. Speech recognition results with language models, improved with FidaPLUS text corpus.

The first type (bigram1, trigram1) of language models in table 9 was built in such a way that FidaPLUS text corpus was added to other baseline text corpora. In the second type (bigram2, trigram2), the FidaPLUS was added, but the Večer text corpus was deleted from the set as it is already included in the FidaPLUS corpus in great extent. The inclusion of FidaPLUS text corpus significantly improved the speech recognition results. The accuracy was increased by 3.6% absolute from 67.5% to 71.1%. In case of these experiments the speech decoder's vocabulary was identical for all four cases. This is the probable cause for the degraded speech recognition performance in case of bigram2 set. In this set the Večer text corpus was excluded from building the language models, but words from this corpus were still present in the lexicon. The frequencies of bigrams from Večer as subcorpus in the FidaPLUS text corpus were not high enough to significantly influence the probabilities in the resulting bigram2 language model.

system:	Correct [%]	Accuracy [%]
bigram1, MFCC, 32ms	70.0	67.4
bigram1, MFCC, 25ms	70.4	67.8
bigram1, PLP, 32ms	70.9	68.0
bigram1, PLP, 25ms	70.5	67.7
trigram1, MFCC, 32ms	73.6	71.0
trigram1, MFCC, 25ms	73.5	71.0
trigram1, PLP, 32ms	73.9	70.9
trigram1, PLP, 25ms	73.6	70.7

Table 10. Speech recognition results using different types of feature extraction and various frame lengths.

The table 10 shows comparison between two different feature extraction frame lengths – baseline 32 ms and 25 ms. There is a small difference between comparable configurations (feature extraction type, language models) for two frame lengths, but it is statistical insignificant.

Various feature extraction configurations were used in combination with the bigram1 and trigram1 language models. The evaluation results are presented in table 11. The increased number of filters in filter bank decreased the speech recognition performance by 0.5% (bigrams) and 0.3% (trigrams). When only 8 mel-cepstral coefficients (8+1 case in table 11) were used, the accuracy decreased, as it was anticipated. The decrease was 4.0% with bigram language model and 3.6% with trigram language model. The advantage with using this configuration was the reduced decoding time, due to lower feature complexity. When bigram language models were applied the decoding time decreased by approximately 16%. The decrease with the trigram language models was approximately 19%. Such faster configuration with decreased accuracy can be successfully included in a speech recognition system with two iterations.

system:	Correct [%]	Accuracy [%]
bigram1, MFCCm	70.9	68.1
bigram1, MFCCm, FB42	70.3	67.6
bigram1, MFCCm, 8+1	66.0	64.1
trigram1, MFCCm	74.0	71.3
trigram1, MFCCm, FB42	73.7	71.0
trigram1, MFCCm, 8+1	69.7	67.7

Table 11. Speech recognition evaluation for various feature extraction configurations.

8. Conclusion

Speech recognition of Broadcast News is a very difficult and resource demanding task. The development of UMB BNSI system is a long-continued project.

The chapter described statistically significant improvements of UMB BNSI system. The analysis of speech recognition results showed the importance of acoustic and language models in speech recognition systems in broadcast news domain. A significant effort was devoted to reducing the complexity of the system. We succeeded to speed up the system by small loss of accuracy to prepare the system for the second pass with lattice rescoring. Our results suggest that these methodologies are well suited to the challenges presented by the Broadcast News domain.

The future work will be focused on implementing a second iteration of speech recognition with increased complexity. The analysis of results namely showed the possibility of overtraining in some evaluation steps, when only one speech recognition iteration was carried out.

We are still far from perfect recognition, the ultimate goal, nevertheless our current technology is able to drive a number of very useful applications, where perfect recognition is not needed, for example audio archive indexing.

9. Acknowledgements

The work was partially funded by Slovenian Research Agency, under contract number P2-0069, Research Programme "Advanced methods of interaction in telecommunication".

10. References

Arhar, Š., Gorjanc, V., (2007). Korpus FidaPLUS: nova generacija slovenskega referenčnega korpusa. Jezik in slovstvo 52/2., 95--110.

Batliner, A., Kiessling, A., Burger, S., Nöth, E., (1995). Filled pauses in spontaneous speech. *In Proc. International Congress of Phonetic Sciences*, Stockholm, Sweden.

Brousseau, J., Beaumont, J.F., Boulianne, G., Cardinal, P., Chapdelaine, C., Comeau, M., Osterrath, F., Ouellet, P., (2003). Automatic Closed-Caption of Live TV Broadcast News in French, *Proc. Eurospeech 2003*, Geneva, Switzerland.

Byrne, W., Hajic, J., Ircing, P., Khudanpur, F., McDonough, J., Peterek, N., Psutka, J.(1999). Large vocabulary speech recognition for read and broadcast Czech, *Proc. Workshop on Text Speech and Dialog*, Plzen, Czech Republic, 1999, Lecture Notes in Artificial Intelligence, Vol. 1692

Byrne W., Hajič J., Ircing P., Krbec P. in Psutka J. (2000). Morpheme Based Language Models for Speech Recognition of Czech, *TSD 2000*, 2000.

Duchateau, J., T. Laureys, P. Wambacq, (2004). Adding Robustness to Language Models for Spontaneous Speech Recognition, *In Proc. ISCA Workshop on Robustness Issues in Conversational Interaction*, Norwich, UK.

Fitzgerald, E., K. Hall, F. Jelinek, (2009). Reconstructing False Start Errors In Spontaneous Speech Text. *In Proc. of the 12th Conference of the European Chapter of the ACL*, pp.255–263, Athens, Greece.

Geuntner P. (1995). Using Morphology Towards Better Large-Vocabulary Speech Recognition Systems, *ICASSP*, pp. 445-448, Detroit, 1995.

Geuntner P., Finke M., Scheytt P., Waibel A. in Wactlar H.(1998). Transcribing Multilingual Broadcast News Using Hypothesis Driven Lexical Adaptation, *DARPA Broadcast News Transcription and Understanding Workshop*, Lansdowne, 1998.

Godfrey, J., Holliman, E., McDaniel, J., (1992). Switchboard: Telephone speech corpus for research and development. *In: Proc. International Conference on Acoustics, Speech and Signal Processing*, Vol. I, San Francisco, USA, pp. 517–520.

Honal, M., T. Schultz, (2005). Automatic Disfluency Removal On Recognized Spontaneous Speech - Rapid Adaptation To Speaker-Dependent Disfluencies. *Proc. of ICASSP, 2005*, vol 1, pp. 969-972.

Imai, T., Kobayashi, A., Sato, S., Tanaka, H., and Ando, A., (2000). Progressive 2-pass decoder for real-time broadcast news captioning, *Proceedings of International Conference on Acoustics, Speech and Signal Processing*, pp.1937-1940, Istanbul, Turkey.

Kemp, T., Waibel, A., (1999). Unsupervised Training Of A Speech Recognizer: Recent Experiments, *In Proc. Eurospeech 1999*, Budapest, Hungary.

Lambourne, A., J. Hewitt, C. Lyon, S. Warren, (2004). Speech-Based Real-Time Subtitling Services, *International Journal of Speech Technology*, Vol. 7, Issue 4, pp. 269-279.

Lamel, L., Gauvain, J., and Adda, G., (2002). Lightly supervised and unsupervised acoustic model training, *Computer Speech and Language*, Volume 16, Issue 1, , January 2002, 115--129.

Leggetter, Woodland, (1995). Maximum likelihood linear regression for speaker adaptation of continuous density hidden Markov models. *Comput. Speech Lang.* v9 i2. 171-185.

Maddi, A., A. Guessoum, D. Berkani, (2006). Noisy Speech Modelling Using Recursive Extended Least Squares Method, *WSEAS TRANSACTIONS on SIGNAL PROCESSING*, Issue 9, Volume 2, September 2006.

Marvi, H., (2006). Speech Recognition Through Discriminative Feature Extraction, *WSEAS TRANSACTIONS on SIGNAL PROCESSING*, Issue 10, Volume 2, October 2006.

Maučec, M. S., Kačič, Z., Horvat, B. (2004). Modelling highly inflected languages. *Inf. sci.*, Oct. 2004, Issue 1/4, Volume 166, pp. 249-269

Maučec, M. S., Rotovnik, T., Kačič, Z., Brest, J.(2009). Using data-driven subword units in language model of highly inflective Slovenian language. *Int. j. pattern recogn. artif. intell.*, Mar. 2009, Volume 23, Issue 2, pp. 287-312.

Nouza, J., Nejedlova, D., Zdansky, J., Kolorenc, J.,(2004). Very Large Vocabulary Speech Recognition System for Automatic Transcription of Czech Broadcast Programs, *Proc. ICSLP 2004*, Jeju Island, Korea.

Peters, J., (May 2003). Lm studies on filled pauses in spontaneous medical dictation. *In: Proc. Human Language Technology conference/North American Chapter of the Association for Computational Linguistics Annual Meeting*, Edmonton, Canada, pp. 82–84.

Quimbo, F.C., Kawahara, T., Doshita, S., (1998). Prosodic analysis of fillers and self-repair in Japanese speech. *In: Proc. International Conference on Spoken Language Processing*, Sydney, Australia, pp. 3313–3316.

Rangarajan, V., S. Narayanan, (2006). "Analysis of disfluent repetitions in spontaneous speech recognition", *Proc. EUSIPCO 2006*, Florence, Italy.

Rotovnik T., Maučec M. S., Horvat B., Kačič Z., (2002). Large vocabulary speech recognition of Slovenian language using data-driven morphological models, TSD 2002.

Rotovnik T., Maučec M. S., Horvat B., Kačič Z., (2003). Slovenian large vocabulary speech recognition with data-driven models of inflectional morphology, *ASRU 2003*, U.S. Virgin Islands, 2003. pp. 83-88, 2003.

Rotovnik T., Maučec, M. S., Kačič Z., (2007). Large vocabulary continuous speech recognition of an inflected language using stems and endings, *Speech communication*, 2007, vol. 49, iss. 6, pp. 437-452.

Schwartz, R., H. Jin, F. Kubala, and S. Matsoukas, (1997). Modeling those F-Conditions - or not, in *Proc. DARPA Speech Recognition Workshop 1997*, pp 115-119, Chantilly, VA.

Seiichi, N., K. Satoshi, (2007). Phenomena and acoustic variation on interjections, pauses and repairs in spontaneous speech, *The Journal of the Acoustical Society of Japan*, Vol.51, No.3, pp. 202-210.

Siu, M., Ostendorf, M., (1996). Modeling disfluencies in conversational speech. *In: Proc. International Conference on Spoken Language Processing*, Vol. I, Atlanta, USA, pp. 386-389.

Stolcke, A., Shriberg, E., (1996). Statistical language modeling for speech disfluencies. In: *Proc. International Conference on Acoustics, Speech and Signal Processing*, Vol. I, Atlanta, USA, pp. 405-408.

Stolcke, A. (2002). *SRILM an Extensible Language Modeling Toolkit*. Proc. of the ICSLP, Denver, Colorado, September 2002.

Stouten, F., Martens, J.-P., (2003). A feature-based filled pause detection system for Dutch. *In: Proc. IEEE Automatic Speech Recognition and Understanding Workshop*, Virgin Islands, USA, pp. 309-314.

Stouten, F., J. Duchateau, J.P. Martens, P. Wambacq, (2006). "Coping with disfluencies in spontaneous speech recognition: Acoustic detection and linguistic context manipulation". *Speech Communication* 48(11): 1590-1606.

Woodland, P.C., Povey, D.,(2000). Large Scale Discriminative Training For Speech Recognition, *In ISCA ITRW Automatic Speech Recognition: Challenges for the Millennium*, pages 7-16, Paris, 2000.

Žgank, A., Kačič, Z., Horvat, B, (2001). Large vocabulary continuous speech recognizer for Slovenian language. *Lecture notes computer science, 2001*, pp. 242-248, Springer Verlag.

Žgank, A., Horvat, B., Kačič Z., (2005). Data-driven generation of phonetic broad classes, based on phoneme confusion matrix similarity. *Speech Communication* 47(3): 379-393.

Žgank, Andrej, Verdonik, Darinka, Zögling Markuš, Aleksandra, Kačič, Zdravko, (2005). BNSI Slovenian broadcast news database - speech and text corpus, *9th European conference on speech communication and technology*, September, 4-8, Lisbon, Portugal. Interspeech Lisboa 2005, Portugal.

Žgank, A., Rotovnik, T., Maučec Sepesy, M., Kačič Z., (2006). Basic Structure of the UMB Slovenian Broadcast News Transcription System, *Proc. IS-LTC Conference*, Ljubljana, Slovenia.

Žgank, A., Rotovnik, T., Sepesy Maučec, M., (2008). Slovenian Spontaneous Speech Recognition and Acoustic Modeling of Filled Pauses and Onomatopoeas, *WSEAS TRANSACTIONS on SIGNAL PROCESSING*, Issue 7, Volume 4, July 2008.

12

Wake-Up-Word Speech Recognition

Veton Këpuska[1]

Florida Institute of Technology, ECE Department
Melbourne, Florida 32931
USA

1. Introduction

Speech is considered one of the most natural forms of communications between people (Juang & Rabiner, 2005). Spoken language has the unique property that it is naturally learned as part of human development. However, this learning process presents challenges when applied to digital computing systems.

The goal of Automatic Speech Recognition (ASR) is to address the problem of building a system that maps an acoustic signal into a string of words. The idea of being able to perform speech recognition from any speaker in any environment is still a problem that is far from being solved. However, recent advancements in the field have resulted in ASR systems that are applicable to some of Human Machine Interaction (HMI) tasks. ASR is already being successfully applied in application domains such as telephony (automated caller menus) and monologue transcriptions for a single speaker.

Several motivations for building ASR systems are, presented in order of difficulty, to improve human-computer interaction through spoken language interfaces, to solve difficult problems such as speech-to-speech translation, and to build intelligent systems that can process spoken language as proficiently as humans. Speech as a computer interface has numerous benefits over traditional interfaces using mouse and keyboard: speech is natural for humans, requires no special training, improves multitasking by leaving the hands and eyes free, and is often faster and more efficient to transmit than the information provided using conventional input methods.

In the presented work, in Section 2, the concept of Wake-Up-Word (WUW) is being introduced. In Section 3, the definition of the WUW task is presented. The implementation details and experimental evaluations of the WUW-SR system are depicted in Section 4. The WUW recognition paradigm partially applied to general word recognition is presented in Section 5. A developed data collection system from the DVD's of movies and TV series is presented in Section 6. Concluding remarks and future work is provided in Section 7.

2. Wake-up-Word paradigm

In the recent developments (Këpuska & Klein, 2009) were focused on the **Wake-up-Word (WUW)** Speech Recognition paradigm. WUW has the following unique requirement: *Detect*

---

[1] vkepuska@fit.edu

a single word or phrase when spoken in an alerting context, while rejecting all other words, phrases, sounds, noises and other acoustic events with virtually 100% accuracy including the same word or phrase of interest spoken in a non-alerting (i.e. referential) context (Këpuska, Carstens, & Wallace, 2006)(Këpuska V. , 2006).

One of the goals of speech recognition is to allow *natural* communication between humans and computers via speech, where *natural* implies similarity to the ways humans interact with each other. A major obstacle to this is the fact that most systems today still rely to some extent on non-speech input, such as pushing buttons or clicking with a mouse. However, much like a human assistant, a natural speech interface must be *continuously listening* and must be robust enough to recover from any communication errors without non-speech intervention. Problem with present SR system is that they solely relay on push-to-talk and non-speech intervention paradigms.

1. Push-to-Talk - Speech recognizers deployed in *continuously listening* mode are continuously monitoring acoustic input and do not necessarily require non-speech activation. This is in contrast to the *push- to- talk* model, in which speech recognition is only activated when the user "pushes a button". Unfortunately, today's *continuously listening* speech recognizers are not reliable enough due to their insufficient accuracy, especially in the area of correct rejection. For example, such systems often respond erratically, even when no speech is present. They sometimes interpret a background noise as speech, and they sometimes incorrectly assume that certain speech is addressed at the speech recognizer when in fact it is targeted elsewhere (context misunderstanding). These problems have traditionally been solved by the *push- to- talk* model: requesting the user to push a button immediately before or during talking or similar prompting paradigms. This action in fact represents an explicit triggering of the recognizer while in all other times the recognizer remains inactive, hence avoiding false triggers.

2. Non-Speech Intervention - Another problem with traditional speech recognizers is that they cannot recover from errors gracefully, and often require non-speech intervention. Any speech-enabled human-machine interface based on natural language relies on carefully crafted dialogues. When the dialogue fails, currently there is no good mechanism to resynchronize the communication, and typically the transaction between human and machine fails by termination. A typical example is a SR system which is in a dictation state, when in fact the human is attempting to use command-and-control to correct previous dictation error. Often the user is forced to intervene by pushing a button or keyboard key to resynchronize the system.

3. Current SR systems that do not deploy the *push- to- talk* paradigm use *implicit context switching*. For example, a system that has the ability to switch from "dictation mode" to "command mode" does so by trying to infer whether the user is uttering a command rather than dictating text. This task is rather difficult to perform with high accuracy, even for humans. The *push- to- talk* model uses *explicit context switching*, meaning that the action of pushing the button (or similar paradigm) explicitly sets the context of the speech recognizer to a specific state.

To achieve the goal of developing a natural speech interface, it is first useful to consider human to human communication. Upon hearing an utterance of speech a human listener must quickly make a decision whether or not the speech is directed to him or her. This decision determines whether the listener will make an effort to "process" and understand the utterance. Humans can make this decision quickly and robustly by utilizing visual, auditory, semantic, and/or additional contextual clues.

Visual clues might be gestures such as waving of hands or other facial expressions. Auditory clues are attention grabbing words or phrases such as the listener's name (e.g. John), interjections such as "hey", "excuse me," and so forth. Additionally, the listener may make use of prosodic information such as pitch and intonation, as well as identification of the speaker's voice.

Semantic and/or contextual clues are inferred from interpretation of the words in the sentence being spoken, visual input, prior experience, and customs dictated by the culture. Humans are very robust in determining when speech is targeted towards them, and should a computer SR system be able to make the same decisions its robustness would increase significantly.

Wake-Up-Word is proposed as a method to *explicitly request* the attention of a computer using a spoken word or phrase (Këpuska V. , Elevator Simulator Screen Perspective, 2009), (Këpuska V. , Elevator Simulator User Perspective, 2009). The WUW must be spoken in the context of requesting attention, i. e.alerting context and should not be recognized in any other context.   After successful detection of WUW and its alerting context, the speech recognizer may safely interpret the following utterance as a command. The WUW is analogous to the button in *push to talk*, but the interaction is completely based on speech. Therefore it is proposed to use *explicit context switching* via WUW. Furthermore, this is similar to how context switching occurs in human to human communication as well.

3. WUW definition

WUW technology solves three major problem areas:

1. **Detecting WUW Context –** The WUW system must be able to notify the host system that attention is required in certain circumstances and with high accuracy. Unlike keyword-spotting, see for example (Juang & Rabiner, 2005), in which a certain keyword is recognized and reported during *every* occurrence, WUW dictates these occurrences only be reported during an *alerting context*. This context can be determined using features such as leading and trailing silence, difference in the long term average of speech features, and prosodic information (pitch, intonation, rhythm, etc.). This is still active research area (Këpuska & Chih-Ti, 2010)

2. **Identifying WUW –** After identifying the correct context for a spoken utterance, the WUW paradigm shall be responsible for determining if the utterance contains the pre-defined Wake-up-Word to be used for command (e.g. "Computer") with a high degree of accuracy, e.g., > 99% (Këpuska & Klein, 2009).

3. **Correct Rejection of Non-WUW –** Similar to identification of the WUW, the system shall also be capable of filtering speech tokens that are *not* WUWs with practically 100% accuracy to guarantee 0% false acceptances (Këpuska & Klein, 2009).

4. Wake-Up-Word system

The concepts of WUW have been most recently expanded in (Këpuska & Klein, 2009). Currently, the system is implemented in C++ as well as Objective C, and provides four major components for achieving the goals of WUW for use in a real-time environment.

1. **WUW Front End** – This system component is responsible for extracting *features* from the input audio signal. The current system is capable of extracting Mel-Filtered Cepstral Coefficients (MFCC), Linear Predictive Coding coefficients (LPC), and enhanced MFCC features.
2. **Voice Activity Detector (VAD)** – A large portion of the input audio signal to the system are *non-speech events* such as silence or environmental noise. Filtering this information is critical in order to ensure the system is only listening during speech events of interest. Areas of audio that are determined to be speech-related are then forwarded to the later stages of the WUW system.
3. **WUW Back End** – The Back End performs a complex recognition procedure based on Hidden Markov Models (HMMs). HMMs are continuous densities HMM's.
4. **SVM Classification** - The final system component is responsible for classifying speech signals as In-Vocabulary (INV) or Out-of-Vocabulary (OOV) using Support Vector Machines (SVMs). In the WUW context, the only INV word is the one selected for command and control of the host system. Any other word or sound is classified as OOV.

The following diagram illustrates the top-level workflow of the WUW system:

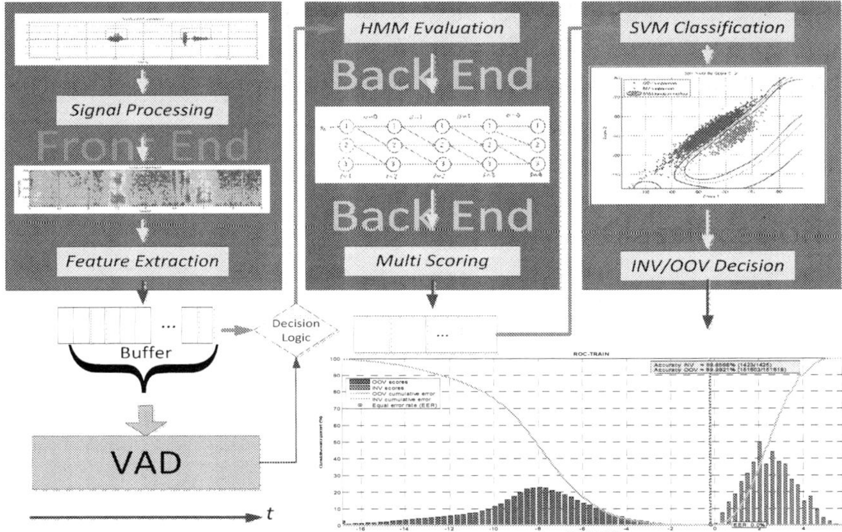

Fig. 1. WUW System Architecture.

4.1 Wake-Up-Word Front End

The front end is responsible for extracting features out of the input signal. Three sets of features are extracted: Mel-Filtered Cepstral Coefficients (MFCC), LPC (Linear Predictive Coding) smoothed MFCCs, and Enhanced MFCCs.

The following image, Figure 2, shows a waveform superimposed with its VAD segmentation, its spectrogram, and its enhanced spectrogram.

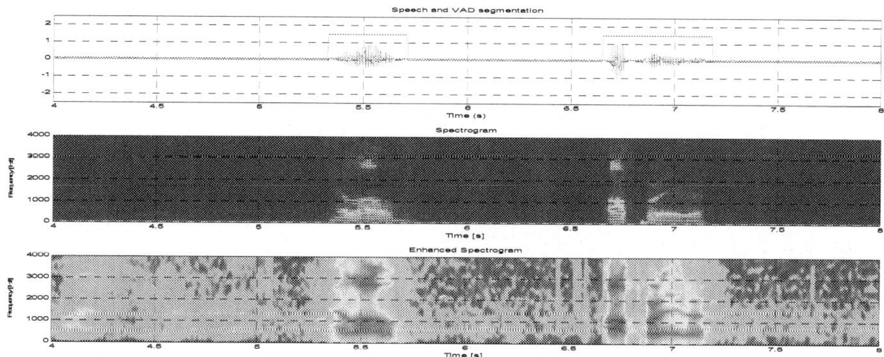

Fig. 2. Speech signal with VAD segmentation, spectrogram, and enhanced spectrogram generated by the Front End module. (Këpuska & Klein, 2009).

The MFCCs are computed using the standard algorithm as presented in the Figure 3:

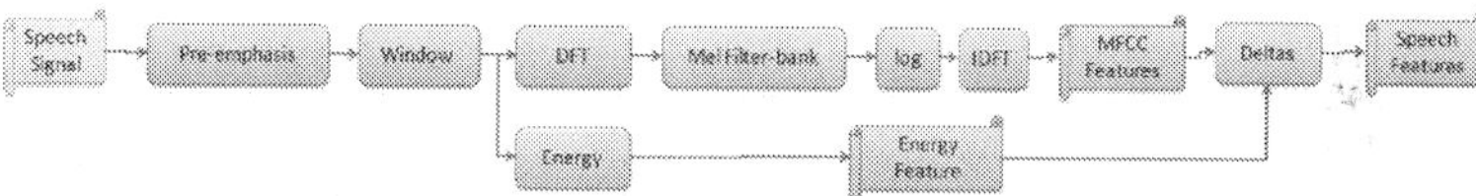

Fig. 3. Feature Extraction Workflow

Pre-emphasis – This stage is used to amplify energy in the high-frequencies of the input speech signal. This allows information in these regions to be more recognizable during HMM model training and recognition.

Windowing – This stage slices the input signal into discrete time segments. This is done by using window N milliseconds typically 25 ms wide and at offsets of M milliseconds long. A Hamming window is commonly used to prevent edge effects associated with the sharp changes in a Rectangular window. Equation 1 and Figure 5 show the equation for the , typiccally 10 ms or 5 ms Hamming window and its effect when it is applied to a speech signal, respectively:

$$w[n] = \begin{cases} 0.54 - 0.46 \cos \dfrac{2\pi n}{L} & 0 \leq n \leq L-1 \\ 0 \end{cases} \tag{1}$$

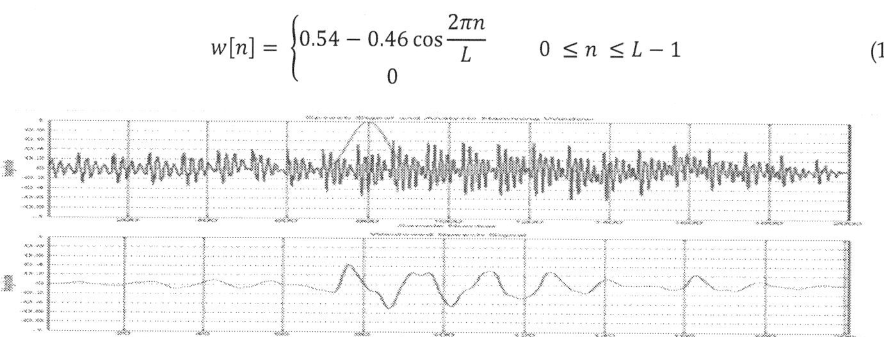

Fig. 4. Original Speech Signal and Windowed Speech Signal

Discrete Fourier Transform – DFT is applied to the windowed speech signal, resulting in the magnitude and phase representation of the signal. The log-magnitude of an example speech signal is depicted in Figure 4.

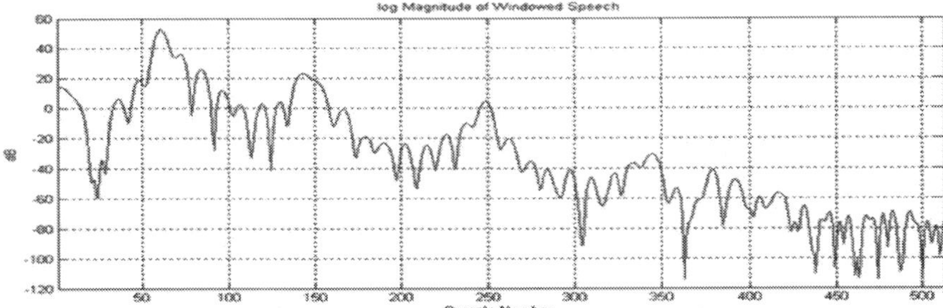

Fig. 5. Log Magnitude of Speech Signal DFT.

Mel Filter Bank – While the resulting spectrum of the DFT contains information in each frequency, human hearing is less sensitive at frequencies above 1000 Hz. This concept also has a direct effect on performance of ASR systems; therefore, the spectrum is warped using a logarithmic **Mel** scale (see Figure 6. below). A Mel frequency can be computed using equation 3. In order to create this effect on the DFT spectrum, a bank of filters is constructed with filters distributed equally below 1000 Hz and spaced logarithmically above 1000 Hz. The Figure 7 displays an example filter bank using triangular filters. The output of filtering the DFT signal by each Mel filter is known as the **Mel spectrum**.

$$mel(f) = 1127 \ln(1 + \frac{f}{700}) \tag{2}$$

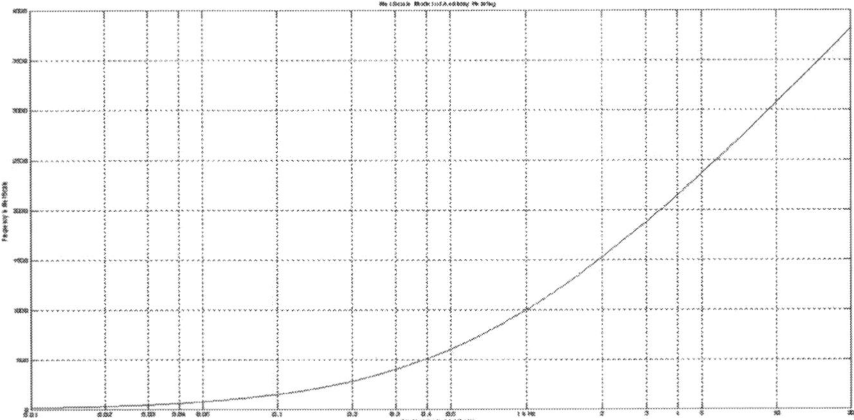

Fig. 6. Mel Scale.

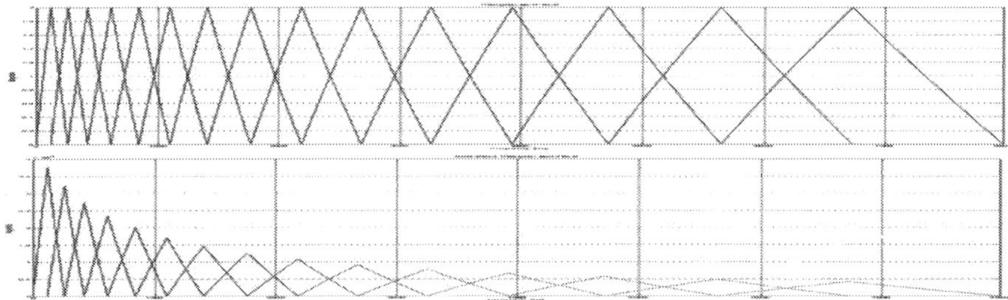

Fig. 7. Mel Filter Bank filters. The bottom figure shows normalized filters.

Inverse DFT – The IDFT of the Mel spectrum is computed, resulting in the **cepstrum**. This representation is valuable because it separates characteristics of the source and vocal tract from the speech waveform. The first 12 values of the resulting cepstrum are recorded.

Additional Features -

i.   **Energy Feature** – This step is performed in parallel with the MFCC feature extraction and involves calculating the total energy of the input frame.

ii. **Delta MFCC Features** – In order to capture the changes in speech from frame-to-frame, the first and second derivative of the MFCC coefficients are also calculated and included.

The LPC (Linear Predictive Coding) smoothed MFCCs, and Enhanced MFCCs are described in (Këpuska & Klein, 2009). Those triple features are used by the *Back End* to score each with its corresponding HMM model.

4.2 VAD classification

In the first phase, for every input frame VAD decides whether the frame is speech-like or non-speech-like. Several methods have been implemented and tested to solve this problem.

In the first implementation, the decision was made based on three features: log energy difference, spectral difference, and MFCC difference. A threshold was determined empirically for each feature, and the frame was considered speech-like if at least two out of the three features were above the threshold. This was in effect a Decision Tree classifier, and the decision regions consisted of hypercubes in the feature space.

In order to improve the VAD classification accuracy, research has been carried out to determine the ideal features to be used for classification. Hence, Artificial Neural Networks (ANN) and Support Vector Machines (SVM) were tested for automatic classification. One attempt was to take several important features from a stream of consecutive frames and classify them using ANN or SVM. The idea was that the classifier would make a better decision if shown multiple consecutive frames rather than a single frame. The result, although good, was too computationally expensive, and the final implementation still uses information from only a single frame.

4.2.1 First VAD phase – single frame decision

The final implementation uses the same three features as in the first implementation: log energy difference, spectral difference, and MFCC difference; however, classification is performed using a linear SVM. There are several advantages over the original method. First, the classification boundary in the feature space is a hyperplane, which is more robust than the hypercubes produced by the decision tree method. Second, the thresholds do not have to be picked manually but can be trained automatically (and optimally) using marked input files. Third, the sensitivity can be adjusted in smooth increments using a single parameter, the SVM decision threshold. Recall that the output of a SVM is a single scalar, $u = \mathbf{w} \cdot \mathbf{x} - b$ (Klein, 2007). Usually the decision threshold is set at $u = 0$, but it can be adjusted in either direction depending on the requirements. Finally, the linear SVM kernel is extremely efficient, because classification of new data requires just a single dot product computation. The following figures show the training data scattered on two dimensional planes, followed by a 3 dimensional representation which includes the SVM separating plane.

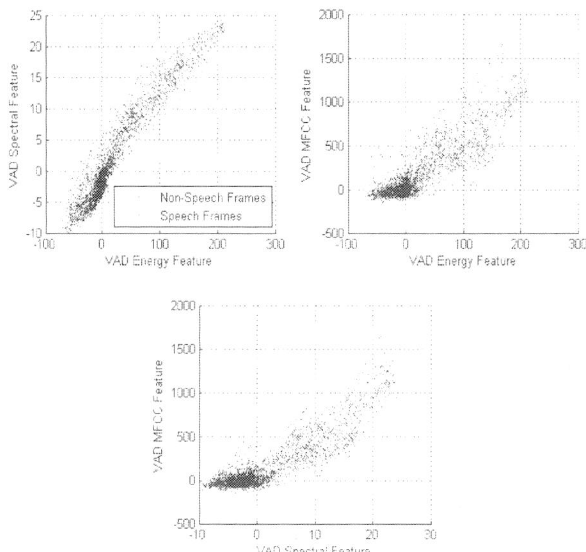

Fig. 8. VAD features in two dimensional space

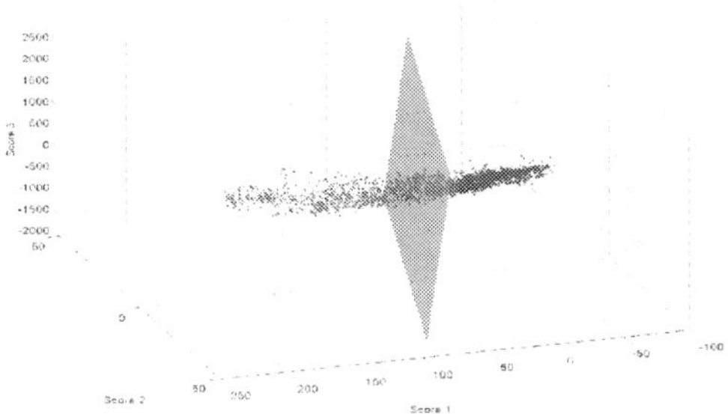

Fig. 9. VAD features with linear SVM

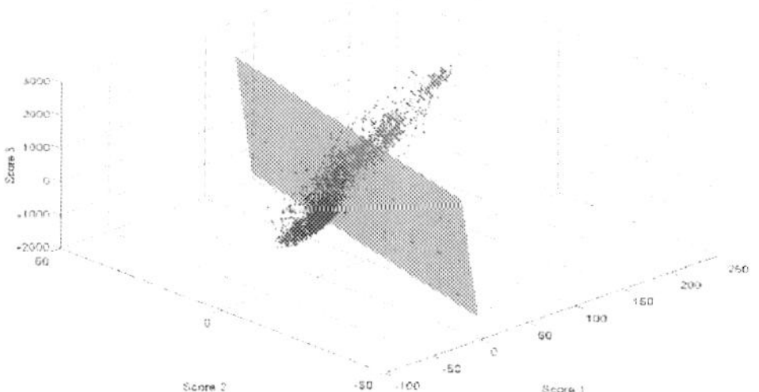

Fig. 10. VAD features with linear SVM (different perspective)

In the figures above, the red points correspond to speech frames while the blue points correspond to non-speech frames, as labeled by a human listener. It can be seen that the linear classifier produces a fairly good separating plane between the two classes, and the plane could be moved in either direction by adjusting the threshold.

4.2.2 Second VAD phase – final decision logic

In the second phase, the VAD keeps track of the number of frames marked as speech and non-speech and makes a final decision. There are four parameters: MIN_VAD_ON_COUNT, MIN_VAD_OFF_COUNT, LEAD_COUNT, and TRAIL_COUNT. The algorithm calls for a number of consecutive frames to be marked as speech in order to set the state to VAD_ON; this number is specified by MIN_VAD_ON_COUNT. It also requires a number of consecutive frames to be marked as non-speech in order to set the state to VAD_OFF; this number is specified by MIN_VAD_OFF_COUNT. Because the classifier can make mistakes at the beginning and the end, the logic also includes a lead-in and a trail-out time. When the minimum number of consecutive speech frames has been observed, VAD does not indicate VAD_ON for the first of those frames. Rather it selects the frame that was observed a number time instances earlier; this number is specified by LEAD_COUNT. Similarly, when the minimum number of non-speech frames has been observed, VAD waits an additional number of frames before changing to VAD_OFF, specified by TRAIL_COUNT.

4.3 Back end - plain HMM scores

The Back End is responsible for scoring observation sequences. The WUW-SR system uses a Hidden Markov Models for acoustic modeling, and as a result the back end consists of a HMM recognizer. Prior to recognition, HMM model(s) must be created and trained for the word or phrase which is selected to be the Wake-Up-Word.

When the VAD state changes from VAD_OFF to VAD_ON, the HMM recognizer resets and prepares for a new observation sequence. As long as the VAD state remains VAD_ON, feature vectors are continuously passed to the HMM recognizer, where they are scored using the novel triple scoring method. If using multiple feature streams, recognition is performed for each stream in parallel. When VAD state changes from VAD_ON to VAD_OFF, multiple scores (e.g., MFCC, LPC and E-MFCC Score) are obtained from the HMM recognizer and are sent to the SVM classifier. SVM produces a classification score which is compared against a threshold to make the final classification decision of INV or OOV.

For the first tests on speech data, a HMM was trained on the word "operator." The training sequences were taken from the CCW17 and WUW-II (Këpuska & Klein, 2009) corpora for a total of 573 sequences from over 200 different speakers. After features were extracted, some of the erroneous VAD segments were manually removed. The INV testing sequences were the same as the training sequences, while the OOV testing sequences included the rest of the CCW17 corpus (3833 utterances, 9 different words, over 200 different speakers). The HMM was a left-to-right model with no skips, 30 states, and 6 mixtures per state, and was trained with two iterations of Baum-Welch.

The score is the result of the Viterbi algorithm over the input sequence. Recall that the Viterbi algorithm finds the state sequence that has the highest probability of being taken while generating the observation sequence. The final score is that probability normalized by the number of input observations, T. The Figure 8 below shows the result:

The distributions look Gaussian, but there is significant overlap between them. The equal error rate of 15.5% essentially means that at that threshold, 15.5% of the OOV words would be classified as INV, and 15.5% of the INV words would be classified as OOV. Obviously, no practical applications can be developed based on the performance of this recognizer.

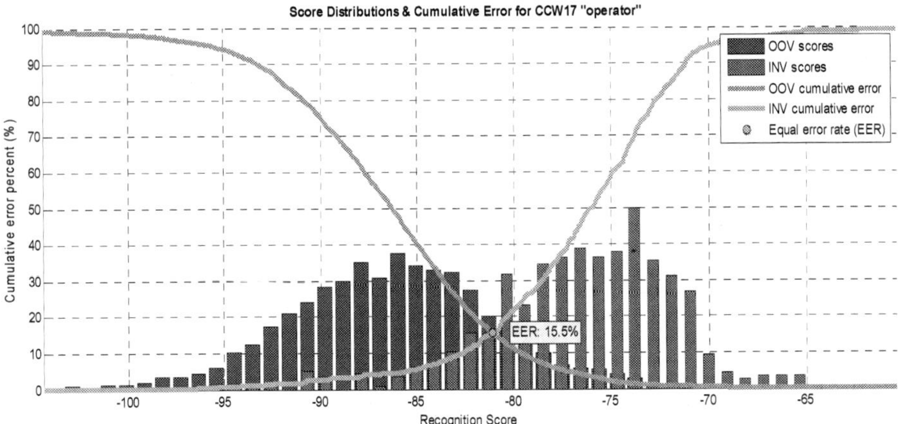

Fig. 11. Score distributions for plain HMM (Këpuska & Klein, 2009)

4.4 SVM classification

After HMM recognition, the algorithm uses two additional scores for any given observation sequence (e.g., MFCC, LPC and e-MFCC). When considering the three scores as features in a three dimensional space, the separation between INV and OOV distributions increases significantly. The next experiment runs recognition on the same data as above, but this time the recognizer uses the triple scoring algorithm to output three scores (Këpuska & Klein, 2009).

4.4.1 Triple scoring method

The figures below show two-dimensional scatter plots of Score 1 vs. Score 2, and Score 1 vs. Score 3 for each observation sequence (e.g., MFCC, LPC and e-MFCC). In addition, a histogram on the horizontal axis shows the distributions of Score 1 independently, and a similar histogram on the vertical axis shows the distributions of Score 2 and Score 3 independently. The histograms are hollowed out so that the overlap between distributions can be seen clearly. The distribution for Score 1 is exactly the same as in the previous section, as the data and model haven't changed. Any individual score does not produce a good separation between classes, and in fact the Score 2 distributions have almost complete overlap. However, the two dimensional separation in either case is remarkable. When all three scores are considered in a three dimensional space, their separation is even better than either two dimensions as depicted in Figure12 and Figure 13.

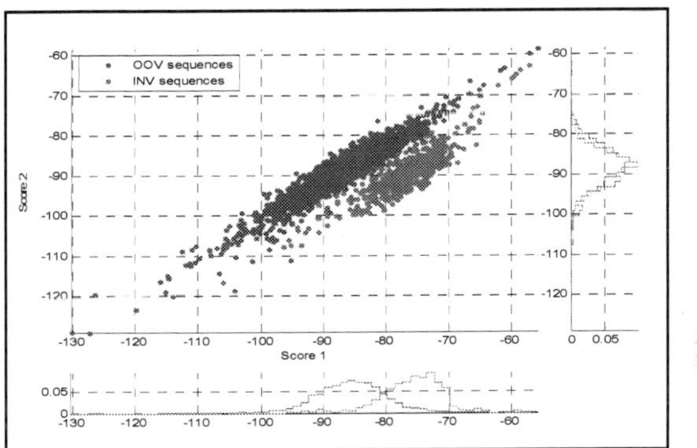

Fig. 12. Triple scoring, score 1 vs. score 2 (Këpuska & Klein, 2009)

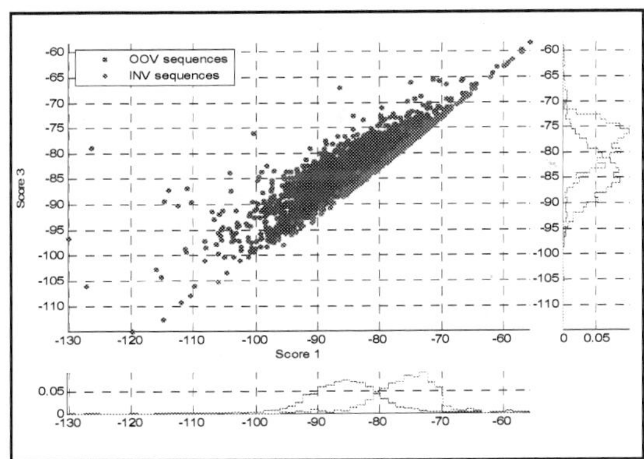

Fig. 13. Triple scoring, score 1 vs. score 3 (Këpuska & Klein, 2009)

In order to automatically classify an input sequence as INV or OOV, the triple score feature space, $\mathcal{R}^3$, can be partitioned by a binary classifier into two regions, $\mathcal{R}_1^3$ and $\mathcal{R}_{-1}^3$. The SVMs have been selected for this task because of the following reasons: they can produce various kinds of decision surfaces including radial basis function, polynomial, and linear; they employ Structural Risk Minimization (SRM) (Burges, 1998) to maximize the margin which has shown empirically to have good generalization performance.

4.4.2 SVM parameters

Two types of SVMs have been considered for this task: linear and RBF. The linear SVM uses a dot product kernel function, $K(x,y) = x \cdot y$, and separates the feature space with a hyperplane. It is very computationally efficient because no matter how many support vectors are found, evaluation requires only a single dot product. Figure 14 above shows that the separation between distributions based on Score 1 and Score 3 is almost linear, so a linear SVM would likely give good results. However, in the Score 1/Score 2 space, the distributions have a curvature, so the linear SVM is unlikely to generalize well for unseen data. The figures below show the decision boundary found by a linear SVM trained on Score 1+2, and Score 1+3, respectively.

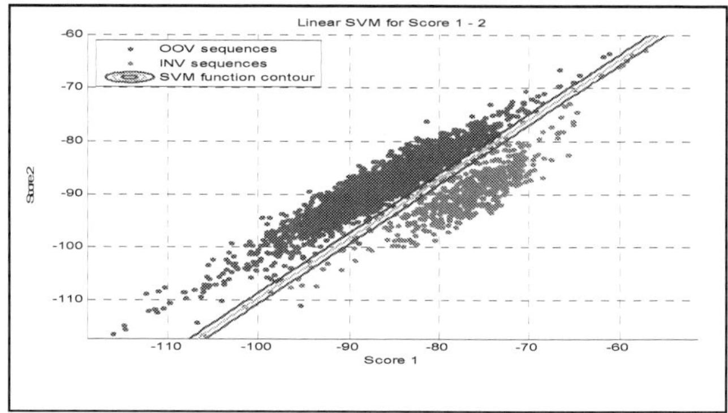

Fig. 15. Linear SVM, scores 1-2 (Këpuska & Klein, 2009)

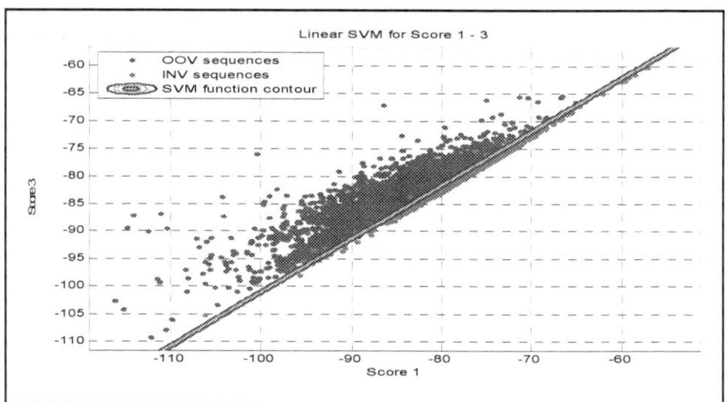

Fig. 16. Linear SVM, scores 1-3 (Këpuska & Klein, 2009)

The line in the center represents the contour of the SVM function at $u = 0$, and outer two lines are drawn at $u = \pm 1$. Using 0 as the threshold, the accuracy of Scores 1 - 2 is 99.7% Correct Rejection (CR) and 98.6% Correct Acceptance (CA), while for Scores 1 – 3 it is 99.5% CR and 95.5% CA. If considering only two features, Scores 1 and 2 seem to have better classification ability. However, combining the three scores produces the plane shown below from two different angles.

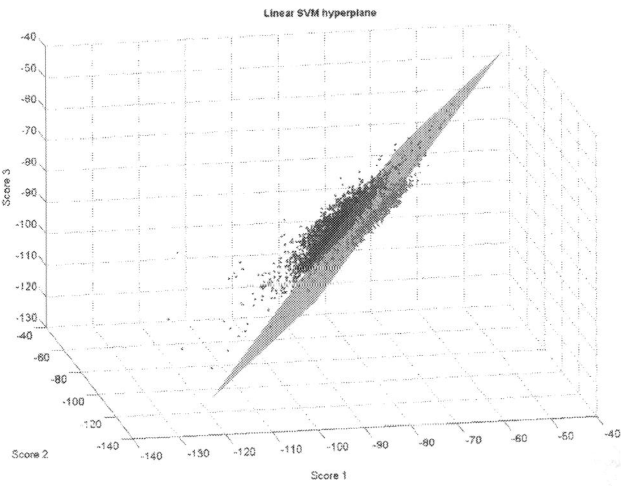

Fig. 17. Linear SVM, 3D view 1 (Këpuska & Klein, 2009)

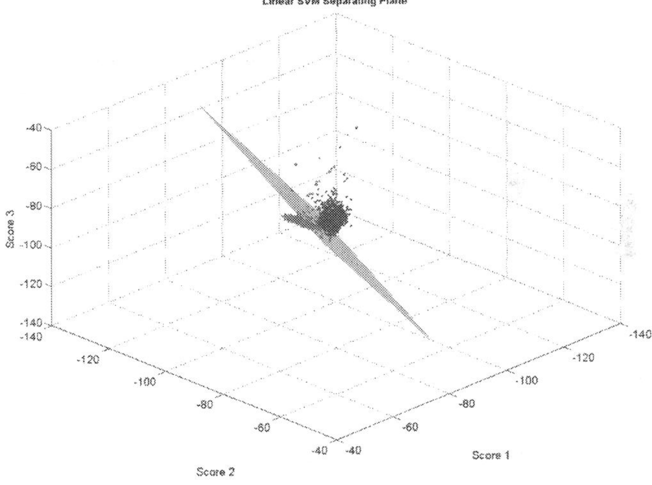

Fig. 18. Linear SVM, 3D view 2 (Këpuska & Klein, 2009)

The plane split the feature space with an accuracy of 99.9% CR and 99.5% CA (just 6 of 4499 total sequences were misclassified). The accuracy was better than any of the 2 dimensional cases, indicating that Score 3 contains additional information not found in Score 2. The classification error rate of the linear SVM is shown below:

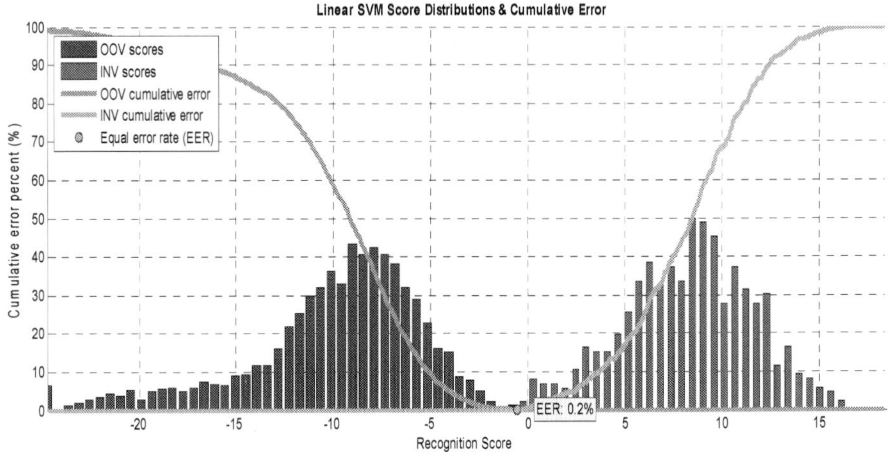

Fig. 19. Score distributions for triple scoring and linear SVM (Këpuska & Klein, 2009)

The conclusion is that using the triple scoring method combined with a linear SVM decreased the equal error rate on this particular data set from 15.5% to 0.2%, or in other words increased accuracy by over 76.5 times (i.e., error rate reduction of 7650%)!

In the next experiment, a Radial Basis Function (RBF) kernel was used for the SVM. The RBF function, $K(x,y) = e^{-\gamma|x-y|^2}$, maps feature vectors into an infinitely dimensional Hilbert space and is able to achieve complete separation between classes in most cases. However, the γ parameter must be chosen carefully in order to avoid overtraining. As there is no way to determine it automatically, a grid search may be used to find a good value. For most experiments $\gamma = 0.008$ gave good results. Shown below are the RBF SVM contours for both two-dimensional cases.

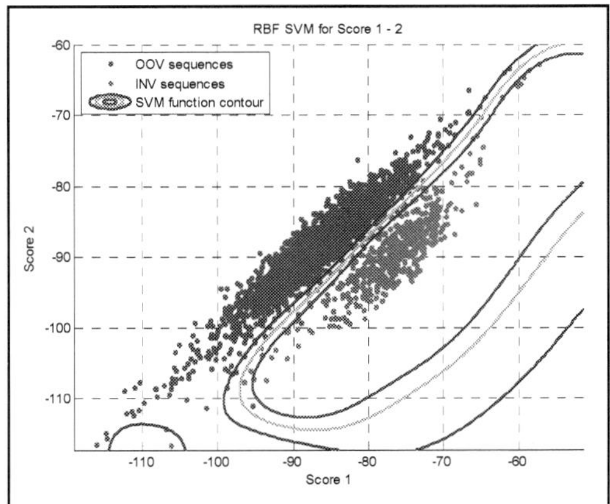

Fig. 20. RBF kernel, scores 1-2 (Këpuska & Klein, 2009)

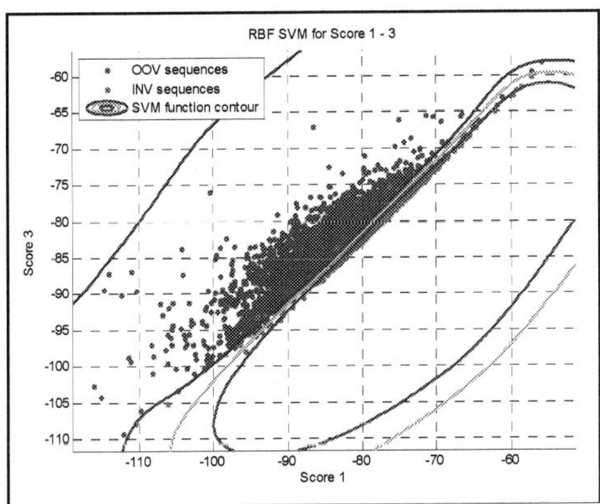

Fig. 21. RBF kernel, scores 1-3 (Këpuska & Klein, 2009)

At the $u = 0$ threshold, the classification accuracy was 99.8% CR, 98.6% CA for Score 1-2, and 99.4% CR, 95.6% CA for Score 1-3. In both cases the RBF kernel formed a closed decision region around the INV points (Recall that the SVM decision function at $u = 0$ is shown by the green line).

Some interesting observations can be made from these plots. First, the INV outlier in the bottom left corner of the first plot caused a region to form around it. SVM function output values inside the region were somewhere between -1 and 0, not high enough to cross into the INV class. However, it is apparent that the RBF kernel is sensitive to outliers, so the γ parameter must be chosen carefully to prevent overtraining. Had the γ parameter been a little bit higher, the SVM function output inside the circular region would have increased beyond 0, and that region would have been considered INV.

Second, the RBF kernel's classification accuracy showed almost no improvement over the linear SVM. However, it is expected that due to the RBF kernel's ability to create arbitrary curved decision surfaces, it will have better generalization performance than the linear SVM's hyperplane.

The figure below shows a RBF kernel SVM trained on all three scores.

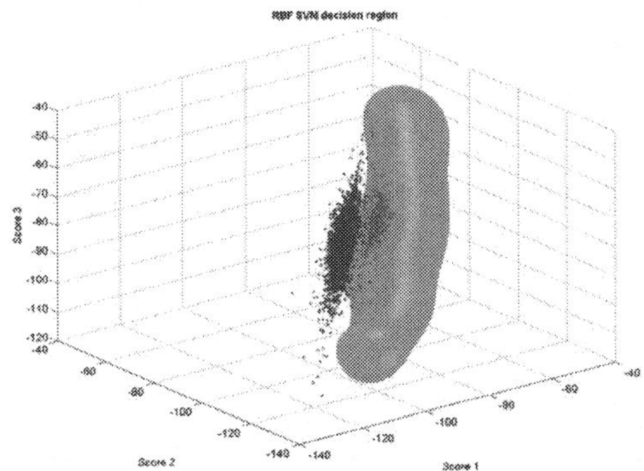

Fig. 22. RBF kernel, 3D view 1 (Këpuska & Klein, 2009)

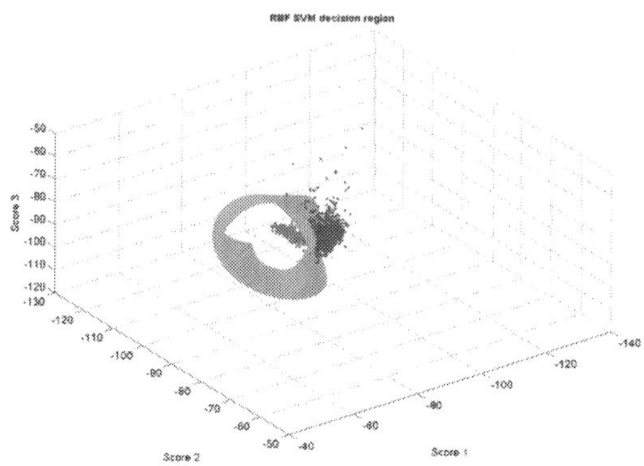

Fig. 23. RBF kernel, 3d view 2 (Këpuska & Klein, 2009)

The RBF kernel created a closed 3-dimensional surface around the INV points and had a classification accuracy of 99.95% CR, 99.30% CA. If considering $u = 0$ as the threshold, the triple score SVM with RBF kernel function shows only little improvement over the linear SVM for this data set. However, as shown below, the SVM score distributions are significantly more separated, and the equal error rate is lower than the linear SVM; from 0.2% to 0.1%.

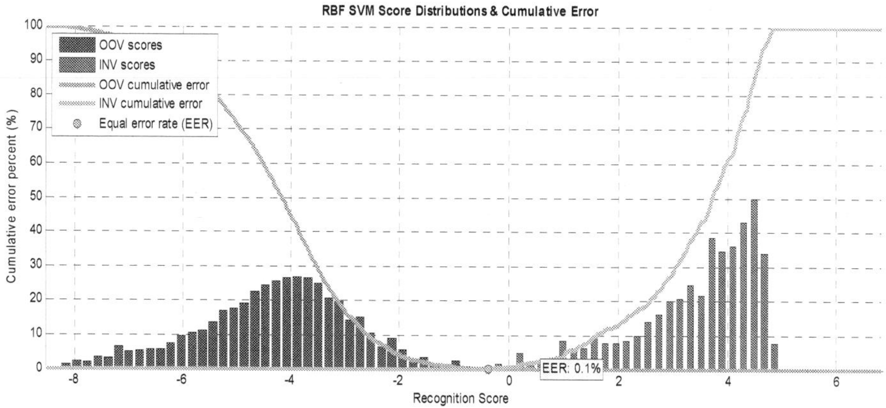

Fig. 24. Score distributions for triple scoring and RBF kernel (Këpuska & Klein, 2009).

Final results when combining all three features using all the available data for testing and training (Callhome, Phonebook, WUW and WUWII Corpora, CCW17) provides a clear superiority of the presented method (Figure 25). In this test the INV accuracy of only two **(2)** errors out of **1425** operator utterances or **99.8596%** and OOV accuracy of twelve **(12)** errors on **151615** tokens or **99.9921%**.

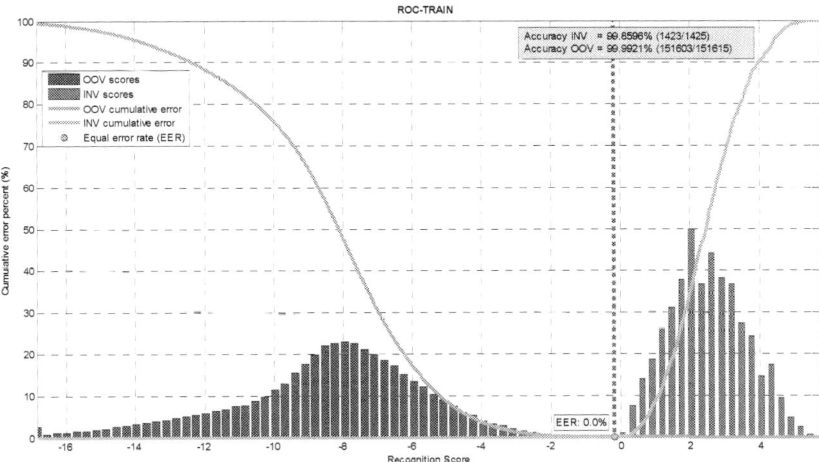

Fig. 25. Overall recognition rate of WUW-SR utilizing Callhome, Phonebook, WUW, WUWII and CCW17 corpora.

The chart above demonstrates WUW-SR's improvement over current state of the art recognizers. WUW-SR with three feature streams was several orders of magnitude superior to the baseline recognizers in INV recognition and particularly in OOV rejection. Of the two OOV corpora, Phonebook was significantly more difficult to recognize for all three systems due to the fact that every utterance was a single isolated word. Isolated words have similar durations to the WUW and differ just in pronunciation, putting to the test the raw recognition power of ASR system. HTK had 8793 false acceptance errors on Phonebook and the commercial SR system had 5801 errors.

WUW-SR demonstrated its OOV rejection capabilities by committing just total of **12** false acceptance errors on all the corpora (**151615 tokens**) used for OOV rejection testing while maintaining high recognition rate by committing only **2** false rejection errors for **1425** INV words. This result is not being biased to optimize against neither false rejection nor false acceptance. If biasing is necessary it can be easily accomplished by shifting the threshold factor of SVM from zero toward -1 to reduce false rejection or toward +1 to reduce false acceptance.

5. Scoring experiments using the TIMIT corpus and the HTK

In order to show the versatility of the approach taken in the whole word HMM scoring with WUW-SR paradigm the next set of experiments applied a phonetic modeling approach. The experiments rely on the **Texas Instruments and Massachusetts Institute of Technology (TIMIT)** corpus. TIMIT is a standard data set that is designed to provide speech data for acoustic-phonetic studies and for the development and evaluation of ASR systems (John S. Garofolo, 1993). TIMIT contains recordings of 630 speakers in 8 dialects of U.S. English. Each speaker is assigned 10 sentences to read that are carefully designed to contain a wide range of phonetic variability. Each utterance is recorded as a 16-bit waveform file sampled at 16 KHz. The entire data set is split into two portions: *TRAIN* to be used to generate an SR baseline, and *TEST* that should be **unseen** by the experiment until the final evaluation.

5.1 Data selection

TIMIT contains time-aligned transcriptions on both the whole word and phonetic level. Each transcription is hand-verified for proper time-boundary markings.[2] TIMIT also includes a phonetic dictionary containing the transcriptions for all words. The combined, unique word count of each utterance in TIMIT is ~**6220 words**. However, valid training and evaluation can only be performed on individual words that have a reasonable amount of occurrences within the *TEST* portion of the data set.

It is important to note that the selected test set contains the *most common* pronunciation of the word. The difference in phoneme choices for the alternate pronunciation is not considered for the experiments.

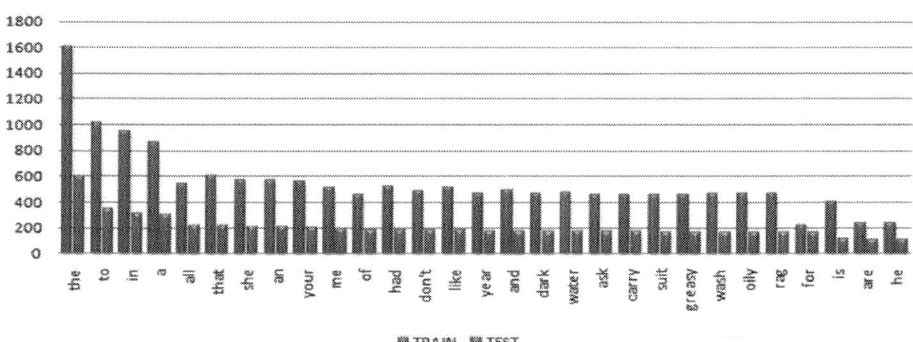

Fig. 26. TIMIT Word Occurrences

5.2 Baseline score

Using the two-score method and a properly trained SVM model, the Total Error Rate is reduced from 2.45% (standard scoring using HTK) to 0.97%; a recognition rate that is **2.55** times better.

The developed single-word recognition system has the following techniques that will be evaluated against the 25-word TIMIT *TEST* subset. Each technique will be assigned a code that will be referred to in the presented results.

1.   (**Score 1**) Standard Acoustic Score Classification (Code: "Score 1")
2.   (**Score 1 + Score 2**) Classification With Two-Class SVM (Code: "CSVM No Dur.")
3.   (**Score 1 + Score 2 + Duration**) Classification With Two-Class SVM (Code: "CSVM")
4.   (**Score 1 + Score 2 + Duration**) Classification With One-Class SVM (Code: "OSVM")

All acoustic scores will be generated using **16-Mixture Monophone HMMs**. The Total Error Rate metric will be the primary criterion of performance for each method described above. The Relative Error Rate Reduction (RERR) and Error Rate Ratio (ERRR) will be calculated and used to compare performance between two methods. They are computed as:

---

[2] While useful, the accuracy of many of the time boundary markings in TIMIT is questionable.

$$\mathrm{RERR} = \frac{B - N}{N} * 100\%; \ \mathrm{ERRR} = \frac{B}{N} \tag{3}$$

where B is the baseline Total Error Rate and N is the new Total Error Rate.

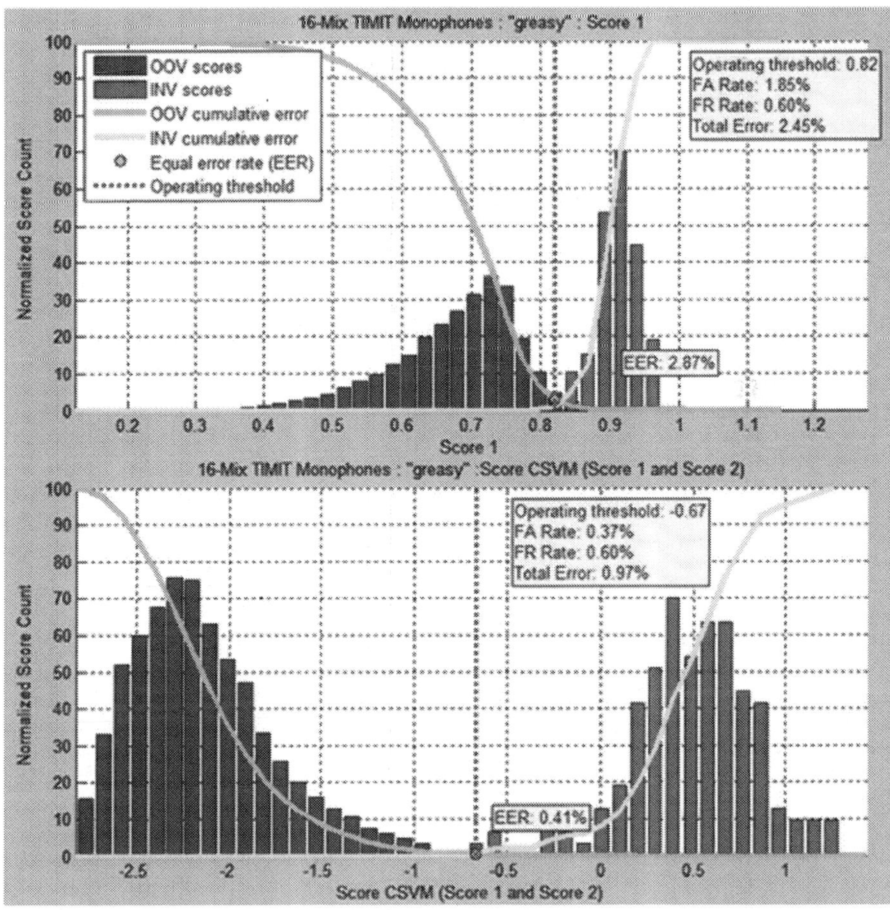

Fig. 27. SVM Classifier Scores for TIMIT word "greasy". Top viewgraph uses standard score (Score 1), the second viewgraph uses Score1 and Score2.

5.3 Summary results

The entire TIMIT test set results are shown in Figure 28 and Figure 29. The word list is sorted by increasing Total Error Rates for the usual, standard "Score 1", classifier and broken into two groups for clarity. The Table 1 and Table 2 summarize the RERR gains for each method. Table 2 also shows the average RERR gain across *all* words considered in the TIMIT test set.

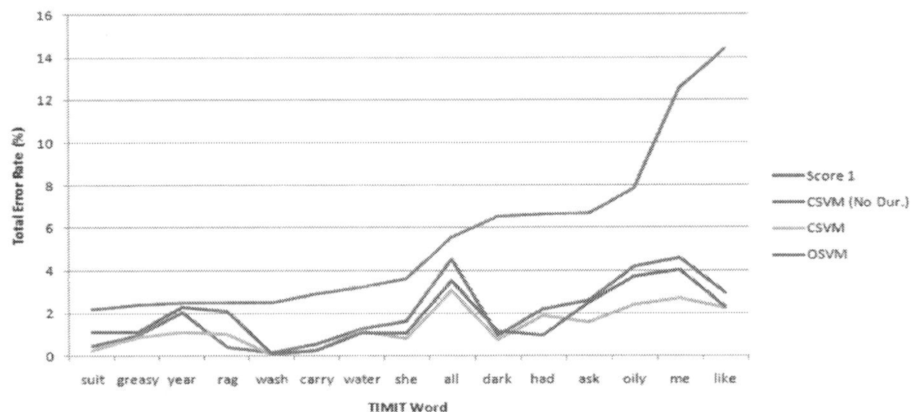

Fig. 28. Error Rates – for TIMIT Test Set (Part 1)

Word	RERR (%) CSVMND	ERRR CSVMND	RERR (%) CSVM	ERRR CSVM	RERR (%) OSVM	ERRR OSVM
suit	391%	4.91	723%	8.23	90%	1.90
greasy	146%	2.46	172%	2.72	117%	2.17
year	23%	1.23	126%	2.26	8%	1.08
rag	518%	6.18	147%	2.47	19%	1.19
wash	1432%	15.32	4303%	44.03	2249%	23.49
carry	407%	5.07	1152%	12.52	1152%	12.52
water	156%	2.56	180%	2.80	197%	2.97
she	124%	2.24	344%	4.44	245%	3.45
all	22%	1.22	82%	1.82	59%	1.59
dark	590%	6.90	737%	8.37	465%	5.65
had	205%	3.05	253%	3.53	575%	6.75
ask	158%	2.58	324%	4.24	169%	2.69
oily	89%	1.89	228%	3.28	111%	2.11
me	175%	2.75	368%	4.68	211%	3.11
Like	389%	4.89	538%	6.38	522%	6.22

Table 1. Summary of RERR Gains for the WUW Recognizer – TIMIT Test Set (Part 1)

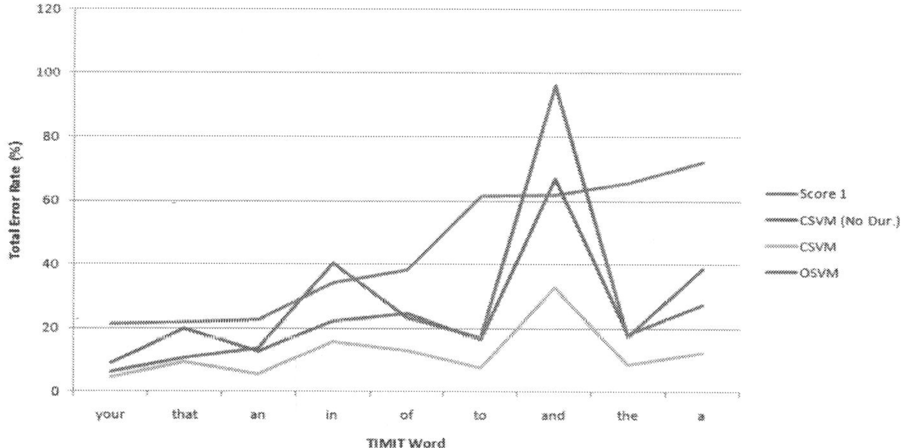

Fig. 29. Error Rates – for TIMIT Test Set (Part 2)

Word	RERR (%) CSVMND	ERRR CSVMND	RERR (%) CSVM	ERRR CSVM	RERR (%) OSVM	ERRR OSVM
your	251%	3.51	360%	4.60	137%	2.37
that	106%	2.06	133%	2.33	10%	1.10
an	64%	1.64	301%	4.01	79%	1.79
in	-15%	0.85	116%	2.16	53%	1.53
of	65%	1.65	198%	2.98	55%	1.55
to	261%	3.61	725%	8.25	278%	3.78
and	-36%	0.64	88%	1.88	-8%	0.92
the	275%	3.75	673%	7.73	258%	3.58
Average	245%	3.45	532%	6.32	301%	4.00

Table 2. Table Summary of RERR Gains for *the WUW* Recognizer – TIMIT Test Set (Part 2)

The final results in Table 6 show an average Relative Error Rate Reduction of **532%** using Two-Class SVM Scoring with the Duration feature. This leads to a word recognition system capable of performing with an overall average Total Error Rate of **5.4%** as compared to the baseline of **20.6%**. The highest gain was found using the TIMIT word "wash": the baseline Total Error Rate was **2.51%** and the Two-Class SVM with Duration Total Error Rate was **0.06%**; a RERR of **4303%**!

The results also shows that One-Class SVM is indeed a viable method for significantly reducing recognizer error, with an average RERR of **301%** which still outperforms Two-

Class SVM without the Duration feature. Note that Once-Class SVM is necessary if the OOV data is not available.

The McNemar test for statistical significance, presented in (Gillick & Cox, 1989), was performed to compare results between the Score 1 recognizer and the Two-Class SVM with Duration recognizer. Two tests were performed to characterize the error rates of correct recognition (INV) and correct rejection (OOV). Across all TIMIT test data, on average, both the INV and OOV showed statistical relevance, with INV P= 4.67E-01 and OOV P = 2.25E-04. In other words, the probability of the null hypothesis (that both methods are statistically the same) for an INV test is on average 47% and for OOV is 0.02%. Note that the test for INV data is skewed due to some difficult short words.

6. Data collection system

The idea of corpus generation from DVDs of movies and TV series is inspired from the study of prosodic analysis of Wake-Up-Word technology (Placeholder1) (Këpuska & Shih, 2010) and (Këpuska, Sastraputera, & Shih, Discrimination of Sentinel Word Contexts using Prosodic Features, Submitted 2010). A need for obtaining natural and inexpensive speech corpora for prosodic analysis and in general study for any speech recognition had inspired the research for the data collection system from DVDs of movies and TV series. The C# .NET Framework application Data Collection Toolkit was developed to facilitate this research.

6.1 Components of data collection system

The data collection system consists of five components. The first step of the data collection system begins from selecting a DVD of a movie or TV series. The audio will then be extracted from the video of the DVD. The text from the subtitles will be converted into text transcriptions. The subtitles will also be used for cutting the extracted audio file into small utterances (audio segmentation). The text transcriptions and utterances are then combined into a basic speech corpus.

There are two optional components in the data collection system that can be used with the corpora generated from the DVDs for more specific tasks. First is the language analysis: this component takes a text from a transcription and finds the relationship of each word. This analysis can be used for the study of Wake-Up-Word's context detection. Another component is the force alignment: which can be used for generating time markers of each individual word in the selected utterance. The force alignment can also be used for filtering and/or trimming utterances to ensure that they match with the corresponding text transcriptions. The Figure 30 shows an overview of the data collection system.

The Data Collection Toolkit provides a tool called TIMIT Corpus Browser, which allows a user to load and view TIMIT corpus in a form that is more organized and easier to view TIMIT's utterances as shown in Figure 31. It also provides options to play an audio of any utterance and its individual words using time markers labeled by TIMIT or SAPI Force Alignment (if available). There is also an option to export the information of the TIMIT corpus into a Comma Separated Value (CSV) file to perform further data analysis such as drawing graphs, histograms, or any other numerical computation using Microsoft Excel spreadsheet.

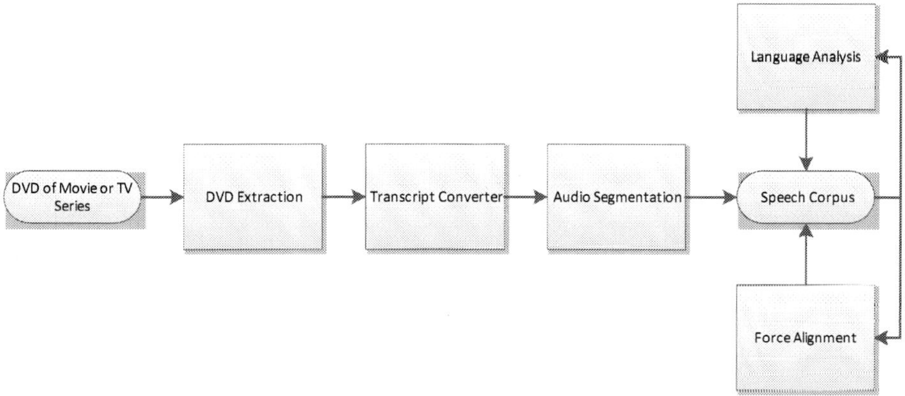

Fig. 30. Overview of Data Collection System

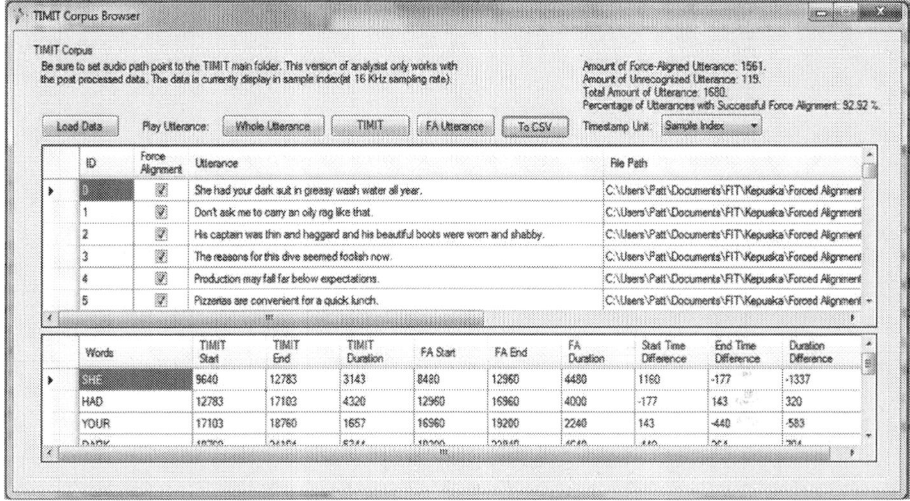

Fig. 31. Screenshot of TIMIT Corpus Browser

6.2 Performance evaluation of the system

To compare the time markers, the TIMIT Corpus Browser tool can export the information into the CSV file. The content of this file is then loaded into Microsoft Excel and used for drawing histograms as shown in Figure 32. Based on these histograms, the most of the frequency difference values of the time markers and word durations are located between -50 to 50 milliseconds and the largest frequency is at 0. Some extreme differences values turned out to be that the time markers of either from TIMIT corpus or SAPI Force Alignment's results have included the silence in them.

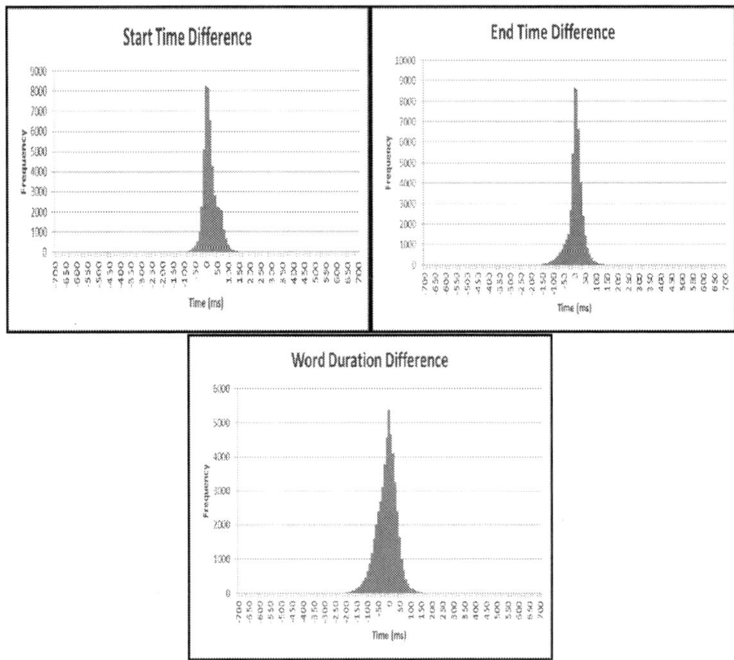

Fig. 32. Start and End Time as well as Word Duration Difference between TIMIT and SAPI Force Alignment

7. Conclusion

The WUW-SR system developed in this work provides for efficient and highly accurate speaker independent recognitions at performance levels not achievable by current state of the art recognizers. Extensive testing demonstrates accuracy improvements superior by several orders of magnitude over the best known academic speech recognition system, HTK, as well as a leading commercial speech recognition system. Specifically, the WUW-SR system correctly detects the WUW with **99.98%** accuracy. It correctly rejects non-WUW with over **99.99%** accuracy. The WUW system makes **12** errors in **151615** words or less than **0.008%**. Assuming speaking rate of **100 words per minute** it would make **0.47** false acceptance errors **per hour**, or **one false acceptance** in **2.1 hours**.

Comparison of WUW performance in detection and recognition performance is **2525%**, or **26** times better than HTK for the same training & testing data, and **2,450%**, or **25** times better than Microsoft SAPI 5.1 recognizer. The out-of-vocabulary rejection performance is over **65,233%**, or **653** times better than HTK, and **5900%** to **42,900%**, or **60** to **430** times better than the Microsoft SAPI 5.1 recognizer.

In order to achieve these levels of accuracy, the following innovations were accomplished:

*   Hidden Markov Model triple scoring with Support Vector Machine classification
*   Combining multiple speech feature streams (MFCC, LPC-smoothed MFCC, and Enhanced MFCC)

- Improved Voice Activity Detector with Support Vector Machines classification

To show that the presented WUW paradigm can be applied to Large Vocabulary Continuous Speech Recognition (LVCSR), the experiments using HTK framework using TIMIT corpus and partial WUW paradigm (e.g., Score1 and Score2) were conducted. The results show superior performance of the recognition compared to the HTK: an average Relative Error Rate Reduction of **532%** using Two-Class SVM Scoring with the Duration feature was obtained.

Finally, the data collection frame work from the DVD's of movies and TV series was described. It provides a good source of data against expensive data collection systems. The system was evaluated against TIMIT's manually labeled time markers that showed no statistical difference. In the future it is planned to apply the developed data collection system for further data collection that will serve for future development of a LVCSR system.

8. References

AoAMedia.Com. (2009). AoA Audio Extractor.

Burges, C. J. (1998). A Tutorial on Support Vector Machines for Pattern Recognition. *Data Mining and Knowledge Discovery*.

Cambridge University Engineering Department. (n.d.). *HTK 3.0*. Retrieved 2007, from http://htk.eng.cam.ac.uk

Carnegie Mellon University. (n.d.). Retrieved April 2007, from The CMU Pronouncing Dictionary: http://www.speech.cs.cmu.edu/cgi-bin/cmudict

Chang, C.-C., & Lin, C.-J. (2001). *LIBSVM : A Library for Support Vector Machines*. Retrieved from http://www.csie.ntu.edu.tw/~cjlin/libsvm

CMU Sphinx. (2010). *CMU Sphinx: Open Source Toolkit for Speech Recognition*. Retrieved 8 13, 2010, from http://cmusphinx.sourceforge.net/

Daniels, G. (Director). (2005). *The Office Season 1* [Motion Picture].

Fan, R.-E., Chen, P.-H., & Lin, C.-J. (2005). Working Set Selection Using Second Order Information for Training Support Vector Machines. *Journal of Machine Learning Research 6*, pp. 1889-1918.

Garofolo, John S., et al. (1993). TIMIT Acoustic-Phonetic Continuous Speech Corpus. Philadelphia, Pennsylvania, USA.

Gillick, L., & Cox, S. (1989). Some Statistical Issues in the Comparison of Speech Recognition Algorithms. *International Conference on Acoustics*. Newton.

Hemming, C., & Lassi, M. (2010). *Copyright and the Web as Corpus*. Retrieved October 27, 2010, from Swedish National Graduate School of Language Technology: http://hemming.se/gslt/copyrightHemmingLassi.pdf

John S. Garofolo, e. a. (1993). *TIMIT Acoustic-Phonetic Continuous Speech Corpus*. Philadelphia: Linguistic Data Consortium.

Juang, B. H., & Rabiner, L. R. (2005). *Automatic Speech Recognition - A Brief History of the Technology Development*. Elsevier Encyclopedia of Language and Linguistics.

Këpuska, V. (2006). Wake-Up-Word Application for First Responder Communication Enhancement. *SPIE*. Orlando, Florida: SPIE.

Këpuska, V. (2009). *Elevator Simulator Screen Perspective*. Retrieved from YouTube: http://www.youtube.com/watch?v=OQ8eyBTbS_E;

Këpuska, V. (2009). *Elevator Simulator User Perspective*. Retrieved from YouTube: http://www.youtube.com/watch?v=j5CeVtQMvK0;

Këpuska, V. Z. (2006, January 3). *Patent No. 6983246*. USA.

Këpuska, V. Z. (2006, April 1). *Patent No. 7085717*. USA.

Këpuska, V. Z., & Klein, T. B. (2009). A novel Wake-Up-Word speech recognition system, Wake-Up-Word recognition task, technology and evaluation. *Nonlinear Analysis: Theory Methods and Applications.*, e2772–e2789.

Këpuska, V., & Shih, C. (2010). Prosodic Analysis of Alerting and Referential context of Sentinel Words. Orlando: AIPR.

Këpuska, V., Carstens, D. S., & Wallace, R. (2006). Leading and Trailing Silence in Wake-Up-Word Speech Recognition. *Industry, Engineering & Management Systems 2006*. Cocoa Beach.

Këpuska, V., Gurbuz, S., Rodriguez, W., Fiore, S., Carstens, D., Converse, P., et al. (2008). uC: Ubiquitous Collaboration Platform for Multimodal Team Interaction Support. *Journal of International Technology and Information Managment*, 264-284.

Klein, T. B. (2007). *Triple Scoring of Hidden Markov Models in Wake-Up-Word Speech Recognition*. Thessis, Florida Institute of Technology, Melbourne.

LDC, University of Pennsylvania. (2009, October 19). *Top Ten Corpora*. Retrieved September 22, 2010, from Linguistic Data Consortium: http://www.ldc.upenn.edu/Catalog/topten.jsp

MSDN. (2010). *Microsoft Speech API 5.3*. Retrieved 8 7, 2010, from MSDN: http://msdn.microsoft.com/en-us/library/ms723627%28VS.85%29.aspx

NCH Software. (2010). Switch Audio File Converter Software.

OpenCog Wiki. (2010). *RelEx Dependency Relationship Extractor*. Retrieved September 13, 2010, from OpenCog Wiki: http://wiki.opencog.org/w/RelEx

Ramdhan, R., & Beharry, X. (2009). Movie Transcript Parser.

Rojanasthien, P. (2010). *Data Collection System for Prosodic Analysis and Acoustic Model Training for Wake-Up-Word Speech Recogntion*. Thessis, Electrical and Computer Engineering, Melbourne.

Rudnicky, A. (2010). *lmtool*. Retrieved Oct 1, 2010, from Sphinx Knowledge Base Tools: http://www.speech.cs.cmu.edu/tools/lmtool.html

Sastraputera, R. (2009). *Discriminating alerting and referential context from prosodic features*. Thessis, Florida Institute of Technology, Melbourne.

Shih, C.T. (2009). *Investigation of Prosodic Features for Wake-Up-Word Speech Recognition Task*. Thessis, Florida Institute of Technology, Melbourne.

Zuggy, T. V. (2009). SubRip 1.20/1.50b: DVD Subtitles Ripper.

13

Syllable Based Speech Recognition

Rıfat Aşlıyan
Adnan Menderes University
Turkey

1. Introduction

Speech recognition is the process of converting speech signals to the text. Studies on speech recognition have increased very fast for the last twenty-five years. Most of these studies have used phoneme and word as speech recognition units. Namely, in phoneme based speech recognition systems, all phonemes in a language have been modelled by a speech recognition method, and then the phonemes can be detected by these models. The recognized words are constructed with concatenating these phonemes. However, word based systems model the word utterances and try to recognize the word as a text unit. Word based systems have better success rate than phoneme based systems. As a rule, if a speech recognition system has longer recognition unit than sub-word units, it has better success rate on recognition process. In addition, phoneme end-point detection is quite difficult operation, and this effects the success of the system.

Turkish, that is one of the least studied languages in the speech recognition field, has different characteristics than European languages which require different language modelling technique. Since Turkish is an agglutinative language, the degree of inflection is very high. So, many words are generated from a Turkish word's root by adding suffixes. That's why, word based speech recognition systems are not adequate for large scaled Turkish speech recognition. Because Turkish is a syllabified language and there are approximately 3500 different Turkish syllables, speech recognition system for Turkish will be suitable to use syllable (sub-word unit) as a speech recognition unit.

Turkish speech recognition studies have increased in the past decade. These studies were based on self organizing feature map (Artuner, 1994), DTW (Meral, 1996; Özkan, 1997), HMM (Arısoy & Dutağacı, 2006; Karaca, 1999; Koç, 2002; Salor & Pellom, 2007; Yılmaz, 1999) and Discrete Wavelet Neural Network (DWNN) and Multi-layer Perceptron (MLP) (Avcı, 2007).

In a simplified way, speech recognizer includes the operations as preprocessing, feature extraction, training, recognition and postprocessing. After the speech recognizer takes the acoustic speech signal as an input, the output of the recognizer will be the recognized text.

The most common approaches to speech recognition can be divided into two classes: "template based approach" and "model based approach". Template based approaches as Dynamic Time Warping (DTW) are the simplest techniques and have the highest accuracy when used properly. The electrical signal from the microphone is digitized by an analog-to-digital converter. The system attempts to match the input with a digitized voice sample, or template. The system contains the input template, and attempts to match this template with the actual input. Model based approaches as Artificial Neural Network (ANN), Hidden Markov Model (HMM) and Support Vector Machine (SVM) tend to extract robust representations of the speech references in a statistical way from huge amounts of speech data. Model based approaches are currently the most popular techniques. However, when the size of the vocabulary is small and the amount of training data is limited, template based approaches are still very attractive.

Speech recognition system can be speaker dependent or speaker independent. A speaker dependent system is developed to operate for a single speaker. These systems are usually more successful. A speaker independent system is developed to operate for any speaker. These systems are the most difficult to develop, most expensive and accuracy is lower than speaker dependent systems.

The size of vocabulary of a speech recognition system affects the complexity, processing requirements and the accuracy of the system. Some applications only require a few words such as only numbers; others require very large dictionaries such as dictation machines. According to vocabulary size, speech recognition systems can be divided into three main categories as small vocabulary recognizers (smaller than 100 words), medium vocabulary recognizers (around 100-1000 words) and large vocabulary recognizers (over 1000 words).

Speech recognition studies started in the late 1940s. Dreyfus-Graf (1952) designed his first "Phonetographe". This system transcribed speech into phonetic "atoms". Davis et al. (1952) designed the first speaker dependent, isolated digit recognizer. This system used a limited number of acoustic parameters based on zero-crossing counting. In Bell Laboratories, a word recognizer is designed with a phonetic decoding approach using phonetic units (Dudley & Balashek, 1958). Jakobson et al. (1952) developed the speaker independent recognition of vowels. At RCA laboratories, phonetic approach was used in the first "phonetic typewriter" which recognizes syllables by a single speaker (Olson & Belar, 1956).

The first experiments on computer based speech recognition were started in the late 1950s. The studies as speaker independent recognition of ten vowels (Forgie & Forgie, 1959), phoneme identification (Sakai & Doshita, 1962), and digit recognition (Nagata et al., 1963) have been made at this period.

Dynamic time warping using dynamic programming was proposed by Russian researchers (Slutsker, 1968; Vintsyuk, 1968). Reddy (1966) developed continuous speech recognition by dynamic tracking of phonemes.

Several systems such as HARPY (Lowerre, 1976), HEARSAY II (Lesser et al., 1975), HWIM (Wolf & Woods, 1977), MYRTILLE I (Haton & Pierrel, 1976) and KEAL (Mercier, 1977) have been implemented in 1970s.

Statistical modelling methods as Hidden Markov Models (HMM) (Ferguson, 1980; Rabiner, 1989) were used in 1980s. Neural networks as perceptron were proposed in 1950s. In 1980s, neural network approaches were presented again (Lippmann, 1987).

Support Vector Machine (SVM) was presented as a novel method for solving pattern recognition problems (Blanz et al., 1996; Cortes & Vapnik, 1995; Osuna et al., 1997). SVM has been successfully used for implementation speech recognition systems in 1990s and 2000s.

This chapter is organized as follows. In the next section, system databases, preprocessing operation, word and syllable end-point detection, feature extraction, dynamic time warping, artificial neural network and postprocessing operation have been explained. In Section 3, how to detect misspelled words using syllable n-gram frequencies is presented in detail. The experimental results of the developed systems have been given in Section 4. The final section concludes the chapter.

2. Implementation of syllable based speech recognition

In this study, speaker dependent isolated word speech recognition systems using DTW and ANN have been designed and implemented, and the speech signal features as mfcc, lpc, parcor, cepstrum, rasta and the mixture of mfcc, lpc and parcor have been used for the speech recognition approaches.

The speech recognition applications have been executed on the computer which has the following features: Pentium Centrino 1.6 CPU, 768 MB RAM, 40 GB harddisk, Windows XP Operating System, a sound card and a microphone. The codes of the applications have been written with Matlab 6.5.

2.1 System databases

System dictionary consists of 200 different Turkish words (Aşlıyan, 2010). Using this dictionary, two databases have been constructed (Aşlıyan, 2010). One database has been used for training and the other is for testing of the system.

The training speech database (approximately 2.7 hours of 250 MB speech material) involves 5000 Turkish word utterances (25x200) which were recorded by a male speaker. Each word in the dictionary was recorded 25 times.

The testing speech database was constructed by recording every word 10 times in the dictionary. Total number of utterances is 2000 (about 1.1 hours of 100 MB speech material).

The recording procedure took place in a noise-free environment. A head-mounted close-talking microphone was used. The format of the file recording is WAVE file format. The waveforms of the utterances are encoded using Pulse Code Modulation (PCM) coding format, 11025 Hz sampling rate, 2 bytes per sample. The utterances are recorded in 2 seconds time duration.

2.2 Preprocessing operation

After the digitization of the word speech signal, preemphasis filter has been applied to spectrally flatten the signal. For the speech signal the syllable end-point detection is applied. After that each syllable utterance is divided into frames of 20 ms by frameblocking. To reduce the signal discontinuity at the ends of each block, Hamming window is applied for each frame.

2.3 Word and syllable end-point detection

An important problem in speech processing is to detect the presence of speech in a background of noise. This problem is often referred to as the end-point location problem (Rabiner & Sambur, 1975). The accurate detection of a word's start and end-points means that subsequent processing of the data can be kept to a minimum.

A major cause of errors in isolated-word automatic speech recognition systems is the inaccurate detection of the beginning and ending boundaries of test and reference patterns (Junqua et al., 1997). It is essential for automatic speech recognition algorithms that speech segments are reliably separated from non-speech.

The reason for requiring an effective end-point algorithm is that the computation for processing the speech is minimum when the end-points are accurately located (Savoji, 1989). In syllable end-point detection operation, the speech signals are taken and after processing them, the number of syllables and the indexes of syllable end-points have been detected. Namely, the beginning and end indexes are computed on the digital speech signal.

After sampling the sound wav files, the mean of the speech signal as a vector is calculated and translated to $y = 0$ axis. Assume that y_n is a speech signal. The new speech signal, which is focused on $y = 0$ axis, is $y'_n = y_n - mean(y_n)$. After that, the voiced and unvoiced parts of the speech signal are approximately computed with the slope between the beginning value of the digital sound and the maximum value of the sound. This slope is the threshold slope. The utterance is divided into windows which have 350 samples. If the slope, which is calculated between two windows, which are one after the other, is greater than the threshold slope, this means that the voiced part of the sound begins at the index. However, these beginning and end index of the voiced part are nearly true, but not certain value. The distance data of zero-crossing index of sound vector has been used because of obtaining more accurate results. A new vector which represents the zero-crossing distances, has been constructed, then a threshold has been defined (say zero-crossing threshold=100). The beginning index is found earlier but not certainly true index. Now this index goes on one by one to the first index if the zero-crossing distance is between 1 and zero-crossing threshold. Zero values of the vector are not taken into account. In the same way, the end index of the voiced part is calculated. At the end, the voiced part is found exactly.

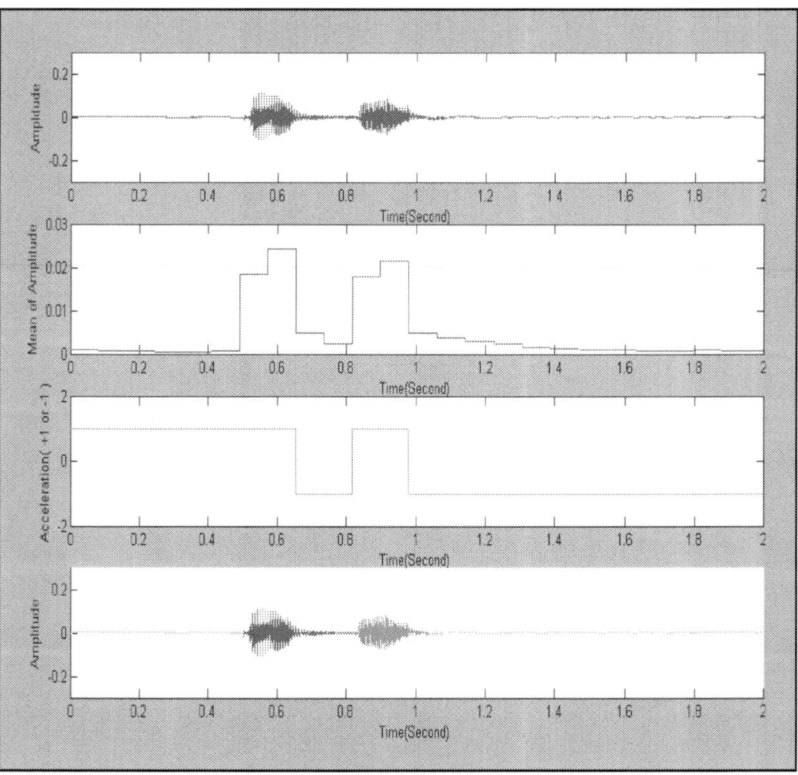

Fig. 1. The process of syllable endpoint detection

To discover syllable end-points, the windows that consist of 900 samples are generated without overlapping. The mean values of these windows are computed and assembled for constructing a new mean vector as shown in Figure 1. The slope between one element and the next element of the mean vector is determined, and if the slope is zero or greater than zero, a new vector's value is +1. Otherwise, the value is -1. Using these vectors, the boundaries of syllables on the sound vector are obtained approximately. The samples between 500 samples backward and 500 samples forward from the found syllable end-points are divided into windows which include 20 samples. After that, the middle index of the window which has the minimum mean is syllable end-point. Finally, the beginning and end index of the syllables can be calculated for each word before processing them. Now we have the number of syllables of the word and their end-point indexes.

According to the number of syllables in a word using syllable end-point detection algorithm which is mentioned in Subsection 2.3.2, it is found that the accuracy result is approximately 99%. For example, the word which has five syllables is successfully divided into five syllables and the end-points of the syllables are detected.

2.3.1 Word end-point detection algorithm

Step 1. x in Equation 1 is digital sound vector. $N = 22050$ (N is the number of samples in the utterance)

$$x = (x_1, x_2, x_3 ..., x_N) \tag{1}$$

Step 2. λ is the mean of the values of first 200 samples in x. $\tilde{x}$ is a vector which translated to the axis $y = 0$.

$$\lambda = (\sum_{i=1}^{200} x_i) / 200 \tag{2}$$

$$\tilde{x} = x - \lambda = (x_1 - \lambda, ..., x_N - \lambda) = (\tilde{x}_1, \tilde{x}_2, ..., \tilde{x}_N) \tag{3}$$

Step 3. M is the maximum value of the vector $\tilde{x}$. I is the index of maximum value of the vector $\tilde{x}$. E_b and E_s are the beginning and end threshold values respectively.

$$[M, I] = \max(\tilde{x}) \tag{4}$$

$$E_b = M / I \quad E_s = M / (N - I) \tag{5}$$

Step 4.   The vector $\tilde{x}$ is divided into windows which consist of 350 samples. The vector $\overline{x}$ is the mean vector of above windows.

$$\overline{x} = (\overline{x}_1, \overline{x}_2, ..., \overline{x}_p) \text{ and } p = N / 350 \tag{6}$$

$$\overline{x}_i = \left(\sum_{k=i*350}^{(i+1)*350-1} \tilde{x}_k \right) / 350 \ , i = 1, 2, ..., p \tag{7}$$

Step 5. For $i = 1, 2, ..., p-1$, $\bar{x}_E$ and $\bar{x}_{E_i}$ are calculated as shown in Equation 8.

$$\bar{x}_E = (\bar{x}_{E_1}, \bar{x}_{E_2}, ..., \bar{x}_{E_{p-1}}) \text{ and } \bar{x}_{E_i} = \bar{x}_{i+1} / \bar{x}_i \tag{8}$$

Step 6. S_b is the beginning index of the sound vector.

For $r = 1$ to $p-1$

   if $\bar{x}_{E_r} > E_b$ then $S_b = r * 350$

End

Step 7. S_s is the end index of the sound vector.

For $r = x_{E_{p-1}}$ DownTo 1

   if $1 / \bar{x}_{E_r} > E_s$ then $S_s = r * 350$

End

Step 8. The beginning and end indexes are approximately determined from Step 6 and 7. To decide exactly the end-points of the sound, the zero-crossing indexes are fixed. Using the sound vector $\tilde{x} = (\tilde{x}_1, \tilde{x}_2, ..., \tilde{x}_N)$, the zero-crossing vector $z = (z_1, z_2, ..., z_{N-1})$ is generated.

For $k = 2$ To N

  if $\tilde{x}_{k-1} / \tilde{x}_k < 0$ then

$$z_{k-1} = 1$$

  else

$$z_{k-1} = 0$$

End

Step 9. After the distances between one after the other zero-crossing indexes are computed, new distance vector of zero-crossing $\tilde{z}_k = (\tilde{z}_1, \tilde{z}_2, ..., \tilde{z}_{N-1})$ is calculated as the followings.

For $k = 1$ To $N-1$

if $z_k = 1$ and after the index k, its first value of the following indexes is 1,

$(z_h = 1)$ then

$\tilde{z}_k = h - k$

else

$\tilde{z}_k = 0$

if $z_k = 0$ then $\tilde{z}_k = 0$

End

Step 10. The threshold value of zero-crossing is accepted as $T = 100$. SB is the value at the index which the sound begins.

$SB = S_b$

For $k = S_b$ DownTo 1

if $\tilde{z}_k > 0$ and $\tilde{z}_k < T$ then $SB = k$

if $\tilde{z}_k = 0$ then continue

if $\tilde{z}_k > T$ then break

End

Step 11. SS is the value at the index which the sound ends.

$SS = S_s$

For $k = S_s$ To $N - 1$

if $\tilde{z}_k > 0$ and $\tilde{z}_k < T$ then $SS = k$

if $\tilde{z}_k = 0$ then continue

if $\tilde{z}_k > T$ then break

End

2.3.2 Syllable end-point detection of the word utterances

After detecting the end-points (SB and SS) of the words, the end-points of the syllables in the words are determined with the following algorithm.

Step 1. $n = (n_1, n_2, ..., n_k) = (\tilde{x}_{SB}, \tilde{x}_{SB+1}, ..., \tilde{x}_{SS})$

Step 2. The vector n is divided into windows, which have 900 samples, without overlapping. The vector $\bar{n}$ is the mean vector of each window above.

$\bar{n} = (\bar{n}_1, \bar{n}_2, ..., \bar{n}_p)$ and $p = k / 900$

$$\bar{n}_i = \left(\sum_{m=i*900}^{(i+1)*900-1} n_m \right) / 900 , i = 1, 2, ... p \tag{9}$$

Step 3. The slope vector is composed by computing the slopes between the values of the vector $\bar{n}$ which follow one after another.

$$\bar{n}_E = (\bar{n}_{E_1}, \bar{n}_{E_2}, ..., \bar{n}_{E_{p-1}}) \text{ and } \bar{n}_{E_i} = \bar{n}_{i+1} / \bar{n}_i , i = 1, 2, ..., p - 1 \tag{10}$$

Step 4. Using the slope vector, we calculate the vector $a = (a_1, a_2, ..., a_{p-1})$ which has the values, +1 and -1. Namely, the increasing and decreasing positions are determined.

For $k = 1$ To $p - 1$

if $n_{E_k} \geq 0$ then $a_k = 1$

else $a_k = -1$

End

Step 5. H is the number of syllables in the word.

$H = 0$

For $k = 2$ To $p - 1$

if $a_{k-1} = 1$ and $a_k = -1$ then $H = H + 1$

End

Step 6. The values of the middle indexes, which include the value -1 in the vector a, are approximately the end-points of syllables. There are $H - 1$ syllable end-points. The syllable end-point vector $s = (s_1, s_2, ..., s_{H-1})$ is calculated as shown in the following. The values s_i are the indexes which are the values of the vector $\tilde{x}$.

For $k = 1$ To $H - 1$

if the middle index of the indexes, which have the k-th value -1 that follows one after the other, is w then

$$s_k = SB + 900 * w$$

End

Step 7. Until now, the beginning point SB and end point SS is detected. The vector s represents the end-points of syllables. To find the syllable end-points more accurately the following algorithm is performed, and the vector $\tilde{s} = (\tilde{s}_1, \tilde{s}_2, ..., \tilde{s}_{H+1})$ is attained.

$$\tilde{s}_1 = SB \text{ and } \tilde{s}_{H+1} = SS$$

For $i = 1$ To $H - 1$

The windows with 20 samples between $s_i - 500$ and $s_i + 500$ are constructed, and the mean values are computed for each windows.

if the middle index of the window, which has the smallest mean, is q

then

$$\tilde{s}_{i+1} = q$$

End

Step 8. The vector $\tilde{s}$ which represents the syllables end-points in the word sound vector $\tilde{x}$ is decided accurately. There are H syllables in the word. The beginning index of k-th syllable is $\tilde{s}_k$ and the end index is $\tilde{s}_{k+1}$.

2.4 Feature extraction

After preprocessing the speech signal, we have the syllable end-points of the word. The syllable utterances are framed with Hamming window. The length of one frame is 20 ms with 10 ms shift (overlapping time=10 ms). 10 features are computed from each frame. These features are lpc, parcor, cepstrum, mfcc and rasta. The number of frames is not constant, but the number of frames is normalized to 30 frames with the length of 10 as shown in Figure 2. The normalized features are used only for the speech recognition method as ANN. $s(n)$ is the syllable feature vector. $x(10, m)$ is the syllable feature matrix. For normalized features, m is 30 as illustrated in Figure 2. In Figure 3, the time duration for each speech feature is shown, and the fastest speech feature extraction algorithm among these features is mfcc.

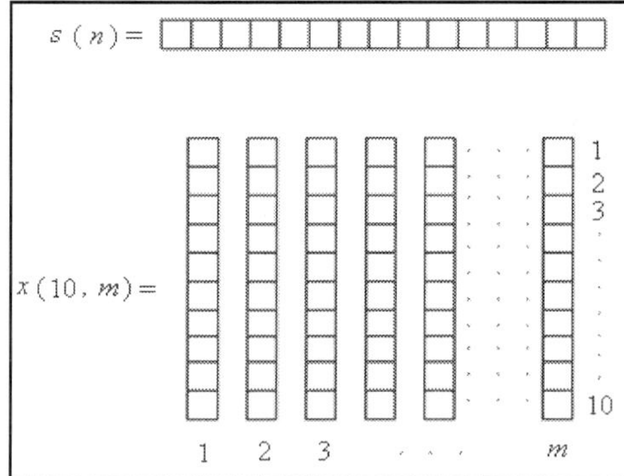

Fig. 2. Feature extraction

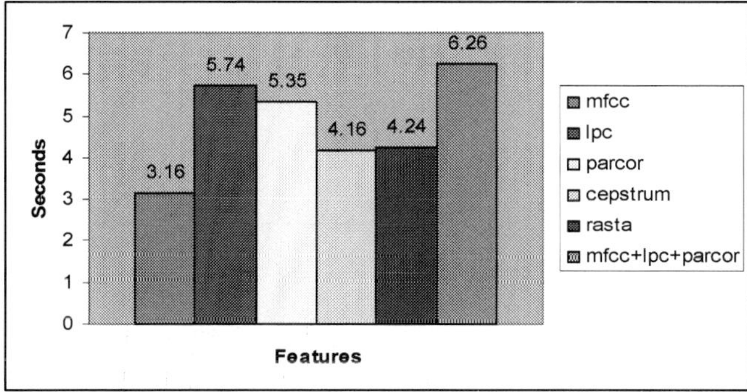

Fig. 3. Feature extraction time duration

2.5 Dynamic Time Warping

Dynamic Time Warping (DTW) (Fornés et al., 2010; Myers et al., 1980 ; Sankoff & Kruskal, 1999) is a template-based classification technique which has the principle of matching a input speech signal converted into a feature matrix against reference templates. The templates are simply feature matrix examples of each syllable of a word or syllable in the vocabulary of the system. Consequently, DTW is normally used for recognition of isolated words or syllables. The similarity between a template and the unknown speech feature matrix is assumed to be inversely proportional to the minimum cost alignment. This is normally evaluated by calculating a local distance between each input features and all feature matrices of the reference template. Calculating the minimum cost alignment is then a matter of finding the optimal path from the bottom left-hand to the top right-hand corner of the matrix. Namely, the path that accumulates the lowest sum of local distances and does not stray too far away from the diagonal.

If we define two time series $S = s_1, s_2, ..., s_n$ and $T = t_1, t_2, ..., t_m$, then DTWCost(S, T) calculates the distance between these two time series (S and T). Using dynamic programming DTW[i, j] is computed as DTW[i, j] = C + Minimum(DTW[i-1, j], DTW[i, j-1], DTW[i-1, j-1]) where C= Distance(s_i, t_j). As shown in the following, the warping path is found by detecting the minimum cost index pairs (i, j) form (0, 0) to (n, m).

2.5.1 Dynamic Time Warping algorithm

The following algorithm takes two speech feature matrices (inputs) to calculate the distance of them. The output of this algorithm is the distance of these two features. These two matrices consist of n and m frames respectively. Each frame has been assumed to get ten speech features. ∞ stands for infinity.

DTW_Cost (S[1..10, 1..n], T[1..10, 1..m])

   DTW[0..n, 0..m] as a matrix variable

   $i, j, Cost$ as integer variables

   For i=1 To m

      DTW[0, i] = ∞

   end

   For i=1 To n

```
    DTW[i, 0] = ∞
end
DTW[0, 0] = 0
For i=1 To n
   For j=1 To m
      Cost = Calculate Distance(S[1..10, i], T[1..10, j])
      DTW[i, j] = Cost + Find Minimum(DTW[i-1, j], DTW[i, j-1], DTW[i-1, j-1])
   end
end
Return DTW[n, m]
```

2.6 Artificial neural networks

A Neural Network (NN) is a computer software that simulates a simple model of neural cells in humans. The purpose of this simulation is to acquire the intelligent features of these cells.

Backpropagation networks are a popular type of network that can be trained to recognize different patterns including images, signal, and text. Backpropagation networks have been used for this speech recognition system.

2.6.1 Sigmoid function

The function as Equation 11 is called a Sigmoid function. The coefficient a is a real number constant. In NN applications, a is usually chosen between 0.5 and 2. As a starting point, we can use $a=1$ and modify it later when we are fine-tuning the network. Note that $s(0) = 0.5$, $s(\infty) = 1$, $s(-\infty) = 0$ (The symbol ∞ means infinity).

$$s(x) = \frac{1}{(1 + e - ax)} \tag{11}$$

The Sigmoid function will convert values less than 0.5 to 0, and values greater than 0.5 to 1. The Sigmoid function is used on the output of neurons.

In NNs, a neuron is a model of a neural cell in humans. This model is simplistic, but as it turned out, is very practical. The neuron has been thought as a program or a class that has one or more inputs and produces one output. The inputs simulate the signals that a neuron gets, while the output simulates the signal which the neuron generates. The output is calculated by multiplying each input by a different number which is called weight, adding them all together, then scaling the total to a number between 0 and 1.

Figure 4 shows a simple neuron with:

a. Three hundred inputs $[x_1, x_2, x_3, ..., x_{300}]$. The input values are usually scaled to values between 0 and 1.

b. 300 input weights $[w_1, w_2, w_3, ..., w_{300}]$. The weights are real numbers that usually are initialized to some random numbers. The weights are variables of type real. We can initialize to a random number between 0 and 1.

c. One output z. A neuron has only one output. Its value is between 0 and 1, it can be scaled to the full range of actual values.

$$d = (x_1 * w_1) + (x_2 * w_2) + (x_3 * w_3) + ... + (x_{300} * w_{300}) \tag{12}$$

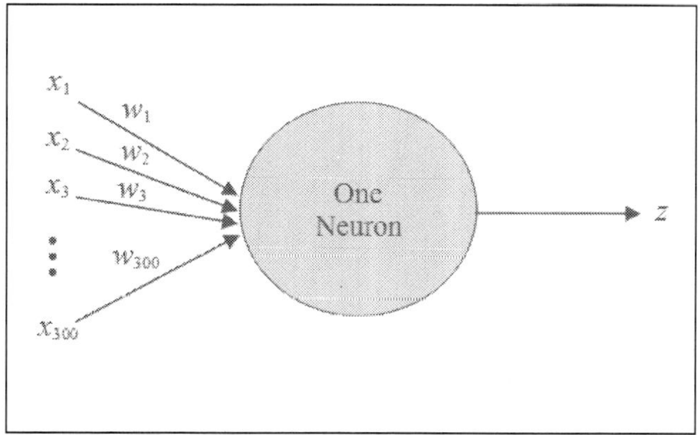

Fig. 4. One neuron structure

In a more general manner, for n number of inputs, d is defined as Equation 13.

$$d = \sum_{i=1}^{n} x_i * w_i \tag{13}$$

Let θ be a real number which is known as a threshold. Experiments have shown that best values for θ are between 0.25 and 1. θ is just a variable of type real that is initialized to any number between 0.25 and 1.

$$z = s(d + \theta) \tag{14}$$

In Equation 14, the output z is the result of applying the sigmoid function on $(d + \theta)$. In NN applications, the challenge is to find the right values for the weights and the threshold.

2.6.2 Backpropagation

The structure of the system is shown in Figure 5. This NN consists of four layers: Input layer with 300 neurons, first hidden layer with 30 neurons, second hidden layer with 10 neurons and output layer with one neuron.

The output of a neuron in a layer goes to all neurons in the following layer. Each neuron has its own input weights. The weights for the input layer are assumed to be 1 for each input. In other words, input values are not changed. The output of the NN is reached by applying input values to the input layer, passing the output of each neuron to the following layer as input. The Backpropagation NN must have at least an input layer and an output layer. It could have zero or more hidden layers.

The number of neurons in the input layer depends on the number of possible inputs while the number of neurons in the output layer depends on the number of desired outputs. In general, the addition of a hidden layer could allow the network to learn more complex patterns, but at the same time decreases its performance.

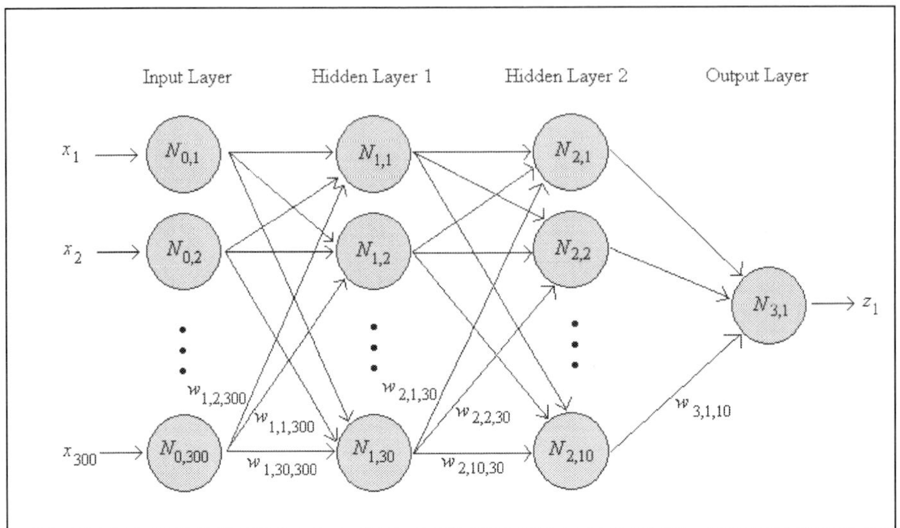

Fig. 5. Backpropagation network of the system

2.6.3 Supervised learning

The Backpropagation NN works supervised training. The training can be summarized as the following algorithm.

Step 1. Start by initializing the input weights for all neurons to some random numbers between 0 and 1.

Step 2. Apply input to the network.

Step 3. Calculate the output.

Step 4. Compare the resulting output with the desired output for the given input. This is called the error.

Step 5. Modify the weights and threshold θ for all neurons using the error.

Step 6. Repeat the process until the error reaches an acceptable value (the error, 0.006), which means that the NN was trained successfully, or if we reach a maximum count of iterations, which means that the NN training was not successful.

The challenge is to find a good algorithm for updating the weights and thresholds in each iteration (Step 5) to minimize the error.

Changing weights and threshold for neurons in the output layer is different from hidden layers. For the input layer, weights remain constant at 1 for each input neuron weight.

For the training operation, the followings are defined.

The Learning Rate, λ : A real number constant, 0.02 for the system.

The change, Δ : For example Δx is the change in x.

2.6.3.1 Output layer training

Let z be the output of an output layer neuron. Let y be the desired output for the same neuron, it should be scaled to a value between 0 and 1. This is the ideal output which we like to get when applying a given set of input. Then the error, e, will be as Equation 15.

$$e = z * (1 - z) * (y - z) \tag{15}$$

$$\Delta\theta = \lambda * e \tag{16}$$

$$\Delta w_i = \Delta\theta * x_i \tag{17}$$

$\Delta\theta$ represents the change in θ. Δw_i is the change in weight i of the neuron. In other words, for each output neuron, calculate its error e, and then modify its threshold and weights using Equation 15, 16 and 17.

2.6.3.2 Hidden layer training

Consider a hidden layer neuron as shown in Figure 6. Let z be the output of the hidden layer neuron. Let m_i be the weight at neuron N_i in the layer following the current layer. This is the weight for the input coming from the current hidden layer neuron. Let e_i be the error e at neuron N_i. Let r be the number of neurons in the layer following the current layer. (In Figure 6, $r = 3$).

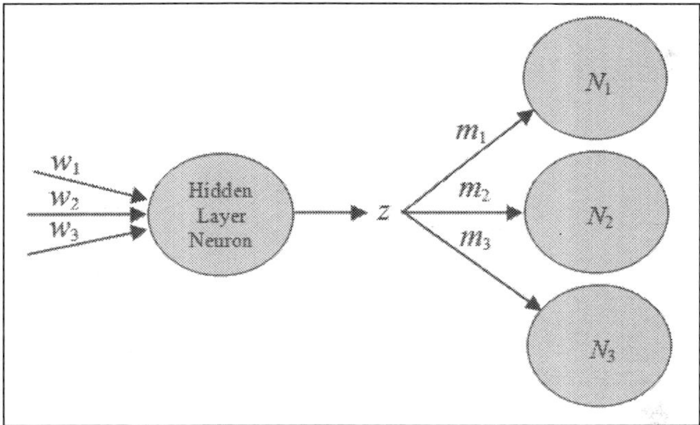

Fig. 6. Hidden layer training

$$g = \sum_{i=1}^{r} m_i * e_i \tag{18}$$

$$e = z * (1 - z) * g \tag{19}$$

$$\Delta\theta = \lambda * e \tag{20}$$

$$\Delta w_i = \Delta\theta * x_i \tag{21}$$

e is the error at the hidden layer neuron. $\Delta\theta$ is the change in θ. Δw_i is the change in weight i. In calculating g, we use the weight m_i and error e_i from the following layer, which means that the error and weights in this following layer should have already been calculated. This implies that during a training iteration of a Backpropagation NN, we start modifying the weights at the output layer, and then we proceed backwards on the hidden layers one by one until we reach the input layer. It is the method of proceeding backwards which gives this network its name Backward Propagation.

2.7 The postprocessing of the system

After the syllables of the word utterance are recognized using the speech recognition method, and the most similar 10 syllables are put in order, the recognized syllables are concatenated and generated the recognized word. We can find the most similar words in order by concatenation of the most similar syllables. From the uppermost recognized words, it can be determined whether or not the word is Turkish. If the word is Turkish, it is the recognized word of the system. If these words are not Turkish, the system does not recognize any word.

For example, as shown in Table 1, the recognized syllables are ordered. Hence, the most similar syllables as "kı", "tap" and "lik" have been found. These syllables are concatenated, and the most similar word as "kıtaplik" is constructed. But, the system decides that the word is not Turkish word. Then, the next most similar word is concatenated, and it is determined whether or not the word is Turkish. This process is continued until a Turkish word is found in these concatenated words. In this example, the word "kitaplık" which is generated from the syllables "ki", "tap" and "lık" is detected by the system. Therefore, it is the recognized word using the postprocessing.

The order of the most similar syllables	Recognized Syllables		
	"ki"	"tap"	"lık"
1.	kı	tap	lik
2.	ki	tap	lak
3.	ki	tep	lık
4.	ki	ta	lik
5.	kı	ta	lık

Table 1. The most similar syllables

3. Detecting misspelled words using syllable n-gram frequencies

To detect misspelled words in a text is an old problem. Today, most of word processors include some sort of misspelled word detection. Misspelled word detection is worthy in the area of cryptology, data compression, speech synthesis, speech recognition and optical character recognition (Barari & QasemiZadeh, 2005; Deorowicz & Ciura, 2005; Kang & Woo, 2001; Tong & Evans, 1996). The traditional way of detecting misspelled words is to use a word list, usually also containing some grammatical information, and to look up every word in the word list (Kukich, 1992) from dictionary.

The main disadvantage of this approach is that if the dictionary is not large enough, the algorithm will report some of correct words as misspelled, because they are not included in the dictionary. For most natural languages, the size of dictionary needed is too large to fit in the working memory of an ordinary computer. In Turkish this is a big problem, because Turkish is an agglutinative language and too many new words can be constructed by adding suffixes.

To overcome this difficulties, a new approach has been proposed for detecting misspelled words in Turkish text. For that, Turkish syllable *n*-gram frequencies which are generated from several Turkish corpora have been used. From the corpora, syllable monogram, bigram and trigram frequencies have been extracted using TASA (Aşlıyan & Günel, 2005). These *n*-gram frequencies have been used for calculating a word probability distribution. After that the system has decided whether a word is misspelled or not. This approach does not need any word list.

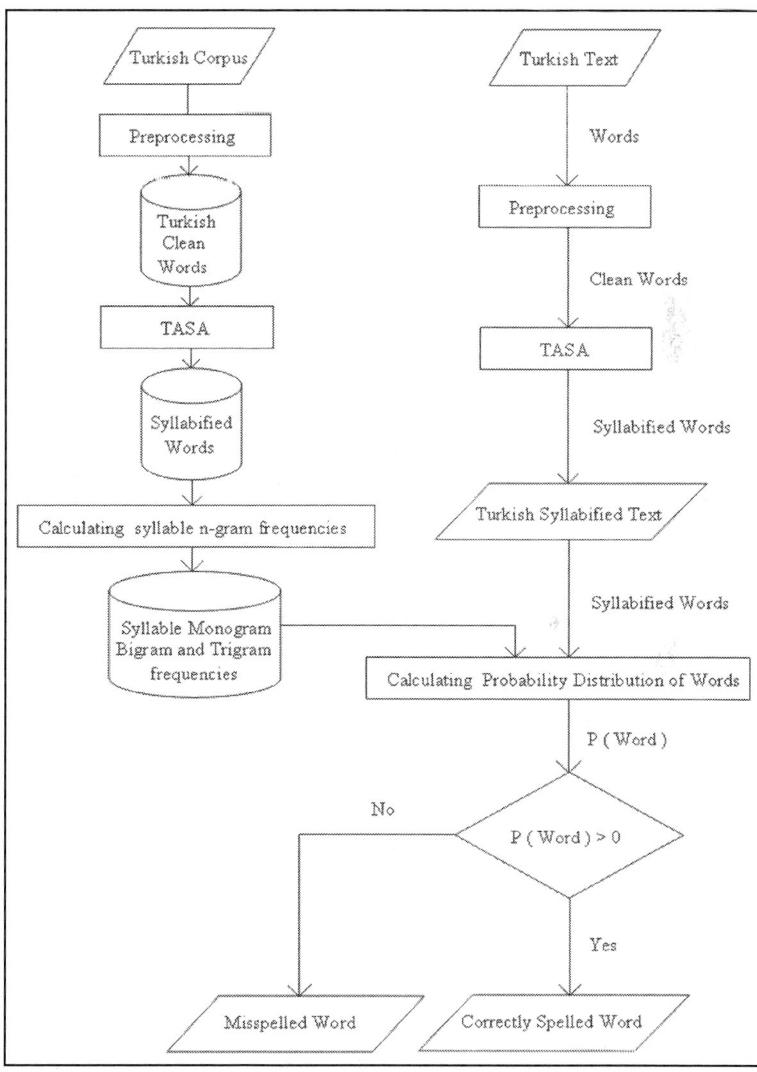

Fig. 7. The system architecture

3.1 System architecture

The system consists of three main components. First component is preprocessing which cleans a text. Second component is TASA, and third component is calculating probability distribution of words. As shown in Figure 7, the system takes words in Turkish text as input and gives the result for each word as "Misspelled Word" or "Correctly Spelled Word".

In preprocessing component of the system, punctuation marks are cleaned. All letters in the text are converted to lower case. Blank characters between two successive words are limited with only one blank character.

In second component, TASA takes the Turkish clean text as an input and gives the Turkish syllabified text. The system divides words into syllables putting the dash character between two syllables. For example, the word "kitaplık" in Turkish text is converted into the syllabified word "ki-tap-lık" in Turkish syllabified text.

In third component, the probability distribution is calculated for each syllabified word. The system uses syllable monogram, bigram and trigram frequencies to find this probability distribution.

3.2 Calculation of the probability distribution of words

An n-gram is a sub-sequence of n items from a given sequence. n-grams are used in various areas of statistical natural language processing and genetic sequence analysis. The items in question can be letters, syllables, words according to the application.

An n-gram of size 1 is a "monogram"; size 2 is a "bigram"; size 3 is a "trigram"; and size 4 or more is simply called an "n-gram" or "$(n-1)$-order Markov model" (Zhuang et al., 2004).

An n-gram model predicts x_i based on $x_{i-1}, x_{i-2}, x_{i-3}, ..., x_{i-n}$. When used for language modelling independence assumptions are made so that each word depends only on the last n words. This Markov model is used as an approximation of the true underlying language. This assumption is important because it massively simplifies the problem of learning the language model from data.

Suppose that a word W in Turkish syllabified text consists of the syllable sequence $s_1, s_2, s_3, ..., s_t$. This word has t syllables. To obtain the n-gram probability distribution (Jurafsky & Martin, 2000) of the word W, we have used in Equation 22.

$$P(W) = P(s_1, s_2, ..., s_t) = \prod_{i=1}^{t} P(s_i \mid s_{i-n+1}, s_{i-n+2}, ..., s_{i-1}) \tag{22}$$

In n-gram model, the parameter $P(s_i \mid s_{i-n+1}, s_{i-n+2}, ..., s_{i-1})$ in Equation 22 can be estimated with Maximum Likelihood Estimation (MLE) (Aşlıyan & Günel, 2005) technique as shown in Equation 23.

$$P(s_i \mid s_{i-n+1}, s_{i-n+2}, ..., s_{i-1}) = \frac{C(s_{i-n+1}, s_{i-n+2}, ..., s_{i-1}, s_i)}{C(s_{i-n+1}, s_{i-n+2}, ..., s_{i-1})} \tag{23}$$

So, it is concluded as Equation 24.

$$P(W) = P(s_1, s_2, ..., s_t) = \prod_{i=1}^{t} \frac{C(s_{i-n+1}, s_{i-n+2}, ..., s_{i-1}, s_i)}{C(s_{i-n+1}, s_{i-n+2}, ..., s_{i-1})} \tag{24}$$

In Equation 23 and Equation 24, $C(s_{i-n+1}, s_{i-n+2}, ..., s_{i-1}, s_i)$ is the frequency of the syllable sequence $s_{i-n+1}, s_{i-n+2}, ..., s_{i-1}, s_i$. Furthermore, $C(s_{i-n+1}, s_{i-n+2}, ..., s_{i-1})$ is the frequency of the syllable sequence $s_{i-n+1}, s_{i-n+2}, ..., s_{i-1}$. The frequencies of these syllable sequences can be calculated from some Turkish corpora.

For bigram and trigram models, probability distribution $P(W)$ can be computed as shown in Equation 25 and Equation 26 respectively.

$$P(W) = P(s_1, s_2, ..., s_t) = \prod_{i=1}^{t} P(s_i \mid s_{i-1}) = \prod_{i=1}^{t} \frac{C(s_{i-1}, s_i)}{C(s_{i-1})} \tag{25}$$

$$P(W) = P(s_1, s_2, ..., s_t) = \prod_{i=1}^{t} P(s_i \mid s_{i-2}, s_{i-1}) = \prod_{i=1}^{t} \frac{C(s_{i-2}, s_{i-1}, s_i)}{C(s_{i-2}, s_{i-1})} \tag{26}$$

For example, according to bigram model it can be calculated the probability distribution of a word in Turkish text. Assume that we have a text which includes some words as "... Bu gün okulda, şenlik var...". This text is converted to syllabified text as "... Bu gün o-kul-da, şen-lik var...". Syllables in the words are delimited with dash character. Assume that the word W="okulda" in the text is taken for computing its probability distribution and W can be written as the syllable sequence $W = s_1, s_2, s_3$ = "o", "kul", "da". Here, s_1 = "o", s_2 = "kul", s_3 = "da". Blank character is accepted as a syllable. This syllable is called as λ. So, assume that syllable monogram frequencies are $C("\lambda")$=0.003, $C("o")$=0.002, $C("kul")$=0.004 and syllable bigram frequencies are $C("\lambda", "o")$=0.0001, $C("o", "kul")$=0.0002, $C("kul", "da")$=0.0003. $P("okulda")$ has been calculated using bigram model. It can be found that the probability distribution of the word "okulda" is 0.0002475 as shown in Equation 27.

$$P(W) = P("okulda") = P(s_1, s_2, s_3) = P("o", "kul", "da")$$
$$= \prod_{i=1}^{3} P(s_i \mid s_{i-1}) = \prod_{i=1}^{3} \frac{C(s_{i-1} \mid s_i)}{C(s_{i-1})} \tag{27}$$
$$= \left(\frac{C("\lambda", "o")}{C("\lambda")} \right) \left(\frac{C("o", "kul")}{C("o")} \right) \left(\frac{C("kul", "da")}{C("kul")} \right)$$

3.3 Testing and evaluation of the system

Two systems have been designed and implemented to detect misspelled words in Turkish text. One uses monogram and bigram frequencies. The size of monogram database is 41 kilobytes and the monogram database consists of 4141 different syllables. The sizes of bigram and trigram databases are 570 and 2858 kilobytes respectively. While the bigram database includes 46684 syllable pairs, the trigram database consists of 183529 ternary syllables. The other uses bigram and trigram frequencies. These two systems have been tested for two Turkish texts. One is correctly spelled text which includes 685 correctly spelled words. The other is misspelled text which has 685 misspelled words. These two texts have same words. Namely, misspelled words are generated with putting errors on the correctly spelled words. These error types are substitution, deletion, insertion, transposition and split word errors. The system takes correctly spelled and misspelled texts as input and gives the results for each word as "correctly spelled word" or "misspelled word". Probability distributions are calculated for each word. If the probability distribution of a word is equal to zero, system decides that the word is misspelled. If it is greater than zero, system decides that the word is correctly spelled.

Firstly, the system on the correctly spelled text has been tested using monogram and bigram frequencies. The system determines 602 correctly spelled words from the correctly spelled text, so the words are correctly recognized with 88% success rate. Also, 589 misspelled words within the misspelled text are decided successfully by the system. Namely, the system which is tested on the misspelled text correctly recognized the words with 86% success rate.

Then the system on the correctly spelled text has been tested using bigram and trigram frequencies. The system determines 671 of 685 correctly spelled words from the correctly spelled text. The success rate on correctly recognition of the words is 98%. Furthermore, 664 of 685 misspelled words within the misspelled text are decided successfully by the system. Thus, the system which is tested on the misspelled text correctly recognized the words with 97% success rate. The system can analyze 75000 words per second.

4. Experimental results

In this section, the extperimental results of the developed syllable based speech recognition have been given according to DTW and ANN approach, and the success rates of the systems have been compared.

The most widely used evaluation measure for speech recognition performance is Word Error Rate (WER) (Hunt, 1990; McCowan et al., 2005). The general difficulty of measuring the performance lies on the fact that the recognized word sequence can have different length from the reference word sequence. The WER is derived from the Levenshtein distance, working at word level instead of character.

This problem is solved by first aligning the recognized word sequence with the reference sequence using dynamic string alignment. The word error rate can then be computed as in Equation 28.

$$WER = 100\left(\frac{E}{N}\right) \tag{28}$$

where E is the number of wrongly detected words, and N is the number of words in the reference set.

In Figure 8, the WER results are given for dynamic time warping. If we evaluate the system, we can say that the best result for DTW is obtained with the mfcc feature. It is followed by rasta feature. The system accuracy rate is increased with postprocessing operation about 9% using DTW.

In Figure 9, the WER results are given for artificial neural network. If we evaluate the system, it can be said that the best result for ANN is obtained with the mfcc feature. The system accuracy rate is increased with postprocessing operation about 15% using ANN.

According to the results of WER of the system, the most successful feature and speech recognition method are mfcc and DTW (5.8% WER) respectively. The postprocessing improves approximately 14% of the system accuracy.

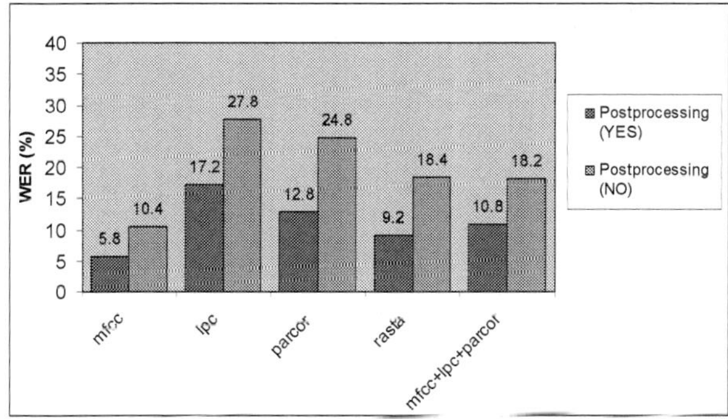

Fig. 8. WER results of system using DTW

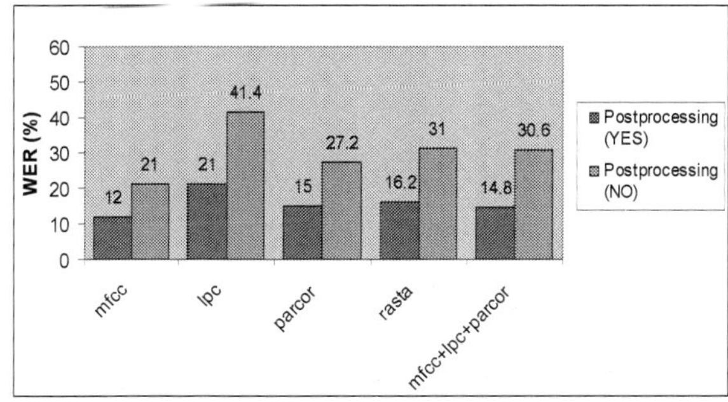

Fig. 9. WER results of system using ANN

DTW does not need training operation. It uses the extracted features. The best feature is mfcc because its extraction time duration is the lowest. ANN needs training, and it constructs a model for each syllable in words using training. As shown in Table 2, the average training time for ANN is about 1102.5 seconds.

Table 3 displays average testing time duration. Average testing time duration of ANN (7.4 seconds) is quite shorter than that of DTW.

Methods	Training Time (Seconds)
ANN	1102.5

Table 2. Average training time for one syllable

Methods	Testing Time (Seconds)
DTW	57.3
ANN	7.4

Table 3. Average testing time for one syllable

5. Conclusion

In this study, syllable based isolated word Turkish speech recognition systems using the speech recognition methods as DTW and ANN have been designed and implemented. These speaker dependent systems use the features as mfcc, lpc, parcor, cepstrum, rasta and the mixture of mfcc, lpc and parcor. Syllable models of the words in the dictionary are constructed syllable databases to compare the word utterence. The system firstly recognizes the syllables of the word utterence. Recognized word is found by the concatenation of the recognized syllables.

To use in postprocessing stage of the system, firstly, TASA have been designed and implemented. TASA's correct spelling rate is about 100%. Then, Turkish syllable n-gram frequencies for some Turkish corpora have been calculated. In addition, using syllable n-gram frequencies, a system which decides whether or not a word is misspelled in Turkish text has been developed. The system takes words as inputs. The system produces two results for each word: "Correctly spelled word" or "Misspelled word". According to the system designed with bigram and trigram frequencies, the success rate is 97% for the misspelled words, and 98% for the correctly spelled words.

In postprocessing operation, after the recognized word is constructed by concatenating of the recognized syllables, the system decides whether it is Turkish word or not. If the word is Turkish word, then it is new recognized word. This postprocessing increases the accuracy rate of the system approximately 14%.

After testing of the middle scaled speech recognition system, the most successful method is DTW whose word error rate is about 5.8%. It can be said that the best feature for the speech recognition is mel frequency cepstral coefficients.

For future work, Support Vector Machine and Hidden Markov Model can be applied for syllable based speech recognition, and we can compare among the results obtained using these speech recognition methods.

6. Acknowledgment

The author would like to thank the Scientific Research Unit (BAP) of Adnan Menderes University.

7. References

Arısoy, E. & Dutağacı, H. (2006). A unified language model for large vocabulary continuous speech recognition of Turkish. *Signal Processing*, Vol.86, No.10, pp. 2844-2862

Artuner, H. (1994). *The design and implementation of a Turkish speech phoneme clustering system*, PhD Thesis, Hacettepe University, Ankara, Turkey

Aşlıyan, R. & Günel, K. (2005). Design and implementation for extracting Turkish syllables and analysing Turkish syllables, *INISTA (International Symposium on Innovations in Inttelligent Systems and Applications)*, pp. 170-173, ISBN 975-461-400-8, İstanbul, Turkey, 15-18 June 2005

Aşlıyan, R.; Günel, K. & Yakhno, T. (2007). Detecting misspelled words in Turkish text using syllable n-gram frequencies. *Lecture Notes in Computer Science (LNCS)*, Vol.4815, pp. 553-559

Aşlıyan, R. (December 2010). Speech Recognition System Databases, 15.01.2011, Available from http://web.adu.edu.tr/akademik/rasliyan/speech/sdw.html

Avcı, E. (2007). An automatic system for Turkish word recognition using discrete wavelet neural network based on adaptive entropy. *Arabian Journal for Science and Engineering*, Vol.32, pp. 239-250

Barari, L. & QasemiZadeh, B. (2005). CloniZER spell checker adaptive language independent spell checker, *AIML 05 Conference CICC*, pp. 19-21, Cairo, Egypt

Blanz, V.; Schölkopf, B., Bulthoff, H., Burges, C., Vapnik, V. N. & Vetter, T. (1996). Comparison of view-based object recognition algorithms using realistic 3D models, *Lecture Notes in Computer Science (LNCS)*, Vol.1112, pp. 251-256

Cortes, C. & Vapnik, V. N. (1995). Support vector network. *Machine Learning*, Vol.20, pp. 1-25

Davis, K.; Biddulph, R., & Balashek, S. (1952). Automatic recognition of spoken digits. *J. Acous. Soc. Ame.*, Vol.24, pp. 3-50

Deorowicz, S. & Ciura M. G. (2005). Correcting spelling errors by modelling their causes. *International Journal of Applied Mathematics and Computer Science*, Vol.15, No.2, pp. 275-285

Dreyfus-Graf, J. (1952). Letyposonographe phonetique ou phonetographe. *Bulletin Technique Des PTT Suisses*, Vol.12, pp. 363-379

Dudley, H. & Balashek, S. (1958). Automatic recognition of phonetic patterns in speech. *J. Acoustic Soc. Am.*, Vol.30, pp. 721-733

Ferguson, J. (1980). *Hidden Markov Models for speech*, IDA-CRD, Princeton, New Jersey

Forgie, J. & Forgie, C. (1959). Results obtained from a vowel recognition computer program. *J. Acoust. Soc. Ame.*, Vol.31, pp. 1480-1489

Fornés A.; Lladós J., Sánchez G. & Karatzas D. (2010). Rotation invariant hand-drawn symbol recognition based on a dynamic time warping model. *International Journal on Document Analysis and Recognition*, Vol.13, No.3 pp. 229-241

Haton, J. P. & Pierrel, J. M. (1976). Organization and operation of a connected speech understanding system at lexical, syntactical and semantical levels. In : *ICASSP*, pp. 430-433

Hunt, M. J. (1990). Figures of merit for assessing connected word recognisers. *Speech Communication*, Vol.9, pp. 229-236

Jakobson, R.; Fant, G., & Halle, M. (1952). *Preliminaries to speech analysis*, MIT Press, ISBN 0-262-60001-3 Cambridge, MA

Junqua, J. C.; Mak, B. & Reaves, B. (1997). A robust algorithm for word boundary detection in the presence of noise. *IEEE Transactions on Speech and Audio Processing*, Vol.2, No.3, pp. 406-412

Jurafsky, D. & Martin, J. H. (2000). *Speech and language processing*, Prentice Hall, ISBN 0-13-095069-6 New Jersey

Kang, S. S. & Woo, C. W. (2001). Automatic segmentation of words using syllable bigram statistics, *Proceedings of the Sixth Natural Language Processing Pacific Rim Symposium*, pp. 729-732, Tokyo, Japan

Karaca, N. (1999). *Realization of a Turkish isolated word speech recognition system under noisy environments*, PhD Thesis, Hacettepe University, Ankara, Turkey

Koç, A. (2002). *Acoustic feature analysis for robust speech recognition*, MSc Thesis, Boğaziçi University, İstanbul, Turkey

Kukich, K. (1992). Techniques for automatically correcting words in text. *ACM Computing Surveys*, Vol.24, No.4, pp. 377-439

Lesser, V.; Fennell, R., Erman, L., & Reddy, D. (1975). Organization of the HEARSAY II speech understanding system. *IEEE Trans. ASSP*, Vol.23, No.1, pp. 11-23

Lippmann, R. (1987). An introduction to computing with neural nets. *IEEE Trans. ASSP Magazine*, Vol.4, No.2, pp. 4-22

Lowerre, B. (1976). *The harpy speech recognition system*, Technical Report, Carnegie Mellon University

McCowan, I.; Moore, D., Dines, J., Gatica-Perez, D., Flynn, M., Wellner, P., et al. (2005). *On the use of information retrieval measure for speech recognition evaluation*, IDIAP, IDIAP-RR 73

Meral, O. (1996). *Speech recognition based on pattern comparison techniques*, MSc Thesis, İstanbul Technical University, İstanbul

Mercier, G. (1977). A multipurpose speech understanding system, In: *ICASSP*, pp. 815-818

Myers, C.; Rabiner, L. & Rosenberg, A. (1980). Performance tradeoffs in dynamic time warping algorithms for isolated word recognition. *IEEE Transactions on Acoustics, Speech, and Signal Processing*, Vol.6, pp. 623-635

Nagata, K.; Kato, Y., & Chiba, S. (1963). Spoken digit recognizer for Japanese language. *NEC Res. Develop.*, Vol.6, No.2

Olson, H. & Bellar, H. (1956). Phonetic typewriter. *J. Accous. Soc. Ame.*, Vol.2, pp. 1072-1081

Osuna, E.; Freud, R. & Girosi, F. (1997). Training support vector machines: An applications to face detection, In : *CVPR97*, pp. 130-136

Özkan, Ö. (1997). *Implementation of speech recognition for connected numerals*, MSc Thesis, Middle East Technical University, Ankara, Turkey

Rabiner, L. & Sambur, M. R. (1975). An algorithm for determining the end-points of isolated utterances. *The Bell System Technical Journal*, Vol.54, No.2, pp. 297-315

Rabiner, L. (1989). A tutorial on hidden markov models and selected applications in speech recognition. *Proc. IEEE*, Vol.77, No.2, pp. 257-286

Reddy, D. (1966). An approach to computer speech recognition by direct analysis of the speech wave, Technical Report, Stanford University

Sakai, T. & Doshita, S. (1962). The phonetic typewriter. In: *IFIP Congress*, pp. 445-449

Salor, Ö & Pellom, B. L. (2007). Turkish speech corpora and recognition tools developed by porting SONIC: Towards multilingual speech recognition. *Computer Speech and Language*, Vol.21, No.4, pp. 580-583

Sankoff, D. & Kruskal, J. (1999). *Time Warps, String Edits, and Macromolecules–The Theory and Practice of Sequence Comparison*, The David Hume Series, Stanford, CA

Savoji, M. H. (1989). End-pointing of speech signals. *Speech Communication*, Vol.8, No.1, pp. 46-60

Slutsker, G. (1968). Nelinejnyp method analiza recevych signalov. *Trudy NIIR*, Vol.2, pp. 76-82

Tong, X. & Evans, D. A. (1996). A statistical approach to automatic OCR error correction in context, *Proceedings of the Fourth Workshop on Very Large Corpora*, pp. 88-100, Copenhagen, Denmark

Vintsyuk, T. (1968). Speech discrimination by dynamic programming. *Cybernetics (Kibernetika)*, Vol.4, No.1, pp. 81-88

Wolf, J. & Woods, W. (1977). The HWIM speech understanding system. In: *ICASSP*, pp. 784-787

Yılmaz, C. (1999). A large vocabulary speech recognition system for Turkish, M. S. Thesis, Bilkent University, Ankara, Turkey

Zhuang, L.; Bao, T., Zhu, X.,Wang, C. & Naoi, S. (2004). A chinese OCR spelling check appoarch based on statistical language models, *IEEE International Conference on Systems, Man and Cybernetic*, pp. 4727-4732

14

Phone Recognition on the TIMIT Database

Carla Lopes[1,2] and Fernando Perdigão[1,3]
[1]Instituto de Telecomunicações,
[2]Instituto Politécnico de Leiria,
[3]Universidade de Coimbra
Portugal

1. Introduction

In the information age, computer applications have become part of modern life and this has in turn encouraged the expectations of friendly interaction with them. Speech, as "the" communication mode, has seen the successful development of quite a number of applications using automatic speech recognition (ASR), including command and control, dictation, dialog systems for people with impairments, translation, etc. But the actual challenge goes beyond the use of speech in control applications or to access information. The goal is to use speech as an information source, competing, for example, with text online. Since the technology supporting computer applications is highly dependent on the performance of the ASR system, research into ASR is still an active topic, as is shown by the range of research directions suggested in (Baker et al., 2009a, 2009b).

Automatic speech recognition – the recognition of the information embedded in a speech signal and its transcription in terms of a set of characters, (Junqua & Haton, 1996) – has been object of intensive research for more than four decades, achieving notable results. It is only to be expected that speech recognition advances make spoken language as convenient and accessible as online text when the recognizers reach error rates near zero. But while digit recognition has already reached a rate of 99.6%, (Li, 2008), the same cannot be said of phone recognition, for which the best rates are still under 80% [1],(Mohamed et al., 2011; Siniscalchi et al., 2007).

Speech recognition based on phones is very attractive since it is inherently free from vocabulary limitations. Large Vocabulary ASR (LVASR) systems' performance depends on the quality of the phone recognizer. That is why research teams continue developing phone recognizers, in order to enhance their performance as much as possible. Phone recognition is, in fact, a recurrent problem for the speech recognition community.

Phone recognition can be found in a wide range of applications. In addition to typical LVASR systems like (Morris & Fosler-Lussier, 2008; Scanlon et al., 2007; Schwarz, 2008), it can be found in applications related to keyword detection, (Schwarz, 2008), language recognition, (Matejka, 2009; Schwarz, 2008), speaker identification, (Furui, 2005) and applications for music identification and translation, (Fujihara & Goto, 2008; Gruhne et al., 2007).

The challenge of building robust acoustic models involves applying good training algorithms to a suitable set of data. The database defines the units that can be trained and

---

[1] Phone recognition using TIMIT Database, [9]

the success of the training algorithms is highly dependent on the quality and detail of the annotation of those units. Many databases are insufficiently annotated and only a few of them include labels at the phone level. So the reason why the TIMIT database (Garofolo et al., 1990) has become the database most widely used by the phone recognition research community is mainly because it is totally and manually annotated at the phone level.

Phone recognition in TIMIT has more than two decades of intense research behind it and its performance has naturally improved with time. There is a full array of systems, but with regard to evaluation they concentrate on three domains: phone segmentation, phone classification and phone recognition. While the first reaches rates of 93% [2], (Hosom, 2009), the second reaches around 83% (Karsmakers et al., 2007) and the third stays at roughly 79%, (Mohamed et al., 2011; Siniscalchi et al., 2007). Phone segmentation is a process of finding the boundaries of a sequence of known phones in a spoken utterance. Determining boundaries at phone level is a difficult problem because of coarticulation effects, where adjacent phones influence each other. Phonetic classification is an artificial but instructive problem in ASR, (Sha & Saul, 2006). It takes the correctly segmented signal, but with unknown labels for the segments. The problem is to correctly identify the phones in those segments. Phone models compete against each other in an attempt to set their label to the respective segment. The label of the winning model is compared with the corresponding TIMIT label and a hit or an error occurs. Nevertheless, phone classification allows a good evaluation of the quality of the acoustic modelling, since it computes the performance of the recognizer without the use of any kind of grammar, (Reynolds & Antoniou, 2003). Phone recognition obeys harder and more complex criteria. The speech given to the recognizer corresponds to the whole utterance. The phone models plus a Viterbi decoding find the best sequence of labels for the input utterance. In this case a grammar can be used. The best sequence of phones found by the Viterbi path is compared with the reference (the TIMIT manual labels for the same utterance) using a dynamic programming algorithm, usually the Levenshtein distance, which takes into account phone hits, substitutions, deletions and insertions.

The use of hidden Markov models (HMMs) is widespread in speech recognizers, at least for event time modelling. After decades of intensive research everything indicates that the performance of HMM-based ASR systems has reached stability. In the late 1980s artificial neural networks (ANNs) (re)appeared as an alternative to HMMs. Hybrid HMM/ANN methods emerged and achieved results comparable, and sometimes superior, to those of HMMs. In the last decade two new techniques have appeared in the machine learning field, with surprising results in classification tasks: support vector machines (SVMs) and, more recently, conditional random fields (CRFs). But the best results in TIMIT are achieved with hybrid ANN/HMM models, (Rose & Momayyez, 2007; Scanlon et al., 2007; Siniscalchi et al., 2007), and hybrid CRF/HMM models, (Morris & Fosler-Lussier, 2008).

This chapter will focus on the TIMIT phone recognition task and cover issues like the technology involved, the features used, the TIMIT phone set, and so on. It starts by describing the database before looking at the state-of-art regarding the relevant research on the TIMIT phone recognition task. The chapter ends with a comparative analysis of the milestones in phone recognition using the TIMIT database and some thoughts on possible future developments.

---

[2] Boundary agreement within 20 ms

2. TIMIT Acoustic-Phonetic Continuous Speech Corpus

The DARPA TIMIT Acoustic-Phonetic Continuous Speech Corpus (TIMIT - Texas Instruments (TI) and Massachusetts Institute of Technology (MIT)), (Garofolo et al., 1990), described in (Zue et al., 1990), contains recordings of phonetically-balanced prompted English speech. It was recorded using a Sennheiser close-talking microphone at 16 kHz rate with 16 bit sample resolution. TIMIT contains a total of 6300 sentences (5.4 hours), consisting of 10 sentences spoken by each of 630 speakers from 8 major dialect regions of the United States. All sentences were manually segmented at the phone level.

The prompts for the 6300 utterances consist of 2 dialect sentences (SA), 450 phonetically compact sentences (SX) and 1890 phonetically-diverse sentences (SI).

TIMIT Corpus documentation suggests training ($\approx$ 70%) and test sets, as described in Table 1. The training set contains 4620 utterances, but usually only SI and SX sentences are used, resulting in 3696 sentences from 462 speakers. The test set contains 1344 utterances from 168 speakers. The core test set, which is the abridged version of the complete testing set, consists of 192 utterances, 8 from each of 24 speakers (2 males and 1 female from each dialect region). With the exception of SA sentences which are usually excluded from tests, the training and test sets do not overlap.

Set	# speakers	#sentences	#hours
Training	462	3696	3.14
Core test	24	192	0.16
Complete test set	168	1344	0.81

Table 1. TIMIT Corpus training and test sets

TIMIT original transcriptions are based on 61 phones, presented in Table 2. The alphabet used – TIMITBET – was inspired by ARPABET. Details of transcription and manual alignment can be found in (Zue & Seneff, 1996) and phonetic analysis in (Keating et al., 1994). The 61 TIMIT phones are sometimes considered a too narrow description for practical use, and for training some authors compact the 61 phones into 48 phones. For evaluation purposes, the 61 TIMIT labels are typically collapsed into a set of 39 phones, as proposed by Lee and Hon, (Lee & Hon, 1989).

This speech corpus has been a standard database for the speech recognition community for several decades and is still widely used today, for both speech and speaker recognition experiments. This is not only because each utterance is phonetically hand labelled and provided with codes for speaker number, gender and dialect region, but also because it is considered small enough to guarantee a relatively fast turnaround time for complete experiments and large enough to demonstrate systems' capabilities.

2.1 Standard evaluation phone recognition metrics

In ASR systems, the most common phone recognition evaluation measures are phone error rate (PER), or the related performance metric, phone accuracy rate. The latter is defined by the following expression:

$$Accuracy = \frac{(N_T - S - D - I)}{N_T} \times 100\%$$

(1)

	Phone Label	Example		Phone Label	Example		Phone Label	Example
1	iy	beet	22	ch	choke	43	en	button
2	ih	bit	23	b	bee	44	eng	Washington
3	eh	bet	24	d	day	45	l	lay
4	ey	bait	25	g	gay	46	r	ray
5	ae	bat	26	p	pea	47	w	way
6	aa	bob	27	t	tea	48	y	yacht
7	aw	bout	28	k	key	49	hh	hay
8	ay	bite	29	dx	muddy	50	hv	ahead
9	ah	but	30	s	sea	51	el	bottle
10	ao	bought	31	sh	she	52	bcl	b closure
11	oy	boy	32	z	zone	53	dcl	d closure
12	ow	boat	33	zh	azure	54	gcl	g closure
13	uh	book	34	f	fin	55	pcl	p closure
14	uw	boot	35	th	thin	56	tcl	t closure
15	ux	toot	36	v	van	57	kcl	k closure
16	er	bird	37	dh	then	58	q	glotal stop
17	ax	about	38	m	mom	59	pau	pause
18	ix	debit	39	n	noon	60	epi	epenthetic silence
19	axr	butter	40	ng	sing			
20	ax-h	suspect	41	em	bottom	61	h#	begin/end marker
21	jh	joke	42	nx	winner			

Table 2. 61 TIMIT original phone set.

where N_T is the total number of labels in the reference utterance and S, D and I are the substitution, deletion and insertion errors, respectively. $PER = 100\% - Accuracy$. Another measure is correctness, which is similar to accuracy, but where insertion errors are not considered. The number of insertion, deletion and substitution errors is computed using the best alignment between two token sequences: the manually aligned (reference) and the recognized (test). An alignment resulting from search strategies based on dynamic programming is normally used successfully for a large number of speech recognition tasks, (Ney & Ortmanns, 2000). Speech recognition toolkits, such as HTK, (Young et al., 2006), include tools to compute accuracy and related measures on the basis of the transcribed data and recognition outputs using this dynamic programming algorithm.

3. Overview of current and past research on TIMIT phone recognition task

In spite of the advances made in recent decades, the TIMIT phone recognition task is still a challenging and difficult task. Many attempts have been made to improve phone recognizer performance, including the use of better features or multiple feature sets, improved statistical models, training criteria, pronunciation modelling, acoustic modelling, noise handling, language modelling, and others.

Regarding the approaches of statistical models, they can be broadly placed in two main categories: generative and discriminative. Phone recognition consists of finding the best possible sequence of phones (Ph) that fit a given input speech X. It is a search problem involving finding the optimal phone sequence Ph^* given by

$$Ph^* = \arg\max_{Ph} P(Ph \mid X) \tag{2}$$

Generative approaches apply Bayes rule on

arriving to $Ph^* = \arg\max_{Ph} P(X \mid Ph)P(Ph)$. This expression relies on a learned model of the conditional probability distribution of the observed acoustic features X, given the corresponding phone class membership. The name 'generative' came about because the model "generates" input observations in an attempt to fit the model Ph. Generative approaches are those involving HMMs, segmental HMMs, hidden trajectory models, Gaussian mixture models (GMMs), stochastic segment models, Bayesian networks, Markov random fields, etc. The probabilistic generative models based on maximum likelihood have long been the most widely used in ASR. The major advantage of generative learning is that it is relatively easy to exploit inherent dependency or various relationships of data by imposing all kinds of structure constraints on generative learning, (Jiang, 2010).

In contrast, discriminative approaches, such as those based on maximum entropy models, logistic regression, neural networks (multi-layer perceptron (MLP), time-delay neural networks (TDNN) or Boltzmann machines), support vector machines (SVMs) and conditional random fields (CRFs), instead of modelling the distribution of the input data assuming a target class, aim to model the posterior class distributions, maximizing the discrimination between acoustically similar targets.

The relevant research on TIMIT phone recognition over the past years will be addressed by trying to cover this wide range of technologies.

One of the first proposals involving phone recognition on the TIMIT database was presented by Lee and Hon, (Lee & Hon, 1989), just after TIMIT was released in December 1988. Their system is based on discrete-HMMs. The best results were achieved with phones being modelled by means of 1450 diphones (right–context) using a bigram language model. Three codebooks of 256 prototype vectors of linear prediction cepstral coefficients were used as features. They achieved a correctness rate of 73.80% and an accuracy rate of 66.08% using 160 utterances from one test set (TID7). They propose that their results should become a TIMIT phone recognition benchmark. In fact, their paper has become a benchmark not only because of the performance but also because of the phone folding they proposed. These authors folded the 61 TIMIT labels into 48 phones for training purposes. For evaluation purposes, they collapsed the 61 TIMIT labels into 39 phones, which has become the standard for evaluation. Table 3 describes this folding process and the resultant 39 phone set. The phones in the left column are folded into the right column's labels. 23 phone labels disappear and the label "sil" is added to the set. The remaining phones from the original 61-set are left intact.

Also in 1989, Steve Young presented the first version of HTK (hidden Markov model toolkit), (Young et al., 2006). This software package, developed in Cambridge University, allows the construction and manipulation of hidden Markov models and lead to a notable increase in the area of speech recognition. In (Young, 1992) the author presents the concept of HMM state tying using triphone models (left and right context). The goal is to produce a compact set of context dependent HMMs, showing that state tying significantly reduces the number of physical triphone models in training. They generate triphones from a phone set with 48 elements. The experimental conditions are similar to those established by Lee and

Hon (Lee & Hon, 1989), except that they used standard Mel-frequency cepstral coefficients (MFCCs) features and log energy and their first order regression coefficients (deltas - Δ). The best results presented are 73.7% for correctness and 59.9% for accuracy, using the 39 phone set proposed in (Lee & Hon, 1989) and 160 sentences randomly taken from the test set.

aa, ao	aa
ah, ax, ax-h	ah
er, axr	er
hh, hv	hh
ih, ix	ih
l, el	l
m, em	m
n, en, nx	n
ng, eng	ng
sh, zh	sh
uw, ux	uw
pcl, tcl, kcl, bcl, dcl, gcl, h#, pau, epi	sil
q	-

Table 3. Mapping from 61 classes to 39 classes, as proposed by Lee and Hon, (Lee & Hon, 1989). The phones in the left column are folded into the labels of the right column. The remaining phones are left intact. The phone 'q' is discarded.

In 1991 Robinson and Fallside (Robinson & Fallside, 1991) developed a phone recognition system using a recurrent error propagation network that achieved an astonishing result: 76.4% for correctness and 68.9% for accuracy using the same Lee and Hon evaluation set (Lee & Hon, 1989). These results rise to 76.5% and 69.8% for correctness and accuracy, using the complete test set. The authors point out even higher rates (71.2% for accuracy), but the set of phones is no longer the traditional 39; they used a set of 50 phones. In 1993, (Robinson & Fallside, 1991) Robinson et al coupled the recurrent network with an HMM decoder, where the network is used for HMM state posterior probability estimation. This system was tested with the Wall Street Journal database. The TIMIT results came from a hybrid RNN/HMM in 1994, (Robinson, 1994). The inputs to the neural network are features extracted using a long left context. The network is trained using a softmax output under a cross-entropy criterion. The network outputs were trained as a function of the 61 original TIMIT labels. Results regarding the 39 classical phone set achieved 78.6% for correctness and 75% for accuracy. This result is still above recent publications! The paper also presents an interesting comparison of several works on the phone recognition task.
In 1993 Lamel and Gauvain (Lamel & Gauvain, 1993) reported their research on speaker-independent phone recognition using continuous density HMMs (CDHMM) for context-dependent phone models trained with maximum likelihood and maximum a posteriori (MAP) estimation techniques. The feature set includes cepstral coefficients derived from linear prediction coefficients (LPC) plus Δ and $\Delta\Delta$ cepstrum (second order regression coefficients). Using the complete test set the results were 77.5%/72.9% (correctness/accuracy).
Halberstadt and Glass (Halberstadt & Glass, 1998), as a result of PhD research, (Halberstadt, 1998) proposed a system in 1998 where several classifiers are combined. The training was performed to maximize the acoustic modelling via multiple heterogeneous acoustic measurements. Each classifier is responsible for identifying a subset of the original TIMIT

labels. Separately, 6 classifiers train 60 TIMIT phone labels (they do not consider the glottal stop /q/). There are 3 additional classifiers combining the information from previous classifiers. Table 4. shows the phones trained in each classifier.

Phone Class	# TIMIT labels	TIMIT labels
Vowel/Semivowel (VS)	25	aa ae ah ao aw ax axh axr ay eh er ey ih ix iy ow oy uh uw ux el l r w y
Nasal/Flap (NF)	8	em en eng m n ng nx dx
Strong Fricative (SF)	6	s z sh zh ch jh
Weak Fricative (WF)	6	v f dh th hh hv
Stop (ST)	6	b d g p t k
Closure (CL)	9	bcl dcl gcl pcl tcl kcl epi pau h#
Sonorant (SON)	33	Vowel/Semivowel + Nasal/Flap
Obstruent (OBS)	18	Strong Fric + Weak Fric + Stop
Silence (SIL)	9	Same as Closure

Table 4. Broad classes of phones used in the multiple classifier system proposed in (Halberstadt, 1998).

Classification uses the SUMMIT[3] segment-based recognizer, (Robinson et al., 1993). Gaussian mixture models are used and different phone sets use different features: MFCCs, perceptual linear prediction cepstral coefficients, and a third MFCC-like representation that the authors call "discrete cosine transforms coefficients". They also used windows of different lengths, temporal features, deltas, etc. Phone recognition is achieved by means of two different approaches: one hierarchical and another parallel. The results exceeded those of all the systems existing at the time. Accuracy, using the core test set, reached 75.6%! The long list of tests performed allowed the authors to conclude that better results are achieved using combinations of classifiers trained separately, rather than a single classifier trained to distinguish all the phones or using all the classifiers. The best results achieved were given by a combination of only five of the eight classifiers available.

In 2003 Reynolds and Antoniou (Reynolds & Antoniou, 2003) proposed training a modular MLP. On a first level they trained the 39 phones but used different feature sets (MFCCs, perceptual linear prediction coefficients, LPC and combinations of them). As a result, they collected several predictions for the same phone that are later combined in another MLP. The best results were achieved by optimizing the number of hidden nodes and also using information from seven broad classes, whose composition is shown in Table 5.

In the detection of these broad classes, several context sizes of the input features were tested, and a context of 35 frames (350ms) was found to be the best. With a slightly different test set (they took the core test set out of the complete test set), they report an accuracy of 75.8% for the 39 TIMIT standard phone test set. The paper also gives a good overview of prior work on TIMIT phone recognition and classification.

---

[3] SUMMIT is a speech recognition system developed at MIT. This speech recognizer uses a landmark-based approach for modelling acoustic-phonetic events and uses finite-state transducer (FST) technology to efficiently represent all aspects of the speech hierarchy including: phonological rules, lexicon, and probabilistic language model.

Phone Class	# TIMIT labels	TIMIT labels
Plosives	8	b d g p t k jh ch
Fricatives	8	s sh z f th v dh h
Nasals	3	m n ng
Semi-vowels	5	l r er w y
Vowels	8	iy ih eh ae aa ah uh uw
Diphthongs	5	ey aw ay oy ow
Closures	2	sil dx

Table 5. Broad classes of phones used in the system proposed by Reynolds and Antoniou, (Reynolds & Antoniou, 2003).

Sha and Saul (Sha & Saul, 2006) present a system which, while its performance is not very competitive, does introduce an interesting idea. They trained GMMs discriminatively, using the SVM's basic principle: attempt to maximize the margin between classes. With MFCCs and deltas as features and using 16 Gaussian mixtures they achieved an accuracy rate of 69.9%.

The result of a study undertaken at Brno University on the use of TRAPs (TempoRAl Patterns) was a paper on the hierarchical structures of neural networks for phone recognition (Schwarz et al., 2006). The focus was to exploit the contribution that the temporal context can make to phone recognition. The system relies on two main lines:

- The TRAP system – a set of MLPs where each neural network receives features of a single critical band as input. The TRAP input feature vector describes the temporal evolution of critical band spectral densities within a single critical band. The MLPs are trained so as to classify the input patterns in terms of phone probabilities. The phone probabilities of all these MLPs (one for each critical band) are given to another MLP – a probability merger – whose output gives a final posterior probability of each phone.
- Temporal context split system– also based on MLPs, assumes that two parts of a phone may be processed independently: one considering left context and the other right context. Two MLPs are trained to produce phone posteriors for left and right contexts. The outputs of these MLPs feed another MLP whose outputs give a final posterior probability for each phone.

The authors compared several input feature sets, networks with outputs giving posterior probabilities of phones and HMMs states, and also tried to find the best number of frequency bands to analyze. The best result achieved 75.16% accuracy. Tuning the number of the MLP's hidden nodes; using a bigram language model and using 5 context blocks (instead of only left and right) they reached an interesting improvement (4.5% relative), resulting in 78.52% accuracy.

The Brno recognizer is based on 39 phones, which are not exactly the standard TIMIT phones. Closures were merged with their burst instead of with silence (bcl b → b) suggesting that it is more appropriate for features which use a longer temporal context such as theirs. Looking at the utterance transcriptions in 87% of the [bcl] occurrences the closure is followed by [b], but not in the other 13% (e.g.: bcl t, bcl el, bcl ix, etc), and the same happens with the other closures. The paper does not make it clear if the closures also merge with the following phone in these situations. Because these speech units are not the standard TIMIT, some authors argue that their results would be probably worse if they use the standard speech units, (Mohamed et al., 2011).

Interesting results are reported by a Microsoft research group devoted to the study of hidden trajectory models (HTM). Deng et al's HTMs are a type of probabilistic generative model which aims to model the speech signal dynamics and add long-contextual-span capabilities that are missing in the hidden Markov models (Deng el al., 2005). A detailed description of the long-contextual-span of hidden trajectory model of speech can be found in (Dong el al., 2006). The model likelihood score for the observed speech data is computed from the estimate of the probabilistic speech data trajectories for a given hypothesized phone sequence, which is given by a bi-directional filter. The highest likelihood phone sequence is found through the A* based lattice search. A rescoring algorithm was specially developed for HTM. In (Deng & Yu, 2007), the results reached 75.17% for accuracy and 78.40% for correctness. Joint static cepstra and their deltas are used as acoustic features by the HTM model.

Rose and Momayyez, (Rose & Momayyez, 2007), use the outputs of eight phonological feature detectors to produce sets of features to feed HMM recognizers. The detectors are time delay neural networks whose inputs are standard MFCC features, with deltas and delta-deltas. The HMM recognizers defined over the phonological feature streams are combined with HMMs defined over standard MFCC acoustic features through a lattice rescoring procedure. For the complete test set they achieved an accuracy of 72.2%.

Knowing that phone confusions occur within similar phones (Halberstadt & Glass, 1998), Scanlon, Ellis and Reilly (Scanlon et al., 2007) propose a system where information coming from a base system is combined with information coming from a set of broad phone class experts (broad phonetic groups). The base system is a hybrid MLP/HMM using PLP features with 1st and 2nd derivatives. The MLP is trained to discriminate the 61 original TIMIT phone set. The broad phonetic groups are presented in Table 6. They trained only four networks' experts: vowels (25 phones), stops (8 phones), fricatives (10 phones) and nasals (7 phones).

Since each broad-class phone's characteristics are quite different, they use, in each MLP expert, different sets of features found by Mutual Information criteria. The number of outputs of each MLP network is the same as the number of TIMIT labelled phones of the corresponding broad phonetic group.

The output of a broad phonetic group detector (also an MLP which, for each frame, gives a probability of the frame belong to a group) is combined with the output of a phone classifier. If they agree (the phone recognized by the phone classifier belongs to the broad phonetic group given by the broad class detector) they patch the phone posteriors given from the broad phonetic group detector onto the phone classifier predictions. This merged information is then given to an HMM decoder. After tuning the system they achieved 74.2% accuracy for the 39 TIMIT standard phone set, using the complete TIMIT test.

Broad Phonetic Groups	TIMIT – labelled phones
Vowels	aa, ae, ah, ao, ax, ax-h, axr, ay, aw, eh, el, er, ey, ih, ix, iy, l, ow, oy, r, uh, uw, ux, w, y
Stops	p, t, k, b, d, g, jh, ch
Fricatives	s, sh, z, zh, f, th, v, dh, hh, hv
Nasals	m, em, n, nx, ng, eng, en
Silences	h#, epi, pau, bcl, dcl, gcl, pcl, tcl, kcl, q, dx

Table 6. Broad classes of phones used in the system proposed by Scanlon, Ellis and Reilly (Scanlon et al., 2007).

In 2004, a 4-institute research project in the ASR field, named ASAT (automatic speech attribute transcription), (Lee et al., 2007) generated several ideas for the phone recognition task, (Morris & Fosler-Lussier, 2006, 2007, 2008; Bromberg et al., 2007). The main goal of ASAT is to promote the development of new approaches based on the detection of speech attributes and knowledge integration. In 2007 in a joint paper (Bromberg et al., 2007) , several approaches are presented on the detection of speech attributes. The overall system contains a front-end whose output gives predictions for the detected attributes as a probability. This front-end is followed by a merger, which combines predictions of several speech attributes and whose output is given to a phone based HMM decoder.

Methods of Detection	Front-end Processing (Features)	Speech Attributes Detected
MLP (Sound Pattern of English)	13 MFCCs 10ms frames	vocalic, consonantal, high, back, low, anterior, coronal, round, tense, voice, continuant, nasal, strident, silence. (14 attributes)
SVM	13 MFCCs 9 context frames 10ms frames	coronal, dental, fricative, glottal, high, labial, low, mid, nasal, round minus, round plus, silence, stop, velar, voiced minus, voiced plus, vowel. (17 attributes)
HMM	13 MFCCs+Δ+$\Delta\Delta$ 10ms frames	
Multi-class MLPs	13 PLPs+Δ+$\Delta\Delta$ 9 context frames 10ms frames	Sonority: obstruent, silence, sonorant, syllabic, vowel; Voicing: voiced, voiceless, NA; Manner: approximant, flap, fricative, nasal, flap, stop-closure, stop, NA; Place: alveolar, dental, glottal, labial, lateral, palatal, rhotic, velar, NA; Height: high, low-high, low, mid-high, mid, NA; Backness: back, back-front, central, front, NA; Roundness: nonround, nonround-round, round-nonround, round, NA; Tenseness: lax, tense, NA. (44 atributes)

Table 7. ASAT project (Bromberg et al., 2007): features used in the front-end and the speech attributes detected as a function of the detection method.

The acoustic-phonetic attribute detectors were achieved using several technologies: MLPs, SVMs, HMMs, TDNNs. Depending on the classifier, different sets of features were used (MFCCs, PLPs, and derivatives). The set of attributes also differs in each classifier, in number and in the detected acoustic-phonetic feature. Table 7 shows the features used in the front-end and the detected speech attributes as a function of detection method in the ASAT project.

In order to provide higher-level evidence of use for speech recognition, the attributes were combined. Conditional Random Fields (CRFs) and knowledge-based rescoring of phone lattices were used to combine the framewise detection scores for TIMIT phone recognition. Several configurations of speech attribute detectors as inputs to the CRF were tested. The best result was achieved combining 44 MLP attribute predictions with 17 HMM predictions - 69.52% accuracy and 73.39% correctness.

Morris and Fosler-Lussier in (Morris & Fosler-Lussier, 2006) used eight MLPs to extract 44 phonetic attributes as depicted in Table 8. After decorrelating these 44 features with a Karhunen-Loeve transform, they are modelled by conventional HMMs with Gaussian mixtures and by CRFs. The best results came from a TANDEM architecture (attributes are used as input features for the HMMs) with triphones modelled with 4 Gaussian mixtures: 72.52%/66.69% (correctness/accuracy). With the CRF system the performance is a bit lower 66.74%/65.23% (correctness/accuracy), but better than the TANDEM HMM with monophones modelled by a single Gaussian.

The same authors published another work in 2008 (Morris & Fosler-Lussier, 2008), where the TANDEM architecture combined with the use of triphones trained with 16 Gaussian mixtures increased accuracy to 68.53%. The best results using the core test set is 70.74% for accuracy, and using a set of 118 speakers (speakers in the core test set as well as the rest of the speakers from the TIMIT test set that are not among the speakers in the development set) the reported accuracy rate rose to 71.49%. These results were attained using CRFs with 105 input features: 61 corresponding to the posterior probabilities of the TIMIT phones given by a single MLP classifier and the remaining 44 features are phonetic attributes originating in 8 MLP classifiers of the phonetic classes described in Table 8. All MLP classifiers were trained using PLPs plus their deltas and delta-deltas.

Attribute	Possible output values
sonority	vowel, obstruent, sonorant, syllabic, silence
voice	voiced, unvoiced, n/a
manner	fric.; stop, closure, flap, nasal, approx.; nasal flap, n/a
place	lab.; dent.; alveolar, pal.; vel.; glot.; lat.; rhotic, n/a
height	high, mid, low, lowhigh, midhigh, n/a
front	front, back, central, backfront, n/a
round	round, nonround, round-nonround, nonround-round, n/a
tense	tense, lax, n/a

Table 8. Phonetic attributes extracted by the MLPs in (Morris & Fosler-Lussier, 2006).

Linking knowledge from Brno University of Technology and the Georgia Institute of Technology, we get one of the best reported results on the phone TIMIT recognition task.

The authors, Siniscalchi, Schwarz and Lee, (Siniscalchi et al., 2007) report 79% for accuracy in the complete TIMIT test set. The proposed system is similar to that described by Schwarz, Matejka, and Cernocky in (Schwarz et al., 2006) and can be seen as a TANDEM architecture of MLPs ending in a HMM decoder. The left and right signal contexts are processed separately with windowing and DCT transform and each is applied to a different neural network. The outputs of these two neural networks feed another neural network. Finally, an HMM decoder is then used to turn these last neural network outputs, which are frame-based, into a signal that is segmented in terms of phones.

An extra knowledge-based module to rescore the lattices is included in (Siniscalchi et al., 2007). The lattice rescoring is done in two phases. In the first, the decoder generates a collection of decoding hypotheses. It is followed by a rescoring algorithm that reorders these hypotheses at the same time as it includes additional information. The additional information comes from a bank of speech attribute detectors which capture articulatory information, such as the manner and place of articulation. The bank of speech attribute detectors uses HMMs to map a segment of speech into one of the 15 broad classes, i.e. fricative, vowel, stop, nasal, semi-vowel, low, mid, high, labial, coronal, dental, velar, glottal, retroflex, and silence.

A log-likelihood ratio (LLR) at a frame level is taken as the measure of goodness-to-fit between the input and the output of each detector. A feed-forward ANN is then trained to produce phone scores for each set of LLR scores. These phone scores are then used in the lattice rescoring process changing the value of the arcs as a weight sum between the original values, with these last coming from the attribute detectors. The set of phones used in this system is the same as in (Rose & Momayyez, 2007).

In early 2009, Hifny and Renals (Hifny & Renals, 2009) presented a phonetic recognition system where the acoustic modulation is achieved by means of augmented conditional random fields. The results, using the TIMIT database, are very good. They reach 73.4% for accuracy using the core test set and 77% in another test set which includes the complete test set and the SA sentences.

A new automatic learning technique for speech recognition applications has recently been presented (Mohamed & Hinton, 2010). The authors, Mohamed and Hinton, apply Restricted Bolzmann Machines (RBMs) to phonetic recognition. Boltzmann machine is a type of stochastic recurrent neural network. As a real generative model, the Trajectory-HMM overcomes a major weakness of using HMMs in speech recognition, which is the conditional independence assumption between state outputs. With respect to the TIMIT database the authors observe that RBMs outperform a conventional HMM based system in 0.6% of PER. Regarding accuracy and using the core test set the result is 77.3%. A recent publication (Mohamed et al., 2011) reports the use of neural networks for acoustic modelling, in which multiple layers of features are generatively pre-trained. The outcome is, to the best of our knowledge, the highest TIMIT results reported so far in the core test set, 79.3% accuracy.

Although a fair comparison cannot be always made, Table 9 summarizes some of what we believe are the most important systems, considered as milestones in TIMIT phone recognition over the past twenty years. The systems differ considerably in terms of features, test material, phone set, acoustic modelling etc.; which make their comparison harder. A timeline survey, including the speech technology involved, the achieved rates and the test set used is then presented.

Year	System	Speech Technology	%Corr	%Acc	Test Set
1989	(Lee & Hon, 1989)	HMM	73.80	66.08	160 utterances (TID7)
1991	(Robinson & Fallside, 1991)	Recurrent Error Propagation Network	76.4 76.5	68.9 69.8	160 utterances (TID7) Complete Set
1992	(Young, 1992)	HMM	73.7	59.9	160 utterances randomly selected
1993	(Lamel & Gauvain, 1993)	Triphone Continuous HMMs	77.5	72.9	Complete Set
1994	(Robinson, 1994)	RNN	78.6 77.5	75.0 73.9	Complete Set Core Set
1998	(Halberstadt & Glass, 1998)	Heterogeneous input features. SUMMIT. Broad classes	-	75.6	Core Set
2003	(Reynolds & Antoniou, 2003)	MLP, Broad Classes	-	75.8	1152 utterances
2006	(Sha & Saul, 2006)	GMMs trained as SVMs	-	69.9	Complete Set
2006	(Schwarz et al., 2006)	TRAPs and temporal context division	-	78.52	Complete Set
2007	(Deng & Yu, 2007)	Hidden Trajectory Models	78.40	75.17	Core Set
2007	(Rose & Momayyez, 2007)	TDNN, phonological features HMM		72.2	Complete Set
2007	(Scanlon et al., 2007)	MLP/HMM	-	74.2	Complete Set
2007	ASAT, (Bromberg et al., 2007)	MLP/HMM	73.39	69.52	-
2007	(Siniscalchi et al., 2007)	TRAPs, temporal context division + lattice rescoring	-	79.04	Complete Set
2008	(Morris & Fosler-Lussier, 2006)	MLP/CRF	- 74.76	70.74 71.49	Core Set 944 utterances
2009	(Hifny & Renals, 2009)	Augmented CRFs	-	77.0	Complete Set + SA
2010	(Mohamed & Hinton, 2010)	Boltzmann Machines	-	77.3	Core set
2011	(Mohamed et al., 2011)	Monophone Deep Belief Networks	-	79.3	Core set

Table 9. Milestones in phone recognition using the TIMIT database. The percentages of correctness (%Corr) and accuracy (%Acc) are given.

4. Conclusions and discussion

This chapter focuses on how speech technology has been applied to phone recognition. It contains a holistic survey of the relevant research on the TIMIT phone recognition task, spanning the last two decades. This survey is intended to provide baseline results for the TIMIT phone recognition task and to outline the research paths followed, with varying success, so that it can be useful for researchers, professionals and engineers specialized in speech processing when considering future research directions.

The previous section described several approaches for phone recognition using the TIMIT database. Fig. 1 shows the chronology of the milestones in TIMIT phone recognition performance. Over the past 20 years the performance improved about 13%, mainly in the first 5 years of research. Improvement in the last 15 years has been very slight. Several approaches, covering different original technologies have been taken, none of them entirely solving the problem. It is hard to extrapolate future improvements from the graph in Fig. 1, but it appears that an upper bound of about 80% for accuracy will be hard to beat.

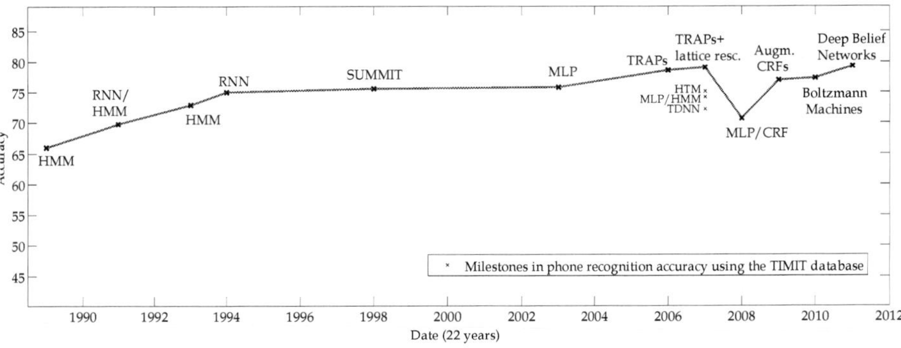

Fig. 1. Progress of the performance of TIMIT phone recognizer milestones.

Is there room for further improvement? Or does TIMIT database itself not allow it? The TIMIT hand-labelling was carefully done, and the labels have been implicitly accepted by the research community. Nevertheless, some authors (Keating et al., 1994; Räsänen et al., 2009) have pointed out issues related to TIMIT annotation. In (Keating et al., 1994) phonetic research on TIMIT annotations is described, drawing a parallel between standard and normative descriptions of American English. In spite of raising a question about the theoretical basis of the segmental transcriptions, the authors still found them useful. Another issue relates to label boundaries. In TIMIT 21.9% of all boundaries are closer than 40 ms to each other, (Räsänen et al., 2009). This may potentiate deletion errors, as a typical frame rate is 10ms, resulting in phones with less than 4 frames. Does this have an impact on the systems' performance, restricting room for improvement? Maybe, but we think that the long tradition of using the TIMIT test sets as a way of comparing new systems and approaches in exactly the same conditions will prevail.

Although the data in Fig. 1 indicate that there is limited room for improvement, new challenges must be taken up so as to uncover the full potential of speech technology. Until now, the main research issues rely on discriminative approaches and on the use of additional information, mainly wider feature temporal context, as well as speech attributes, broad phonetic groups, landmarks, and lattice rescoring. The acoustic and phonetic information in the speech signal might already be fully exploited. One way to create a breakthrough in performance might be by adding syntactic (although language models are often used) or higher linguistic knowledge. Decoding the "meaning" of the words will probably help to improve word recognition, implying a top down approach or even avoiding classification at the phone level.

5. Acknowledgment

Carla Lopes would like to thank the Portuguese foundation, Fundação para a Ciência e a Tecnologia, for the PhD Grant (SFRH/BD/27966/2006).

6. References

Baker, J. M.; Deng, L.; Glass, J.; Khudanpur, S.; Lee, C.; Morgan, N. & O'Shaugnessy, D. (2009a). Research Developments and Directions in Speech Recognition and Understanding, Part 1. *IEEE Signal Processing Magazine*, vol. 26, no. 3, (May 2009), pp. 75-80, ISSN 1053-5888.

Baker, J. M.; Deng, L.; Glass, J.; Khudanpur, S.; Lee, C.; Morgan, N. & O'Shaugnessy, D. (2009b). Updated MINDS Report on Speech Recognition and Understanding, Part 2. *IEEE Signal Processing Magazine*, vol. 26, no. 4, (July 2009), pp. 78-85, ISSN 1053-5888.

Bromberg, I.; et al.. (2007). Detection-based ASR in the automatic speech attribute transcription project. *Proceedings of Interspeech2007*, ISSN 1990-9772, Belgium, August, 2007.

Deng, L. & Yu, D. (2007). Use of differential cepstra as acoustic features in hidden trajectory modelling for phonetic recognition. *Proceedings of IEEE International Conference on Acoustics, Speech, and Signal Processing (ICASSP)*, Hawaii, April, 2007.

Deng, L.; Yu, D. & Acero, A. (2005). A generative modeling framework for structured hidden speech dynamics. *Proceedings of NIPS Workshop on Advances in Structured Learning for Text and Speech Processing*, Canada, December 2005.

Dong , Y.; Deng, L. & Acero, A. (2006). A lattice search technique for a long-contextual-span hidden trajectory model of speech. *Speech Communication*, 48: pp: 1214-1226, ISSN 0167-6393.

Fujihara, H. & Goto, M. (2008). Three Techniques for Improving Automatic Synchronization between Music and Lyrics: Fricative Detection, Filler Model, and Novel Feature Vectors for Vocal Activity Detection. *Proceedings of IEEE International Conference on Acoustics, Speech, and Signal Processing (ICASSP)*, pp.69-72, USA, April 2008.

Furui, S. (2005). 50 Years of Progress in Speech and Speaker Recognition Research. *Proceedings of ECTI Transactions on Computer and Information Technology*, vol. 1, no. 2, 2005.

Garofolo, J.; Lamel, L.; Fisher, W.; Fiscus, J.; Pallett, D.; & Dahlgren, N. (1990). DARPA, TIMIT Acoustic-Phonetic Continuous Speech Corpus CD-ROM. National Institute of Standards and Technology, 1990.

Gruhne, M.; Schmidt, K.; Dittmar, C. (2007). Phone recognition in popular music. *Proceedings of 8th International Conference on Music Information Retrieval*, Austria, September 2007.

Halberstadt, A. K. (1998). Heterogeneous Acoustic Measurements and Multiple Classifiers for Speech Recognition. *Ph.D. thesis*, Department of Electrical Engineering and Computer Science, Massachusetts Institute of Technology, 1998.

Halberstadt, A. & Glass, J. (1998). Heterogeneous measurements and multiple classifiers for speech recognition. *Proceedings of International Conference on Spoken Language Processing (ICSLP)*, Australia, November 1998.

Hifny Y. & Renals S. (2009). Speech recognition using augmented conditional random fields. *IEEE Transactions on Audio, Speech & Language Processing*, vol. 17, no. 2, 2009, pp. 354–365, ISSN 1558-7916.

Hosom, J.-P. (2009). Speaker-independent phoneme alignment using transition-dependent states. *Speech Communication*, vol. 51, no. 4, 2009, pp. 352–368, ISSN 0167-6393.

Jiang, H. (2010). Discriminative training of HMMs for automatic speech recognition: A survey. *Computer Speech & Language*, Vol. 24, No. 4, October 2010, pp. 589-608, ISSN 0885-2308.

Junqua, J.-C. & Haton J.-P. (1996). Robustness in Automatic Speech Recognition: Fundamentals and Applications". Boston: *Kluwer Academic Publishers*. ISBN 0792396464.

Karsmakers, P.; Pelckmans, K.; Suykens, J.; Van Hamme, H. (2007). Fixedsize kernel logistic regression for phone classification. *Proceedings of Interspeech2007*, ISSN 1990-9772, Belgium, August, 2007.

Keating, P.A.; Byrd, D.; Flemming, E. & Todaka Y. (1994). Phonetic analyses of word and segment variation using the TIMIT corpus of American English, *Speech Communication*. 14, 131-142, ISSN 0167-6393.

Lamel L. & Gauvain J. L. (1993). High Performance Speaker Independent Phone Recognition using CDHMM. *Proceedings of Eurospeech*, Germany, September, 1993.

Lee, C.-H.; Clements, M. A.; Dusan, S.; Fosler-Lussier, E.; Johnson, K.;. Juang, B.-H and Rabiner, L. R. (2007). An Overview on Automatic Speech Attribute Transcription (ASAT). *Proceedings of Interspeech2007*, ISSN 1990-9772, Belgium, August, 2007.

Lee, K. & Hon, H. (1989). Speaker-independent phone recognition using hidden Markov models. *IEEE Transactions on Acoustics, Speech, and Signal Processing*, vol.37 (11), November 1989, pp. 1642-1648, ISSN: 0096-3518.

Li, J. (2008). Soft Margin Estimation for Automatic Speech Recognition. *PhD thesis*, Georgia Institute of Technology, School of Electrical and Computer Engineering, 2008.

Matejka, P. (2009). Phonotactic and Acoustic Language Recognition. *PhD thesis*, Brno University of Technology, Faculty of Electrical Engineering and Communication, 2009.

Mohamed, A.; Dahl, G.; Hinton, G. (2011). Acoustic Modeling using Deep Belief Networks", *IEEE Transactions on Audio, Speech, and Language Processing*, 2011, ISSN 1558-7916.

Mohamed, A.-R.; Hinton, G. (2010). Phone recognition using Restricted Boltzmann Machines. *Proceedings of IEEE International Conference on Acoustics, Speech, and Signal Processing (ICASSP)*, USA, March 2010.

Morris, J. & Fosler-Lussier, E. (2008). Conditional Random Fields for Integrating Local Discriminative Classifiers. *IEEE Transactions on Audio, Speech, and Language Processing*, 16:3, March 2008, pp 617-628. , ISSN 1558-7916.

Morris, J. & Fosler-Lussier, E. (2007). Further experiments with detector-based conditional random fields in phonetic recognition. *Proceedings of IEEE International Conference on Acoustics, Speech, and Signal Processing (ICASSP)*, Hawaii, April 2007.

Morris, J. & Fosler-Lussier, E. (2006). Combining phonetic attributes using conditional random fields. *Proceedings of Interspeech2006*, USA, September 2006.

Ney, H. & Ortmanns, S. (2000). Progress in Dynamic Programming Search for LVCSR. *Proceedings of the IEEE, 88(8):1224-1240*, 2000.

Räsänen, O.; Laine, U. & Altosaar, T. (2009). An Improved Speech Segmentation Quality Measure: the R-value. *Proceedings of Interspeech2009*, U.K.; September 2009.

Reynolds, T.J. & Antoniou, C.A. (2003). Experiments in speech recognition using a modular MLP architecture for acoustic modelling. *Information Sciences*, vol 156, Issue 1-2, 2003, pp 39 – 54, ISSN 0020-0255.

Robinson T. & Fallside F. (1991). A Recurrent Error Propagation Network Speech Recognition System. *Computer Speech & Language*, 5:3, 1991, pp. 259-274, ISSN 0885-2308.

Robinson, T. (1994). An application of recurrent nets to phone probability estimation. *IEEE Transactions on Neural Networks*, vol. 5, no. 2, March 1994, ISSN 1045-9227.

Robinson, T.; Almeida, L.; Boite, J. M.; Bourlard, H.; Fallside, F.; Hochberg, M.; Kershaw, D.; Kohn, P.; Konig, Y.; Morgan, N.; Neto, J. P.; Renals, S.; Saerens, M.; & Wooters, C. (1993). A neural network based, speaker independent, large vocabulary, continuous speech recognition system: The wernicke project. *Proceeding of Eurospeech93*, Germany, September 1993.

Rose, R.; Momayyez, P. (2007). Integration Of Multiple Feature Sets For Reducing Ambiguity In ASR". *Proceedings of IEEE International Conference on Acoustics, Speech and Signal Processing, 2007 (ICASSP)*, Hawaii, April 2007.

Scanlon, P.; Ellis, D. & Reilly, R. (2007). Using Broad Phonetic Group Experts for Improved Speech Recognition. *IEEE Transactions on Audio, Speech and Language Processing*, vol.15 (3) , pp 803-812, March 2007, ISSN 1558-7916.

Schwarz, P. (2008). Phone recognition based on long temporal context. PhD thesis, Brno University of Technology, Faculty of Information Technology, 2008.

Schwarz, P.; Matejka, P. & Cernocky, J. (2006). Hierarchical structures of neural networks for phone recognition. *Proceedings of IEEE International Conference on Acoustics, Speech and Signal Processing, 2006 (ICASSP)*, France, May 2006.

Sha, F. & Saul, L. (2006). Large margin Gaussian mixture modelling for phonetic classification and recognition. *Proceedings of IEEE International Conference on Acoustics, Speech and Signal Processing, 2006 (ICASSP)*, France, May 2006.

Siniscalchi, S. M.; Schwarz, P. & Lee, C.-H.; (2007). High-accuracy phone recognition by combining high-performance lattice generation and knowledge based rescoring. *Proceedings of IEEE International Conference on Acoustics, Speech and Signal Processing, 2007 (ICASSP)*, Hawaii, April 2007.

Young, S. J. (1992). The general use of tying in phone-based hmm speech recognizers. *Proceedings of IEEE International Conference on Acoustics, Speech and Signal Processing, 1992 (ICASSP)*, USA, March 1992.

Young, S. J.; et al. (2006). The HTK book. Revised for HTK version 3.4, *Cambridge University Engineering Department*, Cambridge, December 2006.

Zue, V. & Seneff, S. (1996). Transcription and alignment of the TIMIT database. *In Hiroya Fujisaki (Ed.), Recent research toward advanced man-machine interface through spoken language.* Amsterdam: Elsevier, pp 464-447, 1996.
Zue, V.; Seneff, S. & Glass J. (1990). Speech database development at MIT: TIMIT and beyond. *Speech Communication*, Vol. 9, No. 4, pp. 351-356, ISSN 0167-6393.

15

HMM Adaptation Using Statistical Linear Approximation for Robust Speech Recognition

Berkovitch Michael[1] and Shallom D.Ilan[1,2]
[1]Ben Gurion University
[2]AudioCodes
Israel

1. Introduction

Automatic Speech Recognition (ASR) systems, show degraded recognition performance when train and operate on mismatched environments. This mismatch can be caused due to different microphones, noise conditions, communication channels, acoustical environment etc.

This work is motivated, in part, by the Distributed Speech Recognition (DSR) architecture. The DSR uses ASR server that provides speech recognition services to different devices that may operate in different environments (i.e. mobile devices). Thus, the ASR server must implement environment compensation techniques. The traditional ASR environment compensation techniques use filtering and noise masking, spectral subtraction and multi microphones array. These techniques are usually implemented in the ASR front end and aims to provide clean speech samples to the ASR engine. State of the art ASR systems use Hidden Markov Models (HMM) to represent the stochastic nature of the speech features. These statistical models achieves high recognition rate when trained and tested at the same environmental condition. To add noise robustness for these models, methods such as Maximum Likelihood Linear Regression (MLLR) and Parallel Model Combination (PMC) had been developed. These methods perform an adaptation of the ASR engine to better fit the recognition environment. The main drawback of these methods is there computational complexity and the need of large adaptation data, which makes them not suitable for real-time application.

The environment compensation technique, presented in this chapter, is an extension of the Statistical Linear Approximation (SLA) method originally applied in the feature space to the model space. Using this environment compensation technique, new adapted HMMs set are created Using the clean speech HMMs and the noise model. The adapted HMMs are then used for the recognition of the degraded speech. The proposed robustness method is highly attractive for the Distributed Speech Recognition (DSR) architecture, since there is no impact on the Front End structure and neither on the ASR topology. Experiments, using this method, show high recognition rates in various noise conditions, close to the case of matched training (i.e. recognition and training performed in the same degraded environment).

2. Technique for Robust Speech Recognition

Techniques for Robust Speech Recognition can be divided into three categories.

- Extraction of environmental invariant (robust) features out of the input speech waveform.
- Data compensation ("cleaning") methods of either the input speech or its features .
- Model compensation methods which manipulate the acoustic models to better fit the noise environment .

These noise robustness techniques and there locations in the ASR decoder are shown in the following figure.

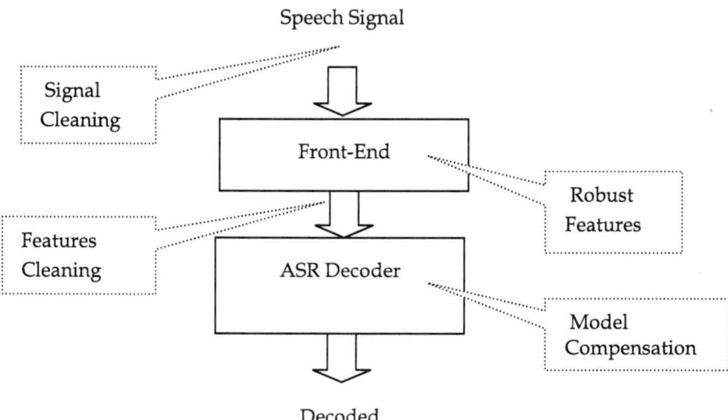

Fig. 1. Techniques for noise robustness scheme

2.1 Environmental robust features

Cepstral Mean Normalization (CMN) is a popular method for channel robust features. CMN efficiently reduce the effects of unknown linear filtering in the absence of additive noise CMN uses the fact that convolutive distortion is additive in the cepstral domain, shown in Eq.(1).

$$y_c = x_c + h_c \tag{1}$$

Here, yc, xc and hc are the corrupted, clean and channel cepstral coefficients respectively.

$$\hat{x}_c = y_c - E[y_c] \tag{2}$$

The CMN subtracts the long-term average of cepstral vectors from the incoming cepstral coefficients, resulting with estimation of the clean cepstral by Eq. (2). CMN can be seen as high-pass filtering of the cepstral coefficients, making them less sensitive to channel and speaker variation. Practically, the non-zero residuals of the mean reflect the channel distortion and speakers variability. This simple and effective procedure is applied to both the training and testing data.

2.2 Data compensation

Data Compensation refers to the process of restoring the clean speech signal or features from the degraded data. Data compensation methods were first introduced to the field of speech enhancement and then were adapted to robust ASR.

Spectral Subtraction is a popular additive noise suppression method. The basic assumption of spectral subtraction is that the effects of the additive noise can be modeled as a bias in the spectrum domain. The corrupted speech expected power spectrum can then be written as

$$|Y_i|^2 = |X_i|^2 + |N_i|^2 \tag{3}$$

The noise bias is estimated using a section of the signal that contains only background noise.

$$|\bar{N}|^2 = \frac{1}{M} \sum_{i=0}^{M-1} |Y_i|^2 \tag{4}$$

The clean speech power spectrum is then estimated using Eq.(5).

$$|\hat{X}_i|^2 = \max\left\{ \left(|Y_i|^2 - \alpha|\bar{N}|^2 \right), \beta|\bar{N}|^2 \right\} \tag{5}$$

Where α and β are adjustment factors.
Spectral Normalization was introduced by stockham et al to compensate for the effects of linear filtering. This algorithm estimates the average power spectra of speech in the training data and then applies the linear filter to the testing speech to "best" convert its spectrum to that of the training speech.
Another well known data compensation method is the Minimum Mean Squared Error (MMSE) uses a-priory statistical model of speech features to derive with a point estimate $\hat{x}$ for the clean speech features [22]. MMSE is defined in its general form using Eq.(6)

$$\hat{x}_{mmse} = \int x \cdot p(x \mid y)dx = \int x \cdot p(x,n,h \mid y)dxdndh \tag{6}$$

Where y, x represents the corrupted and clean speech, n, h represents the additive and convolutive noise and $p(x,n,h \mid y)$ is the joint conditional distribution. To estimate the clean speech we first need to formulate the relation between the clean and noisy speech signals. This relation is assumed in its general form as

$$y = x + f(x,n,h) \tag{7}$$

Therefore the MMSE estimation can be written as

$$\hat{x}_{mmse} = y - \int f(x,n,h) \cdot p(x,n,h \mid y)dxdndh \tag{8}$$

The joint conditional distribution is approximate using Vector Taylor Series (VTS), moreno had introduced this method to the log-spectral domain.

2.3 Model compensation
In Acoustical Model compensation we accept the presence of noise in the feature domains, and adapt the pattern recognition models to match the new acoustic environment, taking into account the noise statistics and the speech models (trained in the reference clean environment). The recognition is then performed using the models adapted to the noise conditions. Some well known model compensation techniques are the parallel Model compensation and multi-pass retraining.

Parallel Model Combination (PMC) is widely used for HMM compensation, it uses the fact that in the linear domain the corrupted speech is expressed as a summation of the additive noise and clean speech. Thus, the clean speech and additive noise cepstral model parameters (i.e. means and covariance) are transformed into the linear domain. There, they are combined and transformed back into the cepstral domain, as illustrated in Figure 2. Mathematically, the transformation of the mean vector and the covariance matrix between the cepstral-domain and the linear-spectral domain is defined in two steps, first the cepstral coefficients are transformed to the log-spectral using

$$\underline{\mu}^{\log} = C^{-1}\underline{\mu}^{cep}$$
$$\Sigma^{\log} = C^{-1}\Sigma^{cep}\left(C^{-1}\right)^{T} \tag{9}$$

Then they are transformed to the linear-spectral domain using

$$\mu_{i}^{lin} = \exp\left(\mu_{i}^{\log} + 0.5 \cdot \Sigma_{ii}^{\log}\right) \quad 0 \le i < N$$
$$\Sigma_{ij}^{lin} = \mu_{i}^{lin}\mu_{j}^{lin}\left(\exp\left(\Sigma_{ij}^{\log}\right) - 1\right) \quad 0 \le i,j < N \tag{10}$$

In the linear domain the noise and clean speech distribution is log-normal, in this domain the corrupted speech is summation of the noise and clean speech. Although summation of log-normal distributions is not log-normal, the PMC assumes it is log-normal. The corrupted speech means and covariance are then transformed back to the Log domain using the following inverse transform

$$\mu_{i}^{\log} = \log(\mu_{i}^{lin}) - 0.5\log\left(\frac{\Sigma_{ii}^{lin}}{\left(\mu_{i}^{lin}\right)^{2}} + 1\right) \quad 0 \le i < N$$
$$\Sigma_{ij}^{\log} = \log\left(\frac{\Sigma_{ij}^{lin}}{\mu_{i}^{lin}\mu_{j}^{lin}} + 1\right) \quad 0 \le i,j < N \tag{11}$$

Multi/Single Pass Retraining is an off-line model compensation method. In this method the speech models are retrained using speech database recorded in the corrupted environment. If the corrupted recognition environment is known a-priory, one can create off-line synthetic database to retrain the speech models. Since ASR maximizes their performance when trained and tested under the same environment condition, this is probably the best one can do. Unfortunately, this method is not applicable for real-time adaptation.

2.4 Model compensation motivation
Figure 3 illustrates the relations between data and model compensation robustness techniques. Using data compensation we pass in the feature space from the noisy data to the clean data. Using model compensation we pass in the model space from the clean model to

the noisy model. Therefore, using "clean model" with data compensation in the feature space
and using noisy data with noise compensated models can be viewed as a symmetric process.

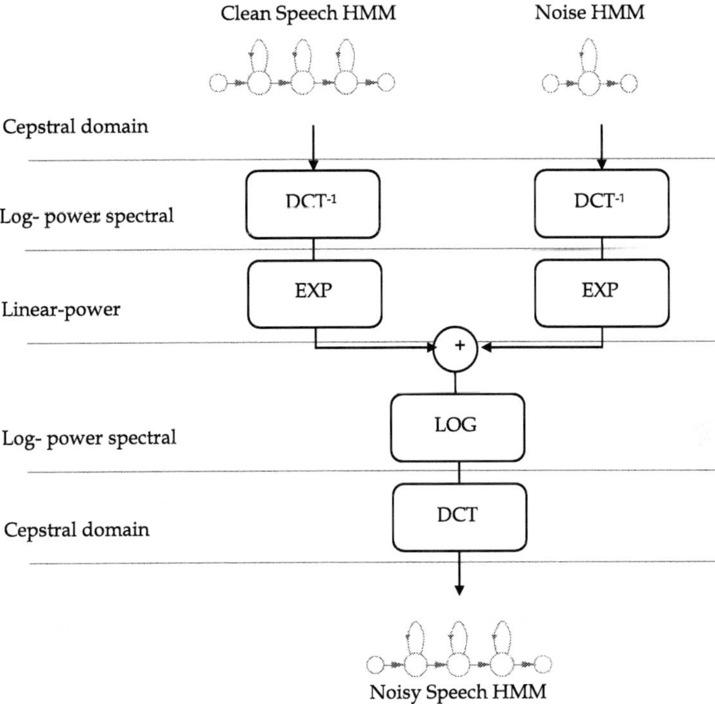

Fig. 2. Parallel Model Combination (PMC) block diagram

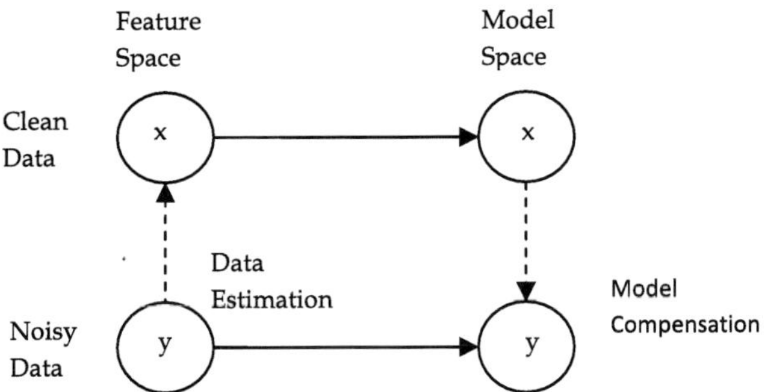

Fig. 3. Model compensation vs. feature estimation.

To illustrate these two noise robustness techniques, we will use a simple binary classifier.
The objective of this classifier is to associate each input vector x to one of the two classes A,B

$(A, B \in S)$ each with Gaussian pdf, seen in Figure 2.10. The classification problem can be written as

$$\frac{p(x|S=A) \cdot p(S=A)}{p(x|S=B) \cdot p(S=B)} = \begin{cases} >1 & x \in A \\ <1 & x \in B \end{cases} \tag{12}$$

When no noise is added, the error probability of the classifier, i.e. selecting A when B or vice versa, is given by

$$Err(x) = p(A) \cdot \int_{x \in B} p(x|S=A)dx + p(B) \cdot \int_{x \in A} p(x|S=B)dx \tag{13}$$

In the case of noisy observation, x becomes a hidden variable, the classifier job is to overcome the noise, and derive with the correct classification. Data compensation algorithms such as MMSE is used to derive with a point estimation $\hat{x}_{mmse}$ of this hidden variable by

$$\hat{x}_{mmse} = \int_x x \cdot p(x|y)dx \tag{14}$$

And then uses the "clean" classifier. In this case the classifier error probability is

$$Err(\hat{x}_{mmse}) = p(A) \int_{\hat{x}_{mmse} \in B} p(\hat{x}_{mmse}|S=A)dx + p(B) \int_{\hat{x}_{mmse} \in A} p(\hat{x}_{mmse}|S=B)dx \tag{15}$$

Model compensation method are used to derive with a new probability model $p(y|s)$, the classifier error probability is then

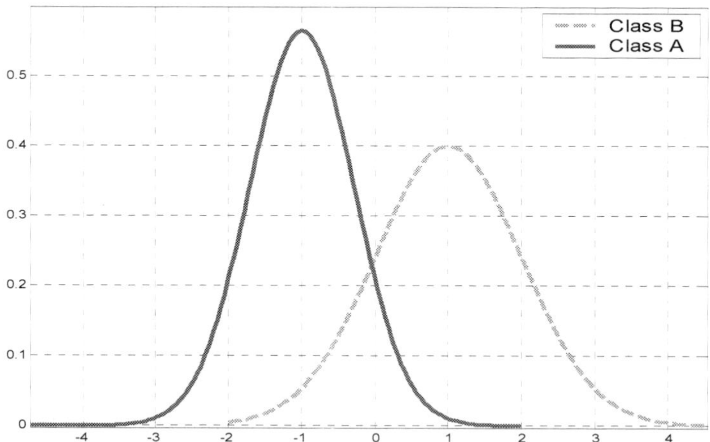

Fig. 4. The binary classification problem

$$Err(y) = p(A) \int_{y \in B} p(y|S=A)dy + p(B) \int_{y \in A} p(y|S=B)dy$$

$$Err(y) = p(A) \int_{y \in B x} \int p(y|x)p(x|S=A)dxdy \tag{16}$$

$$+p(B) \int_{y \in A x} \int p(y|x)p(x|S=B)dxdy$$

The advantage of using model compensation rather than data compensation is reducing the computational load, since data compensation requires a sampled or frame based compensation, where model compensation requires adaptation only when the noise conditions are changed. Speech recognition in noise can be seen as a complicated version of the binary classifier. The complications arise from the stochastic representation of speech (HMM) and the non-linear effect of noise on speech features.

3. The environment model

The environment model shown in Figure 5, assumes that clean speech (x[m]) is first passes through a transfer channel (h[m]) and then degraded by a additive noise (n[m]), resulting with a corrupted speech (y) expressed by

$$y[m] = x[m] * h[m] + n[m] \tag{17}$$

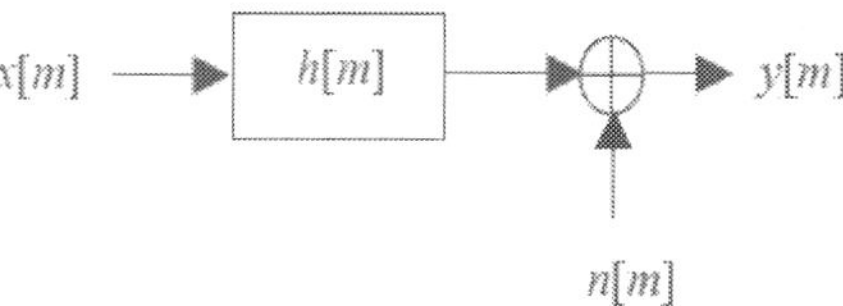

Fig. 5. The environment model.

State of the art ASR uses Mel-Frequency Cepstral Coefficients (MFCC) as their features. MFCC are obtained by passing the spectral magnitude of the noisy speech through a mel-scaled filter bank, taking its logarithm and applying the Discrete Cosine Transform (DCT). Thus, the effect of the environment in the MFCC feature spaces results with the well known environment function

$$y_c = x_c + h_c + C \cdot g(C^{-1}x_c, C^{-1}n_c, C^{-1}h_c) + err \tag{18}$$

Where y_c, x_c, n_c and h_c are the MFCC representation of degraded speech, clean speech, noise and channel respectively. C and C^{-1} are the DCT and inverse DCT matrix. The non-linear function $g(n,x,h)$ is presented by

$$g(x,n,h) = \log(1 + \exp(n - x - h)) \tag{19}$$

The term err in Eq.(18) represents a small amount of residual error due to the neglecting of the cross-correlation between the noise and clean speech.

Figure 6 and Figure 7 shows the effects of additive noise channel on speech in the MFCC domain. One can see that the additive noise changes the contour of the MFCC in non-linear manner. The lower the SNR the more noticeable is the non-linear effect. On the other hand, the channel effect in the MFCC domain can be seen as a-bias tilt, where the lower frequencies are attenuated, while higher frequencies are amplified. These plots also illustrate the de-convolutive property of the DCT transform.

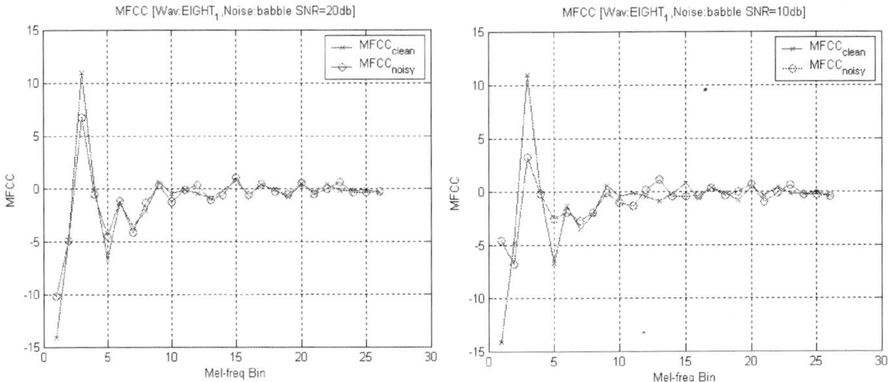

Fig. 6. Effect of additive noise on the MFCC

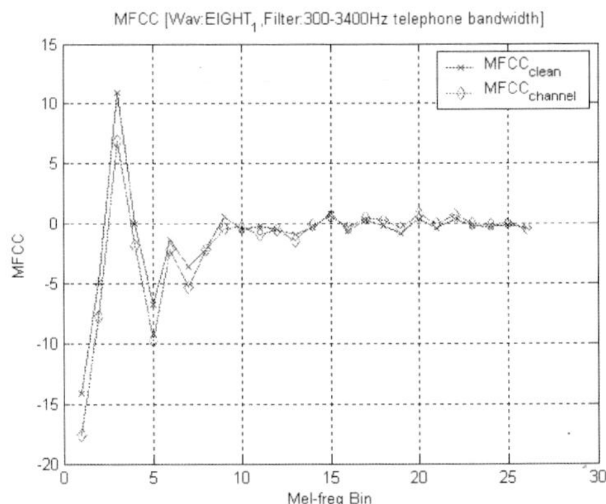

Fig. 7. Effect of linear filtering on the MFCC and Log-spectral features

It can be seen that the degraded speech MFCC is a non-linear transformation of the clean speech, noise and channel MFCC. This non-linearity makes it difficult to find a close analytical solution for the statistics of the degraded signal. The SLA method, shown in this chapter, is used to approximate this non-linearity, and by that, to derive an approximation for the statistics of the degraded speech

3.1 Effect of the environment model on MFCC distribution

When using model compensation it is important to understand the environment effect on the MFCC distribution. Clean speech, noise and channel MFCCs has Gaussian distribution but the degraded speech MFCCs distribution is no longer Gaussian. Nevertheless, the degraded speech MFCCs distribution could still be approximated using Gaussian distribution by

$$\mu_{y_c} = E\left[x_c + f(x_c, n_c, h_c)\right] = \mu_{x_c} + E\left[f(x_c, n_c, h_c)\right]$$

$$= \mu_{x_c} + \iiint_{x_c, n_c, h_c} p(x_c)p(n_c)p(h_c)f(x_c, n_c, h_c)dx_c dn_c dh_c \qquad (20)$$

$$\Sigma_{y_c} = E\left[\left(x_c + f(x_c, n_c, h_c)\right)\left(x_c + f(x_c, n_c, h_c)\right)^T\right] - \mu_{y_c}\left(\mu_{y_c}\right)^T$$

Where

$$f(x_c, n_c, h_c) = h_c + C\log\left(1 + \exp\left(C^{-1}(n_c - x_c - h_c)\right)\right) \qquad (21)$$

To evaluate the degraded speech MFCCs distribution, a Monte-Carlo simulation had been used.Large number of points, drawn from the clean speech and noise models, were combined together using Eq.(17) to produce the corrupted MFCC. Figure 8 illustrate the corrupted MFCC "true" distribution (solid line) and its Gaussian estimation (dotted line) for different values of Σx. The noise model was set to be Gaussian with $\mu n=0$ and $\Sigma n=4dB$, the clean data was also model using Gaussian with fix mean $\mu x=10$ and different covariance $\Sigma x=100, 20, 10$ and $5dB$. The degraded speech MFCCs distribution is clearly non-Gaussian. Though for small Σx values it can be well model using Gaussian distribution. For large Σx values the resulting corrupted distribution can be model using mixture of Gaussians Fortunately, ASR contains GMM thus each Gaussian mixture has small covariance values. Typical value range for the clean speech Gaussian mixture variance is 5-20dB.

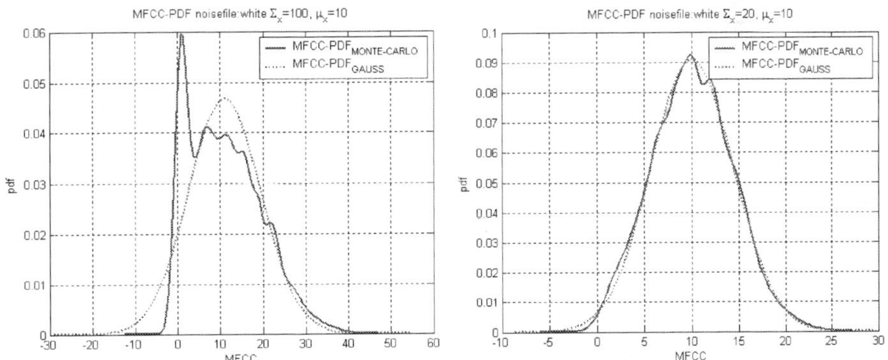

Fig. 8. Effect of the environment function on the distribution of cepstral coefficient

Figure 9 shows the effects of babble noise on the distribution of the third cepstrum coefficient (MFCC3) of the digit /eight/ for different SNRs. The noise affects both the mean and variance, resulting with mean shift and variance reduce. One can see that the lower the SNR the greater is the dissimilarity between the clean and corrupted MFCC PDFs. The effect of noise over MFCC features distribution is evident. Thus, the distributions representing clean speech features do not represent appropriately the corrupted speech features. The following paragraphs introduce the SLA-HMM method to approximate the effect of noise on the clean speech distribution and compensates for it, to achieve high noise robustness.

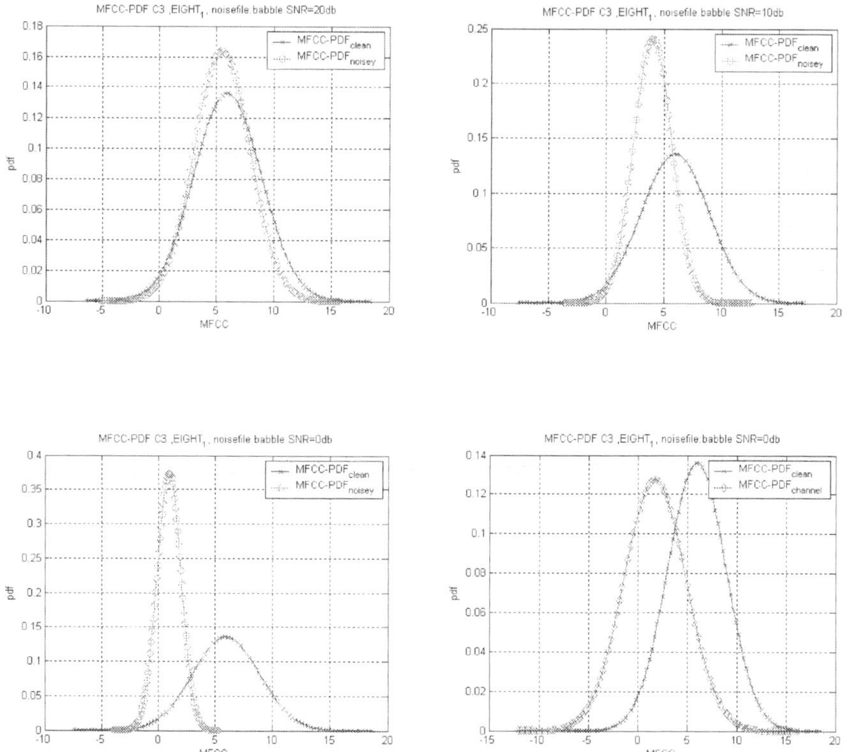

Fig. 9. Clean speech MFCC pdf vs. noisy speech MFCC for different SNRs

4. HMM adaptation for noise robustness

4.1 Statistical linear approximation

The Statistical Linear Approximation (SLA) method, used to approximates a nonlinear function with a linear combination of it variables, around a fix point. This method, assumes that the non-linear function variables are independent random variables with Gaussian distribution. To derive with the formulation of the SLA approximation, lets define g(x,n,h) as an arbitrary non-linear function with three independent variables, e.g. the clean speech, noise and channel respectively. Define $\tilde{g}(x,n,h)$ to be a linear approximation of $g(x,n,h)$ around a fix point (x$_0$, n$_0$, h$_0$,) given by

$$\tilde{g}(x,n,h) = a^m \cdot (x - x_0) + b^m \cdot (n - n_0) + c^m \cdot (h - h_0) + d^m \tag{22}$$

Where {a^m,b^m,c^m,d^m} are the linearization coefficients that need to be evaluate. Using the SLA method an optimal, in the Mean Square Error (MSE) sense, linearization coefficients can be found.

The m order Taylor series expansion of the non-linear function $g(x,n,h)$, around a fix point (x_0,n_0,h_0) is written by the following polynomial

$$P_g^m(x,n,h) = \sum_{k=0}^{m} \frac{1}{k!}\left((x-x_0)\frac{d}{dx}+(n-n_0)\frac{d}{dn}+(h-h_0)\frac{d}{dh}\right)^k \cdot g(x_0,n_0,h_0)$$

$$= \sum_{k=0}^{m}\sum_{j=0}^{k}\sum_{i=0}^{j} \zeta_{k,j,i} \cdot (x-x_0)^i (n-n_0)^{j-i} (h-h_0)^{k-j} \tag{23}$$

Where $\zeta_{k,j,i}$ define as

$$\zeta_{k,j,i} = \frac{1}{i! \cdot (j-i)! \cdot (k-j)!} \cdot \frac{d^k g(x_0,n_0,h_0)}{dx^i \, dn^{j-i} \, dh^{k-j}} \tag{24}$$

The linear coefficients are then found by minimizing the MSE between the m order Taylor series expansion and the linear approximation, given the assumptions about the variables x, n, h.

$$\varepsilon_{rr} = \arg\min_{a^m,b^m,c^m,d^m} \left(E[(P_g^m - \tilde{g})^2]\right)$$

$$\varepsilon_{rr} = E[(P_g^m)^2] + E[(\tilde{g})^2] - 2 \cdot E[P_g^m \tilde{g}]$$

$$\varepsilon_{rr} = E[(P_g^m)^2] + E[\tilde{g}^2] - 2 \cdot E[(a^m(x-x_0)+b^m(n-n_0) \tag{25}$$

$$+c^m(h-h_0)+d^m) \cdot P_g^m]$$

The error function around $(x_0,n_0,h_0) = (\mu_x,\mu_n,\mu_h)$ Expressed by

$$\varepsilon_{rr} = E[(P_g^m)^2] + \left(a^m \Sigma_x \left(a^m\right)^T + b^m \Sigma_n \left(b^m\right)^T + c^m \Sigma_h \left(c^m\right)^T + \left(d^m\right)^2\right)$$

$$-2\left(a^m E[(x-\mu_x)P_g^m] + b^m E[(n-\mu_n)P_g^m] + c^m E[(h-\mu_h)P_g^m] + d^m E[P_g^m]\right) \tag{26}$$

The linearization coefficients, which minimizes the MSE, are found by solving the following equations

$$
\frac{d\varepsilon_{rr}}{da^m} = 2a^m \Sigma_x - 2E[(x-\mu_x) \cdot P_g^m] = 0
$$

$$
\frac{d\varepsilon_{rr}}{db^m} = 2b^m \Sigma_n - 2E[(n-\mu_n) \cdot P_g^m] = 0
$$

$$
\frac{d\varepsilon_{rr}}{dc^m} = 2c^m \Sigma_h - 2E[(h-\mu_h) \cdot P_g^m] = 0
$$
(27)
$$
\frac{d\varepsilon_{rr}}{dd^m} = 2d^m - 2E[P_g^m] = 0
$$

After some algebra, the following expressions to the linearization coefficients are derived

$$
a^m = \Sigma_x^{-1} \sum_{k=0}^{m} \sum_{j=0}^{k} \sum_{i=0}^{j} \zeta_{k,j,i} \cdot E[(x-\mu_x)^{i+1}(n-\mu_n)^{j-i}(h-\mu_h)^{k-j}]
$$

$$
b^m = \Sigma_n^{-1} \sum_{k=0}^{m} \sum_{j=0}^{k} \sum_{i=0}^{j} \zeta_{k,j,i} \cdot E[(x-\mu_x)^{i}(n-\mu_n)^{j-i+1}(h-\mu_h)^{k-j}]
$$
(28)
$$
c^m = \Sigma_h^{-1} \sum_{k=0}^{m} \sum_{j=0}^{k} \sum_{i=0}^{j} \zeta_{k,j,i} \cdot E[(x-\mu_x)^{i}(n-\mu_n)^{j-i}(h-\mu_h)^{k-j+1}]
$$

$$
d^m = \sum_{k=0}^{m} \sum_{j=0}^{k} \sum_{i=0}^{j} \zeta_{k,j,i} \cdot E[(x-\mu_x)^{i}(n-\mu_n)^{j-i}(h-\mu_h)^{k-j}]
$$

This is further simplified by using the well-known property for Gaussian PDF shown in Eq.(29), where all variables assume to be independent Gaussian.

$$
E[(y-\mu_y)^m] = \begin{cases} 0 & m\_odd \\ 1\cdot 3\ldots\cdot(m-1)\Sigma_y^{m/2} & otherwise \end{cases}
$$
(29)

One can see that for m=1 the SLA linear approximation is the same as the Taylor expansion. Higher order of m introduces more statistical information to the approximation, making the approximation more accurate.

4.2 Statistical linear approximation for HMM adaptation

The SLA-HMM adaptation framework, shown in Figure 10, uses the pre-trained clean speech HMMs and the noise model (both in the MFCC feature space), to update each HMM state PDF, using the SLA method. The output of this process is a set of new robust HMMs. These robust HMM have the same structure as the clean HMM, but with updated states distributions.The additive noise is modeled using single Gaussian, which is good approximation for stationary noise. For none stationary noises multi-mode Gaussian can be used. The noise model is trained during the non-voice periods, and updated to reflect the noise

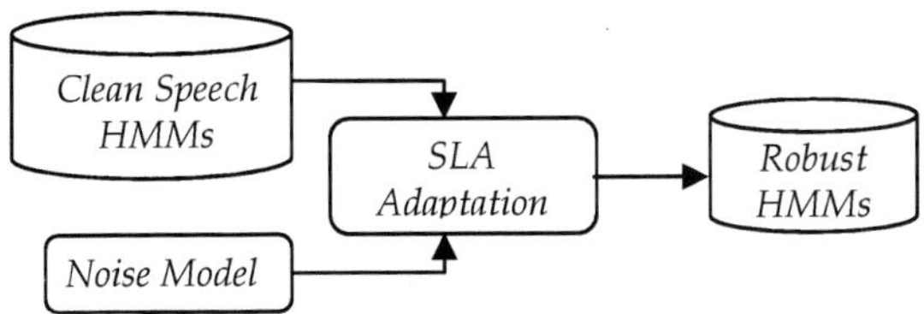

Fig. 10. SLA- HMM adaptation scheme.

To derived with the SLA approximation of the noise robust HMM, we start with an approximation of the environment function, in the MFCC domain, as given by Eq.(30)

$$\underline{y}_c = \underline{x}_c + \underline{h}_c + C \cdot g_l(C^{-1}\underline{x}_c, C^{-1}\underline{n}_c, C^{-1}\underline{h}_c)) \tag{30}$$

Using Eq.(22) the linear approximation of Eq.(30) is

$$\underline{y}_c \approx \underline{x}_c + \underline{h}_c + A^m(\underline{x}_c - \underline{\mu}_{x_c}) + B^m(\underline{n}_c - \underline{\mu}_{n_c})$$
$$+ C^m(\underline{h}_c - \underline{\mu}_{h_c}) + Cd^m \tag{31}$$

Where the matrices {A^m,B^m,C^m} are given by

$$A^m = C \cdot diag(\underline{a}^m) \cdot C^{-1}$$
$$B^m = C \cdot diag(\underline{b}^m) \cdot C^{-1} \tag{32}$$
$$C^m = C \cdot diag(\underline{c}^m) \cdot C^{-1}$$

Using Eq.(32) one can write an approximation to the noise speech mean and covariance matrix as follows

$$\underline{\mu}_{y_c} = \underline{\mu}_{x_c} + \underline{\mu}_{h_c} + C \cdot d^m$$
$$\Sigma_{y_c} = (I + A^m)\Sigma_{x_c}(I + A^m)^T + B^m\Sigma_{n_c}(B^m)^T + \tag{33}$$
$$(I + C^m)\Sigma_{h_c}(I + C^m)^T$$

ASR also uses the MFCC first and second derivative. Therefore, their means and covariance matrices need to be approximate. The delta and delta-delta MFCC are calculated using

$$\Delta x_c(t) = x_c(t+2) - x_c(t-2)$$
$$\Delta\Delta x_c(t) = \Delta x_c(t+2) - \Delta x_c(t-2) \tag{34}$$

The delta MFCC related to the MFCC by $\Delta x_c \approx \dfrac{dx_c}{dt}$ 0. Thus, the noisy speech delta MFCC

can be written as

$$\Delta y_c \approx \frac{dy_c}{dt} = (I + A^m)\frac{dx_c}{dt} + B^m \frac{dn_c}{dt} \tag{35}$$

Here we use the assumption that h is constant through the speech utterances. The delta and delta-delta MFCC approximated means and covariance matrices are then can be written by

$$\mu_{\Delta y_c} = (I + A^m)\mu_{\Delta x_c} + B^m \mu_{\Delta n_c}$$
$$\mu_{\Delta\Delta y_c} = (I + A^m)\mu_{\Delta\Delta x_c} + B^m \mu_{\Delta\Delta n_c} \tag{36}$$

$$\Sigma_{\Delta y_c} = (I + A^m)\Sigma_{\Delta x_c}(I + A^m)^T + B^m\Sigma_{\Delta n_c}(B^m)^T$$
$$\Sigma_{\Delta\Delta y_c} = (I + A^m)\Sigma_{\Delta\Delta x_c}(I + A^m)^T + B^m\Sigma_{\Delta\Delta n_c}(B^m)^T \tag{37}$$

To evaluate the SLA-HMM approximation, the "true"(using Monte-Carlo simulation) and approximated HMM PDFs were compared using the Kullback-Leibler Divergence (KL). The approximated PDFs derived using the proposed SLA method. Figure 11 shows the resulting KL-measure for SLA order 1-3 as a function of μ_{x_c} where $\sigma_{x_c} = 5$, $\mu_{n_c} = 0$ and $\sigma_{n_c} = 2$.

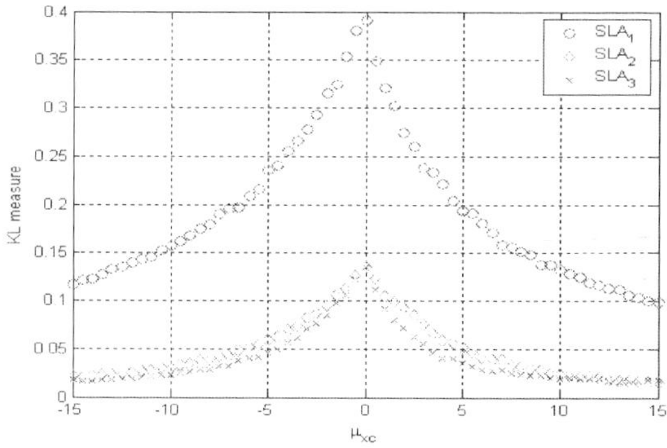

Fig. 11. Kullback-Leibler measure for different SLA order.

The triangular-like shape of the KL-measure indicates that, the larger the distance between the clean and noise MFCC means the more accurate is the approximation, i.e. for $\mu_x >> \mu_n$ the noise can be neglect, resulting with the clean speech PDF and vice versa. One can see that SLA of order 2, 3 yield with more accurate approximation then the VTS, shown by SLA1

5. Experimental results

To investigate the performance of the HMM adaptation algorithm, the well established TIDIGIT speech corpus was used. The TIDIGIT consists of 4480 utterances of isolated digits spoken by men and women for training and testing. Care was taken to balance the training material with respect to an equal number of male and female speakers and equal number of training utterances for all digits.

All speech utterances were recorded without background noise. The noisy speech data-base was created artificially by adding noise sources to the clean speech. The noise sources were taken from the NOISEX-92 database. For each noise source, the average log power of the low (0-1500Hz) and high frequencies band (1500-4000Hz) was calculated. The noise source had been divided into three test groups. Test group A contains high average log power at the low frequency band. Test group B contains high average log power at the high frequency band. Test group C contains non-stationary noises (i.e. babble, machinegun). Figure 12 depict the three noise test groups.

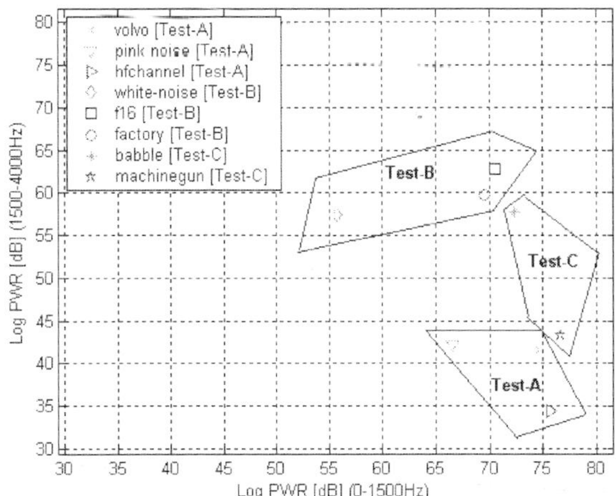

Fig. 12. Test sets noises low-band log power vs. high-band log power

HTK software tool kit had been used to perform all the recognition tests. The ASR HMM structure consists of 4 states, with 4-8 Gaussians per state depending on the available training data. These HMMs were trained using 13-dimensional MFCC feature vector and its delta and delta-delta derivative. The baseline ASR was trained using clean training data. The Baseline ASR HMMs were then retrained, using the noisy speech training data, creating the matched ASR HMMs. For HMM model adaptation algorithm evaluation, the baseline ASR and a matched trained ASR word error rate (WER), can be considered as the upper and Lower performance bounds respectively. The performance of the proposed SLA-HMM adaptation needs to be compare to the performance of matched trained recognizer. Table 1 shows the average WER results of the baseline recognizer for the different noise groups and SNRs.

For the baseline ASR, the lack in noise robustness is highly noticeable especially in the case of wide-band noise (test-b). One can see that for SNRs lower than 10 dB the ASR performance "breaks" for all noise groups.

Table 2 shows the average WER results of the matched recognizer. As expected, the matched ASR yields with high noise robustness, comparing to the base line recognizer. Nevertheless, at SNRs lower than 5dB the performance improvement starts to fail. Thus, it is expected that at low SNRs the proposed model compensation method will show the same behavior . One of the reasons for this ASR behavior is that at low SNR , ASR model topology changes may be require.

SNR [dB]	Test-A	Test-B	Test-C
Clean	0.7	0.9	0.6
20	1.0	3.4	1.4
15	2.2	11.4	4.9
10	7.3	38.0	17.1
5	19.0	67.2	34.0
0	30.5	86.8	41.8
-5	42.0	89.6	49.6
Avg	14.7	42.5	21.3

Table 1. Baseline ASR WER[%]

SNR [dB]	Test-A	Test-B	Test-C
Clean	0.6	0.9	0.8
20	0.5	0.9	1.2
15	0.7	1.8	2.6
10	1.6	5.2	5.0
5	3.6	15.0	12.4
0	8.4	42.0	36.1
-5	2.6	11.0	9.7
Avg	0.6	0.9	0.8

Table 2. Matched ASR WER[%]

5.1 Evaluation of SLA-HMM adaptation

For the evaluation of the SLA-HMM adaptation algorithm, the baseline HMMs were used to represent the clean speech models. The noise was model using a mixture of gaussian (up to four), trained by the noisy speech utterances first 20 frames, which contains noise only. To evaluate the SLA-HMM performance, the SLA-HMM ASR word error rate (WER) measurements were compared to the matched HMM ASR WER. The following figures present the average WER results attained using the SLA-HMM algorithm at different noise conditions. Each figure presents different noise group average WER results versus SNR. Results attained using high order SLA-HMM (three and above) had been omitted, as they show no or little performance improvement.

One can see that the proposed noise robustness algorithm improves the ASR performance in all of the tested noise conditions. The proposed algorithm shows high noise robustness, with performance results close to the matched trained ASR (represented by the solid line).

The experiments show that SLA-HMM of order 3 yields with the highest recognition rates, outperforming the VTS algorithm (represents by SLA-HMM of order 1). Thus, high order SLA approximation increases the algorithm accuracy, as expected.

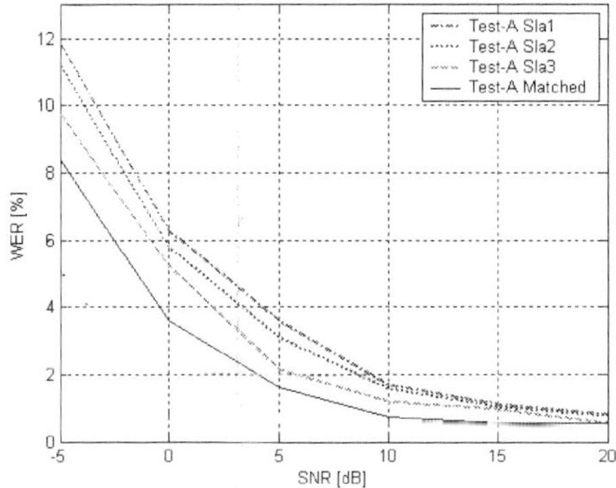

Fig. 13. SLA-HMM average WER vs. SNR using Test-A

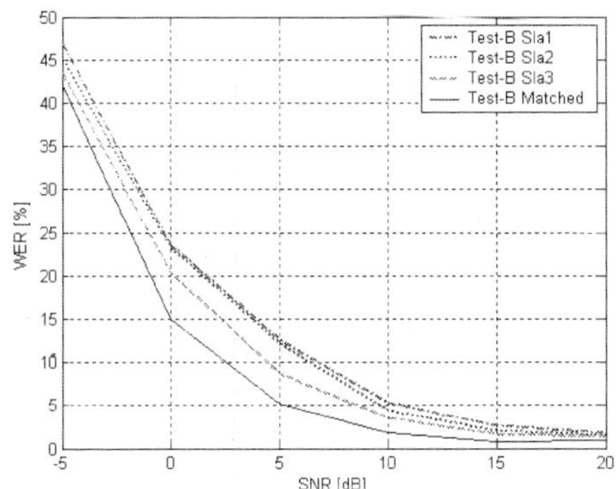

Fig. 14. SLA-HMM average WER vs. SNR using Test-B

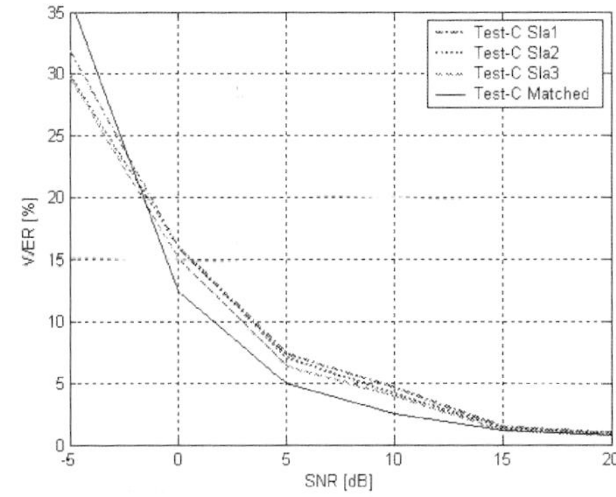

Fig. 15. SLA-HMM average WER vs. SNR using Test-C (noise model 4-GMM)

6. Conclusion

This chapter presents a robust ASR method based on model adaptation using the Statistical Linear Approximation. The proposed SLA-HMM model adaptation had achieving an average of 70% WER improvement with respect to the baseline ASR. The proposed algorithm achieves high robustness performance in variety of environmental conditions compared to the baseline recognizer. The proposed model-compensation had also shown good performance compare to the matched trained ASR

The proposed robustness algorithm has an advantage in Distributed Speech Recognition (DSR), since no changes are required to the front-end terminals and to the ASR topology, as the adaptation is done on HMMs models on the server side.

Further work will put emphasis on improving the robustness performance at very low SNR, where this algorithm had shown some decrease in performance. This performance decrease can be cope by Appling changes to the HMM topology. The proposed noise robustness algorithm had been tested using isolated word recognizer, the same algorithm can be evaluated using phone level continues speech recognizer

7. References

Acero, L., (1993). Acoustical and Environmental Robustness in Automatic Speech Recognition. Kluwer Academic Publishers

Acero, L., Kristjansson, T. & Zhang, J. (2000). Hmm Adaptation using Vector Taylor Series for Noisy Speech Recognition. *Proc ICSLP*, Vol.3, pp. 869-872

Deng, L.; Acero, A.; Jiang, L.; Droppo, J. & Hunag, X.-D. (2001). High-perfromance robustspeech recognition using stereo training data. *Proceedings of ICASSP*, Vol.4, pp. 301-304

Fujimoto M. & Ariki Y., (2004). Robust Speech Recognition in Additive and Channel Noise Environments Using GMM and EM Algorithm. *Proceedings of ICASSP*, Vol. 1, pp. 941-944

Gales, M. J. F. & Young, S. J. (1996). Robust continuous speech recognition using parallel model combination. *IEEE Trans. Speech and Audio Proc,* pp. *352-359*

Hamaguchi S.,; Kitaoka N., & Nakagawa S., (2005). Robust Speech Recognition under Noisy Environments based on Selection of Multiple Noise Suppression Methods, *IEEE-EURASIP (NSIP2005)*, pp.308–313

Kim, N. S., (1998). Statistical linear approximation for environment compensation. *IEEE Signal Processing Letters*, Vol. 5, pp. 8-10

Martin, F.,; Shikano K. & Minami Y. (1993). Recognition of noisy speech by composition of hidden Markov models, *Proceedings of. EuroSpeech,* Vol.4, pp. 1031–1034

Macho, D.,; Mauuary, L.,; Noe, B.,; Cheng, Y. M.,; Ealey, D.,; Jouvet, D.,; Kelleher, H.,; Pearce, D. & Saadoun, F. (2002). Evaluation of a Noise-Robust DSR Front-End on Aurora Databases. *Proceedings of ICSLP*, pp. 17-20

Moreno, P., (1996). Speech Recognition in Noisy Environments, Ph.D. thesis. Carnegie Mellon University

Varga, A. P.,; Steeneken, H. J. M.,; Tomlinson, M., & Jones, D., (1992). The NOISEX-92 Study on The Effect of Additive Noise on Automatic Speech Recognition. Technical Report DRA Speech Research Unit

Young, S. J.,; Evermann, G.,; Gales, M.,; Hain, T.,; Kershaw, D.,; Liu, X.,; Moore, G.,; Odell, J.,; Ollason, D.,; Povey, D.,; Valtchev, V. & Woodland, P. C., (2006). The HTK Book (for HTK Version 3.4), University of Cambridge

16

Speech Recognition Based on the Grid Method and Image Similarity

Janusz Dulas
Opole University of Technology
Poland

1. Introduction

The problem of communication between a man and a machine is very old. First constructors had to decide how to transmit information from a man to machine and vice versa. This problem still exists and each engineer who designs a new device must decide how the communication between operator and a machine will be done. Simple devices use buttons and Light Emit Diodes [LED], more complicated – keyboards and screens. Fast technical development and numerous scientific research allowed to use also voice for this purpose. Here there are two different problems: voice producing and voice recognition. The first one is not very difficult, in the simplest case the machine could record a set of words which would be used for communication. Nowadays there are specialised integrated circuits (speech processors) which enable recording and reproducing whole words and sentences. The second problem – voice recognition is more complicated. First of all people are different and say the same words in a different way. Secondly, the way of speaking depends on many aspects like health of the speaker, his mood or emotion. Thirdly, we are living in noisy environment so usually together with speech signal we also obtain different noises. There are a lot of different methods used for automatic speech recognition. The most popular is HMM – Hidden Markov Model (Junho & Hanseok, 2006; Wydra, 2007; Kumar & Sreenivas 2005; Ketabdar at al., 2005) , which uses sequences of events (states), where the probability of being in each state and the probability of transition to the other states are counted. Each state is described by many, mostly spectral parameters. There are also other, less popular methods used for automatic speech recognition like Neural Network Method (Vali at al., 2006; Holmberg at al.,2005; Togneri & Deng, 2007), Audio-visual Method (Seymour at al., 2007; Hueber at al., 2007) and many others (Nishida et al., 2005). Nowadays there is a possibility to achieve more than 90% accuracy in automatic speech recognition. HMM method, although the most popular, is very complicated. Each state is described by the matrix with many spectral, cepstral and linear prediction parameters. It causes the need for many analyses and calculations during the automatic recognition process. In this chapter the author shows a new approach to this problem. The new method described here is simpler and faster than HMM method and gives similar or better results in speech recognition accuracy. Although it was tested in Polish, the rules can be adopted to other languages.

2. Some interesting voice signal properties

Usually the voice signal which will be analysed is first converted into the electric signal by the microphone. The most popular are dynamic and condenser microphones. No matter which one is used, we obtain a signal with frequency of between dozen or so hertz and some kilohertz. Figure 1 shows time characteristic for word "zero" spoken by the man.

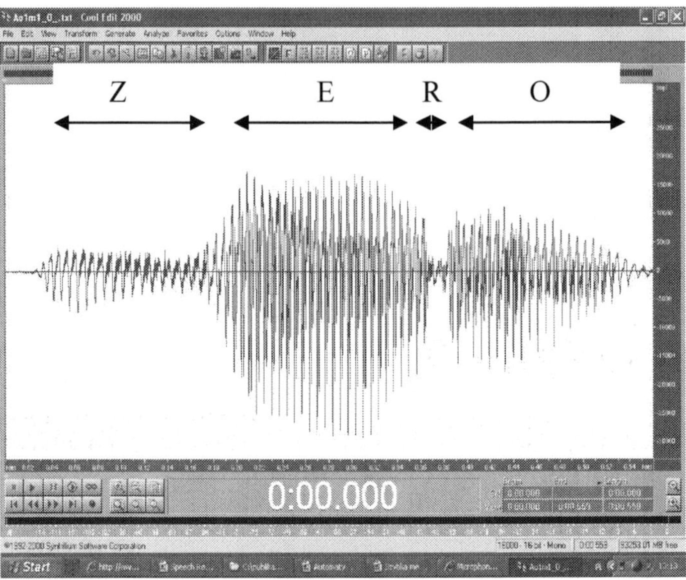

Fig. 1. The electric signal time characteristic for word "zero"

As is well known, each word could be divided into the smallest parts called phonemes. In Polish there are 37 phonemes which can built 95% of all words. Usually they are well visible in time characteristic. In figure 1 it is easy to find four phonemes for example by listening tests of different parts of this record. As is easy to observe, the phonemes could have different duration. For example in figure 1, the "R" phoneme has the smallest duration. They could also have different amplitudes. In figure 1 phonemes "E" and "O" have greater amplitudes than phonemes "Z" and "R". As the theory said – phonemes could be voiced and unvoiced. All vowels and some consonants are voiced. Voiced phonemes are easy to find because they include many repeatable basic periods inside of them. These periods have similar duration (between 2 and 10 ms) which is dependent on the speaker's sex and age. Men have bigger basic periods duration (usually 7...10ms) than women and children (usually 2..5ms). The shape of the signal in neighbouring basic periods is similar. Let's look at the magnifying part of the phoneme's "O" time characteristic (figure 2).

There are many basic periods with similar signal's shape and similar duration (about 7ms). Because the duration equals 7ms, it means this is the man's voice record. Another interesting voice feature is the envelope shape. In figure 3 there are shown three time characteristics of the word "zero" spoken by the man, woman and child.

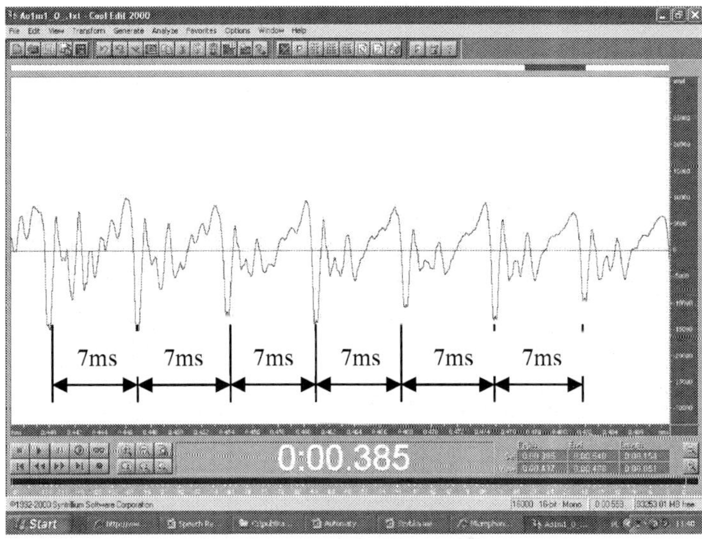

Fig. 2. Magnifying part of phoneme "O" time characteristic.

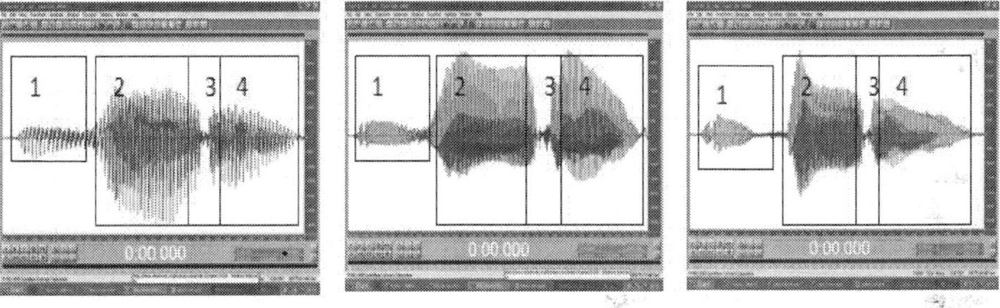

Fig. 3. The word "zero" spoken by the man, woman and child

In rectangles there are included four different parts of the records. The first has rather small amplitude, the second's amplitude is bigger, the third's smaller and the fourth's bigger. Although these records come from different speakers, the same amount of different parts is included inside them. Maximum duration of each part could vary and is difficult to find but there is a possibility of finding the minimum duration what has been proven in authors research.

Another voice feature is fluently changing the signal shape between neighbouring phonemes. It is not just one point but the zone, which possible duration of many milliseconds.

In figure 4 there is shown such a zone between phonemes "z" and "e" in word "zero".

As is shown in figure 4 the transient zone duration in this case equals about 30ms.

Another group of phonemes are noisy phonemes. These phonemes don't include basic periods in their time characteristics but many irregular signals. In Polish there are some such phonemes. The example of noisy phoneme time characteristic is shown in figure 5.

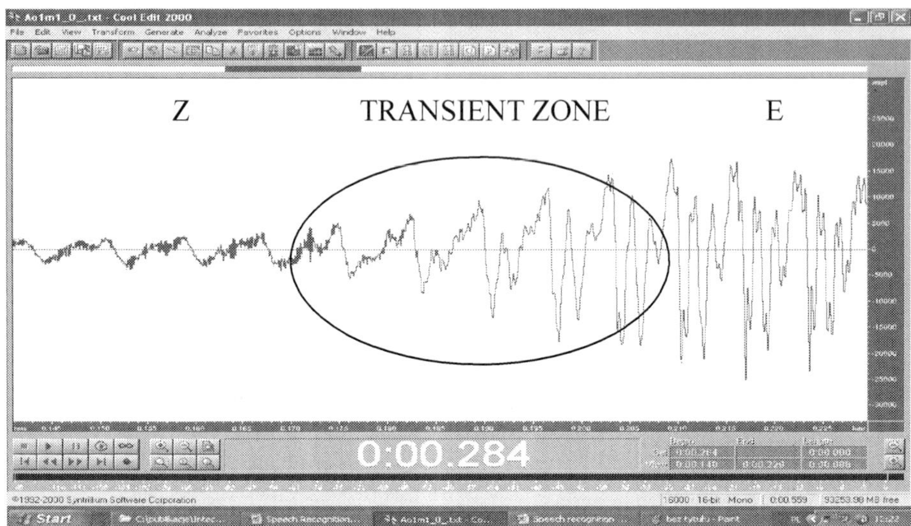

Fig. 4. Transient zone between phonemes "z" and "e" in word "zero"

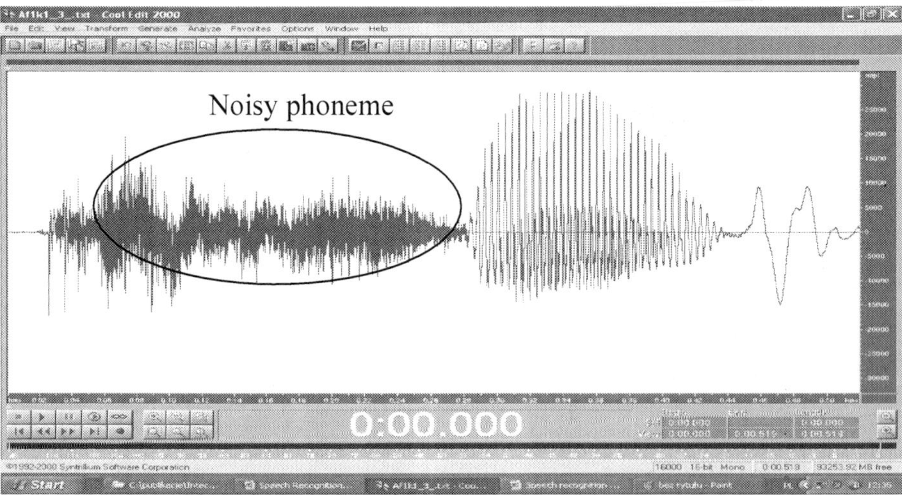

Fig. 5. The word spoken in Polish including a noisy phoneme.

The magnifying part of noisy phoneme from figure 5 is shown in figure 6.

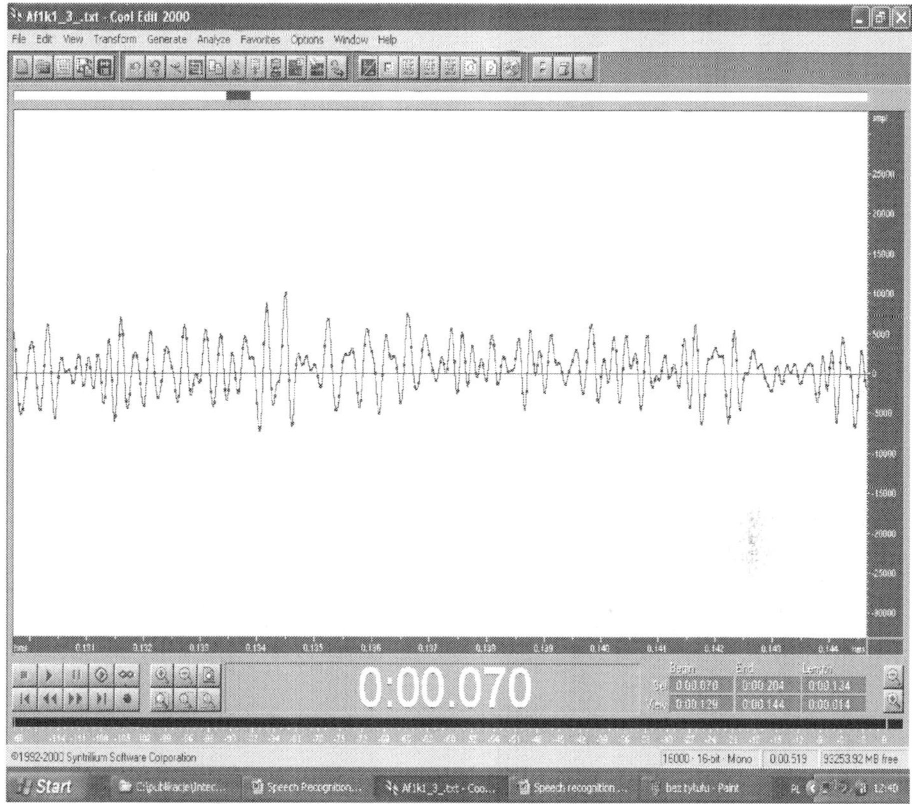

Fig. 6. A magnifying part of noisy phoneme time characteristic

As is easy to notice here there are no repeatable similar basic periods. The signal changes it's amplitude very often. Sometimes the stronger signals appear but the moments of these events are accidentally.

3. Envelope similarity analyses

As was mentioned in section 2, the envelopes of the same word spoken by different speakers have similar shapes. This feature will be used for automatic speech recognition. There are a lot of possibilities of the envelope shape describing. In author's research, each word (digits from 0 to 9 names spoken in Polish) was described by number of unique parts, their minimum durations and amplitude range. This operation was made on the 500 records set from speakers different sex and age. As results showed, this approach allowed to build envelope patterns of all digits names for all speakers. They are shown in table 1.

As was shown in table 1 each digit has its own envelope pattern with a defined number of unique parts (column 3), their minimum durations (column 4) and amplitude ranges (column 5). The amplitude values are defined in per cents of the maximum signal's value for

Digit	Envelope's shape	Number of parts	Minimum durations	Amplitude ranges
0	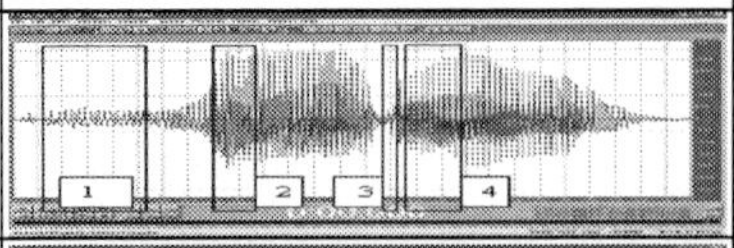	4	1.80ms 2.30ms 3.10ms 4.50ms	1.A<50% 2.A>53% 3.5-64% 4.A>31%
1	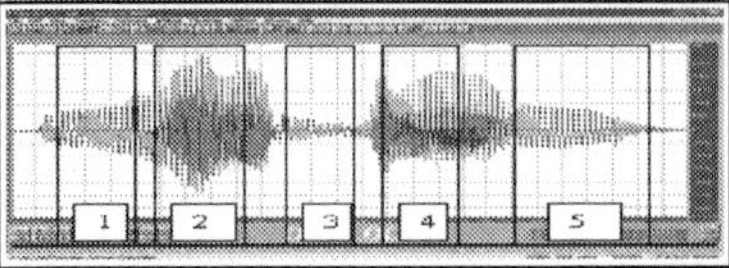	5	1.60ms 2.70ms 3-50ms 4-60ms 5-100ms	1.A<62% 2.A>44% 3-1%<A<26% 4-A>25% 5-A<50%
2	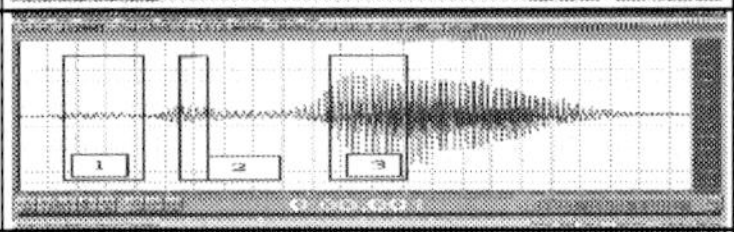	3	1.50ms 2.20ms 3.50ms	1.A<30% 2.A>29% 3.A>43%
3	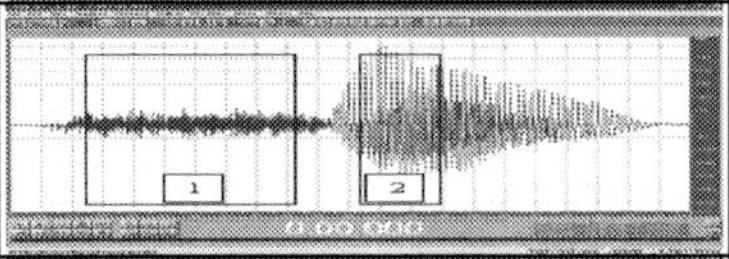	2	1.130ms 2.40ms	1.6%<A<32% 2.A>68%
4	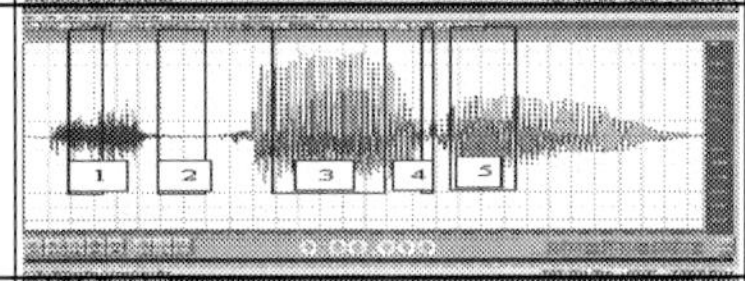	5	1.30ms 2.40ms 3.100ms 4.10ms 5.60ms	1.A>1% 2.A<4% 3.A>40% 4.3%<A<35% 5.A>13%
5	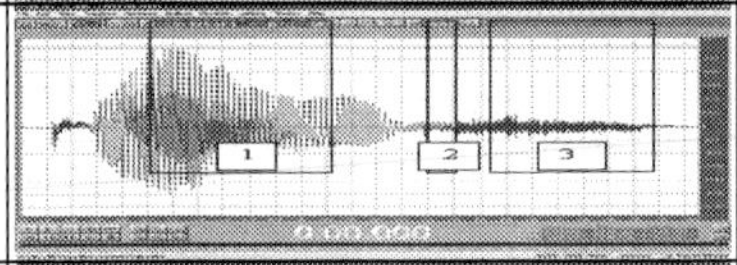	3	1.140ms 2.20ms 3.110ms	1.A>29% 2.A<23% 3.A>0%
6	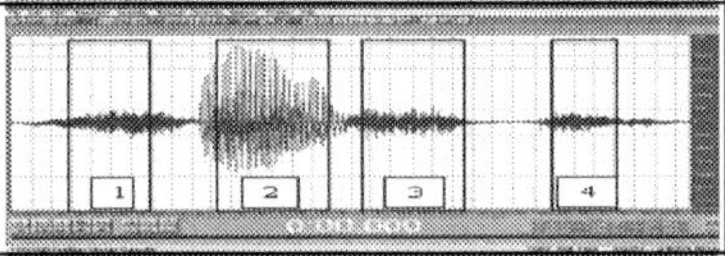	4	1.80ms 2.100ms 3.100ms 4.70ms	1.2%<A<35% 2.A>26% 3.1%<A<56% 4.A>1%
7	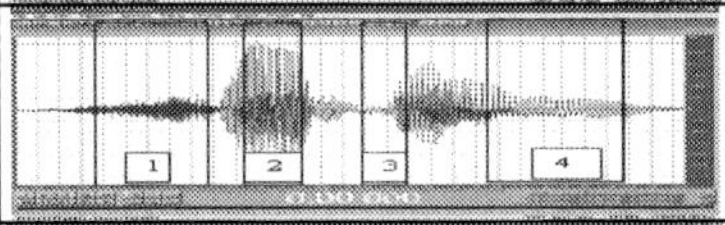	4	1.100ms 2.50ms 3.30ms 4.110ms	1.3%<A<65% 2.A>36% 3.2%<A<28% 4.6%<A<59%
8	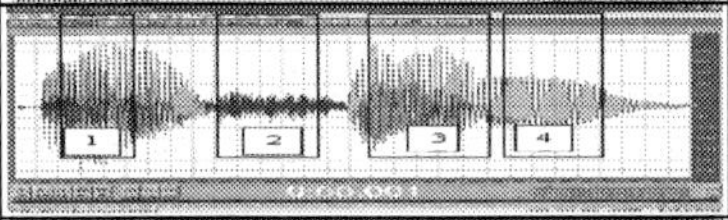	4	1.70ms 2.90ms 3.100ms 4.90ms	1.A>46% 2.6%<A<61% 3.16%<A<92% 4.5%<A<43%
9	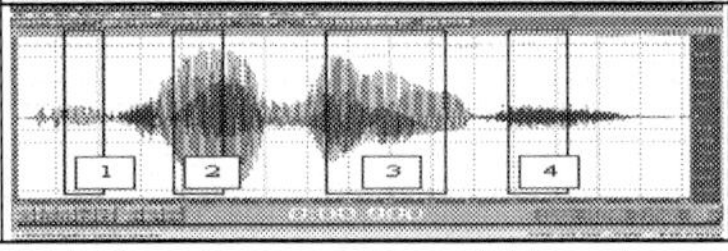	4	1.40ms 2.70ms 3.150ms 4.80ms	1.1%<A<45% 2.A>46% 3.A>9% 4.A<50%

Table 1. Envelope patterns together with unique parts parameters

the whole words. As is easy to observe, the number of unique parts is different for different digits and their values are between 2 and 5 (for Polish). These patterns were tested on 500 records and all of them are compatible with them.

4. The grid method

The word's phonemes structure could be very important for automatic speech recognition . For digits' recognition it could be simplified to recognition of voiced phonemes and noisy phonemes. Table 2 shows simplified phonemes structure for digits 0-9 spoken in Polish.

Digit	Simplified phonemes structure (V-voiced phoneme, N-noisy phoneme)
0	V+V+V
1	V+V+V+V
2	V+V+V
3	N+V
4	N+V+V
5	V+V+N
6	N+V+N
7	N+V+V+V+V
8	V+N+V+V
9	V+V+V+V+V+N

Table 2. Simplified phonemes structure for digits 0-9 spoken in Polish

According to table 2 some digits include noisy phonemes (3, 4,5 ,6 ,7 ,8 ,9) and some don't (0, 1, 2). Also the number of voiced phonemes is different (from 1 to 5). For finding voiced phonemes the author's Grid method was used.

4.1 The basic periods finding

The first step according to the grid method is finding basic periods included in voiced phonemes. At the beginning the algorithm tests 100ms signal before the beginning of the recorded word. This way the mean value of the noises are computed and "zero" level of the signal is found. Then, all samples of the signal are tested and local minimums are found. Three criteria are used here:
1.   The sample is a minimum if the next sample's value and the previous sample's value is greater than the tested sample.
2.   The time between the previous sample and tested sample must be greater than 2ms
3.   The tested sample's value must be lower than the "zero" level.
This way, the local minimums are found and written to the matrix as a number of samples in which they were found.
Figure 7 shows the result of this operation. The local minimums were matched by the circles.

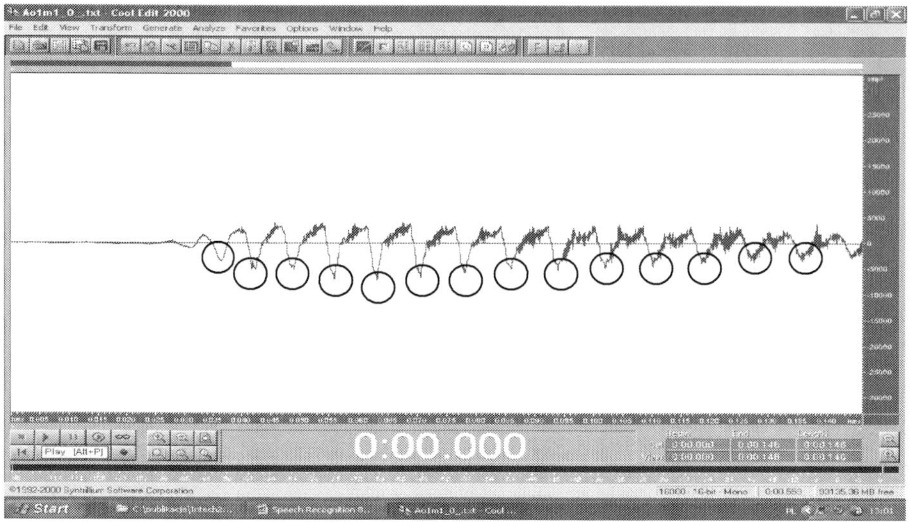

Fig. 7. Local minimums found in the speech signal

4.2 The grids fitting

The next step is coding each basic period in the matrix. This is made by putting grids on them. The rule is showed in figure 8. In cells of the grid "1's" or "0's" are automatically written. Ones – if there is a signal inside a cell, zeros – if there is no signal.

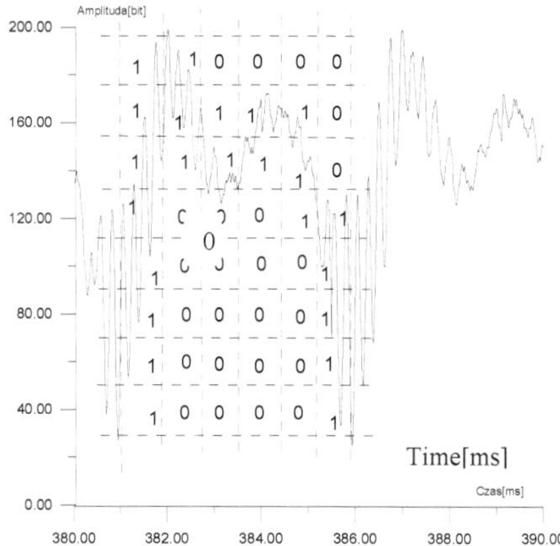

Fig. 8. The basic period coding

The size of each grid is automatically fitted into the signal. The highest – to the signal's amplitude and the widest – to the basic period duration. This way the shape of the signal is coded independently of the personal speaker's voice feature. If the amplitude or duration change the size of each cell is changes proportionally. Finally, the binary matrix is obtained. Fig.9 shows this matrix for signal from Fig.8.

$$\begin{bmatrix} 1 & 1 & 0 & 0 & 0 & 0 \\ 1 & 1 & 1 & 1 & 1 & 0 \\ 1 & 1 & 1 & 1 & 1 & 0 \\ 1 & 0 & 1 & 0 & 1 & 1 \\ 1 & 0 & 0 & 0 & 0 & 1 \\ 1 & 0 & 0 & 0 & 0 & 1 \\ 1 & 0 & 0 & 0 & 0 & 1 \\ 1 & 0 & 0 & 0 & 0 & 1 \end{bmatrix}$$

Fig. 9. The binary matrix obtained from the grid

4.3 The similarity coefficients computing

For one word there is a possibility to obtain even some hundred binary matrixes. This amount depends on the phonemes' number in this word and the speaker's sex. For the same length of the word women and children records have more grids than the men. This is because of the less basic periods duration for women and children voices. After the binary matrixes obtaining, the similarity among them is computed. Each matrix is automatically compared with the five matrixes before it and the five matrixes after it (all bits on the same position of matrixes are compared). If more than 88% bits are the same, the grid is matched as "similar" if not as "not similar". This way, all the grids get their similarity coefficients. This coefficients could have value between 1 (there is no similar grids around it, so it is only one such matrix) and 11 (there are 5 similar matrixes before and after tested matrix plus this matrix).As author's research showed, if there 1 or more similarity coefficients one after another, with value higher than 27% of the maximum similarity coefficient in the word, which last (together) at least 10ms it means that there is a voiced phoneme. The lower number of such coefficients means that there is no phoneme (break) , unvoiced phoneme or noisy phoneme. It could also show the zone where one voiced phoneme is finishing and another starting. This is a very important observation because it allows to find all voiced phonemes inside each word. This parameter (number o phonemes) will be used in the automatic speech recognition process. The same research showed that the brake between phonemes insists if three conditions are performed simultaneously:

1.   Duration of grids coming one after another, with similarity coefficient lower than 27% of the maximum similarity coefficient in the word, must be greater than 14ms.

2.   Time between the previous break and tested grid must be greater than 88ms

3.   Time between the beginning of the last voiced phoneme and tested grid must be greater than 42ms

The example of the similarity coefficients for word "zero" is shown in table 3.

As is easy to observe in table 3, grids from 7 to 20 have similarity coefficients greater than 2, so there is a voiced phoneme. Then there are grids with smaller coefficients, although sometimes there is a grid with the bigger one. As was mentioned earlier – one or more grids lasted more than 10ms (in this case at least 3 grids) with coefficients greater than 2 (27%×11=2,97) depict the voiced phoneme, so one or two such a grid means nothing. This is the part of the record where the one voiced phoneme (z) changing to another (e), so this is the transient zone. The grids from 40 to 82 have again greater similarity coefficients so it means that another voiced phoneme (e) was found . Grids from 83 to 89 have small

Number of grid	Similarity coefficients	Phoneme	Number of grid	Similarity coefficients	Phoneme	Number of grid	Similarity coefficients	Phoneme
1	1		39	2		77	7	E (continuation)
2	1		40	5		78	11	
3	3		41	4		79	11	
4	1		42	3		80	10	
5	2		43	4		81	9	
6	2		44	3		82	8	
7	5		45	5		83	2	
8	8		46	4		84	3	
9	7		47	6		85	1	
10	8		48	5		86	2	
11	11		49	6		87	1	
12	10		50	4		88	1	
13	10	Z	51	7	E	89	1	
14	9		52	8		90	3	
15	9		53	8		91	5	
16	7		54	10		92	6	
17	7		55	11		93	5	
18	3		56	11		94	6	
19	3		57	11		95	6	
20	7		58	9		96	5	
21	2		59	9		97	6	O
22	4		60	10		98	6	
23	2		61	11		99	4	
24	1		62	11		100	6	
25	2		63	11		101	8	
26	3		64	11		102	7	
27	2		65	11		103	7	
28	1		66	11		104	8	
29	2		67	11		105	9	
30	1		68	10		106	11	
31	1		69	9		107	11	
32	1		70	11		108	11	
33	1		71	11		109	11	
34	3		72	11		110	11	
35	2		73	11		111	11	
36	3		74	11		112	6	
37	6		75	11		113	7	
38	1		76	11		...	...	...

Tabele 3. Similarity coefficient in word "zero" and found voiced phonemes

coefficients, but this time it is because the unvoiced phoneme "r" is found. Grids from 90 to 113 have greater coefficients what means that another voiced phoneme (o) was found. This way, using only similarity coefficients, three voiced phonemes were found. This method was used for finding a number of voiced phonemes for digit's from 0 to 9 records (50 records for each digit = 500 records). Another example for digit "1" (in Polish "JEDEN") is shown in table 4.

Number of grid	Simila-rity coeffi-cients	Phoneme	Number of grid	Simila-rity coeffi-cients	Phoneme	Number of grid	Simila-rity coeffi-cients	Phoneme
1	4		25	2		49	8	
2	4		26	5		50	8	
3	4	J	27	8	E Continu-ation	51	5	
4	7		28	8		52	7	
5	5		29	7		53	6	
6	6		30	6		54	7	
7	2		31	6		55	7	
8	1		32	1		56	7	
9	1		33	1		57	6	
10	1		34	1		58	6	
11	2		35	1		59	1	
12	1		36	1		60	5	
13	3		37	2		61	7	
14	2		38	1		62	5	
15	2		39	2		63	7	
16	2		40	1		64	8	
17	4		41	1		65	10	E-N Continu-ation
18	3		42	1		66	10	
19	6	E	43	2		67	8	
20	1		44	1		68	7	
21	5		45	4		69	6	
22	8		46	4		70	6	
23	8		47	7	E-N	71	1	
24	10		48	7		...	...	

Table 4. Similarity coefficient in word "jeden" and found voiced phonemes

Here 4 phonemes were recognized ('D' phoneme hadn't basic periods). Two last phonemes (E-N) are not divided by the small coefficients so there is a transient zone. As research shown such a zones are present if the phoneme last at least 100ms and inside of it there are grids with similarity coefficients less than 70% of the maximum similarity in the word, and before, and behind them there are grids with higher than 70% similarity coefficients. Another example of digit "8" (in Polish "OSIEM') is shown in table 5.

In this case (tab.5) there is one noisy phoneme between voiced phoneme "O" and "E" and one break between phonemes "E" and "M". This break is only 15ms long but it is enough (according to the rules mentioned above the break exist if the duration of the grids with less than 27% of the maximum similarity coefficients is bigger than 14ms). This record was made by the man whose basic periods equal 7,5ms. More details about noisy phoneme finding is placed in section 5.

Number of grid	Similarity coefficients	Phoneme	Number of grid	Similarity coefficients	Phoneme	Number of grid	Similarity coefficients	Phoneme
1	3		25	4	Noisy Phoneme (continu-Ation)	49	7	
2	3		26	4		50	3	
3	2		27	2		51	1	Break
4	2		28	1		52	1	
5	3	O	29	6		53	3	M
6	5		30	2		54	4	
7	5		31	3		55	6	
8	5		32	1		56	2	
9	4		33	2		57	7	
10	3		34	2		58	8	
11	1	Noisy Phoneme	35	2		59	4	
12	1		36	1		60	10	
13	2		37	3		61	7	
14	3		38	2		62	8	
15	3		39	2		63	6	
16	5		40	6	E	64	5	
17	2		41	6		65	4	
18	2		42	6		66	3	
19	2		43	3		67	4	
20	4		44	4		68	6	
21	2		45	5		69	3	
22	5		46	6		70	3	
23	5		47	7		71	2	
24	5		48	8		...	...	

Table 5. Similarity coefficient in word "jeden" and found voiced phonemes

5. A noisy phoneme finding

As was mentioned in point 4, digits from 3 to 9 spoken in Polish include noisy phonemes. In figure 10 there is a time characteristic for digit "3" spoken in Polish by the woman.

As the author's research showed the duration of the noisy phoneme is usually bigger than 50ms, there are no basic periods inside them and they could be placed in different parts of the word once or more times. Figures 11-13 show different possibilities.

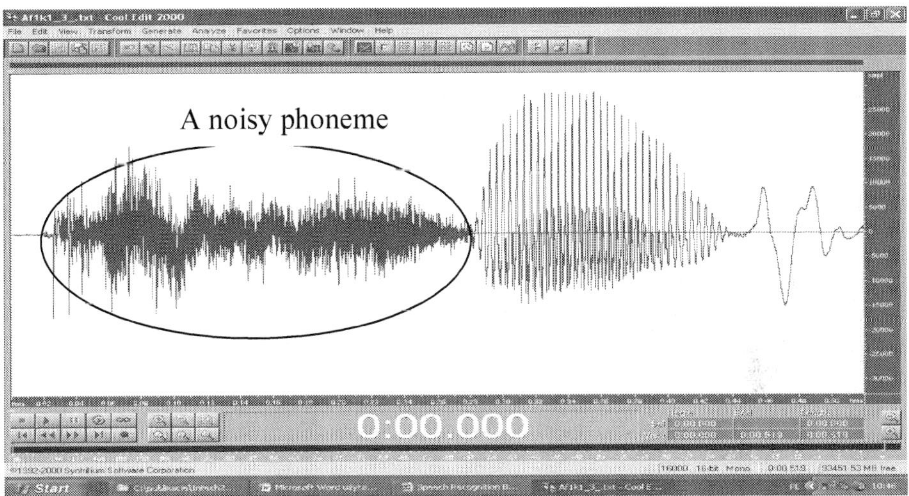

Fig. 10. Digit's three name spoken in Polish be the woman

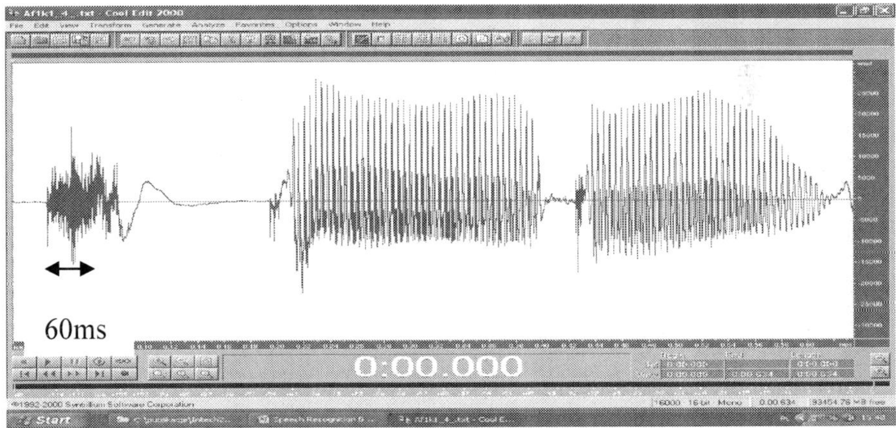

Fig. 11. The word with e noisy phoneme placed at the beginning of the word (digit 4 spoken in Polish)

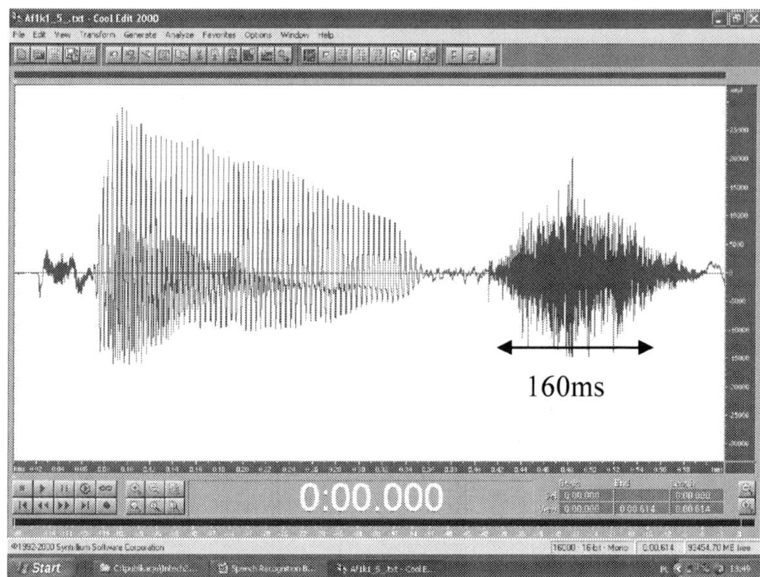

Fig. 12. The word with noisy phoneme placed at the end of the word (digit 5 spoken in Polish)

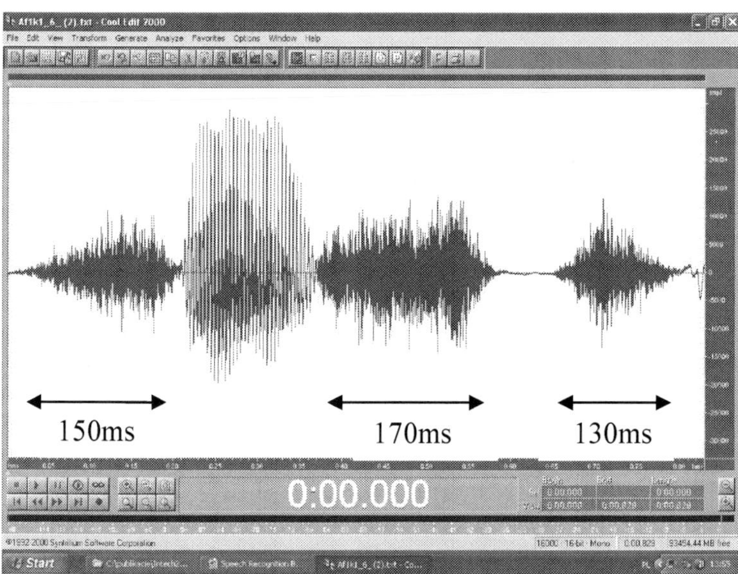

Fig. 13. The word with a noisy phonemes placed at the beginning and at the end of the word (digit 6 spoken in Polish)

Sometimes the noisy phoneme has a very small amplitude that could be mistaken with outside noises. (Fig.14)

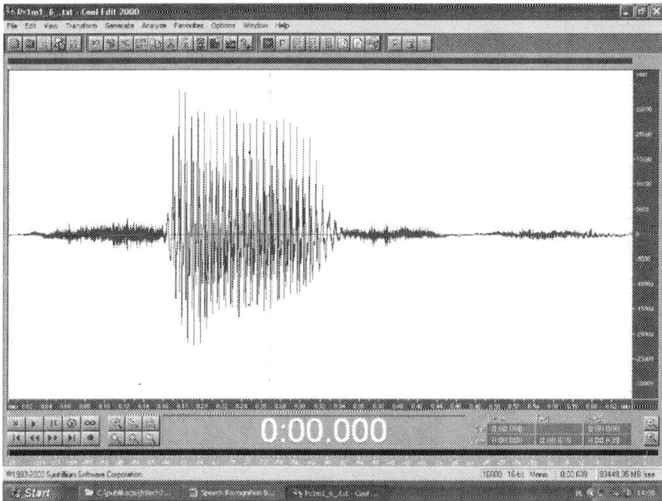

Fig. 14. A word with small amplitude noisy phonemes.

Another noisy phoneme's interesting feature is a big number of local extremes placed in small distances one after another. Figure 15 shows an enlarged part of the noisy phoneme's time characteristic.
As is easy to observe (in fig.15)The time between neighbouring extremes is usually less than 0,5ms.

Fig. 15. A big number of local extremes inside the noisy phoneme.

6. The automatic digit's names recognition algorithm

All features described in the previous units were used for constructing an automatic digit's name recognition algorithm. It was implemented in Delphi software and automatically computed all necessary parameters. The complete algorithm is showed in figure 16. At the beginning the file with the recorded word should be loaded. Then the signal's "zero level" is found. Next, the local minimums are found and borders of the basic periods are computed. Then, the grids with 5×7 cells are automatically fitted to the basic periods. From here the binary matrixes are obtained. Next, the similarity coefficients are computed. According to them the number of the voiced and noisy phonemes is calculated. The next step is constructing of the word's phoneme structure. Here the voiced and noisy phonemes are placed in the right order, depending on their starting and ending time.

The received word's phoneme structure is compared with 9 structures (number of voiced phonemes for digit "0" and "2" for Polish is the same). If no one of them is the same, the word is treated as "unrecognizable" and the algorithm finishes its work. If the word's structure is the same as one of the 9-s shown in the table, the respective envelope pattern is compared with the recorded signal. Now there are two possibilities. If the envelope pattern agrees with the signal envelope the algorithm gives as a result the right digit, if not the word is treated as an unrecognized. As is easy to observe the envelope analyses is more important for digits "0" and "2" than for the others because of their the same phoneme's structure. For other digits this analyses result makes the recognition process more exact. The rules presented in the algorithm could be modified. For example instead of treating the word as "unrecognized" the algorithm could calculate the percentage similarity to all possible structures. The same could be made for the envelope analyses. Also here the similarity calculations are possible. As a result the algorithm always could find the solution but the user should be informed if the result is reliable or percentage calculated.

7. The way of research making

The envelope analyses was made in some steps. First, the time characteristics for each digit and different speakers was reviewed. From here the number of units was obtained. Then each unit was described by a minimum duration and amplitude range. Next, for another record these two values were tested and corrected in order to achieve properly the units number. This method is shown in figure 17.

In the similar way the number of voiced and unvoiced phonemes was found and corrected. After each change which improve the recognition results for any digit the previous digits were tested. This way the algorithm was tested for each digit. About 30% of records weren't used for parameter correction because their recognition results were proper from the beginning, also sometimes any correction in one parameter improved the recognition results for some speakers.

8. Results of research

During the author's research 500 records of digits from 0 to 9 spoken in Polish were used. They include men's, women's and children's voices. For all these records the envelope patterns were found. As the results show it was possible to find the envelope pattern for each digit (10 patterns) which are common for all speakers. Then the new method of the

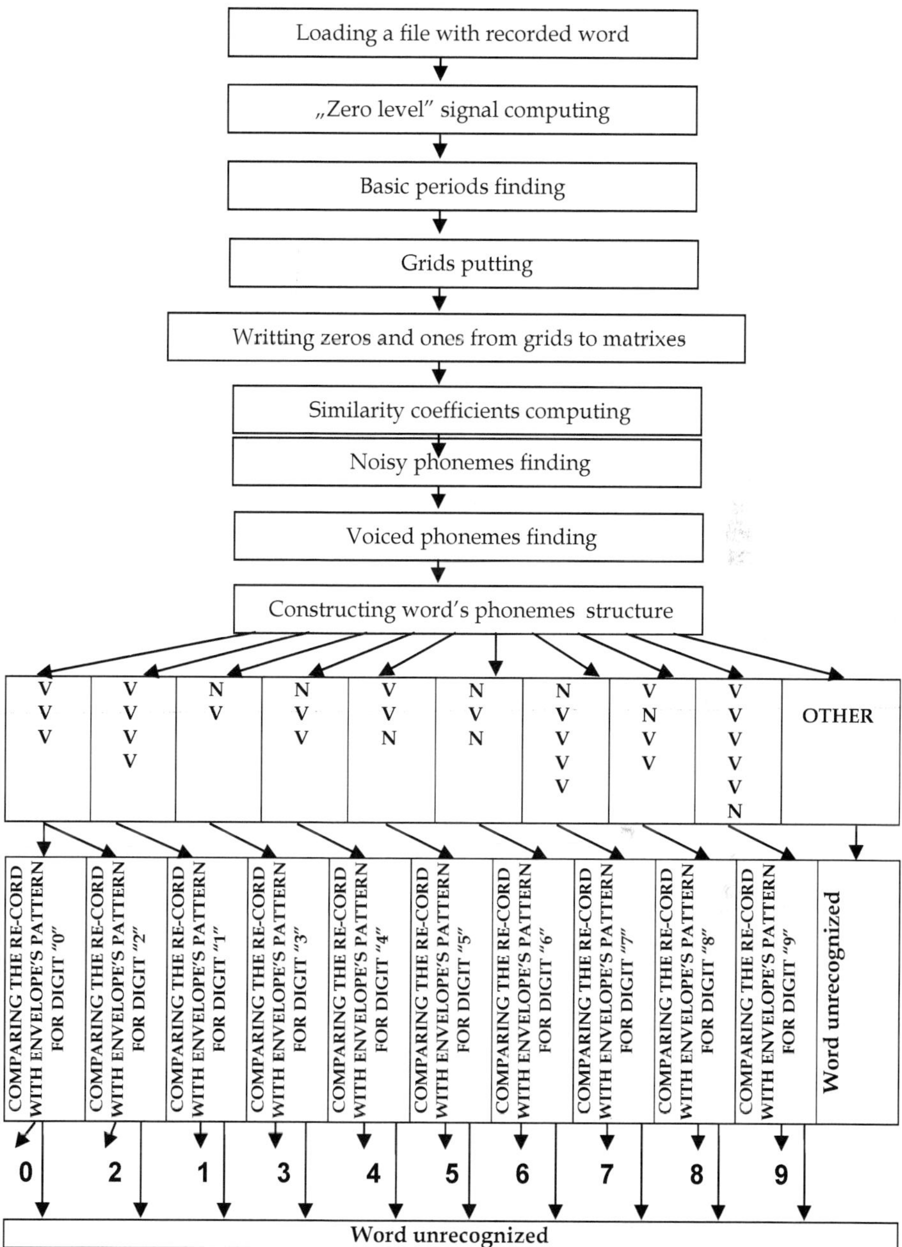

Fig. 16. The automatic speech recognition algorithm (for Polish)

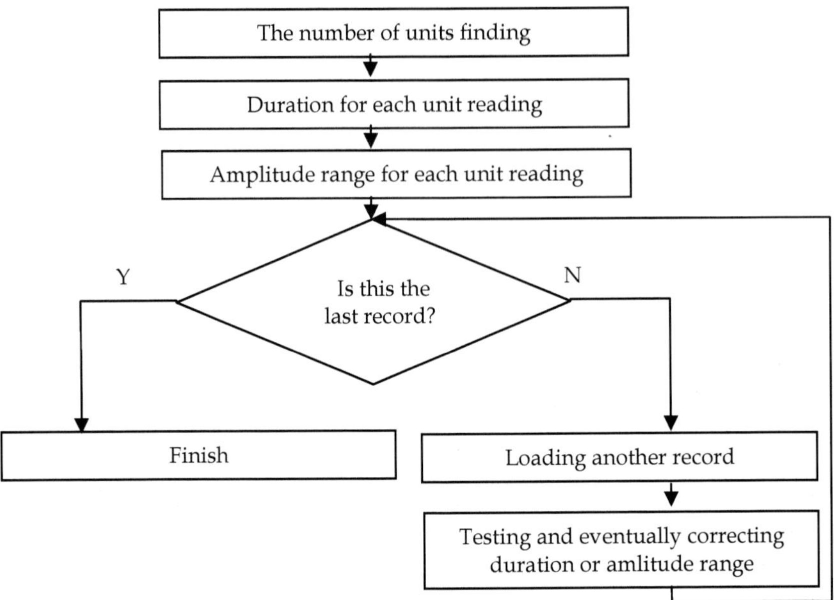

Fig. 17. The envelope patterns finding

phonemes recognition was worked out. It allowed to find voiced and noisy phonemes inside each word. From here the simplify phonemes structure for each word was obtained. At present this algorithm works properly for digits 0-9. In table 6 there are placed the results of recognition of author's system and HMM based system (Wydra, 2007).

Parameter	Author's method	HMM method
Number of recognizing words	10	20
Number of speakers	35	30
Recognition quality for digit "0"	100%	94%
Recognition quality for digit "1"	100%	98%
Recognition quality for digit "2"	100%	100%
Recognition quality for digit "3"	100%	100%
Recognition quality for digit "4"	100%	100%
Recognition quality for digit "5"	100%	98%
Recognition quality for digit "6"	100%	98%
Recognition quality for digit "7"	100%	96%
Recognition quality for digit "8"	100%	100%
Recognition quality for digit "9"	100%	100%

Table 6. Recognition results for author's and HMM based system for Polish.

As table 6 shows the recognition results of the author's system are the same or better than for HMM based system. Very important is also the fact that the recognition result in the author's system was achieved with lower amount of calculations and without a spectrum analyses. It means that it is faster and needs less memory and microprocessors operations, so it could be implemented in almost every simple microprocessor system.

9. Summary

Presented algorithm works properly for a small amount of word's systems. For bigger ones more parameters should be implemented. The new approach presented here is based on the electrical signal image recognition which is a source for all existing speech recognition methods. This signal includes all information necessary for reliable speech recognition. The main problem is what operation will be done in order to achieve the best recognition results. The most popular HMM method is based on the spectral and cepstral analyses which are complicated and difficult for implementation in simple processor systems. Here the signal processors should be used and conversion the signal from the time to frequency domain must be done. As the author's research showed, for small systems such as dialing a telephone number, changing the TV channel, choosing a level in the lift and many others, the systems based on the image recognition could be cheaper and more exact.

10. References

Holmberg, M.; Gelbard, D.; Ramacher, U.; Hemmert, W.(2005). *Automatic speech recognition with neural spike trains,* Interspeech, pp.1253-1256, Lisbon, Portugal

Hueber, T.; Chollet, G.; Denby, B.; Deryfus, G.; Stone, M.(2007).*Continous-speech phone recognition from ultrasound and optical images of the tongue and lips,* Interspeech, pp.658-661, Antwerp, Belgium

Junho, P.; Hanseok, K.(2006). *A new state-dependent phonetic tied-mixture model with head-body-tail structured HMM for real time continous phoneme recognition system,* Interspeech , pp. 1583-1586, Pittsburg, USA, 2006

Ketabdar, H.; Vepa,J.; Bengio, S.; Bourlard, H. (2005). *Developing and enhancing posterior based speech recognition systems,* Interspeech, pp.1461-1464, Lisbon, Portugal

Kumar, S.; Sreenivas T.(2005).*Speech Enhancement using Markov Model of Speech Segments,* Interspeech, pp.2069-2072, Lisbon, Portugal

Nishida, M.;Horiuchi, Y., Ichikawa A. (2005). *Automatic speech recognition based on adaptation and clustering using temporal-difference learning,* Interspeech, pp.285-288, Lisbon, Portugal

Seymour, R.; Stewart, D.; Ming, J.(2007).*Audio-visual integration for robust speech recognition using maximum weighted stream posteriors,* Interspeech, pp.654-657, Antwerp, Belgium

Togneri, R.;Deng, L.(2007).*A structured speech model parametrized by recursive dynamics and Neural Networks,* Interspeech, pp.894-897, Antwerp, Belgium

Vali, M.; Salehi, S.; Karimi, K.(2007). *Robust speech recognition by modifying clean and telephone feature vectors using bidirectional neural network,* Interspeech, pp.2554-2557, Pittsburgh, USA

Wydra, S. (2007). *Recognition Quality Improvement in Automatic Speech Recognition System for Polish*, Eurocon, pp.218-223, Warsaw, Poland, 2007

Part 3

Applications

17

Improvement of Sound Quality on the Body Conducted Speech Using Differential Acceleration

Masashi Nakayama[1,3], Shunsuke Ishimitsu[2] and Seiji Nakagawa[3]
[1]Kagawa National College of Technology,
[2]Hiroshima City University
[3]National Institute of Advanced Industrial Science and Technology,
Japan

1. Introduction

During recent years, applications using speech recognition have been developed to aid dictation during lectures and to advance voice-prompted car navigation systems. Research in speech recognition has been conducted to improve recognition performance and spoken document processing (Nakagawa, 2007). However, even with developments in speech recognition technology, high recognition performance can be compromised due to noisy environments. Standard rate scales, such as CENSREC (Kitaoka et al., 2006) and AURORA (Hirsch and Pearce, 2000), are typically used for evaluating speech recognition performance in noisy environments and have shown that speech recognition rates are approximately 50–80% when under the influence of noise, demonstrating the difficulty of achieving high recognition percentages. To achieve a high recognition performance, background noise should be minimal, and normal speech should be clear, because the system estimates recognition using a feature vector from its signal. This signal can be affected by sound quality or by an utterance style due to noise in the surrounding environment.

When the noise level is low, sound quality becomes clear. However, when the noise level is high, the speech is buried in the noise, causing a change in the speaker's utterance style, termed the Lombard effect. This change causes the basic frequency to rise because a speaker does not hear the feedback sound from the ear. The method of extracting normal speech under these complex conditions because environment always changes. Several methods have been investigated to extract clear speech under these conditions, such as a noise reduction method, the use of a microphone array or a body-conducted signal. Of these, noise reduction is most commonly used for retrieving a noisy signal and can extract clear speech effectively as long as the background noise is not too high. The microphone array is typically combined with noise reduction. Body-conducted speech is a robust signal extraction method that differs from the other techniques, because it provides a solid signal that propagates through skin and bone.

Previously, we built a body-conducted speech recognition system to recognize speech in a noisy environment (98 dB SPL), specifically in the engine room of Oshima-maru, a training ship in Oshima National College of Maritime Technology (Ishimitsu et al., 2004). We found that this system exhibited an average recognition rate of greater than 95 %. However, the recognition for body-conducted speech needs the suitable acoustic model to achieve a high recognition performance. Here, we aimed to extract a clear signal using body-conducted speech and to evaluate its efficacy by signal frequency characteristics and recognition performance. Though body-conducted speech gives a robust signal, it does not have a clear quality.

Conventional retrieval methods for body-conducted speech include Modulation Transfer Function (MTF), Linear Predictive Coefficients (LPC), direct filtering and the use of a throat microphone. However, these methods need the direct input of speech (Tamiya and Shimamura, 2006; Vu et al., 2006; Liu et al., 2004; Dupont et al., 2004). Additionally, a conventional microphone does not extract speech in a noisy environment. Thus, we proposed retrieval methods with only body-conducted speech.

2. Body-conducted speech

2.1 Characteristics of body-conducted speech

Speech is an air-conducted signal and is easy to influence with surrounding noise. In contrast, body-conducted speech is a solid propagated signal and is less influenced by noise. Figures 1 and 2 demonstrate the word, "Asahi", obtained from the database of JEIDA which contains 100 local place words (Itahashi, 1991). They were uttered by a 20-year-old male. Speech was measured 30 cm from the mouth using a microphone, and body-conducted speech was extracted from the upper lip with an accelerator. This microphone position is commonly used for a speech input of the car navigation system. The upper lip, as a signal extraction position, can provide the best cepstral coefficient characteristic as a feature vector for recognition (Ishimitsu et al., 2004). The signals were recorded at 16 kHz and 16 bits. Table 1 shows the recording environments used in this research. Speech generally provides a clear signal; however, body-conducted speech is not always clear because it lacks a high frequency component (2 kHz or more). Thus, the recognition performance can be low when its signal is used for the recognition directory.

Recorder	TEAC RD-200T
Microphone	Ono Sokki MI-1431
Microphone amplifier	Ono Sokki SR-2200
Microphone position	30cm (Between mouth and microphone)
Accelerator	Ono Sokki NP-2110
Accelerator amplifier	Ono Sokki PS-602
Accelerator position	Upper lip

Table 1. Recoding environments

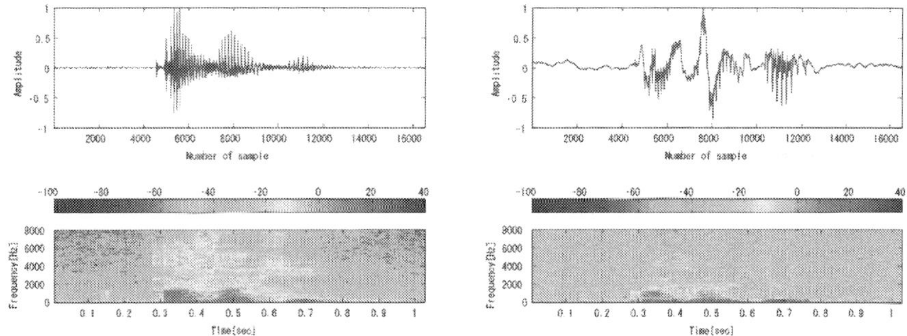

Fig. 1. Speech   Fig. 2. Body-conducted speech

2.2 Differential acceleration

Because body conducted speech does not exhibit a high frequency component, conventional retrieval techniques may also be needed to extract clear speech. However, speech is not well measured with a microphone in noisy environments. Therefore, we aimed to investigate the signal retrieval from body-conducted speech itself. To improve the sound quality, we focused on a high frequency component of 2 kHz or more, however this signal has little gain and includes an effective frequency. Subsequently, we developed for a novel signal retrieval method using differential acceleration calculated from the difference of body-conducted speech in each sample. Even with the changing of sampling frequency and speaker, it was not necessary to design a new filter because the proposed technique allowed signal retrieval with only differential procedure.

Figure 3 shows the differential acceleration signal estimated from Figure 2. Figure 3 becomes a emphasized signal however the stationary noise was included. For this reason, differential acceleration involving a retrieval signal introduces conventional noise reduction (Gong, 1995). To obtain a signal that approximates natural speech and includes effective frequencies components, conventional noise reduction techniques were employed for the differential acceleration.

3. Noise reduction for differential acceleration

3.1 Spectral subtraction method

The spectral subtraction method subtracts the spectrum of the noise sections from the average of spectrum of the noisy signal (Gong, 1995). Equations (1) and (2) describe this method.

$$x(i) = s(i) + n(i) \tag{1}$$

$$S(\omega) = \left(|X(\omega)| - |N(\omega)| \right) \exp^{j \arg X(\omega)} \tag{2}$$

It is assumed that differential acceleration $x(i)$ consists of the speech signal $s(i)$ and the noise signal $n(i)$. An estimated spectrum $S(\omega)$ can be obtained using the spectral subtraction method from Equation (2). The phase information on the input signal spectrum,

$X(\omega)$, is represented by $\arg X(\omega)$. Figure 4 shows the results from the spectral subtraction method when the filtering was repeated seven times with a setting frame width of 128 samples. The stationary noise is not removed completely. The characteristics of the high frequency component cannot be fully recovered because musical noise is produced in the signal (Nomura et al., 2006; Yamashita et al., 2005). So we concluded that it was difficult to recover frequency characteristics with this method.

3.2 Wiener filtering method

The Wiener filtering method is a technique which estimates a speech spectrum envelope from noisy speech (Li and O'Shaughnessy, 2003). The speech spectral envelope is estimated using linear prediction coefficients to obtain a clear signal that nears the frequency component of speech. The following equation describes the Wiener filtering method.

$$H_{Estimate}(\omega) = \frac{H_{Speech}(\omega)}{H_{Speech}(\omega) + H_{Noise}(\omega)} \tag{3}$$

The estimated signal spectrum, $H_{Estimate}(\omega)$, is calculated from the noisy speech, $H_{Speech}(\omega)$, and noise spectrum, $H_{Noise}(\omega)$. $H_{Estimate}(\omega)$ is expressed as a transfer function that converts a noisy signal to a clear signal. To estimate $H_{Estimate}(\omega)$, autocorrelation functions and linear prediction coefficients by the Levinson Durbin algorithm are required (Durbin, 1960). Noise spectrum, $H_{Noise}(\omega)$, is then estimated by autocorrelation functions and is used as a noise signal in differential acceleration. Figure 5 shows the result of each signal when the coefficient of both linear prediction coefficients and autocorrelation functions were equal to 1, frame width was 764 sample, and repetition was three times.

To estimate $H_{Speech}(\omega)$ and $H_{Noise}(\omega)$, the number of the linear prediction coefficients and autocorrelation function used the same number because this setting allows us to solve the problem simply and easily. The number of coefficients was changed from 1 to 32, the frame width was changed from 128 to 4,096, and the number of repetitions was also changed from 1 to 5. The best results were obtained using the conditions shown in Figure 5. We confirmed the recovery of frequency components at 2 kHz or more when using the Wiener filtering method, and musical noise was not found. Next, we compared the signal difference using spectrograms. The experimental results showed that the Wiener filtering method was suitable for differential acceleration.

4. Improvement using a combination between the proposed method and conventional method

We attempted to extract a clear signal using a combination of differential acceleration and the Wiener filtering method. We next evaluated the combination of the proposed method with various conventional methods including the cross spectrum method and the adaptive filter method. These results are shown in the following sub-sections.

4.1 Cross spectrum method

The cross spectrum method (Morise et al., 2007) was introduced using the auto spectrum of body-conducted speech, $H_{BCS}(\omega)$, and the cross spectrum between normal speech and body-conducted speech, $H_{Speech-BCS}(\omega)$. To estimate the retrieval signal, $H_{BCS_{Estimate}}(\omega)$, the following equation was used.

$$H_{BCS_{Estimate}}(\omega) = \frac{H_{Speech-BCS}(\omega)}{H_{BCS}(\omega)} \qquad (4)$$

Figure 6 shows the retrieval signal using a transfer function in a word estimated by the cross spectrum method. Sufficient recovery of the frequency characteristic was not observed when processed by the cross spectrum method. Since a transfer function is estimated by the signal in a word that contains two or more phonemes and syllables, it is difficult to retrieve sound quality. However, it is possible to improve sound quality using a transfer function for sub-word, because sub-word is a minimum unit of uttered speech (Ishimitsu et al., 2007).

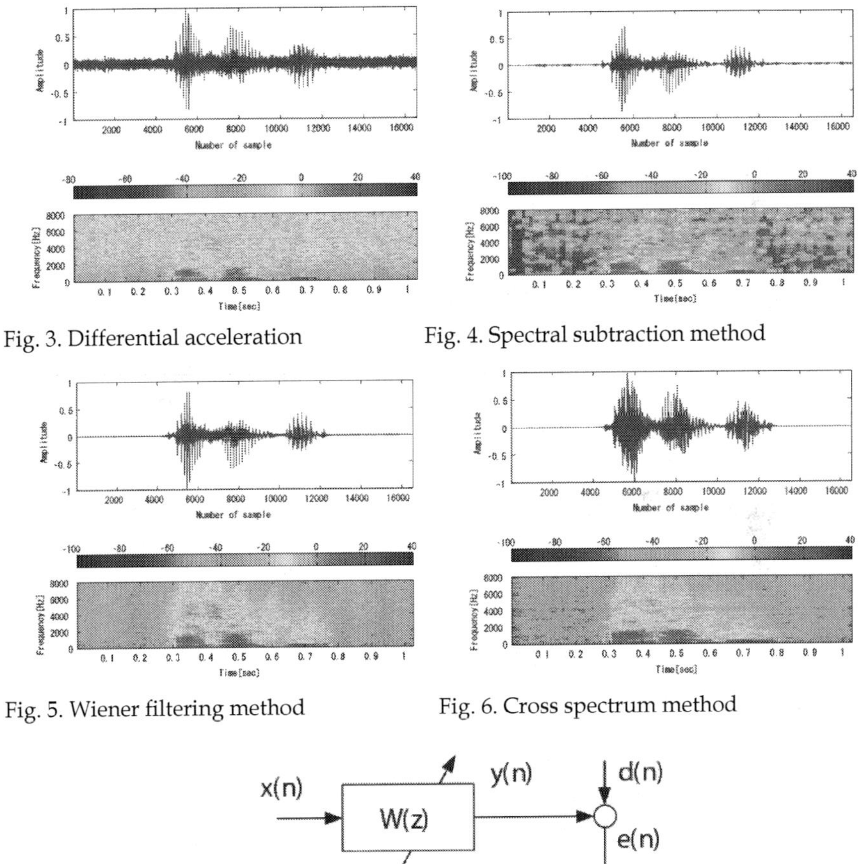

Fig. 3. Differential acceleration

Fig. 4. Spectral subtraction method

Fig. 5. Wiener filtering method

Fig. 6. Cross spectrum method

Fig. 7. LMS algorithm

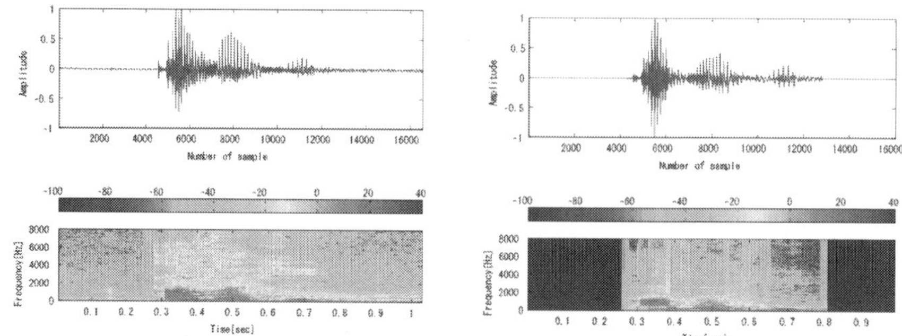

Fig. 8. Adaptive filter for word unit   Fig. 9. Adaptive filter for sub-word unit

4.2 Adaptive filter method for word unit

In previous research (Ishimitsu et al., 2004), the adaptive filter method (Haykin, 1996) was not enough to recover a sufficient frequency characteristic when body-conducted speech was used as a reference signal. The result in previous research is not improved the frequency characteristic because bodyconducted speech is low quality (Ishimitsu et al., 2004). However, since a retrieval signal using differential acceleration is clear, the estimation of clearest signal can be expected by using the retrieval signal and adaptive filter (Haykin, 1996). The updated filter method is shown in the following equation and in Figure 7.

$$w(n+1) = w(n) + \mu \cdot e(n) \cdot x(n) \tag{5}$$

where, $w(n+1)$ is new filter, μ is the convergence coefficient, and n is time index, respectively. Output signal $y(n)$ is provided by input signal $x(n)$ and current filter $w(n)$. And then, error signal $e(n)$ is calculated from the difference between the input signal and the output signal. By using an error signal, the system can be used to estimate a new filter part using Equation 5. Figure 8 shows the retrieval signal using an adaptive filter when the convergence coefficient was set to 0.01, and the filter length of taps was 16,384. Subsequently, the coefficients of the final stage of updated adaptive filter were used. Thus, a clear signal was produced using an adaptive filter. Moreover, the formant was not observed in the retrieval signal with the cross spectrum method. And it was also confirmed in the spectrogram.

4.3 Adaptive filter method for sub-word unit

The result of previous sub-section confirmed the efficacy of the proposed method. Next, we proposed the use of an adaptive filter using a sub-word unit. Previously, we constructed the speech support system that used a transfer function for sub-word to create a clear speech from body-conducted speech (Ishimitsu et al., 2007). Thus, the sound quality was improved by a transfer function for a sub-word.

Consequently, we experimented whether supervised speech recognition could be achieved by this system. The proposed system would be able to estimate the boundary of a sub-word or a word using the recognition decoder. The continuous sub-word unit recognition decoder is made by Julian that is the Large vocabulary continuous speech recognition system (Kawahara et al., 1999; Lee et al., 2001). Our subjects are Japanese, so we choose the Mora unit as a sub-word. The Mora unit is constructed of a vowel or consonant and a vowel.

There is a problem in length of sample because the length of an adaptive filter for a sub-word is very short. So adaptive filter for sub-word unit could not be estimated by conventional methods. As a result, the adaptive filter for sub-word unit is required the long sample. The input signal can be a long sample using following equation.

$$x = iN \qquad (6)$$

where x is the length of long sample; i is the number of each sub-word sample, and N is the number of connection. Figure 9 shows the results of using a adaptive filter for a sub-word. A convergence coefficient of 0.3 and number of connection of 6 times were used. It was possible to recover the high frequency components and the formant frequencies. Additionally, since an impulsive noise was mixed at the boundary of each sub-word, the calculated results always include the errors. The adaptive filter for word unit compared with the adaptive filter for sub-word unit, so we decided that the adaptive filter for word unit is suitable for retrieval signal with differential acceleration.

5. Investigation of characteristics difference

To evaluate the efficacy of the retrieval signals, the following signals were compared with speech:

- Body-conducted speech (BCS)
- Differential acceleration with the spectral subtraction method (SS)
- Differential acceleration with the Wiener filtering (Wiener)
- Retrieval signal with Wiener filtering and the cross spectrum method (Cross)
- Retrieval signal with Wiener filtering and the adaptive filter for word (Adaptive 1)
- Retrieval signal with Wiener filtering and the adaptive filter for sub-word (Adaptive 2)

Figure 10 shows the difference between speech and body-conducted speech using a time-frequency representation. Figure 11 shows the difference between speech and the signal retrieves by the spectral subtraction method, and Figure 12 represents the difference between speech and the signal retrieves using Wiener filtering. As shown in Figure 10, there was a large difference between speech and body-conducted speech, including the formant frequencies greater than 2 kHz. However, body-conducted speech had no formant frequencies which are characteristic of the Japanese vowels. Comparing Figures 11 and 12, there was little difference in the frequency component. Particularly, as shown in Figure 12, the difference of formant frequencies was minimal. Wiener filtering was used to calculate the linear predictive coefficients, and the stationary noise was then reduced. This technique worked effectively because the predictive coefficients provided suitable parameters in each retrieval phase. Therefore, we concluded that the most suitable noise reduction method was Wiener filtering combined with differential acceleration.

Figures 13, 14 and 15 demonstrate the differences between speech and each retrieval signal that was used in combination with a conventional method. These include the retrieval signals obtained using differential acceleration calculated from the cross spectrum method or an adaptive filter for a word or for a sub-word. Each figure was compared with its original signal obtained with Wiener filtering. In the lower range of 1.5 kHz, there is a large difference in spectrograms between speech and retrieval signal with cross spectrum method. The difference was similarly extended in Figure 15. The retrieval signal calculated from the adaptive filter for a sub-word could not extract a clear signal from the body-conducted speech because the number of samples was reduced in each sub-word duration. However, there was a marginal difference of spectrograms in all frequencies of Figure 14. Therefore, the adaptive filter for a word was confirmed as the most suitable retrieval method when it was combined with retrieval signal of differential acceleration.

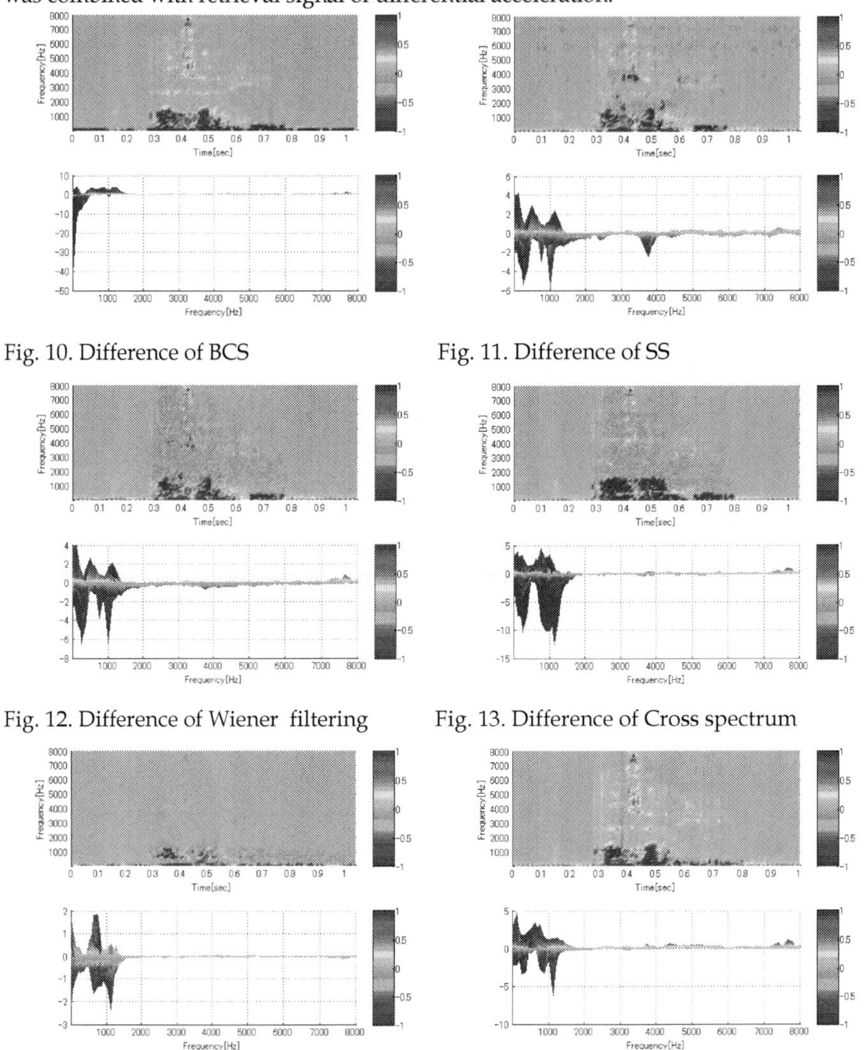

Fig. 10. Difference of BCS   Fig. 11. Difference of SS

Fig. 12. Difference of Wiener filtering   Fig. 13. Difference of Cross spectrum

Fig. 14. Difference of Adaptive 1   Fig. 15. Difference of Adaptive 2

6. Recognition experiment

Next, we evaluated the performance of the proposed method with an isolated word recognition experiment. In previous research, we constructed the body-conducted speech recognition system, which could perform in noisy environments, specifically in the engine room of a training ship (Ishimitsu et al., 2004). Here, to obtain a high recognition performance, the acoustic model needed to re-estimate the parameter using body-conducted speech. Because it is possible to estimate a speech from body-conducted speech, it expects that the retrieval signal can be directory used to speech recognition. The recognition performance can be improved when its signal becomes a clear speech. Therefore, to perform an objective experiment with statistical analysis, the recognition rate of isolated word recognition was evaluated using an acoustic model for unspecified speakers built with a speech. Generally, a subjective listening experiment is often used to evaluate the sound quality however it needs many people and much data as a admitting result.

Speech recognition was matched with the feature vector of each signal. The model parameters were able to approximate a natural speech when the recognition rate compared with body-conducted speech to each retrieval signal. Additionally, because HMM is an acoustic model that evaluates each feature vector using the output of a multi-dimensional normal distribution, it can be evaluated statistically. Thus, HMM can confirm whether the speech nearness characteristic is acquired at the feature parameter level by comparing word recognition rates.

Table 2 shows the experimental environments for isolated word recognition. The recognition decoder, Julius (Kawahara et al., 1999; Lee et al., 2001), was used in this experiment. Because Julius is a decoder for large vocabulary continuous speech recognition, it can be changed into isolated word recognition. Thus, it became possible to recognize words without a language model. JEIDA 100 local place words were used as candidates for word recognition (Itahashi, 1991). The words consisted of a database of Japanese place names after consideration of phoneme balance. The acoustic model was the context-dependent type tri-phone model in a word for unspecified speakers. The differential acceleration was processed with the parameter used in the previous chapter. The candidates for recognition in this experiment included each of the following signals:

- Speech : Speech
- BCS : Body-conducted speech
- ret. BCS : Retrieval signal with Wiener filtering

The body-conducted speech was compared with the retrieval signal from the recognition experiment. It was expected that the recognition performance would improve if the signal approximated natural speech from the body-conducted speech. Tables 3 - 5 show the recognition rate in each speaker. And Table 6 shows the average of all speakers. There was an improvement of 3 - 9 % in Speakers B and C but little improvement in Speaker A. About 5 % of the improvement was obtained through average of the recognition rate. From Table 6, the retrieval signals with differential acceleration become clear signals compare to original body-conducted speeches. Using an adaptation technique to estimate the new parameter in an acoustic model, the recognition performance increased to greater than 95 %. Here, we focused on the investigation of the signal retrieval, so the feature vectors in the acoustic models did not need new parameters in this experiment. Though the improvement was marginal, this result demonstrated the effectiveness for signal retrieval without speech. We expect that these recognition rates can be greatly improved by fine-tuning parameters for each speaker using an adaptation technique.

Speaker	two 20 and one 37 years old male
Number of data sets	100 words × 3 set/person
Vocabulary	JEIDA 100 local place names
Recognition system	Julius-3.4
Acoustic model	gender dependent triphone model
Model conditions	16 mixture gaussian, clustered 3000 states
Feature vectors	MFCC(12)+ΔMFCC(12)+ΔPow(1)=25 dim.
Training condition	20,000 sample and more (Itou et al., 1999), HTK 2.0 (Young et al.,2000)

Table 2. Experimental environments

Signal type	Set 1	Set 2	Set 3	Average
Speech	90%	90%	91%	90.3%
BCS	63%	56%	61%	60.0%
ret. BCS	62%	57%	63%	60.7%

Table 3. Speaker A (20 years old male)

Signal type	Set 1	Set 2	Set 3	Average
Speech	93%	94%	92%	93.0%
BCS	53%	50%	48%	50.3%
ret. BCS	63%	57%	58%	59.3%

Table 4. Speaker B (20 years old male)

Signal type	Set 1	Set 2	Set 3	Average
Speech	92%	94%	92%	92.7%
BCS	60%	68%	61%	63.0%
ret. BCS	65%	68%	65%	66.0%

Table 5. Speaker C (37 years old male)

Signal type	Average
Speech	92.0%
BCS	57.8%
ret. BCS	62.0%

Table 6. Recognition results of all speakers

7. Investigation of body-conducted speech in a noisy environment

7.1 Signal recording in a noisy environment

In order to acquire, a noisy environment, we used the engine room of the 'Oshima-maru' training ship from the Oshima National College of Technology, Japan. Noise within the engine room, under the two conditions of anchorage and cruising, were 93 and 98 dB SPL, respectively, and the SNR measurements from microphone. There was –20 and –25 dB SNR, respectively. The signals of 100 words, from the database of JEIDA were read three times in each environment by three males aged 20, 20 and 37 years old. For body-conducted speech extraction, measurements were taken from the upper lip. In this study, we experimented under anchorage condition to estimate retrieval signals.

Figures 16 and 17 demonstrate the word "Ageo" that was obtained from the database of JEIDA. Figures 16 and 17 exhibit speech and body-conducted speech signals from the engine room of the Oshima-maru. Because body-conducted speech is a structure bone sound, it is less influenced by noise than normal speech. Unlike body-conducted speech, normal speech signals do not detect the utterance of speakers. Comparing Figures 2 and 17, there was little difference of frequency characteristic between quiet and noisy environment, so it expects that the proposed method for signal retrieval can apply to the signal in noisy environment.

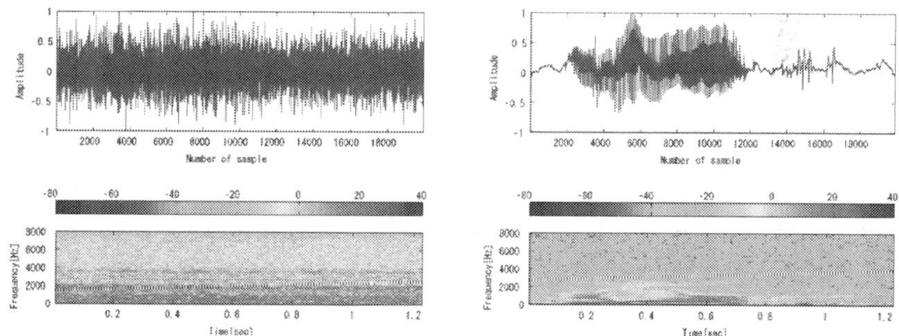

Fig. 16. Speech in noise   Fig. 17. Body-conducted speech in noise

7.2 Differential acceleration in a noisy environment

The signals can be a clear with same setting of signal retrieval in quiet room with proposed method. Difference in signals characteristics between speech and body-conducted speech are little because that reason is shown a difference of Figures 2 and 17. Thus, we also estimate the differential acceleration directory which the difference between the signals is calculated. Figure 18 shows the differential acceleration estimated from Figure 17. Body-conducted speech was extracted with an accelerator from the noisy environment. The signal level in each frequency is low compares to signal in quiet environment. Therefore, differential acceleration in the noisy environment exhibited a clearer signal compared with that extracted in the quiet environment.

7.3 Signal retrieval for body-conducted speech in a noisy environment

The signal characteristic of body-conducted speech in a noisy environment is not affected by noise; however, the basic frequency of the signal rises by the Lombard effect. Generally, since the decoder only uses spectral envelopes as recognition parameters, the problem is a matter of no importance.

Figures 19, 20 and 21 show the retrieval signals using the proposed methods that differ in the number of Wiener filtering repetitions. The signals exhibited frequency characteristics of 2 kHz and more. The estimated signal rejected stationary noise from the differential acceleration completely. The effect of repetitions was also clearly observable. We found that three repetitions allowed stationary noise to be completely reduced. In this study, parameter settings in Wiener filtering were the same as for a quiet room because difference in signal characteristic between quiet and noise is little. From Figure 21, we expect that performance of speech recognition can also be improved.

8. Decoding algorithm for differential acceleration

8.1 Problem of recognition for differential acceleration

The differential acceleration exhibited a distorted signal when a consonant was present. Consonants were removed together with the stationary noise because its signal level is low. However, the signal levels of vowels are high because of the formant frequencies. Thus, vowels were kept intact. The stationary noise level changed according to the environment of

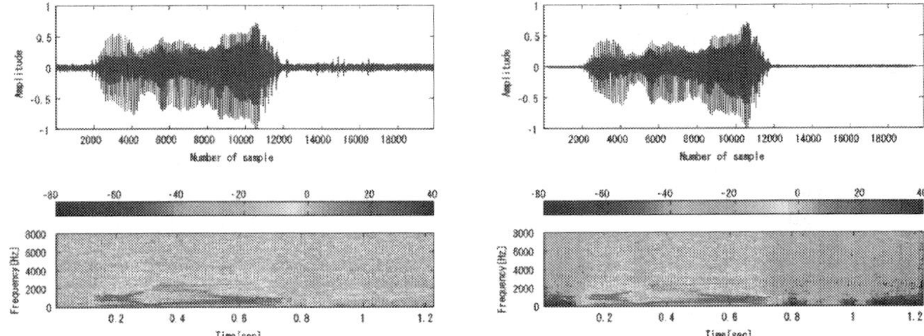

Fig. 18. Differential acceleration in noise   Fig. 19. Retrieval signal with Wiener 1

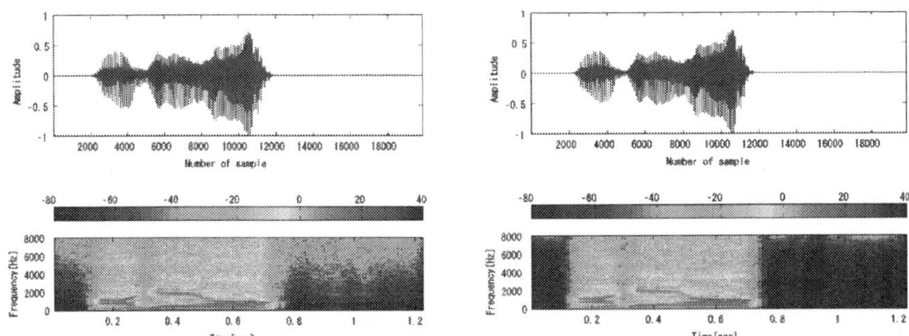

Fig. 20. Retrieval signal with Wiener 2   Fig. 21. Retrieval signal with Wiener 3

the recording signal, so the number of the suitable repetitions should be selected appropriately for recognition with the proposed retrieval method and noise environment. The recognition performance decreases if the repetitions are not sufficient when the stationary noise level is changed.

To solve the problem, we have to invent decision method for number of repetition in Wiener filtering. Then, we focused on the recognition system that calculates the likelihood between signal and model in recognition parameter. The algorithm chooses the clearest signal because it is appeared a highest likelihood from the recognition decoder. So we apply this idea to the decoding algorithm for differential acceleration.

8.2 Fundamental speech recognition

The fundamental speech recognition is described as follows briefly (Rabiner, 1993). Speech were recorded with a microphone and sampled at 16 kHz and 16 bits. As part of the recognition parameters, speech data were converted to the feature vectors as cepstrum coefficients. Speech recognition systems often use cepstrum techniques that consist of LPC and melfrequency cepstral coefficients (MFCCs) (Davis and Mermelstein, 1980). MFCCs were used in 12 dimensions computed every 10 ms. The differences in coefficients (ΔMFCC) and power (ΔLogPow) were also incorporated into the feature vectors. Thus, the feature vectors in each frame consisted of 25 (= 12 + 12 + 1) variables. The recognition system then uses these parameters to discriminate sub-word or word unit candidates. Each sub-word or word unit model consists of hidden Markov models (HMM) (Rabiner, 1993), which have transition probability and output probability distributions. A neural network (NN) is also used in speech recognition previously. However ANN is applied to other application (Rivara et al., 2009), speech recognition systems uses only HMM recently. Usually, the HMM's state transitions are in a left-to-right model, and the initial and final states are limited. This system calculates the likelihood (nearness of each acoustic model to an input parameter) using feature vectors and HMM. From the highest likelihood, the system can determine the candidate word/sub-word HMM. Generally, likelihood of acoustic models is computed with Viterbi algorithms. This recognition system includes dictionary and acoustic models, however no language models. The dictionary indicates the sub-word sequence for a word, because a word consists of the sub-word unit acoustic model. Equation (6) shows the fundamental formulation of this isolated word/sub-word recognition.

$$\hat{w} = \arg\max_{w \in W} P(X \mid w) \tag{6}$$

In equation (6), $\hat{w}$ is an estimated candidate, W is set of all candidates, w represents each candidate in W, and $X = x_1, x_2, \cdots, x_n$ are feature vectors. $P(X \mid w)$ is likelihood from the acoustic model. Generally, the acoustic model represents the sub-word or word unit. The system determines the estimated candidate by the likelihood from each HMM.

8.3 Proposed algorithm

To avoid decreasing of the recognition performance, the decoder algorithm was improved for signal retrieval using differential acceleration. The proposed algorithm using differential acceleration is shown in Figure 22 and represents three input signals. First, the speaker uttered a word, and its signal was then extracted with the accelerator. Thus, the signals $X_1, X_2, \cdots, X_N$ were performed for speech recognitions as input signals. The signals of

Figure 22 represent original body-conducted speech, differential acceleration and retrieval signals using Wiener filtering. This experiment focused on the body-conducted speech recognition in a noisy environment, so the speech signal is removed in this experiment. Although the recognition performance is improve that its decoder combines speech as input signal when the noise level is low. Equation (7) was applied for speech recognition with signals of differential acceleration.

$$w_i = \arg\max_{w \in W} P(X_i \mid w) \tag{7}$$

The recognition decoders give the recognition results that are the candidates of words $w_1, w_2, \cdots, w_N$. The parameters of the frame lengths and acoustic scores differ in scale for each signal because Wiener filtering causes a problem in sample length. To compare the acoustic scores, it was necessary to regulate the number of samples. The regulated acoustic score was calculated by the acoustic score and flame length. With equation (8), each score was compared and then the decoder determined the final candidate using the regulated acoustic scores.

$$w_{final} = \arg\max_{\substack{w \in W \\ i=1,\cdots,N}} \left\{ \frac{P(X_i \mid w)}{l_i} \right\} \tag{8}$$

8.4 Experimental setup

Finally, we evaluated the signal retrieval from body-conducted speech in a noisy environment with conventional decoding and the decoding algorithm for differential acceleration. The following signals and decoding algorithms were performed in this experiment:

- BCS: body-conducted speech
- Diff. Acc.: differential acceleration of BCS
- Wiener 1: differential acceleration using Wiener filtering that is repeated one time
- Wiener 2: differential acceleration using Wiener filtering that is repeated two times
- Wiener 3: differential acceleration using Wiener filtering that is repeated three times
- Max: the decoding algorithm for differential acceleration using regulated acoustic scores from the retrieval signals and body-conducted speech.

To evaluate the performance of signal retrieval using differential acceleration, the Julian (Kawahara et al., 1999; Lee et al., 2001), the Japanese speech recognition system that consists of grammar and an acoustic model, was used as the recognition decoder. The experimental environments are shown Table 2.

The improvement efficacy was evaluated by the following measurements:

$$Correct = \frac{Correct\ words}{Rercognition\ words} \times 100\,[\%] \tag{9}$$

$$Relative\ Improvement = \frac{Correct\ rate\ B - Correct\ rate\ A}{100 - Correct\ rate\ A} \times 100\,[\%] \tag{10}$$

Equation (9) is a word correct rate, which calculates a result whether the word is recognized or not. Equation (10) is relative improvement, depicting major improvements above base line levels.

8.5 Recognition results

Retrieval signals with Wiener filtering exhibited marginal improvement with a decrease in recognition because the algorithm rejects a stationary noise and consonant frequency. This problem is described in Section 8.1. We speculated that the noise reduction made improved the recognition performance when the stationary noise level was louder. Clear body-conducted speech retrieval using differential acceleration is not always associated with noisy environment, because the environment often varies according to factors such as the speaker, equipment. Tables 7-9 are shown the recognition results of each speaker. And Table 10 is the result of average of all speakers. The meaning of each data is described in Section 5. In all speakers, the recognition performances are improved on 'Diff. Acc.' and 'Max' however Wiener's results are little improvement. 'Diff. Acc.' becomes a clear signal in this experiment because it does not produce a stationary noise from differential acceleration. And 'Max' is worked on the recognition experiment correctly, so it is proven by Table 10 that the effectiveness of the combination method using retrieval method of signal and its decoding algorithm. So, the recognition performances are improved about 3-4% in word correct rate and about 10-19% in relative improvement.

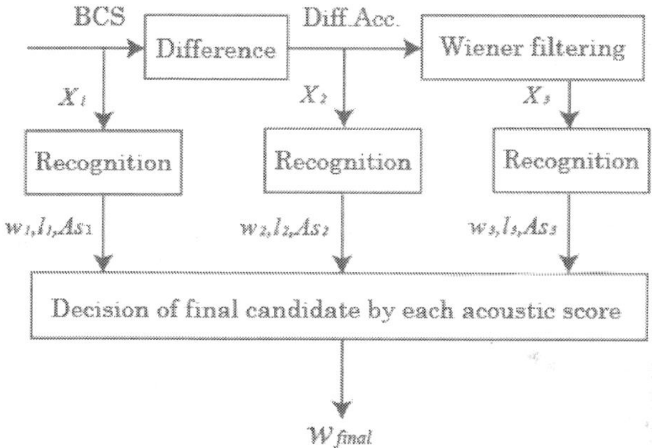

Fig. 22. Decoding algorithm for differential acceleration

	Set 1	Set 2	Set 3	Average	RI
BCS	72%	67%	75%	71.3%	-
Diff. Acc.	76%	74%	80%	76.7%	18.6%
Wiener 1	65%	69%	80%	71.3%	0.0%
Wiener 2	70%	71%	79%	73.3%	7.0%
Wiener 3	60%	74%	81%	71.7%	1.2%
Max	76%	71%	80%	75.7%	15.1%

Table 7. Recognition results of Speaker A in noisy environment

	Set 1	Set 2	Set 3	Average	RI
BCS	70%	71%	71%	70.7%	-
Diff. Acc.	71%	72%	77%	73.3%	9.1%
Wiener 1	67%	65%	72%	68.0%	-9.1%
Wiener 2	68%	65%	70%	67.7%	-10.2%
Wiener 3	72%	67%	72%	70.3%	-1.1%
Max	72%	72%	77%	73.7%	10.2%

Table 8. Recognition results of Speaker B in noisy environment

	Set 1	Set 2	Set 3	Average	RI
BCS	84%	76%	75%	78.3%	-
Diff. Acc.	86%	79%	79%	81.3%	13.8%
Wiener 1	87%	74%	76%	79.0%	3.1%
Wiener 2	88%	69%	77%	78.0%	-1.5%
Wiener 3	86%	74%	77%	79.0%	3.1%
Max	86%	74%	77%	79.0%	3.1%

Table 9. Recognition results of Speaker C in noisy environment

	Average	RI
BCS	73.4%	-
Diff. Acc.	77.1%	13.8%
Wiener 1	72.8%	-2.5%
Wiener 2	73.0%	-1.7%
Wiener 3	73.7%	0.8%
Max	76.1%	10.0%

Table 10. Recognition results of all speakers in noisy environment

9. Conclusions and future work

Here, we investigated a signal retrieval from body-conducted speech using differential acceleration combined with conventional noise reduction methods. Specifically, differential acceleration was used to emphasize the high frequency component of body-conducted speech. Additionally, this method is little cost in calculation. Although the differential acceleration of body-conducted speech became a retrieval signal when stationary noise was present. Thus, it was possible to remove noise effectively using conventional noise reduction methods i.e. spectral subtraction or Wiener filtering. From the experimental results, the Wiener filtering method proved to be a suitable noise reduction method for differential acceleration, as evidenced by the difference between normal speech and each retrieval signal. So, this method can be used to estimate a clear speech using only body-conducted speech. Thereafter, we combined the proposed method and conventional signal retrieval methods to make a clear signal. Combined methods using an adaptive filter for a word, its effectiveness is shown the results in the difference of spectrograms between each signal and speech. Thus, it appears that the proposed method was effective when pre-processing for the conventional signal retrieval techniques existed. The recognition experiment using the differential acceleration followed by the Wiener filtering method, demonstrated the efficacy of differential acceleration that the recognition performance improved 3 - 5 % in isolated word recognition. These results suggest that the retrieval signal approximated natural speech. So we concluded that the proposed method was able to estimate clear speech from body-conducted speech in quiet room.

As a next step of the proposed method, we applied the noise reduction methods to body-conducted speech in a noisy environment. From the experimental results, the Wiener filtering method proved to be a suitable noise reduction method for differential acceleration as evidenced by comparing spectrograms with normal speech and each retrieval signal in a noisy environment. To decide the suitable number of repetitions on Wiener filtering, we proposed a decoding algorithm that was used to regulate the acoustic scores. From the recognition experiments, the differential acceleration signals exhibited the most improvement, and the proposed algorithms improved when compared with base-line body-conducted speech signals. Furthermore, the system does not depend on the environments and speakers because the system chose the highest likelihood from the signals.

As a future works, we will be examined as a pre-processing for the speech support system using body-conducted speech for disorders that converts a clear speech from body-conducted speech of disorders (Ishimitsu and Nakayama, 2009). And, the signal retrieval using differential acceleration is applied to body-conducted speech in noisy environments. Furthermore, we will also construct the microphone using body-conducted speech and differential acceleration for noise environment.

10. References

S. Nakagawa (2007). To spoken document processing from spontaneous speech transcription, in proc. 2007 Autumn Meeting ASJ CD-ROM, pp.1-4

N. Kitaoka, T. Yamada, S. Tsuge, C. Miyajima, T. Nishiura, M. Nakayama, Y. Denda, M. Fujimoto, K. Yamamoto, T. Takiguchi S. Kuroiwa, K. Takeda, and S. Nakamura (2006). CENSREC-1-C: Development of evaluation framework for voice activity detection under noisy environment, in IPSJ SIG Technical Report, 2006-SLP-63, pp.1-6

H. Hirsch and D. Pearce (2000). The AURORA experimental framework for the performance evaluation of speech recognition systems under noisy conditions, in proc. ISCA ITRW ASR2000, pp. 181-188

S. Ishimitsu, M. Nakayama, and Y. Murakami (2004). Study of Body-Conducted Speech Recognition for Support of Maritime Engine Operation, in Journal of the JIME, Vol.39 No.4, pp.35-40

T. Tamiya and T. Shimamura (2006). Improvement of Body-Conducted Speech Quality by Adaptive Filters, in IEICE Technical Report, SP2006-191, pp.41-46

T. T. Vu, M. Unoki, and M. Akagi (2006). A STUDY ON RESTORATION OF BONE-CONDUCTED SPEECH WITH LPC-BASED MODEL, in IEICE Technical Report, SP2005-174, pp.67-78

Z. Liu, Z. Zhang, A. Acero, J. Droppo, and X. Huang (2004). Direct Filtering for Air- and Bone-Conductive Microphones, in proc. IEEE International Workshop on Multimedia Signal Processing (MMSP'04), pp.363-366

S. Dupont, C. Ris, and D. Bachelart (2004). Combined use of closetalk and throat microphones for improved speech recognition under non-stationary background noise, in proc. COST278 and ISCA Tutorial and Research Workshop (ITRW) on Robustness Issues in Conversational Interaction, paper31

S. Itahashi (1991). A noise database and Japanese common speech data corpus, in Journal of ASJ, Vol.47 No.12, pp.951-953

Y. Gong (1995). Speech recognition in noisy environments: A survey, Speech Communication 16, pp.261-291

Y. Nomura, H. Tozawa, J. Lu, H. Sekiya, and T. Yahagi (2006). Musical Noise Reduction by Spectral Subtraction Using Morphological Process, in Trans. of IEICE on information and systems, Vol.89 No.5, pp.991-1000

K. Yamashita, S. Ogata, and T. Shimamura (2005). Improved Spectral Subtraction Utilizing Iterative Processing, in Trans. of IEICE on Inst. of Electronics, Information and Communication Engineers, Vol.J88-A No.11, pp.1246-1257

D. Li and D. O'Shaughnessy (2003). Speech Processing: A Dynamic and Optimization - Oriented Approach, Marcel Dekker Inc

J. Durbin (1960). The Fitting of Time-Series Models, Review of the International Statistical Institute, Vol.28 No.3, pp.233-244

M. Morise, T. Irino, and H. Kawahara (2007). Error Evaluation of Impulse Response Estimation by Cross Spectral Method Using Speech Signal, in the Journal of IEICE, Vol.J90-A N0.7, pp.559-566

S. Ishimitsu, M. Nakayama, and K. Oda (2007). Study of Speech Support System for Disorders Using Body-Conducted Speech Recognition, in proc. 2007 Autumn Meeting ASJ CD-ROM, pp.715-716

S. Haykin (1996). Adaptive filter theory (3rd ed.), Prentice-Hall, Inc.

T. Kawahara, A. Lee, T. Kobayashi, K. Takeda, N. Minematsu, K. Itou, A. Ito, M. Yamamoto, A. Yamada, T. Utsuro, and K. Shikano (1999), Japanese Dictation Toolkit -1997 version-, in Journal of ASJ, Vol.20 No.3, pp.233-239

A. Lee, T. Kawahara, and K. Shikano (2001). Julius - an open source real-time large vocabulary recognition engine, in Proc. European Conference on Speech Communication and Technology (EUROSPEECH), pp. 1691-1694

K. Itou, M. Yamamoto, K. Takeda, T. Takezawa, T. Matsuoka, T. Kobayashi, K. Shikano, and S. Itahashi (1999). JNAS: Japanese speech corpus for large vocabulary continuous speech recognition research, in Journal of ASJ, Vol.20, No.3, pp.199-206

S. Young, J. Jansen, J. Odell, and P. Woodland (2000). The HTK Book for V2.0, Cambridge University

L. Rabiner (1993). Fundamentals of Speech Recognition, Prentice Hall

S.B. Davis and P. Mermelstein (1980). Comparison of parametric representations for monosyllabic word recognition in continuously spoken sentences, IEEE Trans. Acoustics, Speech Signal Proc., ASSP-28, Vol. 4, pp.357–366

N. Rivara, P.B. Dickinson, and A.T. Shenton (2009). Constrained variance control of peak-pressure position by spark-ionisation feedback for multi-cylinder control', *International Journal of Advanced Mechatronic Systems (IJAMechS)*, Vol. 1, No. 4, pp.242–250

S. Ishimitsu and M. Nakayama (2009). Construction of Speech Support System Using Body-Conducted Speech Recognition for Disorders, in proc. of The Third International Conference on Innovative Computing, Information and Control (ICICIC2008), CD-ROM

18

Frequency Lowering Algorithms for the Hearing Impaired

Francisco J. Fraga[1], Leticia Pimenta C. S. Prates[2],
Alan M. Marotta[3] and Maria Cecilia Martinelli Iorio[4]
[1]Universidade Federal do ABC (UFABC),
[2]Universidade Federal de Minas Gerais (UFMG),
[3]Centro Federal de Educação Tecnológica de Minas Gerais (CEFET/MG),
[4]Universidade Federal de São Paulo (UNIFESP)
Brazil

1. Introduction

Hearing, as a complex function, requires perfect cochlea and auditory pathways and any interference in this system may compromise its performance. Hearing aids have made great advances in hearing rehabilitation. However, audiology professionals still face failures, usually related to speech discrimination. This is a common situation in sloping sensorineural hearing loss, which is often associated with marked difficulties in word recognition, especially in detection and discrimination of fricative phonemes, even using hearing aids.

There is a consensus that the main difficulty related to hearing loss refers to communication, with the loss in the ability of speech discrimination and recognition. However, the increase on acoustic information available through hearing aids does not always provide the complete restoration of these abilities. Some patients present little or no benefit with amplification, particularly those with severe high frequencies hearing loss. Several studies demonstrate the contribution of high frequencies on speech intelligibility. Consequently, the sloping sensorineural hearing loss is related to the difficulty in understanding speech, even with the use of hearing aids.

Hearing loss is more common for high–frequency and mid–frequency sounds (1 to 3 kHz) than for low–frequency. Frequently, there are only small losses at low frequencies (below 1 kHz) but almost absolute deafness above 1.5 or 2 kHz. A considerable percentage of the hearing impaired with moderate/severe hearing loss has audiograms where the losses are profound for high frequencies, severe for medium frequencies and mild or moderate for low frequencies.

Such problems lead researchers to lower the spectrum of speech in order to match the residual low-frequency hearing of listeners with high-frequency impairments. For these patients, lowering the high-frequency speech spectrum to the frequencies where the losses are mild or moderate could be a good processing tool to be added in the implementation of a digital hearing aid device. In this section we will provide a brief review of frequency transposition and frequency compression algorithms developed for hearing aid users along the past three decades.

Given the difficulties encountered on amplification of high frequencies, frequency lowering has been suggested by some authors in an attempt to provide speech cues contained in high frequencies (Hicks et al., 1981; Reed et al., 1983; Reed et al., 1985).

Speech playback at a slower sampling rate and reduction of zero-crossing rate are some of the frequency lowering methods that were used in surveys conducted before the eighties, as reported by Hicks et al. (1981). All these methods involve signal distortion, more or less noticeable, usually dependent on the degree of spectral change. Such schemes perceptually modify important speech characteristics such as rhythmic and time patterns, psychophysical frequency (pitch) sensation, and duration of segmental elements. In their paper (Hicks et al., 1981), authors presented a remarkable investigation on frequency lowering. Their technique involves monotonic compression of short-time spectrum, without pitch alteration, while avoiding some problems observed in other methods.

Reed et al. (1983) conducted an experimental study to evaluate human speech recognition, using linear and nonlinear frequency compression, according to the method proposed by Hicks et al. (1981). Initially, the study was conducted with six normal hearing individuals, performing consonant discrimination experiments on these normal listeners and results were compared with the control condition, using low-pass filtering. They have observed that Hick's frequency lowering scheme presented better performance for fricative and affricate sounds if compared with low pass filtering to an equivalent bandwidth. On the other hand, the performance of the low pass filtering was better for vowels, semivowels and nasal sounds. For plosive sounds, both methods have shown similar results. In general, the performance on the best frequency–lowering conditions was almost the same to that obtained on low pass filtering to an equivalent bandwidth.

Subsequently, in another study (Reed et al., 1985) authors applied the frequency compression test in individuals with mild to severe hearing loss and sloping audiograms. Non-linear frequency compression was used and results were compared with conventional sound amplification. They reported that frequency compression was not beneficial in any condition.

Turner and Hurtig (1999) commented that the frequency region where the hearing loss occurs, as well as its extent, are determining factors in word discrimination. In general, hearing loss exceeding 60 dB HL at frequencies above 2-3 kHz causes a reduction in speech discrimination. Therefore, they believe that the perception of high frequencies speech cues can be improved by changing the high frequency components to low-frequency regions, since the hearing sensitivity in these regions is greater than 60 dB HL.

The authors hypothesized that, in hearing loss above 60 dB HL for high frequency sounds, the auditory system loses the ability to discriminate the articulation point, as this information is contained in higher frequencies (above 1 kHz) of the speech spectrum. Thus, they suggest that only patients with hearing loss at frequencies above 2 kHz and hearing thresholds better than 60 dB HL in the frequencies below 2 kHz have the potential to benefit from frequency compression.

McDermott and Dean (2000) evaluated speech recognition in individuals with sloping hearing loss whose tone thresholds at low frequencies were better than 30 dB HL, while in medium and high frequencies presented profound hearing loss. Twenty six subjects were evaluated through a task of speech recognition in noise, in free-field at 65 dB A, with the signal/noise ratio of 6 dB. Upon testing, subjects were not using their hearing aids. The results were similar to those obtained in a previous experiment - which used the same speech material and procedures - performed with normal hearing individuals with a hearing loss simulation using similar low-pass filters and cutoff frequencies. The authors affirmed that using normal hearing subjects on this type of experiment is advantageous because it ensures that evaluation of the algorithm is not influenced by other factors associated with sensorineural hearing loss.

Simpson et al. (2005) developed a frequency compression algorithm for hearing aids. They used a nonlinear compression method, increasing progressively the compression ratio for high frequency sounds. To evaluate the algorithm, they conducted a study on recognition of monosyllabic words in quiet, with 17 hearing aids users with moderate to severe sloping sensorineural hearing loss. Their objective was to compare phoneme recognition using conventional hearing aids and those with the frequency compression algorithm embedded. Of the 17 participating subjects, eight had improvement in recognition of phonemes using frequency compression; eight showed no differences regarding the amplification used and one subject presented significantly lower performance with the algorithm. Fricative sounds were the most favoured by frequency compression.

Using the same algorithm developed in their earlier studies, authors (Simpson et al., 2006) studied frequency compression in seven individuals with hearing loss suggestive of cochlear dead regions, defined as regions in the cochlea that have no inner hair cells or adjacent functional neurons (Moore et al., 2000). In general, performance in the task of speech in quiet with conventional amplification was similar to performance with frequency compression. The authors commented that it is possible that frequency compression has brought benefits in the discrimination of some phonemes and detriment of others, so the final score did not change. For example, fricative phonemes /ʃ/ and /ʒ/ were more correctly identified by frequency compression than by conventional amplification. On the other hand, recognition of phoneme /s/ was reduced. Fricatives /ʃ/, /z/ and /v/ were the most selected when frequency compression was used.

Kuk (2007) gave a brief discussion about benefits and applicability of frequency transposition. In that article, he presents the frequency transposition algorithm developed by Widex, available on the Inteo hearing aid. Continuing the previous study, Kuk et al. (2007) discussed the importance of experience with the frequency transposition algorithm to fitting success. According to authors, on the first experience, some users do not like the sound quality provided by this algorithm, referring to sound harsh or unnatural. They concluded that the great sound change caused by frequency transposition account for this negative reaction, requiring a long-term use so that a reorganization of the cortical tonotopic representation may occur.

Robinson et al. (2007) considered severe high frequency hearing loss when average of pure tone thresholds at 4.0, 6.0 and 8.0 kHz was less than 75 dB HL, and stressed that this loss is prevalent in 24% of individuals over 60. The authors presented a new method of frequency transposition applied only on sounds that have significant energy at high frequencies. They set the dead region frequency edge considering this feature a fundamental key in the individual formatting of the frequency transposition algorithm. They concluded that the benefit observed in the use of frequency transposition was reduced by the confusion generated between phonemes. Thus, they hypothesized that frequency transposition, instead of improving discrimination of consonants, improves detection of fricatives. The authors evaluated the new algorithm to detect the phonemes /s/ and /z/ in final word position. They used 24 pairs of words that differed by the presence or absence of /s/ and /z/ in final syllables, recorded by a single female speaker. The assessment was performed by seven subjects with hearing loss and cochlear dead regions at high frequencies. Participants were instructed to select visually one of the words of the pair. As a result, authors found that frequency transposition significantly improved task performance, compared to the control condition.

In next sections we present some frequency compression and transposition algorithms we developed and evaluated for helping the hearing impaired with severe high frequency hearing loss.

2. Comparison of two frequency lowering algorithms for digital hearing aid

In this section we present a new frequency-lowering algorithm that uses frequency transposition instead of frequency compression. Furthermore, the frequency transposition is applied only over fricatives and affricates, leaving the other speech sounds untouched, as previous works have shown that frequency lowering only benefits high frequency phonemes. To perform comparison, we have also implemented a frequency compression algorithm based on Hick's method (Hicks et al., 1981).

Results of subjective preference (considering speech quality) indicate better performance of our frequency transposition method compared to Hick's frequency compression method. We also present subjective intelligibility tests over 20 subjects, showing that in this case performance (now considering speech intelligibility) depends on which are the specific phonemes being processed by these two algorithms.

2.1 Audiometric data acquisition and processing

The first step of both frequency-lowering algorithms consists in audiometric data acquisition of the hearing impaired subject. The audiometric exam is employed for measuring the degree of the hearing impairment of a given patient. In this exam, the listener is submitted to a perception test by continuously varying the sound pressure level (SPL) of a pure sinusoidal tone in a discrete frequency scale. The frequency values most frequently used are 250 Hz, 500 Hz, 1 kHz, 2 kHz, 4 kHz, 6 kHz and 8 kHz. For each of these frequencies, the minimum SPL in dB for which the patient is capable of perceiving the sound is registered in a graph.

The audiogram is the result of the audiometric exam, which is presented by a graph with the values in dB SPL for each of the discrete frequencies. This graph is done separately for each subject's ear. Since the level of 0 dB SPL is considered the minimum sound pressure level for normal hearing, the positive values in dB registered on the vertical axis of the audiogram can be considered as the hearing losses of the patient's ear.

If the average loss at frequencies of 500, 1000 and 2000 Hz is equal or inferior to 20 dB, the subject is considered as having normal hearing. From 21 to 40 dB, hearing loss is classified as mild. Average loss greater than 40 dB but inferior to 70 dB is considered moderate. From 71 to 90 dB, we consider that patient has severe hearing loss and more than 95 dB of loss is classified as profound.

The threshold of discomfort, for normal or impaired listeners, is always below 120 dB SPL. Indeed, commonly the threshold of discomfort for the hearing impaired is lower than for normal hearing subjects. Although less common, some audiograms bring both the threshold of discomfort and the threshold of hearing (Alsaka & McLean, 1996), as one can observe in Fig. 1. In this figure, points of audiogram corresponding to the right ear are signalled with a round mark and those corresponding to the left ear are signalled with an X mark. These marks are worldwide used in this way by audiologists. The dynamic range of hearing for each frequency is the threshold of discomfort minus the threshold of hearing.

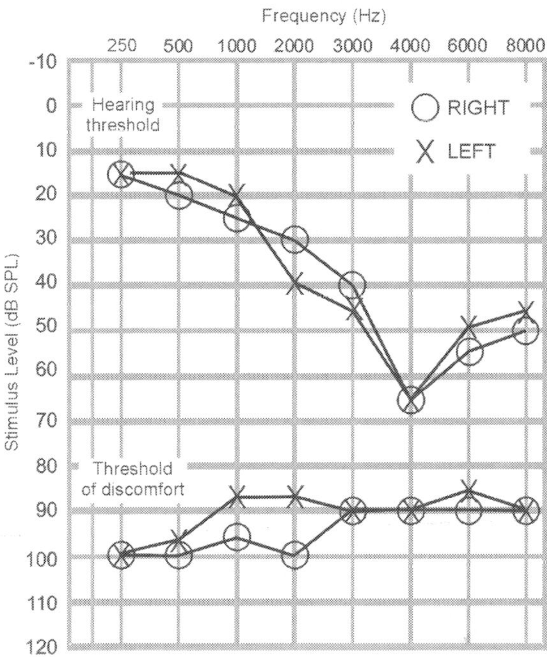

Fig. 1. Sloping sensorineural hearing loss case

Based on the acquired audiometric data, the algorithm analyses the range of frequencies where there is still some residual hearing. The criterion used is the following: first, it is verified if patient has a ski–slope kind of losses, i.e., if the losses are increasing with frequency. Only patients with this type of impairment can be aided by any frequency lowering method.

After that, the first frequency where there is a profound loss is determined. If this frequency is between 1.2 kHz and 3.4 kHz, a destination frequency to which the high–frequency spectrum will be transposed is calculated. Otherwise, no frequency transposition is needed (residual hearing above 3.4 kHZ) or profitable (residual hearing below 1.2 kHZ). This destination frequency is considered as the geometrical mean between 900 Hz and the highest frequency where there is still some residual hearing. The geometrical mean was empirically chosen because it provides a good trade-off between minimum spectrum distortion and maximum residual hearing profit. In order to obtain more accuracy in the losses thresholds, audiogram points are linearly interpolated.

As will be explained further, tests were done first in normal hearing people, simulating hearing losses by means of low-pass filtering. In this case, for destination frequency calculation as well as for definition of other algorithm parameters (see 2.2), the low-pass filter cut-off frequency is considered as the highest frequency where there is still some residual hearing.

2.2 Speech data acquisition and processing

Speech signals are sampled at 16 kHz and Hamming windowed with 25 ms windows. These windows are 50% overlapped, what means that the signal is analyzed at a frame rate of 1/12.5 kHz. A 1024-point FFT is used for representing the short–time speech spectrum in the frequency domain.

If in the previous audiometric data analysis a ski–slope kind of loss was detected and the frequency transposition criterion was matched, a destination frequency has already been determined. Then, we have to find out (in a frame–by–frame basis) if the short–time speech spectrum presents significant information at high frequencies that justify the frequency transposition operation. The criterion used for transposing or not the short–time spectrum of each speech frame depends on a threshold. When the signal has high energy in high frequencies the algorithm transposes high frequency information to lower frequencies. The threshold is set for suppressing the processing of all vowels, nasals and the semivowels, while activating frequency transposition for fricatives and affricates.

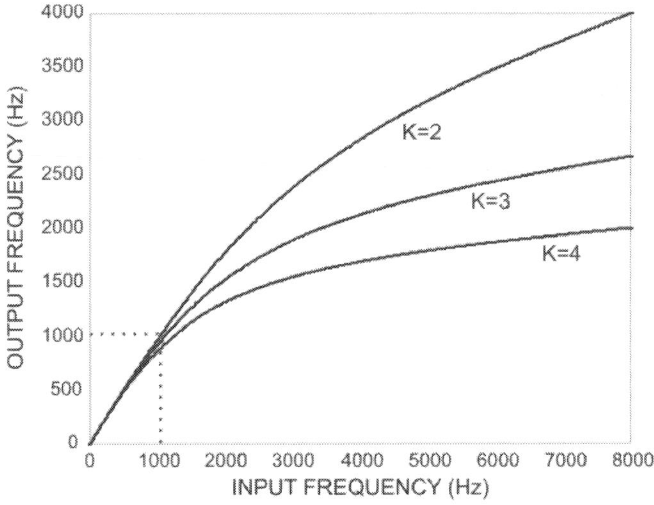

Fig. 2. Input-output frequency compression curves

To decide which part of the spectrum will be transposed, the energy of 500 Hz bandwidth sliding windows are calculated with 100 Hz spacing, from 1 kHz to 8 kHz (Nyquist frequency). This is done with the aim of find out an origin frequency. The origin frequency is the frequency 100 Hz below the beginning of the 500 Hz bandwidth window with maximum energy. The part of the spectrum that will be transposed corresponds to the range of all frequencies above the origin frequency. This empirical criterion guarantees that the unavoidable distortion due to the frequency lowering operation will be profitable. Because in this way the most important part of high–energy spectrum will be transposed to lower frequencies, maintaining untouched low–frequency information.

For comparison, the Hick's frequency compression scheme was already implemented, but now only when the same frequency lowering criterion (high/low frequency energy ratio) used for transposition was matched, i. e., only for fricatives and affricates. The frequency compression was done by means of the same equation used by Reed et al. (1983). But in practice, it is more useful to implement its inverse equation, which is

$$\frac{f_{IN}}{f_s} = \frac{1}{\pi}\tan^{-1}\left[\left(\frac{1-a}{1+a}\right)\tan\left(K\pi\frac{f_{OUT}}{f_s}\right)\right] \quad , \quad a = \frac{K-1}{K+1} \tag{1}$$

where f_{IN} is the original frequency, f_{OUT} is the corresponding compressed frequency, K is the frequency compression factor, a is the warping parameter and f_s is the sampling rate. For minimum distortion at low frequencies, the warping parameter must be chosen by the ratio defined in second part of equation (1).

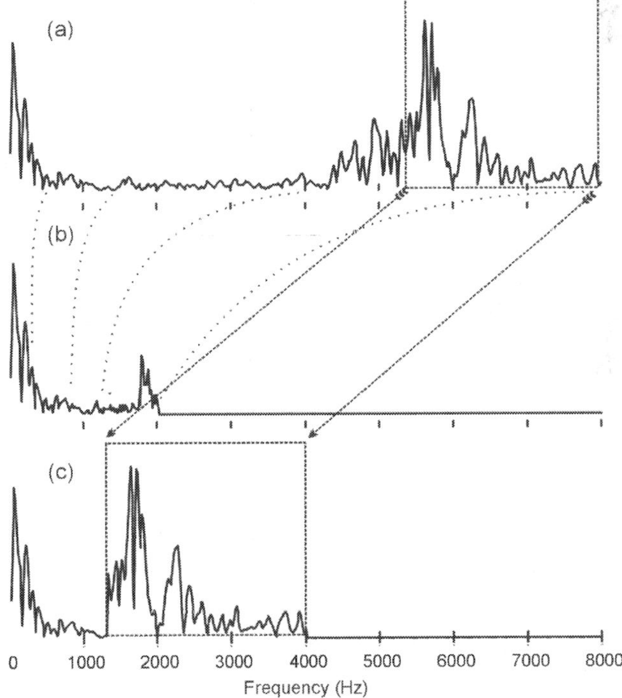

Fig. 3. Comparison of frequency lowering schemes: compression (b) versus transposition (c)

As it occurs with the destination frequency calculation (see 2.1), the compression factor K was determined according to the listener's loss degree. Fig. 2 shows the curves of equation (1) for K = 2, 3 and 4. In this figure we can see that low frequency spectral content (below 1000 Hz) is barely compressed.

For better understanding and comparison of frequency transposition and frequency compression spectral effects, in part (a) of Fig. 3 one can see the original short-time spectrum of a speech frame taken from a female pronunciation of phoneme /s/, in part (b) the same frame is shown compressed by a factor K = 4 and part (c) presents the frame after frequency transposition. It is easy to observe that frequency transposition preserves the spectral shape, what does not occur in the case of frequency compression, where one can clearly note a great amount of shape distortion at high frequencies, but still preserving low frequency spectral content.

2.3 Preliminary qualitative test

Both frequency lowering algorithms (frequency compression and frequency transposition) were not already tested with hearing impaired subjects. But we got some preliminary results with normal listeners, first considering only qualitative aspects of processed speech. In this case, a simple low pass filtering process simulates the losses above the frequency where there is no more residual hearing. In this preliminary qualitative test, cut-off frequency was fixed to 2 kHz.

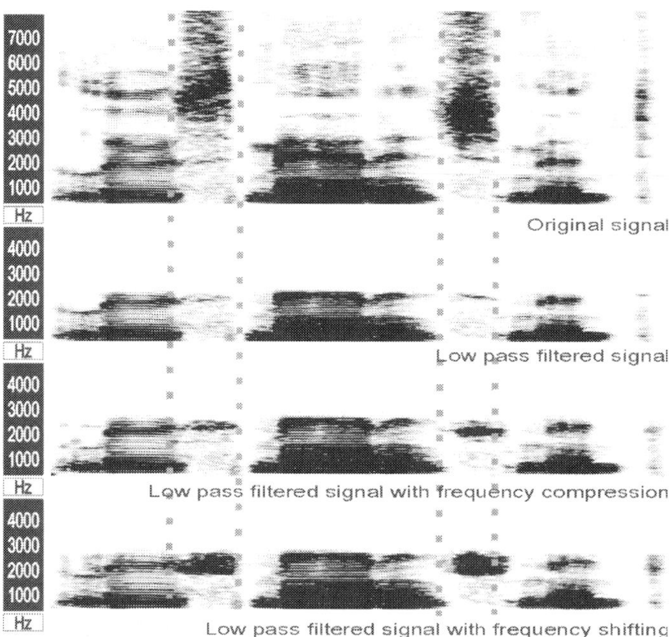

Fig. 4. Spectrograms of "loose management"

The experiment we have carried out consists of submitting the low-pass filtered speech signal to both frequency lowering algorithms. After, two normal hearing adults (one male and one female) listened to the processed speech signals, as well as to the control condition (low-pass filtering only). Listeners are not previously informed regarding signals' processing schemes and are asked for ranking the three speech sounds according to their subjective quality.

In this preliminary test, only two different speech signals were submitted to the algorithms. The original and processed spectrograms of one of these speech signals (a male pronunciation of the words 'loose management') are shown in Fig. 4, where we can appreciate again the visual difference between the two frequency lowering algorithms. It is important to remark that both listeners are native speakers of Brazilian Portuguese and are not used to listen to English words in their everyday tasks. This is important because in this way we intend to separate speech quality from speech intelligibility, although both aspects are correlated and cannot be perfectly assessed by subjective evaluation.

According to our prevision, only fricative speech sounds were frequency lowered in both algorithms. The unique exception is the phoneme / l /, which is not fricative but lateral approximant. But in this case, its pronunciation had high frequency energy, as we can observe in the spectrogram of the original speech signal (see Fig. 4).

Listeners' preferences were listed in Table 1. In this table, 'Signal 1' is the Portuguese word "pensando" (which means 'thinking'), pronounced by a Brazilian Portuguese native speaker (male), and 'Signal 2' is the English words 'loose management', the latter corresponding to the spectrograms of Fig.4.

Speech signal	Male listener	Female listener
Signal 1 – low pass filtering (control)	1st	3rd
Signal 1 – frequency compression	3rd	2nd
Signal 1 – frequency transposition	2nd	1st
Signal 2 - low pass filtering (control)	2nd	2nd
Signal 2 – frequency compression	3rd	3rd
Signal 2 – frequency transposition	1st	1st

Table 1. Listener's preferences

One can observe that listeners' preference are more consistent when listening to foreign words (english, in this case), where speech quality can be easily separated from speech inteligibility. These preliminary results indicate that the frequency shifting (or transposition) method was preferred by the listeners when compared to the frequency compression method. But it is important to remark that the subjective difference between the low pass filtered signal, the frequency–compressed signal and the frequency-shifted signal is very slight, as perceived by normal listeners.

2.4 Preliminary intelligibility test

We perform a syllable identification test over 42 normal hearing subjects, 31 male and 11 female; a simple low pass filtering process simulates the losses above the frequency where there is no more residual hearing. Speech material consists of 21 different CV phonetic syllables, which are composed with the seven Brazilian Portuguese fricative phonemes ([f], [v], [ʒ], [ʃ], [s], [z], [x]) followed by three vowels ([a], [i], [u]).

Six Brazilian Portuguese native speakers, three female and three male, pronounced once all these syllables. After processing, each utterance generates nine speech signals: low-pass filtered syllable (control), frequency compressed syllable and frequency transposed syllable. Previously to frequency lowering, all signals passed through three different low–pass filters with cutoff frequencies of 1.5, 2 and 2.5 kHz, thus forming a final speech database composed by 1134 WAVE files.

After has heard three times a phonetic syllable at random, the listener must choose one written syllable from a list of seven possibilities, because only syllables with the correct vowel is presented. Due to the random choice of the syllables that were presented to the listeners, there were some syllables that were less listened than others. But each of the 63 different processed fricatives was presented at least 5 times to each listener, and any of them was presented more than 15 times.

Processed Syllable	None	Compression	Shifting
[f] 1500	61,5	72,7	62,5
[f] 2000	40,0	44,4	69,2
[f] 2500	85,7	53,3	58,3
[v] 1500	78,6	80,0	81,8
[v] 2000	100,0	71,4	66,7
[v] 2500	77,8	61,5	90,9
[ʒ] 1500	25,0	28,6	33,3
[ʒ] 2000	50,0	81,8	86,7
[ʒ] 2500	69,2	62,5	77,8
[ʃ] 1500	0,0	20,0	45,5
[ʃ] 2000	44,4	62,5	55,6
[ʃ] 2500	77,8	100,0	84,6
[s] 1500	53,8	50,0	8,3
[s] 2000	73,3	36,4	33,3
[s] 2500	76,9	41,7	25,0
[z] 1500	57,1	46,7	75,0
[z] 2000	70,0	60,0	40,0
[z] 2500	44,4	60,0	33,3
[x] 1500	66,7	40,0	12,5
[x] 2000	46,2	21,4	38,5
[x] 2500	55,6	38,5	75,0

Table 2. Listener's correct decisions (%).

The results of this test are shown in Table 2, where column None means no processing further than low pass filtering, Compression means frequency compression and Shifting means frequency shifting (transposition). In the first column we have all the possible fricatives for each (three) filter cutoff frequencies. In the table, numbers signaled in boldface correspond to the greatest percentage of correct decisions made for each processing type.

2.5 Discussion and conclusions

The slight perceived difference in the quality observed by both male and female listeners among the processed signals may be due to the fact that the disparity between the original signal (with frequencies up to 8 kHz) and the low pass filtered (2 kHz) signals is large. But for the impaired subject, that never (or for a long time) had any perception of sounds with frequencies above 2 kHz, may be the difference between the processed signals was not so slight.

Relatively to the results of the intelligibility test, results are difficult to analyze if we consider the set of syllables as a whole. But it is interesting to analyze each fricative sound in particular. For example, we can conclude from the results that for phone [s] the better is to do no further processing, but if we consider phone [ʃ] we conclude just the opposite: no processing leads to zero percent correct identification when the highest audible frequency is 1.5 kHz, but it improves to 45,5% when submitted to frequency transposition (shifting). In the case of fricative sound [ʒ], the better results are also obtained with our frequency shifting algorithm, independently of the signal bandwidth. For all other situations, the optimal solution depends on the specific phone and cutoff frequency considered.

Considering the set of phonemes as a whole, based on the preliminary syllable identification test, we observed that there was no statistical significance between both frequency lowering algorithms when compared to low-pass filtering ($p > 0.05$), as well as compared to eachother ($p > 0.07$). But considering invidual phonemes, we can conclude that if we incorporate a simple automatic phoneme classifier in the system, it is possible to choose the better frequency lowering algorithm to be applied for each specific phone, given the maximum frequency where there is some residual hearing. This is not difficult to do, considering the advances observed in the performance of automatic phoneme recognition algorithms over the last years (Scanlon et al., 2007). Finally, it is important to remark that both algorithms have demonstrated to be fast enough to enable their usage in digital hearing aid devices.

3. Frequency compression and its effects on human speech recognition

In this section we present the development and evaluation of the same frequency compression algorithm described in section 2, but with some modifications. This is a pilot study where the modified algorithm was applied to a list of monosyllabic words to be recognized and replicated by normal hearing subjects, considering the compression ratio applied (3:1, 2:1, 1:1) for a subsequent study in deaf individuals. The purpose of this research was to conduct a descriptive analysis of results in normal individuals, considering the compression ratio applied and the familiarity with the words of the test.

3.1 Methods

This study was conducted at the Department of Integrated Care, Research and Teaching on Hearing (NIAPEA), Federal University of São Paulo - PaulistaSchool of Medicine, after approval by the Research Ethics Committee of the Federal University of São Paulo / Hospital São Paulo, under the protocol 0150. All participants signed the free and informed consent form.

The study included 18 normal listeners of both genders, with ages between 21 and 42 years. Of the participants, eight were Speech-Language Pathologists/Audiologists and were familiar with the list of words contained in the applied test. The other ten participants were companions of patients of the clinic, without any prior knowledge of the words on the list.

Thus, two groups were defined: group F, composed by Speech-Language Pathologists/Audiologists and group P, composed by the remaining participants.

Participants had hearing thresholds better than 20 dB in the frequencies from 250 to 8000 Hz, measured before the beginning of the evaluation. Speech material used in this study consisted of monosyllabic words applied through TDH 39 headphones at 60 dB NA intensity, in silence, monotic task, both ears. The subjects were instructed to repeat, exactly, the monosyllables presented. The word recognition rate (WRR) was established by counting the number of words repeated correctly and dividing by the number of words heard.

For the word recognition test (WRT) we used a list of 25 monosyllabic words phonetically balanced (Pen & Mangabeira, 1973) and available on CD (Pereira & Schochat, 1997). A new organization of the words list was played in another CD in three different sequences of the same words, to reduce the listener learning effect.

To determine the pure tone and speech tests thresholds, we used the Aurical™ audiometer from Madsen Electronics™, coupled to a personal computer. The speech procedures were applied in a sound proof booth using a portable compact disc player, model 4147 from Toshiba™, coupled to the Aurical™ audiometer and TDH 39 headphones, besides the CD containing speech samples.

The words in the lists had the speech spectrum modified by frequency compression. We performed all speech processing using Matlab™, at the Engineering and Modeling Center of the ABC Federal University (UFABC. After processing, speech material were assembled in a computer and recorded on CD.

Frequency compression was performed by non-linear method - i.e. performing smaller compression in low frequencies and further compression on high frequencies (6). Speech signals are sampled at 16 kHz and Hamming windowed with 25 ms windows. These windows are 50% overlapped, what means that the signal is analyzed at a frame rate of 1/12.5 kHz. A 1024-point FFT is used for representing the short–time speech spectrum in the frequency domain.

Three following compression ratios were used (or compression factor - K) in the words lists: 1:1 (K = 1), 2:1 (K = 2) and 3:1 (K = 3), thus composing three lists of frequency compressed words. Compression ratio of 1:1 (or the compression factor K = 1) refers to the absence of compression, i.e. the words were presented in a natural form, providing the whole spectrum of speech in the signal sampled at 16 kHz. Compression ratios of 2:1 and 3:1 (or compression factor K = 2 and K = 3) mean application of frequency compression in different proportions.

The higher the compression ratio is, the greater the degree of frequency lowering - which creates major changes on the speech spectrum. The frequency compression curves used in this study can be observed in Figure 1. These curves were implemented directly in the frequency domain, in a frame-by-frame basis, using the equation shown in the lower right corner of the figure, where variable a controls the degree of nonlinearity of the curves (a = 0 turns the curve into a straight line). Speech processing back to the time domain were performed by the well-known overlap-and-add method (Nawab & Quatieri, 1998).

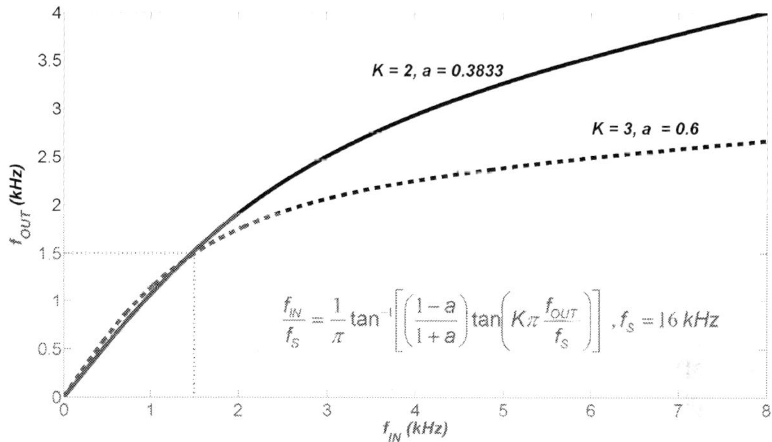

$$\frac{f_{IN}}{f_S} = \frac{1}{\pi}\tan^{-1}\left[\left(\frac{1-a}{1+a}\right)\tan\left(K\pi\frac{f_{OUT}}{f_S}\right)\right], f_S = 16\,kHz$$

Fig. 5. Frequency compression curves used in the pilot study. Horizontal axis depicts the frequency range of input (original) signal and vertical axis the frequency range of output (processed) signal for the compression factors K = 2 (full line) and K = 3 (dashed line).

The total lack of compression corresponds to K = 1 and a = 0. When a = 0 and K = 2 for example, the compression is linear (a = 0) in the ratio of 2:1 (K = 2). This means, in this example, that output frequencies (of processed signal) correspond exactly to half the values of input frequencies (of original signal). That is, if the original signal has a frequency component at 2000 Hz, this will correspond to 1000 Hz in the processed signal.

On the algorithm originally proposed (6), the curves were approximately linear and with no compression in the range from 0 to 1 kHz. In this study, the approximate range of linearity (and no compression) was extended up to 1.5 kHz, aiming to reduce as most as possible the perceptual distortion of main pitch harmonics and formants of the original speech signal.

Figure 6 displays the spectrogram of the Portuguese monosyllable "jaz" (/ʒas /, male speaker) in three situations evaluated in this study: K = 1 and a = 0 (i); K = 2 and a = 0.3833 (ii); K = 3 and a = 0.6 (iii). A fourth situation (not evaluated in this study), which corresponds to the linear compression, with K = 2 and a = 0 (iv) is also presented. Comparing the Figures 2-ii to 2-iv, one can clearly observe the difference between the spectrogram obtained with the non-linear and the linear compression.

The lists of words were heard in order of difficulty, starting the list with K = 3 and ending with K = 1. This was done in order to not provide clues that could facilitate the recognition of words, once all lists are composed by the same words arranged in different forms.

The results were treated statistically through the Wilcoxon and Mann-Whitney non-parametric tests. To complement the descriptive analysis, confidence intervals of the means were calculated. The significance level adopted was 5%. We use an asterisk (*) to characterize statistical significance.

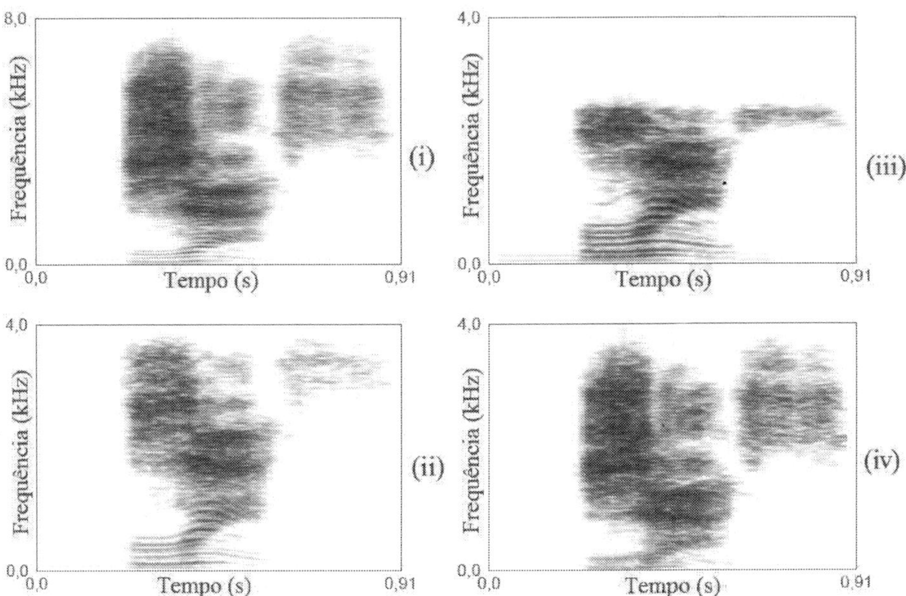

Fig. 6. Spectrograms of /ʒas / (male speaker): (i) original (K = 1 and a = 0); (ii) non-linear compression with K = 2 and a = 0.3833; (iii) nonlinear compression with K = 3 and a = 0.6; and (iv) linear compression, with K = 2 and a = 0 (situation not assessed in this study).

3.2 Results
In Table 3, we present the mean WRR values obtained in the WRT, with compression ratios of 3:1 (K = 3), 2:1 (K = 2) and 1:1 (K = 1) for groups of Speech-Language Pathologists/Audiologists (F) and companions of patients (P). Results of right and left ears are compared.

As there were no statistically significant differences between the WRR obtained for the right and the left ear in both groups, as demonstrated by the p-values at bottom line of Table 3, we chose to perform the remaining analysis considering the values of both ears. Thus, the samples are doubled, making the results statiscally more reliable.

Thus, in Figure 7 we show the WRR average values obtained in groups P and F (joining both ears), considering the compression ratio (compression factor K).

3.3 Discussion
Evaluation of human speech recognition using frequency compression has been proposed by many authors in studies dating from the 70's or earlier. What differs among these studies

is how the algorithm is processed. However, despite the divergent and often disappointing results, even today, many researchers focus on the same methods as an attempt to improve speech recognition, especially for the hearing impaired with losses at high frequencies.

	Group P						Group F					
	K3		K2		K1		K 3		K 2		K 1	
	OD	OE	OD	OE	OD	OE	OD	OE	OD	OE	OD	OE
Mean	42,40	44,40	74,00	74,40	92,00	93,20	68,50	67,50	91,50	91,00	98,00	98,00
Median	42	42	74	76	92	94	78	74	94	96	100	100
SD	15,23	12,57	8,27	10,70	3,27	4,24	19,18	16,06	9,90	9,50	3,02	3,02
CV	35,9%	28,3%	11,2%	14,4%	3,5%	4,5%	28,0%	23,8%	10,8%	10,4%	3,1%	3,1%
Q1	32	37	69	65	89	89	53	54	87	83	96	96
Q2	51	44	76	80	95	96	80	77	100	97	100	100
N	10	10	10	10	10	10	8	8	8	8	8	8
IC	9,44	7,79	5,13	6,63	2,02	2,63	13,29	11,13	6,86	6,58	2,10	2,10
p-value	0,509		0,862		0,180		0,480		0,655		1,000	

Wilcoxon Test Note: SD: Standard Deviation; VC: variation coefficient; Q1: first quartile; Q2: second quartile; N: sample size; CI: confidence interval

Table 3. Descriptive analysis of WRT results (%WRR) of the group of Speech-Language Pathologists/Audiologists (F) and companions of patients (P) with compression factors K = 3, K = 2 and K = 1, for right and left ear separetely.

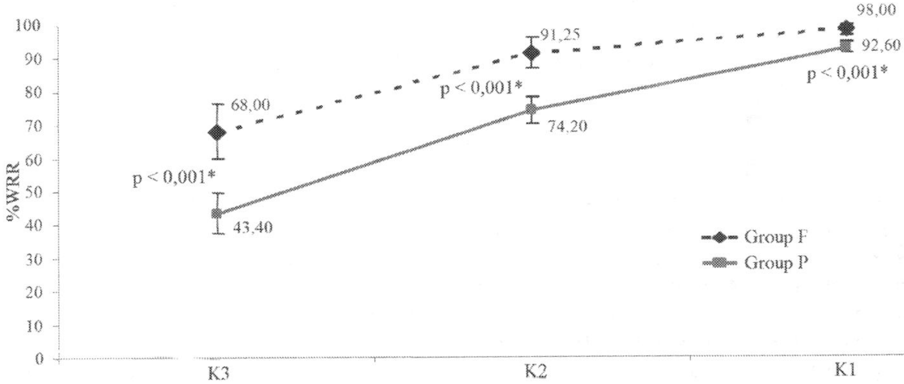

Fig. 7. Comparative graphic of average WRR values obtained in groups P and F, with compression factors K = 3, K = 2 and K = 1, now considering both ears (joined). Statistical significance (p-values) was established with Mann-Whitney Test.

With the discovery of dead regions in the cochlea (Moore et al., 2000), and successive studies demonstrating its negative impact on the ability of word recognition (Gordo & Iorio, 2007), the frequency compression is again investigated with a reinvigorated proposal that, having all technology for sound amplification available, seems to be an effective outcome in improving speech discrimination of the hearing impaired with presence of cochlear dead regions.

The purpose of this study was to develop a frequency compression algorithm and to assess, in normal individuals, the word recognition rate (WRR) using this algorithm. With the aim of conducting a pilot study, we used frequency compression in three distinct ratios: 3:1 (K= 3), 2:1 (K = 2) and 1:1 (K = 1), changing the degree of distortion of the recorded words. Furthermore, it was also evaluated whether the familiarity with the words of the test facilitated their recognition.

As expected, we found poorer performance on tests of word recognition the higher the compression ratio was in both groups evaluated. Figure 7 shows that group F presented better performance in all compression ratios evaluated ($p < 0.001$). Based on this result, we can state that familiarity with the words of the test facilitated their recognition at all compression ratios studied. This leads us to believe that prior training using a hearing aid with this algorithm embedded can be a way to improve word recognition by the hearing impaired.

Still in Figure 3, it can be noticed by the crescent lines a gradual improvement in WRR as the compression ratio decreases. This trend could be observed for both groups. A study conducted with normal hearing participants using a linear frequency compression algorithm showed that compression ratios equal or greater than 1.43: 1 (i.e. K< 1.43) did not alter the performance in speech recognition (Turner & Hurtig, 1999). However, the authors investigated only the compression ratios of 2:1 (K = 2), 1.66:1 (K = 1.66), 1.43:1 (K = 1.43), 1.25:1 (K = 1.25) and 1.11: 1 (K = 1.11), which are much smaller than those used in this study, with less signal distortion.

Moreover, in the present work we used non-linear frequency compression, while this study used only the linear compression. Other authors (Turner & Hurtig, 1999; Simpson et al., 2005; Baskent & Shannon, 2006) concluded that frequency lowering algorithms should be implemented cautiously, in order to avoid strong signal distortion. Almost all authors believe that prior training with the algorithm facilitates the recognition of words because the patient learns how to listen to new speech clues.

In contrast, the perceived effects of distortions in speech spectrum caused by frequency lowering are greater in normal hearing individuals as compared to hearing impaired subjects, once normal hearing are not accustomed to listen to degraded speech signals.

The idea of conducting a pilot study with normal hearing subjects allowed evaluating the variables that could influence the test applied in hearing impaired ones. It is intended, in future, to continue this study applying frequency compression for the hearing impaired with dead regions in the cochlea. As this was just a pilot study, we can and should be questioning the methodology applied. We believe that we used too high frequency compression ratios and, therefore, it would be important to study lower compression ratios to promote less distortion in the speech signal, as other authors suggest (Turner & Hurtig, 1999).

Moreover, we believe it will be necessary to use speech material more appropriate to the proposal of this study, with a larger sample, using recordings from both male and female speakers (Baskent & Shannon, 2006). Also, it would be important to design a WRT with more repetitions of the same phonemes, enabling us to analyze the recognition of phonemic groups separately (Simpson et al., 2005). This would allow the study of frequency compression effects for each sound in particular and the precise benefits and harms of this algorithm for human word recognition.

3.4 Conclusions

1. The frequency compression ratios of 2:1 and 3:1 difficult speech recognition in normal hearing subjects.
2. The higher the frequency compression ratio is the worse the speech recognition is.
3. Familiarity with listened words facilitates their recognition even when these words are distorted by frequency compression.

4. Frequency compression/transposition of fricative consonants for the hearing impaired with high-frequency dead regions

Moore et al. (2000) called Dead Regions (DR) those parts of the cochlear basilar membrane with complete absence of inner hair cells. They alerted that simple sound amplification (by a hearing aid) over a dead region may be unbeneficial and may even impair speech intelligibility. Face to this difficulty, frequency compression or transposition have been suggested by many authors in the attempting to bring the high-frequency speech information to lower frequencies.

An overview of more recent studies in frequency compression/transposition is provided by Robinson et al. (2007). They developed a new frequency transposition method too, applied only to fricative and affricate sounds. But their results showed that there was no statistical significant improvement for fricatives discrimination. They concluded that the increasing in the confusion between some fricative phonemes have canceled the effect of the better recognition of others. Based on these negative results, the primary target of this research was the development of a frequency compression algorithm to be applied only to fricative consonants and that does not increase the confusion between them. We have also not observed in previous works a direct concern in making frequency compression according to the average spectral shape of fricatives or any other speech sound.

In this section, we present the design of our original piecewise linear frequency compression/transposition curve was made taking into account the average short-time spectrum of the most frequent Brazilian Portuguese (BP) fricatives. In the first phase of our research, which is described in this section, the dead regions were simulated by low-pass filtering of the speech material presented to normal hearing listeners.

4.1 Piecewise linear frequency compression

The frequency compression/transposition algorithm was implemented with Matlab™. The signal analysis computations are made in the frequency domain and the processed speech is re-synthesized in the time domain using the well-known overlap-and-add technique (Nawab & Quatieri, 1998). After normalizing the dynamic range of the speech signals (each recorded utterance should has the same rms value), they were divided in frames of 50 ms (800 samples) with an overlap of 75% between adjacent frames.

Then a 2048-point FFT is applied to each speech frame, which was previously multiplied by a Hamming window in the time domain. For the control condition, we just eliminate the frequency domain samples corresponding to the simulated dead region (low-pass filtering).

In our algorithm, the frequency compression curve should be applied only over non-vocalic speech sounds, i.e., just for noise-like consonants (fricative and affricates). To perform such sound classification, we calculate the Spectral Flatness Measure (SFM) of each signal frame, which is used to determinate the noise-like or tone-like nature of a given speech frame. We develop a method based on the original work of Johnston (1998) but with some modifications.

In a recent published research on frequency transposition (Robinson et al., 2007) it was used a much simpler criterion to do the same task, which is based in the energy ratio between high-frequency and low-frequency power. In a previous work, which was presented in section 2, we also used this same simple criterion and we have actually tried to use it again, but we did not achieve a hundred percent efficiency in the frame classification task. Experimentally we have observed that the straightforward high-frequency to low frequency energy ratio criterion has failed sometimes to classify correctly a noise-like speech sound, mainly in the case of voiced fricatives. Otherwise, using our method (based on SFM), all speech frames of all fricative consonants from our database were properly classified as noise-like ones. In addition, any frame belonging to a vowel or a silence segment in the speech material was misclassified.

Applying our SFM criterion, it was possible to verify whether a short-time spectrum of the audio signal has a noise-like or tone-like nature. This means, in practice, that the frequency compression curve acted only and always on fricative phonemes –voiceless or voiced.

SFM calculation consisted on the following steps:

1. Power spectrum of each frame was obtained by multiplying each FFT sample by its complex conjugate;
2. The geometric mean (G_q) of the power spectrum of the current speech frame q was calculated including only the frequency range from 800 to 2800 Hz;
3. The arithmetic mean (A_q) of the power spectrum of the current frame q was calculated including only the frequency range from 800 to 2800 Hz;
4. SFM of the current frame q was calculated in decibels, according to (1)

$$SFM_{dB} = 10\log_{10}\left(\frac{G_q}{A_q}\right) \tag{2}$$

5. The factor a_q of the actual frame was defined and calculated by (2)

$$\alpha_q = \min\left(\frac{SFM_{dB}}{-40}, 1\right) \tag{3}$$

6. The a_m factor was calculated as the output of a moving average filter applied to the factor a of the last P frames:

$$\alpha_m = \frac{1}{P}\sum_{p=0}^{P-1}\alpha_{q-p} \tag{4}$$

7. Similarly, the same moving average filter was applied to the last P values of arithmetic mean A_q:

$$A_m = \frac{1}{P}\sum_{p=0}^{P-1}A_{q-p} \tag{5}$$

8. If the a_m factor was greater or equal to the tonality threshold a_T, the current frame was considered of tone-like nature and the mean tone-like average A_T was updated with the value of the arithmetic mean A_q of the current power spectrum;

9. If the a_m factor was lower than the tonality threshold a_T, the current frame was considered of noise-like nature if, additionally, the arithmetic mean A_q was at least four times lower than the mean tonal value A_T.

Experimentally, it was verified that the values $P = 4$ and $a_T = 0.03$ were the ones that produced the best results. For these values, the algorithm achieved 100% efficiency on the speech classification task (tone-like or noise-like nature) of frames of fricative consonants when applied on 192 recorded monosyllables. Thus, the frequency compression algorithm was only applied on the current speech frame if it was classified as a noise-like nature signal by the above described method.

Considering the spectral characteristics of studied sounds, the SFM calculation was applied only in the frequency range between 0.8 and 2.8 kHz to allow the detection of sounds of a non-tonal (noise-like) nature without changing the identity of the remaining sounds. It is well known that the presence or absence of voicing is expressed mainly at low frequencies (Russo & Behlau, 1993; Robinson et al., 2007). So, in order to correct classifying the voiced fricatives as noise-like nature signals, the frequencies in the range between 0 and 0.8 kHz were not considered for the SFM calculation as the compression of all fricatives, both voiced and voiceless, was desired. The sounds above 2.8 kHz were also excluded from the SFM calculation because the main vowel formants correspond to frequencies between 500 and 3000 Hz (Behlau, 1984) and consequently the harmonic structure of vowel sounds is stronger in this frequency range.

Based on our own experiments as well as in literature about the average spectral distributions of Britain English, European Portuguese and Spanish fricatives (Jesus 2001; Manrique & Massone, 1981), we confirmed that spectral cues for discrimination between fricatives with different articulation places are all above 2000 Hz. This fact is the major reason behind the difficulty in the fricatives differentiation observed in patients presenting high-frequency dead regions in the cochlea. Joining this result from literature with our own, we designed the piecewise linear frequency compression curve shown in Figure 8.

Following, the compression curve is described justifying each designed part (I, II and III) with their respective compression ratios (CR) according to the frequency ranges of the original speech signal:

i.   From 0.0 to 0.5 kHz: To preserve the pitch perception of voiced fricatives, this frequency regions remains untouched;

ii. From 0.5 to 3.0 kHz: In this part of the spectrum, only the fricatives /ʃ/ and /ʒ/ offer cues for phoneme identification. But these cues (basically an increase of spectral power) continue until 6500 Hz approximately. Thus, we applied a strong compression (CR = 0.2) to this region since there is no relevant information for fricative discrimination;

iii. From 0.5 to 3.0 kHz: For this frequency range the CR becomes 0.67 in order to preserve the original speech information, because most of the cues for fricative discrimination belong to this region. Just for clearness reasons, we divide this frequency range in two parts: from 3.0 to 4.5 kHz, which will be mapped to 1.0-2.0 kHz after compression (see Figure 3), and from 4.5 to the Nyquist frequency, mapped to 2.0-4.33 kHz after compression. The main purpose of this research is help the hearing impaired with dead regions above 1.5 or 2.0 kHz, so the first part of this region is the major one. We hypothesize that the transposition of these frequencies to the frequency range from 1.0 to 2.0 kHz will be effective to improve the perception and discrimination of fricative consonants, mainly for /ʃ/ and /ʒ/. For /f/

and /v/ we do not expect significant differences in perception after compression due to their spectral flatness in this frequency range.

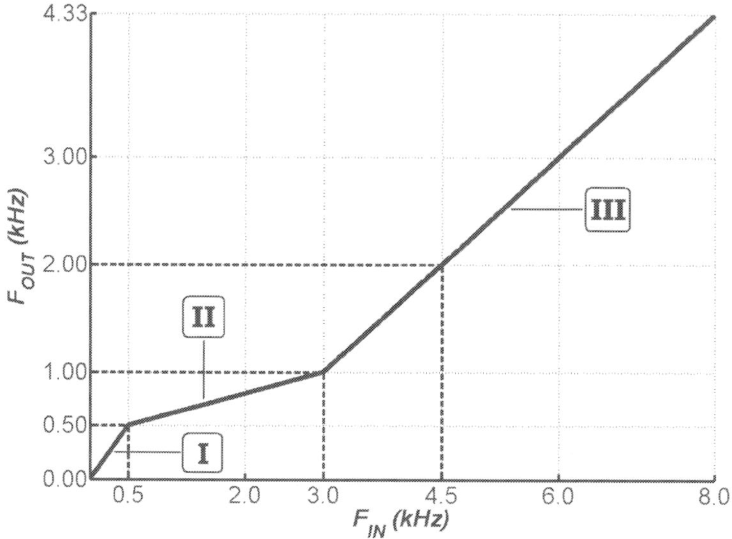

Fig. 8. Frequency compression curve designed and used in this work, with two knee points delimiting regions I, II and III with different compression ratios: (1:1), (5:1) and (1.5:1), respectively

Considering dead regions above 2.0 kHz, for example, the frequency range from 3.0 to 4.5 kHz (first subpart) is transposed to the range from 1.0 to 2.0 kHz. This is actually one of the strengths of this new algorithm: to obtain an effect of frequency transposition by means of a frequency compression curve with two knee points.
In order to facilitate the visualization of the effect of this two knees frequency compression curve on voiced fricatives, these three frequency ranges (I, II and III) are delimited by vertical grey lines in Figure 9.

4.2 Speech test material

We have designed an experiment for simultaneously evaluate consonant discrimination (fricatives in initial syllabic position) and fricative detection (in final syllabic position). In this paper we will focus only in the results of the consonant discrimination test.
The vocabulary for the speech recognition test was formed by the combination of the six most used BP fricative phonemes (/s/, /z/, /f/, /v/, /ʃ/, /ʒ/) with the vowels /a/ and /i/ and a final /s/ in half the situations, forming the set of 24 CV and/or CVC Brazilian Portuguese syllables shown in Table 1. From these, 19 monosyllables form known words in Portuguese, but the remaining 5, marked with ᴺ in the table, are nonsense syllables. In Table 4, the articulation places and voicing manner of course refer only to the consonant in initial syllabic position, because the final one (when it exists) is always the post alveolar unvoiced fricative /s/.

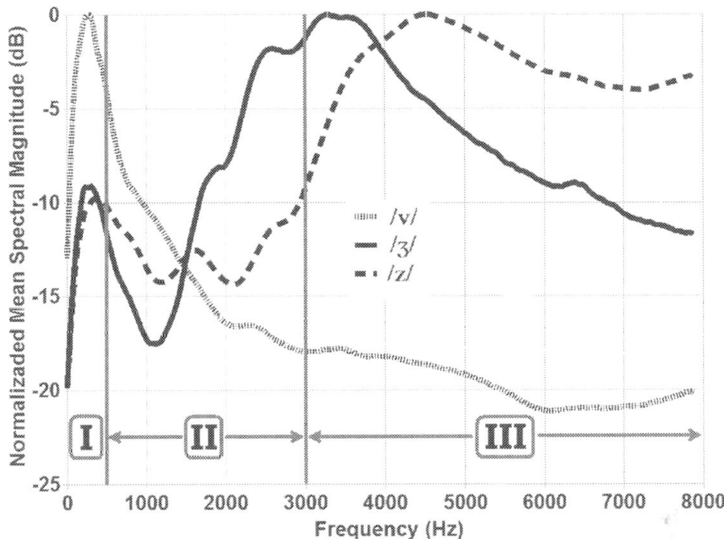

Fig. 9. Average spectral distributions of voiced fricative phonemes /v/ (dotted line), /ʒ/ (continuous line), and /z/ (dashed line), pronounced by male and female speakers. The two knee-point frequencies of the frequency compression curve delimiting the three frequency ranges (I, II and III, see Figure 8) are shown by vertical grey lines.

These words were recorded from 8 speakers, 4 female and 4 male, which pronounced once each different monosyllable. Thus, the original database was composed by 192 utterances, digitized at a 16 kHz sampling rate and stored in separated WAV files.
All utterances were then processed by the same frequency compression/transposition algorithm, which will be presented in the next section. In order to simulate 3 different high-frequency dead regions, both the processed and unprocessed (original) speech material was low-pass filtered at the cutoff frequencies of 1.5, 2.0 and 3.0 kHz. Thus, the final speech database was formed by 3 sets of WAV files, stored in different folders containing 192 processed and 192 unprocessed utterances (control condition) for each simulated dead region.

Labiodentals		Alveolar		Post alveolar	
unvcd.	voiced	unvcd.	voiced	unvcd.	voiced
/fas/	/vas/	/ʃas/	/ʒas/	/sas/^{N}	/zas/
/fa/	/va/	/ʃa/	/ʒa/	/sa/	/za/
/fis/	/vis/	/ʃis/	/ʒis/	/sis/^{N}	/zis/^{N}
/fi/	/vi/	/ʃi/	/ʒi/^{N}	/si/	/zi/^{N}

Table 4. Brazilian Portuguese monosyllables used in the fricatives identification and detection experiment.

4.3 Results

Ten normal hearing volunteers, 5 men and 5 women, all Brazilian native speakers between 23 and 30 years old, have been selected to participate. All listeners did the test first for the simulated DR above 2.0 kHz and after for the DR above 1.5 kHz, in order to offer an ever-increasing level of difficulty in the consonant discrimination task. For each listener, the test was applied in a different day for each simulated DR and the average running time spent in the sessions was 67 minutes. The subjects have to choice the written form of the word they have just listened to, in a computer screen. Before deciding, it was necessary to listen at least 3 times to each word, automatically chosen by specific software in a random sequence among 384 utterances (192 processed and 192 unprocessed).

Two-way repeated measures ANOVA were performed over the speech recognition results of the 10 listeners, in terms of correctness (%) in the identification of fricatives in initial syllabic position. The data analysis was done separately according to the speaker gender, using as fixed factors the processing type (COMP versus FILT) and the simulated DR size (above 1500 versus above 2000 Hz). Using Tukey simultaneous tests it was verified that the performance of our original frequency compression algorithm (COMP) was significantly superior (p-value = 0.00005 for female and p-value = 0.007 for male speakers) compared to the simple low-pass filtering (FILT) results, for both simulated dead regions.

4.4 Conclusion

The two-way ANOVA results have shown that our piecewise linear frequency compression curve, applied only to fricative sounds, has presented a statistical significant better performance than low-pass filtering (control condition) in all situations, for both male and female speakers.

5. References

Hicks, B.L., Braida, L.D., Durlach, N.I. (1981). Pitch invariant frequency lowering with non–uniform spectral compression. Proceedings of the IEEE International Conference on Acoustics, Speech, and Signal Processing (ICASSP 81), 6, 121-124.

Reed, C.M., Hicks, B.L., Braida, L.D., et al. (1983). Discrimination of speech processed by low-pass filtering and pitch-invariant frequency-lowering. J Acoust Soc Am, 74(2), 409-491, ISSN: 0001-4966

Reed, C.M., Schultz, K.I., Braida, L.D., et al. (1985). Discrimination and identification of frequency-lowered speech in listeners with high-frequency hearing impairment. J Acoust Soc Am, 78(6), 2139-2141, ISSN: 0001-4966

Turner, C.W., Hurtig, R.R.(1999). Proportional frequency compression of speech for listeners with sensorineural hearing loss. J Acoust Soc Am, 106(2), 877-886, ISSN: 0001-4966

Simpson, A., Hersbach, A.A., McDermott, H.J. (2005). Improvements in speech perception with an experimental nonlinear frequency compression hearing device. Int J Audiol, 44, 281-292, ISSN 1499-202

Simpson, A., Hersbach, A.A., McDermott, H.J. (2006). Frequency-compression outcomes in listeners with steeply sloping audiograms. Int J Audiol, 45, 619-629, ISSN 1499-202

McDermott, H.J., Dean, M.R.(2000) Speech perception with steeply sloping hearing loss: effects of frequency transposition. Br J Audiol, 34(6), 353-361, ISSN: 0300-5364

Moore, B.C.J., Huss, M., Vickers, D.A., et al. (2000). A test for the diagnosis of dead regions in the cochlea. Br J Audiol, 34, 205-224, ISSN: 0300-5364

Kuk, F. (2007) Critical factors in ensuring efficacy of frequency transposition. Part 1: individualizing the start frequency. Hearing Review [serial online]. 2007, Mar. Available from http://www.hearingreview.com

Kuk, F., Keenan, D., Peeters, H., Lau, C. and Crose, B. (2007) Critical Factors in Ensuring Efficacy of Frequency Transposition Part 2: Facilitating Initial Adjustment. Hearing Review [serial online]. 2007, Apr. Available from http://www.hearingreview.com

Robinson, J.D., Baer, T., Moore, B.C.J.(2007). Using transposition to improve consonant discrimination and detection for listeners with severe high-frequency hearing loss. Int J Audiol, 46(6), pp. 293-308, ISSN 1499-202

Alsaka, Y. A., McLean, B. Spectral Shaping for the Hearing Impaired (1996). Proceedings of the IEEE Southeastcon '96, pp 103-106, ISBN: 0-7803-3088-9, Tampa, FL , USA, 11-14 Apr, 1996

Scanlon, P., Ellis, D.P.W., Reilly, R.B. Using broad phonetic group-experts for improved speech recognition, Ieee Transactions on Audio, Speech and Language Processing, Vol. 15, No. 3 (March 2007), pp 803-812, ISSN: 1558-7916

Gordo A, Iorio MCM. (2007) Zonas mortas na cóclea em freqüências altas: implicações no processo de adaptação de prótese auditivas. Rev. Bras. Otorrinolaringol. 2007 May-June 73(3):299-307, ISSN: 0034-7299

Baskent D, Shannon RV. (2006). Frequency transposition around dead regions simulated with a noise band vocoder. J Acoust Soc Am. 2006;119(2):1156-63, ISSN: 0001-49

Johnston, J.D. (1998). Transform Coding of Audio Signals Using Perceptual Noise Criteria. IEEE Journal on Selected Areas in Communications, vol. 6,. N.o 2 (February 1988), ISSN: 0733-8716

Russo, I.C.P., Behlau, M. (1993). Percepção da fala: análise acústica do português brasileiro (1st ed.). São Paulo: Lovise, ISBN: 85-7241-404-5

Behlau, M. (1984). Uma análise das vogais do português brasileiro falado em São Paulo: perceptual, espectrográfica de formantes e computadorizada de freqüência fundamental. [PhD thesis]. São Paulo: Universidade Federal de São Paulo

Jesus, L.M.T.(2001). Acoustic phonetics of European Portuguese fricative consonants [PhD thesis] Southampton: University of Southampton

Manrique, A.M., Massone, M.I.(1981). Acoustic analysis and perception of spanish fricative consonants. J Acoust Soc Am, 69(4), pp. 1145-1153, ISSN: 0001-4966

Pen M, Mangabeira-Albernaz PL (1973). Desenvolvimento de testes para logoaudiometria - discriminação vocal. Anales Del Congreso Pan-americano de Otorrinolaringologia y Broncoesofagia, Lima - Peru; 1973, pp. 223-226.

Pereira LD, Schochat E. (1997), Manual de avaliação do processamento auditivo central. São Paulo: Lovise; 1997, ISBN: 8585274441

Nawab, S.H. and Quatieri, T.F. (1998). Short-time Fourier transform. Advanced Topics in Signal Processing, Chapter 6, ed. by J.S. Lim and A.V. Oppenheim, Prentice-Hall, ISBN: 0471446785

19

The Usability of Speech and Eye Gaze as a Multimodal Interface for a Word Processor

T.R. Beelders and P.J. Blignaut
University of the Free State
South Africa

1. Introduction

Communication between humans and computers is considered to be two-way communication between two powerful processors over a narrow bandwidth (Jacobs and Karn, 2003). Most interfaces today utilise more bandwidth with computer-to-user communication than vice versa, leading to a decidedly one-sided use of the available bandwidth (Jacobs and Karn, 2003). An additional communication mode will invariably provide for an improved interface (Jacobs, 1993) and new input devices which use passive measurements to capture data from the user both conveniently and at a high speed are well suited to provide more balance in the bandwidth disparity (Jacobs and Karn, 2003). In order to better utilise the bandwidth between human and computer, more natural communication which concentrates more on parallel and not sequential communication is required (Jacobs, 1993).

Furthermore, the user interface is the connection between the user and the computer and as such plays a vital role in the success or failure of an application. Modern-day interfaces are entirely graphical and require users to visually acquire and manually manipulate objects on screen (Hatfield and Jenkins, 1997) and the current trend of Windows, Icons, Menu and Pointer (WIMP) interfaces has already been around since the 1970s (van Dam, 2001). Unlike their command line counterparts, these graphical user interfaces are not in the least accessible to users with disabilities and it has become essential that viable alternatives to mouse and keyboard input are found (Hatfield and Jenkins, 1997). Specially designed applications which take users with disabilities into consideration are available but these do not necessarily compare with the more popular applications. This chapter therefore aims to investigate various ways to provide alternative means of input which could facilitate use of the mainstream product by disabled users.

These alternative means should also enhance the user experience for novice, intermediate and expert users. Findings from previous studies (Beelders, 2006; Blignaut, Dednam and Beelders, 2007) show that while novice users of word processors experience a number of obstacles in acceptance and usage of the application that are unique to the demographic, alternative pictorial icons, text buttons and translation of the interface into the native language of the user all failed to lessen the learning curve significantly or to increase usability significantly. However, these findings should not discourage researchers but should serve as encouragement to find more innovative and creative means of alleviating the burden on these users. Particularly since these users show remarkable eagerness and enthusiasm to learn, greater effort should be made to accommodate them to become mainstream users. Although the main focus could be to narrow the gap between novice and expert users, the means to achieve this should not alienate or disrupt the smooth flow of work that an expert user is capable of achieving. Rather, the improvements should serve not only the novice users but also provide an alternative means for experts as a way to improve their interaction with the product. The study that is reported in this chapter therefore proposes to be an extension or continuation of these aforementioned studies, and investigate further ways to improve the interface of a word processor for all user groups.

The eye-tracker has steadily become more robust and reliable and cheaper and therefore, presents itself as a suitable tool for this use (Jacobs and Karn, 2003). However, much research is still needed to determine the most convenient and suitable means of interaction before the eye-tracker can be fully incorporated as a meaningful input device (Jacobs and Karn, 2003). However, the disadvantages associated with eye-tracking as an input device mean that it should be used with caution or as suggested by Istance, Spinner and Howarth (1996), it should ideally be combined with other input modalities which will provide a means to overcome the limitations of eye-tracking, such as speech. As it is, Microsoft Office already comes bundled with an in-built speech engine which makes speech recognition available in all Office packages. There are also a number of affordable alternative speech engines available on the market. Eye-trackers may eventually become cost-effective enough to be a standard feature in future computing devices (Isokoski, 2000). However, given that the hardware and software is available, the task remains to prove that the eye-tracker improves the quality of human-computer interaction as validation for the inclusion in future devices (Isokoski, 2000). Although neither eye-tracking nor speech recognition is new to usability studies or as a potential source of increased usability, few studies have been found that use a combination of the two in a single package as a means of usability improvement.

Therefore, the aim of this study was to determine whether a multimodal interface, using non-traditional input means could be created for a word processing application. In this way, this popular application can cater for a more diverse group of users through a highly customisable interface. The following section will provide some background literature which serves as a foundation on which this study was based.

2. Background

This section will discuss some of the available literature which was used as a foundation for the study.

2.1 Advantages for users

The high incidence of afflictions such as tendonitis, carpal tunnel syndrome and repetitive strain injuries provides ample motivation to reduce typing requirements and device manipulation (Klarlund, 2003). Automatic speech recognition (ASR) offers an interaction means capable of replacing conventional typing.

Moreover, the most sensible way of empowering disabled users is to provide them with a means to be able to use the same software applications as any other computer user, which requires that input devices specifically tailored for these users will have to be developed (Istance, Spinner and Howarth, 1996). Eye movement is ideal for such situations as it requires no additional training, is high-speed and the majority of motor impaired individuals still retain ocular motor abilities (Istance, Spinner and Howarth, 1996).

2.2 Eye-tracking and human-computer interaction

Eye-tracking has been used as an alternative input means in a number of applications (for example Gips and Olivieri, 1996; Hornof, Cavender and Hoselton, 2004; Kumar, 2007). The use of eye-tracking can be facilitated in a number of ways, for example dwell time (Isokoski, 2000), look and shoot (Isokoski, 2000) or eye gestures. The use of dwell time requires the user to look at a target for a certain amount of time before the target is activated. Alternatively, look and shoot requires an additional mechanism to be triggered whilst gazing at the desired target. For example, the user may be required to press a key on the keyboard to activate the target under the eye gaze. Gaze gestures require the users to complete a predefined set of eye movements to activate a command (Drewes and Schmidt, 2007). Gaze gestures have been used to successfully map the entire alphabet, thereby allowing users to type text using only their eye gaze (Wobbrock, Rubinstein, Sawyer and Duchowski, 2008). All of these selection methods will be incorporated into the proposed multimodal interface to allow for maximum customisation of the interface to suit the needs of the user at any given time.

The role of feedback is also vital in the development of eye gaze applications (Hyrskykari, Majarants and Räihä, 2003) and serves to increase the user efficiency and enjoyment (for example, Miniotas, Špako and Evreinov, 2003). Therefore, during this study visual feedback will always be given when eye gaze is used as an interaction technique.

Furthermore, even with advances in technology and continued research, most interfaces which are gaze sensitive are designed with oversized interface elements to facilitate easier acquisition and activation of the element (Ashmore, Duchowski and Shoemaker, 2005). The use of oversize targets impacts negatively on screen real estate as a lot of free space is now occupied by icons, buttons etc. To counteract both the impact on available screen real estate and to exploit the properties of Fitts' Law several target expansion mechanisms have been proposed and implemented for both eye pointing and manual input (Ashmore, Duchowski and Shoemaker, 2005). These include expansion of the target in motor space, expanding or zooming into the entire display uniformly or expanding a portion of the display through the use of a fisheye lens (Ashmore, Duchowski and Shoemaker, 2005). Expansion of the targets can be either visible or invisible when it occurs strictly in motor space, implying the user is not aware of the expansion. The idea behind invisible expansion is to create a larger selection area around the target without visual feedback. This allows room for error and slight displacement of the eye during target selection. Buttons used during this study for text input will be larger than the standard icons in Windows. Even so, invisible expansion of buttons will also be used for the onscreen keyboard. This invisible expansion will be referred to as a gravity well as the actual selectable area of the button will be larger than the physical size of the button. Once the eye gaze is detected within the bounds of the enlarged area of expansion, the button will become selectable, thus creating the impression that the eye gaze is drawn onto the button. Additional visible expansion capabilities, in the form of magnification triggered by the position of the eye gaze, will also be provided.

2.3 Eye-tracking and speech recognition in combination

The limitations created by the lack of accuracy of eye-tracking equipment can be overcome by the simultaneous use of speech recognition (Castellina, Corno and Pellegrino, 2008). Insofar as can be ascertained these particular modalities are often used in isolation. When used in such a manner, these are often ambiguous but when appropriately used in combination they could result in effective interaction methods (Oviatt, 1999). This would create a multimodal interface, which is an interface that uses several input and output modalities in combination in an effort to assist human-computer communication through utilising natural human communication channels (Pireddu, 2007) such as voice and gaze.

The underlying foundation of this research undertaking is the view that while eye gaze and speech recognition are prone to ambiguity when used in isolation, using them in combination may allow much of the problems to be overcome. User intent can be inferred by providing a means for the user to gaze at certain objects and then issue verbal commands which can then be executed to create a hands-free application (Hatfield and Jenkins, 1997). In this way it is envisaged that the strengths of one interaction technique will be able to compensate for the weaknesses of the other and together speech and vision should provide a better interaction experience than each in isolation. Given the inherent problems associated with target selection via eye gaze, such as accuracy, stability and the Midas touch (everything the user gazes at is selected as the user is not accustomed to an interface which reacts to eye gaze) problem, it seems plausible that an additional modality might make selection easier and more feasible even though to date there have been very few empirical studies conducted to explore this phenomenon. One such study did determine that there is high accuracy of target selection using eye gaze and speech to such an extent that user performance approaches that of manual pointing (Miniotas, Špakov, Tugoy and MacKenzie 2006). Furthermore, integration of voice and speech for a multimodal interaction was shown to be a feasible option and an option that works well with robust eye trackers (Pireddu, 2007).

EyeTalk is a voice and vision integrated application which allows a user to gaze at an object and issue a verbal command which is then captured and merged into a single message and passed to the current application as a mouse click or keyboard event (Hatfield and Jenkins, 1997). EyeTalk is application independent and can therefore be used with a multitude of standard applications. Users are able to fixate on an object, which causes the mouse cursor to move to that position, and then issue a command to execute a mouse click (Hatfield and Jenkins, 1997). Initial results with EyeTalk showed positive feedback and indicated that users were able to operate the system with high efficiency after just a few moments of getting accustomed to the system (Hatfield and Jenkins, 1997). A promising consequence of the EyeTalk application is the indication that a stand-alone application can be developed to interact with any Windows application without any need to re-engineer the entire existing application (Hatfield and Jenkins, 1997).

3. Developed application

The premise of the study that is reported in this chapter - to test the feasibility and usability of a multimodal interface for a word processor – necessitated that an application be developed for these purposes. Since Microsoft Word® enjoys the highest market penetration (Bergin, 2006) and also leads the way as the *de facto* interface standard; it was the focus of the study. Consequently, there were two options available, a complete application could be developed that emulated the look, feel and functionality of Word or the Word application itself could be used with data capturing capabilities being provided.

Since Visual Studio for Office (VSTO) allows .NET developers to customise not only the interface of the Office suite but also to add functionality that is required (Anderson, 2009) it was decided to rather use the tried and tested application and add the required components.

Therefore, VSTO was used to manipulate Microsoft Word to make a multimodal interface within a well-known environment. The integrated development environment (IDE) of Visual Studio 2008 was used for development with C# as the programming language.

The Tobii Studio Software Development Kit (www.tobii.com) was used to add eye gaze functionality to the application and the Microsoft Speech Application Programming Interface (www.microsoft.com) was used to add speech capabilities. MagniGlass Pro® (http://magnifying-glass-pro.softutopia.com) was used for magnification purposes as it was fairly inexpensive and was the only tool that was found to allow interaction on the magnification itself. This means that the user could click on the magnified area and did not first have to close the magnification before being able to click, which defeats the purpose of using magnification for selection of small targets.

Figure 1 shows the tab called "Multimodal Add-Ins" that was added to the ribbon in Word 2007. The magnifier button allows the magnifying capabilities to be toggled on and off. Following this are the buttons to show and hide the onscreen keyboards. An alphabetic or standard QWERTY keyboard layout can be chosen. The onscreen keyboards are used for hands-free text entry using eye gaze and speech recognition. The next button group manages the speech engine. The speech engine can be turned on and off, a trained speech profile can be selected and automatic speech recognition (ASR) can be used for either command or dictation purposes. The final group manages the eye gaze interaction technique. The first step when using eye gaze is to calibrate the eye-tracker. The calibration process has a significant effect on the accuracy of the eye gaze interaction technique. The gaze type can then be set. Dwell time (linked to the sensitivity setting), blinking and look

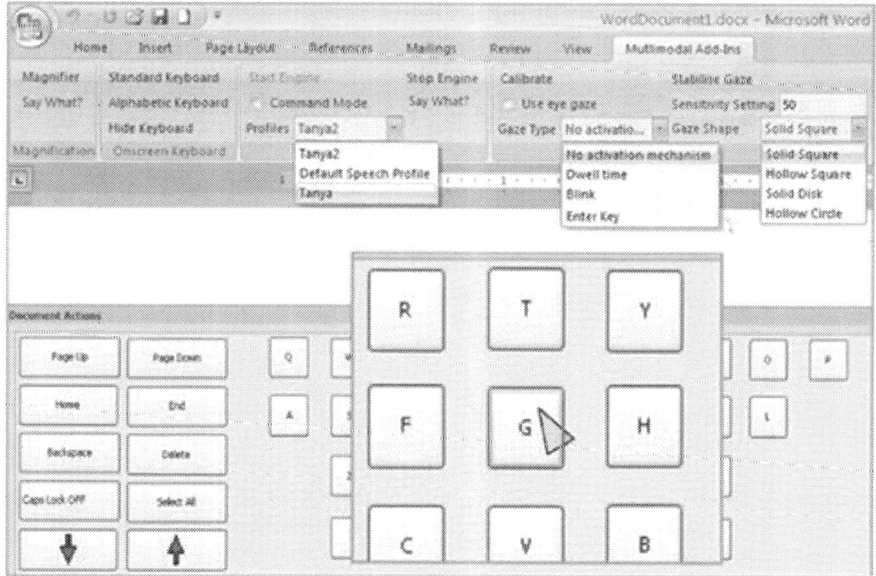

Fig. 1. Multimodal Add-Ins tab in Microsoft Word

and shoot (with the Enter Key) are all available. When the "no activation mechanism" is chosen, then eye gaze can be used in combination with speech recognition. The gaze shape dropdown allows the user to select the shape of the visual feedback cue on the letters of the onscreen keyboard.

The editable region of the document is shown in the figure as a much smaller area than what it was in reality. At the bottom of the screen, the onscreen QWERTY keyboard can be seen with the area directly under the current eye gaze being magnified. The yellow arrow indicates the exact position of the eye gaze.

Speech recognition can be used for both dictation and command purposes. A simple grammar containing common formatting commands (for example bold, italic and underline), cursor movement (for example right, left, up and down) and text selection (for example, select a line, select a word, select whole document) commands was built. In this way it became possible to move around the document or select and manipulate text contained in the document without using either the mouse or the keyboard.

The dwell time can be set by the user to a length of time with which they are comfortable. Blinking requires the user to blink in order to activate the object currently being fixated on. Since blinking is a natural occurrence, the blink required for this activation must be more pronounced. Finally, eye gaze can be used in combination with speech recognition as a text entry method using an onscreen keyboard. When the eye gaze is stable and directed at a certain key, the key is framed with a green square, or the selected shape (see Figure 2). This gives a visual cue/feedback to the user so that they know the key can now be activated. The user can then issue one of several verbal commands in order to type the selected letter to the document at the cursor position. The keys of the onscreen keyboard had a gravity well of 20 pixels on all sides.

Fig. 2. Onscreen keyboard framed in green when selected

By providing all these functions and settings, a highly customisable interface was built within the well-known environment of Word.

4. User testing

The scope of the project did not allow full-scale user testing to be conducted on all the interaction techniques, such as dwell time and blinking. Therefore, the user testing only concentrated on testing the combination of eye gaze and speech when used in a word processor. These interaction techniques could be used for two specific purposes, namely to issue commands in order to perform basic word processing tasks and to enter text within the document. These two types of tasks will be reported on separately within this chapter.

Longitudinal testing was conducted over a ten week period with each participant attending one session per week at the same time and on the same day. During the first session, participants each trained their speech profile using the Microsoft speech training wizard. The participants were then introduced to the multimodal Word that they would be using for the next few weeks and were given a brief tutorial of the speech grammar which was available for use in Word. The participants were then encouraged to interact with the application and to use all the verbal commands as well as attempting to type a full sentence using the onscreen keyboard and the interaction technique of eye gaze and speech. Every subsequent session followed the same procedure, which was to complete the list of preset task as quickly and correctly as possible.

4.1 User testing of speech commands

The use of speech commands and how their performance compares with that of the mouse and keyboard will be investigated first.

4.1.1 Participants

In total there were 25 participants who participated in the longitudinal study. They were all undergraduate students who were completing their studies at the University of the Free State, South Africa. A pre-requisite for participation in the study was sufficient computer literacy as well as word processor expertise.

There were 17 male participants and 8 female participants with an average age of 21.1 (standard deviation = 1.9). Six participants indicated that English was their first language, 7 Afrikaans and the remainder (12) were African language speakers. Since the University employs a parallel medium tuition policy where classes are offered in either English or Afrikaans, all students are comfortable in either English or Afrikaans. Therefore, each session was conducted in the tuition language of the participant.

4.1.2 Tasks

Participants had to complete 20 tasks, five of which were typing tasks. The majority of the other tasks, for example selection and formatting, had to be completed using the traditional means of a mouse or keyboard. A similar task then had to be repeated using speech recognition. The tasks were set up in such a way that the same types approximately required an equal number of minimum actions to complete it successfully. A summary of the tasks is tabulated below (with typing tasks omitted):

Task Description	Shortened task description	Keyboard	Speech
Select three lines and apply formatting such as bold or italics	Line selection and formatting	1	1
Select all text in the document and remove it by deleting or cutting	Select all text and remove	1	1
Select two words and make them bold	Select words and format	1	1
Paste previously copied text at the current cursor position	Paste	1	1
Undo the previous action	Undo	1	1
Select a single word and copy it	Select word and copy	1	1
Position the cursor at a certain position in the document and paste the previously copied text	Position and paste	1	1

Table 1. Grouped tasks as divided between interaction techniques

4.1.3 Measurements

The measurements that will be analysed are the time taken to complete the task as well as the number of actions that were required to complete the task. The number of errors was also considered as a means to determine how effective the interaction technique is. However, since there are multiple ways to complete a task, it became very difficult to pinpoint exactly what was an erroneous action, particularly where the mouse or keyboard was used. For the speech, the commands that could complete the task could be isolated as an acceptable set of commands for that task and then any command issued that is not a member of that set can be flagged as an error command. However, since there is considerable risk for potentially flagging an action as an error when it might not be, it was decided that the percentage of the task completed correctly were better indicators of the effectiveness of the interaction techniques.

4.1.4 Time to complete a task

The time to complete the task was measured from when the task was started to when the task was considered by the participant to be completed. This time included the time it took the participant to read the description of the task. Since similar tasks had virtually identical wording it was assumed that they would require the same amount of time to read and that, therefore, the time to read would not have an effect on the time required to complete the task.

The charts below (Figures 3-6) plot the least square means for both interaction techniques over all sessions. The least squares means are the means of interest when interpreting significant results of a factorial design (StatSoft, 2010) and will therefore be provided as a visual representation of the descriptive statistics. The vertical bars denote a 95% confidence interval. The blue line plots the completion time for the speech and the red line that of the keyboard.

As can clearly be seen from the graphs above, in some instances the keyboard maintained a faster average completion time and in others the speech interaction technique could surpass the performance of the keyboard.

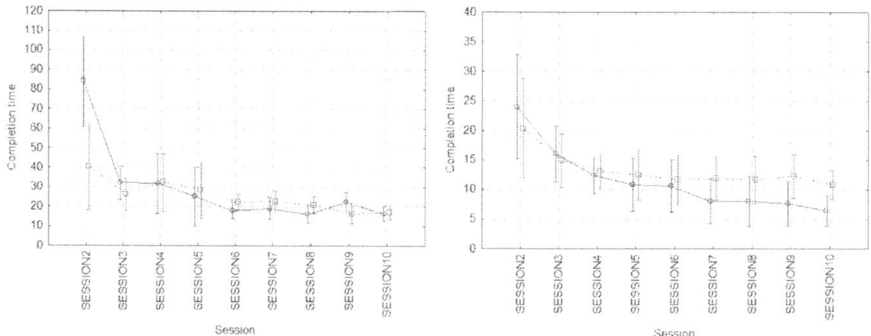

Fig. 3. Average completion times for (a) line selection and formatting and (b) select all and remove

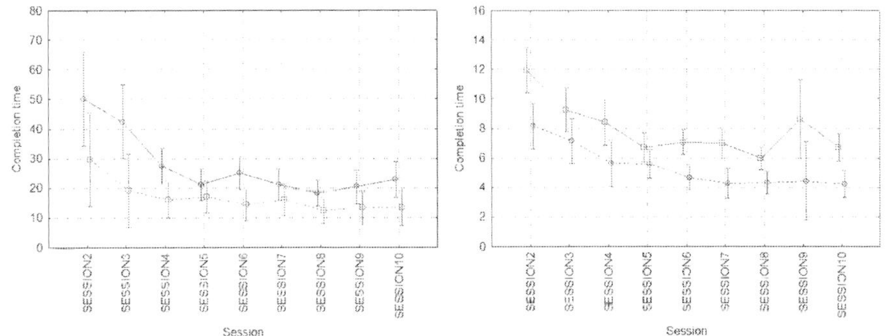

Fig. 4. Average completion times for (a) select words and format and (b) paste

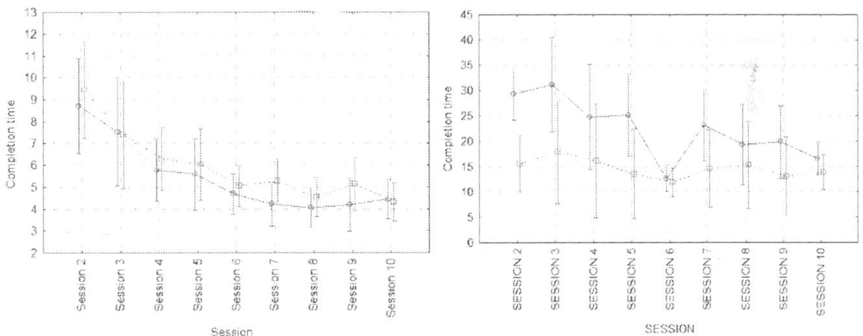

Fig. 5. Average completion times for (a) undo and (b) select word and copy

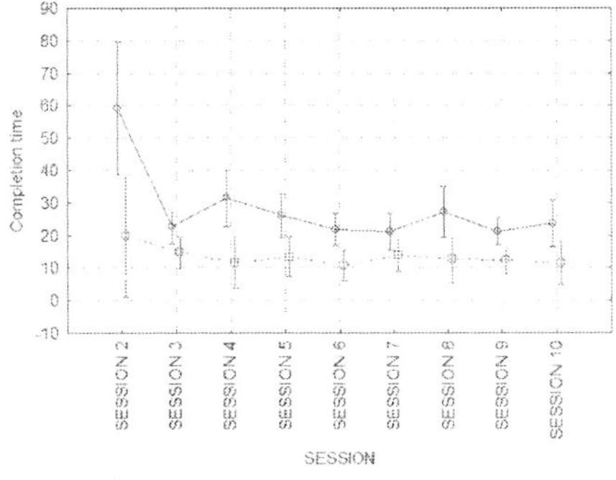

Fig. 6. Average completion times for position and paste

The time measurements were in seconds and there were a vast number of instances in which the normality tests fail for the data. In order to combat this, the time measurement was converted to 1/time.

For each of the tasks, the following hypotheses were formulated:

1. $H_{0,1}$: There is no difference between the time required to complete the tasks when using the mouse and keyboard or speech commands.
2. $H_{0,2}$: Participants did not improve over time with regard to the time taken to complete the tasks.

A repeated-measures within-subjects ANOVA was performed to analyse the aforementioned hypotheses. Where necessary, the adjusted corrections of Geisser-Greenhouse and Huyn-Feldt were applied to the degrees of freedom in the cases where the assumption of sphericity was not met. The table below shows only the results of the original ANOVAs and not, for the sake of brevity, the results of the adjusted corrections. For the Paste task, there was significant interaction between the factors of interaction technique (keyboard and speech) and improvement over time (session) the two hypotheses had to be examined in isolation.

	$H_{0,1}$	$H_{0,2}$
Line selection and formatting	$F(1, 23) = 0.286$, $p > 0.05$	$F(8, 184) = 14.040$, $p < 0.05$
Select all and remove	$F(1, 23) = 4.328$, $p < 0.05$	$F(8, 184) = 15.197$, $p < 0.05*$
Select words and format	$F(1, 26) = 10.447$, $p < 0.05$	$F(8, 208) = 9.487$, $p < 0.05$
Paste		
Undo	$F(1, 24) = 0.001$, $p > 0.05$	$F(8, 192) = 22.148$, $p < 0.05$
Select word and copy	$F(1, 22) = 3.655$, $p > 0.05$	$F(8, 176) = 3.470$, $p < 0.05$
Position and paste	$F(1, 22) = 15.448$, $p < 0.05$	$F(8, 176) = 5.123$, $p < 0.05$

Table 2. Results of ANOVA for time of speech commands

The first null hypothesis could be rejected for the task which required all text to be selected and removed. In this instance, it was the speech commands which averaged a faster completion time. Conversely, the keyboard was significantly faster for the task where words had to be selected and formatted as well as for the position and paste task. This finding could imply that the speech command to select all text was fairly intuitive and easy to learn, which facilitated a faster completion time than using the mouse or keyboard. However, selection of individual words was less intuitive and took longer than when using the keyboard or mouse. It could also mean that participants did not use the keyboard shortcut to select all text as this is the fastest way of selecting all text in a document. Analysis of the number of actions should provide more clarity in this regard.

For those tasks where the second null hypothesis could be rejected, it was under the majority of cases the first few sessions which differed significantly from the last sessions. This provides a very encouraging finding that there is a significant effect of learning which occurs as the amount of exposure to the application is increased.

When a repeated-measures within-subjects ANOVA was performed for the paste task, it was found that there was significant interaction between the two factors of session and interaction technique ($F(8, 192) = 2.356$, $p < 0.05$). Therefore, it was imperative that each factor was isolated and analysed separately to preclude the interaction with the other factor having an effect on the analysis. Firstly, $H_{0,1}$ was evaluated by isolating each session individually and testing for a difference between interaction techniques. For brevity's sake, the actual results of the ANOVA will not be reported here. Suffice it to say that, at an α-level of 0.05, there was a significant difference between the interaction techniques in every session. Therefore, the completion time is significantly better for speech than for the keyboard and mouse throughout all the sessions. Secondly, $H_{0,2}$ was evaluated using a repeated-measures within-subject ANOVA but testing each interaction technique separately. Consequently, it was found that $H_{0,2}$ could be rejected for both the speech interaction technique ($F(8, 96) = 17.727$, $p < 0.05$) and the keyboard and mouse ($F(8, 96) = 6.883$, $p < 0.05$).

4.1.5 Number of actions

The next measurement to be analysed was the number of actions that were performed during task completion. Actions were defined as any mouse click, button press or speech command that was issued during completion of the task. The number of actions were measured per interaction technique and per session for each participant and then, as always, outliers were removed from the data set prior to analysis.

The underlying hypotheses were formulated to analyse the actions for this task:

$H_{0,1}$: The interaction technique does not significantly affect the number of actions required to complete the task.

$H_{0,2}$: Participants did not improve over time with regard to the number of actions required to complete the task.

The charts below (Figures 7-10) plot the number of actions for each interaction technique over all sessions. The red line plots the keyboard and mouse actions, while the blue plots the speech commands.

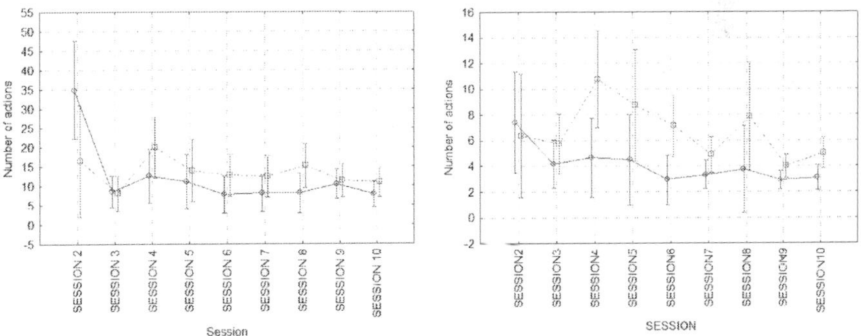

Fig. 7. Average number of actions for (a) line selection and formatting and (b) select all and remove

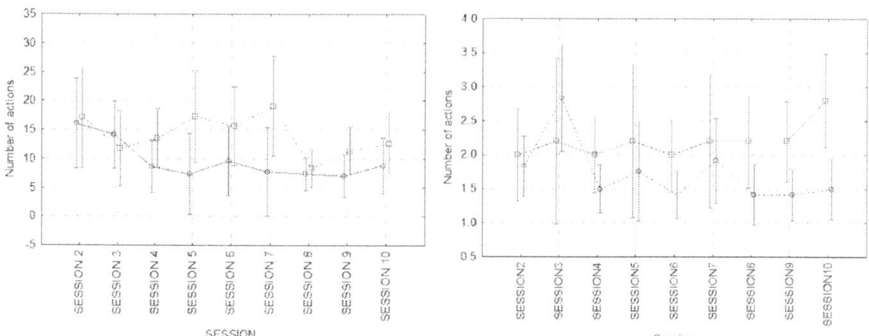

Fig. 8. Average completion times for (a) select words and format and (b) paste

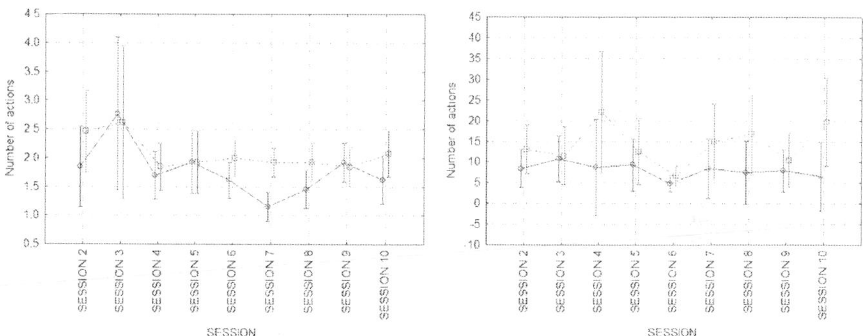

Fig. 9. Average completion times for (a) undo and (b) select word and copy

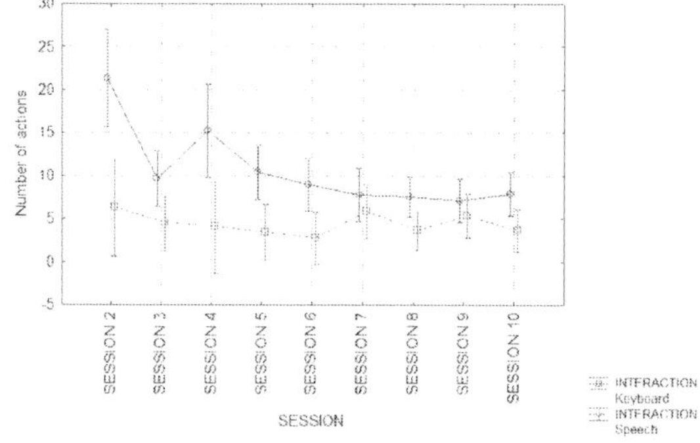

Fig. 10. Average completion times for position and paste

The graphs clearly show that in most instances the use of the keyboard and mouse resulted in more actions being performed. It was only when participants were required to position the cursor and paste previously copied text that the speech commands required more actions. The table below summarises the results of the repeated-measures within-subjects ANOVA for each task.

	$H_{0,1}$	$H_{0,2}$
Line selection and formatting		
Select all and remove	$F(1, 18) = 8.574$, $p < 0.05$	$F(8, 144) = 2.562$, $p < 0.05$
Select words and format	$F(1, 23) = 2.598$, $p > 0.05$	$F(8, 184) = 2.234$, $p < 0.05$
Paste	$F(1, 15) = 6.287$, $p < 0.05$	$F(8, 120) = 1.297$, $p > 0.05$
Undo	$F(1, 24) = 2.294$, $p > 0.05$	$F(8, 192) = 2.934$, $p < 0.05$
Select word and copy	$F(1, 19) = 3.498$, $p > 0.05$	$F(8, 152) = 1.378$, $p > 0.05$
Position and paste		

Table 3. Results of ANOVA for actions of speech commands

In the two instances where there was a significant difference between the interaction techniques, it was the speech commands which required significantly less actions than the keyboard. This result for the selection and removal of all text and the paste task corresponds with the findings that the speech commands were also more efficient, in terms of the time required to complete a task, for these tasks.

For the task which requires that words be selected and formatted, session 2 had a significantly higher number of actions than any other session. During the undo task, session 3 resulted in a significantly larger number of actions than the other sessions.

The two tasks for which there are no results in the above table had significant interaction between the two factors. This meant that individual analyses had to be performed in order to counteract the effect of one factor on another. For the line selection and formatting task, the two interaction techniques differed significantly from one another during the second and eighth session. During the other sessions the number of actions for the two interaction techniques was comparable to one another. The second null hypothesis could be rejected for the keyboard, where a significantly higher number of actions were performed during session 2 than all the other sessions, but not for the speech commands. Closer inspection of the analysis revealed that some participants resorted to using longer methods of text selection when using the keyboard. For example, they would select the text one character at a time instead of using the efficient means which were available. Since it appears that the majority of the participants used the mouse for selection purposes, the fact that there was a minority who employed this very inefficient means was not cause for great concern but cognisance was taken thereof.

For the task where the cursor had to be positioned and text pasted at that specific location, speech required significantly more actions than the keyboard during all the sessions. Even though the number of actions decreased over the sessions, which indicates learning, the learning did not allow the speech to perform on a comparable level to the keyboard. The higher number of actions for the speech interaction technique could be explained by the types of commands that were issued. Therefore, an analysis was conducted to determine which commands were issued during the completion of this task. This showed a high incidence of the command 'Right' which could be used to move the cursor to the right. This indicated that the participants resorted to moving the cursor to the correct position one character at a time. Obviously very few participants realised that they could use the command 'Select word' and then 'Right' to move the cursor to the right a word at time. Since the keyboard and mouse offers the alternative of simply clicking the mouse pointer at the correct position this could account for the significant difference between the two interaction techniques. This finding could mean that the participants do not seek to find the most efficient method of task completion.

The ANOVA performed to evaluate $H_{0,2}$ for the speech commands showed that there was a significant difference between the sessions ($F(8, 64) = 5.820$, $p < 0.05^*$). Post-hoc tests indicated that there was significant improvement between session 2 and the remainder of the sessions.

4.1.5 Discussion

The speech interaction technique performed relatively well when compared with the keyboard and mouse, in some instances even surpassing the performance of the traditional input methods. Clearing of all text in the document and pasting were even faster and completed with less actions than when using the keyboard and mouse. It is only when positioning within the document must occur that the keyboard outperforms the speech interaction technique in terms of both the time that it takes and the number of commands that are issued.

While this finding was very encouraging, the most promising finding was that there was continued improvement in the efficiency with which the task was completed. Even though the improvement between subsequent sessions was not always significant the fact there is continual improvement hints at the possibility that the two interaction techniques could eventually compete on a comparable level for all tasks or that the speech interaction technique could eventually perform better.

Since there are often multiple options available to the user to complete the task when using the traditional means, the most effective method was not always chosen. This was also noticed when using speech to move the cursor. Rather the user chooses the method which results in an intermediate action which is closer to the final result when in reality there is a shorter method that can be used.

The fact that the speech commands resulted in less actions for most of the tasks, may be attributed to the fact that the grammar was fairly simple and provided commands to complete basic operations only. The complexity of the options provided by Word is much higher than accommodated in the grammar. When using Word in the normal capacity there is, more often than not, at least 3 different ways to complete a task which may place an added burden on the user of the application. However, the goal of the study was not to provide a complete alternative to the keyboard and mouse but rather to determine whether common word processing tasks could be achieved using an alternative interaction technique. Therefore, by the very nature of the study, the grammar was required to be simple in composition.

4.1.6 Further research

The tasks that were chosen for this part of the study were chosen as some of the more common tasks that may occur in the word processing application. Therefore, they may be viewed as some of the less complex tasks and other tasks may require less intuitive commands and more complex commands. However, this will parody the nature of any other system which provides access to common tasks "at your fingertips", for example the Home tab in Office while lesser used tasks or more complex tasks require further navigation and perhaps a heavier burden on one's memory. It may be possible to extend the grammar to encompass many more tasks within the word processor application. Another consideration would be to use a default smaller grammar and an optional extended grammar that can be activated on request.

The results of the study indicate that interaction through speech could dramatically increase the efficiency of end-users. However, it remains to be seen if this result holds when the user is free to use the grammar in a normal setting. This would require that the participants would not be given small separate tasks but rather that they would have to compile a document from scratch with pre-defined formatting.

Whether or not an extended grammar is considered, further research will have to be done where the exposure to the application is lengthened in order to determine whether the learning effect can continue to an even greater degree. This study could use a smaller sample as it has already been established that it is possible to use this interaction technique effectively.

4.2 User testing of text input

As previously mentioned, the longitudinal testing also included tasks which required that the participants input text using either the keyboard or eye gaze and speech recognition. This section is a discussion of the comparative study between these two text input methods.

4.2.1 Participants

The participants for this analysis were the same as in the previous section. There were, however, three of the 25 participants who were unable to type using eye gaze and speech for various reasons and they were excluded from the analysis. Fourteen of the remaining participants were male and 8 were female, 6 were English-speaking, 6 Afrikaans-speaking and the remainder (10) had an African language as their first language. The average age of participants was 21.1 (standard deviation = 2.0).

4.2.2 Tasks

In total there were two typing tasks using the keyboard and three using the eye gaze and speech. The tasks required participants to type phrases that were randomly selected from a set of 35 preselected tasks, which were in turn selected from the 500 everyday commonly used phrases as determined by MacKenzie and Soukoreff (2003).

When using eye gaze and speech the size of the buttons was set to 60×60 ($\approx$1.55° visual angle) pixels. Buttons were spaced 60 pixels apart with a gravity well of 20 pixels on all sides of each button. Although there were three typing tasks using these settings, only the last two of each session were included in the analysis. This was due to the fact that the first one was viewed more as a practice typing task to reacclimatise the participants to typing using eye gaze and speech. The participants were not told that the first task would not count towards the analysis and were instructed to complete all tasks to the best of their ability.

In order to investigate the effect of size and spacing between targets, additional typing tasks were added from the fifth session onwards. Within these additional typing tasks, the first one had to be completed using the originally sized and spaced buttons. The next two had to be completed with buttons that were 50×50 (≈1.29° visual angle visual angle at a viewing distance of 600 mm) pixels in size and spaced 70 pixels apart. Following this there were another two tasks which had to be completed using buttons that were also 50×50 pixels in size but were spaced 60 pixels apart. For all typing tasks a gravity well of 20 pixels on all sides of the buttons were employed.

4.2.3 Measurements

Since both input methods (the keyboard and eye gaze and speech recognition) were character based, the measurements that were selected for analysis were the character error rate and the characters typed per second. The character error rate (CER) measures how many insertions, deletions and substitutions have to be done to convert the presented text to the text as entered by the participant (Read, 2005). This measurement is synonymous with the Levenshtein distance between two strings (Levenshtein, 1966) divided by the number of characters that were typed (Read, 2005; MacKenzie and Soukoreff, 2002). This error rate measurement will be used in this section to analyse the effectiveness of the interaction techniques.

For the efficiency of the interaction techniques, the measurement of characters per second (CPS) will be used. This measurement divides the number of characters that were typed by the time taken in seconds. Similar to previous studies (MacKenzie, 2002), the time taken was measured from the time when the first character was typed to the time the last character was typed. This excludes the time required to read the question, including the sentence that must be typed, and the time taken to locate the first character that must be typed. As a consequence, the number of characters becomes n-1.

4.2.4 Results

The initial analysis will only include the data from the original typing tasks using the originally sized buttons.

The leftmost chart below shows the average error rate for input through eye gaze and speech (blue line) and the keyboard (red line). The chart on the right shows the characters per second that were achieved with both interaction techniques and for all sessions. Clearly, the technique of eye gaze and speech results in far more errors than the keyboard when used for text entry while the keyboard facilitates a faster typing speed. Although the error rate of eye gaze and speech declines as exposure increases, the typing speed does not increase significantly. This could indicate that either more practice is required to increase typing speeds or that the typing speed quickly reaches a plateau which cannot be breached. Observation of the participants during their interaction with the system would suggest that more practice is required to increase the efficiency of the text entry.

Using a confidence interval of 95%, it was found that the interaction technique had a significant effect on the number of errors made ($F(1, 21) = 6.516$, $p < 0.05$) but that there was also a significant difference between the sessions ($F(8, 168) = 2.278$, $p < 0.05$). In particular, sessions 9 and 10 differed significantly from sessions 2 and 3. This shows a measure of improvement in the error rate as time went by and would suggest that participants were becoming more accustomed to using eye gaze and speech for text input purposes.

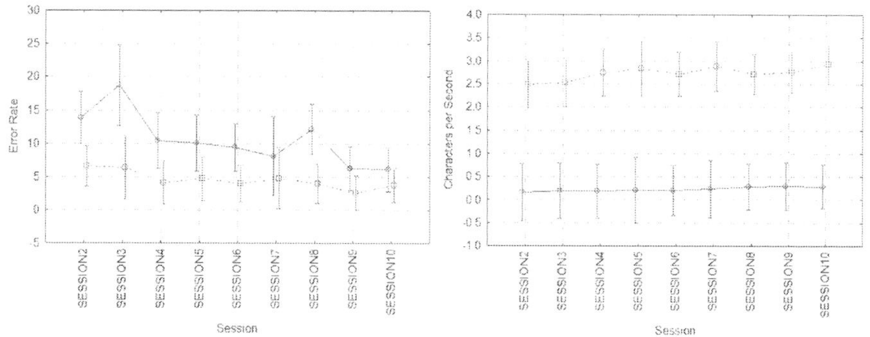

Fig. 11. Least squares mean plot of character error rate and characters per second

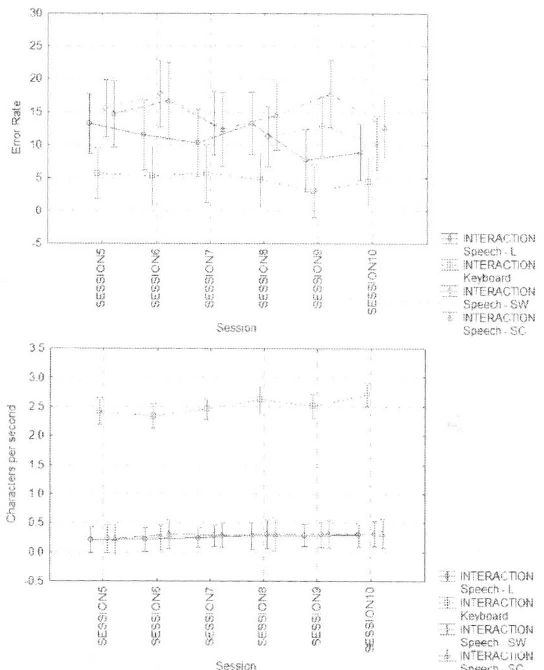

Fig. 12. Least squares mean plot of character error rate and characters per second for all typing tasks

Similarly, the interaction technique (F(1, 21) = 54.704, p < 0.05) had a significant effect on the characters typed per second but there was no significant difference between the sessions (F(8, 168) = 1.385, p > 0.05). Therefore, using eye gaze and speech for typing is significantly slower than when typing with the keyboard but there is no significant improvement in typing speed as exposure to the system increases.

The next step was to analyse text input that includes the additional tasks and differently sized and spaced buttons. Since the additional tasks were only completed from session 5 onwards. The analysis was done for these sessions only. In order to distinguish between the different sized buttons, results for the originally sized and spaced buttons will be referred to as speech-L, the smaller widely spaced buttons as speech-SW and the smaller closely spaced buttons as speech-SC.

Figure 12 plot the error rate and characters per second for each of the text entry methods for the sessions during which they were tested.

The keyboard has the lowest error rate of all the interaction techniques and it also has the highest typing speed. Regarding the error rate and typing speed of the eye gaze and speech, the three different methods are virtually indistinguishable from one another.

The interaction technique $(F(3, 44) = 4.100, p < 0.05)$ causes a significant difference in the error rate but there is no significant difference between the error rates of the various sessions $(F(5, 220) = 1.056, p > 0.05)$. Post-hoc tests indicate that there is a significant difference between the error rates of the keyboard and those of the speech-SW interaction technique. In terms of typing speed, the interaction technique $(F(3, 44) = 148.369, p < 0.05^*)$ significantly affects this measurement as does the session $(F(5, 15) = 3.002, p < 0.05^*)$. As could be expected the keyboard results in a significantly faster typing speed than all other interaction techniques. The typing speeds in the last session were also significantly faster than the speeds of the first two sessions which indicates some measure of learning.

4.2.5 Discussion

It was found that the eye gaze and speech interaction technique causes a significantly higher error rate than the keyboard. There was no difference between the error rates of speech-L, speech-SW and speech-SC and they all differed from the keyboard at some stage. However, the interaction technique of speech-L did seem to offer the most improved error rate as it did not differ from the keyboard when analysed for the later sessions only. In some instances there was improvement over the sessions, which indicates some measure of learning when using eye gaze and speech. If the learning effect can be maintained, more practice could possibly lead to an effectiveness measurement which is comparable to that of the keyboard.

In terms of efficiency (characters per second), the keyboard outperformed the eye gaze and speech interaction technique. The efficiency of eye gaze and speech also did not improve as exposure increased. This could either indicate that more practice is needed to achieve increased speed or that the typing speed quickly reaches the fastest achievable rate. Neither the size of the buttons nor the spacing between buttons affected the efficiency of the eye gaze and speech.

4.2.6 Further research

Further research can be conducted whereby the participants receive more practice with using eye gaze and speech as a text input mechanism. This will allow more detailed analysis to be performed in order to determine whether a much longer period of exposure would serve to increase the effectiveness and efficiency of the interaction technique. Furthermore, future studies could incorporate the correction of errors so that the character error rate could determine the eventual correctness of the transcribed text in conjunction with the transcribed text before corrections were applied.

Since it was found that neither the size of the buttons nor the spacing between the buttons influenced the usability of the interaction technique, further tests can be conducted to determine whether an increase in the gravity well will impact performance. Although the decrease of physical size and increase of gravity well result in a selectable area with the same size as a large button, the *perceived* accuracy with smaller buttons could serve to boost the confidence, and therefore satisfaction, of end-users.

5. Conclusion

This chapter reported on the results of similar word processing tasks which were compared when they were completed using the mouse and keyboard or when using speech commands. The measurements which were analysed were time to complete the task and the number of actions that were performed during completion of the task. For the majority of the tasks it was found that the interaction techniques could compete on a comparable level, particularly as the participant gained experience. This indicates that the application was indeed learnable. These results indicate that the proposed use of speech commands within a word processor application is viable.

This chapter also reported on the results of the use of eye gaze and speech for text input when compared to a traditional keyboard. Measurements of effectiveness, namely the error rate, and efficiency, namely characters typed per second were analysed. It was found that when using eye gaze and speech for text input, neither the size of the buttons nor the spacing between the buttons affected the performance of the interaction technique. The performance of the keyboard for both these usability measures far outstrips that of the eye gaze and speech. Even with extended exposure to the eye gaze and speech interaction techniques, the effectiveness and efficiency could not reach levels which were equivalent to those achieved by the keyboard.

6. References

Ashmore, M., Duchowski, A.T. & Showmaker, G. (2005). Efficient Eye Pointing with a Fisheye Lens. In *Proceedings of Graphics Interface 2005*

Beelders, T.R. (2006). A comparative study on users' responses to graphics, text and language in a word processor interface. M.Sc dissertation, University of the Free State, Bloemfontein, South Africa

Bergin, T.J. (2006). The Origins of Word Processing Software for Personal Computers: 1976 – 1985. *IEEE Annals of the History of Computing.* 28(4), pp. 32-47

Blignaut, P.J., Dednam, E.H. & Beelders, T.R. (2007). Die opleiding van persone uit benadeelde groepe in rekenaargebruik: Is die agterstand nie té groot om te oorbrug nie? *Suid-Afrikaanse Tydskrif vir Natuurwetenskap en Tegnologie,* 26(3)

Castellina, E., Corno, F., & Pellegrino, P. (2008). Integrated Speech and Gaze Control for Realistic Desktop Environments. In *Proceedings of ETRA 2008*

Drewes, H. & Schmidt, A. (2007). Interacting with the Computer using Gaze Gestures. In *Proceedings of the 11th IFIP TC13 International Conference on Human-Computer Interaction, INTERACT 2007, Rio de Janeiro, Brazil, September 2007*

Gips, J. & Olivieri, P. (1996). EagleEyes: An Eye Control System for Persons with Disabilities. In *Proceedings of The Eleventh International Conference on Technology and Persons with Disabilities,* Los Angeles, March 1996

Hatfield, F. & Jenkins, E.A. (1997). An interface integrating eye gaze and voice recognition for hands-free computer access. In *Proceedings of the CSUN 1997 Conference*

Hornof, A., Cavender, A & Hoselton, R. (2004). EyeDraw: A system for drawing pictures with eye movements. *ASSETS 2004*

Hyrskykari, A., Majaranta, P. & Räihä, K-J. (2003). Proactive response to eye movements. In M. Rauterberg et al. (Eds.), *Human-Computer Interaction -- INTERACT'03*, IOS Press, pp. 129-136

Isokoski, P. (2000).Text input methods for eye trackers using off-screen targets. In *Proceedings of ETRA 2000*

Istance, H.O., Spinner, C. & Howarth, P.A. (1996). Providing motor impaired users with access to standard Graphical User Interface (GUI) software via eye-based interaction. In Proceedings of *1st European Conference on Disability, Virtual Reality and Associated Technology*, Maidenhead, UK

Jacobs, R. J. (1993). Advances in Human-Computer Interaction, Vol. 4. In H.R. Hartson and D. Hix (eds.), *Eye Movement-Based Human-Computer Interaction Techniques: Toward Non-Command Interfaces*, pages 151–190. Ablex Publishing Co

Jacob, R.J.K. & Karn, K.S. (2003). "Eye Tracking in Human-Computer Interaction and Usability Research: Ready to Deliver the Promises (Section Commentary)," in J. Hyona, R. Radach, and H. Deubel (eds.), *The Mind's Eye: Cognitive and Applied Aspects of Eye Movement Research*, pp. 573-605, Amsterdam, Elsevier Science

Klarlund, N. (2003). Editing by Voice and the Role of Sequential Symbol Systems for Improved Human-to-Computer Information Rates. In *Proceedings of ICASSP*

Kumar, M. (2007). Gaze-enhanced user interface design. PhD Thesis, Stanford University.

Miniotas, D., Špakov, O. & Evreinov, G. (2003). *Symbol Creator: An alternative eye-based text entry technique with low demand for screen space*. In M. Rauterberg et al. (Eds.) Human Computer Interaction – INTERACT '03, pp. 137-143

Miniotas, D., Špakov, O., Tugoy, I. & MacKenzie, I.S. (2006). Speech-Augmented Eye Gaze Interaction with Small Closely Spaced Targets. In *Proceedings of the 2006 symposium on Eye tracking research and applications (ETRA)*, San Diego, California, pp. 67-72

Oviatt, S. (1999). Mutual disambiguation of recognition errors in a multimodal architecture. In *Proceedings of the ACM SIGCHI 99*, Pittsburgh, Pennsylvania, United States, pp. 576 – 583. New York: ACM Press

Pireddu, A. (2007). Multimodal Interaction: An integrated speech and gaze approach. Thesis submitted at Politecnico di Torino

Van Dam, A. (2001). *Post-Wimp user interfaces: The human connection*. In R. Earnshaw, R. Guedj, A. van Dam and J. Vince (Eds), Frontiers of human-centred computing, online communities and virtual environments (pp. 163-178). London, Great Britain:Springer-Verlag

Wobbrock, J.O., Rubinstein, J., Sawyer, M.W. & Duchowski, A.T. (2008). Longitudinal evaluation of discrete consecutive gaze gestures for text entry. In *Proceedings of the 2008 Symposium on Eye Tracking Research and Applications (ETRA)*, Savannah, Georgia, United States of America, pp. 11-18

20

Vowel Judgment for Facial Expression Recognition of a Speaker

Yasunari Yoshitomi, Taro Asada and Masayoshi Tabuse
Kyoto Prefectural University
Japan

1. Introduction

To better integrate robots into society, a robot should be able to interact in a friendly manner with humans. The aim of our research is to contribute to the development of a robot that can perceive human feelings and mental states. A robot that could do so could, for example, better take care of an elderly person, support a handicapped person in his or her live, encourage a person who looks sad, or advise an individual to stop working and take a rest when he or she looks tired.

Our study concerns the first stage of the development of a robot that has the ability to detect visually human feelings or mental states. Although a mechanism for recognizing facial expressions has received considerable attention in the field of computer vision research (Harashima et al., 1989; Kobayashi & Hara, 1994; Mase, 1990, 1991; Matsuno et al., 1994; Yuille et al., 1989), currently it still falls far short of human capability—especially from the viewpoint of robustness under widely varying lighting conditions. One of the reasons for this is that the nuances of shade, reflection, and localized darkness—as the result of the inevitable changes in gray levels—influence the accuracy of the discernment of facial expressions.

To develop a robust method of facial expression recognition applicable under widely varied lighting conditions, we do not use a visible ray (VR) image, instead we use an image produced by infrared rays (IR), which show temperature distributions of the face (Fujimura et al., 2011; Ikezoe et al., 2004; Koda et al., 2009; Nakano et al., 2009; Sugimoto et al., 2000; Yoshitomi et al., 1996, 1997a, 1997b, 2000, 2011a, 2011b; Yoshitomi, 2010). Although a human cannot detect IR, a robot can process the information contained in the thermal images created by IR. Therefore, as a new mode of robot vision, thermal image processing is a practical method that is viable under natural conditions.

The timing for recognizing facial expressions also is important for a robot because processing can be time consuming. We adopted an utterance as the key to expressing human feelings or mental states because humans tend to say something to express their feelings (Fujimura et al., 2011; Ikezoe et al., 2004; Koda et al., 2009; Nakano et al., 2009; Yoshitomi et al., 2000; Yoshitomi, 2010). In conversation, we utter many phonemes. We have selected vowel utterances for use as timings to recognize facial expressions because the number of vowels is very limited, and the waveforms of vowels tend to have a bigger amplitude and a longer utterance period than consonants. Accordingly, the timing range of each vowel can be relatively easily decided by a speech recognition system.

In this paper, we briefly look at a proposed method (Koda et al., 2009) for recognizing the facial expressions of a speaker. For this facial expression recognition, we select three image timings: (i) just before speaking, and speaking (ii) the first vowel and (iii) the last vowel in an utterance. To apply the proposed method (Koda et al., 2009), three subjects spoke 25 Japanese given names that provide all combinations of first and last vowels. These utterances were used to prepare the training data and then the test data.

2. Speech recognition system

We use a speech recognition system called Julius (Kawahara et al., 2010b) to save as a wav file the timing positions of the start of speech, and the first and last vowels (Koda et al., 2009; Yoshitomi, 2010; Fujimura et al., 2011; Yoshitomi et al., 2011a).

Julius has been widely used by researchers and engineers, especially in Japan. Julius can achieve typically real-time dictation of a 20,000-60,000 word vocabulary with an accuracy of about 90% on a PC (Kawahara et al., 2010a). In the references (Kawahara et al., 2010a, 2010b; Lee & Kawahara, 2009), Julius is explained in detail. Based on these references, we briefly explain the characteristics of Julius.

Julius has been developed as a research software for large-vocabulary continuous speech recognition (LVCSR) since 1997, and is distributed under an open license together with source codes. Julius is an open-source software for Japanese LVCSR. Word N-gram, context-dependent Hidden Markov Model (HMM), tree lexicon, N-gram factoring, crossword context dependency handling, enveloped beam search, Gaussian pruning, and Gaussian selection are used as the main techniques in Julius. According to the references (Kawahara et al., 2010a, 2010b; Lee & Kawahara, 2009), the main characteristics of Julius are:

- Real-time, high-speed, recognition based on a two-pass strategy.
- Live audio input recognition via microphone/input socket.
- Less than 32 M Bytes required for work area in memory.
- Supports language model (LM) of N-gram, grammar, and isolated words.
- Any LM in standard ARPA format and acoustic models in HTK ascii hmmdefs format can be used.
- Set various search parameters. Alternate decoding algorithm can be chosen.
- Triphone HMM/tied-mixture HMM/phonetic tied-mixture HMM with any number of states, mixtures and models are supported in HTK.
- Most mel-frequency cepstral coefficients and their variants are supported in HTK.

Figure 1 shows examples of outputs by Julius. The figure shows the timing position at the start of speech, and each trimming range of the first and last vowels for the utterance of "Shinnya" pronounced by Subject A while expressing the emotions "angry," "happy," "neutral," "sad," and "surprised."

	Angry	Happy	Neutral	Sad	Surprised
Silent	0-35 frame	0-12	0-64	0-43	0-48
Consonant	36-56	13-38	65-75	44-66	49-67
Vowel(/i/)	57-73	39-53	76-83	67-74	68-76
Consonant	74-91	54-69	84-110	75-99	77-97
Vowel(/a/)	92-103	70-84	111-129	100-117	98-117
Silent	104-191	85-191	130-191	118-191	118-191

Fig. 1. Examples of outputs by Julius

3. Method for recognizing facial expressions

Figure 2 is a flowchart of the proposed method. We have two modules in our system. The first is for speech recognition and dynamic image analysis, and the second is for learning and recognition. In the module for learning and recognition, we embedded the module for for front-view face judgment, which is not described in this paper because it is not directly related to speech recognition. The procedure used, except for the pre-processing module for front-view face judgment (Fujimura et al., 2011), is explained below.

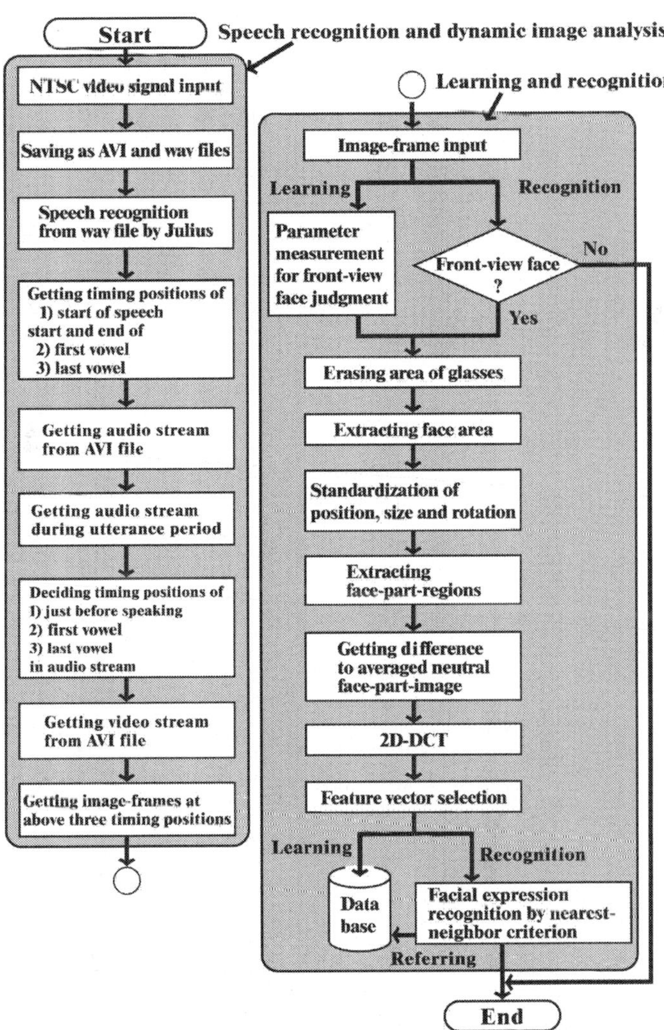

Fig. 2. Flowchart of proposed method (Fujimura et al., 2011)

3.1 Speech recognition and dynamic image analysis

Figure 3 shows the waveform of the Japanese given name "Taro;" the timing position of the start of speech, and the timing ranges of the first vowel (/a/) and the last vowel (/o/) were decided by Julius. By using these three timing positions obtained from a wav file, three thermal image frames are extracted from an AVI file. For the timing position just before speaking, we use 84 ms, as determined in a previously reported study (Nakano et al., 2009). As the timing position of the first vowel, we use the position where the absolute value of the amplitude of the waveform is the maximum while speaking the vowel. For the timing position of the last vowel, we apply the same procedure used for the first vowel.

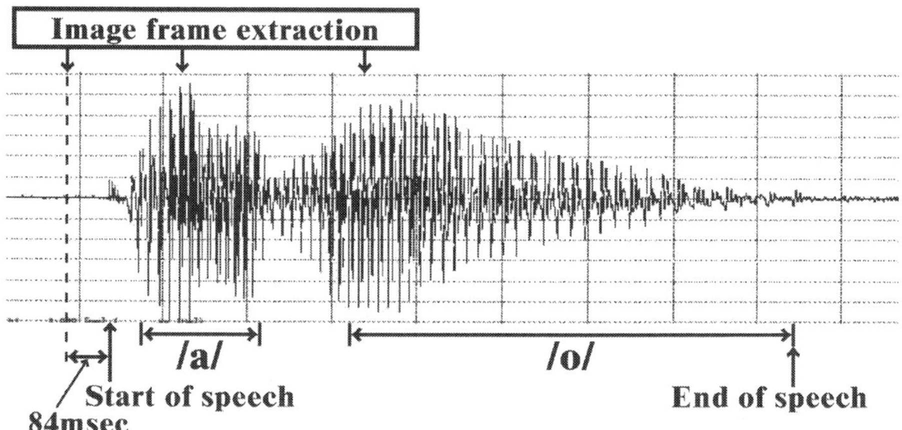

Fig. 3. Speech waveform of "Taro" and timing positions for image frame extraction (Koda et al., 2009)

3.2 Learning and recognition

For the static thermal images obtained from the extracted image frames, the process of erasing the area of the glasses, extracting the facial area, and standardizing the position, size, and rotation of the face are performed according to the method described in our previously reported study (Nakano et al., 2009). Figure 4 shows the blocks for extracting the facial areas in a thermal image of 720 × 480 pixels. In the next step, we generate difference images between the averaged neutral face image and the target face image in the extracted facial areas to perform a two-dimensional discrete cosine transform (2D-DCT). The feature vector is generated from the 2D-DCT coefficients according to a heuristic rule (Ikezoe et al., 2004; Nakano et al., 2009).

The Julius speech recognition system used in our study sometimes makes a mistake in recognizing the first and/or last vowel(s). For example, /a/ for the last vowel is sometimes misrecognized as /o/. We correct this misrecognition for the training data, however, corrections cannot be made for the test data. For example, in the experiment described later, when Julius correctly judges the first vowel of the utterance of "Ayaka," but misjudges the last vowel as /o/, the training data in speaking "Taro" are used for recognition instead of those for speaking "Ayaka." The facial expression is recognized by the nearest-neighbor criterion in the feature vector space by using the training data just before speaking and while uttering the phonemes of the first and last vowels.

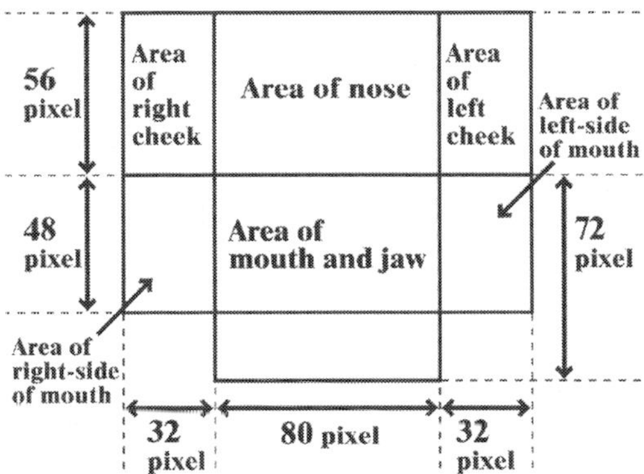

Fig. 4. Blocks for extracting facial areas from a thermal image

4. Experiments

4.1 Conditions

The thermal image produced by a thermal video system (Nippon Avionics TVS-700) and the sound captured by an electret condenser microphone (Sony ECM-23F5), amplified by a mixer (Audio-Technica AT-PMX5P), were transformed into a digital signal by an analogue/digital converter (Thomson Canopus ADVC-300) and input into a computer (DELL Optiplex GX620, CPU: Pentium IV 3.4 GHz, main memory: 2.0 GB, OS: Windows XP (Microsoft)) with an IEEE1394 interface board (I·O Data Device 1394-PCI3/DV6). We used Visual C++ 6.0 (Microsoft) as the programming language. To generate a thermal image, we set the conditions so the thermal image had 256 gray levels for the detected temperature range. This range was decided independently for each subject in order to best extract the facial area. We saved the visual and audio information in the computer as a Type 2 DV-AVI file, in which a frame had a spatial resolution of 720 × 480 pixels and an 8-bit gray level, and the sound was saved in a PCM format as stereo, 48 kHz, 16-bit file. The version 4.0 of Julius was used in the current study.

All subjects exhibited, in alphabetical order, each of the intentional facial expressions of "angry," "happy," "neutral," "sad," and "surprised," while speaking the semantically neutral utterance of each of the Japanese given names listed in Table 1. There were three subjects. Subject A was a male without glasses. Subject B was a male with glasses. Subject C was a female without glasses. Figures 5, 6, and 7 show images of Subjects A, B, and C, respectively.

		First vowel				
		a	i	u	e	o
Last vowel	a	ayaka	shinnya	tsubasa	keita	tomoya
	i	kazuki	hikari	yuki	megumi	koji
	u	takeru	shigeru	fuyu	megu	noboru
	e	kaede	misae	yusuke	keisuke	kozue
	o	taro	hiroko	yuto	keiko	tomoko

Table 1. Japanese given names used in the experiment (Yoshitomi et al., 2011a)

	Just before speaking	In speaking firstvowel (/i/)	In speaking last vowel (/a/)
Angry	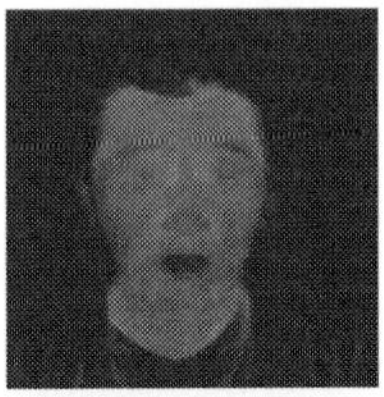	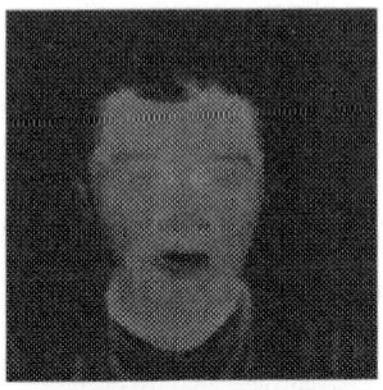	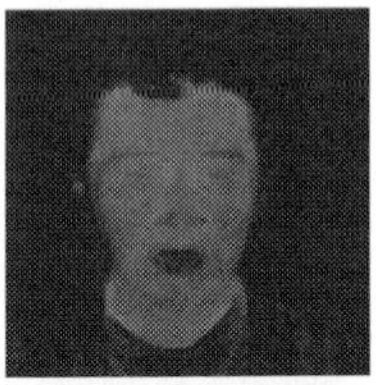
Happy	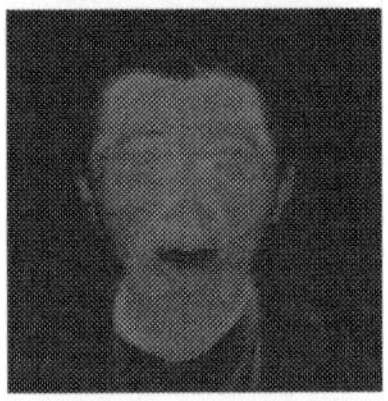		
Neutral		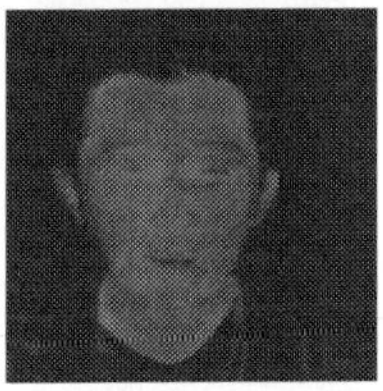	
Sad	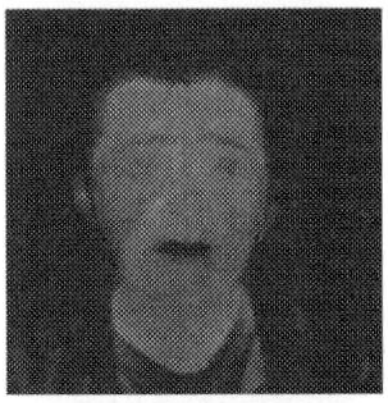		
Surprised		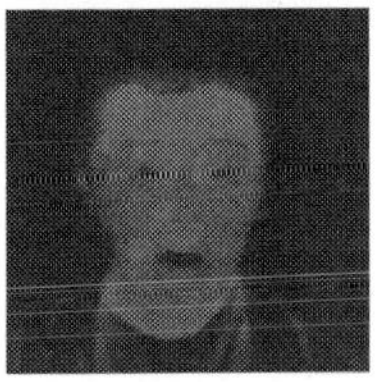	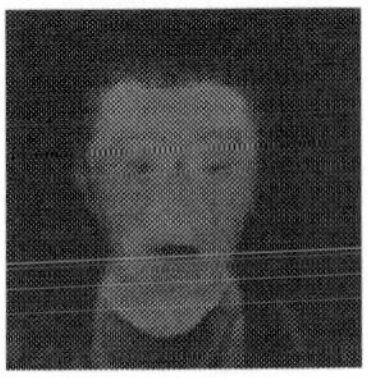

Fig. 5. Thermal images of Subject A expressing all facial expressions when speaking "Shinnya"

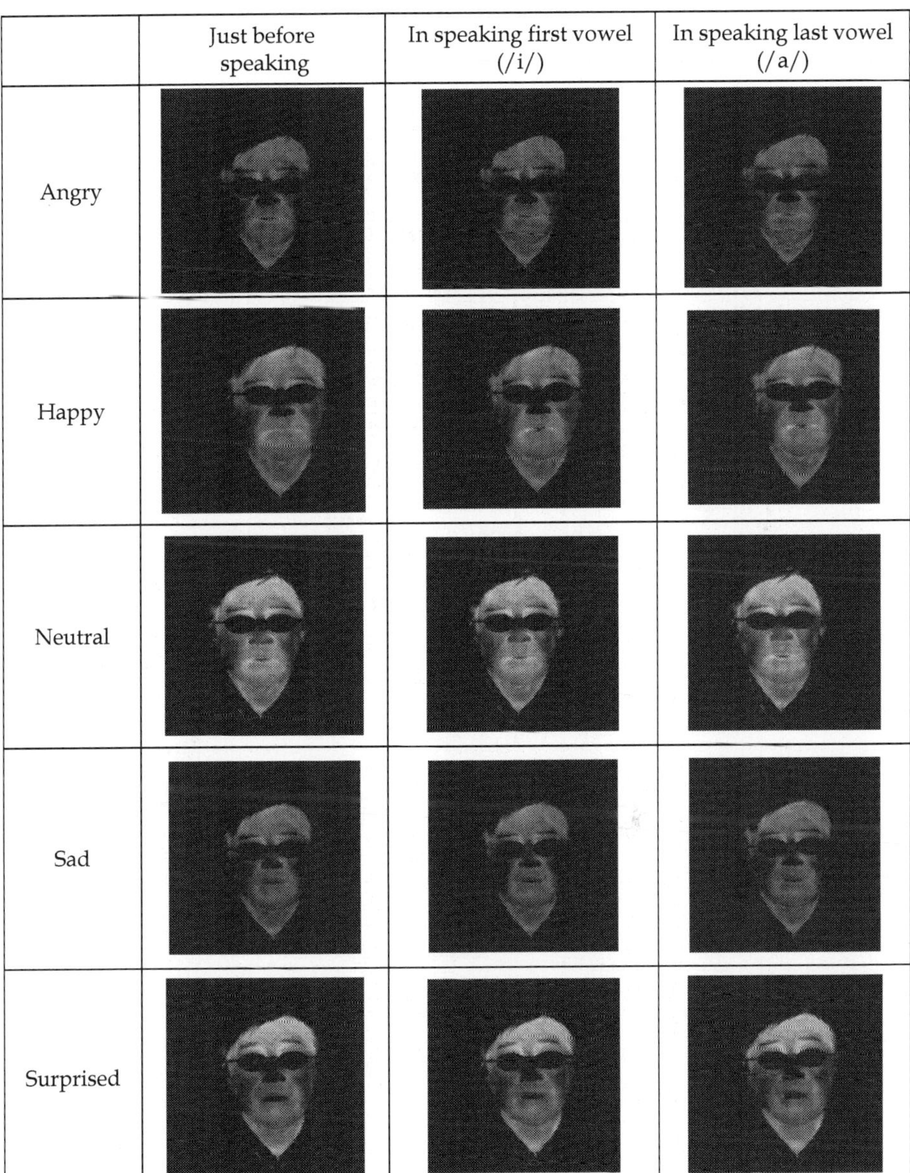

Fig. 6. Thermal images of Subject B expressing all facial expressions when speaking "Shinnya"

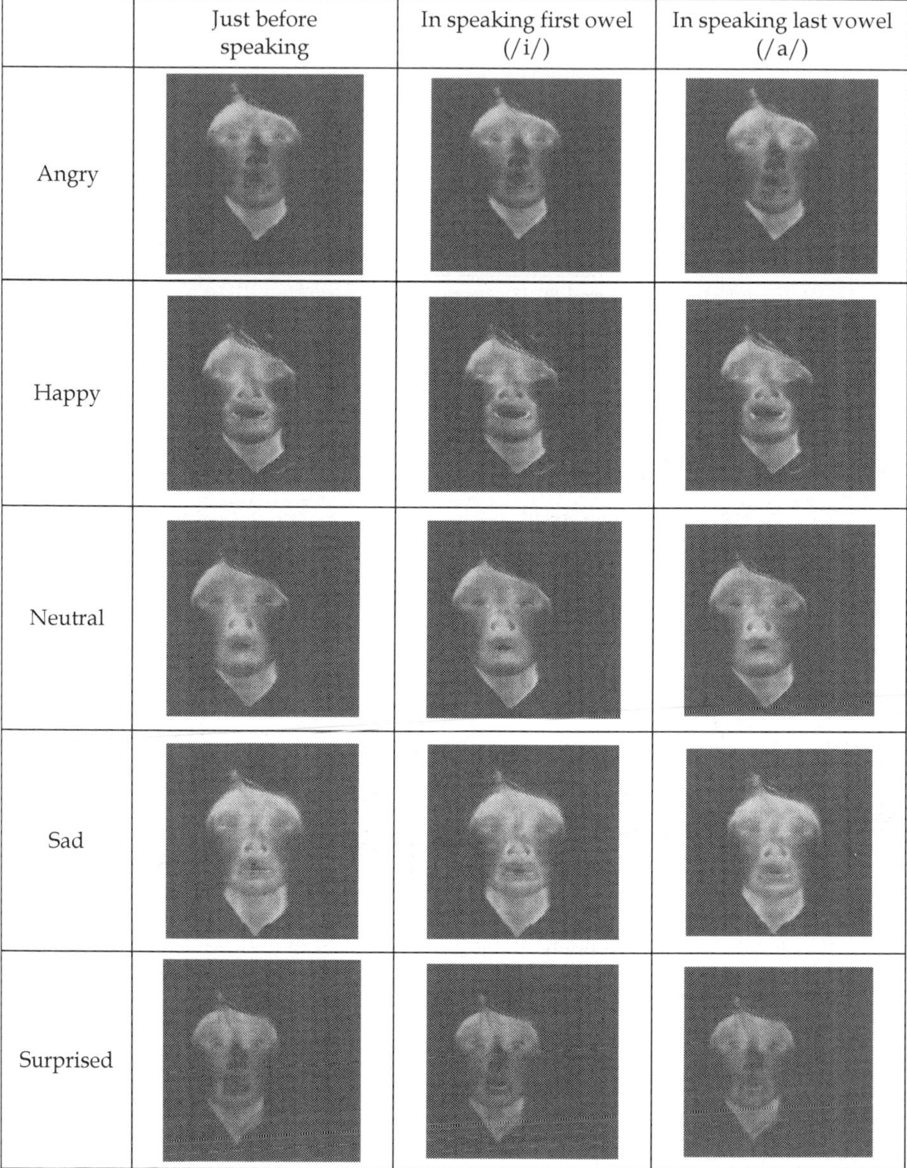

Fig. 7. Thermal images of Subject C expressing all facial expressions when speaking "Shinnya"

In the experiment, all subjects kept intentionally the front-view faces in the AVI files saved as both the training and test data. Accordingly, the pre-processing module for front-view face judgment (Fujimura et al., 2011) was not used in the experiment. We assembled 20 samples as training data and 10 samples as test data. From one sample, we obtained three images at the timing positions of just before speaking, and just speaking the phonemes of the first and last vowels. We obtained training data for all combinations of vowel type of the first and last vowels.

4.2 Results and discussion

The mean values for the recognition accuracy of Subject A in speaking 25 names with five emotions were 94.1% for the first vowel and 87.0% for the last vowel. Those of Subject B were 87.4% for the first vowel and 80.4% for the last vowel. Those of Subject C were 84.7% for the first vowel and 70.8% for the last vowel. For all subjects, Julius recognized the first vowel more accurately than the last vowel. Tables 2, 3 and 4 show the recognition accuracy for both the first and last vowels of Subjects A, B, and C, respectively. In Tables 2, 3 and 4, the recognition accuracy means the ratio in percentage of cases in which both the first and last vowels are correctly recognized. The mean values for the recognition accuracy for both the first and last vowels of Subject A in speaking 25 names with each emotion were 82.0% for "angry," 87.2% for "happy," 82.0% for "neutral," 83.6% for "sad," and 76.4% for "surprised." Those of Subject B were 54.2% for "angry," 74.5% for "happy," 98.0% for "neutral," 69.2% for "sad," and 62.0% for "surprised." Those of Subject C were 54.4% for "angry," 47.4% for "happy," 74.0% for "neutral," 63.6% for "sad," and 55.6% for "surprised." For both Subjects B and C, the mean value of the recognition accuracy for both the first and last vowels in speaking 25 names with the emotion of "neutral" was higher than that with other emotions, while the difference of emotion did not have much of an influence on the mean value of the recognition accuracy for both the first and last vowels in speaking 25 names in the case of Subject A, who could clearly pronounce the names selected in the study with all of the emotions.

Table 5 shows the mean values for the recognition accuracy for both the first and last vowels in speaking each name while expressing all five emotions. The highest value, 98.7%, as the mean value of all subjects was obtained for the name "Shinnya" where the first and last vowels are /i/ and /a/, respectively, while the lowest, 42.0%, was obtained for "Yuki" where the first and last vowels are /u/ and /i/, respectively. Moreover, the mean values of the recognition accuracy for both the first and last vowels with five emotions depended remarkably on the name to be pronounced, especially with Subject C. Figure 8 shows the waveforms for "Shinnya" pronounced by Subjects A, B, and C while expressing each emotion. All of the first and last vowels whose waveforms are shown in Fig. 8 were correctly recognized by Julius. Figure 9 shows the waveforms of "Koji" pronounced by Subjects A, B, and C for each emotion. In Fig. 9, all of the first and last vowels pronounced by Subject A were correctly recognized by Julius. As shown in Fig.9, some of the first and last vowels pronounced by Subject B and C were misrecognized by Julius. Julius tends to correctly recognize an utterance when it is clearly pronounced.

Table 6 shows facial expression recognition accuracy as mean values over all combinations of first and last vowels. The mean recognition accuracy of the facial expressions of all subjects was 79.8%. The mean recognition accuracy of the facial expressions was 85.5% for Subject A, 74.1% for Subject B, and 79.7% for Subject C. As stated in Section 3.2, Julius sometimes makes a mistake in recognizing the first and/or last vowel(s). For example, /a/ for the last vowel is sometimes misrecognized as /o/.

First-last vowel	Angry	Happy	Neutral	Sad	Surprised	Mean
a-a	50	100	100	80	0	66.0
a-i	100	100	100	90	80	94.0
a-u	90	0	100	100	70	72.0
a-e	80	100	100	90	100	94.0
a-o	80	60	100	90	80	82.0
i-a	100	100	100	100	100	100.0
i-i	100	80	100	100	60	88.0
i-u	100	80	100	100	90	94.0
i-e	30	100	70	40	0	48.0
i-o	100	100	30	20	100	70.0
u-a	80	70	40	70	60	64.0
u-i	100	90	20	10	100	64.0
u-u	90	100	70	70	100	86.0
u-e	100	100	100	100	100	100.0
u-o	100	100	70	100	100	94.0
e-a	50	100	80	100	10	68.0
e-i	100	100	100	100	100	100.0
e-u	30	40	100	100	90	72.0
e-e	50	80	100	90	90	82.0
e-o	100	100	60	100	90	90.0
o-a	80	80	100	100	60	84.0
o-i	100	100	100	100	100	100.0
o-u	100	100	100	100	100	100.0
o-e	100	100	100	100	70	94.0
o-o	40	100	10	40	60	50.0
Mean	82.0	87.2	82.0	83.6	76.4	82.2

Table 2. Accuracy (%) of speech recognition for Subject A (Yoshitomi et al., 2011b)

First-last vowel	Angry	Happy	Neutral	Sad	Surprised	Mean
a-a	30	100	100	100	60	78.0
a-i	40	60	100	70	33	60.6
a-u	50	90	100	56	80	75.2
a-e	67	90	90	70	60	75.4
a-o	30	90	100	60	20	60.0
i-a	100	100	100	100	100	100.0
i-i	40	90	100	90	20	68.0
i-u	20	40	100	78	0	47.6
i-e	70	75	100	70	67	76.4
i-o	0	90	90	90	60	66.0
u-a	50	100	100	100	80	86.0
u-i	70	10	90	10	70	50.0
u-u	100	60	100	90	100	90.0
u-e	50	78	100	67	100	79.0
u-o	10	40	100	20	90	52.0
e-a	80	90	90	90	80	86.0
e-i	100	90	100	70	100	92.0
e-u	0	40	100	50	30	44.0
e-e	89	80	90	90	90	87.8
e-o	50	60	100	90	90	78.0
o-a	80	100	100	80	0	72.0
o-i	60	30	100	10	60	52.0
o-u	40	90	100	10	50	58.0
o-e	30	90	100	80	100	80.0
o-o	100	80	100	90	10	76.0
Mean	54.2	74.5	98.0	69.2	62.0	71.6

Table 3. Accuracy (%) of speech recognition for Subject B

First-last vowel	Angry	Happy	Neutral	Sad	Surprised	Mean
a-a	100	78	100	50	80	81.6
a-i	80	100	100	100	40	84.0
a-u	0	0	40	40	0	16.0
a-e	60	60	90	30	100	68.0
a-o	89	40	100	80	100	81.8
i-a	100	100	100	80	100	96.0
i-i	0	56	100	10	30	39.2
i-u	0	0	0	50	0	10.0
i-e	90	90	100	80	50	82.0
i-o	70	20	100	80	80	70.0
u-a	70	100	100	90	90	90.0
u-i	10	0	50	0	0	12.0
u-u	0	0	0	10	0	2.0
u-e	70	80	100	80	50	76.0
u-o	40	0	60	80	10	38.0
e-a	90	60	100	60	100	82.0
e-i	100	100	100	100	100	100.0
e-u	0	0	10	70	10	18.0
e-e	90	100	100	100	90	96.0
e-o	40	30	100	100	100	74.0
o-a	90	70	100	90	50	80.0
o-i	0	0	0	0	0	0.0
o-u	0	0	10	10	30	10.0
o-e	100	20	90	100	90	80.0
o-o	70	80	100	100	90	88.0
Mean	54.4	47.4	74.0	63.6	55.6	59.0

Table 4. Accuracy (%) of speech recognition for Subject C

First-last vowel	Sbject A	Subject B	Subject C	Mean
a-a	66.0	78.0	81.6	75.2
a-i	94.0	60.6	84.0	79.5
a-u	72.0	75.2	16.0	54.4
a-e	94.0	75.4	68.0	79.1
a-o	82.0	60.0	81.8	74.6
i-a	100.0	100.0	96.0	98.7
i-i	88.0	68.0	39.2	65.1
i-u	94.0	47.6	10.0	50.5
i-e	48.0	76.4	82.0	68.8
i-o	70.0	66.0	70.0	68.7
u-a	64.0	86.0	90.0	80.0
u-i	64.0	50.0	12.0	42.0
u-u	86.0	90.0	2.0	59.3
u-e	100.0	79.0	76.0	85.0
u-o	94.0	52.0	38.0	61.3
e-a	68.0	86.0	82.0	78.7
e-i	100.0	92.0	100.0	97.3
e-u	72.0	44.0	18.0	44.7
e-e	82.0	87.8	96.0	88.6
e-o	90.0	78.0	74.0	80.7
o-a	84.0	72.0	80.0	78.7
o-i	100.0	52.0	0.0	50.7
o-u	100.0	58.0	10.0	56.0
o-e	94.0	80.0	80.0	84.7
o-o	50.0	76.0	88.0	71.3
Mean	82.2	71.6	59.0	70.9

Table 5. Accuracy (%) of speech recognition for Subjects A, B, and C

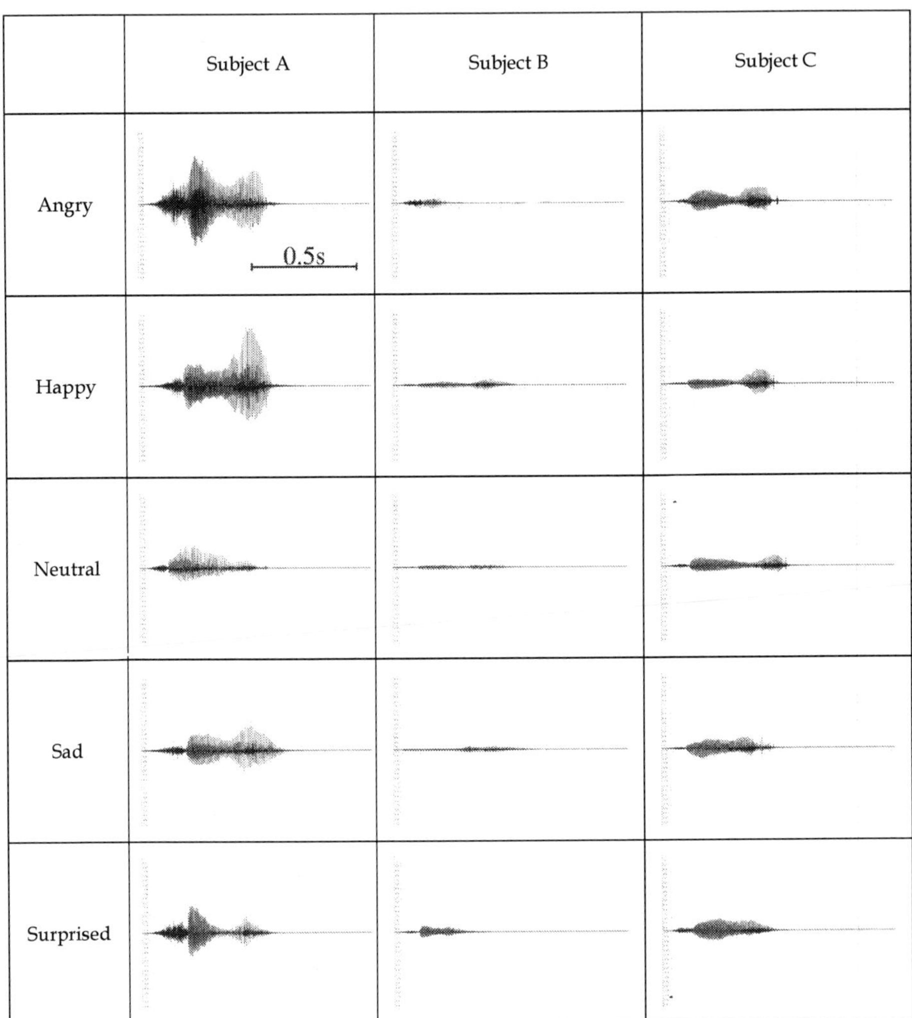

Fig. 8. Waveforms for each subject when speaking "Shinnya", whose vowels are /i/ for the first and /a/ for the last, while expressing each emotion

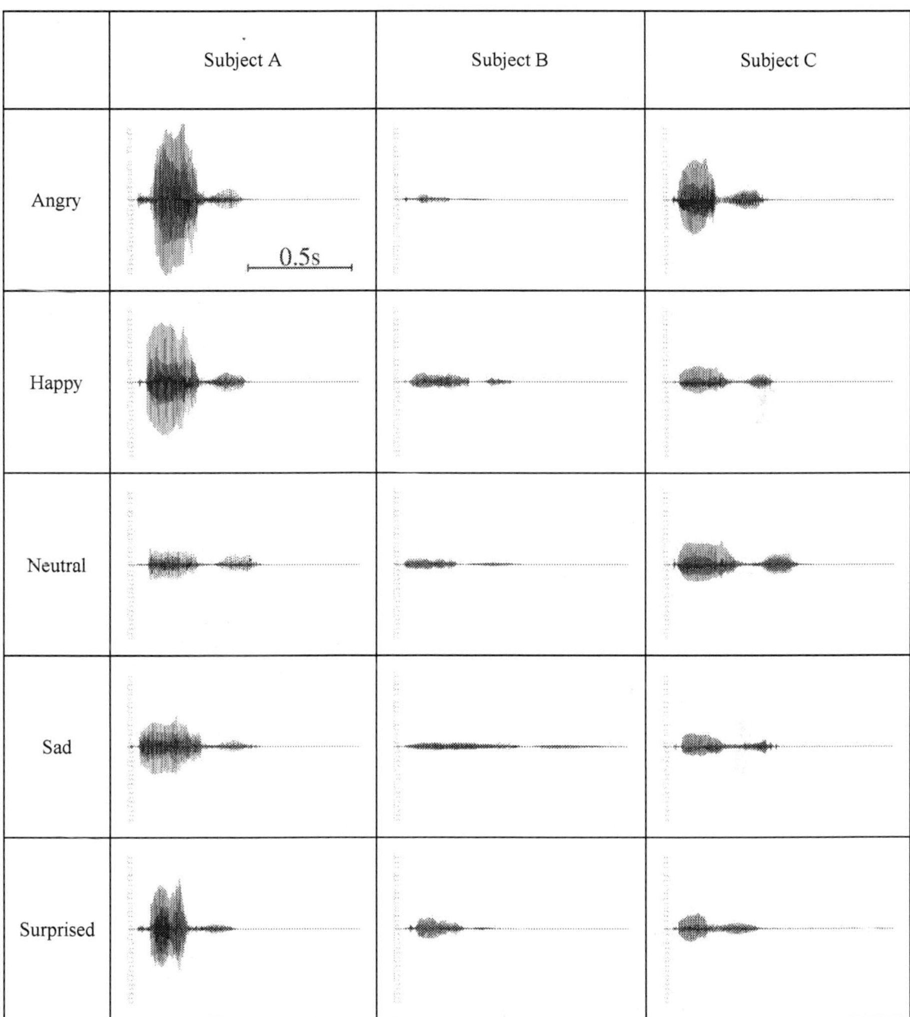

Fig. 9. Waveforms for each subject when speaking "Koji", whose vowels are /o/ for the first and /i/ for the last, while expressing each emotion

In order to estimate the effect of improving the recognition accuracy of vowel(s), we manually corrected the misrecognition of vowel(s) when Julius made a mistake in recognizing the first and/or last vowel(s). In this case, for example, when Julius correctly judged the first vowel at the utterance of "Ayaka" but misjudged the last vowel as /o/, the training data in speaking "Ayaka" were used for facial expression recognition after manually correcting /o/ into /a/on the speech recognition of the last vowel. Table 7 shows the accuracy in recognition of facial expressions as mean values for all combinations of first and last vowels after correcting the misrecognition of vowel(s). Each value in Table 7 means one obtained in the case of perfect recognition of both the first and last vowels. In such a case, the mean recognition accuracy of the facial expressions of all subjects was 87.0%, and the mean recognition accuracy of the facial expressions was 89.7% for Subject A, 82.5% for Subject B, and 88.7% for Subject C. Accordingly, improving the recognition of the first and last vowels would improve the mean value of facial expression recognition by up to 7.2%.

The mean values of the recognition accuracy of all subjects in speaking 25 names while expressing all five emotions were 88.7% for the first vowel and 79.4% for the last vowel. The recognition accuracy of vowels pronounced while expressing various emotions might be high enough to decide the timing of facial expression recognition using the speech recognition system. Accordingly, as a continuation of our work, we will use the proposed method for recognizing facial expressions in daily conversation.

Subject A		Input facial expression				
		Angry	Happy	Neutral	Sad	Surprised
	Angry	90.4	0.4	0.0	6.0	2.4
	Happy	3.6	94.8	9.6	4.8	7.2
	Neutral	0.0	0.0	87.2	0.0	0.0
Output	Sad	0.4	2.8	0.4	78.8	14.0
	Surprised	5.6	2.0	2.8	10.4	76.4

Subject B		Input facial expression				
		Angry	Happy	Neutral	Sad	Surprised
	Angry	64.1	5.2	5.2	6.7	9.2
	Happy	10.8	77.2	0.8	7.3	13.4
	Neutral	0.0	4.0	83.6	0.0	0.0
Output	Sad	7.2	7.6	2.0	78.0	9.7
	Surprised	17.9	6.0	8.4	8.0	67.7

Subject C		Input facial expression				
		Angry	Happy	Neutral	Sad	Surprised
	Angry	78.8	4.4	7.2	5.2	0.8
	Happy	2.4	77.1	3.6	2.4	0.0
	Neutral	10.8	2.0	71.9	3.2	2.0
Output	Sad	2.8	11.3	12.9	78.8	5.2
	Surprised	5.2	5.2	4.4	10.4	92.0

Table 6. Accuracy (%) of facial expression recognition (Yoshitomi et al., 2011b)

Subject A		Input facial expression				
		Angry	Happy	Neutral	Sad	Surprised
Output	Angry	91.6	0.4	0.0	4.8	1.2
	Happy	3.2	94.8	2.4	4.8	3.2
	Neutral	0.0	0.0	97.6	0.0	0.0
	Sad	0.4	2.8	0.0	79.2	10.4
	Surprised	4.8	2.0	0.0	11.2	85.2
Subject B		Input facial expression				
		Angry	Happy	Neutral	Sad	Surprised
Output	Angry	79.2	2.8	4.4	3.7	3.6
	Happy	5.6	85.2	2.8	3.6	11.9
	Neutral	0.0	4.0	83.6	0.0	0.0
	Sad	2.4	4.0	1.2	89.1	9.2
	Surprised	12.8	4.0	8.0	3.6	75.3
Subject C		Input facial expression				
		Angry	Happy	Neutral	Sad	Surprised
Output	Angry	88.4	2.4	4.8	3.6	0.4
	Happy	0.4	92.8	2.8	1.6	0.0
	Neutral	4.8	0.8	79.1	2.0	0.4
	Sad	1.6	1.6	10.5	86.0	2.0
	Surprised	4.8	2.4	2.8	6.8	97.2

Table 7. Accuracy (%) of facial expression recognition for perfect speech recognition of both first and last vowels

5. Conclusion

We have developed a method for recognizing the facial expressions of a speaker by using thermal image processing and a speech recognition system. To implement the proposed method, three subjects spoke 25 Japanese given names that provided all combinations of first and last vowels. These subjects were used to prepare training data and then test data for all combinations of the first and last vowels. The mean values of the recognition accuracy of all subjects in speaking 25 names while expressing five emotions were 88.7% for the first vowel and 79.4% for the last vowel. Using the proposed method, the facial expressions of three subjects were discernable with an accuracy of 79.8% when the subject exhibited one of the intentional facial expressions of "angry," "happy," "neutral," "sad," and "surprised." Improving the recognition of the first and last vowels could improve the mean value of facial expression recognition by up to 7.2% The recognition accuracy of vowels pronounced with various emotions might be high enough to decide the timing of facial expression recognition using the speech recognition system. We expect the proposed method to be applicable for recognizing facial expressions in daily conversation.

6. Acknowledgment

We would like to thank Mr. K. Shimada of Nova System Co. Ltd for his valuable cooperation while he was a student at Kyoto Prefectural University (Yoshitomi et al., 2011a, 2011b). We would like to thank all the subjects who cooperated with us in the experiments. This work was supported by KAKENHI (22300077).

7. References

Fujimura, T.; Yoshitomi, Y.; Asada, T. & Tabuse, M. (2011). Facial Expression Recognition of a Speaker Using Front-view Face Judgment, Vowel Judgment, and Thermal Image Processing, *Proceedings of 16th International Symposium on Artificial Life and Robotics*, pp. 219-224, ISBN 978-4-9902880-5-1, Beppu, Oita, Japan, January 27-29, 2011

Harashima, H.; Choi, C. S. & Takebe, T. (1989). 3-D Model-based Synthesis of Facial Expressions and Shape Deformation, *Human Interface*, Vol.4, pp. 157-166 (in Japanese)

Ikezoe, F.; Ko, R.; Tanijiri, T. & Yoshitomi, Y. (2004). Facial Expression Recognition for Speaker Using Thermal Image Processing, *Transaction of Human Interface Society*, Vol.6, No.1, (February 2004), pp. 19-27 (in Japanese)

Kawahara,T.; Lee, A.; & Kiyohiro Shikano, K. (2010). Julius: Open-source software toolkit for large vocabulary continuous speech recognition. In S.Itahashi and C-Y.Tseng, editors, *Computer Processing of Asian Spoken Languages*, Consideration Books, pp.305-308. 2010

Kawahara, T. et al. (December 2010). Open-Source Large Vocabulary CSR Engine Julius Julius rev.4.1.5.1 http://julius.sourceforge.jp/

Kobayashi, H. & Hara, F. (1994). Analysis of Neural Network Recognition Characteristics of 6 Basic Facial Expressions, *Proceedings of 3rd IEEE International Workshop on Robot and Human Communication*, pp. 222-227, ISBN 0-7803-2002-6, Nagoya, Japan, July 18-20, 1994

Koda, Y.; Yoshitomi, Y.; Nakano, M. & Tabuse, M. (2009), Facial Expression Recognition for a Speaker of a Phoneme of Vowel Using Thermal Image Processing and a Speech Recognition System, *Proceedings of 18th IEEE International Symposium on Robot and Human Interactive Communication*, pp. 955-960, ISBN 978-4244-5081-7, ISSN 1944-9445, Toyama, Japan, September 29 - October 1, 2009

Lee, A. & Tatsuya Kawahara, T. (2009), Recent Development of Open-Source Speech Recognition Engine Julius, *Proceedings of Asia Pacific Signal and Information Processing Association Annual Summit and Conference*, pp. 131-137, Sapporo, Japan, October 4-7, 2009

Mase, K. (1990). An Application of Optical Flow – Extraction of Facial Expression, *Proceedings of IAPR Workshop on Machine Vision and Application*, pp. 195-198, Kokubunji, Tokyo, Japan, November 28-30, 1990

Mase, K. (1991). Recognition of Facial Expression from Optical Flow. *Transaction of IEICE*, Vol.E74, No.10, (October 1991), pp. 3474-3483

Matsuno, K.; Lee, C.; & Tsuji, S. (1994). Recognition of Facial Expressions Using Potential Net and KL Expansion, *Transaction of IEICE*, Vol.J77-D-II, No.8 , pp. 1591-1600 (in Japanese)

Nakano, M.; Ikezoe, F.; Tabuse, M. & Yoshitomi, Y. (2009). A Study on the Efficient Facial Expression Using Thermal Face Image in Speaking and the Influence of Individual Variations on Its Performance, *Journal of IEEJ*, Vol.38, No.2, (March 2009), pp. 156-163, ISSN 0285-9831 (in Japanese)

Sugimoto, Y.; Yoshitomi, Y.; & Tomita, S. (2000). A Method for Detecting Transitions of Emotional States Using a Thermal Face Image Based on a Synthesis of Facial expressions, *Journal of Robotics and Autonomous Systems*, Vol.31, No.3, (May 2000), pp. 147-160, ISSN 0921-8890

Yoshitomi, Y.; Kimura, S.; Hira, E. & Tomita, S. (1996). Facial Expression Recognition Using Infrared Rays Image Processing, *Proceedings of the Annual Convention IPS Japan*, Vol.2, pp. 339-340, Osaka, Japan, September 4-6, 1996

Yoshitomi, Y.; Kimura, S.; Hira, E. & Tomita, S. (1997). Facial Expression Recognition Using Thermal Image Processing, *IPSJ SIG Notes*, Vol.CVIM103-3, pp. 17-24, Kyoto, Japan, January 23-24, 1997

Yoshitomi, Y.; Miyawaki, N.; Tomita, S. & Kimura, S. (1997). Facial Expression Recognition Using Thermal Image Processing and Neural Network, *Proceedings of 6th IEEE International Workshop on Robot and Human Communication*, pp. 380-385, ISBN 0-7803-4076-0 (Softbound Edition), 0-7803-4077-9 (Microfiche Edition), Sendai, Japan, September 29 - October 1, 1997

Yoshitomi, Y.; Kim, S.-Ill; Kawano, T., & Kitazoe, T. (2000). Effect of Sensor Fusion for Recognition of Emotional States Using Voice, Face Image and Thermal Image of Face, *Proceedings of 6th IEEE International Workshop on Robot and Human Interactive Communication*, pp. 178-183, ISBN 0-7803-6273-X, Osaka, Japan, September 27-29, 2000

Yoshitomi, Y. (2010). Facial Expression Recognition for Speaker Using Thermal Image Processing and Speech Recognition System, *Proceedings of 10th WSEAS International Conference on Applied Computer Science*, pp. 182-186, ISBN 978-960-474-231-8, ISSN 1792-4863, Appi Kogen, Iwate, Japan, October 4-6, 2010

Yoshitomi, Y.; Asada, T. ; Shimada, K. & Tabuse, M. (2011). Facial Expression Recognition of a Speaker Using Vowel Judgment, and Thermal Image Processing, *Proceedings of 16th International Symposium on Artificial Life and Robotics*, pp. 225-230, ISBN 978-4-9902880-5-1, Beppu, Oita, Japan, January 27-29, 2011

Yoshitomi, Y.; Asada, T. ; Shimada, K. & Tabuse, M. (2011). Facial Expression Recognition of a Speaker Using Vowel Judgment, and Thermal Image Processing, *Proceedings of Journal of Artificial Life and Robotics*, Vol. 16, to appear

Yuille, A. L.; Cohen, D. S.; & Hallinan, P. W. (1989). Feature Extraction from Faces Using Deformable Templates, *Proceedings of IEEE Conference on Computer Vision and Pattern Recognition*, pp. 104-109, ISBN 0-8186-1952-X, San Diego, California , USA, June 4-8, 1989

21

Speech Research in TUSUR

Roman V. Meshchryakov
*Tomsk State University of Control Systems and
Radioelectronics (TUSUR)*
Russia

1. Introduction

In article results of researches in TUSUR are show. Researches proceed more than 20 years. The basic consumers of production are medical institutions

Researches in the field of speech technologies in TUSUR are spent more than 20 years. Among the basic directions definition of the announcer, speech synthesis on printing text are allocated the adaptive analysis of a speech signal for the decision of problems of the analysis and speech recognition. Important applied value is medical appendices for support of the doctor-logopedist, and also on carrying out of procedures of rehabilitation of vocal and speech functions at the person.

2. Processing of a speech signal

For processing of a speech signal the hierarchical model was used. The information is used from various levels of speech system hierarchy. It allows to use the information presented in various scales for the full-function analysis and synthesis of a speech signal.

Elements at each level are thus allocated, their properties, possible transformations are defined. It is besides defined that elements at the bottom levels of hierarchy of speech system under certain conditions form configurations which are elements of top levels.

Thus conditions of a regularity of the configurations defining calculations are formed. In turn at synthesis of a speech signal elements of top levels will be transformed to configurations of elements of the bottom levels of hierarchy of speech system.

2.1 Speech signal analysis

The acoustic model of speech perception system has been developed for carrying out of researches of a speech signal. Its maintenance is represented by original mathematical model and algorithms of processing. Masking is simultaneous allows to eliminate redundancy in the speech signal, connected with features of delay of reaction sensor's systems after peaks in frequency area. Frequency masking allows to eliminate surplus information on a frequency spectrum which isn't perceived by the person since it disappears behind other frequencies.

In a complex of simultaneous and frequency masking the volume of the processed information on a speech signal at what the information isn't lost is considerably reduced, and its quality only improves, raises it informative.

In fig. 1 results on research of a site of a speech signal are presented. At the left results FFT, on the right – are presented at use of the developed model. It allows to spend segmentation of a speech signal on vocal and non-vocal sequence. They are used for the parametrical description of a speech signal.

Besides, on vocal sequence fundamental frequency with split-hair accuracy in comparison with other algorithms is defined.

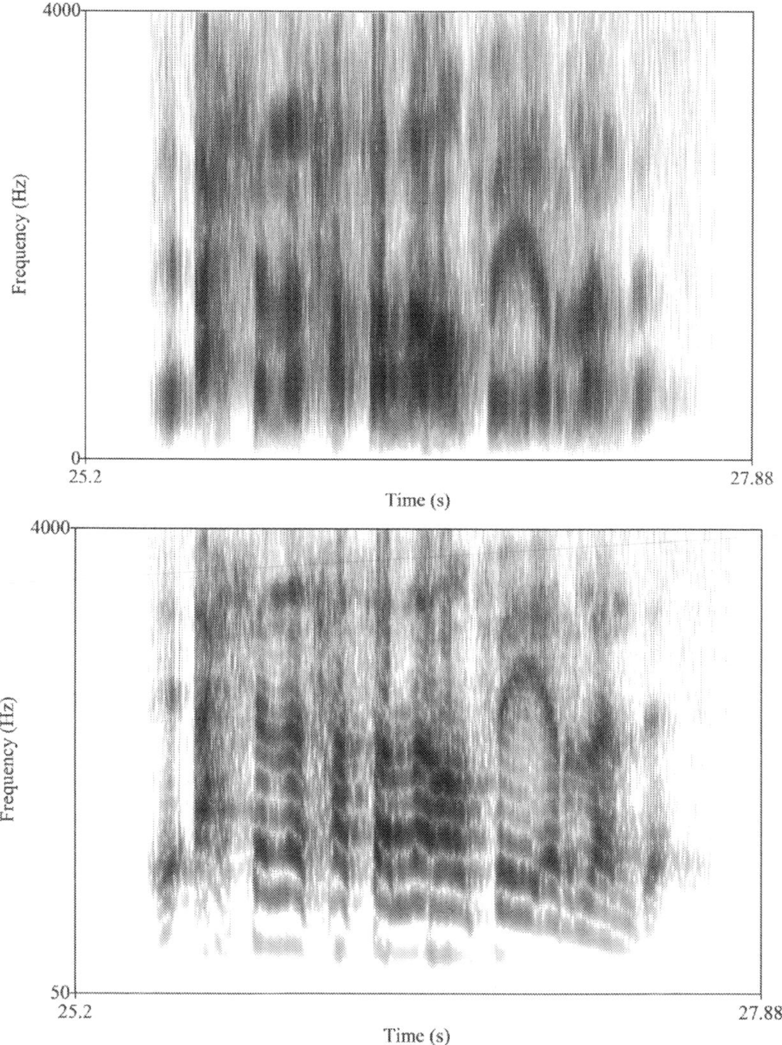

Fig. 1.

2.2 Medical research

Medical researches go in a direction of quality improvement of diagnosis statement and times reduction of patients rehabilitation. The first developed information system shows to the doctor-logopedist of speech signal feature (on a spectrum) and prompts infringements of speech formation bodies of patient.

The second component allows to form with use of biological feedback esophagus voice. To patients cut throat and form artificial vocal folds in a gullet. In fig 2 anatomic features after removal of a throat and to formation of a new vocal path are presented

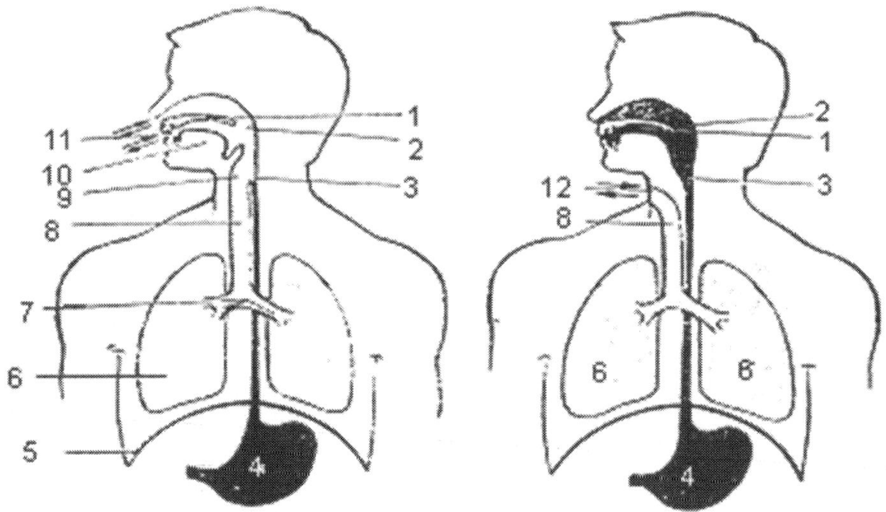

Fig. 2.

In fig. 3 basic elements of man-machine system are presented. In it the logopedist forms the task for the patient. The patient spends trainings on formation or restoration of vocal function about use of a hardware-software complex. The hardware includes a microphone with which help the data and the monitor on which process of interaction with the patient and its results is displayed are entered. Program and algorithmic maintenance forms contains mathematical model and functions of processing of a speech signal, interaction with the patient, and as history of speech rehabilitation.

Using biocontrol at first it is formed phonation, then the patient is trained to operate vocal folds (stability of fundamental frequency, duration phonation, etc.).

In figure 4 the photo from scientific research institute of oncology of Russian Academy of Medical Science on which base medical researchers are conducted is presented. Active participation is accepted by professor Balatskaja L.N., professor Chojnzonov L.T., logopedist Krasavina E.A. In TUSUR Bondarenko V. P, Kornilov A.J., Kotsubinsky V.P. were engaged and engaged in Konev A.A., Kostjuchenko E.J., Kvasov A.N. in the given problem

In figure 5 results of change of frequency of the basic tone at stages of vocal rehabilitation are presented (a) - Fundamental frequency, b) - Deviation fundamental frequency, c) - Sound duration [a]).

speech therapist
Algorithms and
soft-ware
Vocal source
model
Corrective
action
(positive reward)
Biological
parameters
(voice)
Hardware
Patient

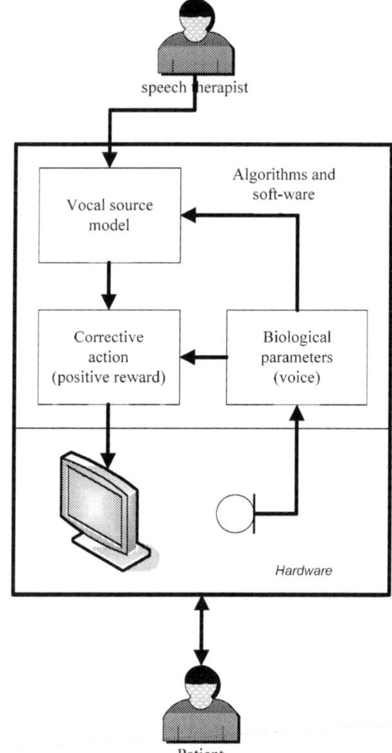

Fig. 3.

Fig. 4.

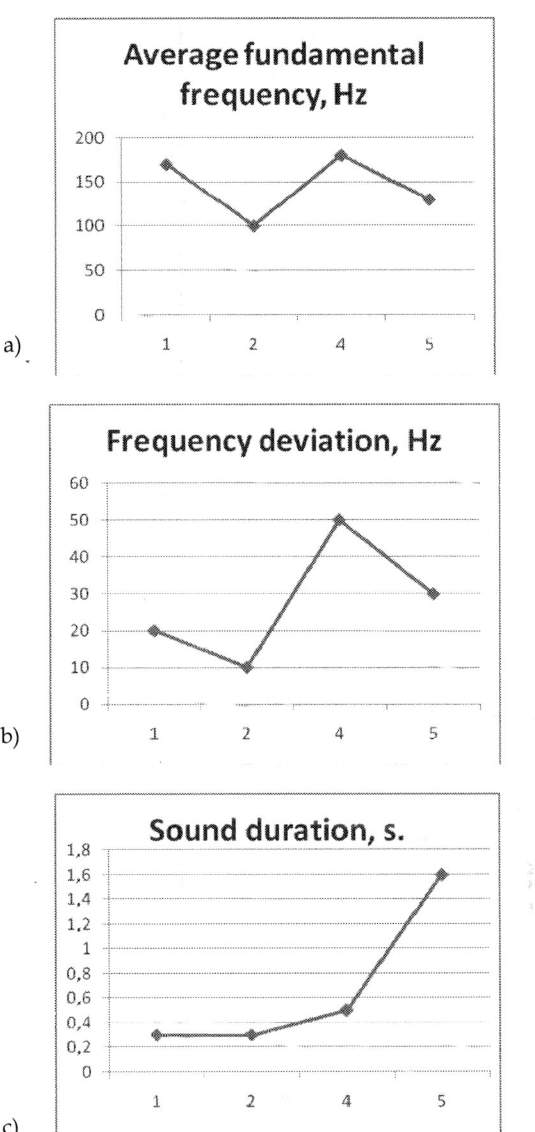

Fig. 5.

It is obvious that the base investigated characteristic is fundamental frequency. Measurements at various stages logorestore experts were spent:
1.   prior to the beginning of complex rehabilitation;
2.   in the beginning of complex rehabilitation;

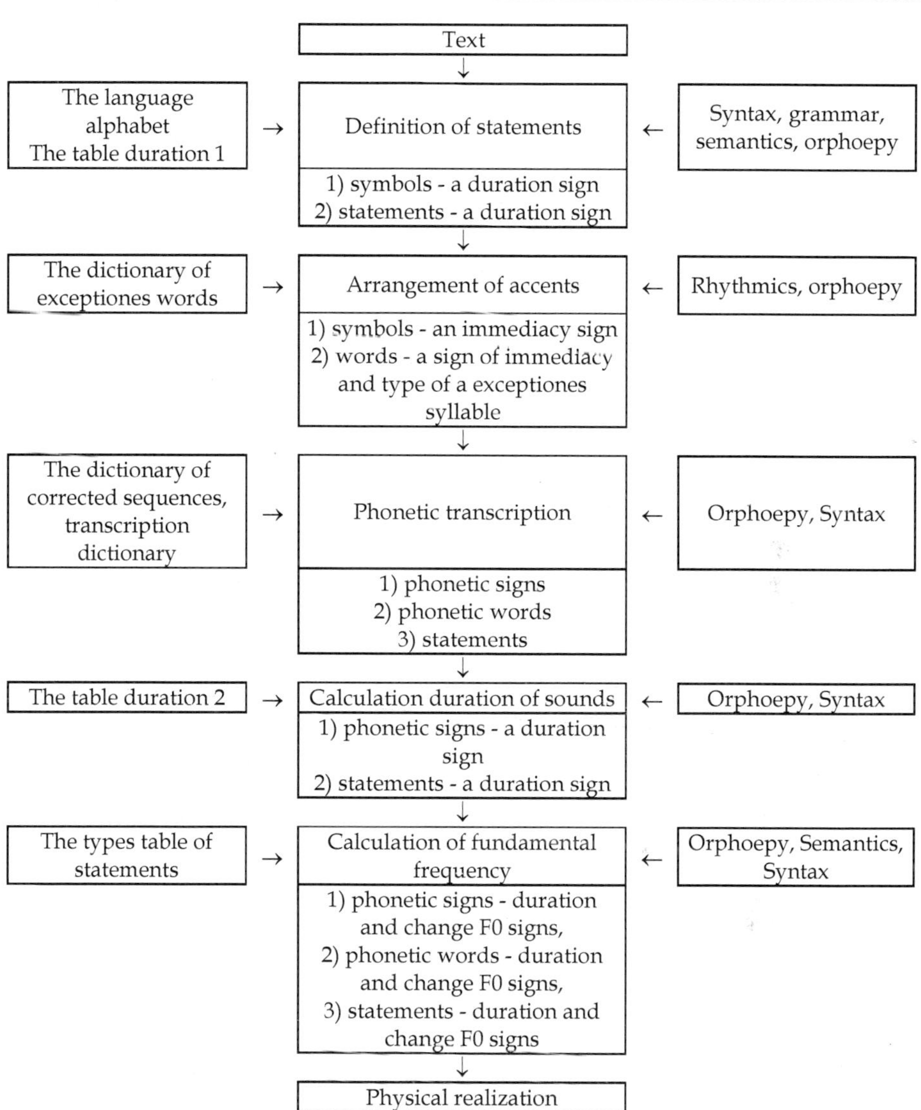

Fig. 6.

On the basis of the scheme resulted in figure 6 and the received practical results it is possible to make recommendations about the organization of knowledge bases for language systems:

1. Any speech system should be preliminary considered for revealing of the most informative blocks influencing result. By results of the analysis the criteria differentiating the information on significance values should be created. In particular, it is necessary to use criterion of efficiency of the transferred information.

2. All information necessary for transformation, it is expedient to divide into base data (tables and dictionaries) and rules according to which transformation is made.
3. For the information which can't be formalized it is presented in the form of rules dictionaries are used. The size of dictionaries is limited to demanded quality and admissible quantity of objects. In the given model 3 dictionaries and 5 sets of the rules considering both language, and parameters of the announcer are used.
4. For the information unequivocally defined by object it is expedient to use tables, in conformity with which on demanded object its sign is defined. For example, the table duration.
5. The general parameters of a speech signal should be based on physiological parameters speech formation systems of the person. It allows to adjust system of synthesis of speech on the announcer and to receive natural speech.
6. Introduction of criteria of efficiency is necessary both at the various intermediate stages, and on resultant. Their task can be as in obvious, and implicitly in the form of restrictions. Thus, we receive a control system of speech signal reception.

3. Conclusion

Now there is a development in the field of realization of effective algorithms. Researches on cases of various languages are conducted.

4. Acknowledgment

The collective long time was headed by professor Vladimir Bondarenko. Two students: Evgenie Kostjuchenko and Evgenie Shchipunov have received grants ASA (2008, 2010).

5. References

Meshchryakov, Roman & Bondarenko Vladimir (2008) Dialogue as a basis for construction of speech systems. *Cybernetics and Systems Analysis*, Vol.44, No.2 (March 2008), pp. 175-184, ISSN: 1060-0396

Meshcheryakov, Roman, Ronzhin Andrey, Karpov Alexey, Zelezny Milos, Hoffmann Ruediger Development of Multimodal Applications for Disabled People. Proc. of the Eighth All-Ukrainian International Conference, Kyiv, Ukraine, August 28−31, 2006, pp. 163-166.

Bondarenko V.P., Meshcheryakov R.V., Konev A.A. Biologic feedback formation by vocal rehabilitation Proceedings of the International Workshop SPEECH and COMPUTER (SPECOM'2006) St.Peterburg, Russia 25-29 June 2006 pp 251-257

Meshcheryakov R.V., Bondarenko V.P., Kotsubinsky V.P. Peculiarities of vocal sounds generational speech synthesis by rules Proceedings of the Ninth International Conference "SPEECH and COMPUTER" (SPECOM'2004) Saint-Petersburg, Russia 20-22 September 2004, 726p., pp 575-577

Taylor Paul, Text-to-Speech Synthesis: Cambridge University Press, 2009. – 597p.